SOCIAL WELFARE INSTITUTIONS

A Sociological Reader

Social Welfare Institutions

A SOCIOLOGICAL READER

EDITED BY *Mayer N. Zald*

Department of Sociology and Anthropology
Vanderbilt University

John Wiley & Sons, Inc., New York · London · Sydney

HV
31
.Z3

To Joan, a professional who knows

the value of theory in practice

PREFACE

ONE of the hallmarks of modern industrialized society is the development of private and public welfare institutions. These institutions care for and attempt to change those individuals that a humane society perceives as needing help.

As welfare institutions have developed it has become abundantly clear that they are complexly related to the societies of which they are a part. Furthermore, it is clear that simple ideological explanations are inadequate in accounting for either the emergence of welfare institutions or their successes and failures. Yet, few sociologists and other social scientists have devoted much attention to explaining the development, structure, and operation of welfare institutions and organizations. In this collection of readings I have attempted to bring together articles and essays that will contribute to a basic understanding of modern welfare institutions.

May I make it clear at the beginning that this book is not a reader on social problems, or even on welfare problems. The literature on social problems, social disorganization, the causes of poverty, and so on, is extensive and deep. Instead of dealing with that phase, this volume focuses on the response of society to social welfare needs and problems—on society's attempt to meet these problems through purposive programs and organizations.

Nor have I tried to establish what should be the current social policy. My purpose has been to present a positivistic description and explanation of the growth, structure, and recurring problems of welfare institutions. Of course, I should like the description and explanation to contribute to sound thinking about social policy, but my prime objective has been to develop an analytic framework, and to collect related essays and studies that will help in understanding the structure and operation of welfare institutions.

This book is intended for several audiences. The first one is students. An increasing number of schools of social work attempt to leaven their curriculums with sociological concepts of culture, society, community, large-scale organization, and interpersonal relations. Yet, often the material used has only an indirect relation to the social welfare field. In this regard, this volume is fashioned as a two-edged teaching tool: it is designed to aid the teaching of basic sociological concepts as well as the teaching of the structure and operation of welfare institutions. From the same perspective, the book can be used appropriately in presocial work courses at the senior level. Although these courses are often taught in sociology departments, they frequently have little sociological content. A second major audience that I hope for is the informed and concerned public. There are large numbers of people who are concerned about the operation of our welfare institutions. This collection of articles views those institutions from a broad and systematic perspective. Finally, this book is aimed at the growing number of workers, teachers, and researchers in the welfare field for whom it will provide a convenient summary and framework of one line of approach to welfare institutions.

The idea for this presentation took root when I was a graduate student at the University of Michigan. I was working on a research project directed by my iconoclastic teachers, Morris Janowitz of the Department of Sociology and Robert Vinter of the School of Social Work. The project was housed at the School of Social Work, which had just inaugurated its Doctoral Program in Social Work and Social Science. In the heady atmosphere created by this vital group of people—especially Henry Meyer, Edwin Thomas, and Eugene Litwak—the need for a sociology of social welfare "struck home," and the concept of this book began to germinate.

Several of the Michigan group have provided useful suggestions for this volume. Also I have been ably counseled by Alan Blum, Charles Perrow, Rosemary Sarri, David Street, Irving Spergel, Edward Schwartz, Thomas Sherrard, Joseph Eaton, and Martin Rein. Morris Janowitz nurtured my original idea and provided me with sage and always provocative advice. But I take responsibility for the faults of the final product, and gratefully share with my advisers and contributors the credit for its achievements.

MAYER N. ZALD

Nashville, Tennessee, 1965

CONTENTS

INTRODUCTION

THE emergence of the modern systems of social welfare has been rife with controversy. Competitive philosophies of the nature of man and the good society have offered alternative approaches to welfare organization and welfare services. The topic that is often obscured by polemic is the relationship of welfare services and organizations to the structure of society. All societies provide for the care of the lame and sick; all societies establish conditions for participation in the society's bounty and, if the society is at all above the subsistence level, it assigns different shares of the bounty to various groups; all societies make provision for handling the socially deviant. Societies differ, however, in the way in which they are organized to handle welfare problems, in the resources committed to handling different kinds of problems, and in the values attached to different types of programs and allocations.

Compared with less differentiated and less complex societies, modern society separates many welfare functions from the family unit. Yet, although we possess fairly well-developed sociologies of other major institutional focuses—such as the sociology of religion, of the family, of education, and of industry—no comparable body of literature exists for the sociology of social welfare.

This lack of literature is all the more surprising when we consider the early and important association, in the last century, of sociology with the development of social welfare reform and professional social work. Empirical sociology is based on the use of social statistics, and the use of social statistics was advanced by the problems of measuring poverty.

But just as it seems to some observers that social work, in its drive toward professionalization, deserted the poor, so, too, sociology, in its pursuit of scientific status, deserted the value-laden problems of social welfare. Almost in a "reaction formation," social problems and welfare problems became taboo topics for sociology; only general topics or topics without polemic overtones were acceptable for research. Of course, many

1

researchers continued to study social and welfare problems (the two are not necessarily the same) but, nevertheless, the study was not quite intellectually respectable.

However, since World War II, sociological theory and research have been applied more and more to social welfare problems. For one thing, sociologists have become less concerned with preserving their intellectual purity. First, many sociologists believe that by making value judgments explicit, biases can be controlled. Second, even if the sociologist is still concerned about the biasing effects of value judgments, the process of research replication and of scientific criticism acts as a safeguard against potential bias in research. Third, for a variety of political and social reasons, there has been an increasing concern about America's domestic problems, especially those of poverty. Finally, the sociologist has come to realize that the welfare sector represents an arena that is as good as any other for the testing of general sociological theories and concepts.

At the same time, welfare administrators, social workers, philanthropic foundations, and government agencies have become dissatisfied with self-justifying assertions about the impact of different programs, and have begun to demand systematic research as one part of the process of evaluating welfare programs. Furthermore, the need to modify and, in some cases, reject individualistic models of change has led to a quest for sociological answers to welfare problems. Both of these developments— the change in sociology and the change in welfare perspectives—have created an opportunity for the rapid development of the sociology of welfare.

A fully developed sociology of social welfare would have two central features: in common with any branch of sociology, it would attempt to *explain* the pattern of institutional development and organization; and, in the light of this knowledge, it would aid in the development of a more effective knowledge base for professional practice. This latter feature sets apart the sociology of welfare from many branches of sociology. The body of knowledge that emerges about welfare institutions may be value-free, but the operating sociologist will often be asked to make recommendations for the *solutions* of welfare problems. The first task of a sociology of social welfare obviously is to help explain the pattern of development of welfare institutions, but the second task of developing a more effective knowledge base for professional practice will always be at least a subsidiary aspect of the sociologist's job.

In this book of readings we present a preliminary approach to the sociological study of welfare institutions. A framework for the study of social welfare obviously hinges on the distinctive characteristics of welfare as contrasted with other kinds of social institutions. In order to isolate the distinctive characteristics of welfare institutions it is necessary to formulate an adequate analytic definition of social welfare. But it is not easy to develop a connotative definition of social welfare and social welfare institutions that will cover those activities that have come to be described as such in common parlance and, at the same time, will exclude those social services not so considered.

In common parlance, social welfare often refers to the helping of individuals or groups who, for one reason or another, are "needy"; that is, those who are unable to attain a defined minimum level of living or of personal functioning. Furthermore, the common conception of social welfare suggests that the adult or child is in some way incapacitated so that he cannot attain this minimum level of functioning by his own effort or the efforts of his family or friends. Rather than discussing in detail the problem of defining social welfare institutions, let us advance the following heuristic definition: social welfare institutions are the patterned collection of positions and organizations whose primary manifest purpose is to restore and/or maintain members of the society at a minimum level of personal and social functioning.

Such a definition excludes some organizations that have a *latent* social welfare function. For instance, it excludes political machines which, in distributing food baskets and the like, have helped the poor.

Our definition also excludes some other organizations and institutional complexes that are sometimes considered as a part of the social welfare complex. For instance, we exclude medical institutions whose primary manifest function involves the maintenance and restoration of *physical* functioning. In essence, our definition suggests that specialized social welfare programs and organizations come into play in many areas of modern life in order to maintain a minimum adequate level of living. Individuals and groups may fall below this minimum for many reasons— failure of the economy, inadequate socialization (training), high rates of geographic mobility, family disorganization, and poor articulation of the educational system with economic needs. Regardless of the cause of the problem, once a group is defined as falling below the minimum adequate level, social welfare institutions will be called into play.

Our definition also suggests that social welfare institutions and programs will often cut across other institutional areas because personal and social malfunctioning may occur in disparate areas of social life. For instance, as children drop out of school their educational failure becomes a social welfare problem. Similarly, as workers drop out of the labor force, their care becomes a social welfare problem.

Finally, our definition bypasses the question of the recipient's payment for service. Sometimes welfare organizations are envisioned as those institutions in which the organization helps to maintain or restore individuals or groups to minimum levels of functioning *without* the recipient paying full costs. We prefer not to restrict our definition to those institutions in which unreciprocated exchange is a dominant feature. Although many welfare recipients may not pay money for the service that they receive, they may pay much more: gratitude, political acquiescence, and the like. Thus, the lack of reciprocity depends upon the specification of coin. As we shall see, while unreciprocated exchange is not the defining characteristic of welfare organizations, it is an important element in their operation. Furthermore, some social welfare programs are almost fully funded by recipients. The Old Age Survivor's Insurance program and workmen compensation laws are legally regulated efforts of a massive cooperative sort in which recipients participate in protecting themselves against later dependency.

Accepting as valid our definition of welfare institutions, how can we group the major kinds of welfare tasks? There are at least three major tasks that welfare institutions deal with: (1) the task of insuring adequate income support and maintenance, (2) the task of providing adequate levels of deviance prevention and rehabilitation, and (3) the task of providing adequate levels of social participation and integration. Income support and maintenance programs range from social security insurance to vocational retraining programs designed to enable people with below-standard skills to earn acceptable minimum wages. Deviance prevention and rehabilitation programs range from those designed to rechannel the energies of delinquents to casework with mothers of illegitimate children. Programs to insure adequate levels of participation and integration range from language classes for immigrants to senior-citizen centers and youth-club programs.

The operating programs and organizational structures of agencies designed to deal with these different kinds of welfare goals or tasks vary widely and, at first, appear to have little in common. However, there are at least four important problems and structural characteristics which, although not common to all welfare programs, are common to many, and are related to the basic nature of welfare institutions. These problems are listed below.

(1) Welfare goals and minimum standards are subject to debate and continuing modifications.

(2) Welfare programs are usually operated by nonprofit organizations and the clients' contribution of money, if any, does not cover the cost of service.

(3) The clientele is heavily dependent on the organization.

(4) If the clientele is to be changed and maintained by other than money grants, interpersonal relationships are the "technologies" through which the change is induced.

The above aspects in the operation of welfare programs create some of the distinctive problems of welfare organizations, and will come up repeatedly in the main body of this reader.

Now we shall briefly discuss the above four aspects and some of the consequences of each.

(1) *Definition of welfare goals.* In American society, welfare goals are a matter of continuing debate. There may be a consensus on the highly abstract definitions of welfare goals—such as "freedom from want" or "the ability to lead useful and psychologically satisfying lives"—but, in implementing any abstract goal, there is likely to be a good deal of debate over both the means to the goal and the concrete referents of the goal. Regardless of the question of who is to provide welfare services—organs of the state or private organizations—there is debate about what should be the minimum level of personal and social functioning. This is a question that is raised for each type of welfare task—income maintenance, deviance prevention, and social participation. Furthermore, the minimum standards can, in no sense, be thought to be absolute. The poor of today, typically, have a much higher real income than the poor of a previous era, but they also have higher expectations. Not only the poor, but the rest of the society has higher standards. In other words, adequate levels of income are not defined in absolute terms but in social psychological terms relative to standards and values in the society.

Not only is there a changing definition of income adequacy, but there are changing minimum standards in the areas of deviance reform and of social participation. Social welfare advocates have argued that the task involves not only the elimination of negative deviance but the rehabilitation of the deviant to a more satisfying mode of life. In the area of social participation and integration, welfare goals often seem to be that everybody should be able to have enjoyable human relations and that nobody should be socially isolated. Certainly, previous generations have not always had organizations that focused on such goals. Since welfare goals are in a state of flux and are subject to debate, the sociology of welfare institutions must attend to the processes and conditions under which welfare goals are defined and changed.

(2) *Financial support.* Rarely do welfare organizations raise enough money from client fees to cover their operating costs. Indeed, in the case of many welfare organizations, client fees are either negligible or nonexistent. Thus, unlike businesses, the people who use the organization, who gain the immediate benefits of the organization and program, do not pay for the total cost of service.

In general, the funds for welfare organizations and programs are provided by the agents of society or by some subgroup in the society. Since the people and groups that pay for the service do not themselves usually receive the service, there is a complex process of justification of the "need" for the service by the recipients and by the society at large. If the welfare agency is "privately" financed, a complex fund-raising machinery develops to generate support and commitment. If the agency is supported through public channels, it must compete with a host of other departments and bureaus that give direct service to taxpayers and organized interest groups.

Since welfare organizations tend to be money-short, several consequences follow. First, their personnel problems are legion. Welfare organizations have a tough time competing with other organizations for personnel and, consequently, have a high rate of personnel turnover. Second, departures from traditional programs are hard to support because the organization rarely has surplus funds. Thus, elaborate justifications are required in order to experiment with new programs. In both cases the effectiveness of welfare organizations is limited by their fund-raising ability.

(3) *Clientele of welfare programs.* The clientele of most welfare organizations is, by definition, functioning below the minimum levels that are considered adequate in the society. Since the clients rarely pay meaningful fees, they do not come to the organization as equal citizens but as supplicants. Sometimes the organization is legally responsible for its clients' actions; sometimes the financial status of the clients makes them heavily dependent on the welfare organization; and sometimes the clients' psychological status makes them incapable of independent action.

Whether for psychological, legal, or financial reasons, the client usually has few controls or sanctions over the agency. Therefore, only professional commitment and special modes of supervision can insure that the clients' interests are, indeed, served.

Not only are clients supplicants, but they often come to the organization without the personal skills or makeup that will lead them to change easily their level of functioning. Thus, welfare organizations may have the task of compensating for deeply engrained deficits of personal functioning created over many years. And, what is even more difficult: these organizations may have to try to change the conditions that cause such deficits.

(4) *Interpersonal technologies for change.* To change the characteristics of clients, social welfare organizations are dependent on the interpersonal relationships between staff and client. Certainly, programs that have rehabilitative goals must often attempt to induce changes in attitudes and skill levels. The dependence upon interpersonal technologies for achieving these goals leads welfare institutions to a set of programs which are difficult to evaluate and which do not have clearly specified procedures. First, it is difficult to evaluate effectiveness until several years after "treatment" is concluded. Second, the specific aspects of interpersonal relationships that lead to change are difficult to evaluate. In particular, both casework and group work, as welfare technologies, are not easy to evaluate. Organizations that are dependent on interpersonal technologies are often subject to continuing debates over the relative efficacy of different procedures. Of course, many clients of welfare organizations may not be changeable; they may be permanent clients. Even in these cases

the goals of a humane society require that the attempt be made to maintain these permanent clients in a dignified fashion. Here, too, interpersonal technologies for support are used.

These four aspects of the operation of welfare institutions—the debate over goals, the problems of financial support, the clientele characteristics, and the interpersonal technologies—are discussed in several sections of the volume. For instance, the debate over goals is considered primarily in Section I, "The Historical and Societal Context of Welfare" and also in Section III, Part A, "Goals Setting and Organizational Requirements." However, this book is not organized around these four recurring aspects of the operation of welfare institutions. Instead, the selections have been organized according to a conception of the major determinants of the structure and problems of welfare services.

OVERVIEW OF THE READER

The institutions of social welfare exist within and are determined by the framework of a larger cultural and social milieux—they are a function of the "macrosociological" processes and structures, including the structure of the economy, the political system, and the basic value patterns of the culture. At the same time, the character of welfare services reflects the "microsociological" processes of role relations and of specific organizational decisions. Both in selecting the articles and in organizing their sequence we have attempted to articulate the larger macrosociological concerns as well as the more immediate microsociological processes.

The readings have been selected with several basic criteria in mind. First, we sought articles that exemplified basic sociological concepts and processes such as the nature of ruling elites, value patterns, role conflict, organizational structure, professionalism, and the like. Although all of the articles were not written by authors who are professional sociologists (selections by historians, political scientists, economists, anthropologists, social workers, and psychiatrists have been included), the articles were essentially chosen because they help to explain underlying sociological processes. We also sought articles that show how social science research and concepts might aid in increasing institutional effectiveness. This latter criterion has been used for only a few articles, and they have been so noted.

Finally, and most important, we sought articles that illuminate some of the distinctive problems of welfare organizations. Although our goal was to use basic sociological concepts, we wished to do so only in so far as they were linked to the operation of welfare institutions. While a few articles do not deal with social welfare, there usually is a clear link between their analyses and their implications for welfare organizations.

The selections have been *arranged* to move from the "macro," or societal processes, to the "micro," or interpersonal processes in the functioning of welfare institutions in modern society. We discuss the content and implication of each article in our introduction to the particular part of the section in which it appears. Here, we briefly survey the over-all structure of the reader.

The three major sections of the volume—Section I, "The Historical and Societal Context of Welfare"; Section II, "Welfare Organizations in the Community"; and Section III, "Goals, Internal Organization, and Client Relations"—present a flow of analysis from the societal-level determinants of welfare organization and ideology to the staff-client determinants of actual services. That is, we turn from the broad social forces determining the shape and level of welfare service to the immediate environment of welfare organizations and, finally, we examine the actual interpersonal relationships between the recipients of service and welfare organizations.

The over-all purpose of Section I is to explore the societal context of welfare services, not only in terms of the historical changes that have occurred but also in terms of the basic components of the society that affect policy and the organization of welfare services. The selections in Part A, "The Historical Background of Modern Welfare," deal with the societal transformation in both America and Britain necessary for and accompanying the rise of modern welfare systems. The selections in Part B, "Comparative Elites and Social Structure," take a comparative view of the ways in which different societies have industrialized and have developed their welfare systems. This part focuses upon the role of elites, political structures, and economic development in shaping welfare institutions. Part C, "Beliefs and Values," deals with the impact of beliefs, ideology, and values on the organization of welfare services. Beliefs, ideologies, and values are the components of the cultural system, which help to determine the pace of welfare development and to condition the debates over what kind of services will be provided.

Parts D and E of Section I present articles on the social-movement processes and processes of social-policy formulation by which demands for welfare services are finally translated into welfare programs. These articles differ from the selections in Parts A to C of Section I in that they move away from the *context* of the development of welfare institutions to the processes by which policies are actually formed. Part D, "Social Movements and Demands for Change," presents articles concerning the way that demands for service feed into the broader process by which decisions are made to provide welfare services. The articles in Part E, "The Formation and Consequences of Policy," analyze the relation of social structure to policy formation in the United States and elsewhere. These selections also examine the complexity of developing consistent policies in a modern society.

With a few exceptions, the articles in Section I deal with the factors that shape welfare institutions, organizations, and policy at the societal or national level. There is little concern with specific organizations operating in specific organizational environments.

In Section II, "Welfare Organizations in the Community," we step down a level and consider the external relations of organizations. Part A, "The Community Context of Welfare Services," focuses on the urban context in which most welfare goals are sought. Depending upon such factors as the local elite structure, economic conditions, and other aspects of communities, we would expect to find differences in welfare problems of communities and differences in the ability of organizations to grapple with such problems. Part B, "Support Bases for Welfare Organizations," deals with some of the factors leading to more, or less, support for specific welfare goals and organizations. What leads some organizations to be supported and others not to be? Why do some people who are not employed by welfare organizations, such as volunteer fund raisers, give the organizations a great deal of their time and energy? Both social psychological analyses of motivation and analyses of organizational prestige are relevant here. The selections in Part C, "Interdependence and Coordination among Welfare Organizations," deal with the problems of coordinating agencies. Among welfare experts, there has long been an interest in achieving better coordination. However, there may also be conditions under which the costs of coordination are too great.

Section III, "Goals, Internal Organization, and Client Relations," deals with the problem of welfare organizations actually attempting to achieve their goals. How are welfare institutions organized? What are some of the crucial organizational dilemmas, and how are the goals of the organizations implemented? The articles in Part A, "Goal Setting and Organizational Requirements," serve as a bridge between the material in Section II and Section III. On the one hand, goals are set in relationship to external needs, community support, and in competition with other organizations. On the other hand, goal setting also reflects internal capabilities and leads to internal structures to achieve goals.

Part B of Section III, "Organizational Structure," presents material on the relationship of goals to structure and the relationship of organizational structure to workers' conceptions of their jobs. Part C, "Professions and Organizations," deals with the problem of integrating professionals with knowledge-based standards into organizations whose standards and methods of proceeding may be based on practical criteria that are different from those learned by professionals. This part also deals with some of the problems involved in professional change. The last two parts of Section III (Parts D and E) apply the material from the earlier parts (A to C) to the problem of the relationships between welfare organizations and their clientele. The articles in Part D, "Client Relations," focus on the general problem of welfare organization-client relations. The articles in Part E, "Social Welfare Organizations and Lower-Class Clientele," focus on the relationship of welfare organizations to clientele drawn from the lower, or working, class. These articles question the effectiveness of welfare organizations in reaching lower-class clientele, and suggest ways of increasing effective service. In the material on organization-client relations (Part D), we are concerned with the consequences of the organization of services for the clients *and* the consequences of different types of clients for the organization.

Taken together, the selections in this volume deal with many of the major sociological concepts necessary for the analysis of welfare institutions.

Before beginning Section I and our analysis of the articles in that section, we present an introductory article, "Conceptions of Social Welfare," by Harold L. Wilensky and Charles N. Lebeaux. It is a discussion of the conception of social welfare in an industrial society that is held by various scholars. The authors discuss the differences between a "residual" and an "institutional" view of the social welfare sector. The residual view sees welfare institutions as designed to handle the abnormal or pathological problems created by modern society, while the institutional view sees modern social welfare institutions as a means by which the society tries to insure individual fulfillment. Wilensky and Lebeaux delineate criteria for distinguishing welfare organizations from other kinds of organizations. Note that the two conceptions of social welfare discussed in this article are those used by people working in the welfare field, not by sociologists analyzing welfare institutions on theoretical grounds. Our purpose in including this article is to explore alternate ways of conceptualizing and delineating welfare institutions. The book in which this chapter appeared is a general treatment of urban-industrial society, the roots of its social problems, and the welfare response.

Conceptions of Social Welfare

Harold L. Wilensky and Charles N. Lebeaux

What is meant by social welfare? Is it relief, and just for the poor? Is social insurance included? What of public recreation and parks? And if these are social welfare, why not public highways and the Tennessee Valley Authority? How about private industry's pension plans? And what of fee-charging social agencies and the "private practice" of social work?

We are not concerned here with formulating a view of what social welfare ought ideally to involve, but rather with its existing outlines and trends in the United States. Specifically, we will: (1) point out what seem to be the currently dominant concepts of welfare, and (2) state some criteria for delineating social welfare. Later chapters will discuss the implications of the dominant American conceptions of social welfare for the services and for the professional practice of social work.

CURRENT CONCEPTIONS

Two conceptions of social welfare seem to be dominant in the United States today: the *residual* and the *institutional*. The first holds that social welfare institutions should come into play only when the normal structures of supply, the family and the market, break down. The second, in contrast, sees the welfare services as normal, "first line" functions of modern industrial society. These are the concepts around which drives for more or for less welfare service tend to focus. Not surprisingly, they derive from the ethos of the society in which they are found. They represent a compromise between the values of economic individualism and free enterprise on the one hand, and security, equality, and humanitarianism on the other. They are rather explicit among both social welfare professionals and the lay public.

The residual formulation is based on the premise that there are two "natural" channels through which an individual's needs are properly met:

Harold L. Wilensky and Charles N. Lebeaux, *Industrial Society and Social Welfare*, Chapter VI, "Conceptions of Social Welfare," Russell Sage Foundation: New York, 1958; Paperbound Edition, New York: The Free Press, A Division of Macmillan, 1965, pp. 138–147.

the family and the market economy. These are the preferred structures of supply. However, sometimes these institutions do not function adequately: family life is disrupted, depressions occur. Or sometimes the individual cannot make use of normal channels because of old age or illness. In such cases, according to this idea, a third mechanism of need fulfillment is brought into play—the social welfare structure. This is conceived as a residual agency, attending primarily to emergency functions, and is expected to withdraw when the regular social structure—the family and the economic system—is again working properly. Because of its residual, temporary, substitute characteristic, social welfare thus conceived often carries the stigma of "dole" or "charity."

The residual concept was more popular in the United States before the Great Depression of 1929 than it is now. That it is consistent with the traditional American ideology of individual responsibility and by-your-own-bootstrap progress is readily apparent. But it does not reflect the radical social changes accompanying advanced industrialization, or fully account for various aspects of contemporary social welfare activity.

The second major formulation of social welfare is given in a widely used social work textbook as "the organized system of social services and institutions, designed to aid individuals and groups to attain satisfying standards of life and health. It aims at personal and social relationships which permit individuals the fullest development of their capacities and the promotion of their well-being in harmony with the needs of the community." [1] This definition of the "institutional" view implies no stigma, no emergency, no "abnormalcy." Social welfare becomes accepted as a proper, legitimate function of modern industrial society in helping individuals achieve self-fulfillment. The complexity of modern life is recognized. The inability of the individual to provide fully for himself, or to meet all his needs in family and work settings, is considered a "normal" condition; and the helping agencies achieve "regular" institutional status.

---

[1] Friedlander, Walter A., *Introduction to Social Welfare,* Prentice-Hall, New York, 1955, p. 4. Cf. Kraus, Hertha, *Common Service Resources in a Free Society,* Association for the Study of Community Organization, New York, 1954 (mimeographed). This is a typically vague definition of the "institutional" view. Contemporary definitions of welfare are fuzzy because cultural values regarding the social responsibilities of government, business, and the individual are now in flux. The older doctrines of individualism, private property and free market, and of minimum government provided a clear-cut definition of welfare as "charity for unfortunates." The newer values of social democracy—security, equality, humanitarianism—undermine the notion of "unfortunate classes" in society. All people are regarded as having "needs" which *ipso facto* become a legitimate claim on the whole society. Business and government as channels to supply these needs have vastly broadened their responsibilities. Both the older and newer doctrines coexist today, creating conflicts and ambiguities in values which are reflected in loose definitions of social welfare.

While these two views seem antithetical, in practice American social work has tried to combine them, and current trends in social welfare represent a middle course. Those who lament the passing of the old order insist that the second ideology is undermining individual character and the national social structure. Those who bewail our failure to achieve utopia today, argue that the residual conception is an obstacle which must be removed before we can produce the good life for all. In our view, neither ideology exists in a vacuum; each is a reflection of the broader cultural and societal conditions described in Part I; and with further industrialization the second is likely to prevail.

CRITERIA FOR DELINEATING SOCIAL WELFARE

Keeping in mind this ideological dualism, we can now look at the substance of social welfare. What are the main distinguishing characteristics of activities which fall within the range of welfare practice in America today?[2]

1. Formal Organization

Social welfare activities are formally organized. Handouts and individual charity, though they may increase or decrease welfare, are not organized. Likewise, services and help extended within such mutual-aid relationships as family, friends and neighbors, kinship groups, and the like are not included in the definition of social welfare structure. It is recognized that there is a continuum running from the most informal to the most formal, and that in-between cases—the mutual-aid welfare services of a small labor union, church, or fraternal society—cannot be precisely classified. The distinction is clear in principle, however, and important.

Modern social welfare has really to be thought of as help given to the stranger, not to the person who by reason of personal bond commands it without asking. It assumes a degree of social distance between helped and helper. In this respect it is a social response to the shift from rural to urban-industrial society. Help given within the family or friendship group is but an aspect of the underlying relationship. Welfare services are a different kind of "help." We must think here of the regular, full-time, recognized agencies that carry on the welfare business.

[2] All institutions, of course, undergo change over time, both in form and function. However, some continuing identity is usually clear. Thus, the historical continuity and interconnection of social welfare institutions can be traced—from hospitals first designed as a place for the poor to die, to modern community hospitals serving the health needs of all; from sandpiles for the children of working mothers, to the tennis courts and baseball tournaments of a modern recreation program; from poorhouses to Social Security.

2. Social Sponsorship and Accountability

Social auspice—the existence of socially sanctioned purposes and methods, and formal accountability—is the crucial element in social welfare service versus comparable service under profit-making auspices. If mobilization of resources to meet needs is not accomplished by the family or through the market economy, some third type of organization must be provided, and this is typically the society as a whole acting through government (city, state, federal), or a smaller collectivity operating through a private social agency.[3]

Some mechanism for expressing the public interest and rendering the service accountable to the larger community is an essential part of social sponsorship. For public welfare services in a democratic society, the mechanism is simply the representative structure of government. For voluntary agencies accountability is typically, though less certainly, achieved through a governing board. That some of these boards are self-perpetuating, unresponsive to changing needs and isolated from constituencies, does not deny the principle of accountability, any more than oligarchy denies it in the public welfare arena. The principle is acknowledged in privately as well as publicly sponsored organizations.

3. Absence of Profit Motive as Dominant Program Purpose

Just as the needs-service cycle within the family is excluded from the concept of social welfare, so generally are those needs which arise and are fulfilled within the bounds of the free enterprise system. The services and goods produced by the market economy and purchased by individuals with money derived from competitive participation in that economy are not social welfare. Profitable and most fee-for-service activities are excluded. But there are cases difficult to classify.

Social welfare objectives can be intimately associated with what is basically profit-making enterprise, as when a private business provides recreation facilities, pension plans, or nurseries for its employees. The view may be taken, on the one hand, that since such services attend human wants quite peripheral to the purpose of the organization, they neither share in nor alter the nature of the underlying profit-making activity. The latter remains nonwelfare, while the former are essentially social welfare programs under business auspices. This view gains support from the observation that separate structures for the administration of welfare services often develop within the business enterprise, and constitute a kind of "social auspice." An industrial pension plan, for instance, usually has a trust fund separate from the financial operations of the company; a separate office with its own physical facilities will be set up

[3] United Nations, Department of Social Affairs, *Training for Social Work: An International Survey*, Columbia Univ. Press, New York, 1950, p. 13.

to administer it; the policy-making group—board or committee—will often have employee or union representation, especially if the plan is collectively bargained; and its operation will likely come under some degree of government regulation.

On the other hand, the view may be taken that industry-sponsored welfare programs are simply part of the conditions of employment, a substitute for wages. Industries provide restrooms and run recreational programs to compete for a labor supply and maintain employee morale and efficiency. Pensions, in this view, are a kind of deferred wage. Programs are often administered not through separate administrative offices, but by the business accounting or personnel office. Even when separate administrative structures are created, this does not alter the underlying program purpose of facilitating production.[4]

Thus, the degree to which an industrial welfare program may be considered social welfare varies inversely with extent of emphasis on a contractual relationship between two parties seeking a mutually rewarding arrangement, and directly with extent of social sponsorship and control. It is clear, nevertheless, that industrial welfare programs affect the development of social welfare institutions. The Supplemental Unemployment Benefits scheme, for instance, creates pressure for expanded unemployment insurance, and private pension plans are integrated with OASI in planning for retirement.

Some aspects of professional fee-for-service practice are also difficult to classify. Most Americans probably would think—and without derogatory implication—that professions as well as trades are primarily ways of making a living (often a kind of small business), and thus nonwelfare in nature. Yet it is a fact that many individual professional practitioners—physicians, lawyers, and dentists particularly—observe what appears to be a semi-social welfare practice of scaling fees according to ability to pay. Fee-scaling in private practice, however, is often a professional norm, part of a formal code of ethics. As such, its meaning and nature derive from a different context—professionalism—and it can be seen as a device by which a group with a monopoly of an indispensable service protects its fee-taking privilege. Where the professional "charges what the traffic will bear," there is no ambiguity, and his activity is clearly nonwelfare in nature.

To the extent that the private practice of social casework resembles other fee-for-service professions, it, too, is rather clearly outside the field

---

[4] It is true that men's motives vary; and businessmen are not an exception. What we are talking about here is not individual motives but organizational purposes. Many business leaders may acquire a sense of trusteeship going beyond their obligations to the shareholders. Thus, multi-plant companies have been known to avoid shutdown of an unprofitable unit because of major disruption to the local community. But one cannot say that the enterprise purpose is to save declining communities, any more than one can call dropping 50 cents in a blind man's hat Aid to the Blind.

of social welfare. Solo practice of social work is as yet so little developed, however, that it cannot be seen how close it will hew to the model of the other professions.

4. Functional Generalization: An Integrative View of Human Needs

Since almost any of the gamut of culturally conditioned human needs may be unmet and since human capacities which can be developed are many, welfare services to meet needs and enhance capacities will be varied. Placing babies in foster homes, operating a recreation program, administering social insurance, developing medical service in a rural community—the substantive activities here have little in common; a great variety of activities may take on a social welfare aspect. From the standpoint of the welfare structure as a whole, these activities are properly described as "functionally generalized"; that is, welfare services are found attached to, or performing in place of, medical institutions, the family, education, industry—wherever there is "unmet need." It will be noticed that this concept is closely related to that of residuality discussed above; what other institutions do not do, it is the job of welfare to do. To the extent that it is the function of social welfare to come in and "pick up the pieces" in any area of need, it must lack attachment to any given area.

From this characteristic derives, in part at least, the comprehensive view of human needs and personality that distinguishes social work from other professions. An international study by the United Nations of training for social work concludes that social work seeks to assist

> . . . individuals, families and groups in relation to the many social and economic forces by which they are affected, and differs in this respect from certain allied activities, such as health, education, religion, etc. The latter . . . tend to exclude all save certain specific aspects of the socio-economic environment from their purview. . . . The social worker, on the other hand, cannot exclude from his consideration any aspect of the life of the person who seeks help in solving problems of social adjustment . . . [or any] of the community's social institutions that might be of use to the individual. . . .[5]

Individual agencies are, of course, specialized and limited in function; but the welfare field is inclusive. It is because social welfare is "functionally generalized" that we exclude the school system, which tends to be segmental in its approach to its clientele.

5. Direct Concern with Human Consumption Needs

Finally, how are government welfare services to be distinguished from other government services, since all are socially sponsored? It is possible

[5] Ibid.

to place governmental activities on a continuum which ranges from services primarily concerned with the functional requisites of the society and only indirectly with the fate of the individual, to those which provide direct services to meet immediate consumption needs of individuals and families. At the "indirect" end of this continuum, following the analysis of Hazel Kyrk, are government activities "inherent in the nature of the state . . . such as the national defense, the preservation of law and order, the administration of justice, the exercise of regulatory functions. . . ." Intermediate are road building, flood control, forest conservation, and other such services, "the benefits of which are so remote in time or diffused among the population that they will not be privately provided." At the direct services end are those where "specific beneficiaries can be identified, although there are also general benefits. . . . Schools and universities, recreational facilities, libraries, museums, concerts, school books and lunches, subsidized housing, medical and hospital services. In this last group of services described are those which are distinctly for consumer use and enjoyment." [6]

In the last group fall the welfare services. Of course, social welfare programs serve the needs of both the larger social structure and the individual consumer. The unemployment compensation program in the United States, for example, has been designed as an anti-depression weapon as well as a means of alleviating the individual distress accompanying unemployment. But it is the latter, rather than the former, aspect of the program which from the present point of view qualifies it as a social welfare activity.

A nineteenth century view of government in the United States saw its functions restricted to "activities inherent in the nature of the state." The veto of Dorothea Dix's mental hospital bill in 1854, it will be remembered, was based on President Pierce's belief that the life conditions of individuals were no proper concern of government. Today many government services are directed specifically to individuals, and it is these which tend to be identified as social welfare.

[6] Kyrk, Hazel, *The Family in the American Economy*. University of Chicago Press, Chicago, 1953, pp. 148–49. An interesting parallel to the distinction Kyrk makes here has been noted with respect to Soviet state institutions where, since "everything is government," it might also be expected that everything would be social welfare. Sociologist Vucinich observes, however, that in the U.S.S.R.: "Soviet experts in jurisprudence make a sharp distinction between social institutions . . . and Soviet enterprises. Institutions (post offices, telegraphic services, scientific laboratories, schools, and the like) are, in the economic sense, nonproductive units which draw their funds from the state budgets and are not considered independent juridical persons. Enterprises, on the other hand, have their 'own' budgets . . . their 'own' basic capital (machines, tools, etc.) and working capital." Vucinich, Alexander S., *Soviet Economic Institutions: The Social Structure of Production Units*. Stanford University Press, Stanford, California, 1952, pp. 9–10.

It is thus an additional distinguishing attribute of social welfare programs that they tend to be aimed directly at the individual and his consumer interests, rather than at the general society and producer interests; that they are concerned with human resources as opposed to other kinds of resources. Soil conservation, subsidy of the merchant marine, development of water power resources, much as these redound ultimately to human welfare, are not typically defined as social welfare; but feeding the hungry, finding homes for dependent children, even provision of recreational facilities are so defined. This is the point of the stipulation in the definition of welfare given by Kraus,[7] that welfare services have "direct effects on welfare and health of individuals and families," and of Cassidy's definition of the social services as "those organized activities that are primarily and directly concerned with the conservation, the protection, and the improvement of human resources."[8]

In sum, the major traits which, taken together, distinguish social welfare structure in America (made explicit here as criteria to define the field of analysis) are:

1. Formal organization
2. Social sponsorship and accountability
3. Absence of profit motive as dominant program purpose
4. Functional generalization: integrative, rather than segmental, view of human needs
5. Direct focus on human consumption needs

The major weakness in definition occurs in the area of socially sponsored, nonprofit services which affect nearly everyone in the society. It would seem, for instance, that public education might be classed among the social services, as it is in England (and by a few American welfare experts, for example, Ida C. Merriam). In the U.S. there is apparently a tendency to exclude from the welfare category any service, no matter how identified with welfare it may have been in origin, which becomes highly developed, widespread in its incidence among the population, and professionally staffed by persons other than social workers. Helen Witmer notes social insurance as an example of a welfare service which has tended to move out of the welfare area after it became a "usual institutional arrangement."[9] This seems to be consistent with the residual conception and its view of the welfare services as emergency, secondary, peripheral to the main show. As the residual conception becomes weaker, as we

---

[7] At a meeting of the United States Committee of the International Conference of Social Work, New York City, June 17, 1955.

[8] Cassidy, Harry M., *Social Security and Reconstruction in Canada*, Bruce Humphries, Inc., Boston, 1943, p. 13.

[9] Witmers, Helen L., *Social Work: An Analysis of a Social Institution*, Farrar and Rinehart, New York, 1942, pp. 484–486.

believe it will, and the institutional conception increasingly dominant, it seems likely that distinctions between welfare and other types of social institutions will become more and more blurred. Under continuing industrialization all institutions will be oriented toward and evaluated in terms of social welfare aims. The "welfare state" will become the "welfare society," and both will be more reality than epithet.

Section I

The Historical and Societal Context of Welfare

Part A

The Historical Background of Modern Welfare

THE primary purpose of this section is to give analyses of the context in which welfare services develop and are administered, to provide a background understanding of the societal forces leading to the development of the contemporary welfare scene. At the same time, concepts are introduced which can be utilized to analyze current developments, both in American society and in other societies.

Modern society is an industrialized society, and the development of contemporary welfare institutions is directly linked to industrialization. First, as the level of industrialization increases, the over-all resources and standards of living increase. Thus, industrialization leads to higher minimum standards of human welfare. Higher minimum standards are reflected through the demands of potential recipients, professional groups, and the general public for greater welfare services. Second, as industrialization increases, many welfare functions that were previously handled by the family become the function of differentiated welfare institutions— "needs" that were previously met by the family, or not at all, become collective responsibilities. Third, as industrialization increases, the degree of societal interdependence and differentiation increases. On the one hand, welfare policies and programs become nationwide in scope. On the other hand, effective policies and programs must be adapted to the many types and categories of dependencies and needs created by the increased complexity of the social system.

Although industrialization and the companion process of urbanization lead to the growth of welfare institutions, the nature and timing of welfare developments are contingent on a host of historical, ideological, and structural patterns. In the first three parts of this section we examine the historical, ideological, and structural context of welfare in modern society.

The two articles in Part A, "The Historical Background of Modern Welfare," briefly set forth the historical context of the development of modern welfare. The first selection, "Shifting Attitudes," by Robert Bremner, discusses the changing attitudes toward poverty in the United States during the nineteenth century. This change in attitude preceded the widespread adoption of organized welfare services. As Bremner notes, there had to be shifts in the then-current political, economic, and religious thinking regarding the sources of and responsibility for the poverty of individuals before the society could attempt to alleviate poverty on a mass scale. As America changed from an agricultural to an industrial economy, and from a society with an open frontier to a settled urban society, professors, journalists, settlement workers, and ministers identified problems of poverty and their consequences, and by their publicity created the attitudinal conditions for social reforms.

In the second article, "The Welfare State in Historical Perspective," Asa Briggs analyzes the role of the state in welfare activities in Britain and, to a lesser extent, elsewhere. Starting with the assumption that it is historically naive to believe that the government's involvement in welfare is of recent origin, he traces the political processes which, in the nineteenth century, led to a government involvement in a wide range of welfare activities. He also examines the shifting standards of welfare and the changing definition of welfare problems.

Shifting Attitudes

Robert Bremner

> I think the best way of doing good to the poor, is, not making them
> easy *in* poverty, but leading or driving them *out* of it.
>
> BENJAMIN FRANKLIN, On the Price of Corn,
and Management of the Poor.

> Write a sermon on Blessed Poverty. Who have done all the good in the
> world? Poor men. "Poverty is a good hated by all men."
>
> RALPH WALDO EMERSON, Journals, entry for
May 12, 1832.

In the latter half of the nineteenth century the American attitude toward
poverty was a somewhat incongruous composite of two sharply contrasting points of view. Mindful of Christ's dictum, "The poor always ye have
with you," traditional religion taught that poverty was a visitation upon
men of God's incomprehensible but beneficent will. Although inescapable,
poverty was a blessing in disguise, for it inspired the rich to acts of loving
charity and led the poor into the paths of meekness, patience, and gratitude. In contradiction to these teachings American experience indicated
that poverty was unnecessary. When there was work for all, no man who
was willing to do his share need want. Indigence was simply the punishment meted out to the improvident by their own lack of industry and
efficiency. Far from being a blessed state, poverty was the obvious consequence of sloth and sinfulness.

More or less unconsciously the nineteenth-century American combined
these divergent views into a creed that ran approximately as follows:
Poverty is unnecessary (for Americans), but the varying ability and virtue
of men make its presence inevitable; this is a desirable state of affairs,
since without the fear of want the masses would not work and there would
be no incentive for the able to demonstrate their superiority; where it

Robert Bremner, "Shifting Attitudes," *From the Depths: The Discovery of Poverty in
the United States,* Chapter 2, New York University Press, Washington Square, N.Y.,
1956, pp. 16–30.

exists, poverty is usually a temporary problem and, both in its cause and cure, it is always an individual matter.

This creed both followed and departed from the traditional religious view. It accepted the inevitability of want and need but attributed their cause to man rather than to God. It recognized the value of differences in economic status, not so much as a spiritual discipline in generosity and humility, but as a goad to spur the ambitious to success and as a penalty for failure in the competitive struggle. It did not deny the obligation of the fortunate to aid the unfortunate, but it so emphasized the responsibility of each individual to look out for his own interests that it promoted a kind of social irresponsibility. Despite its hardheaded practicality, it left uncertain whether poverty was to be regarded as the soil from which Lincoln and Carnegie had sprung, or the breeding ground of the dangerous classes.

The individualistic interpretation of poverty, like its corollary the individualistic interpretation of wealth, was based on a revolutionary concept of man, society, and religion. It was not a new thing to exhort the masses to work; throughout the centuries toil had been their lot. By tradition, however, labor was an onerous duty attaching to the lowborn. It had never been highly regarded, well rewarded, or entirely free. The boast of Americans, the characteristic that made American life seem so vulgar to older civilizations, was that here, for almost the first time in history, labor was prized for its own sake. The promise of America was not affluence, but independence; not ease, but a chance to work for oneself, to be self-supporting, and to win esteem through hard and honest labor.

The gospel of self-help was well suited to the needs and circumstances of American life in the earlier part of the nineteenth century. Then, in a very real sense, a man's ability to take care of himself was a social asset, and inability to do so a liability. In sparsely settled, rapidly growing communities, where labor was scarce, there was substantial truth in the assumption that willingness to work brought material well-being, while failure implied some personal defect in the sufferer. The experience of countless immigrants and native-born Americans alike substantiated the national confidence in the common man's ability to achieve the good life through his own exertions. As one writer expressed it, the founding fathers may have intended the United States to be an asylum for the distressed peoples of the Old World; but it was a workhouse that they had prepared, not a refuge for idlers.[1]

The era of self-help in economics coincided with a similarly oriented period in religion. In the first half of the nineteenth century salvation through personal regeneration was a dynamic and still relatively novel theological doctrine. Americans embraced the belief that the door to heaven was open to all who made themselves worthy to enter with the same enthusiasm that characterized their faith in free enterprise and manhood suffrage. The new religious currents infused a spirit of optimism into discussions of economic no less than of religious questions. Previously the weight of ecclesiastical authority had more often than not been cast on the side of passive acceptance of inequality of status; for, as already suggested, the churches taught that providence decreed the existence of poverty among men. The Universalists, the Unitarians, and the numerous revivalistic sects, however, proclaimed that neither earthly want nor eternal damnation was foreordained for the masses of men. On the contrary, they asserted, just as any man could purify himself of sin, so he could purge himself of the bad habits that led to indigence.

Emancipation from the authoritarian puritanical theology and acceptance of religious creeds that emphasized the dignity and perfectibility of man loosed a tumult of energy for the cause of moral and humanitarian reform. It is not surprising that when this energy was directed toward the problem of poverty the initial impulse was to attack those individual vices, such as intemperance and immorality, that were regarded as barriers both to salvation and to temporal prosperity. Nor is it surprising that enlightened philanthropists in the nineteenth century should have deemed almsgiving as of less benefit to the poor than guidance into the path of morality and self-discipline.[2]

The individualistic interpretation of poverty began as a hopeful and essentially radical doctrine. Well before the end of the century, however, it had been converted into a formidable bulwark of that strange brand of conservatism espoused by the dominant business classes. Like the other principles of *laissez-faire* economics, the individualistic interpretation was given a supposedly scientific basis by the teachings of Herbert Spencer and his American disciples, and also by the early application of Darwinian biology to social thought. If, as the Spencerians and Social Darwinists asserted, competition was the law of life, there was no remedy for poverty except individual self-help. The poor who remained poor must pay the price exacted by nature from all the unfit. Any interference in their behalf, whether undertaken by the state or by unwise philanthropists, was not only pointless but absolutely dangerous. Protecting the weak in the struggle for existence would only permit them to multiply and could lead to no other result than a disastrous weakening of the species; it would thwart nature's plan of automatic, evolutionary progress toward higher forms of social life.[3]

Although the pseudoscientific assignments advanced to justify inequality and to condone misery never went unchallenged, the theory that poverty was caused exclusively by personal frailty was not easily supplanted. Endowed with a new aura of authority, this theory retained a loyal following long after the disappearance of the peculiar circumstances that had once given it a certain practical validity, and despite the emergence of conditions that strongly indicated the need for different hypotheses. For many years the problems of tenement dwellers in large cities, or of unemployed workmen in the breadlines, continued to be discussed as though the people involved were ne'er-do-wells in a frontier community. Nevertheless, under the impact of social and industrial changes the inadequacies and fallacies of the individualistic explanation became more obvious, and its critics gradually became more numerous and outspoken.

Herman Melville, writing in 1854, scoffed at the slander of the poor by the prosperous. "Of all the preposterous assumptions of humanity over humanity," he wrote, "nothing exceeds most of the criticisms made on the habits of the poor by the well-housed, well-warmed, and well-fed." In Melville's opinion, poverty was no blessing, actual or potential, but "a misery and infamy, which is, ever has been, and ever will be, precisely the same in India, England, and America." He felt that the mental anguish of the native American poor was more intense than that of any similar class in the rest of the world. This was because in the rich new land a sense of shame was attached to poverty, producing repugnance toward charity at all social levels; and also because there was an appreciation, on the part of the American poor, of "the smarting distinction between their ideal of universal equality and their grindstone experience of the practical misery and infamy of poverty. . . ." [4]

At the same time as Andrew Carnegie and Horatio Alger were preaching that poverty in youth was the key to prosperity in age, other observers were recalling Theodore Parker's warning that the destruction of the poor was their poverty. The findings of British students were quoted to prove that bitter need was a lesson in improvidence rather than in thrift; and that if intemperance led to poverty it was equally true that being poor drove men to drink.[5] Ira Steward, labor reformer and early advocate of the eight-hour workday, contended that "Poverty crams cities and their tenement houses with people whose conduct and votes endanger the republic." In his opinion, the problems that disturbed and perplexed mankind were incapable of solution while the masses remained poor.[6]

Americans long took comfort in the belief that the boundless opportunities offered by a rich and relatively unpeopled continent afforded a sure cure for the economic ills of the discontented classes. Orestes Brownson's warning, voiced in 1840, that the wilderness had receded so far that the new lands were already beyond the reach of the mere laborer, went unheeded.[7] Much more typical was the assurance given the Boston Society for the Prevention of Pauperism in 1844: "Untilled fields are around us; unhewn forests before; and growing villages and cities are springing up upon every side."[8] For half a century "the West" was the medicine prescribed for all those who wished to better their condition.

Joseph Kirkland's *Zury* (1888), although more consciously realistic than most pictures of frontier life, began in a characteristic vein:

> In the prairies, Nature has stored, and preserved thus far through the ages, more life-materials than she ever before amassed in the same space. It is all for man, but only for such men as can take it by courage and hold it by endurance. Many assailants are slain, many give up and fly, but he who is sufficiently brave, and strong, and faithful and fortunate, to maintain the fight to the end, has ample reward.[9]

Even as Kirkland wrote, however, "the myth of the garden" was being exposed to critical scrutiny. A contributor to *The Forum* dealt realistically with the practical obstacles that made it extremely unlikely that the masses in Eastern cities could improve their lot on Western homesteads; and Henry Demarest Lloyd declared in 1884: "Our young men can no longer go west; they must go up or down."[10]

Meanwhile, other critics denied the truth of another tenet of American individualism: the opportunity available to all to rise from a lower to a higher social class. The youthful John R. Commons declared in 1894:

> Class lines have become more rigid, and the individual, if his lot be in the unpropertied class, is destined, as a rule, to remain there. His economic resources determine, by relentless pressure, what shall be his social environment.[11]

Josiah Strong also contended that wealth and poverty were becoming more and more matters of inheritance and less and less products of character.[12] William Dean Howells took an even darker view of the situation. "Here and there one will release himself from it," he wrote of poverty, "and doubtless numbers are alway[s] doing this, as in the days of slavery there were always fugitives; but for the great mass captivity remains."[13]

It was particularly difficult for nineteenth-century Americans to accept the fact that in a complex economy individuals were no longer such independent agents as they had seemed to be but a few decades earlier. By the 1890's, however, numerous students were pointing out that not clerk nor factory hand nor farmer was as free as formerly to determine, by his own efforts, whether his labor would be well or ill rewarded, or even whether there would be a place for him in the productive processes of the nation. An impersonal element had invaded economics with the result that personal virtue, or the lack of it, counted for little in determining whether men were rich or poor. On the contrary, it was increasingly apparent that individuals suffered as often from the misdeeds and miscalculations of others as from their own failings. In the year before the panic of 1893 President E. B. Andrews of Brown University

wrote prophetically that the worst vice of modern industry was that it
frequently visited curses on men through events which they had no
part in originating. Under existing circumstances, said Andrews, "a great
many men are poor without the slightest economic demerit. They are
people who do the best they can, and always have done so. . . . Yet
they are poor, often very poor, never free from fear of want." [14] Josephine
Shaw Lowell wrote of the people rendered jobless by the depression of
1893 that the causes of their distress were "as much beyond their power
to avert as if they had been natural calamities of fire, flood, or storm." [15]

Hard times on the farm, where the heaviest work, the plainest living,
and the most abundant harvest sometimes brought but scant profit to the
cultivator of the soil gave many Americans firsthand experience with the
impersonal causes of poverty. Hamlin Garland's stories in *Main-Travelled
Roads* (1891) were peopled by men and women who, like Garland's own
parents, had nothing to show for years of drudgery except lined faces
and gnarled hands. In "Under the Lion's Paw" he told of a farmer who
saw the fruit of his toil consumed in one year by a plague of grasshoppers
and in another by the equally voracious greed of a land speculator.
Despite their traditional reliance on self-help, the farmers were among
the first occupational groups in the United States to renounce the individualistic interpretation. They saw and felt the effects of poverty-
producing factors with which individuals were unable to deal, not only in
natural disasters such as drought, but in railroad abuses, the sharp practices of middlemen and moneylenders, and in governmental currency and
fiscal policies. They did not hesitate to demand relief for sufferers from
the acts of God, regulation of private businesses that affected the public
welfare, and other legislation that ran counter to the assumed natural laws
of *laissez faire*.[16] The agrarian parties were the radical ones of the seven-
ties, eighties, and nineties because they proposed social remedies for the
impersonal forces that imposed hardship on a large proportion of the
nation's people.[17]

According to the creed of self-help it was as reprehensible to obtain
wealth without working for it as to be poor because of laziness. In practice, criticism of the idle rich was less frequently voiced than condemnation of the shiftless poor, but it was by no means lacking. In a novel
entitled *The Wreckers* (1886), George T. Dowling asserted that the most
dangerous elements in society were "the rich who do not know how to
use their riches." Several years later the author of an article in *Scribner's
Magazine* declared: "The opulent who are not rich by the results of their
own industry . . . suffer atrophy of virile and moral powers, and, like
paupers, live on the world's surplus without adding to it or giving any
fair equivalent for their maintenance." [18]

Grover Cleveland's vetoes of pension bills and his messages urging
reduction of tariff duties directed public attention, not only to the specific

issues at hand, but also to the broader question of the extent to which some persons profited through circumstances unrelated to their own merit. In his Fourth Annual Message, delivered after his defeat in the election of 1888, Cleveland told the Congress "We discover that the fortunes realized by our manufacturers are no longer solely the reward of sturdy industry and enlightened foresight, but that they result from the discriminating favor of the government and are largely built upon undue exactions from the masses of our people." Later in the same message he cautioned that

> . . . the communism of combined wealth and capital, the outgrowth of overweening cupidity and selfishness, which insidiously undermines the justice and integrity of free institutions, is not less dangerous than the communism of oppressed poverty and toil, which, exasperated by injustice and discontent, attacks with wild disorder the citadel of rule.[19]

Subsequently numerous critics of the plutocratic drift cited both the lavish bestowal of Civil War pensions and the granting to favored industries of unwarrantedly high tariff protection as largely responsible for the rise of "the pauper spirit" in American life.[20] The tariff controversy remained a heated one for many years and, by provoking a more critical study of the sources of wealth, fostered the development of a more realistic approach to the problem of poverty. By the turn of the century tariff reformers had convinced some Americans that the rich, to an even greater extent than the poor, were guilty of seeking "something for nothing."

No single figure in the last two decades of the nineteenth century was more successful than Henry George in arousing public opinion to an awareness of the social origins of wealth and poverty. Yet there was nothing new in his assertion that land values were created by the growth and needs of the community rather than by efforts of the proprietor; that was precisely the principle which canny land speculators had taken for granted ever since colonial days. Several years before the publication of *Progress and Poverty* (1879) the theory of unearned increment had been expounded in homespun dialect by a character in Edward Eggleston's popular novel *The Hoosier Schoolmaster:*

> Jack, he's wuth lots and gobs of money, all made out of Congress land. Jack didn't get rich by hard work. Bless you, no! Not him. That a'n't his way. Hard work a'n't, you know. 'Twas that air six hundred dollars he got along of me, all salted down into Flat Crick bottoms at a dollar and a quarter a acre. . . .[21]

George's contribution was to redirect attention from the individual benefits to the social consequences of private profit in land. He argued that permitting landlords to pocket the socially created value of land actually meant allowing them to take from the public wealth that properly belonged to the community as a whole. As a result, he said, the few were unmeritedly enriched, the many unjustly burdened. Furthermore, he continued, existing laws gave the owners of land and natural resources not only the legal right to fix the terms under which these necessities might be utilized, but also the power to hold them out of productive use. George believed that as long as these extraordinary powers resided in private hands it was inevitable that many citizens should experience involuntary and undeserved privation in the form of unemployment, inadequate wages, and extortionate rents.

The fact that George was an unusually eloquent advocate of free competition helps to explain why his diagnosis of society's ills won wide popular approval. His attack on private profit in land was not essentially different from the earlier *laissez-faire* economists' criticism of monopolies and other vested rights. Like them, George assumed that if monopolistic restraints on industry and trade could be removed, competition between free and unhampered individuals would work an automatic improvement in social conditions. Perhaps George differed from the earlier advocates of *laissez faire* mainly in the complete confidence he placed in competition as a beneficent and direct instrument for the welfare of all levels of society.[22]

The novelty of Georgian economics lay in its optimistic outlook and humanitarian bias. In no sense was George's influence more significant than in the conviction he inspired in the rising generation that poverty was abnormal—contrary to, rather than dictated by, natural law. To George involuntary poverty seemed, not an ineradicable problem, but, on the contrary, one that could be solved by simple and relatively painless social action. Even those who rejected the specific remedies he proposed were encouraged by his example to take up the fight against want.

Not only George's own writings but the protracted argument they excited between his supporters and opponents kindled new interest in all issues affecting human welfare. His contention that, despite all the material progress of the century, the rich were growing richer and the poor poorer provoked several pioneer efforts to estimate the distribution of property in the United States and the relative shares of the national income going to capital and labor. Although crude by later statistical standards, and generally unreliable since there was at the time no public or private registry of profits, these ventures were far from useless. If nothing else they revealed the need for more factual information on which to posit economic generalizations. In themselves they were evidences of the emergence of an objective, analytical approach to problems that had hitherto been looked at from an almost exclusively subjective and moralistic point of view.[23]

George's adulation of competition was not shared by some of the other students of social institutions who were his contemporaries. Felix Adler confessed that the Single Tax remedy—"a single draught of Socialism with unstinted individualism thereafter"—never attracted him.[24] Henry Demarest Lloyd, Edward Bellamy, George D. Herron, and William Dean Howells each expressed repugnance, not only for sharp business practices, but also for the selfishness which they thought underlay competitive economics. "We are not good enough or wise enough to be trusted with this power of ruining ourselves in the attempt to ruin others," cried Lloyd in 1884. Like the old antislavery agitator, Theodore Parker, Lloyd and the other critics of competitive capitalism insisted that the purpose of life was to live, not to amass property.[25] They rejected competition because they thought it produced an atmosphere of insecurity in which conscience and kindness were subordinated to the naked instinct of economy. The central idea of Edward Bellamy's *Looking Backward* (1888) was the comparison of a kindly and efficient cooperative society with a blundering, helplessly cruel competitive way of life. Helen Campbell, a forerunner of the muckrakers, wrote a series of newspaper articles on New York sweatshops in 1886 in which she cited instances of well-intentioned employers who were forced, by the intense competition prevailing in the needle trades, to choose between giving up their scruples and getting out of business.[26] E. B. Andrews pursued the same theme when he alleged that under competition one could not obey conscience without becoming a martyr. "The best men in a trade do not fix its maxims," he asserted, "but the worst. . . . Out of this murderous competition there is survival not of the fittest but of the unfittest, the sharpest, the basest." [27]

The moral objection to competition arose in large part from a feeling that such savage strife as individualism implied was not only unseemly, but unnecessary. Said George D. Herron: "There is enough in this world for all to have and enjoy in abundance, if there were a system by which there could be an equitable distribution of that abundance upon the principle of the divine economy." [28] To men such as Herron, who thought that capitalism was unchristian, the so-called personal causes of poverty appeared insignificant in comparison with the larger problem of a fantastically inefficient system of economics. "What other result can we expect under our present organization than that great numbers of persons should be poor?" "Our economic order is not intended to serve any social purpose, but only to enrich individuals." Poverty was far from seeming an insoluble problem to the Christian Socialists, but they did not expect any significant improvement in conditions until society saw fit to adopt a system of production and distribution better suited to its physical and ethical needs.

Those who opposed competition on ethical grounds scorned what seemed to them the parvenu conception of society as a mere bundle of distinct and irresponsible individuals. Instead, they gave their allegiance to the much older ideal of society as an organism. Not only religion, but also the realities of contemporary industrial society made them think it was necessary to regard society as a unit. Josiah Strong used the analogy of an ocean liner to illustrate the unity of social interest. If the steerage goes to the bottom, he said, so does the cabin; if pestilence rages among third-class passengers, first-class travelers cannot afford to be indifferent. "Modern civilization is fast getting us all into one boat," wrote Strong, "and we are beginning to learn how much we are concerned with the concerns of others. . . ." [29]

The emphasis they so often placed upon the organic unity of society helps to explain why even the most vigorous critics of contemporary social conditions at the turn of the century refused to endorse violent methods of eliminating the evils they denounced. The idea of competing classes was no less repugnant to them than that of competing individuals; and they were convinced that drastic and revolutionary purges were useless to remedy the ills of society. If a house has fallen into ruin, said Washington Gladden, the sensible course may well be to tear it down and build another. But society is not an inanimate thing; it is a living organism, more like a tree than a house. And if a tree is pining we cannot cure its sickness by overturning it. "It may need pruning, and its life may need invigorating by the addition of fertilizers to the soil in which it grows: it cannot be pulled down and rebuilt." [30]

Recognition of the unwholesome results of individualism in economics was accompanied by a lessening emphasis upon individualism in religion. In the earlier years of the century an authoritarian theology had been rejected in favor of a more democratic creed of salvation through individual regeneration. That change, as we have seen, had produced a zeal for the elimination of the personal vices that made salvation impossible. By the eighties and nineties it was becoming apparent that environmental factors and external economic pressures made the task of individual moral improvement extremely difficult. Even good men, pious church members, and solid citizens were seen to be involved in the impersonal cruelties dealt out by corporate enterprise. Rich and poor alike appeared, to some observers, at least, to be enmeshed in an amoral system that too often rewarded cunning more than character and made men indifferent to their fellows. At the end of the century Washington Gladden was telling Yale divinity students that "one man can no more be a Christian alone than one man can sing an oratorio alone"—and entitling the collected volume of his addresses to them *Social Salvation*.[31] Gladden's view, which was by no means peculiar to him, was that society, even more than individuals, stood in need of regeneration.

Earnest reformers such as Theodore Parker and Stephen Colwell had demanded just such a reorientation of religious approach even before the Civil War, but it was not until the last two decades of the century that any considerable number of Protestant clergymen began to devote their attentions to the various problems growing out of rapid industrial and urban growth. The social gospel which then emerged had its roots in the religio-humanitarian movements of a half century earlier. It was in part a conscious effort to counteract the alienation of the working class from organized religion.[32] Examined from a slightly different angle, however, the social gospel may be interpreted as an attempt by conscientious pastors to shake their predominantly middle-class congregations out of complacent self-righteousness and make them realize their own responsibility for social injustice. There are more important moral questions than Sabbath breaking, card playing, and intemperance, urged the followers of the social gospel. The conditions under which men and women work and the circumstances in which they spend their lives are moral questions, too. Gladden warned that unless the churches became thoroughly aroused about these issues and used their influence to promote fundamental reform, they would cease to be religious bodies and degenerate into institutions for the preservation of meaningless rites and superstitions.

The Roman Catholic Church, adhering more closely than the Protestant sects to the traditional religious interpretation of poverty, was frankly critical of individualism whether in religion or economics. Catholicism took poverty for granted; it did not deny that some men were impoverished by lives of sin or habits of improvidence; but it also recognized that others were permitted to live in indigence by the mysterious dispensation of God. To Catholics, man was at best a weak vessel; his failings were an object of pity and an outlet for charity rather than a cause for scorn. Although holding to the idea that poverty was permanent and ineradicable—and perhaps because of this belief—Catholic doctrine was more tolerantly disposed toward the poor than was the case in some of the more individualistic Protestant denominations. Moreover, in view of the predominance of working-class families in many Catholic congregations, influential Catholic leaders such as Cardinal Gibbons recognized that the Church could not afford to take an implacably hostile attitude toward labor unions and collective bargaining.[33] The papal encyclical on the condition of the working class, *Rerum novarum* (1891), condemned socialism and defended private property; but it also upheld the principle of unionism, sanctioned moderate social legislation, and denounced the tendency of *laissez faire* to treat labor as a commodity to be bought cheaply and used hard.[34]

Clergy and laymen of all denominations were inspired by the example of the Salvation Army to take a more sympathetic interest in the people at the bottom of the social heap. A Boston settlement worker, Robert A.

Woods, observed that "more than any other type of person in these days" members of General Booth's Army seemed "moved by a passion for the outcast and distressed." [35] The deeds of soldiers of the Army and of the bonneted lassies who moved "like sweet angels among the haunts of the lost" demonstrated to respectable folk that even the most desperate and vicious of the poor might be saved. No place was Godforsaken to the Army, no man or woman sunk so low as to be excluded from God's bounty.[36] In 1893 Josiah Strong wrote admiringly that "Probably during no hundred years in the history of the world have there been saved so many thieves, gamblers, drunkards, and prostitutes as during the past quarter of a century through the heroic faith and labors of the Salvation Army." [37] The Army's dramatic and apparently successful methods of dealing with the dangerous classes aroused new support for slum evangelization in the old-line churches. As will be shown in the next two chapters this work had not been wholly neglected before General Booth's organization came to the United States, but never before had the need and the opportunity been so effectively publicized.

No less significant than the impetus the Salvation Army's work gave to evangelical crusades was the interest it awakened in social reform. Charles R. Henderson, professor of sociology at the University of Chicago, saw in the Army's program a salutary reminder "that they who touch the soul must minister to the body, as Jesus did." [38] The publication in 1890 of General Booth's *In Darkest England* (ghost written by the journalist William T. Stead) did much to popularize the idea that the moral improvement of the poor was dependent upon the amelioration of their economic condition. This view, of course, was exactly the reverse of the individualistic assumption that if only the poor could be taught to lead moral lives their economic problems would disappear. The young economist Richard T. Ely hailed the book as "a trumpet blast calling men to action on behalf of the poorest and most degraded classes in modern society." [39] Booth himself was primarily concerned with the rescue of souls, but he insisted that as a first step "society, which by its habits, its customs, and its laws, has greased the slope down which these poor creatures slide to perdition," must be brought to mend its ways.[40]

At the close of the century political, economic, and religious influences were undermining popular allegiance to the individualistic interpretation of poverty. The idea that want was primarily the result of laziness, thriftlessness, and immorality was by no means moribund, but to a considerable body of Americans this view no longer seemed to square with the facts of real life. In its place there was emerging a more sympathetic attitude toward the poor which frequently described persons in need as victims rather than as culprits.

REFERENCES

1. Eugene Lawrence, "The New Year—The Poor," *Harper's Weekly*, XXVIII (1884), 35.
2. The contribution of religion to the reform philosophy of the 1830's and 1840's is discussed in Merle Curti, *The Growth of American Thought* (New York, 1943), pp. 380–82. On the influence of William Ellery Channing and Unitarianism on the "philanthropic renaissance" of the decade 1830–40 see Francis G. Peabody, "Unitarianism and Philanthropy," *The Charities Review*, V (1895–96), 25–26. Channing's views on the cause and cure of poverty are outlined in "On the Elevation of the Laboring Classes," *The Works of William E. Channing, D.D.* (Boston, 1889), pp. 58–60. There are interesting comments on the general problem of the relationship of religion to philanthropy in Henry Bradford Washburn, *The Religious Motive in Philanthropy* (Philadelphia, 1931), pp. 7–8 and 172.
3. On the influence of Spencer and the conservative Social Darwinists see Richard Hofstadter, *Social Darwinism in American Thought* (Philadelphia), 1944, pp. 18–37; and Stow Persons, ed., *Evolutionary Thought in America* (New Haven, 1950), particularly the essays by Robert E. L. Faris (pp. 160–80) and Edward S. Corwin (pp. 182–99).
4. "Poor Man's Pudding and Rich Man's Crumbs" in *The Complete Stories of Herman Melville*, ed. by Jay Leyda (New York, 1949), pp. 176–77. This story was originally published in *Harper's New Monthly Magazine*, June, 1854.
5. Theodore Parker, *Sermon on the Perishing Classes in Boston* (Boston, 1846), p. 10. Similar views are expressed in F. A. Walker, "The Causes of Poverty," *The Century Illustrated Monthly Magazine*, LV (1897–98), 216; and Carroll D. Wright, *Outline of Practical Sociology* (New York, 1899), p. 323. For British opinion see London Congregational Union, *The Bitter Cry of Outcast London, An Inquiry into the Condition of the Abject Poor* (Boston, 1883), p. 5; and John A. Hobson, *Problems of Poverty* (7th edition, London, 1909), p. 12. Hobson's book was first published in 1891.
6. Ira Steward, *Poverty* (Boston, 1873), p. 3.
7. Brownson's views are set forth and discussed in Arthur M. Schlesinger, Jr., *Orestes A. Brownson, A Pilgrim's Progress* (Boston, 1939), p. 91 and note 46, pp. 91–92.
8. R. C. Waterston, *An Address on Pauperism, Its Extent, Causes, and the Best Means of Prevention* (Boston, 1844), p. 10.
9. Joseph Kirkland, *Zury: The Meanest Man in Spring County. A Novel of Western Life* (Boston and New York, 1888), p. 1.
10. Rodney Welch, "Horace Greeley's Cure for Poverty," *The Forum*, VIII (1889–90), 586–93. Henry Demarest Lloyd, "The Lords of Industry," *North American Review*, CXXXVIII (1884), 552. The "Myth of the Garden" is examined in Henry Nash Smith, *Virgin Land. The American West as Symbol and Myth* (Cambridge, 1950), p. 189 *et seq.*
11. John R. Commons, *Social Reform and the Church* (New York, 1894), p. 34.
12. Josiah Strong, *The New Era or The Coming Kingdom* (New York, 1893), p. 156.
13. William Dean Howells, *Impressions and Experiences* (New York, 1896), p. 149.
14. E. B. Andrews, "The Social Plaint," *The New World*, I (1892), 206 and 212–13.
15. Josephine Shaw Lowell, "Methods of Relief for the Unemployed," *The Forum*, XVI (1893–94), 659.
16. The instructive series of legal decisions known as the Seed and Feed Cases, which reveals a gradually broadening concept of poverty as it affected farmers, is printed in Edith Abbott, *Public Assistance* (Chicago, 1940), pp. 73–96. On this

point see also Grover Cleveland's veto of a bill authorizing distribution of seeds to drought sufferers in Texas, February 16, 1887, in James D. Richardson, comp., *A Compilation of the Messages and Papers of the Presidents* (11 vols. [New York], 1910), VII, 5142–43.

17. There are interesting comments on agrarian attitudes toward political action in the late nineteenth century in Richard Hofstadter, *The Age of Reform* (New York, 1955), p. 46 *et seq.*

18. George T. Dowling, *The Wreckers: A Social Study* (Philadelphia, 1886), p. 224; and Oscar Craig, "The Prevention of Pauperism," *Scribner's Magazine,* XIV (1893), 121.

19. Richardson, comp., *A Compilation of the Messages and Papers of the Presidents,* VII, 5359 and 5361.

20. Richard T. Ely, *Problems of Today. A Discussion of Protective Tariffs, Taxation and Monopolies* (3rd edition, New York, 1890), p. 65; and Washington Gladden, "The Problems of Poverty," *The Century,* XLV (1892–93), 256.

21. Edward Eggleston, *The Hoosier Schoolmaster* (New York, 1871), p. 29.

22. The main ideas of George's *Progress and Poverty* are analyzed in Charles Albro Barker, *Henry George* (New York, 1955), pp. 265–304.

23. Thomas G. Shearman defended George's position in *The Forum,* VIII (1889–90), 40–52 and 262–73. For the contrary view of Edward Atkinson see Harold Francis Williamson, *Edward Atkinson, The Biography of an American Liberal, 1827–1905* (Boston, 1934), pp. 260–66. See also Strong, *New Era,* pp. 151–52; and Andrews, "The Social Plaint," p. 209.

24. Felix Adler, *An Ethical Philosophy of Life Presented in Its Main Outlines* (New York, 1929), p. 44.

25. Lloyd, "The Lords of Industry," p. 552. For a discussion of Theodore Parker's attitude toward competition and other economic issues see Daniel Aaron, *Men of Good Hope. A Story of American Progressives* (New York, 1951), pp. 38–50.

26. Helen Stuart Campbell, *Prisoners of Poverty* (Boston, 1887), pp. 254–55. This book is a compilation of Mrs. Campbell's articles which first appeared in the *New York Daily Tribune* on October 24, 1886, and at weekly intervals thereafter.

27. Andrews, "The Social Plaint," 215.

28. George D. Herron, *The New Redemption* (New York, 1893), p. 29.

29. Strong, *The New Era,* p. 347.

30. Washington Gladden, *Social Salvation* (Boston and New York, 1902), p. 5.

31. *Ibid.,* p. 7.

32. The development of the social gospel is treated in Aaron Ignatius Abell, *The Urban Impact on American Protestantism, 1865–1900* (Cambridge, 1943); Charles Howard Hopkins, *The Rise of the Social Gospel in American Protestantism, 1865–1915* (New Haven, 1940); and Henry F. May, *Protestant Churches and Industrial America* (New York, 1949).

33. On this point see Henry J. Browne, *The Catholic Church and the Knights of Labor* (Washington, D.C., 1949).

34. *Rerum novarum* is printed in Donald O. Wagner, *Social Reformers* (New York, 1947), pp. 617–37. For comment on the encyclical see Jacques Maritain, *Ransoming the Time* (New York, 1941), p. 208; Arthur Mann, *Yankee Reformers in the Urban Age* (Cambridge, 1954), pp. 47–48; and Harvey Wish, *Society and Thought in Modern America* (New York, 1952), p. 171.

35. Robert A. Woods, "The Social Awakening in London," *Scribner's Magazine,* XI (1892), 407.

36. On the refusal of the Salvation Army to discriminate between the worthy and the unworthy, see St. John Ervine, *God's Soldier: General William Booth* (2

vols., New York, 1935), II, 709; and Walter Besant, *The Autobiography of Sir Walter Besant* (New York, 1902), pp. 256–60.

37. Strong, *The New Era*, pp. 351–52.
38. Charles Richmond Henderson, *The Social Spirit in America* (Chicago, 1905), p. 319. This book was first published in 1897.
39. Richard T. Ely, "Pauperism in the United States," *North American Review*, CLII (1891), p. 395.
40. William Booth, *In Darkest England and the Way Out* (London, 1890), p. 48.

The Welfare State in Historical Perspective

Asa Briggs

I

The phrase "welfare state" is of recent origin. It was first used to describe Labour Britain after 1945. From Britain the phrase made its way round the world. It was freely employed, usually but not exclusively by politicians and journalists, in relation to diverse societies at diverse stages of development. Historians also took over the phrase. Attempts were made to re-write nineteenth and twentieth century history, particularly British history, in terms of the "origins" and "development" of a "welfare state."

Much of the political talk and the international journalism was loose and diffuse. The phrase "welfare state" was seldom defined. It was used to cover both social and economic changes. Among the social changes the demand for more comprehensive social security—"freedom from want" —was linked, often with little thought, with the demand for greater "equality of opportunity" through educational reform. The differences between the two goals, differences which had been noted by earlier writers, were not usually stressed. It was only in the aftermath of change that the social implications of "meritocracy" were disentangled from the social implications of other aspects of legislation. There was confusion also on critical issues concerning social change and economic power. The most important economic changes which found a place in British

Asa Briggs, "The Welfare State in Historical Perspective," *European Journal of Sociology*, Vol. 2, No. 2, 1961, pp. 221–258.

"definitions" of the "welfare state" were those which seemed to entail direct and immediate social consequences—the "abolition of poverty" and the "conquest of unemployment."

The historical writing dwelt primarily on the contrast between the nineteenth and twentieth centuries. The "night-watchman state," condemned by Lassalle, had become as obsolescent, it was argued, as *laissez faire* itself. Emphasis on "political rights" had given way naturally, as the nineteenth century went by, to the demand for "social rights." The year 1848 was a landmark on the continent: Chartism was a landmark movement in Britain. Democracy had become completely meaningful only as it had taken the form of "social democracy." "Welfare states" were fruits of "social democracy." One strain in this historiography was a modern counterpart of the "Whig" historiography of nineteenth-century Britain with the concept of "welfare" substituted for the concept of representative government. The past was seen as leading inevitably and inexorably along a broad highway with the "welfare state" as its destination.

Already the early journalism appears dated and the history looks slanted. Increasing emphasis has recently been placed in Britain, the home of the phrase, on the contemporary social influence not of legislation but of an affluent market economy. Both critics and admirers of the welfare state have been driven to concern themselves with "affluence." There has been talk of "myths" of the "welfare state," including a "myth of the welfare state for the working classes" which has persuaded (against much factual evidence) both politicians and voters that most, if not all, contemporary social problems have been solved since 1945. The inhibiting effects of the "myth" have received as much attention from critics as the liberating effects of the legislation. At the same time recent writings from all sides make it abundantly clear that the ideals which inspired the achievement of a "welfare state" are now no longer universally shared. Comprehensive notions of a "welfare state" based on complete "equality of citizenship" no longer receive universal assent (or lip service). Against a background of recurring fiscal crises, "paying for services" has replaced "fair shares for all" as a current political slogan. The switch may only be temporary and it has already met with resistance, but it is a sign that what only recently seemed to be fixed is far from fixed, that the post-1945 "welfare state" was not in itself a final destination. "Beyond the welfare state" has become a slogan for socialists. On the other side a number of writers, some of them influential, have reverted to older and more limited ideas of a "social service state" where limited services are provided for a limited section of the population. That section is the least well-off section of the community. The state services liquidate themselves, it is claimed, as more and more people rise above the level of a minimum standard of living to reach "freedom" to buy for themselves the services (health, education, etc.) which they want.

While political attitudes have been changing not only in Britain but even more markedly in other parts of the world, a small number of British historians and sociologists have begun to make a more searching examination of the "background" and "benefits" of the "welfare state." As a result of their continuing labours, the significance of each of the great "turning points" of British "welfare state" history is already being re-assessed. The stark contrast between the nineteenth and twentieth centuries has been qualified. Landmark legislation such as the National Health Insurance Act of 1911, which hitherto had been treated generally or symbolically, has been re-interpreted in the light of newly discovered or hitherto neglected evidence. The pressures have been more carefully scrutinized, and the setbacks have been examined as well as the successes. Many of the "reforms" were designated as remedies for specific problems: they were certainly not thought of as contributions to a "trend" or a "movement." The sources of inspiration were multiple—socialism was only one of several strands—and this very multiplicity added to later complications and confusions. The old poor law, from which social services emerged both directly and by reaction, was not so much broken up, as its critics had wished, as eroded away by depression, war, unemployment and the introduction piecemeal of remedial legislation. The social welfare legislation of the Labour government of 1945–50, the climax of fifty years of social and political history, has itself begun to be viewed historically. The pre-suppositions which underlay it can now be seen to have been the products of a particular set of circumstances, circumstances which have already changed. Among those circumstances the experience of war seems to have been as relevant as the appeal of socialism in determining the practicability and the popularity of introducing comprehensive welfare proposals.

So far, however, the re-interpretation and the rewriting have largely been insular. Relatively little attention has been paid, in consequence, to the comparative history of welfare legislation. Specialists in social administration have collected comparative data, but they have naturally enough used them more frequently for practical than for historical purposes. The "uniqueness" of Britain has been emphasized to the neglect of the study of trends and tendencies in other countries.

In certain respects British experience has been unique, as foreign writers as different as Halévy and Schumpeter, have recognized. The uniqueness can only be appreciated, however, when the experience of several countries is taken into account. The trends and tendencies which led journalists, politicians and historians to apply the label "welfare state" to Britain may be noted in all modern industrialised communities. They have influenced non-industrialised communities also. The "causes" of the "welfare state," as of nineteenth-century *Sozialpolitik*, are to be found, therefore, in far more general phenomena than the programmes of the

British Labour party or the persistent prodding of the British "liberal conscience."

It was the International Labour Office, a mine of invaluable factual information and a source of inspiration in international social service development, which noted in 1950 at a time when the term "welfare state" was being generally applied to Britain, that a "new conception" was transforming the pre-war systems of social insurance in many countries. "There is a movement everywhere," one of its reports stated, "towards including additional classes of the population, covering a wider range of contingencies, providing benefits more nearly adequate to needs and removing anomalies among them, loosening the tie between benefit right and contribution payment, and, in general, unifying the finance and administration of branches hitherto separate." [1] In other words, a "quest for universality" was transforming the pre-war "social service state" into some kind of "welfare state."

The "new conception" reflected changing attitudes towards citizenship as well as changing views about the proper role of the state. Some of these attitudes and views had taken shape during the Second World War when talk of "four freedoms" was thought to have universal application, and the International Labour Conference at Philadelphia in 1944 dwelt on "the deep desire of men to free themselves from the fear of want." "The meaning which can be given to 'international society,' it was argued, will be judged in terms of human benefit and welfare." [2] The I.L.O. report of 1950 went on to state that "the transformation of social insurance is accompanied by the absorption or coordination of social assistance, and there begins to emerge a new organization for social security, which we can describe only as a public service for the citizenry at large. This new organization now concerns society as a whole, though it is primarily directed to the welfare of the workers and their families. It tends, therefore, to become a part of national government, and social security policy accordingly becomes coordinated closely with national policy for raising the standard of welfare and, in particular, for promoting the vitality of the population."

This international report touches on matters which had already been discussed at length in British contexts. During the Second World War, the historian of British social policy writes, "it was increasingly regarded as a proper function or even obligation of government to ward off dis-

---

[1] I.L.O., International Labour Conference, 34th Session, *Objectives and Minimum Standards of Social Security* (1950), pp. 3–4. See also "Survey of Post-War Trends in Social Security" in *International Labour Review,* June, July, August, September, 1949.

[2] I.L.O., *Approaches to Social Security* (1942), p. i; *Objectives and Advanced Standards of Social Security* (1952); D. Thomson, A. Briggs, E. Meyer, *Patterns of Peacemaking* (1945), p. 340, ch. VII, appendix II.

tress and strain not only among the poor but among all classes of society. And because the area of responsibility had so perceptibly widened, it was no longer thought sufficient to provide through various branches of social assistance a standard of service hitherto considered appropriate for those in receipt of poor assistance." [3] The disassociation of "welfare" from poor law stigmas inevitably meant a raising of standards. Concern for the "citizenry at large" meant taking account of democratic demands not simply seeking to satisfy assessed needs.

There were many instances in Britain of changing notions of what was "appropriate." One of the most striking was a revolution in school meals policy. School meals had developed during the nineteenth century as a charitable service for "necessitous children" (private charity outside the scope of the poor law). The private charities providing them were at pains to make sure that they were not catering for the children of "undeserving and worthless parents." [4] The Education (Provision of Meals) Act of 1906, which brought the state directly into this area of social welfare policy, was a highly controversial measure. It drove A. V. Dicey, the noted British lawyer and writer, to complain that it was altogether wrong that fathers of children fed by the state should retain the right of voting for members of parliament. "Why a man who first neglects his duty as a father and then defrauds the state should retain his full political rights," he went on tendentiously, "is a question easier to ask than to answer." [5] Dicey, like a number of his conservative contemporaries, was concerned that social service legislation would follow a "slippery slope" in which each generation would fall more sharply than its predecessor. The statesmen who had passed the Education Act of 1870, creating the first public-provided schools, would probably have been quite unwilling to have passed the 1891 Act relieving parents of the necessity for paying for any part of their children's elementary education. The people who passed the 1891 Act would in their turn have baulked at the School Meals Act of 1906. Dicey was right in implying that the men of 1906 would certainly have stopped far short of the "school meals revolution" of the Second World War. A Board of Education circular of 1941 completely abandoned old precepts that cheap school meals should be provided only to children who were both "necessitous" and "undernourished." Already during the previous year the number of school meals provided had doubled. By 1945 1,650,000 dinners were taken on every school day in England and Wales, about fourteen percent being free and the rest costing the parents a nominal sum. This figure compared with 130,000 in 1940 and 143,000 in the depressed conditions of the mid-1930s. In

---

[3] R. M. Titmuss, *Problems of Social Policy* (1950), p. 506.
[4] C. L. Mowat, *The Charity Organization Society, 1869–1913* (1961), p. 75.
[5] A. V. Dicey, *Law and Public Opinion in England during the Nineteenth Century* (1914 edn.), p. 1.

round figures one child in three was fed at school in 1945 in place of one
child in thirty in 1940.

The distribution of milk, fruit juice and "welfare foods" was regulated
on social grounds throughout the Second World War. The same principles were carried from nutritional policy to social security policy.[6] "In
a matter so fundamental," a government White Paper of 1944 stated, "it
is right for all citizens to stand in together, without exclusion based on
differences of status, function or wealth."[7] The argument was not simply
that administrative problems would be simplified if structures were "comprehensive" or "universal" but that through "universal schemes" "concrete expression" would be given to the "solidarity and unity of the
nation, which in war has been its bulwark against aggression and in
peace will be its guarantee of success in the fight against individual want
and mischance."

This White Paper, like the equally significant White Paper of 1944
(Cd. 6527) accepting the need for social action to prevent unemployment, was the product of a coalition government, pledged to national
unity. The strains and stresses of total war forced politicians to consider
the "community" as a whole: the hopes of "re-construction" (the term
was used with particular fervour during the First World War) were held
out to inspire the public in years of trial. There was thus a close association between warfare and welfare. Moreover, the knowledge that large
sums of money, raised through taxation at a level without precedent,
were being used to wage war led without difficulty to the conclusion that
smaller sums of money could produce a "welfare state" in times of peace.
All parties were interested in this line of argument. The Conservative
partner in the war-time coalition, the predominant political partner,
published as late as 1949 a pamphlet, *The Right Road for Britain*, which
stated unequivocally that "the social services are no longer even in theory
a form of poor relief. They are a cooperative system of mutual aid and
self-help provided by the whole nation and designed to give to all the
basic minimum of security, of housing, of opportunity, of employment
and of living standards below which our duty to one another forbids us
to permit any one to fall."

By 1949, when this pamphlet was published, the legislation introduced
by the Labour government of 1945 to 1950, particularly the health service
legislation, was freely talked of as "welfare state" legislation. Much of
it went beyond the ideas of "comprehensiveness" or "cooperation" as such
and reflected socialist philosophies of "equality." Attempts had been
made to raise the standards of service to meet the claims of "equal citi-

[6] Titmuss, *op. cit.* pp. 509–10.
[7] Cd. 6550 (1944) § 8, § 33. See also Cd. 6404 (1942) and A. Briggs, "The Social
Services" in *The British Economy, 1945–50* (ed. G. D. N. Worswick and P. Ady,
1952), pp. 365–80.

zenship." "Homes, health, education and social security, these are your birthright," exclaimed Aneurin Bevan. Sociologists as well as socialists explained the new policies in terms of the fabric of citizenship. Hitherto, they suggested, social service policy had been thought of as a remedial policy to deal with the basement of society, not with its upper floors. Now the purpose was extended. "It has begun to re-model the whole building, T. H. Marshall wrote in 1949, and it might even end by converting a skyscraper into a bungalow" or at least into a "bungalow surmounted by an architecturally insignificant turret." [8]

The changes in mood since 1949 have already been noted: they can be explained in narrowly fiscal or broadly socio-political terms and they constitute the background of current controversies. The object of this paper is to go back beyond the current controversies, beyond the relatively recent experience of total war, to the historical matrix within which the idea of a "welfare state" has taken form. Before going back in time, however, it is necessary to attempt a more precise definition of the term "welfare state" than has been common in recent discussions. And the definition itself will suggest certain interesting and relevant lines of historical enquiry.

II

A "welfare state" is a state in which organized power is deliberately used (through politics and administration) in an effort to modify the play of market forces in at least three directions—first, by guaranteeing individuals and families a minimum income irrespective of the market value of their work or their property; second, by narrowing the extent of insecurity by enabling individuals and families to meet certain "social contingencies" (for example, sickness, old age and unemployment) which lead otherwise to individual and family crises; and third, by ensuring that all citizens without distinction of status or class are offered the best standards available in relation to a certain agreed range of social services.

The first and second of these objects may be accomplished, in part at least, by what used to be called a "social service state," a state in which communal resources are employed to abate poverty and to assist those in distress. The third objective, however, goes beyond the aims of a "social service state." It brings in the idea of the "optimum" rather than the older idea of the "minimum." It is concerned not merely with abatement of class differences or the needs of scheduled groups but with equality of treatment and the aspirations of citizens as voters with equal shares of electoral power.

Merely to define the phrase "welfare state" in this way points to a number of historical considerations, which are the theme of this article.

[8] T. H. Marshall, *Citizenship and Social Class* (1949), pp. 47 and 48.

First, the conception of "market forces" sets the problems of the "welfare state" (and of "welfare") within the context of the age of modern political economy. In societies without market economies, the problem of "welfare" raises quite different issues. Within the context of the age of modern political economy an attempt has been made, and is still being made, to create and maintain a self-regulating system of markets, including markets in the fictitious commodities, land, money and labour. The multiple motives lying behind the attempt to control these markets require careful and penetrating analysis.

Second, the conception of "social contingencies" is strongly influenced by the experience of industrialism. Sickness, old age and death entail hardships in any kind of society. Ancient systems of law and morality include precepts designed to diminish these hardships, precepts based, for example, on the obligations of sons to support their parents or on the claims of charity, *obsequium religionis*. Unemployment, however, at least in the form in which it is thought of as a social contingency, is a product of industrial societies, and it is unemployment more than any other social contingency which has determined the shape and timing of modern "welfare" legislation. Before the advent of mass unemployment, "unemployability," the inability of individuals to secure their livelihood by work, was a key subject in the protracted debates on poor law policy. The existence of "chronic unemployment," structural or cyclical, has been a powerful spur from the nineteenth century onwards leading organized labour groups to pass from concentration on sectional interests to the consideration of "social rights" of workers as a class; to philanthropic businessmen wishing to improve the "efficiency" and strengthen the "social justice" of the business system; and to politicians and governments anxious to avoid what seemed to be dangerous political consequences of unemployment. The memories of chronic unemployment in the inter-war years and the discovery of what it was believed were new techniques of controlling it reinforced "welfare state" policies in many countries after the Second World War.

Third, the idea of using organized power (through politics and administration) to determine the pattern of welfare services requires careful historical dating. Why not rely for "welfare" on the family, the church, "charity," "self help," "mutual aid" (gild, trade union, friendly society) or "fringe benefits" (business itself)? Whole philosophies of "welfare" have been founded on each of these ideas or institutions: often the philosophies and the interests sustaining them have been inimical to the suggestion that the state itself should intervene. The possibility of using governmental power has been related in each country to the balance of economic and social forces; estimates of the proper functions and, true or false, of the available resources of the state; effective techniques of influence and control, resting on knowledge (including expert knowledge); and, not least, the prevalence (or absence) of the conviction that societies can be shaped by conscious policies designed to eliminate "abuses" which in earlier generations had been accepted as "inevitable" features of the human condition.

Not only does the weighting of each of these factors vary from period to period, but it also varies from place to place. It was Bentham, scarcely distinguished for his historical sense, who in distinguishing between *agenda* (tasks of government) and *sponte acta* (unplanned decisions of individuals) wrote that "in England abundance of useful things are done by individuals which in other countries are done either by government or not at all . . . [while] in Russia, under Peter the Great, the list of *sponte acta* being a blank, that of *agenda* was proportionately abundant." [9] This contrast was noted by many other writers later in the nineteenth century, just as an opposite contrast between Britain and the United States was often noted after 1945.

If the question of what constitutes "welfare" involves detailed examination of the nature and approach to "social contingencies," the question of why the state rather than some other agency becomes the main instrument of "welfare" involves very detailed examination of a whole range of historical circumstances. The answer to the question is complicated, moreover, by differences of attitude in different countries, to the idea of "the state" itself. Given these differences, a translation of basic terms into different languages raises difficulties which politicians and journalists may well have obscured. For example, is the term *Wohlfahrtsstaat* the right translation of "welfare state"? British and German approaches to "the state" have been so different that they have absorbed the intellectual energy of generations of political scientists. In the nineteenth century there were somewhat similar difficulties (although on a smaller scale) surrounding the translation of the British term "self help." A French translator of Samuel Smiles's book of that title (1859) said that the term "self help" was "*à peu près intraduisible.*"

Fourth, the "range of agreed social services" set out in the provisional definition of "welfare state" is a shifting range. Policies, despite the finalism of much of the post-1945 criticism, are never fixed for all time. What at various times was considered to be a proper range shifts, as Dicey showed, and consequently must be examined historically. So too must changing areas of agreement and conflict. Public health was once a highly controversial issue in European societies: it still is in some other societies. The "sanitary idea" was rightly regarded by the pioneers of public health as an idea which had large and far-reaching chains of consequences. It marked an assault on "fate" which would be bound to lead

[9] J. Bentham, *Works* (ed. J. Bowring, 1843), vol. III, p. 35. Cf. J. M. Keynes's view of the "agenda" of the state in *The End of Laissez Faire* (1926).

to other assaults. Public health, in the administrative sphere of drains, sewers and basic "environmental" services, has been taken outside the politics of conflict in Britain and other places, but personal health services remain controversial. There is controversy, very bitter indeed in the United States, not only about the range of services and who shall enjoy them but about the means of providing them. The choice of means influences all "welfare state" history. "Welfare states" can and do employ a remarkable variety of instruments, such as social insurance, direct provision in cash or in kind, subsidy, partnership with other agencies, including private business agencies, and action through local authorities. In health policy alone, although medical knowledge is the same in all countries of the West and the same illnesses are likely to be treated in much the same kind of way, there is a remarkable diversity of procedures and institutions even in countries which make extensive public provision for personal health services.

Fifth, there are important historical considerations to take into account in tracing the relationship between the three different directions of public intervention in the free (or partially free) market. The demand for "minimum standards" can be related to a particular set of cumulative pressures. Long before the Webbs urged the need in 1909 for government action to secure "an enforced minimum of civilised life," the case for particular minima had been powerfully advocated. Yet the idea of basing social policy as a whole on a public commitment to "minimum" standards did not become practical politics in Britain until the so-called "Beveridge revolution" of the Second World War. The third direction of "welfare" policy, and the distinctive direction of the "welfare state," can be understood only in terms of older logic and more recent history. The idea of separating "welfare" policy from "subsistence" standards (the old minima, however measured) and relating it to "acceptable" standards ("usual work income") provides an indication of the extent to which "primary poverty" has been reduced in "affluent societies." It may be related, however, to older ideas of equality, some of which would lead direct not to state intervention in the market but to the elimination of the market altogether, at least as a force influencing human relationships. A consideration of the contemporary debate is more rewarding if it is grounded in history.

III

Each of these five historical considerations deserves fuller treatment. The texture is often complex. There have been markedly different chronologies of development and different answers have been given in different countries to the same set of leading questions.

By the end of the nineteenth and the beginning of the twentieth century there had been a general reaction against attempts to maintain self-regulating systems of markets. This reaction has been variously described as "the decline of liberalism," "the advent of collectivism" and "the rise of socialism." Fabian writers, who are particularly illuminating on these themes, used all three labels, and after painting a grim picture of a period of capitalist anarchy in the early nineteenth century went on to show how

> in the teeth of the current Political Economy, and in spite of all the efforts of the millowning Liberals, England was compelled to put forth her hand to succour and protect her weaker members [. . .] Slice after slice has gradually been cut from the profits of capital, and thereby from its selling value, by strictly beneficial restrictions on the user's liberty to do what he likes with it [. . .] On every side he is being registered, inspected, controlled, and eventually superseded by the community [. . .] All this has been done by "practical men," ignorant, that is to say, of any scientific sociology, believing Socialism to be the most foolish of dreams [. . .] Such is the irresistible sweep of social tendencies, that in their every act they worked to bring about the very Socialism they despised.[10]

In outlining this development of "our unconscious Socialism" Sidney Webb directed attention to the efforts both of "individuals" and of "municipalities" before he turned explicitly to the state. The "masses" were kept in the background, vague and undifferentiated. So too were the trade unions, the importance of which he discovered only a few years later. The main emphasis was placed on the power of the ballot box as it was by revisionists on the continent. It might have been foreseen, Webb remarked (and it had indeed been foreseen by men like Bagehot), that "individualism could not survive their (the working classes) advent to political power." "Unconscious" or later "conscious" socialism was the necessary corollary of political democracy. The result would necessarily be the emergence of a more active state.

The analysis was historically significant but limited in depth. Another of the Fabian essayists, Hubert Bland, pointed out by implication three of Webb's superficialities. First, state control did not imply socialism, conscious or unconscious. "It is not so much to the thing the State does as to the end for which it does it that we must look before we decide whether it is a Socialist State or not." Sixpenny telegrams organised by a state-run Post Office had nothing to do with socialism or "welfare" in the "welfare state" sense. Second, and in writing in this way Bland was exceptionally percipient about the shape of the future, "it is quite certain that the social programme of our party will become a great fact long before the purely political proposals of the Liberals have received the

10 S. Webb, in *Fabian Essays* ([1889] 1948 edn.), p. 43, p. 46.

royal assent." Third, and here Bland was a better historian than Webb, there had been a far less sharp break than Webb had suggested between the "period of anarchy" of the early nineteenth century and "the present." There was certainly no one single landmark, like Mill's *Political Economy* (1848), which provided a frontier post between an age of individualism on one side and an age of socialism on the other. "There never has been as long as society lasts," Bland went so far as to argue, "and never can be a *parti sérieux* of logical *laissez faire*. Even in the thick of the industrial revolution the difference between the two great parties was mainly one of tendency—of attitude of mind." [11] The simplicities of market political economy could never be consistently applied in practical politics. The attempt to plan *laissez faire* was doomed from the start. If you had to refer to an economist, you would have to fall back upon Adam Smith, a pragmatist, rather than upon more systematic classical theoreticians. When the classical theoreticians were drawn into active politics, their theories immediately became hedged round by an intricate tangle of qualifications.

Bland was more subtle in his approach than Webb (and incidentally more direct in his demand for a new and "definitely Socialist party"). It is clear from more recent academic writings first that there never was a completely "negative state" even in early nineteenth-century Britain, and second that even classical theoreticians were by no means unanimous about the merits of complete *laissez faire*. "The principle of *laissez faire* may be safely trusted to in some things," wrote J. R. McCulloch (1789–1864), but in many more it is wholly inapplicable; and to appeal to it on all occasions savours more of the policy of a parrot than that of a statesman or philosopher." [12] Nassau Senior (1790–1864), the architect of the new poor law of 1834, a substitute for a social policy, yet an innovation from which many new social policies in health and education derived, maintained that

> it is the duty of a government to do whatever is conducive to the welfare of the governed. The only limit to this duty is power [. . .] it appears to me that the most fatal of errors would be the general admission of the proposition that a government has no right to interfere for any purpose except for that of affording protection, for such an admission would be preventing our profiting from experience, and even from acquiring it.[13]

[11] H. Bland, *ibid.* p. 198.

[12] J. R. McCulloch, *Treatise on the Succession to Property vacant by Death* (1848), p. 156.

[13] The passage comes from his Oxford lectures of 1847–8. It is quoted in L. Robbins, *The Theory of Economic Policy* (1953), p. 45. See also for a modern comment on the history of the term *laissez faire*, D. H. McGregor, *Economic Thought and Policy* (1949), ch. III.

Senior stressed, of course, that the power limit to the duty of the state was set not only by the coercive power of the law but by the effective power of the "laws of political economy." A knowledge of the laws of political economy was necessary to legislators, and the new poor law of 1834 with its abandonment of outdoor relief to the poor and its stress on making conditions for indoor relief in workhouses "less eligible" than the worst employment outside was an attempt to rule the poor by the laws of political economy. Later critical writers were to dismiss these economic laws as "gigantic stuffed policemen," [14] and even at the time there were passionate enemies of "political economy" who went far towards envisaging a "welfare state" where politics would have primacy over economics.

In early industrial Britain one of the most influential of the group of anti-political economists was Richard Oastler (1789–1861), a religious man of Tory convictions and a violent critic of the poor law of 1834, who led a working-class agitation during the 1830's for legal limitation of the hours of work of women and children in textile factories. He was known in consequence as "the Factory King." To him "political economy" was "at total variance with every precept of our Holy Religion, every principle of our Constitution, and every security to Rank and Prosperity." The ideal state was what he called the "social state." This state would seek "to secure the prosperity and happiness of every class of society" but it would be particularly concerned with "the protection of the poor and needy, because they require the shelter of the constitution and the laws more than other classes." The "social state" was the true state of history: it was the political economists who were the revolutionaries. Because, however, the actual state in the early nineteenth century was deviating further and further from the ideal (and historic) state, the defence of social rights would have to take the form, if need be, of rebellion.

> If governments are established in this land for the sole purpose of hoarding up large masses of gold and stamping down individual wretchedness, if *that* is the sole interest and sole object of our government, I declare myself a traitor to it, if I die tomorrow for using the word.[15]

Oastler's movement, grounded in toryism, thus merged into Chartism. The idea of the "historic rights of the poor," threatened by 1834, provided a link between "traditionalism" and modern working-class politics. Chartism was a movement with several distinct sources of inspiration: it never-

---

[14] G. Wallas, *Human Nature in Politics* ([1908] 1929 edn.), p. 13. There is a fascinating, if controversial, account of poor law and market in K. Polanyi, *Origins of Our Time* (1946).

[15] *The Fleet Papers* (1842), p. 58; (1841), p. 39; *Leeds Intelligencer*, 10 August 1833.

theless asserted clearly and unequivocally the case for the extension of
the suffrage to the working classes in the name not only of political but
of social rights.

What Marx called "feudal socialism" was one source, therefore, of the
revolt against the market economy, "the laws of political economy" and
"the night-watchman state." Indeed the *Deutsche Allgemeine Zeitung*,
called Oastler a "democratic Tory," a title adopted by his most recent
biographer.[16] It is easy to see how close certain aspects of his thought
were to that of John Ruskin (1819–1900), a social prophet of great influence, who went on (with Marx himself) to shape the thought of William
Morris (1834–1896) and later of J. A. Hobson. Ruskin criticised orthodox
political economy at greater length than Oastler while seeking to evolve
a system of political economy of his own with his own definitions of
"wealth," "illth" and "value" and with a practical concern for the provision of a "living wage." "The first duty of the state," he urged, "is to
see that every child born therein shall be well housed, clothed, fed and
educated until it attains years of discretion." He added the rider that to
do this "the government must have an authority over the people of which
we now do not so much as dream." [17]

Through Ruskin and others, Oastler points forwards as well as back-
wards. His immediate support, however, came from working men, organised in factory committees (he has his place, therefore, in the history
of working-class organisation as well as of social thought) and from a
motley group of clergymen, philanthropists, small squires and Tory
members of parliament. Leading the latter for many years was Lord
Ashley, later the seventh Earl of Shaftesbury, the main parliamentary
spokesman for legislative interference with the working hours of women
and children. It was Ashley's efforts which led to the passing of a number
of factory acts, notably the Ten Hours Act of 1847, which marked a definite breach with *laissez faire*. He was also associated with reforms in
mining, housing and health. Like Oastler, Ashley would have argued that
the breach with *laissez faire* was less significant than the "capitalist"
breach with the past. The "welfare state" was the true historic state. The
Fabians took up this point also. *Laissez faire* was an aberration, "an acute
outbreak of individualism, unchecked by the old restraints." [18] There had
not only been a medieval order—unlike Carlyle, Ruskin and Morris, they
did not dwell on this—but a "mercantilist" order, buttressed by custom
and law. It had disappeared under the weight of the pressure for profit

[16] *Deutsche Allgemeine Zeitung*, 6 July 1843; C. Driver, *Tory Radical* (1946).
[17] The phrase is taken from his *Stones of Venice* (1851). (*Works,* ed. Cook and
Wedderburn, vol. XI, p. 263). The term "living wage" was first used by the English
Cooperator, Lloyd James, in the *Beehive*, July 1874. The term "fair day's wages for
a fair day's work" was older.
[18] H. S. Foxwell, *The Claims of Labour* (1886), p. 249.

during the industrial revolution. According to the Fabians, it was the task of socialists to create a new order appropriate to democracy. The increasing state intervention during the previous forty years seemed to point (although as Bland showed, not always indubitably) towards this destination.

Bland was right to imply that there were intricacies and complications. Ashley, for example, can only be properly understood if his work is related to that of Senior as well as of Oastler. The extension of the powers of the state had a Benthamite as well as a philanthropic or tory inspiration. One of Senior's colleagues in the drafting of the new poor law of 1834 was Edwin Chadwick, Bentham's disciple and "attached friend." Chadwick went on to concern himself with public health and was the author of the important official publication, *The Sanitary Condition of the Labouring Classes* (1842), which had a profound effect on the evolution of British social legislation. When at last in 1848 a General Board of Health was founded under the first national public health act (there had previously been a certain amount of local initiative and legislation), both Chadwick and Ashley were made members. Behind Ashley was the old dream of a traditional "social state," grounded in "responsibility" and strengthened by "charity": Chadwick, selecting from a number of possible Benthamite philosophies that which laid greatest emphasis on the active intervention of the state to suppress "sinister interests" in the name of "the greatest happiness of the greatest number," was a believer in a renovated "administrative state." Such a state would rest on uniformity of procedures and the kind of "centralisation" which Oastler abhorred. "I care more for the good of the service," Chadwick once said in a revealing phrase, "than for putting it in what is called Harmony with the House of Commons." [19]

Ashley and Chadwick worked together closely before, to their mutual regret, the General Board of Health was destroyed by a coalition of enemies in 1854. Yet their sources of inspiration remained quite different. Ashley, tory though he was, looked to the people: he liked crowds. Chadwick looked to the expert. There were, of course, far fewer acknowledged "experts" in the late 1840's and 1850's than there were a hundred years later when the twentieth-century "welfare state" was being fashioned. It is interesting to note also that Chadwick, like Senior, feared the extension of the suffrage to the working classes. Senior had warned against the advocacy of "the political economy of the poor," their belief in the power of human institutions to subvert "the laws of political economy" in the name of "social rights" and "equality": [20] Chadwick feared something

---

[19] Quoted in S. E. Finer, *The Life and Times of Sir Edwin Chadwick* (1952), p. 477.
[20] N. Senior, *Journals Kept in France and Italy* (1843), pp. 150–2. In this journal Senior compared England with Switzerland. The "pure democracies" of small Swiss cantons, he claimed, resisted the spell of "the political economy of the poor" because

worse, that the "quest for popularity" would lead rich men to subvert the poor at election times by offering lavish promises.[21]

These fears, shared by many people of property, were as important, and in some ways more incisive, than other men's hopes in determining the tempo and the pattern of state intervention during the first three quarters of the nineteenth century. For Chadwick and the practical Benthamites, however, the fears were not completely inhibiting. They were constructive men who evolved useful new administrative devices, notably the device of inspection, without which social legislation would have been administratively ineffective. Although the coercive powers of factory, mining and school inspectors were severely limited and most of the early inspectors came from the upper middle classes, the inspectors exerted considerable influence, through their presence as well as through their reports, not only on the way in which existing legislation was administered but on the preparation of new legislative initiatives.[22] In the long run, moreover, Benthamitism itself could be given a democratic tinge. As Professor McGregor has written, "the greatest happiness of the greatest number is an invitation to a continuous review of economic policy; and the greatest number is always the working classes." [23]

The complex detail of nineteenth-century British approaches to state action makes all attempts to divide the century neatly and tidily into "phases" or "epochs" seem grossly over-simplified. The most ambitious of such attempts was A. V. Dicey's large and stimulating *Law and Public Opinion in England in the Nineteenth Century* (1905). Originally a collection of lectures delivered in Harvard in 1898, Dicey's book had polemical as well as historical significance, particularly when it was re-issued in 1914 with a new preface attacking "the trend towards collectivism" which had been especially pronounced since the return of the Liberals to power before the general election of 1906. Dicey placed at 1865 or "roundabouts" the beginning of "collectivism," which he defined as "faith in the benefit to be derived by the mass of the people from the action or intervention of the State." Thereby he ignored the interventionist element in Benthamism, formalized statements both about philanthropy and

---

all their adult males "venerated their clergy, their men of birth and of wealth and their institutions." He did not see that "deference" was as much a feature of nineteenth-century England. Estimates of the likely effect of the extension of suffrage on popular demands for a new political economy were influenced by estimates of the power of "deference." See W. Bagehot, *The English Constitution* (1872 edn.); A. Briggs, *The Age of Improvement* (1959), ch. x.

[21] "Much of that tact which dreads the ballot is a dread of the loss of aristocratical influence which prevails by gold, and of the gain of the influence which prevails by popularity" (Letter of 14 October 1852, quoted in Finer, *op. cit.* p. 478).

[22] For details, see D. Roberts, *Victorian Origins of the British Welfare State* (1960), esp. pp. 152–244.

[23] McGregor, *op. cit.* p. 54.

laissez faire, and confused his own hostility towards "collectivism" with an objective investigation of facts and policies. A recent critic of his work has replaced his tidy phases with a more complex picture of pressures and counterpressures.

> Looking back across the nineteenth century in Great Britain, it is possible to tabulate the parallel developments of *laissez faire* and state intervention almost year by year. What must be kept in mind in spite of our tendency to polarize opposites is that both were exercises of political power, that is, instrumentalities of several kinds of interest. These interests strove to be the state, to use the state for economic and social ends.[24]

Against this background, the extension of the suffrage, which to Webb was decisive, was relevant primarily in that it provided the working classes with an instrument whereby they too *might* attempt to control the state. What Senior, Chadwick (and Bagehot) most feared, Webb, Bland and the Fabians most hoped. Bland noted "the sort of unconscious or semi-conscious recognition of the fact that the word 'state' has taken to itself new and diverse connotations—that the state idea has changed its content." He argued that working people had themselves changed from fearing it as an enemy to regarding it as a "potential saviour." [25] This comment was exaggerated, as we shall see, as a statement of fact but it was a pointer to the politics of the future. In Britain, as in many continental countries, independent labour parties emerged in the late nineteenth century and put forward demands for "the socialisation of politics." The demands included many of the measures which subsequently have been regarded as central to the "welfare state." Just as eighteenth-century civil rights (freedom of meeting, for example, or of the press) were employed to ensure political rights (the right to vote and its corollaries), so political rights were to be employed to secure social rights. Bevan's claim after 1945—"Homes, health, education, and social security; these are your birthright"—would have seemed neither strange nor extravagant to the socialists of 1895. The long intervening period was a period of intermittently intense struggle to secure objects which had already been defined before the beginning of the twentieth century.

Reliance on the state (rather than on trade-union or other kinds of voluntary action) to secure these objects was for a time controversial, as we shall see, yet, as the Fabians pointed out (the Marxists with their

---

[24] J. B. Brebner, *"Laissez faire* and State Intervention in Nineteenth-century Britain" in *Tasks of Economic History,* Supplement VIII (1948) to the *Journal of Economic History.* For the dangers of explaining in terms of Dicey's "abstractions," see also MacDonagh, "The Nineteenth-century Revolution in Government: a Re-appraisal" in the *Historical Journal* (1958).

[25] Bland, *loc. cit.* p. 195, p. 200.

concern for the forms of economic power did not agree), the state against whose interference "the popular party" waged "such bitter war" in the first decades of the nineteenth century [. . .] was "an altogether different thing" from the state whose assistance "the new democracy" was continually invoking and whose power it was bent on increasing. Bland recognized also that if labour parties put forward "welfare" objectives in their electoral programmes, other parties working within a democracy would be forced themselves to put forward policies which would attempt to meet some at least of the labour demands. Tories had advanced social policies earlier in the nineteenth century in the name of "traditionalism" or sometimes of "paternalism": Liberals, some of whom were developing a positive theory of "welfare" of their own, would similarly be forced to advance "welfare" policies, if only in the name of political realism.

> "The Liberals" he held (and he had a clear anti-Liberal bias) were "traditionally squeezable folk" and "like all absorbent bodies" they would be "forced to make concessions and to offer compromises [. . .] Such concessions and compromises will grow in number and importance with each successive appeal to the electorate, until at last the game is won." [26]

This characteristically Fabian conclusion, which attached strategic significance to the working of the parliamentary system, was not shared by those socialists on the continent and in Britain who were sceptical about parliament and drew a sharp distinction between "palliatives" and "fundamental economic and social transformations." Four years before Bland wrote his essay, Joseph Lane in *The Commonweal* put the alternative point of view when he warned his socialist readers that although it was possible that "the governing classes" might offer a "normal working day of eight hours," free meals for children and cumulative taxation on large incomes, "their doing so would certainly put off the revolution which we aim at." [27] The argument has been echoed ever since. In practice, however, non-Fabian socialists, like H. M. Hyndman, who believed not that the "game would be won" but that there would be a "final clash," were prepared to advocate "palliatives," including, for example, free meals for children. Hyndman's Social Democratic Federation refused to take up an "impossibilist" position and instead talked of "palliatives" as "stepping stones" leading in the right direction.[28] The international socialist controversy on this subject, which reached its climax when two rival conferences were held in Paris in 1889, was never completely settled, but the "palliatives" generally agreed upon at the "possibilist" confer-

[26] *Ibid.* p. 200.
[27] Quoted by D. Thompson in "A Note on the Welfare State" in the *New Reasoner*, No. 4, 1948.
[28] See C. Tsuzuki, *H. M. Hyndman and British Socialism* (1961), p. 56, p. 148.

ence, the larger of the two, were all of a kind later to be associated with the "welfare state."

It was argued, and has often been argued since, that the successful achievement of a programme based on individual "palliatives" would represent a victory for "working-class values" within a capitalist, market society. Marx himself had claimed that the passing of the Ten Hours Act of 1847 was the first great occasion on which "in broad daylight the political economy of the middle class" has "succumbed to the political economy of the working class." Certainly the ten hours agitation, led by Oastler and supported by Ashley, marked a genuine stage in a process of conversion of values.

The "social service state" of the twentieth century, "palliative" state or not, in so far as it was a product of working-class efforts and aspirations, was a different phenomenon from the "social state" of Oastler. Like the mercantilists, Oastler founded his theory of the state on a theory of society divided into "proper stations and ranks." "God has appointed the proper stations and ranks for each. He has exhibited Himself in His Word and His Works as the God of Order, and has thus left man without excuse if he should be in want and destitution." In this sense Oastler's was a stationary view of pre-market society. It did not assume a future increase in national income and it looked back to "ancient corporations and gilds" as proper instruments of welfare.

> There were periods in the past when "the labourer's wages were protected by statute, and the common foods of the working people [. . .] were prohibited from being made articles of speculation. Care was then taken that the labourer's hope of reward should not be cut off by the inordinate desire for gain in the capitalists." [29]

When Oastler attacked "acquisitive society," he was speaking the same language which had been taken for granted as a basis of social morality until the long erosion of values described by Max Weber and R. H. Tawney in their studies of puritan religion gave way to fundamental shifts in outlook, organization and not least in real wealth which we associate with the industrial revolution.

The ten hours movement and the later movements for nine-hour and eight-hour days increasingly became movements within the expanding (but fluctuating) industrial market, with *class* bargaining power being used. The late nineteenth-century British and continental labour groups were reacting against the individualism of orthodox "political economy" and capitalist economic organisation not by falling back on ideas of "rank" and "order" but by developing ideas of "class" and "movement." The systems of regulation which they were anxious to establish were

[29] *The Fleet Papers* (1842), p. 190.

not copies of medieval or mercantilist models (although for a time these were familiar and some of them came into later prominence with gild socialism) [30] but new models appropriate to the new "social nexus" of industrialism. Written into them was the ideal not only of "fairness," a link between old and new, but of "equality." The old system, both Fabians and trade unionists saw, was riddled with what Webb called "status and permanent social inequalities." The attack on status, which had been prosecuted by middle-class radicals and Benthamite theorists, was now pursued by working-class socialists and Fabian theorists. There was a real link between Mill and the Fabians. Of course, the attack was local rather than general, intermittent rather than continuous if only because of economic fluctuations, and subject to all kind of manœuvres and diversions.

Once arguments for social reform had shifted from talk of "rank" and "order," it was easier for a section of non-socialist radical opinion to support them. The so-called "new Liberals" of the late nineteenth and early twentieth centuries argued the case for "welfare" from a democratic standpoint within the new market economy. They could condemn certain of the conditions of the market without condemning "capitalism" as a whole, and they could criticize, from a very different standpoint from that of Oastler, the theory of poverty which lay behind the poor law of 1834. They could thus reach substantial, though limited agreement, with trade unionists and socialists about particular social service measures, as was shown during the period of Liberal government from 1906 to 1914.

It is necessary to draw distinctions between the early and the late nineteenth century not only to arrive at historical truth but to dispose of current descriptions of "welfare state" policy in terms of "neo-mercantilism." The "enlargement of welfare" is not adequately so described. "There are elements in it which were not present in mercantilist phases of the history of civilisation [. . .] It issues from a new phase in man's history." [31]

The point is perhaps most clearly demonstrated from the history not of Britain itself but of British settlements in the Antipodes, where there were striking examples before the end of the nineteenth century of what a French observer called "socialism without doctrines." [32] The early

---

[30] Yet Beatrice Webb herself said of her poor law scheme in 1907: "The whole theory of the mutual obligation between the individual and the State [. . .] is taken straight out of the nobler aspect of the medieval manor"; *Our Partnership* (1948), p. 385.

[31] H. L. Beales, "The Making of Social Policy" (*L. T. Hobhouse Memorial Trust Lecture*, 1946), p. 5. The mercantilist parallel usually refers not only to welfare policy but to population policy (which, through such devices as family allowances, has "welfare" implications) and to protection (which also has "labour" implications).

[32] A. Métin, *Le socialisme sans doctrines* (1901). See also A. Siegfried, *Democracy in New Zealand* (1906).

granting of universal suffrage in Australia and New Zealand was followed by the demand for social measures which would guarantee "fairness." Both Australians and New Zealanders had long boasted that they had no poor law—by that they meant that the conditions giving rise to a poor law and to "workhouses" were absent. In fact, however, they had by no means eliminated poverty, and in the last decade of the nineteenth century legislative measures were introduced which went further in certain respects than British legislation. There had been considerable dependence upon the state from the earliest period of colonization (the older British middle-class fear of the state as an "establishment" was missing) and there was little serious challenge to the view that the state machinery was freely available to those groups able to secure possession of it. "The more the state does for the citizen," Pember Reeves, the first New Zealand minister of labour, remarked in 1895, "the more it fulfils its purpose [. . .] The functions of the state should be extended as much as possible [. . .] True democracy consists in the extension of state activity." It was Pember Reeves who coined the phrase "colonial governmentalism." [33]

There was nothing paternalistic, however, about this willingness to delegate powers to the state. The emphasis, though at times it may have been somewhat misplaced, was always egalitarian. There was talk along practical, if extended Benthamite lines, of "the right to work, the right to fair and reasonable conditions of living and the right to be happy." [34] The collective power of the state (not a remote, impersonal state but a close-at-hand, essentially personally manipulated piece of machinery) was to be used to support social rights. These attitudes were reflected in the social service legislation of the Ballance-Seddon-Reeves ministry in New Zealand from 1891 onwards and in the legislation of the Turner government in Victoria from 1895.

Much of this legislation was concerned with the creation of effective departments of labour and the control of sweated industries paying low wages to their workers. In both Australia and New Zealand, however, pensions legislation was either introduced or just round the corner by the end of the nineteenth century. The New Zealand Old Age Pensions Act of 1898 was the first in a British dominion. It provided at state expense pensions to people of good character but with little or no means above the age of sixty-five. New South Wales and Victoria followed the example of New Zealand in 1901, and the new federal constitution of

[33] Métin, *op. cit.* p. 229; J. B. Condliffe, *New Zealand in the Making* (1930), pp. 164–5.

[34] W. K. Hancock, *Australia* (1930), p. 61. For general reflections on the role of the state in Australia, see S. Encel, "The Concept of the State in Australian Politics" in the *Australian Journal of Politics and History,* May 1960.

Australia stated in the same year that the Commonwealth might legislate for old age and invalid pensions. A federal act of 1908 extended the old age pension system to all Australian states and included also pensions for the blind and for permanently disabled persons. In the same year Britain passed its first non-contributory old age pensions act after decades of pressure from philanthropists, societies and even politicians. It was an act hedged round with moral qualifications,[35] but it nonetheless marked, as did dominions legislation, an attempt to get away from the harshness of an all-embracing poor law. "The state was making new provision for welfare, in piecemeal fashion, outside of and parallel to the poor law." This, it has been argued, was "the real beginning of the welfare state in its modern form." [36]

Pember Reeves, who came to England from New Zealand, was a member of the Fabian Society. He divided old age pensions into three classes. "First comes the socialists' ideal," he said, "of a universal and comfortable provision which shall supersede the necessity for petty thrift; next come the various schemes, more or less orthodox in principle, but complicated and burdensome in their nature, for the reward and encouragement of thrift and self-denial; in the third class may be placed the humanitarian proposals, the humble yet not ungenerous aim of which is to soften the bitterness of poverty to those aged who, while unfortunate, are not wholly undeserving." The antipodean legislation, he believed, fell into the third class: "it was designed to offer help to those who need it most." [37] Its inspiration was neither a set of doctrines nor a cluster of ideas: it was a bundle of feelings about how people were treated. In Britain itself Hobson was to argue that the strongest solvent of the Poor Law of 1834 was "a movement along the lines of the strongest human feelings." [38]

It was liberal rather than socialist governments who moved along the lines described above, abandoning in the process many of the ideas which had dominated liberal thought earlier in the century, however much they had been qualified, as we have seen, on particular occasions or by particular writers.

[35] See A. Wilson and G. S. Mackay, Old Age Pensions, An Historical and Critical Study (1941), ch. II, III, IV. See also R. M. Titmuss, Essays on "The Welfare State" (1958), pp. 18–19.
[36] C. L. Mowat, "The Approach to the Welfare State in Great Britain" in the American Historical Review October 1952. It has also been called "an extended form of outdoor relief." See B. Abel-Smith, "Social Security" in Ginsberg (ed.), Law and Opinion in England in the Twentieth Century (1959), pp. 352 ff.
[37] W. Pember Reeves, State Experiments in Australia and New Zealand (1902), vol. II, p. 244. For more recent appraisals, see W. B. Sutch, The Quest for Security in New Zealand (1942); R. Mendelsohn, Social Security in the British Commonwealth (1954).
[38] J. A. Hobson, The Evolution of Modern Capitalism (1902), p. 321.

"When I went up to Oxford," wrote Lord Milner of the early 1870's, "the *laissez faire* theory still held the field. All the recognised authorities were "orthodox" economists of the old school. But within ten years the few men who still held the old doctrines in their extreme rigidity had come to be regarded as curiosities." [39]

One of the liveliest transforming influences was T. H. Green, who argued forcefully that the state ought to remove all obstacles to the development of "social capacity," such as those arising from lack of education, poor health and bad housing.[40]

Hobson himself—and later L. T. Hobhouse—were sensitive students of the changes and initiators of new views. The issues with which late Victorian and Edwardian liberal intellectuals were having to concern themselves were social issues, and the practical politics, as Bland had prophesied, was increasingly pivoting on social politics. "It is not about details that the people care or are stirred," wrote R. B. Haldane, "what they seem to desire is that they should have something approaching to equality of chance of life with those among whom they live." [41] Even old conservative principles of property were reinterpreted in radical terms and in Hobhouse's arguments were converted into instruments of social justice.[42] Individualism itself was increasingly associated with the freeing of the powers of "under-privileged" individuals. In 1909 Hobson commented that "the whole conception of the state disclosed by the new issues, as an instrument for the active adaptation of the economic and moral environment to the new needs of individual and social life, by securing full opportunities of self-development and social service for all citizens, was foreign to the Liberalism of the last generation." [43]

The "welfare measures of the Liberal governments of 1905–14, culminating in the bitterly controversial "budget against poverty" of 1909 and

[39] A. Milner, Introduction to A. Toynbee, *Lectures on the Industrial Revolution* (1923 edn.), p. xxv. Toynbee anticipated the Fabians in these lectures, delivered to workingmen in the early 1880s, by contrasting the age of capitalist anarchy with the age of regulation which had preceded it. For movements in liberal political economy at this time, see T. W. Hutchison, *A Review of Economic Doctrines, 1870–1929* (1953), ch. i.

[40] T. H. Green, *Lectures on the Principles of Political Obligation* (1895 edn.) pp. 206–209.

[41] R. B. Haldane, *Autobiography* (1929), pp. 212–214.

[42] See, in particular, L. T. Hobhouse, *Elements of Social Justice* (1922); *The Labour Movement* (1893); *Democracy and Reaction* (1904), *Liberalism* (1911); "The Philosophical Theory of Property," in *Property, its Duties and Rights* (ed. C. Gore, 1915). For the significance of his work, see J. A. Hobson and M. Ginsberg, *The Life and Work of L. T. Hobhouse* (1931).

[43] J. A. Hobson, *The Crisis of Liberalism* (1909), p. 3. For Hobson, see H. N. Brailsford, "The Life and Work of J. A. Hobson" (*L. T. Hobhouse Memorial Trust Lecture, 1948*).

Lloyd George's national insurance schemes against ill health and unemployment in 1911, were in sharp contrast to the Gladstonian liberalism of only thirty years before. "They are so far removed from the old Liberal individualism," one Liberal historian has written recently, "that they may be called social democracy rather than pure liberalism." [44]

IV

That was the British story, more complex than it is usually told and revealing a multiplicity of motives and inspirations.

German experience in the nineteenth century was in certain important respects different from that of Britain. If before 1900 factory legislation was more advanced in Britain than in any other European country, Germany had established a "lead" in social security legislation which the British liberal governments of 1906 to 1914 tried to wipe out. Bismarck's reforms of the 1880s—laws of 1882, 1884 and 1889 introducing compulsory insurance against sickness, accidents, old age and invalidity—attracted immense interest in other European countries. Just as British factory legislation was copied overseas, so German social insurance stimulated foreign imitation. Denmark, for instance, copied all three German pensions schemes between 1891 and 1898, and Belgium between 1894 and 1903. Switzerland by a constitutional amendment in 1890 empowered the federal government to organise a system of national insurance. In Britain itself a friendly observer noted in 1890 that Bismarck had "discovered where the roots of social evil lie. He has declared in words that burn that it is the duty of the state to give heed, above all, to the welfare of its weaker members." [45]

More recently Bismarck's social policy has been described by more than one writer as the creation of a "welfare state." [46] The term is very misleading. Bismarck's legislation rested on a basic conservatism which Oastler himself would have appreciated [47] and was sustained by a bureaucracy which had no counterpart in Britain except perhaps in Chadwick's imagination. The Prussian idea and history of the state and the British idea and history of the state diverged long before the 1880s, and it is not fanciful to attribute some of the divergences to the presence or absence a century before of "cameralism," the idea of the systematic application to government of administrative routines.

Equally important, the history of political economy in the two countries diverged just as markedly. The development of a school of historical

44 R. B. McCallum, "The Liberal Outlook," in M. Ginsberg (ed.), *Law and Opinion in England in the Twentieth Century*, p. 75.

45 W. H. Dawson, *Bismarck and State Socialism* (1890), p. IX.

46 S. B. Fay, "Bismarck's Welfare State" in *Current History*, vol. XVIII (1950).

47 "A British Bismarck," Professor Driver has written, "would have commanded all his uncritical devotion, but Wellington was no Bismarck" (Driver, *op. cit.* p. 189).

economics provided a powerful academic re-inforcement in Germany for *Sozialpolitik*. The refusal of historical economists to "isolate" economic phenomena, including "economic man," their distrust of "laws of political economy" covering all ages and all societies, their *critique* of the motives and institutions of contemporary capitalism and their underlying belief in a "social order" distinguished them sharply from classical political economists in Britain. Their influence was considerable enough for Schmoller (1838–1917), the most important figure in the history of the school, to argue forcefully that no Smithian was fit to occupy an academic chair in Germany.[48]

Even among the "precursors" of the historical school and among economists who stayed aloof from Schmoller and his circle, there was a powerful tradition linking social reform with conservative views of society.[49] J. K. Rodbertus (1805–75) was a conservative monarchist who combined dislike of the "class struggle" and belief in state socialism. Adolf Wagner (1835–1917) who stayed aloof from Schmoller and admired Ricardo as the outstanding economic "theorist," acknowledged his debt to Rodbertus when he gave a warm welcome to Bismarck's legislation.

According to Wagner Germany had entered a "new social period," characterised by new economic ideas, new political views and new social programmes. National economy (*Volkswirtschaft*) had to be converted into State economy (*Staatswirtschaft*): the foundation of the new economy would have to be "welfare." The idea of regarding "labour power" as a commodity and wages as its price was "inhuman" as well as "un-Christian." Wagner proposed a number of practical measures, some of which went further than those introduced by Bismarck. Schmoller, too, advocated policies aiming at "the re-establishment of a friendly relation between social classes, the removal or modification of injustice, a nearer approach to the principles of distributive justice, with the introduction of a social legislation which promotes progress and guarantees the moral and material elevation of the lower and middle classes." [50]

Bismarck, for whom the idea of insurance had a particular fascination both in his domestic and foreign policies, did not envisage a social policy which would go anywhere near as far as some of the "socialists of the chair" would have wished. He objected, for example, to the limitation by law of the hours of women and children in factories and he was at least as stubborn as any mill owner of the Manchester School when "theorists" talked of state officials interfering with private concerns in agriculture or

[48] J. A. Schumpeter, *History of Economic Analysis* (1954), p. 765.
[49] The pre-history of this approach leads back to Sismondi who has important links with Mill and the English utilitarians. He is a seminal figure in the critique of industrialism and the demand for welfare legislation.
[50] A. Wagner, *Rede über die soziale Frage* (1872), pp. 8–9. G. von Schmoller, *Über einige Grundfragen des Rechts und der Volkswirtschaft* (1875), p. 92.

industry. He also disliked extensions of direct taxation. He wanted the
state, however, to be actively involved in the financing and administering of the insurance schemes which he proposed and he defended the
introduction of these schemes—against both right-wing and left-wing
opposition—in terms of "the positive advancement of the welfare of the
working classes." "The state," it was laid down in the preamble to the
first and unsuccessful bill of 1881, "is not merely a necessary but a
beneficent institution." Bismarck disagreed with Theodor Lohmann, who
drafted his first social insurance legislation, about whether the state
should contribute directly to the costs of insurance. Bismarck got his
way that it should, but the political parties objected and his first attempts
at legislation foundered. It was a measure of his recognition of political
realities that the idea of state contributions was dropped in 1884 when
his accident insurance bill was introduced. The law of 1889, providing
for disability and old age pensions, did entail a flat rate contribution from
the imperial treasury of fifty marks for each person receiving a pension,
but this was a small element in the total cost and fell far short of the
amount Bismarck had originally envisaged.

Many of Bismarck's critics accused him, not without justification, of
seeking through his legislation to make German workers "depend" upon
the state. The same charges have been made against the initiators of all
"welfare" (and earlier, of poor law) policy often without justification, yet
it was Bismarck himself who drew a revealing distinction between the
degrees of obedience (or subservience) of private servants and servants
at court. The latter would "put up with much more" than the former
because they had pensions to look forward to. "Welfare" soothed the
spirit, or perhaps tamed it. Bismarck's deliberate invocation of "subservience" is at the opposite end of the scale from the socialist invocation of
"equality" as the goal of the "welfare state." It is brutally simple, too,
when compared with sophisticated liberal attempts to define the conditions in which liberty and equality may be made to complement each
other.[51] The invocation was, of course, bound up with conscious political
calculation. Bismarck was anxious to make German social democracy less
attractive to working-men. He feared "class war" and wanted to postpone
it as long as possible. His talks with Lassalle in 1863 had ranged over
questions of this kind,[52] and in 1884 he argued explicitly that if the state
would only "show a little more Christian solicitude for the working-man,"
then the social democrats would "sound their siren song in vain." "The
thronging to them will cease as soon as working-men see that the govern-

---

[51] For the background of these attempts, see M. Ginsberg, "The Growth of Social
Responsibility" in *Law and Opinion in England in the Twentieth Century*, pp. 3–26.
[52] See G. Mayer, *Bismarck und Lassalle* (1927).

ment and legislative bodies are earnestly concerned for their welfare." [53] It has been suggested that Bismarck was influenced by Napoleon III's successful handling of social policy as an instrument of politics. He certainly spent time seeking an "alternative to socialism" and it was this aspect of his policy which gave what he did contemporary controversial significance throughout Europe.

His policy also provided a definite alternative to liberalism. During the last years of his life when he was prepared to contemplate insurance against unemployment and when he talked of the "right to work" as enthusiastically as any Chartist, he was reflecting that sharp reaction against economic liberalism which could be discerned, in different forms, in almost every country in Europe. Disraeli's social policy in his ministry of 1874–1880 had somewhat similar features. It also had the added interest of appearing to realize hopes first formulated by Disraeli in the age of Oastler and the Chartists. In 1874 also a royalist and clerical majority in the French National Assembly carried a factory act, limiting hours of work of children below the age of twelve, which went further than a law of 1848 on the same subject. A later and more comprehensive act of 1892 was the work of Conservative Republicans. The nineteenth century closed with a British Money-lenders Act which, Professor Clapham has argued, in effect revived the medieval law of usury, the last remnants of which had been swept away, it was thought for ever, in 1854.[54]

Medieval attitudes to "welfare" were echoed most strongly in Christian apologetics. Papal encyclicals, notably *Rerum Novarum* (1891), were not only manifestos in crusades against liberalism or socialism but were also important documents in the evolution of *Sozialpolitik*. De Mun, Von Ketteler and Von Vogelsang were writers who advocated particular or general "welfare" policies: so did Heinrich Pesch, who has been singled out for special treatment by Schumpeter. Among Protestants also there was renewed call for a "social gospel." It is not without interest that Lohmann, who had advised Bismarck and went on to advise William II in the formulation of the far-reaching Labour Code of 1891, was a deeply religious man, the son of a Westphalian Lutheran pastor. Canon W. L. Blackley (1830–1902), the pioneer of old age pensions schemes not only in Britain but in other parts of the world and the founder of the National Providence League, was an honorary canon of Winchester Cathedral. On the Liberal side—and there was a close association in Britain between religious nonconformity and political liberalism—Seebohm Rowntree

[53] Dawson, *op. cit.* p. 35. This remark was made in 1884. Five years earlier the Emperor, referring to the antisocialist law of 1878, had said, "a remedy cannot alone be sought in the repression of socialistic excesses; there must be simultaneously the positive advancement of the welfare of the working classes" (quoted *ibid.* p. 110).
[54] J. H. Clapham, *An Economic History of Modern Britain*, vol. III (1938), p. 445.

(1871–1954), one of the first systematic investigators of the facts of poverty, was a Quaker. The whole attack on the limitations of the poor law was guided, though not exclusively, by men of strong religious principles.

V

The complexity of the nineteenth-century background contrasts at first sight with the simplicity of the twentieth-century story. For a tangle of tendencies we have a "trend," a trend culminating in greater "order" and simplification. In fact, however, the twentieth-century story has its own complexities, which are now in the process of being unravelled. Professor Titmuss has shown, for instance, that Lloyd George's national health insurance legislation of 1911, a landmark in "trend" legislation, was the culmination of a long and confused period in which doctors had been engaged in a "Hobbesian struggle for independence from the power and authority exercised over their lives, their work and their professional values by voluntary associations and private enterprise." He has maintained that the legislation of 1911 can only be understood if it is related, as so much else in the twentieth century must be related, to the history of hidden pressures from established interests and a sectional demand for an "enlargement of professional freedom." [55] Many of the complexities of twentieth-century history certainly lie buried in the records of the network of private concerns and of professional groups which came into existence in the nineteenth century. There can be no adequate historical explanation which concerns itself in large terms with the state alone. Just as the administration of "welfare" is complicated in practice and can be understood only in detail, so the outline of "welfare state" legislation only becomes fully intelligible when it ceases to be an outline, and when it looks beyond parliamentary legislation to such crucial twentieth-century relationships as those between governments and pressure groups and "experts" and the "public."

Yet there are five factors in twentieth-century "welfare" history (other than warfare, one of the most powerful of factors) which are beyond dispute and dominant enough to need little detailed research. They are, first, the basic transformation in the attitude towards poverty, which made the nineteenth-century poor law no longer practicable in democratic societies; second, the detailed investigation of the "social contingencies" which directed attention to the need for particular social policies; third, the close association between unemployment and welfare policy; fourth, the development within market capitalism itself of "welfare" philosophies

---

[55] R. M. Titmuss, "Health," in Ginsberg (ed.), *Law and Opinion in England in the Twentieth Century*, p. 308. Cf. p. 313: "The fundamental issue of 1911 was not [. . .] between individualism and collectivism, between contract and status; but between different forms of collectivism, different degrees of freedom; open or concealed power."

and practices; and fifth, the influence of working-class pressures on the content and tone of "welfare" legislation.

The first and second of these five factors can scarcely be studied in isolation. The basis of the nineteenth-century British poor law of 1834 was economic logic. That logic was strained when empirical sociologists, like Charles Booth (1840–1916) and Rowntree, showed that a large number of poor people were poor through no fault of their own but because of tendencies within the market system. They pitted statistics against logic by attempting to count how many people were living in poverty and by surveying the various forms that the poverty assumed.[56] Prior to Booth's "grand inquest," Beatrice Webb wrote, "neither the individualist nor the socialist could state with any approach to accuracy what exactly was condition of the people of England." [57] Once the results of the "inquest" had been published "the net effect was to give an entirely fresh impetus to the general adoption of the policy of securing to every individual, as the very basis of his life and work, a prescribed natural minimum of the requisites for efficient parenthood and citizenship."

Booth's thinking about economics was far less radical than his thinking about "welfare," but Rowntree, who drew a neat distinction between "primary" and "secondary" poverty, the former being beyond the control of the wage-earner, went on to advocate specific "welfare" policies, ranging from old-age pensions to family allowances, public-provided housing to supervised "welfare" conditions in factories. The policies which he urged at various stages of his long life were, indeed, the main constituent policies of the "welfare state." [58] Like the "welfare state," however, Rowntree stopped short of socialism. He separated questions of "welfare" from questions of economic power, and remained throughout his life a "new Liberal." The main tenet of his liberalism was that the community could not afford the "waste," individual and social, which was implied in an industrial society divided "naturally" into "rich" and "very poor." Poverty was as much of a social problem as "pauperism." The roots of poverty were to be found not in individual irresponsibility or incapacity but in social maladjustment. Poverty, in short, was not the fault of the poor: it was the fault of society. Quite apart from "socialist pressure," society had to do something about poverty once it was given facts about its extent, its incidence (Rowntree drew attention to the cycle of poverty in families), its ramifications and its consequences. All facts were grist to the mill. They included facts not only about wages but about nutrition:

[56] C. Booth, Life and Labour of the People in London, 17 vols. 1892–1903); B. S. Rowntree, Poverty: A Study of Town Life (1901).
[57] B. Webb, My Apprenticeship (1926), p. 239.
[58] For Booth, see T. S. and M. B. Simey, Charles Booth, Social Scientist (1960); for Rowntree, see A. Briggs, Seebohm Rowntree (1961). See also B. S. Rowntree and G. R. Lavers, Poverty and the Welfare State (1951).

subsistence levels could only be measured when nutritional criteria were taken into account.

Sharp turns of thought about poverty were by no means confined to people in Britain. There were signs of fundamental re-thinking, allied as we have seen to "feeling," [59] both in Europe and the United States at the end of the nineteenth and the beginning of the twentieth century.[60] The survey method, which Booth and Rowntree depended upon, was capable of general applicability.[61] The limitations of systematic "charity" were noted at least as generally as the limitations of unsystematic charity had been at the beginning of the industrial age. It is no coincidence that in Britain and Sweden, two countries with distinct "welfare" histories, there was keen debate about the poor law at almost exactly the same time. In Sweden the Poor Relief Order of 1871, with its checks on poor relief, was criticised by the Swedish Poor Relief Association which was formed at the first General Swedish Poor Law Congress in 1906. A year later the government appointed a committee to draw up proposals for fresh legislation governing poor relief and the treatment of vagrants. In Britain the Royal Commission on the Poor Laws, which was appointed in 1905 and reported in 1909, covered almost all topics in social policy. The issues were clearly stated and both the social contingencies and the necessary policies of social control were carefully examined. Although new direct legislation was slow to come in both countries, there was much indirect legislation and in both countries there were demands for what Beatrice Webb called "an enforced minimum of civilised life." [62]

The main threat to that minimum in the later twentieth century came from "mass involuntary unemployment." This, of course, was a world phenomenon which strained poor law and social service systems in most countries and presented a threat—or a challenge—to politicians and administrators. In Britain, which was the first country to introduce compulsory unemployment insurance (1911; greatly extended in 1920), the system of relief broke down under the stresses of the 1930s. Insurance benefits, linked to contributions, were stringently restricted, and while tussles about

[59] "In intensity of feeling," Booth wrote, "and not in statistics, lies the power to move the world. But by statistics must this power be guided if it would move the world aright" (*Life and Labour, Final Volume, Notes on Social Influences and Conclusion* (1903), p. 178).

[60] See *inter alia* C. L. Mowat, *The Charity Organisation Society;* K. de Schweinitz, *England's Road to Social Security* (1943); C. W. Pitkin, *Social Politics and Modern Democracies,* 2 vols. (1931), vol. II being concerned with France; R. H. Bremner, *From the Depths; The Discovery of Poverty in the United States* (1956).

[61] See M. Abrams, *Social Surveys and Social Action* (1951); P. V. Young, *Scientific Social Surveys and Research* (1950); D. C. Caradog Jones, *Social Surveys* (1955).

[62] The British controversy is well described in U. Cormack, "The Welfare State," *Loch Memorial Lecture* (1953). For Sweden, see The Royal Social Board, *Social Work and Legislation in Sweden* (1938).

the "means test" were leading to extreme differences of outlook between socialists and their opponents, an Unemployment Assistance Board, founded in 1934, was providing a second-line income maintenance service, centrally administered. In Europe there was an extension of unemployment aid schemes, whether by insurance (the Swedes, for example, introduced state-subsidized unemployment insurance in 1934), "doles" or in certain cases "positive" state-run schemes of "public works." In the United States and Canada, where there had been entrenched resistance to government intervention in "welfare" provision, new legislation was passed,[63] while in New Zealand, which had long lost its reputation as a pioneer of "welfare," there was a remarkable bout of state intervention after the return of a Labour government to power in 1935. The Social Security Act of 1938 contained a list of health services and pensions benefits which, while resting on previous legislation, were everywhere hailed as a bold and daring experiment. The Minister of Finance anticipated later "welfare" legislators in other countries by arguing unequivocally that "to suggest the inevitability of slumps and booms, associated as they are with affluence for a limited number during a period, and followed by unemployment, destitution, hardship and privation for the masses, is to deny all conscious progressive purpose." [64] According to the I.L.O., the 1938 New Zealand Act "has, more than any other law, determined the practical meaning of social security, and so has deeply influenced the course of legislation in other countries." [65]

Twentieth-century social security legislation raises many interesting general issues—the relevance of the insurance principle, for example, the relationship between "negative" social policy and "positive" economic policy, and, underlying all else, the nature and extent of the responsibilities of the state. Insurance principles, actuarially unsound though they may be and inadequate though they have proved as instruments of finance at moments of crisis, have been historically significant. They removed the stigma of pauperism from a social service, reconciled "voluntary" and "compulsory" approaches to provision, and facilitated "public approval" of state expenditures which otherwise would have been challenged. They thus served as a link between old ways of thinking ("self-help" and "mutual help") and new. "Positive" economic policy was in the first instance, as in Roosevelt's America, the child of improvisation: its systematic justification had to await revolutions in political economy (Keynes and after) which accompanied shifts in social power. The difference in

[63] Mendelsohn, op. cit., ch. III: J. C. Brown, Public Relief, 1929–39 (1940); E. A. Williams, Federal Aid for Relief (1939); P. H. Douglas, Social Security in the United States (1939 edn.).

[64] Quoted in W. K. Hancock, Survey of British Commonwealth Affairs, vol. II (1940), p. 275.

[65] I.L.O., Social Security in New Zealand (1949), p. 111.

tone and content between two books by William Beveridge—his *Unemployment* (1909) and his *Full Employment in a Free Society* (1944)—is one of the best indications of the change in the world of ideas between the early and middle periods of the twentieth century. "Beveridgism," an important British phenomenon during the Second World War, had sufficient popular appeal to show that the world of ideas and the world of practical politics were not very far apart. For the intellectuals and for the public the magnification of governmental power—and the enormous increase in government expenditure financed from taxation—were taken for granted.

The fourth and fifth factors are also related to each other. In all advanced industrial countries in the twentieth century there has been a movement towards "welfare" in industry—"industrial betterment" it was originally called—which has been accompanied by the emergence of philosophies of "human relations," "welfare management" and industrial and labour psychology.[66] The movement has to be explained in terms of both economics and politics. A "managerial revolution," limited though it may have been in its economic effects, has accelerated the tendencies making for "welfare capitalism." The need to find acceptable incentives for workers, to avoid labour disputes and to secure continuous production, to raise output in phases of technical change and (more recently) to hold labour "permissively" in a period of full employment has often driven where "human relations" philosophies have failed to inspire. "Welfare," a word which was often resented by workers, when it was applied within the structure of the firm, was, indeed, used in a business context before it began to be applied to a new kind of state. Within state schemes of "welfare" employers have made, and are expected to make sizeable contributions. In France and Italy, in particular, obligatory social charges as a percentage of assessable wages constituted the main source of "welfare" expenditure.[67] In the United States business rather than the state was, and is expected, directly to provide a network of "welfare" services. As in all such situations, the provision of "welfare" varies immensely from one firm (giant businesses are at one end of the scale) to another.

In contrast to these countries, such as Great Britain, which appear to regard government (for reasons which have been stated above) merely

[66] See A. Briggs, "The Social Background," in H. Clegg and A. Flanders (eds.), *Industrial Relations in Great Britain* (1955); L. Urwick and E. F. L. Brech, *The Human Factor in Management*, 1795–1943 (1944); E. D. Proud, *Welfare Work, Employers' Experiments for Improving Working Conditions in Factories* (1916); E. T. Kelly (ed.), *Welfare Work in Industry* (1925); P. E. P., "The Human Factor in Industry" (*Planning*, March, 1948).

[67] P. E. P., "Free Trade and Security" (*Planning*, July 1957); "A Comparative Analysis of the Cost of Social Security" in *International Labour Review* (1953).

as the most effective of several possible institutions for the administration of income security programmes or the provision of services, [. . .] a society like the United States that distrusts its government is likely to seek to organise its social security services in such a way as to keep government activity to a minimum.[68]

United States experience, in contrast to the experience described in other countries, shows that this likelihood has been converted into fact.

It is not accidental that the labour movement in the United States has showed little interest in socialism and that its leaders have chosen of their own volition to bargain for "fringe benefits" at the level of the plant. In most European countries, particularly in Britain and in Scandinavia, there has been a tendency for working-class pressures to lead to greater state intervention. In Britain nineteenth-century patterns of "mutual dependence" through "voluntary action," which impressed so many observers from Tocqueville onwards, have become less dominant, except in the field of industrial relations where they have very tenaciously survived.[69]

As we have seen, the demand for state action has been related to the rights of citizenship, to equality as well as to security. During the critical period between the two World Wars, when economic and social conditions were very difficult, "welfare" measures were demanded and provided "piecemeal" with varying conditions of regulation and administration, "a frightening complexity of eligibility and benefit according to individual circumstances, local boundaries, degrees of need and so forth." [70] The Second World War, which sharpened the sense of "democracy," led to demands both for "tidying up" and for "comprehensiveness." It encouraged the move from "minima" to "optima," at least in relation to certain specified services, and it made all residual paternalisms seem utterly inadequate and increasingly archaic. It was in the light of changes in working-class life within a more "equal community" that post-war writers noted the extent to which the social services of the earlier part of the century had been shaped by assumptions about the nature of man, "founded on outer rather than on inner observation," on the "norms of behaviour expected by one class from another." [71] This period of criticism has already ended. The assumptions which shaped the "welfare state" have themselves been criticized,[72] and radical political slogans have con-

---

[68] E. M. Burns, Social Security and Public Policy (1956), p. 274.
[69] For the nature of the nineteenth-century pattern, see J. M. Baernreither, English Associations of Working Men (1893). For industrial relations, see Clegg and Flanders, op. cit.
[70] R. M. Titmuss, Essays on the Welfare State, pp. 21–22.
[71] Ibid. p. 19.
[72] See A. Peacock, "The Welfare Society," Unservile State Papers (1960); R. M. Titmuss, "The Irresponsible Society," Fabian Tracts (1960); J. Saville, "The Welfare State" in The New Reasoner, No. 3 (1957).

centrated more and more on differences of income between "mature" and "under-developed" countries rather than on differences within "mature" countries themselves.

It may well be that in a world setting the five twentieth-century factors discussed in this article will be considered less important than other factors—the total size of the national income in different countries, for example, and the share of that income necessary for industrial (as, or when, distinct from social) investment, or even, on a different plane, the nature of family structure. Is not the making of the industrial "welfare state" in part at least the concomitant of the decline of the large, extended "welfare family"? How far has the pressure of women (or just the presence of women voters) in industrial societies encouraged the formulation of "welfare" objectives? The historian does well to leave such large questions to be answered rather than to suggest that all or even the most important part of the truth is already known.

Part B

Comparative Elites and Social Structure

EVEN though the historical process of modernization and industrialization leads to the growth of differentiated welfare institutions, not all societies take the same paths. What determines the speed with which an industrializing society develops various welfare structures and services? What determines the auspices—governmental or private—under which welfare services are conducted? What determines the kinds of policies that develop? While institutionalized welfare services may represent new organizational forms, they grow out of the social and cultural systems of the society.

There has been little systematic research on comparative elites and social structure. But research on the process of industrialization does suggest that the nature of the "industrializing elite," their beliefs and values, and their relationship to the society in which they exist will have a strong impact on the speed and shape of welfare institutions. By "industrializing elite" is meant the group that takes the leading entrepreneurial role in introducing modern technologies and industrial organizations to a society.

The first selection, "The Industrializing Elites," by Clark Kerr, John T. Dunlop, Frederick H. Harbison, and Charles A. Myers, was originally published as part of the Inter-University Study of Labor Problems and Economic Development sponsored by the Ford Foundation. The work of these authors focuses on the relation of the industrializing elite—middle-class businessmen, dynastic elite, colonial administrators, revolutionary intellectuals, and nationalistic leaders—to the labor force. The relations and responsibilities of management to labor are a crucial determinant of the social security systems that develop in a society. Furthermore, the nature of the industrializing elite will also be related to the relative emphasis on governmental as contrasted with private initiative in a society.

The second article, "Social Security, Incentives, and Controls in the U.S. and U.S.S.R.," by Gaston V. Rimlinger, is also a product of the Inter-University Study of Labor Problems and Economic Development. In terms of the concepts developed by Kerr and his associates, Rimlinger compares social security systems in industrial societies that had a middle-class and a revolutionary intellectual elite, respectively. He raises the very basic question of the relationship of a social security system to the problems of economic development and to the structure of the political system.

Where Rimlinger compares, in great detail, social security programs in two countries, Phillips Cutright, in "Political Structure, Economic Development, and National Security Programs," subjects to statistical tests factors related to the development of welfare programs in 76 countries. Cutright shows that the level of economic development and the stability and representativeness of the political system have independent effects on the number and extent of basic welfare programs. His statistical measure of welfare programs is ingenious. Rather than try to calculate dollar amounts of welfare, which would be difficult to compare from nation to nation, Cutright uses measures based on the number of major welfare programs and on the number of years in which these programs have been developed. The number of major welfare programs reflects the societies' concern for the welfare of people in different life situations. Cutright's article is one of the few quantitative studies of the development of welfare systems.

The Industrializing Elites

Clark Kerr, John T. Dunlop,
Frederick H. Harbison, and Charles A. Myers

Industrialization is introduced by either native or alien minorities, by groups of men who seek to change or to conquer the society through the superiority of the new means of production. A war between the old system and the new takes place whether the conquest is internal or external. The new, in the long run, is always bound to win. The dramatic issue is not whether industrialization will emerge supreme but rather which minority will assume and maintain control of the process and what its strategic approach to the organization of industrialization will be.

The ideological conflict which is so characteristic of our age is a natural accompaniment of the diverse routes taken toward industrial society under the leadership of diverse minorities. Contending ideologies are fashioned as men seek to guide this historical process by conscious effort, to explain it to themselves, and to justify it to others. But the ideologies are used not only to guide, to understand and to justify, but also as weapons of war among the proponents of the several routes; and thus the inherent conflict is sharpened and the lines are hardened. The routes become crusades as well as diverging pathways. Men debate and protest and fight with each other almost every step of the way. This has been a large share of the history of the past century and will be a good share of the history of the next.

THE DYNAMIC ELITES AND SOCIAL CONQUEST

Industrialization is always of necessity undertaken by a minority group —the colonial company, the indigenous entrepreneur, the government agency, the military unit. It cannot come into full bloom overnight except, perhaps, in small societies with unusual natural resources which attract external capital, like Kuwait. Usually industrialization starts in a restricted

Clark Kerr, John T. Dunlop, Frederick H. Harbison, and Charles A. Myers, "The Industrializing Elites," pp. 30–65, in *Industrialism and Industrial Man*, Oxford University Press, New York, 1964.

geographical area or sector as a small subculture, which then spreads until it is the dominating system of production affecting almost all the relations of men within the society.[1]

At the start of the industrialization process there are some important minorities which do not wish to move in this direction at all. They are the static minorities, usually found among the leaders of the older society: the land owners, the "medicine men," the higher artisans, the aristocrats. They can delay and thus affect the location within society of the new initiative, but they cannot prevent the transformation in the long run; and their delaying efforts are only likely to make the inevitable transition more traumatic.

The technology of industrialization requires dynamic elites for its introduction and extension into a society. The human agents who successfully introduce and extend the new technology come to have great influence in the society. They can guide and direct it within reasonable limits to suit their wishes.

Thus a crucial factor in any industrializing society is which elites become the initiators of industrialization, and how they view their role and the nature of the "good society." The universal questions are these:

(1) Who leads the industrialization march?
(2) What is the purpose of the march?
(3) How is the march organized?

The answers to these three basic questions depend in part on the conjuncture of economic and cultural variables that gives rise to the development of a particular elite and that shapes its values and strategies. The answers also depend in some measure on the aspirations of the newly emerging group of industrial employees, ever more numerous and more powerful. They wish progress, and they also wish participation. Some elites promise more of one or the other or of both than do others. Much of the turmoil of the last century was caused, and much of the turmoil of the next century will be caused, as this group debates its preferences, as it changes or is led to change its preferences, and attempts to assert them. The industrial workers, however, are usually a conditioning, not an initiating influence. But they can have a clear impact on the selection, the performance, and the survival of the dynamic elites. The peasants, however, are, except at certain times of crisis, a more passive force in the industrialization process and are also a declining element.

To this point in history there have been five generalized types of elites who may take the leadership of the industrialization process:

(1) The middle class.
(2) The dynastic leaders.
(3) The colonial administrators.

(4) The revolutionary intellectuals.

(5) The nationalist leaders.

The third group, at least in its pure form, is particularly transitory in its span of leadership; and the longer range competitors are probably found among the other four. But they also may turn out to be transient instruments of the transformation; for industrialization is relatively new to man and what form it will take in the more distant future can only be a matter of speculation.

Each of these elite groups may be composed of several elements—political leaders, industrial managers, military officers, religious figures, top civil servants, leaders of labor organizations, associated intellectuals, among others. Thus when we speak of a certain elite we refer more to the character of its central orientation than to the individuals who constitute it at any moment of time.

Each of these elite groups has a strategy by which it seeks to order the surrounding society in a consistent fashion. This strategic perspective, if the society is to end up with a cultural consistency, must pervade the entire culture. Otherwise there is internal tension, conflict, and restlessness. It is partly because the colonial managers do not have in their positions and in their outlooks the possibilities for developing a cultural consistency that they are perishable elements; their base of operation is too foreign and too narrow.

An internal conflict between the new culture, with its dominant theme set by the industrializing elite, and the old culture is inevitably fought on many fronts—the economic, political, religious, intellectual. An external conflict among alternative ideologies of industrialization tends to be fought on all fronts at once. Consistency at home and compatibility abroad, since industrialization will come to be world-wide, are two imperatives felt in greater or lesser degrees by each dominant group; imperatives which press on the instinct to survive. Each industrializing system becomes a "way of life," and a "way of life" demands internal acceptance and external protection. The only ultimate external protection is a world organized along reasonably compatible lines. These are the internal and external aspects of the historical battle over the character of the industrial society.

Management types, protest forms, labor organization typologies, rule-making relationships, taken as individual phenomena may appear largely unrelated to each other and explained singly only by history. But they are all bound more or less firmly together by an internally consistent theme, as set by these five alternative approaches to industrialization, and the elucidation of this consistency is the first step in the analysis of the separate types, forms, typologies, and relationships. All things are not possible in all situations.

To understand the different forms and paces of industrialization and their varying impacts on labor and management, we need first to take a closer look at the five generalized types of elites. What are their distinguishing attitudes and characteristics? How do they typically work—and with what results?

In this initial discussion of these "ideal" types, we describe the major strategies of industrialization as they appear to have emerged to date and are currently discernible. The five types are depicted here essentially as snapshots of a contemporary slice of time—from approximately post-World War I to the present—and in the poses that are relevant for analysis today and for projection from this date forward. These ideal types of industrializing strategies ignore much important detail in individual cases. Most actual cases are mixtures, and several societies have changed and will continue to change their essential type over time. Moreover, some elites have developed at an earlier point in history than others and would be described somewhat differently then than now. Consequently, comparisons at the same point of time impute no "timeless" value judgments relating to each of the strategies. But most individual cases may be understood better in relation to one of these types. They abstract from reality, but by reducing complexity they can also illuminate reality. They give order to our task of comprehending the forms of industrialization and their varying impacts in the area of labor-management-state relationships; and they provide a base for judging the future turn of events in a world embarked on the quest for effective industrial evolution.

THE MIDDLE CLASS AND THE OPEN MARKET

The human agents here are members of a new class rising, as in England, in opposition to the old elite, but able to live in coexistence with it. They are most likely to be drawn initially from existing commercial or artisan groups often composed of religious or national minorities. Such groups, never entirely integrated into the old society, are sensitive to the gains to be had from the new means of production. They do not advance on the wings of a rigid ideology; rather they tend to be pragmatic. They favor a structure of economic and political rules which best permits them to pursue their gains. This brings them into conflict with the old order, but they seek to impose their will piecemeal, and their assault is carried out through concentration on specific issues rather than as an explicit social revolution. In their conflict with the old order, the new group may find allies among the intellectuals wanting more freedom and the workers wanting more opportunity, particularly for political participation.

The middle-class ideology is economically individualistic and politically egalitarian. Each individual is held to be morally accountable to and for himself, within the limits of the law, which is supposed to apply equally to all members of the community. Each man's responsibility begins and ends with the injunction to make the best use of his opportunities. In practice the rigor of this doctrine is softened by the social and religious beliefs embodied in the culture, but the emphasis is on progress and on the individual. Each man is his own "Lord Spiritual." Instead of the old and the community, there is the new and the self.

Upward mobility in society is fairly directly related to knowledge of opportunities and capacity to make use of them. Family background and wealth are important, not for themselves, but only insofar as they tend to affect the range of opportunities open to men. No one is born to rule, but some must manage; and management relies more on policies and rules than it does on personal preference. The system is based heavily on consent, and the appeal in politics and in economics is to self-advantage. Every manager is, in part, a politician adjusting, within the rules of the game but with some rapidity, to the pressures of individuals, groups, and institutions. Mobility and self-interest are at the center of the social process, in practice and in theory.

The "good society" is an indistinct and shifting shadow. It is more a series of means than an end; and the means are reason, self-interest, and a relatively broad toleration of dissent. Relative emphasis is placed on many centers of decision-making power and on a system of checks and balances. The checks and balances in political life involve the separation of church and state and of the legislative, administrative, and judicial authorities. In economic life, economic units are typically separated into discrete and competitive entities.

In industrial relations, the worker is relatively independent and is expected to be self-sufficient economically and politically. ". . . he knows that he is the political equal of his employer and he has no intention of subordinating himself by incurring a debt of gratitude. He is in the workshop by virtue of a business transaction and he does not consider the personnel as a family group of which the entrepreneur should be the patriarchal head." [2] The worker may indeed be in organized opposition to the enterprise manager—some degree of conflict is built into and accepted by the system; and a whole series of economic and political institutions are in fact devised to channel and settle such conflicts. Rule-making may be more or less equally shared—by management, by organizations of workers, and by the state in a pluralistic arrangement.

Progress is taken for granted in the belief that it flows naturally out of the day-to-day decisions of many people. It should not be retarded nor should it be forced unduly by state action. The incentive of self-interest in a competitive and materialistic society is relied upon as a sufficient spur to progress. Thus economic advance is not centrally planned. Such a system will be intermediate in its record of economic growth. It will not be held back by the built-in resistances of some dynastic elite systems but it also is not geared to the forced-draft industrialization of which the revolutionary-intellectual type is capable.

Such a system depends for its more specific aspects on its origin. It may find its origin in an established society (England, Sweden, India). Here there will be more initial conflict between the old elite and the new entrepreneurs,[3] and also more of an attitude of class warfare between capital and labor because of the heritage of ruling-class attitudes. The old generally will have a greater hold and the new will have to struggle harder to gain acceptance. All this conduces to more participation by the state as the arbiter of these conflicts and as the carrier of the aspirations of the working class.

Such a system may originate in a new and relatively classless society (United States, Canada, and New Zealand). From the beginning there is more social mobility and a freer hand for progress. The middle class reigns supreme and eventually nearly everyone is or believes himself to be middle-class; and the market is as open as markets are ever likely to be. This is the more or less pure model of the "middle class and the open market"; and economic progress is likely to be reasonably rapid—the new business and industrial class is given its head. Internal cultural consistency is comparatively readily attained; in contrast to the case of origin in a class society, where as many as three subcultures may develop beside each other—the subcultures of the aristocracy, the business class, and the working class.

The evolution of the new industrial managers may not be the gradual process experienced in England and the United States. It may instead be abrupt, as in Pakistan; and this is an increasingly important phenomenon. In a rapidly industrializing nation, if the state is not to be the universal entrepreneur, private entrepreneurs must be deliberately developed. They are most likely to be drawn from among the larger merchants who have some capital and some managerial experience. Almost overnight, instead of operating a shop, they are running a modern factory. But they have not had time to accumulate experience, and this leads to inefficient use of the new facilities. Nor have they had an opportunity to change their orientation from concentration on a quick profit to the development of a continuing organization concentrating on production, and this leads to an attitude of short-term exploitation of the new situation. Nor has a competitive market grown up around them to restrict greed and compel efficiency, and so the state must step in to control the situation. The state may have an additional claim to control through its partial provision of the necessary capital.

In these cases, the new industrial managers must be as much oriented toward the state as toward the market—toward the bureaucrat as toward the consumer; and stifling bureaucratic controls and the possibility of corruption may be among the most insistent problems. Middle-class leadership so created is subject to special strains—the task of learning its new assignments and new attitudes quickly, the likelihood of worker and consumer protest against "exploitation," and the complications associated with dealing with the state as well as the market. The success of the new class will depend, in part, on how fast the industrialization proceeds and thus how soon the discipline of the market can replace that of the state in controlling prices and forcing efficiency. Only when the market has largely taken over as the regulating mechanism can this new class be certain of its future.

Middle-class leadership, extending as it does from the merchant just reaching into production in a newly industrializing economy to the formally trained manager of the long established enterprise in the highly organized society, covers a wide span of managerial types and attitudes. Both the men and their environments are widely different; but there is the same search for profits, the same acceptance of a role for private initiative, the same emphasis on piecemeal adaptation and change. Managerial performance, worker attitudes, and labor-management relations, however, will vary quite considerably.

THE DYNASTIC ELITE AND THE
PATERNAL COMMUNITY

The members of the dynastic elite are originally drawn from the landed or commercial aristocracy, since agriculture and commerce are usually the pre-existing forms of production. Less often, they are drawn from the military caste (as the samurai were in Japan), a religious hierarchy, the government bureaucracy, or tribal chieftains. This elite group is held together by a common allegiance to the established order. New recruits may be added from time to time from other strata of society, but the emphasis is on a closed system based on family and on class. Its orientation is predominantly toward tradition and the preservation of tradition.

The "realists" within this elite acknowledge the rise of the industrial system and its eventual dominance. They seek to identify the essentials of the past and to preserve them in the face of the new form of production. However, they will make whatever compromises are necessary to permit industrialization to proceed under their guidance. This was essentially the approach taken by the samurai during the Meiji restoration which sparked Japan's drive to industrialize.

By contrast, the "traditionalists" in the group may denounce and seek to fend off the new industrial system as in some Latin American countries such as Peru, or as in Iran, where the "1000 families" resist industrialization's violation of tradition. Thus the "realists" and the "traditionalists" in the early stages may find themselves locked in combat. Only if the "realists" triumph (and they will start out as a minority within the elite) can this elite avoid liquidation at worst or oblivion at best.

A dynastic elite may also include "decadents" who are oriented toward personal indulgence, which may be expressed in high living, corruption, attachment to a foreign culture, or personal security through foreign investment, rather than toward national tradition or national progress. Only if the "realists" are dominant, and are also strong, competent, and patriotic, is a dynastic elite likely to master the industrialization process, as in Japan and Germany.

If the "realists" get control of the industrialization process, their approach to it is quite distinctive.

The emphasis is on personal rule which involves perpetuation of the family which is "born to rule" and of the class within which alliances are made and from which managerial recruits are usually obtained.

The system rests on tradition but ultimately on the use of power. Such a system under sufficient pressure can become fascist in an effort to maintain internal control, since fascism is oriented toward the elite and the use of force and action. But the normal emphasis is on the approach of the patriarch toward his family or the benevolent monarch toward his subjects.

The "good society" cherishes the virtues and the symbols of the past and its institutions—the family, the church, private property, the national state. It changes from past forms only to the extent necessary for survival. Consequently, it is inherently anti-intellectual except for the "Lords Spiritual" who interpret and reinterpret the essence of the past and assess the present in the light of this essence. These "Lords Spiritual" may hold a high place in the society.

Law and order and firm administration are prized in this system, and there are often cartels and a mixture of "private" and "public" affairs in the conduct of economic life.

The political system is paternalistic and so also is the economic system. The worker is to be cared for and in return he is expected to be loyal. He is dependent on the manager for his welfare and his leadership.

The idea of tension between the enterprise manager and the worker is abhorred; and "harmony" is devoutly sought.

Rule-making is held, as far as possible, solely in the hands of management; prerogatives of management are sacred.

The social and economic systems alike have a clearly stratified hierarchy of superiors and subordinates and a reciprocal series of duties and obligations.

Industrial progress will be no faster than necessary to meet the pressures placed on the elite. These pressures may be external or internal, and they may produce quite different results. If external from foreign economic or political and military competition, they may stimulate rapid economic progress. Germany and Japan again come to mind as examples. The dynastic elite, given strong incentives, can select goals and has the mechanism to achieve them. It may exhibit substantial internal change, although the motto is likely to be "no faster and no farther than necessary." If the pressure is internal, it is less likely to arise from economic competition (since the system is usually structured against it) than from political pressure from a class-conscious working class or a strong group of independent and alienated intellectuals, or both. Checked and balanced this way, the dynastic elite may be unable to maintain its control over the total culture or wield enough power to be able to set and attain economic goals. Consequently, internal pressure is likely to be against economic progress. External pressure aids economic progress and internal pressure supports political instability.

THE COLONIAL ADMINISTRATOR
AND THE "HOME COUNTRY"

The colonial elite has been a major instrument for the introduction of industrialization in many areas of the world—supplying capital, techniques, and leadership. The colonial administrator, however, is an alien "alien"; he not only represents a new system of production but also an external society. Consequently he must carry the weight of two justifications—the justification of the new system and also of his personal intrusion into the indigenous culture. Thus his role as prime mover can be an unusually difficult one.

The other aspect of the externality of the colonial approach is the essential service to the home country rather than to the indigenous population. The home country may be served by a supply of raw materials, a market for finished products, a source of profits, an outlet for "younger sons" or surplus population; or by an opportunity to extend an ideology and political and military suzerainty. An alien elite and an alien purpose are the twin features of all colonialism; and because of this foreignness, the use of force is latent or actual in the direction of the society.

We are not concerned here with simple political control (Cyprus),[4] or with the populating and industrializing of largely empty lands (Canada, Australia). Nor are we concerned with foreign investment, foreign management, and foreign technical assistance under the rules and within the system of the indigenous population; for this is a separate phenomenon. Rather our concern is with foreign control and administration of a society in the course of industrialization.

The colonial approach to industrialization has been and is a diverse one, and so it may be better to identify it as a series of approaches related by the theme of external conquest or attempted conquest of an indigenous culture.

Any colonial power must make several basic decisions. First, is its rule a transitional or a permanent one? Its views on this may change from one period to another. Second, should it develop only a segment of the society (the plantations or copper mines) or should it try to absorb and remake the total society? Should it make the natives "Portuguese" or communists? Third, should its nationals reside temporarily in the area, as "expatriates," or should they become permanent "settlers," maintaining their own separate cultural patterns and dominant economic and political power? Immigrants who adopt the indigenous culture are neither expatriates nor settlers. The answers to these questions lead to differing forms of colonialism.

(1) "Segmental colonialism" is the result when the external power develops only a small segment of the society—more often the extractive and commercial rather than the manufacturing segments. The external power may plan to stay only temporarily and to use expatriates. Examples are cocoa exports from Ghana and sugar cane production in the Philippines and the complementary sale of manufactured goods in return. This is the lightest form of colonialism and seldom has severe political repercussions, but it does serve to introduce contact with the irreversible process of industrialization.

Of greater impact is a segmental form of colonialism which aspires to be permanent. The colonial power makes the investment in transportation, communications, a civil service, and the like, which is requisite to permanent participation in the economy but attempts to develop only segments of the productive system (jute in India, sugar cane in the Fiji Islands and Jamaica, tropical fruits in the Ivory Coast). Segmental colonialism has varied considerably in the depths of its penetration; and the depth of penetration is usually related to the prospective advantage to the home country.

(2) Where "settlers" from the home country become an important element, a new and particularly difficult dimension is added to colonialism ("settler colonialism"), for it takes on an aspect of true permanence; and, to service to the home country, is added service to the "settlers" who may have quite contrary interests to those of the home country because their views, of necessity, are more rigidly tied to the *status quo*. Rather than concentrating on profit, settler colonialism comes to concentrate on preservation of the settlers' "way of life." Settler colonialism may seek to encompass only part of an economy (plantations in Indonesia, farms in Kenya) or it may seek to absorb the total society as part of the home country (pre-DeGaulle Algeria). A dual economy and a dual society are created, whereas industrialism requires unity and consensus for its fullest development.

(3) The heaviest form of colonialism occurs when the home country seeks to transform the subject area into its own image, using indigenous

leaders and a few expatriates as its human agents ("total colonialism"). The purpose is the complete assimilation of the economy and society of the indigenous area, and its permanent attachment to the home country. This may happen with fairly general consent (Hawaii) or grudging acceptance (Mozambique) or general resistance (Hungary). If successful, the subject country has been totally conquered. Industrialization and its guiding elite have become indigenous and, after a time, the system ceases to be "colonial."

The characteristic colonialism of the dynastic elite or the middle class is quite different from that of the revolutionary intellectuals. It has been more apt to be directed toward profit or access to raw materials or outlets for "home" products, or to economic advancement for the individual settlers. The revolutionary intellectuals, as we shall see, have been more politically oriented, and through the use of indigenous associates more intent on conquering the cultural totality of the dependent area. The dynastic elite and the middle class are oriented toward the "home market" and the revolutionary intellectuals toward the "home ideology."

All colonial administrators, however, have in common service to the home country or ideology, above all. The power of the government and of the management of enterprises is likely to be great in order to handle an indigenous labor force; the worker is likely to be viewed as in a dependent or at least semidependent status, since the management represents a superior culture. Conflict between labor and management, subject to exacerbation by nationalistic sentiments, is likely to be severely controlled or suppressed. Labor organizations, when they exist, tend to be oriented toward nationalist goals.

The indigenous worker, however, is likely to be treated quite differently from one form of colonialism to another. Settler colonialism allows him to rise until he competes with the settlers; the segmental, until he reaches the level of the expatriates; the total, once he is politically reliable, to the very top. Total colonialism is most interested in full and rapid development of the economy, including manufacturing; and the segmental generally the least. Total colonialism also attacks the old culture most aggressively; while settler colonialism may even insist on the maintenance of the old culture (South Africa), and segmental colonialism may more or less ignore the existing culture.

THE REVOLUTIONARY INTELLECTUALS
AND THE CENTRALIZED STATE

A new class of intellectuals and associated activists may take over the industrializing process and society in its entirety, and sweep away, as fast as it can, the old elite and the old culture. From the beginning it intends to eliminate the former leadership groups and the pre-existing cultural arrangements and to replace them with a new ruling class and a brand new culture. The new wine shall be in totally new bottles. The principal new bottle is the centralized state. The contrast with the middle-class elite is as sharp as the difference in the industrialization approaches of, for instance, Canada and Communist China.

These intellectuals are self-identified for the task of leadership by their acceptance and espousal of a theory of history. This theory of history specifies for them the place to act, the time to act, and the means to act. Acceptance of this theory of history sets them off from other persons. They are, they contend, the bearers of the virtually inevitable historical process, the possessors of an ideology which will make it possible for them to create the future.

The ideology is the cement which holds this class together. It states that the new society is inevitable—a society fully committed to the new technology and the economic and social relations which are thought to be most compatible with its fullest development. Since an ideology is at the center of this class, there must be "high priests" to interpret and apply this ideology to current developments. The faithfulness with which one follows these interpretations is a main determinant of who belongs to the ruling class and who does not. New recruits to the class are drawn on the basis of ability combined with political reliability.

Once the new class has attained full power to control society in a centralized fashion, then the original revolutionary intellectuals within it give way increasingly to high-level political administrators and bureaucrats as the leaders of the system. It is still the new class that controls the new society but over time the new upcoming bureaucrats may run it rather differently than the original revolutionaries. In fact, the revolutionary intellectuals and the bureaucrats to whom they give over power may be almost the antithesis of each other. Emphasis on constant change gives way to greater conservatism; debate over basic policy yields place to reinterpretation of received doctrine. We see something of this happening today in the U.S.S.R.

This transition is of great importance in the evaluation of this system. But, with both the old intellectuals and the new bureaucrats, instead of the self, there is the ideology, the party, and the state. Once the influence of the original, or old, revolutionary intellectuals is gone, the centralized state remains.

If the first type of elite may be said to spring from commerce and the second from the land, then the third finds its source in the manifesto. The "vision" is the animating force along this road to industrialization. The system rests on the cohesive force of a common ideology among the leaders; the manipulation of economic class interests among the masses; and the use of force when necessary at both levels. Collective thinking and collective force are central to the system.

The world conflict is seen in large part as a test of which system can make the best use of the new technology. This society is considered "good" by its proponents because they believe it follows the logic of industrialization to the full and thus has the greatest survival value. Above all, the new technology must be served. This means forced-draft industrialization and the construction of a culture which is consistent with the new technology and its fullest utilization; thus education, labor organization, art and literature must all be geared to the system of production in a single-minded fashion. The centralized state is the only mechanism which can fully conquer the old and create the new culture, and undertake the forced-draft industrialization—the centralized state under a disciplined bureaucracy supported by the political police.

The society, of necessity, is monolithic—there can be no real separation of economic, political, and religious institutions.

Rule-making, generally, and in industrial relations, specifically, is inherently in the hands of the dominant class—the managers of this historical process. The worker is dependent on the enterprise manager, who is in turn dependent on the state, both economically and politically.

The worker's highest attribute is a sense of duty. "The Productivity of Labor, in the final analysis, is the most important, the main tool for the victory of the new order." (This quotation from Lenin appears on the front of a collective agreement in the Soviet steel industry.)[5] The worker is a "citizen" with many duties and few rights.

Overt conflict between the enterprise managers and the workers is suppressed.

History is viewed as a conscious process, subject within limits to central control. History makes its demands in fits and jerks. Not only are there strategic constellations of class interests to be manipulated, but also strategic moments of time; and it is part of the task of the ideology to identify these constellations and these moments. As a consequence, a chiliastic view of history is forced on the followers who must respond to these crucial moments: expectation of the millennium is used as a force in society. This type of society is particularly capable of forced-draft industrialization, and this may turn out to be both its pre-eminent survival characteristic and its greatest historical impact.

The system, however, is subject to a gap between the assertions of the ideology and the aspirations of the masses. Individual variations within this general approach may be identified depending on the attention paid to each of these factors. In the more orthodox version (Soviet Union and China), the ideology and thus the centralized state are pre-eminent. This calls for a heavy-handed bureaucracy and a strong police arm to get rapid industrialization and to control unrest. The original intellectuals are likely to be most committed to this approach.

The orthodox version may have its costs in internal opposition and sabotage and in external criticism; and so a revision of approach may take place where the masses are served to the extent permitted without endangering minimum adherence to the ideology (Poland and Yugoslavia). There is some decentralization of the bureaucracy, some relaxation of police control, some increase in goods and services available to consumers, some more permissive attitudes toward older culture and nationalistic traits, even at the cost of some resultant slowing of the pace of industrialization. But the central commitment remains to the ideology, the party, and the state. This version is likely to be adopted by the more politically and practically oriented members of the new class, but it is viewed by the more orthodox as a miscellany of expedient concessions which will lead over time to a forsaking of the true faith.

THE NATIONALIST LEADER AND
THE GUIDANCE OF THE STATE

The agent of industrialization may also be the nationalist leader, though the mantle of nationalism may be worn by many different types of persons. There is no single social base for nationalism and no single outlook on the nature of the industrial system. Historically important as a mechanism of transition, the nationalist leader may point his society in any one of several directions. Nationalism is more a sentiment than a system of thought, more a method of motivating than of organizing industrial society. Some other element must enter here before the choice can be made and this other element usually is the social orientation of the nationalist leaders. Beyond the fact of nationalism is the great question of who rides to power on its magic carpet. In this sense "nationalism" is more an opening of the gate toward industrial development than a specifically demarcated road toward industrialization.

Still, nationalism does predispose a society in certain directions.

A nationalist revolt against the old order or a campaign against colonialism usually raises a leader or a small group of leaders to the forefront; men who are the symbols of the new independence and who carry with them the aspirations of the populace; men who are, at least at first, national heroes. They are often charismatic personalities. Their personal influence is great and given the unstructured situation at the start of a period of great national development, they can guide or form a society within broad limits in accordance with their will. Some of the newer nations in Africa, in the Middle East, and in South Asia are examples.

Instead of classes of people there tends to be a chiliastic mass—a mass with great expectations for sudden improvement but little appreciation of how that improvement will come about; a mass subject to ecstasy and to despair. And the earlier the stage of economic development and the lower the level of education and material standards of the population, the more chiliastic the mass. The goals are extravagant and the means ignored. The attitude of this mass is open to sudden and erratic change, and thus the total situation is an unstable one.

This chiliastic attitude pervades nationalism. The view of history is a climactic one—that men can "take fortresses of history by storm." [6] There is not only the Man but also the Moment. The act of independence is such a climactic event, and the tendency is to rely on other climactic undertakings (the Aswan Dam approach). This tends to lead industrialization into difficulties arising from an overextension of total efforts and some grave imbalance among individual efforts as the startling advances (a new steel mill or an elaborate new university) are placed ahead of the more prosaic; and industrialization, instead of being a flow, becomes a series of episodes. Political and economic activity is organized around patriotic zeal instead of duty or self-interest.

While nationalism itself has no social philosophy, and is usually more pragmatic than ideological, it does predispose toward state-directed effort. Nationalism initially is negative—against the old order or the external enemy. This is enough of a platform to gain power but not to rule an economy. There may be no theory in advance as to how to proceed, but there must be a practice, a practice which will almost inevitably involve the state as the only available mechanism for a great national effort. This tends to lead to the planned economy, to state or state-sponsored investment, to state-controlled labor organizations, to workers dependent on the state for economic benefits and political direction, to state guidance of the new industrialists, to state appeals for hard work and saving, and to a call for unity.

The nationalist state requires a civil service in a crucial location in society, and the quality and the source of the civil service is a strategic factor in the development of the society.

With the state assuming the responsibility for the guidance of the new industrial managers, the new labor force, and the new labor organizations, rule-making is largely in the hands of the state, the worker is likely to be viewed as a "patriot" serving a national purpose, and labor-management conflict is likely to be controlled or suppressed.

The nationalist leaders may be found among the indigenous hereditary elite, as in Iran; among the liberal-democratic or quasi-socialistic intellectuals, as in India; or among the military commanders, as in Egypt. The first two sets of leaders may be more inclined toward reliance on private capital and initiative and the last toward state capital and initiative; liberal-democratic and quasi-socialistic intellectuals toward freedom for the individual and persuasion, and the hereditary elite and military commanders toward force and discipline and duty and personal rule. Where labor organizations have been important in the independence struggle, as in Indonesia, and particularly if they are under left-wing influence, the emphasis may be additionally upon state activity. In any event, the nationalist economy is likely to be a mixed economy lying somewhere between the private initiative preferred by the middle class and the state control preferred by the revolutionary intellectuals. Where the leaders have risen through nationalist political or military channels and have had little prior contact with the theory or practice of managing a society, they tend to seek out what works best at the time with few preconceived ideas.

The "nationalist society" is particularly a plaything of history. Its recent past is of especial significance. If the nationalist leaders arise out of a violent rejection of a hereditary dynastic elite or of settler colonialism (e.g., Indonesia), the emphasis is particularly likely to be a negative one stressing hates and fears. But if the transition is a more peaceful one, as, for example, a transition out of segmental colonialism (e.g., India), elements of the old system are more likely to be retained and attention to be turned to positive developments. In any event, there is likely to be a negative period when independence from the old and a lack of social discipline (slack work and heavy consumption) will be the dominant themes. The more violent the act of independence, the longer this period is likely to last with its uncertainty and lack of national consensus about anything except distaste for the old, as in Indonesia and Iraq. More fortunate is the society which can move quickly and firmly into a positive program of national economic development. But even here, as in Turkey, there are likely to come periods of rapid forward progress and periods of relative stagnation. The need for clear direction is great. Yet this clear direction is particularly difficult to attain. The leaders come out of a political background rather than a solidly anchored class or group and are "personalities"; and as the leadership shifts so does the "personality." The mass may alternately expect too much and then too little. And there is no single ready-made ideology for the nationalist conduct of an economy. Consequently, the nationalist approach tends to be a wavering one following an unsteady course. This is particularly true if regional, tribal, or religious differences are added to the uncertainty over social direction. If the nationalist approach is to be successful, it must attain a sense of national unity and substantial forward momentum. The tests are how soon the national purpose can be moved from the negative to the positive phase, and then how much effort can be pulled out of the nation, and how sustained that effort will be.

Any society at any moment of time probably needs some reasonably well-settled theme for its development if it is to move ahead, as is so well illustrated by the case of Indonesia, or of Poland when it was immobilized between Stalinism and revisionism. Economic progress awaits a firm decision as to the specific approach to be followed; in the case of

Table 1 *The Industrializing Elites and Their Strategies*

Strategic Concepts	Middle Class	Dynastic	Revolutionary-Intellectuals	Colonial Administrators	Nationalist Leaders
Central strategy of the elite	Individual self-advancement	Preservation of traditional society	Centralization of power in forced-draft industrialization	Servicing the "home country"	National independence and progress
Central characteristic of the society	Open market	Paternal community	Centralized state	Alien system under alien control	State "guided" development
Sources of variations in the approach	Origin in class or classless society; or in rapid industrialization	Nature of external and internal pressures	Comparative responsiveness to ideology, or to desires of masses	Segmental or total approach; and absence or presence of "settlers"	Negative or positive stage of development
Basic rule-making authority in labor-management relations	Employer, union, state	Employer and state	Largely state	Colonial administrator and employer	Largely state
Elite's view of worker	Independent	Dependent	Dutiful producer	Dependent	Patriot
Elite's attitude toward conflict	Accept within rules of game	Suppress	Prohibit	Suppress	Control

the nationalist economy, in particular, how much state guidance there will be. There is no good substitute for a strategic concept.

Table 1 summarizes the major elements in the strategies of the five generalized types of elites.

In order to contrast the major contemporary patterns of industrializing strategies, the foregoing descriptions of the five generalized types of industrializing elites have been essentially static. In actuality, of course, industrialization under any elite leadership is a constantly growing and shifting process. To provide more reality to the portrayal, it is now essential to consider the dynamics of the total situation, and to examine briefly the sources of the several elites and the natural history of their developments.

THE SOURCES OF THE ELITES

Some elites have achieved supremacy in some places and others in others; some for one reason and some for another. How did they happen to get this authority? In each single case the explanation involves a great deal of historical detail. Viewed broadly, however, there appear to have been four major considerations variously involved: the nature of the pre-existing society, the role of geography, the stage of history, and the accidents of history.

The Pre-Existing Society

Industrialization began in Western Europe. It is one of the mysteries of history why it began there and at the time it did. Ancient Greece and Rome and before them Mesopotamia and Egypt had developed a capacity for new ideas and new ways of doing things. In each of these societies, they could build buildings, organize men, engage in elaborate commerce, develop transportation, keep accounts. But they never did develop science or get the machine capable of repetitive operations, nor did they find the secret of constant sources of power other than man or beast. The Chinese and even the Mayan civilizations also had many of the conditions necessary for the start of industrialization; but it never started.

In the cities of Western Europe, commerce and craftsmanship rose to high levels. When the new machines and the new sources of power came along there was already a substantial urban middle class oriented toward profit and sufficiently independent of the older feudal order to undertake the industrializing process. The early industrialization in England and the Lowlands was led by the new middle-class entrepreneurs already accustomed to a market economy and a democratic polity. Here was a new and better way of getting things done and making profit.

The new held no terror for them because they were already in opposition to the old feudal order. No other elite group at this time could so easily and quickly have embraced and encouraged the new productive techniques.[7]

The new industrialization found acceptance elsewhere, and sometimes in the most unlikely places. Dynastic elites still in control of their societies, as in Germany, Japan, and more recently Iran, saw the success of the new technique and came to use it. In Germany with the competition of England, in Japan with its fear of foreign conquest, and in Iran with its fear of social revolution, the obvious hand of the future impelled the established elites to accept the unaccustomed methods while still seeking to preserve as much as they could of the old order. Some dynastic elites elsewhere, however, either refused to come to terms with the new modes of production or were so ineffective they could not make proper use of them. By a strange turn of fate, in recent times, the old has come to embrace the new. The old dynastic elites which once scorned commercial and industrial pursuits have come to seize upon industrial endeavor, as in parts of Latin America and the Arab world, as the source of their salvation. The old dynastic elite has taken the place of the new middle class as carrier of change.

The middle-class and dynastic elites alike, and for much the same reasons, took industrialization into many more primitive societies in the interests of the home country. These societies were sufficiently primitive economically so that they could not develop, or at least had not developed, industrially. In some cases the idea of industrializing was totally new to them. In any event, they did not have the means of effective resistance in the face of the weapons placed in the hands of the colonial powers by their machines. Thus industrialization initially came to Indonesia, India, the Congo, and many other parts of the world under colonial auspices.

In reaction to colonialism or to a resistant or ineffective dynastic elite or a combination of both, nationalist leaders have seized control, as in Egypt, Mexico, Indonesia, and now lead the industrializing process. Again, reacting to precisely the same forces, revolutionary intellectuals have also captured nations for the sake of industrialization; as they took over in Russia from a crumbling aristocracy and in China from a society too often run by war lords in the country and foreign firms in the treaty ports. Never have the nationalist leaders or the revolutionary intellectuals attained control, by means of internal action, from a vigorous middle class or dynastic elite. In areas and times mutually conducive to their ascendancy, the nationalist leaders and the revolutionary intellectuals often stand as alternatives to each other, and are thus inherently competing for power.

Thus a successful commercial society is predisposed toward middle-class leadership of industrialization; a feudal or semifeudal system toward continued leadership by the dynastic elite if it is realistic enough and forceful enough; a truly primitive society toward guidance, although often involuntarily, by the representatives of a colonial power; the evolving colonial or the decaying feudal society toward either nationalist leaders or revolutionary intellectuals. The middle-class leadership attains supremacy by its mere existence and its inherent temperament; the dynastic, by the right of its hereditary authority; the colonial, by virtue of its technical and military superiority; the nationalist and revolutionary intellectuals through the weakness of others and their own will to power.

The Fact of Geography

This factor affects the advent to power of each of the several elites through the influence of propinquity, of discovery, and of conquest. The British system had its impact in Western and Northern Europe, the North American in Latin America, the Soviet in China; in each case both through example and through influence. The British colonized North America and Australia. The British conquered India; the Dutch, Indonesia; the Soviets, Eastern Europe; the Chinese, Tibet. Africa was divided up by Western European powers. Each dominant nation favored its own system of industrialization.

The Stage of History

Before World War I, industrialization was undertaken by middle-class, dynastic, or colonial elites; since World War I, and particularly since World War II, by nationalist leaders and revolutionary intellectuals. They have risen against alien control and against backwardness. By 1918, colonialism had passed its zenith as an international influence and in many colonial countries, with the spread of skills and education, a new class of indigenous leaders was arising. By 1918, industrialization was so obviously the road to power, to better health, to higher standards of living, and to education that it became the goal of mankind and the essence of national aspiration. Turkey was among the first to seek modernization under nationalist leaders.

By 1918, the Bolsheviks had attained power in Russia and set about the successful and rapid industrialization of that country, with visions of ultimate world-wide conquest. Also by 1918, middle-class elements and most dynastic elites which had the vision and the vigor to industrialize their countries had already begun to do so. Thus the large new areas for industrialization since 1918 have fallen under the leadership of the nationalists or the revolutionary intellectuals; except that, as noted earlier, some still reigning dynastic elites have in recent times undertaken industrialization in the interests of self-preservation.

The Accidents of History

Finally, among our four considerations, the accidents of history help explain who seizes the reins. War and depression have determined a great deal of history. The revolutionary intellectuals would not so certainly have taken over Russia except for World War I and China except for World War II. Colonialism came to a quicker end in India and Indonesia because of World War II. The chief beneficiaries of violent eruption have been the nationalists and the revolutionary intellectuals.

THE NATURAL HISTORY OF THE ELITES

The actual industrializing elites are seldom if ever pure or ideal types, as we have noted earlier. They are often both mixed and changing by type. But there is usually enough resemblance to an ideal type to permit differentiation and classification. At this point in mid-twentieth century, we can still identify many countries which adhere to one or another of these types. Each type seems to have its own natural tendencies for evolution, and thus there exist more or less parallel evolutions for countries equally patterned after a certain type.

The Middle Class and the Organization Society

The middle-class system is the most stable of our several types, partly because the middle class is also the mediating class in society and makes its adjustments a little at a time rather than in dramatic bursts. In fact, the middle class once in full control of the industrialization process has never in history lost its authority for internal reasons. This does not mean, nevertheless, that the middle-class system does not itself change significantly.

The size of enterprise becomes larger. A separation takes place between ownership and management. Workers add to their power through their own large-scale organizations. The state takes on ever new duties. It provides social security, regulates competition and industrial conflict, redistributes wealth, assures a minimum level of economic activity and employment, and enters the internal life of private organizations to guarantee equality of treatment and opportunities for participation. It becomes the biggest single employer.

The market loses some of its influence. Decisions are supplied by rules and by group actions as well as by atomistic interchanges in the market place. The worker becomes more closely tied to his particular employment through seniority rules and security benefits. Individual self-advancement gives way increasingly to efforts at group advancement. The middle class becomes less and less a definable leadership elite, as many elements in society share urban middle-class status. The middle class still rules, but less obviously so; and the markets are still major instruments for making decisions, but they are no longer so open.

The Erosion of the Dynastic Elite

Where the dynastic elite governs ineffectually, as it frequently has done, the country will, in modern times, shift either to nationalist or revolutionary intellectual leadership. If it governs effectively, however, it is also subject to changes. As industrialization proceeds, the hereditary elite expands, recruiting new members from lower strata in its society and particularly by the process of selection through the mechanisms of higher education.

Industrialization requires a great deal of mobility in the labor force, from one occupational level to another, from one area to another, from one enterprise to another. This tends to break down the paternal plant community, as does the growth of social services provided by other institutions than the enterprise. Class lines are softened. The political parties and labor organizations of the working class become gradually less ideological, although this can take a long time and involve many conflicts between the traditionalists and the revisionists. Both the managerial and working classes converge toward the upper and lower ranges of the middle class in their habits and beliefs. Tradition and status mean less; competition and contracts mean more. The worker becomes more independent and the manager more professional. Attitudes toward industrial conflict also soften. The labor organizations come to share more of the rule-making authority.

The society is moving toward the middle-class type, as Germany has done and Japan seems to be doing. But it may retain for a long time remnants of the earlier ideological struggle which is so typical of such societies: permanently enhanced power for the state, a heightened attention to the role of occupation in determining the standing of an individual. The society, however, is no longer so traditional and the managers no longer so paternal.

The Fate of All Colonies

The colonial system is the most transient of the several ideal types of elites. "Colonialism spawned its destroyer—nationalism." [8] Segmental colonialism has not penetrated deeply enough to make possible its continuing hold on the economy and the society. It carries the seeds of industrialization and the seeds of its own destruction. It may continue, however, in a new and changed form: a segment for foreign ownership and management in the economy within a compatible political system operated by the indigenous people. The colonial enterprises may retain their profits by giving up their control of the society. Settler colonialism has more tenacity and also creates a greater need for tenacity. Whether it can survive anywhere is still in doubt. Past history would indicate the settlers only survive by ceasing to be "settlers," giving up their separate and dominant "way of life," as in the case of the colonies of ancient Greece. The colonialism with the greatest survival possibilities is total colonialism because it ceases, once it is effective, to be colonialism. It becomes the system of the country itself under its own indigenous leaders.

All colonialism, in the end, is either overthrown by the "natives" or ceases to be colonialism by becoming the "native" system or a component part of it. No advanced industrial society has ever yet been run by aliens.

The "New Class" of Intellectuals

The revolutionary intellectuals are committed to the view that the climactic change through which they seize power is the last great change in social relations. The classless society will emerge, and, according to Marx, the only other really substantial change in prospect is the "withering away of the state." Thus far it has not withered, and it is highly unlikely it ever will. But other changes can and do take place.

There is in communist society, as noted earlier, the great contradiction between the demands of the ideology and the desires of the populace. These desires are particularly hard to deal with if they arise from a subjugated people (Poland, Hungary) who are resistant to essentially alien rule of an alien system. They have their nationalism around which to rally opposition and pressure. Aside from the pressure of nationalism against the "total colonialism" of the communists, there may also be the antagonistic interests of some national minorities, as in the Soviet Union itself.

The desires of the populace, however, are basic under any circumstances, whether encouraged by nationalism or not. The ideology calls for an attack on the old culture, and there are those who cherish it. The ideology requires an immense national effort of hard work and austerity, and there are those who resent it. The ideology calls for a great centralization of power, and there are those who seek to share it. The most persistent drive is probably in the direction of sharing power. The military makes its demands. The scientists and the new managers make theirs. Even the workers, as they get more skill and responsibility, and thus power, can make demands of their own. These groups may come to have their own areas within which they can govern. While they may not share authority over society, they may be able to bring greater influence to bear upon those who do. Universal education, which is an imperative of successful industrialization, may even open up an eventual possibility of diffusing political power widely throughout the society.

The requirement of efficiency itself may force some fractionalization of power. As there are more enterprises and particularly as more enterprises are involved in the production and distribution of a myriad of consumer goods and the provision of an increasing range of personal services, central control becomes less possible. The more successful the process of industrialization, the more reliance has to be placed on localized decisions and on markets, instead of on centralized decisions and plans; and markets bring the middle-class approach in their wake.

The new generations of leaders become more secure, more professional, more bureaucratically interested in standard performance than in all-out effort, further removed from the old ideological considerations and the traditions of the revolution. The wolves give way to the watchdogs. With greater educational opportunities and a less desperate need for trained people, the class stratification of the society declines and a new equality seeps into the society.

The masses also will come to crave more of the product of their own labor; and the drive for more consumers' goods and better housing will change the society too.[9]

The revolutionary intellectuals appeal particularly to the "transitionals"[10] in societies in the very early stages of industrialization. They promise an end to the old ruling elite or the colonial power, to the old tribal or feudal culture, to economic and educational backwardness. They have much less to offer to others than to the "transitionals," and particularly have they little to offer to the members of a developed middle-class society. They may have some continuing appeal to the workers in a class society under a dynastic elite, but if this elite is successful in managing industrialization and moves over time toward the middle-class approach, the appeal lessens. In the nationalists, they meet competitors who offer the same things and can hold the allegiance of the "transitionals" if they are reasonably successful in delivering what they promise.

The revolutionary intellectuals have programs for handling the problems of the transition—rapid commitment of a labor force, the fast buildup of an educational system, the quick encouragement of labor discipline and productivity, the enlargement of the gap between current consumption and current production for the sake of investment, development of an export surplus from the agricultural segment to feed the cities, suppression of industrial conflict.

Again, however, they have much less in the way of programs for an advanced industrial society. They are handicapped, because of the rigidity of their ideology, in handling diversified production, in responding to the insistent calls for fractionalized power, in giving the freedom for inquiry which goes along with highly developed educational and research institutions.

Their historical message may be only to the "transitionals" anxious to leave behind them a decaying feudal or alien colonial society; and their greatest historical impact may be, not the creation of the "classless" society, but the firm, even forceful handling of the economic and political problems in the immediate transition from the traditional to the technological society. They respond to the problems of one stage in history and to the defaults of others in handling those problems. Their rule is neither inevitable nor necessarily everlasting. It may be communism itself that withers away. However that may be, any society they run, despite any reluctant tendency toward gratification of the desires of the masses, will be comparatively disposed toward the managerial state, the use of force, the service of technology, the supremacy of the party and the suppression of conflict so long as their ideology has any hold either in theory or in continued practice and acceptance.

The Nationalists as Experimenters

Nationalism relies heavily on the state, but not so rigidly as the revolutionary intellectuals. Consequently, private enterprise and markets not only have a chance to survive, but the opportunity to take over larger areas of the economy as they are capable of doing so. Nationalism often conduces to one-party rule or domination, but again this is not based on ideology and, as consensus develops in the society and education spreads, a greater distribution of political power can occur. The nationalist leaders, while having many of the same goals as the revolutionary intellectuals, are not bound by an all-pervading ideology. They are opportunists and experimenters. This has its disadvantages and its advantages. The lack of an effective ideology leads to much stumbling and uncertainty in the early stages; but it also helps avoid confining rigidities in the later stages of industrialization. Generally, nationalism, if successful, will tend toward a modified version of the middle-class approach, modified by heavier emphasis on the state; if unsuccessful, however, only the revolutionary intellectuals can readily attain leadership.

The natural history of each of our five types is to change: some completely (colonial), some drastically (dynastic elite and nationalist), and some substantially (middle-class, revolutionary intellectual); but they all do change. Table 2 summarizes the natural history of these ideal types of elites.

THE FLOATING FORCES—THE INTELLECTUALS
AND THE GENERALS

Two forces—one representing ideas and the other power—are inherently socially unattached on any permanent basis in the struggle for supremacy in organizing industrializing societies. Both the politically minded intellectuals and the generals often can and do align themselves now with one and now with another elite and its strategy; and their alignments can be a crucial factor.

The intellectuals (including the university students) are a particularly volatile element, capable of quite rapid shifts of opinion, quickly sensitive as they are to the social climate. They are almost always divided among

Table 2 *The Sources of the Elites and the Natural History of Their Systems*

Industrializing Elite	Middle Class	Dynastic	Revolutionary-Intellectuals	Colonial Administrators	Nationalist Leaders
Pre-existing society	Commercial	Strongly led feudal or quasi-feudal	Weakly led quasi-feudal; or colonial	Primitive	Weakly led quasi-feudal; or colonial
Stage in history	Relatively early	Relatively early	Relatively late	Relatively early	Relatively late
"Normality" of development	"Normal"	"Normal"	Development at a crisis point (war or depression)	Most transient	Development often at a crisis point (war or depression)
Inherent direction of change	More group and state action	Less elitist and paternal	Less ideological; more bureaucratic; more sensitive to the wishes of the masses and of other emerging elites	Nationalism; and occasionally rule by revolutionary intellectuals	More middle-class influence, if successful; revolutionary intellectuals, if unsuccessful
Changing relation to markets	Markets lose some of their influence	Larger role	Larger role	Larger role internally and externally	Markets qualified by nationalist state

themselves. They have no continuing commitment to any single institution or philosophical outlook, and they are not fully answerable for consequences. They are, as a result, never fully trusted by anybody, including themselves as their constant and often bitter doctrinal and policy disagreements and quarrels testify. Yet they have power which can move society.

The intellectuals generate ideas and serve as constant critics of society. They help determine how men think about each other, about history, about the nature of the good society. They spin theories and ideologies; they can turn conflicts into crusades. In the modern world with its perfected communications, they are particularly influential since ideas travel fast. The new invaders are not the hordes breaking across a traditional boundary but ideas riding the air waves and the printed page around the world. What is the quality of the intellectuals on each side and how well are they used? This is an important question for social groups within a nation as well as for the contending systems among nations; and particularly in periods of internal or external crisis. The intellectuals speak the loudest and are heard the most at the crossroads of social history.

Each of the generalized types of elites, even the colonial in Kipling and others, has drawn its intellectual supporters—the romanticists and historicists supporting the dynastic elite and the old culture and the idea of community; the humanitarians and rationalists favoring the liberal-democratic theme and the open society; the revolutionaries aiding communism and destruction of the old order; and the chauvinists elevating the national state and national character. There have also been political intellectuals who have withdrawn to the side in disillusionment and bewilderment into nihilism, existentialism, or some other school of thought standing largely aside from the battle over the transformation of society into its industrial mold.

But intellectuals are not always free to float as they please, for they may be controlled, and the more authoritarian the society the more effective the control; and the communist as the most authoritarian has the most control. It is part of the essence of communism (and fascism) that the intellectuals must serve the ruling order if they are to serve at all. In these instances they are neither free-floating nor much of a force.

The generals influence society not through ideas, but through the ultimate power of the armed forces. In some societies, aside from the power at their command, they are and are recognized to be the best trained and most patriotic elements in the society. They may also be closest to the aspirations of the mass of the people, particularly when the army is one of the few channels for upward social mobility. They often have a reputation for being less corrupt than other elements, for being more dynamic in getting things done, for being able to make decisions, for having trained staff available. They also, like the intellectuals, can transfer their allegiance and support from one group to another, or from one system to another, but are more likely to be attached to the ruling element, whatever it may be. In fact, in some societies the ruling element is by definition the element with the support of the armed forces. The military tend to be more important in societies which rely heavily on force for their sanction—than in the liberal-democratic society which relies more on consent. In the liberal-democratic system, the military almost of necessity must be under civilian control and is not a significant partisan political factor.

The generals normally stand for law and order, and serve as a reserve force either to back the ruling group or to take over from it if it breaks down. But they may also be a force for reform, often of a populist character, for they have a mass base in the soldiery; and so there may be a Cromwell as well as a Franco. Military reform when it comes tends to be nationalist, disciplinary, and responsive to a great mass wish—like independence or land reform—and not to have a full ideology or an intellectual base or even much knowledge of the complexities of civilian life. Whether supporting the ruling group or supplanting it, the military may insist on industrial modernization, as in Japan and Germany, for the sake of the strength of its armies and thus become an influential factor in economic progress.

The generals, like the intellectuals, are a more crucial factor in a critical period. A crisis, whatever else it may do to other groups—heightens the influence of these two elements; and tranquility humbles both. Even if the military remains silent in a crisis, it is taking sides and affecting the outcome; while the intellectual attempting to influence events cannot be silent. Since force is most likely to be used internally in a period of social transition, the armed forces play a special role under such circumstances. The orientation of their leaders becomes a vital factor, and whoever captures the military leaders may well capture the system. This is particularly true in recent times when the armed power of the soldier so far surpasses the unarmed power of the citizen.

The general is more important at some times—the crises—and in some systems—those based on force—than at other times and in other places. Thus, in a dynastic system under severe internal pressure, the communist society in an internal power struggle, the colonial economy subject to unrest, and the nationalist regime looking for national unity, the role of the generals may be the single conclusive factor. This is not to suggest that they will always all see alike—some of the drama may lie in their internal rivalries. Their role, of course, is enhanced by external as well as internal warfare. Only the liberal-democratic system in peace can afford to ignore the generals.

These floating forces—the intellectuals and the generals—guide industrialization mostly when the process is faltering or changing course. On other occasions the guidance of the process is left to the other more persistent elements described earlier.

The middle class offers individual choice; the dynastic elite, continuity; the revolutionary intellectuals, high velocity industrialization; and the nationalist leaders, the integrity and advancement of the nation. None of them, however different their essential emphasis, can escape the imperatives of consensus and assimilation. In each case, starting as a minority, they must get the acceptance of the society and become broadly based within a culture which is compatible with their strategic approach. Once this has been done, internal ideological conflict in a society will slacken, for there is no longer a basic clash over the strategic approach to industrialization.

The decline of ideology in a society marks the rise in acceptance of the dominant strategy. But new minorities will arise from time to time to challenge the accepted strategy; and so the ideological weapons will be kept burnished, if not often actively employed. The decline of ideology in the world will come when there is only one accepted approach to industrialism; and that eventuality, if it ever comes, is still a long distance away.

REFERENCES

1. Everett E. Hagen, "The Process of Economic Development," *Economic Development and Cultural Change* (April 1957), pp. 206–214, and "How Economic Growth Begins: A General Theory Applied to Japan," *Public Opinion Quarterly* (Fall 1958), pp. 373–390.
2. E. Levasseur, *The American Workman* (Baltimore: The Johns Hopkins Press, 1900), pp. 445–446.
3. Reinhard Bendix, *Work and Authority in Industry* (New York: John Wiley & Sons, Inc., 1956), pp. 22–116.
4. A. J. Meyer, *Middle Eastern Capitalism* (Cambridge, Massachusetts: Harvard University Press, 1959), p. 64: ". . . Cyprus is still economically unviable and a ward of the West for its food and clothing."
5. See American Iron and Steel Institute, *Steel in the Soviet Union* (New York: 1959), p. 329.
6. Karl Mannheim, *Ideology and Utopia* (New York: Harcourt, Brace & Co., 1949), p. 219.
7. For a discussion of the sources of industrializing elites, see Everett E. Hagen, "The Process of Economic Development," *Economic Development and Cultural Change* (April 1957), pp. 193–215.
8. John Scott, *Democracy Is Not Enough: A Personal Survey of the Hungry World* (New York: Harcourt, Brace & Company, 1960), p. 19.
9. W. W. Rostow, *The Stages of Economic Growth, A Non-Communist Manifesto* (Cambridge, England: Cambridge University Press, 1960), pp. 103, 133.
10. Daniel Lerner, *The Passing of Traditional Society* (Glencoe, Illinois: The Free Press, 1958), uses this term to denote the people on the margin between traditional and modern society.

Social Security, Incentives, and Controls in the U.S. and U.S.S.R.

Gaston V. Rimlinger

One of the most important developments in the relationship between the state and the individual citizen during the present century has been the growth in the rights of the citizen to claim economic services and cash benefits from the state. Social security programs, which have appeared in nearly every country of the world, are a central feature of this development.[1] Their main purpose has been the prevention of poverty through protection of the individual and his family against loss of income and against certain financial burdens. The growth of these rights, while greatly enriching the status of citizenship, has always been confronted with certain fundamental economic and social questions.[2] What is likely to be the long-run effect on the work habits and productivity of the mass of the

[1] A note on terminology. "Social security" in this paper is used as a generic term for governmental measures designed to protect individual or family income and to provide certain services. It includes social insurance, public assistance, and social service. "Social insurance" is used to refer specifically to programs with work-related benefits which are financed at least in part by specific taxes. "Public assistance" is used for programs financed out of general revenue with benefits given on the basis of need. Most of the discussion will have reference to social insurance programs.

[2] Those opposing social security programs have always stressed presumed harmful effects. Those who favor them are more interested in finding out at what point and under what conditions public income guarantees may have adverse economic effects. T. H. Marshall throws interesting light on this question in tracing the growth of citizenship rights from the acquisition of civil rights in the 18th century, to political rights in the 19th, to social rights in the 20th century. See *Citizenship and Social Class* (Cambridge, 1950).

Gaston V. Rimlinger, "Social Security, Incentives, and Controls in the U.S. and U.S.S.R.," *Comparative Studies in Society and History*, 1961, pp. 104–124, Mouton and Company, The Hague, Netherlands. Research in the area of this paper was done with financial assistance from the Ford Foundation and the Industrial Relations Section of Princeton University. For counsel and helpful criticism I am indebted to Dean J. Douglas Brown, Mr. Robert J. Myers, and my colleague Professor E. O. Edwards. Responsibility for the content rests solely with myself.

people once a nation has eliminated the fear of destitution? Will a growing sense of security increase productivity? Or is it likely that the more surely individuals can count on essential services and minimal incomes, the greater will be the danger of drifting into indifferent work habits? Such a drift would probably take the form of a subtle change in values rather than a dramatic shift in attitude. Whatever the effect may be, it must certainly depend on the nature of the rights granted, social values and attitudes, and a country's economic and socio-political order.

The historic stress on individualistic self-reliance and political freedom and the restrictions on state intervention under American capitalism are often considered polar opposites of the collectivist mentality and institutions of Soviet socialism. The Soviet system is based on highly centralized economic and political control and inevitably fosters the individual's economic dependence on the state. These divergent environments offer an opportunity for a comparative approach to the complex questions raised above. This article uses the comparative method to explore the relationship between social security rights and production implications in the two countries.

Aside from the inherent interest of this question, its discussion is made timely by the remarkable recent increases and anticipated growth in social security expenditures in many countries, including the U.S. and U.S.S.R.[3] How these large sums and the administrative agencies controlling them will affect economic behavior and processes is becoming increasingly important.[4] For purposes of dealing with this question, we may look upon social security as a system of secondary income distribution, a system which is different in its distributive principles and primary objectives from the economy's functional income distribution. Functional income payments go to employed factors of production. They perform their productive function when they attract and allocate these factors in accordance with economic efficiency. Income from social security, on the

[3] In the U.S. public income-maintenance program expenditures rose from $9.149 billions in 1949–50 to $26.146 billions (projected) in 1959–60. The U.S.S.R. state social insurance budget rose from 17.2 billion rubles in 1950 to 70.2 billion rubles (planned) in 1960. Figures for the U.S. are from Ida C. Merrian, "Social Security Status of the American People," *Social Security Bulletin*, XXIII, No. 8 (August 1960), p. 8. U.S.S.R. data are from "Tsentral'noe Statisticheskoe Upravlenie pri Sovete Ministrov SSSR," *Narodnoe Khoziaistvo SSSR v. 1958 Godu* (Moscow, 1959), p. 906, and from A. Larin, "Leninskie Printsipy Sotsial'nogo Strakhovanii, Vottloshchaiutsia v Zhizni," *Okhrana Truda i Sotsialnoe Strakhovanie*, No. 3 (March 1960), p. 9.

[4] The broader implications of social security are stressed particularly in recent German literature. See, for instance, H. Achinger, *Sozialpolitik als Gesellschaftspolitik* (Hamburg, 1958), and H. Hensen, *Die Finanzen der sozialen Sicherung im Kreislauf der Wirtschaft* (= *Kieler Studien*, No. 36) (Kiel, 1955). Myrdal also stresses the need to integrate the social security edifice in Sweden with "the whole system of public policies." G. Myrdal, *Beyond the Welfare State* (New Haven, 1960), p. 66.

other hand, is oriented, at least in the first instance, to the needs of its beneficiaries rather than the requirements of the production process. Social security payments go chiefly to totally or partially unemployed and unemployable persons, in other words, persons who are in the main separated from productive activity. As all income payments, they tend to have an impact on both the supply and the demand side of the economy's output. Social security income affects the economy's level of effective demand; its timing and amount can be designed to contribute to economic stability. To have an effective impact on the supply side, the distributive pattern and eligibility conditions of social security must be coordinated with functional income distribution and with other factors affecting production costs.

Many problems are inherent in the attempt to make social security serve adequately the needs of its beneficiaries and at the same time use it as an instrument of economic incentive and control. To see how the U.S. and the U.S.S.R. differ in their approaches to these problems, we shall begin with an examination of social security rights, since these determine the principles of benefit distribution in the two countries.

SOCIAL SECURITY RIGHTS AND
BENEFIT DISTRIBUTION

The American System

Social security income, unlike functional income, cannot be distributed "blindly" through the working of an impersonal market mechanism. The state has to decide under what circumstances and in what degree individuals and their families will be supported. Such decisions are necessarily interrelated with prevailing views on the powers and duties of the state, the rights and responsibilities of individuals, and on an evaluation of the economic justification of support and its consequences.

The interaction of these factors in the shaping of a country's social security system is a complex historical process. Only a broad outline of major shifts in ideas and attitudes leading to the present American system can be sketched here. The absence of serious social security planning in America until the 1930's was not due to any stifling of widespread demands for such benefits. This absence, a historian points out, "reflected a positive philosophy . . . that it was up to the individual to work, save, and succeed." [5] It was an affirmation of a faith in a certain uniqueness of the country's economic and social system. According to the dominant views, the country was so full of opportunities for economic self-help that

[5] F. L. Allen, "Economic Security: A Look Back and A Look Ahead," in The American Assembly, *Economic Security for Americans* (New York, 1959), p. 14.

support by the state could be largely ignored or rejected as both harmful and unnecessary.

To be sure, insecurity and personal misfortune were not denied, nor could cases of chronic poverty be entirely overlooked. But insecurity was considered an essential stimulus to economic drive, and relief of personal misfortune was a task for voluntary private charity.[6] Chronic poverty, on the other hand, was accounted for largely in terms of character deficiency. The poorest groups were made up mainly of Negroes and recent immigrants. In the explanation of their lot, sociological theories about racial characteristics, which were most in vogue during the decades of heavy immigration, reinforced the arguments about individual shortcomings as a cause of economic distress. So long as shiftlessness, laziness, lack of prudence and forethought, or ungrateful children, which may be evidence of faulty rearing and care by the parent, were regarded as the source of indigence, the poor could have no strong claim against society. On the contrary, to give them assistance might only encourage their "evil" habits and help them escape the "natural" punishment for their weaknesses.

The provision of restricted public assistance to recognized paupers was, of course, part of Anglo-American tradition, and its legitimacy, in the sense of acceptability to the community, was not in doubt while America industrialized. The legitimacy of social insurance, however, was an entirely different matter, for it meant superimposing upon the private enterprise system state planned support of individuals and families, regardless of their need and without deterrent.

The implied dependence on the state was felt to pose serious threats to individual freedom, thrift, and self-help, which have always been considered the backbone of American economic vitality. The presence of these deep feelings about a fundamental incompatibility of such compulsory measures with the American free enterprise system helps to account for the fact that by the early 1930's the United States, the most important industrial power in the world, was at the same time the greatest laggard among industrial countries in the development of social security. For a quarter of a century protection against industrial accidents alone was thought to be an acceptable field for social insurance. And this was made acceptable by an extension of the concept of employer liability and reliance on state police power, rather than on any welfare state concept. Other forms of social insurance were associated with socialism and state paternalism. They were sensed to be the product of class-conscious governments, governments which admit that not all citizens have equal opportunities, that some social groups cannot fully provide for themselves and are therefore entitled to special protection.

[6] The most forceful presentation of this view is probably in William G. Sumner, *What Social Classes Owe to Each Other* (New York, 1883).

Rather interesting shifts in ideas and attitudes occurred when the spectacular distress of the 1930's made massive state relief measures unavoidable. Now it was officially recognized not only that large numbers of people were becoming economically dependent through no fault of their own, but also that this was a permanent rather than merely a temporary problem.[7] While this recognition removed some of the obstacles to the introduction of social security, it did not eliminate the deeply-rooted American dislike for any arrangement which ties the welfare of large numbers of individuals to benefits provided by the state. In defense against latent and overt arguments that such an arrangement threatens individual freedom and economic self-reliance, the framers of the American social security system put great emphasis on the idea that social security, unlike ordinary relief measures, was not at all a government handout but mainly a social mechanism for the realization of the traditional ideals of economic self-help. Professor J. Douglas Brown, a staff member of the Committee on Economic Security appointed by President Roosevelt, has stated recently: "We wanted our government to provide a mechanism whereby the individual could prevent dependency through his own efforts . . . To us social security was a social mechanism for the preservation of individual dignity . . ."[8] According to this view, the American approach to social security is a conservative force which strengthens rather than weakens economic self-help and other individualistic values.

Although social security inevitably involves governmental intervention in the distributive process, the basic concern of the American approach was to keep this intervention as passive as possible. This concern, due to individualistic and equalitarian legacies, accounts for certain fundamental features of American social insurance programs which significantly affect their distributive aspects. First, the extent and levels of benefit have always been geared to an acceptable minimum, rather than to universality of coverage and comprehensiveness of benefit at maximum feasible levels. Second, the programs treat all individuals alike, without relating eligibility to socio-economic status, which until recently was typical of European programs. Third, and most fundamental, benefits under these programs are said to be on a "contributory-contractual" basis.

The stress on the concept of contract has ideological rather than legal significance. Official educational literature at the inception of the system

---

[7] See the President's message to Congress, June 8, 1934, *Congressional Record*, LXXVIII, Part 10, pp. 10769–10771; and the report of the Committee on Economic Security in U.S. House of Representatives, 74th Congress, 1st Session *Hearings Before the Committee on Ways and Means on H. R. 4120* (Washington, D.C., 1935), pp. 19–20.

[8] "The American Philosophy of Social Insurance," *Social Service Review*, XXX, No. 1 (March 1956), p. 3.

emphasized the idea that benefits were not to be a matter of state benevolence, which presumably could subject them to governmental whims, but a "matter of right." Of course, in any country where social security is established by law, individuals who qualify under the law obtain benefits as a matter of statutory right. The American concern with benefits as a "matter of right" has to do with the basis of this right. Many countries, including the Soviet-Union, treat social security as a "constitutional" or "social" right, something to which the individual is conditionally entitled simply because he is a member of the given social collectivity.[9] But the philosophy of social solidarity which underlies this conception of social security clashes hard with traditional American individualism. The guiding idea in American social insurance is that the *individual earns* the right to benefit through payment of contributions by himself and on his behalf. Although workers in many countries pay contributions, these do not usually carry the significance they do in the United States, where they imply a quasi-contractual relationship between the citizen and the state. Nevertheless, the act of contributing, while it has important political advantages, can only bind the government morally, rather than legally, to render specified benefits.

The emphasis on relating benefits to a contributory contractual basis, which precludes financing from general revenue, is an outstanding manifestation of the traditional ideals of self-help and independence carried over into a governmental "mutual help" program. It reflects the desire for a system under which the individual would merely use the governmental mechanism to help himself, without otherwise relying on state aid. It reflects also a desire to safeguard individual independence by establishing a "contractual" relationship which limits governmental discretion in the collection of contributions and distribution of benefits. Thus, the contributory-contractual principle, which is the basic distributive principle of American social insurance, is intimately related to American social values and attitudes. It puts the right to social security on a modified self-help basis, which is in the main a restrictive approach. It restricts benefits to those by or for whom contributions have been paid, while many needy persons may be overlooked.[10]

One implication of a strict interpretation of the principle is that total accumulated contributions should determine the level of the disability or old age pension to which an individual is entitled, but in practice this

---

[9] For a discussion of this idea see C. Marti Bufill, *Tratado comparado de Seguridad Social* (Madrid, 1951), pp. 106 ff.

[10] In a strict legal sense this is not quite correct since an employer's failure to pay social security taxes does not thereby deprive his employees of their right to benefits if their employment is covered by the law. For persons not eligible the American system relies on public assistance, which pays benefits on the basis of demonstrated need.

emphasis on the equitable interest presents many problems and has been progressively diluted in the evolution of Old Age, Survivors and Disability Insurance. Our main concern here, however, is with the restrictions the contributory contractual approach puts on the use of social insurance funds and institutions for purposes of promoting incentive and effecting control. Although individual benefits are only indirectly related to contributions by or for the individual, the U.S. Congress insists that total disbursements of benefits stay within the limits of contributed funds and interest. This approach tends to impose rather inflexible income and expenditure patterns and calls for maintaining definite relationships between contributions and benefits over time. To safeguard the financial integrity of the system, and hence the individual's unhindered right to benefits, it is felt that contributions and disbursements must be governed solely by the internal requirements of the programs. What this implies for economic policy will be discussed after an examination of the exactly opposite Soviet approach.

The Soviet System

If the atomistic concepts of society and the economy underlying nineteenth century capitalism were a hindrance to the introduction of social security, the sense of solidarity and the relationship of state and society in socialist ideology were highly congenial to it. The Soviet citizen's right to social security rests on a historical basis which goes back to the early years of Russian socialism. Although Marx made only an incidental reference in his writings to "funds for those unable to work," [11] Lenin showed repeated interest in this question and has earned, if not all, at least some of the honor done him by Soviet writers in this field. The first record of Lenin's interest in this matter dates to 1895, when he included social security proposals in the reform program he was then preparing.[12] He also is given major credit for the social security demands embodied in the "Labor Program" adopted in 1903 by the Second Congress of the Russian Social Democratic Workers' Party. The measures envisaged at that time called for "State insurance for old people and people completely or partially incapacitated, out of a special fund created by a special levy on the capitalists." [13] Most important, however, was the plan he advanced at the Prague Conference of the Bolshevik Party in 1912, a plan which called for comprehensive insurance of all wage and salary earners against unemployment and all losses of capacity to work. Benefits were to equal

[11] K. Marx, *Critique of the Gotha Programme* (London, 1943), p. 10.
[12] "Leninskaia Strakhovaia Programma," *Okhrana Truda i Sotsial'noe Strakhovanie*, No. 5 (November, 1958), pp. 68–72.
[13] The program is contained in M. Dewar, *Labour Policy in the U.S.S.R. 1917–1928* (London, 1956), pp. 158–159.

the worker's wage and be paid for entirely by the employer and the state, but control of the system was to be completely in the hands of the insured.[14] Although Lenin's program was part of an attempt to belittle the rather limited social insurance scheme then under consideration by the Tsarist government, it nevertheless supplied the foundation for the prominence of social security among the means by which the Soviet state would carry out its welfare policy.

For the Bolsheviks, social security, as the preamble to the 1903 Program indicates, was a means to strengthen the workers' "capacity to fight for their emancipation." [15] Lenin was convinced, and his successors still are, that capitalism is incompatible with genuine social security. He urged his followers to agitate against the "illusory" Tsarist proposals and assured them that "the necessary condition for the realization of insurance reforms that answer the real needs of the proletariat is the definitive overthrow of Tsarism . . ." [16] After the Tsarist government had established its modest insurance scheme, the Bolsheviks urged their followers to participate in its administration and use it for revolutionary purposes.[17] The struggle for the overthrow of Tsarism and capitalism became in part a struggle for the establishment of comprehensive social security, which has been considered one of the main fruits of the "victory of the working class over capitalism." In the very first days of its existence, on November 14, 1917, the Bolshevik government felt compelled to issue a declaration acknowledging that the "Russian proletariat has placed on its banners comprehensive social insurance for all hired workers and for all urban and rural poor," and that the government "shall without delay proceed with the promulgation of decrees for total social insurance." [18] The Declaration also enunciated five principles, of clear Leninist inspiration, on which to base the planned system: (1) inclusion of all wage and salary earners and all urban and rural indigents, (2) coverage of all income hazards, (3) financing entirely by employers, (4) compensation to equal at least full wages in case of loss of work capacity and unemployment, (5) complete self-administration by the insured.

Taken literally, these principles are not a little heroic. They are just as naive as the once prevalent American attitude that any socially guaranteed income scheme is bound to have adverse incentive effects. An almost

[14] V. I. Lenin, *Sochineniia*, 4th ed. (Moscow, 1948), XVII, p. 427.

[15] Dewar, *op. cit.*, p. 158.

[16] Lenin, *op. cit.*, p. 428.

[17] See the resolutions of the Central Committee of the Russian Social Democratic Workers' Party in 1913–1914, in Nauchno-Issledovatel'skii Institut Professional'nogo Dvizheniia, *VKP(b) i Profsoiuzy o Sotsial'nom Strakhovanii* (Moscow, 1934), pp. 44–48.

[18] A. S. Krasnopol'skii, *Osnovnye Printsipy Sovetskogo Gosudartsvennogo Sotsial'nogo Strakhovaniia* (Moscow, 1951), pp. 13–14.

unrestricted promise to wage and salary earners of full wage compensation, combined with "complete self-administration" by those who draw benefits but do not bear the cost, would in time inevitably have adverse effects on work habits. It is not surprising that when these promises were put into the form of concrete programs they were pragmatically trimmed to the dimensions of reality.

It is not possible to consider here the multitude of decrees and directives which began to be issued in 1917. They reflect experimentation in method as well as important shifts in policy in response to changes in the economic situation and in over-all economic policy. Many of the early, generous measures existed mainly on paper and had very limited practical significance in an era of monetary instability. However, the evolution of Soviet social security policy since then is of great interest from the point of view of the questions raised at the beginning of this paper. Having committed itself not only to a comprehensive social security program but also to a government controlled economy, the Soviet rulers soon realized the labor discipline and productivity implications of social security. Somehow they had to decide in what manner the distribution of social security benefits should be guided by the needs of the beneficiaries or by the requirements of the production process.

The evolution of Soviet policy toward extensive use of social security payments and institutions for purposes of economic incentive and control will be considered below. To understand this evolution one must bear in mind not only the character of the Soviet economic and political order but have some acquaintance with basic Soviet social insurance ideas. The government's conception of the citizen's right to benefits enters into many decisions where the interests of beneficiaries and those of the economy in general are not necessarily identical. It influences the determination of eligibility, the fixing of the structure and level of benefits, and administrative practices. In all these areas the government can discriminate between individuals and groups according to its view of their rights and needs and the broader interest of state and country. It was for the express purpose of restricting this kind of discrimination, and the exercise of power over individual welfare it implies, that the founders of the American system stressed the "contributory-contractual" principle and the idea that the individual *earns* his benefits.

The character of Soviet thought in this respect is quite the opposite from the American, although no less ambiguous. It stresses, on the one hand, that benefits are a free gift from the state, an act of governmental benevolence, a manifestation of socialist humanism. Soviet workers have been told by their leaders that every "figure in the state social insurance budget . . . breathes the warmth and paternal care which our leader and teacher Comrade Stalin manifests daily and hourly toward all people, great and small." [19] On the other hand, as was noted earlier, social security is treated also as an historic right of the working population, a right which has been incorporated into the Constitution. Article 120 of the Constitution (1936, as amended) states in part that "Citizens of the U.S.S.R. have the right to maintenance in old age and also in case of sickness and disability." Conditions governing the receipt of benefits and the benefit structure can be quite different depending on the extent to which they are based on the theory that benefits are a free gift or on the theory that they are a basic right of the worker. As a gift benefits can legitimately serve primarily the purpose of the giver, but as a right they definitely limit the freedom of the giver. The possibility of the theoretical conflict suggested here disappears, however, for all practical purposes, when attention is paid to Article 12 of the Constitution, which is an important corollary to Article 120. Article 12 states in part that "Work in the U.S.S.R. is a duty and a matter of honor for every able-bodied citizen, in accordance with the principle: 'He who does not work, neither shall he eat.'"

In the context of the questions raised earlier it is highly significant, and certainly not accidental, that a constitution which guarantees the individual's maintenance also imposes upon him the duty to work. And conversely, the duty to work implies a right to maintenance that goes beyond any individual merit of support, since maintenance of the worker is then more nearly like the maintenance of capital. In fact, the concept of the maintenance of the efficiency of the "human capital" is a basic and highly interesting ingredient of Soviet social insurance thought. "In the society which is founded on labor, where the exploitation of man by man has been eliminated . . . where people are treated as the *most valuable capital* . . . comprehensive care of aged and disabled members is natural and inevitable." [20] Actual practice, as will be seen below, has become more consistent with this revealing statement in recent years than was the case earlier.

Nevertheless, income maintenance rights in the Soviet Union, as in the United States, are conditional rather than absolute. Being a citizen, or a piece of "human capital," is not sufficient for benefit eligibility. Moreover, in neither country do eligible citizens have an equal right to support; both relate benefits to previous wages, in contrast to the more egalitarian British and Swedish systems, which pay mainly flat benefit amounts. [21]

---

[19] Statement by N. M. Shvernik at a meeting of trade union activists, May 25, 1938, quoted in A. S. Krasnopol'skii, "On the Nature of Soviet State Social Insurance," *Current Digest of the Soviet Press, III,* No. 46 (Dec. 29, 1951), 4, translated from his article in *Sovetskoe Gosudarstvo i Pravo,* No. 6 (June 1951), pp. 62–69.

[20] Krasnopol'skii, *Osnovnye Printsipy* . . . p. 54. Italics are mine.

[21] It is noteworthy, however, that in 1959 both Great Britain and Sweden introduced graduated benefits on top of a flat base rate, which is a move away from the traditional income equality aim in favor of incentive considerations.

But even if in the two countries studied differential benefits serve similar incentive purposes, the concepts behind these differentials reveal interesting differences. In America the higher paid worker pays a larger contribution, and, on the basis of the "contributory contractual" principle, is entitled to higher benefits. But the Russian worker cannot "earn" differential benefits in the sense that the American worker does, unless his earnings are somehow related to payment for benefits. But that would undermine the idea that benefits are a gift of the state and would weaken the propaganda value of the system as well as its flexibility in the pursuit of broader economic and political goals. Furthermore, contractual social insurance concepts run counter to Soviet ideas about the nature of the relationships between individuals and the state.

In Soviet thinking, benefits are in the nature of a *reward* for loyal performance of duties, which is not quite compatible with the contractual idea of an *exchange* of benefits for premium payments. Krasnopol'skii, in one of the few theoretical examinations of the Soviet system, puts particular stress on this point:

> . . . mutuality and reciprocity . . . are not to be found in the mutual relations of the parties in state social insurance. The obligation here lies not on both parties, but only on one—the agency of state social insurance is under obligation to issue funds and to set and pay pensions or other forms of subsistence . . . whereas the worker or employee has no reciprocal obligations to the agencies of state social insurance.[22]

This deliberate avoidance of the contract fiction has the virtue of being consistent with the other fiction, that benefits are a gift, but it implies a rejection of the Soviet wage principle "to each according to his work," which would be one way of justifying differential benefits. Krasnopol'skii clearly states the inapplicability of the wage principle to social insurance, for benefits are not a payment for work done. But, he argues, "The level of consumption that the given person has reached is taken into consideration when he is granted disability aid out of the special funds set aside for purposes of socialist mutual aid."[23] Soviet benefits are, in fact, always related to recent earnings, even in the case of old age benefits. The contractual approach would suggest, of course, that they be based on the total amount of contributions paid, that is, on the total period in covered work.

[22] "On the Nature of Soviet State Social Insurance," p. 6. It may be worth pointing out also that while in America a worker may institute a civil suit in a U.S. court to enforce his benefit claim, Soviet courts have no such jurisdiction. This does not mean that a Soviet worker can be arbitrarily deprived of his benefits, but the fact that the trade unions and administrative agencies make final decisions reflects an important difference in the conception of the worker's right. See N. G. Aleksandrov, *Sovetskoe Trudovoe Pravo,* 2nd ed. (Moscow, 1959), pp. 359–363.

[23] Krasnopol'skii, "On the Nature of Soviet State Social Insurance," p. 5.

Nevertheless, just as the American system has never awarded benefits in direct proportion to total contributions, so is it impossible to provide a simple principle of Soviet benefit distribution. The Soviet government has always used the social security system in a highly pragmatic manner, to suit its economic and social planning purposes. It feels free to discriminate between union and non-union members and between individuals with identical earnings engaged in different occupations, industries, or locations. The government also feels free to introduce non-economic eligibility criteria. For instance, an individual may count as part of his work record required for old-age pension eligibility the time he spent in "bourgeois" jails for revolutionary activity and periods he was unemployed for political reasons in "bourgeois" countries. On the other hand, those who committed a crime against the state in enemy occupied territory during the war or as displaced persons may not count their war-time work record toward meeting the required work stage for old-age pension eligibility.[24]

It is apparent from the foregoing analysis that the distributive philosophy of a social security system is a product of historically interacting forces and is necessarily intimately related to a country's economic and political system. American social insurance concepts have developed in an environment with strong individualistic and laissez faire traditions. Consequently, the American system tries to minimize the role of the state and restrict it as much as possible to the passive provision of a legal framework and administrative machinery. The American social insurance system, in effect, is somewhat of a public trustee of the properties of many individuals, which gives it a semi-autonomous existence. It operates mainly in the interests of "insured" individuals, and its overriding purpose is to meet its obligations to them. In the Soviet Union, on the other hand, social security has always been the mainstay of social welfare policy. Attempts, in the early years of the regime, to make it a quasi-independent undertaking were definitively suppressed.[25] By emphasizing the role of the state as a dispenser of "free" benefits and shunning the concept of individual equitable interest, the Soviet system has facilitated the development of social security as an integral part of the command economy.

ECONOMIC OBJECTIVES

The Soviet System

The Soviet Union has demonstrated that, at least in its environment, a comprehensive system of social security, instead of becoming a threat

[24] V. I. Merkulova and I. M. Sakharova, *Pensii po Strarosti* (Moscow, 1957), p. 31.
[25] On administrative developments see G. V. Rimlinger, "The Trade Union in Soviet Social Insurance: Its Historical Development and Present Function," *Industrial and Labor Relations Review* (April, 1961).

to productivity, can be molded into a fairly versatile tool of economic incentive and labor discipline. For that reason it is most convenient to begin the second part of this paper with an examination of Soviet policy and use it as a basis of comparison for American experience.

The development of Soviet policy with regard to economic objectives can be divided into three fairly distinct periods: 1917–1929, 1929–1956, and since 1956. During the first period, especially in the early years, Soviet legislation was rather undiscriminating in seeking to protect individuals and their families. Characteristic of this approach was the decree of December 22, 1917, which entitled all workers to social security, regardless of "the character or length of their work." [26] Technically, this included even the self-employed peasant. In fact, a decree of October 31, 1918, which was apparently valid until 1922, though probably not enforced, defined coverage to include all those "whose means of subsistence is derived only from their own work, without exploiting the work of others." [27] Highly indicative of the initial strength of the idea that any worker had a historic right to social security was the absence of any service requirement as a condition of eligibility. An eight year requirement for sickness and disability benefits introduced in 1921 was quickly found impractical and discarded as far as sickness benefits were concerned. Although it was retained for disability pensions, it seems to have been indifferently enforced in actual practice. The intent of these requirements was not to make eligibility a matter of individual merit but to restrict benefits to bona fide members of the "working population." This spirit was still abroad in 1925, when a regulation appeared providing that a worker was entitled to sickness benefits as long as he held a job, or within a year after he quit working.

By 1926, however, as benefit levels improved, the official mood began to change. A regulation of that year stipulated that a worker would be ineligible for sickness benefits unless he held a job within the last two weeks before making his claim. Furthermore, at the VIIth Trade Union Congress, held in December, 1926, a proposal was debated that sickness benefits be paid only to workers who met a definite service requirement. Such a requirement was enacted into law in March 1928, on the eve of the central plan era. An even more striking indication that from now on the individual, despite his "historic right" to social insurance, must prove his merit, was the 25-year service requirement of the new old-age pension program inaugurated in January 1928. Before then there was no specific old-age pension program, but many aged persons retired on permanent

[26] See L. Ia. Gintsburg, *Trudovoi Stazh Rabochikh i Sluzhashchikh* (Moscow, 1958), p. 74.
[27] The existence of the decree does not mean that in practice self-employed persons actually received benefits. Its significance lies in its attitude toward the right to benefits.

disability pensions which had only an eight-year service requirement, and a retirement age of fifty instead of sixty under the new law.[28]

These were but straws in the wind announcing the new policy line which characterized the second period, from 1929 to 1956. The decision to industrialize at a forced pace compelled all energies to be directed to that central goal, social security payments and institutions included. Official pronouncements on social security had often stressed that its aim was to raise the material well-being of the workers. Until 1929 this seemed to refer merely to the addition benefits made to worker income. In the mounting drive to industrialize, however, this traditional aim changed its meaning. The familiar, direct effects on worker welfare were almost lost sight of as references to raising the standard of well-being became increasingly identified with the objectives of increasing production and supporting the industrialization effort. A Soviet student of social security has aptly summarized the change in policy which was inaugurated by the Central Committee of the Party, in a famed directive (September 28, 1929) that is still quoted as basic policy in official social insurance handbooks:

> The first five-year plan opens a new era in the history of Soviet social insurance. Already in 1929 the social insurance organs were fully confronted with the task of reorganizing their work to achieve every possible support to the growth of labor productivity and every encouragement to shock work and socialist competition, to heighten the struggle against absenteeism and labor turnover, and to aid in the formation of cadres and the strengthening of labor discipline.[29]

This implied much more than the traditional concern with discouraging disincentives, which had preoccupied social insurance planners in other countries but had been rather neglected in Russia. It was a novel departure aiming at the realization of specific production objectives.

A whole series of regulations and decrees were issued during the 1930's to put the new policy into effect.[30] Much of this legislation was of a restrictive and disciplinary character. Changes in the direction of positive incentives usually involved discrimination in favor of shock workers and production workers in basic industries (fuels, metals, chemicals). In the case of sickness benefits, for instance, only industrial production workers and those engaged in rail and water transport were entitled to full wages from the first day of disability, while others collected 75 percent during

---

[28] The development of the service requirements is traced in Gintsburg, *op. cit.*
[29] *Ibid.*, p. 66.
[30] For a more detailed discussion see S. M. Schwarz, *Labor in the Soviet Union* (New York, Praeger, 1952), Chap. vii; A. Abramson, "The Reorganization of Social Insurance Institutions in the U.S.S.R.," *International Labor Review* XXXI, No. 3 (March 1935), 364–382; and "Social Insurance in the U.S.S.R.," *International Labor Review XXXVIII*, No. 2 (August 1938), 226–242.

the first five days and full wages thereafter. Other common forms of discrimination were preferential treatment in the assignment of passes to sanatoria, rest homes, and children's vacation camps, better services, and higher benefit rates and lower service requirements for old-age, survivorship, and disability pensions.

Most important among the measures taken to increase labor discipline and encourage steady work habits were the outright abolition (October 1930) of unemployment insurance, the further extension of service requirements, and the introduction of benefit bonuses based on the work record. An important innovation was the principle of "continuous work," which aimed directly at reducing turnover. Although this implied continuous work for the present employer, it was necessary from the beginning not to treat all work separations as interruptions of the work stage. Subject to such exception, a directive of July 23, 1931 provided that *full* sickness benefits were payable only if a worker presenting a claim had been employed in his present establishment for at least two years and had done at least three years' work in covered employment. Those failing to meet these requirements, which were imposed also on maternity benefits, were entitled to partial payments. Another innovation, which applied to disability pensions, was to take the total length of the work record into account not only to establish eligibility but to compute graduated pensions. By a directive of February 29, 1932, disability pensions were increased by 2 percent of wages for each year worked over 10 and up to 18, and by 3 per cent for each year from 18 to 23. This length of service bonus was replaced in 1938 by a "continuous work" bonus, which reflected an increased campaign to strengthen discipline and reduce turnover. This new kind of bonus was one of the measures introduced by the important directive of December 28, 1938, which was appropriately entitled: "On Measures to Increase Labor Discipline, Improve the Practice of State Social Insurance, and Combat Abuses in this Area." Another, more important, innovation of this directive was to deny cash sickness benefits altogether (as opposed to paying the short-service rate introduced in 1931) to all workers and employees discharged for disciplinary reason, or who quit voluntarily, until they had been reemployed for at least six months (seven months for maternity benefits).

Of fundamental importance among the measures taken to increase production zeal and discipline was the thorough administrative reorganization of the system during the 1930's. The trade unions, for whom the promotion of production zeal and discipline had become more than ever a primary objective in the centrally planned economy, were given full administrative responsibility for social insurance benefits payable to employed persons.[31] They were to make sure that workers were fully aware

[31] See Rimlinger, *loc. cit.*

of the discipline and incentive features of social insurance, to assist them in obtaining the benefits to which they were entitled by law, and to prevent abuses. In addition to the higher benefits payable to workers in favored occupations and industries, the unions were instructed to give these workers more generous quotas of free and subsidized passes to health and vacation resorts, to provide more day-nurseries, kindergartens, and summer camps for their children, and to grant them priority in the payment of benefits, which was significant in part because the funds budgeted for the programs were not always sufficient to pay all eligible claims. Union disciplinary power and prestige were enhanced as well by the fact that non-union workers were entitled to sickness benefits at only 50 percent of the rate applicable to union members. Denial of or expulsion from membership thus became a potentially serious financial loss to the worker. Furthermore, the unions were entitled to deny benefits to "drifters, troublemakers, and shirkers." [32] Finally, involving larger numbers of union members in the day-to-day adjudication, control, and explanation of social insurance rules strengthened the unions' contact with the working masses and their ability to stimulate production zeal and to enforce discipline.

Chiefly as a result of inflation and fixed maximum benefit levels, the social insurance pension program was reduced to little more than an empty shell during the 1930's and 1940's. Before the 1956 reforms the great majority of the workers received only 150 rubles a month, a maximum set for ordinary pensions in 1932 which had become less than a subsistence minimum.[33] Workers in favored industries, under special programs begun in 1947, were given much larger pensions upon reaching retirement age, even though many continued to work. These special programs, made necessary by the failure to adjust the system as a whole to changed price levels, were started in part to accelerate the restoration of high production levels in basic industries which had been severely taxed during the war years. But their very existence highlights how far the welfare of the mass of beneficiaries had been allowed to deteriorate in an era of excessive concern with increasing output.

The re-establishment of a more evenly balanced approach with respect to welfare and production objectives is the main characteristic of the third period in Soviet social insurance. This period began with the enactment of a series of laws, the most important being the new, comprehensive pension law of July 14, 1956.[34] A few months earlier, in April, 1956,

[32] Decree of September 10, 1933. See *Spravochnik Profsoiuznogo Rabotnika* (Moscow, 1958), p. 295.

[33] R. Schlesinger, "The New Pension Law," *Soviet Studies*, VIII, No. 3 (January 1957), p. 308.

[34] For a discussion of the new law, see Schlesinger, *loc. cit.*, and "The New State Pension Law in the U.S.S.R.," *Bulletin of the International Social Security Association*, XI, No. 6 (June 1958), 220–230.

maternity benefits were liberalized,[35] and February, 1957, improvements were made in the cash sickness benefit program.[36] The main significance of the new laws is that they grant considerably larger benefits, especially pensions, and eliminate the glaring inequities that had permeated the system during the piecemeal adjustments of the late 1940's and early 1950's. There has also been a relaxation of eligibility requirements, although the collective farmers are still excluded from state social insurance. But even here a small concession was made by a directive of May 3, 1957 which allows a collective farmer who joins a state farm to count his continuous work years since 1939 toward meeting the service requirement for pension eligibility.[37] A more important liberalization is the decree of the Supreme Soviet of January 25, 1960 which removes the six months' loss of eligibility for sickness benefits for workers who leave their jobs of their own will. Such workers now retain the "continuity" of their work record, and hence remain eligible, if they become re-employed within one month. Disciplinary discharges, of course, will carry the loss of eligibility penalty and partly for that reason are officially recommended in cases of unexcused absenteeism by a decree of April 25, 1956, which remains in force.[38]

In spite of important changes in favor of welfare objectives, the eligibility conditions and benefit levels of Soviet social insurance continue to reflect the system's emphasis on output objectives. Continuous work, a long work record, work in hot, difficult, dangerous, and underground occupations, and employment in remote areas are more highly rewarded than ordinary service at the same wage level. Pensions are now more closely related to wages than formerly and to that extent reinforce a wage structure which is intended to encourage maximum effort. The administration of social insurance also retains the general goal of promoting labor discipline and production, although the nature of specific objectives has changed. Combat of turnover and preferential treatment of shock workers have lost the significance they had in the early years of rapid industrialization. The system has now moved much closer to the goal of "maintaining the human capital." For the trade union social insurance

[35] See *Current Digest of the Soviet Press,* VIII, No. 13 (May 9, 1956), 30–31.
[36] See "New Principles Come into Force for the Award of Sickness Benefits," *Bulletin of the International Social Security Association,* XI, No. 4–5 (April–May, 1958), 197–198. For a recent official collection of laws regulating sickness, maternity, and other short-term benefits see *Gosudarstvennoe Sotsial'noe Strakhovanie (sbornik ofitsial'nykh materialov)* (Moscow, 1959). For compact but highly useful descriptions in English see "Social Security in the Union of Soviet Socialist Republics," *Social Security Bulletin,* XXII, No. 8 (August 1959), 3–7; and Robert J. Myers "Economic Security in the Soviet Union," *Transaction of the Society of Actuaries,* XI (November 1959) 723–745.
[37] Up to date rules on pensions and related matters are contained in *Pensionnoe Obespechenie v SSSR,* 2nd enlarged ed. (Moscow, 1960).
[38] For a comparison of the 1956 and 1960 decrees see *ibid.,* 121–122 and 354–355.

commission and social insurance activists this means primarily keeping the worker on the job, healthy, safe, and fit to work. Accordingly the administration of sickness benefits has been closely integrated with the control of absenteeism, the supervision of labor medical services, the prevention of illness, and health campaigns. Disability benefit administration has been tied to accident prevention and has been coordinated with rehabilitation measures. Union participation in old-age pension administration is used to maintain contact with working and retired pensioners and provides the basis for plans to improve the placement of aged workers and mobilize the skills and experience of those who have retired. Performance in many of these areas is undoubtedly still spotty, but the objectives are untiringly stated and restated by the Government, the Party, and the trade unions.

The American System

The character of American social security and of the American economic and political system is not compatible with the stress of labor discipline and production that has been so prominent in the Soviet Union since 1929. This does not mean that non-insurance economic implications have been left out of consideration. The prevailing system of wage-related benefits has always been defended in part on the ground that it is more conducive to incentive than flat benefit rates. Dean J. Douglas Brown, who has long defended this view, argues also that the provision of a basic level of security encourages work incentives.[39] This argument now seems to have fairly wide support. Professor Galbraith goes so far as to suggest that "the notion that economic insecurity is essential for efficiency and economic advance was a major miscalculation—perhaps the greatest in the history of economic ideas." [40] In his view, "A high level of economic security is essential for maximum production." [41] Some students with long experience in the social security field, including Professor Eveline M. Burns, question the incentive effects of differential benefits, especially in view of the fact that in America the wages on which benefits are based often have little to do with individual incentive and initiative.[42]

Regardless of the merit of these arguments, what matters in the present context is that increasing the incentive to work has never been singled out as a basic goal of American social security. The main concern of those who have molded the American system has been the avoidance of measures which might hurt individual incentive and self-help initiative. Their approach, on balance, has been negative, in the sense that they

[39] J. Douglas Brown, "The Role of Social Insurance in the United States," *Industrial and Labor Relations Review*, XIV, No. 1 (October 1960), 108–109.
[40] J. K. Galbraith, *The Affluent Society* (Cambridge, Mass., 1958), p. 113.
[41] *Ibid.*, p. 115.
[42] See E. M. Burns, *Social Security and Public Policy* (New York, 1956), Chap. iii and pp. 62–63.

have been more inclined to treat incentive aspects as one of the important limiting factors of the scope and level of social security protection than view them as an opportunity which can be exploited for productivity gains. This differs very significantly from the Soviet method of designing eligibility conditions and benefit levels for the express purpose of achieving particular incentives and controls.

An even greater contrast exists with regard to labor discipline. One of the fundamental principles of American social insurance administration is the restriction of administrative discretion to its practical minimum, which implies the exclusion of any personal element in evaluating an individual's eligibility and reliance on objective, measurable standards. These standards are applied by professionally oriented, paid state officials. In the Soviet Union many administrative tasks requiring considerable discretion are executed by unpaid trade union activists whose duty it is to promote labor discipline and production. This is most important, of course, in the area of sickness benefits, where the room for discretion is substantial under the best of circumstances. It is a noteworthy contrast that in the area of unemployment compensation, which has a great potential for labor discipline and inevitably leaves room for administrative discretion, the American social security act of 1935 laid down certain ground rules to ensure the neutrality of the state in the relationship between employer and worker. Section 903 of the act protects the worker, by allowing him to draw benefits instead of insisting that he take a job offer, in cases where he would have to act as a strike breaker, or where he would have to accept substandard wages or working conditions, or where he would be forced to join a company union or resign from or refrain from joining a bona fide union.

Economic objectives which are more compatible with the spirit of American social insurance are those which can be achieved indirectly, through the effect of benefits on aggregate demand. But even these objectives pose problems for the proper functioning of social insurance and have been regarded as no more than possible by-products. The late Professor E. E. Witte, commonly regarded as the intellectual father of American social security, held the opinion, which seems to be shared by many connected with policy formation, that

> It is a perversion of the concept of social security to look upon it as being primarily designed for control of the business cycle, to insure full employment, or to redistribute income and purchasing power. Its effects in these respects should be considered and discussed, but should not overshadow its major objective—the protection of the individual and the family against the immediate hazards confronting them.[43]

[43] E. E. Witte, "What to Expect of Social Security," American Economic Association, Papers and Proceedings, XXXIV, No. 1, Part 2 (March 1944), 217. A more recent

The United States does not readily alter its social insurance system to suit changing secular or cyclical economic objectives. The nature of the economic impact of the system is determined by its basic laws, and these have no provisions for changing the timing and the rate of taxes and benefits in response to changing business conditions. The unwillingness to experiment with provisions of this kind reflects at least in part the American attitude toward the objectives of social insurance and the quasi-autonomous financial status of the various programs. The pension programs, as presently constituted, are especially unadapted to cyclical measures because contribution rates designed to keep them in budgetary balance are fixed on the basis of long-run expectations of income and expenditure patterns. Short run variations of tax and benefit rates would threaten the solvency of the system and might necessitate assistance from general revenue, which conflicts with prevailing ideas on social security financing.

There were of course basic economic considerations which played a role in the original legislation. Most significant was the deep concern with unemployment which helped to shape various features of the system. Arguments and hearings before Congressional Committees brought out the view that making payment of old age insurance benefits contingent upon withdrawal from the labor market would provide an incentive to retire which would leave jobs for younger, unemployed persons. The decision not to build up large reserves in old age insurance financing was strongly colored by the fear of a depressing effect on aggregative demand. In the area of unemployment compensation the prevailing merit rating system, which relates a firm's tax rate to its unemployment record, was supported on the basis that it contributes to the stabilization of employment. The expectation of this result is based in the main on highly limited micro-economic assumptions. In reality, the need to raise the tax rate after a certain amount of unemployment has occurred may accentuate cyclical fluctuations. Technically, at least, it seems reasonable that the unemployment compensation programs could be made more effective anticyclical weapons without violating any basic concept of American social insurance. The lack of serious efforts in this direction illustrates, among other things, the basic American reluctance to use social security programs for purposes of economic control.[44]

---

statement of this position is in his article on "The Objectives of Social Security," *Review of Social Economy*, XVII, No. 1 (March 1959).

[44] On the present status of unemployment compensation financing and its economic implications, see R. A. Lester, "Financing of Unemployment Compensation," *Industrial and Labor Relations Review*, XIV, No. 1 (October 1960), 52–61; and R. A. Lester, "The Economic Significance of Unemployment Compensation, 1948–1959," *Review of Economics and Statistics*, XLII, No. 4 (Nov. 1960), 349–372.

CONCLUSION

The aspiration for economic security is a powerful force in the evolution of an economic system, whether it is centrally planned or organized by markets. How this force is channeled will depend on historically conditioned economic, social, and political factors. A basic lesson of American experience has been to show the weakness of the old argument, closely associated with the puritanical work ethic of early industrial capitalism, that a lessening of insecurity by social means impairs individual incentive and initiative. Many observers, indeed, argue the opposite case. The danger in following this line of argument beyond the context of limited programs is that it leads to the controversial proposition that the structure and levels of social security programs should be designed to promote incentive, labor discipline, and other economic objectives. By comparison with a Soviet-type economy, a democratic capitalistic system does not present a favorable setting for exploiting the economic incentive and control potentials of social security schemes. Although it is often argued that social security serves as a bulwark of the private enterprise system, there is nevertheless a latent conflict between the stress on individual economic responsibility, individual freedom, and reliance on automatic market processes, and the centralized planning against economic insecurity represented by social security. To minimize this conflict and restrict centralized planning and control, the American approach has been to keep social security measures at a minimum acceptable level and think of benefit distribution in quasi-contractual terms. Consequently, American social security gives precedence to the specific rights of insured individuals over general economic objectives.

The pattern of adaptation of social security to the planned Soviet economy is substantially different. Instead of being hampered by individualistic preconceptions, Soviet social security payments and institutions are based on concepts which facilitate the system's integration with central planning and aid in the control and management of the work force. Theoretically, Soviet spokesmen do not recognize any conflict between individual interests and social goals. On the contrary, they see in social welfare measures an unmistakable manifestation of the basic harmony underlying a socialist society and economy. But Soviet experience has revealed two opposite dangers of an unqualified acceptance of this view. It may lead, as it did initially in the Soviet case, to naively generous but economically impractical and hence self-defeating social security programs. Or it may lead, as it did during the industrialization period, to painful sacrifices of individual welfare for the sake of promoting broader economic aims.

Political Structure, Economic Development, and National Social Security Programs

Phillips Cutright

Comparative sociological studies of political systems in modern nations have, in recent years, experienced impressive theoretical development. Attention has been focused on the "functional prerequisites" for political democracies, the structural conditions generating political stability or instability in "democratic" states, and the value structures necessary for a democratic order.[1] A number of excellent studies of political stability in non-democratic nations exist, but when more than one nation is studied, the comparison is usually limited to somewhat similar under-developed nations. When comparisons between democratic and non-democratic nations are made, the number of observations (nations) is severely limited by the absence of scales and indexes relevant to the analytical variables guiding the analysis.[2]

Elsewhere the author has developed and tested a scale of the complexity of national political organization.[3] The development of similar

[1] William Kornhauser (*The Politics of Mass Society* [Glencoe, Illinois: Free Press, 1959]), in particular, gives a detailed discussion of the concept of "representativeness" and democratic pluralism. Robert R. Alford (*Party and Society: The Anglo-American Democracies* [Chicago: Rand McNally & Co., 1963]) examines longitudinal data bearing on the relations between political parties and the social structure of five democracies. S. M. Lipset ("Democracy and the Social System," in Harry Eckstein [ed.], *Internal War: Problems and Approaches* [New York: Free Press of Glencoe, 1964]) develops a framework for analyzing the value patterns that support democratic government.

[2] See Dick Simpson, "The Congruence of Political, Social and Economic Aspects of Development," *International Development Review*, VI (June, 1964), 21–25.

[3] P. Cutright, "National Political Development: Measurement and Analysis," *American Sociological Review*, XXVIII (April, 1963), 253–64. That study also argues the case for scales rather than crude qualitative categories in international studies. See Appendix B for a description of the revised political representativeness index used in this study.

Phillips Cutright, "Political Structure, Economic Development, and National Security Programs," *The American Journal of Sociology*, March 1965. My thanks to E. Palmore for criticism and helpful suggestions.

scales that would increase the number of nations in comparative studies and serve to aid in the selection of a few nations to fit the requirements of special studies is clearly a desirable goal. One aspect of this article is the development of a scale that can be applied to nations throughout the world. It measures the development of national programs to provide populations with insurance against severe loss of income under stated conditions, that is, the general level of social security development in the nations of the world. Because such national programs are an output of government activity, the analytical value would seem to go beyond the concrete phenomena directly measured. The scale can be used as a yardstick against which governments with varying characteristics can be compared.[4] It may allow one to measure, for example, one aspect of what democratic governments *do* that may distinguish them from non-democratic governments.[5]

In this paper we develop an index of the general level of social security in different nations that is a direct consequence of one kind of government activity (i.e., legislation or government order). We then analyze the relationship of this index to an index measuring the political representativeness of nations and to other indicators of economic and social development. The general purpose of the analysis is to assess the importance of representativeness in governmental organization to the social security and welfare of national populations. Our working hypothesis is that governments in nations whose political structures tend to allow for greater accessibility to the people of the governing elite will act to provide greater social security for their populations than that provided by governments whose rulers are less accessible to the demands of the

[4] An inventory of municipal services in Bristol, England, and Seattle, Washington, revealed remarkable similarities "even in two cities where the governmental power is based on different philosophies. In Bristol the Labor (socialist) party holds political dominance with its leaders in almost all key legislative positions. In Seattle, a conservative local government rules (Republican). Yet each city has almost the same amount of municipal ownership and control" (William H. Form and Delbert C. Miller, *Industry, Labor and Community* [New York: Harper & Bros., 1960], p. 501).

[5] There has been relatively little systematic work on the consequences for national populations of living under more or less representative governments. Studies of this sort often compare only totalitarian and democratic governments, highlighting the impact of government activity on the expression of individual freedoms.

Unfortunately, an inventory of the activities of national governments, or even a conceptual scheme to aid in their classification, is not at hand. Comparative studies of the outputs of national governments are limited by the lack of scales of those activities, and relatively little attention has been given to classification of the activities. Available indicators of government activities are not, however, being fully exploited. Thus, studies using measures of education, health, or demographic conditions do not examine these phenomena as though they were related to government activity. For example, we are more likely to see a certain level of education as a requisite for democratic government than to view government activity as vital for the development of national education levels.

population. The theoretical contribution of this analysis is toward an application of the construct of representativeness (or accessibility) to actual government activity.

MEASURING NATIONAL SOCIAL SECURITY

Perhaps one of the more striking developments of the twentieth century has been the effort by national governments to protect that portion of the population that is, for one reason or another, not in the employed labor force. National social-insurance programs, initiated in Europe near the end of the nineteenth century, first dealt with the problem of income loss resulting from industrial work injury, a problem that was greatly intensified by the expansion of industrial activity. As urbanization and industrialization (and their social and political correlates) continued, social-insurance programs covering other types of risks—sickness, old age, unemployment—began to appear.

Although there exists some detailed information on the extent of coverage or the level of benefits provided by various national social-insurance schemes, these data are available for only a few nations. In a study that concentrated on the economic correlates of certain social-insurance programs, Henry Aaron was able to locate adequate detailed data on twenty-two nations—all economically well developed—and subjected these data to an intensive multiple-regression dummy variable analysis.[6] These data on program coverage and benefit levels showed that the most powerful explanatory variables were (1) years of experience with the program (number of decades since its initiation) and (2) various indicators of national economic development. If one knows how long a nation has had certain programs and what its level of economic development is, then one can assess how the nation will rank in coverage and benefit levels relative to the remaining twenty-one nations in the sample. (The homogeneous economic and political character of the nations in Aaron's study should be noted. Correlations are often low within homogeneous groups; the present instance is an exception to this rule.) Aaron suggests that the relationships among his variables may not be the same in less-developed nations; but the question is not whether the regression is the same but whether Aaron's detailed study can be applied to a slightly different type of analysis that will allow us to get around the problem of lack of detailed program data in many nations. If number of years' experience with a program is highly correlated with the total expenditures, benefit levels, and coverage of a program, then the number of years can be used as an indicator of the level of program development.

[6] Henry Aaron, "Social Security in an Expanding Economy" (unpublished doctoral dissertation, Harvard University, 1963).

However, the lack of detailed and comparable data on social security programs is not the only stumbling block in the way of international comparisons. We have also to establish that what we call social security programs are conceptually related. The fact that custom and administrative usage have grouped different types of programs under a common label (social security) is not proof that these programs are interrelated and form a continuum along which nations may be placed in order from high to low social security development. The first task is to offer some evidence that we can talk about the social security development of nations because a definite pattern of program occurrence or non-occurrence exists among the nations of the world.

PATTERNS OF SOCIAL SECURITY
PROGRAM DEVELOPMENT

There are five major types of social security programs.[7] Of the seventy-six nations outside Africa [8] that had achieved independent political status by 1960, seventy-one had begun work-injury programs, fifty-eight had sickness and/or maternity programs, fifty-six had programs grouped under old-age, invalidism, and death, forty had some type of family allowance plan, and twenty-seven had unemployment-insurance programs. This frequency distribution does not, in itself, tell us that a nation with an unemployment program is necessarily more or less advanced toward a social-insurance goal than is a nation with only a work-injury program. There are several ways to approach this question, but perhaps the simplest is with the Guttman scale.[9] If several discrete items, in this case the five types of social-insurance and benefit programs, form a Guttman scale, we can say that the scale is measuring an underlying dimension along which each of the items may be placed in a known order, and that a given combination of items (i.e., social-insurance programs) represents a higher place along a continuum of social-insurance development than some alternative combination.

[7] All data pertaining to social security programs are taken from U.S. Department of Health, Education, and Welfare, Social Security Administration, *Social Security Programs throughout the World, 1961* (Washington, D.C.: Government Printing Office, 1961). Discussion of the characteristics of each type of program can be found in that document.

[8] This part of the analysis is based on research initially focused on the correlates of political development, which for statistical reasons omitted all African nations in order to avoid spuriously high correlations. The seventy-six nations are listed in Appendix A of this article.

[9] S. A. Stouffer et al., *Measurement and Prediction* (Princeton, N.J.: Princeton University Press, 1950), pp. 60–90. For a more recent explication of Guttman scaling see Allen L. Edwards, *Techniques of Attitude Scale Construction* (New York: Appleton-Century-Crofts, 1957), pp. 172–98.

The five major types of social security programs do form a Guttman scale. A nation can have between zero and five programs, and we have six possible perfect-scale types with varying combinations of programs. Twenty-two nations in our sample are in the first perfect-scale type, having all five programs, while the second type contains thirteen nations lacking only unemployment insurance. It is interesting that seven of these thirteen nations were Soviet Russia and its satellites. A third perfect-scale type contains the twelve nations that had neither unemployment nor family allowances, but did have the three other programs. The five nations in the fourth scale type lack, in addition to unemployment and family-allowances programs, a program to provide for the aged, invalidism, and/or death. They have both work-injury and sickness programs. In the fifth scale type are six nations with work-injury programs only, and the final scale type contains five nations with no programs at all. Thus sixty-three of the seventy-six countries are in perfect-scale types. It is worth noting that, had we included African nations, the sixth scale type would have had many more nations, with a resulting increase in the coefficient of reproducibility (CR) to about .98. However, even without this group the CR is .966, considerably above the usually acceptable level of .90.

Because the items do form a Guttman scale, these scale types may be used to rank order the nations of the world according to the extent to which they have developed a social-insurance program. The scale does not necessarily tell us whether a nation in scale type 1 has a better or more comprehensive old-age program than a nation in scale type 2, but it does indicate that the general social security coverage of the population outside the employed labor force is better in scale type 1 than in scale type 2, 3, and so on.

A CUMULATIVE MEASURE OF THE YEARS
OF SOCIAL-INSURANCE PROGRAM EXPERIENCE

Because the programs form a Guttman scale, it is possible to apply a measure that distinguishes more than six levels of social security development. The measure is, simply, the years of experience with social-insurance programs for each of the seventy-six nations for the period 1934–60. This statistic is similar to that used by Aaron for well-developed nations, and from the above analysis it appears applicable to less-developed nations as well.

An index of a nation's social insurance program experience (SIPE) can be computed by totaling the number of years from 1934 through 1960 that the nation had a given type of program in operation. For each of the five programs, a score of from 0 to 27 is possible. A score of 27 on each program would yield a maximum SIPE score of 135.[10]

The following analysis concentrates on the relationship of SIPE scores to various aspects of national political and economic life. The final section focuses on a social-insurance completion index and relates scores on this index to political and economic levels and changes from 1928 to 1960.

SIPE scores are one possible index of the responsiveness of governments to the needs of the governed. A nation that lacks work-injury or old age insurance programs may or may not have the economic base capable of supporting such programs, but the extent to which governments initiate and improve insurance programs may reflect much more than the operation of an automatic and economically triggered mechanism.

Nevertheless, it is also the case that the ability of a government to begin a program is closely related to the nation's level of social and economic development. The SIPE scores of the seventy-six nations have been correlated with 1960 indexes of energy consumption, urbanization, literacy, and political representativeness (PRI), and the full matrix of product-moment correlations is shown in Table 1.

The highest correlation is between energy consumption and SIPE. This correlation of .90 accounts by itself for 81 percent of the variation around the mean SIPE score. It is much higher than the correlation of energy consumption with PRI, literacy, or urbanization. Further, it is considerably higher than the zero-order relationship between literacy and SIPE. This indicates that the level of economic development has a powerful role in determining the level of social-insurance development, and that we must control for level of economic development as measured by energy consumption as well as for level of political development in any analysis of the amount of change in social-insurance programs from the 1930's through the early 1960's.

The high correlations between social security development and energy consumption or political representativeness do not mean, however, that urbanization and the literacy level of the population are not also important correlates of social security development. Quite the opposite is true. In general, nations with high levels of SIPE also have high literacy rates and tend to be highly urbanized. Nations with low levels of urbanization or literacy have less-developed social security programs as well as lower levels of energy consumption and political representativeness.

[10] SIPE scores for each of the seventy-six nations are shown in Appendix A. Data on political structure are available for as early as 1928, and that time is used in analyzing the introduction of new social-insurance programs later in this paper. The base year for computing the years of program experience is 1934 rather than 1928, however. This is the product of error, not design. However, if 1928 had been used, there would be little difference beyond adding five points to the range of the scale; the relationships with other variables would remain the same.

Table 1   *Zero-Order Correlation Matrix of Energy Consumption, Urbanization, Literacy, Political Representativeness, and Years of Social-Insurance Program Experience, 1960* [a]

	Urbanization	Literacy	PRT	SIPE
Energy consumption	72	81	61	90
Urbanization	—	64	58	58
Literacy	—	—	76	83
PRI	—	—	—	74

[a] All variables except SIPE have been T-scored; $N = 76$.

Source: Data for energy consumption, urbanization, and literacy are taken from the U.N. *Demographic Yearbook* and the U.N. *Statistical Yearbook.* The primary source for political data is the *Political Handbook of the World: Parliaments, Parties and Press* (New York: Harper & Bros. [for the Council on Foreign Relations], annual publication 1928–62).

Although this analysis centers on the relationship of economic development and PRI, it should not be assumed that a change in one or both of these variables alone would be sufficient (although it might be necessary) to produce changes in social security. Changes in the levels of literacy and urbanization of the population usually occur concomitantly with changes in PRI or energy consumption. It would appear that the probability of an increase in the level of social-insurance development is greatest when all four variables are rising. This view is compatible with the proposition that changes in major institutional areas of the society do not proceed far without reacting on each other as well as on lesser aspects of life. Institutions are interdependent. The matrix of correlations is evidence in support of this hypothesis—at the level of national social systems.

In the following section we test the hypothesis that the levels of economic development and PRI will have independent and joint effects on SIPE. Economic development was selected because of its high correlation with SIPE and political development because it is central to analysis.

ANALYSIS OF NATIONAL DIFFERENCES IN YEARS OF SOCIAL-INSURANCE PROGRAM EXPERIENCE

Table 2 presents the mean SIPE scores for nations at five levels of economic development—as measured by energy consumption—and four

Table 2 *Mean Years of Social-Insurance Program Experience by Mean 1930–1960 Energy Consumption and 1930 Level of Political Representativeness* [a]

1930 PRI [b]

Mean Energy Consumption 1930–1960	Dependent Nations		Below Mean		Above Mean		Highest Nations		Row Mean	
I	99	(1)	101	(2)	114	(4)	116	(14)	114	(21)
II	25	(3)	93	(4)	100	(5)	102	(3)	83	(15)
III	36	(1)	88	(4)	62	(5)	54	(2)	67	(12)
IV	30	(8)	44	(9)	54	(1)	–		39	(18)
V	18	(5)	7	(4)	63	(1)	–		18	(10)
Column mean	30	(18)	59	(23)	86	(16)	107	(19)	70	

[a] Nations are placed into energy consumption levels according to their *T*-score. Groups I and II are above the mean of 50; Groups III, IV, and V are below the mean. Groups I and V contain nations that were more than 1 standard deviation from the mean.

[b] Number in parentheses = *N*.

levels of political development in 1930. The mean social-insurance experience of these nations and the number of nations is shown.

In the upper left-hand cell is a single nation with 99 cumulative years of program experience and immediately below it are three nations with a mean of 25 years' experience. (The reader may prefer to collapse cells having only one case with adjacent cells before comparing individual cells with column means.) The mean SIPE scores associated with each level of economic development are in the "row mean" column. The twenty-one nations with the highest level of economic development had an average of 114 years of cumulative social-insurance program experience from 1934 through 1960. Nations in the second highest group had an average of eighty-three years' experience while the ten nations at the lowest level had an average of only eighteen years' experience. The same pattern of decreasing length of program experience is found within each column. We may conclude that the level of economic development is related to SIPE; statistical control for political development does not remove the positive association between the two.

The mean SIPE scores associated with each level of 1930 PRI are in the bottom row of Table 2. The scores show a steady gain with increasing PRI levels. The eighteen nations with dependent political status in 1930 have a mean score of thirty years compared to 107 years for the nineteen nations with the highest PRI scores. This pattern of larger SIPE scores with higher PRI levels holds at the first, second, and fourth levels of economic development. The third level does not fit the general pattern—this "deviant" row may explain why the correlation between PRI and SIPE was "only" .74—and the association in the lowest economic level is also of dubious strength.

Controlling first for one and then for the other variable, then, we see that each is related to the SIPE scores. We should note that the ten nations at the lowest level of economic development have considerably lower SIPE scores than the nations at the next highest level of development. For these nations, it is level of economic development rather than level of political development that determines the level of social-insurance program experience. In terms of causal sequence, it appears that before positive change in political structure can bring about positive change in social-insurance program development, a nation must have experienced some economic growth.

Table 2 supports our working hypothesis. In general, governments in nations with more representative political structures have provided greater social security coverage to their populations. Among self-governing nations there is a nearly uniform increase in government social security activities from one level of representativeness to the next. However, nations with the highest PRI scores—those we would normally call "democratic"—do not really differ qualitatively from those nations of parallel economic development that are in the next lowest PRI group. This finding will be discussed at the conclusion of this paper.

In the next section the idea that changes in political structure are associated with changes in years of social-insurance experience will be tested.

CHANGES IN YEARS OF SOCIAL-INSURANCE PROGRAM EXPERIENCE AND CHANGES IN PRI

Table 3 shows the relationship between changes in political representativeness and changes in SIPE. Since the amount of change in PRI is strongly associated with initial level of PRI (as seen in the disproportionately high gains made by the initially lowest PRI group), it is important to control for 1930 PRI level; level of economic development is not controlled. Nations are ranked in each column according to the size of their gain or loss in political representativeness between 1930 and 1960. Reading down the columns, a near-perfect correlation can be seen between changes in PRI and changes in SIPE. Even within the initially highest PRI group, the twelve nations whose political structure remained perfectly stable throughout the period had an average gain of 121 years of experience; the three that ended at the same level as they began but experienced instability in between (Japan, Uruguay, and Costa Rica) had an average increase of eighty-one; and the two that declined in

Table 3   *Mean Change in Social-Insurance Program Experience, 1934–1960, and Size of Change in Political Representativeness Index, 1930–1960* [a]

Ranked PRI Change Interval	1930 PRI											
	Dependent (N = 18)			Below Mean [b] (N = 20)			Above Mean [b] (N = 15)			Highest [b] (N = 17)		
	PRI Gain	N	SIPE Gain	PRI Gain	N	SIPE Gain	PRI Gain	N	SIPE Gain	PRI Gain	N	SIPE Gain
Largest	23	3	63	13	4	97	7	6	114	0	12	121
Second	16	6	31	5	7	56	3	3	70	0	3 [c]	81
Third	11	4	22	3	3	20	−2	3	66	−8	2	76
Fourth	6	5	14	0	6	49	−5	3	65	d	d	d

   [a] Controlled for PRI.
   [b] Soviet satellites (Albania, Bulgaria, Hungary, Poland, Romania, and Czechoslovakia) are omitted from this table as our scoring of PRI changes excluded those caused by external domination. They are included in all other tables.
   [c] These three nations began and ended the period with the highest PRI scores, but were unstable during the period.
   [d] No. cases.

political representativeness (Canada and Colombia) had a gain of only seventy-six years.

We might note that SIPE gains also are strongly associated with initial PRI level. The largest gains in social insurance are found in nations that began the time period with a maximum political-representativeness score. Reading across the rows in Table 3, within each PRI-change interval there is a positive association (slightly reversed in only one case) between 1930 PRI level and SIPE gains.

A NONCUMULATIVE MEASURE OF SOCIAL-INSURANCE DEVELOPMENT

An alternative measure of social-insurance development in a nation is, for some purposes, more satisfactory. Instead of using a cumulative measure of years of program experience, we can examine the political situation surrounding major changes in a nation's social-insurance programs (i.e., each time a new program is launched). An index can then be developed to measure the extent to which a nation is moving toward social-insurance program completion (SIPC). Completion is used here to mean that a nation has begun to tackle the needs associated with the five basic types of social security programs, and not to refer to the extent of coverage of the population by any or all programs. Some examples of how the SIPC index is constructed follow.

If a nation had three programs in 1928, it can introduce only two additional programs. Assume that such a country experiences a positive political change in 1932 and in 1934 adds one program. Between 1932 and 1934 no political changes occur. A score of 50 (i.e., 50 percent of the total change possible in social-insurance program coverage) is awarded to that specific 1932 political change. If, however, the nation experiences a positive change in 1932 and a negative change in 1933 and adds a social-insurance program in 1934, the positive 1932 political change receives a score of zero, and the negative 1933 change a score of 50. The social-insurance-program completion index is, therefore, a measure of the amount of social-insurance change associated with each change in PRI.[11] The mean SIPC change per nation is calculated in the following manner. For positive and negative PRI changes (computed separately), if a nation has more than one change, the sum of the SIPC index scores associated with these changes is divided by the number of changes. Next, the average SIPC scores for each nation are summed and divided by the number of nations to get the mean SIPC change per nation. For nations with no PRI changes, the mean SIPC change per nation is merely the sum of the nations' SIPC scores divided by the number of nations.

It was suggested earlier that social-insurance programs may represent a measure of the responsiveness of government to the social needs of the population. If so, we would expect not only that social-insurance development would be associated with a *high level* of political representativeness but also that a *positive change* in political representativeness would be *followed* by an increase in social-insurance program coverage. The gain in SIPC index should be larger in association with positive political changes than with negative political changes.

Table 4 presents the results of an analysis of SIPC changes associated with political changes of both types. In the time covered, a total of ninety-

[11] One feature of the SIPC index that should be considered in future work is the correlation between economic and political development and the size of the score awarded to a single program change. Since nations at high development levels will also be more likely to have had several programs by 1928, they will also receive "extra" credit when they introduce their next program. Whether it is more difficult for a nation to launch its first than its last program is not the issue here. Comparison of the results using this index as opposed to another is a matter for investigation rather than for debate. Although it might be expected that larger scores would be associated with the economically and politically more-developed nations, this does not justify assuming that high scores should be associated with positive rather than with negative political changes. Controls for economic-development levels will also be introduced to reduce the spurious association between large scores and high economic-development scores.

Table 4   *SIPC Index Gains Associated with Positive, Negative, and No Changes in PRI*

Direction of PRI Change	Mean SIPC Change [a] per PRI Change	Mean SIPC Change per Nation
Positive	22 (98)	38 (56)
Negative	11 (70)	20 (41)
No change	Not applicable	87 (16)

[a] Numbers in parentheses are the number of PRI changes and the number of nations.

eight positive political changes and an average increase in SIPC of twenty-two are found. In the same period, there were seventy negative changes with an increase in SIPC of eleven per negative change; a net gain of eleven points is associated with each positive change.

A slightly different statistic which allows us to consider SIPC changes in nations experiencing *no* political change between 1928 and 1960 is the mean SIPC change per nation. Table 4 shows that fifty-six nations experienced a positive political change, forty-one had negative changes, and sixteen experienced no change. A net advantage of nearly twenty points per nation goes to countries with positive rather than negative changes, but a still larger SIPC increase of eighty-seven is found among nations that had no political change at all. These stable nations are nearly all at the highest level of economic and political development, a condition favorable to maximum SIPC changes.

Table 5 controls for the level of economic development and shows the amount of social-insurance program-completion change associated in any economic level with either positive or negative political changes or with stable political systems.

At the highest level of energy consumption there were five nations that experienced positive political changes with an average social-insurance index increase of eighty, while seven nations that experienced negative changes had an increase of only seventeen per nation. The thirteen nations with completely stable political structures had an increase of ninety-two. At the second level of energy consumption there is no difference in the amount of social-insurance program-coverage gains between countries with positive or negative change, but the two nations (Finland and Italy) with stable PRI experience have a gain of seventy-five. The third level of economic development again shows the expected pattern with a score of forty-seven associated with positive political change compared to a score of twenty-three associated with negative change. In like fashion, the fourth energy-consumption level reveals an increase of thirty-nine associated with positive change and only eleven with negative change, while the single nation with stable government (Saudi Arabia) had an increase of forty. At the lowest level of development, the ten nations with positive increases had an average of only seven in social-insurance program completion. There were very few cases of negative change and no cases of stable governments in this category. Part of the reason for the small number of negative changes is that nations at this level of economic development have minimal PRI scores to begin with and thus have little room to decrease.

If we look down the columns in Table 5, we see some irregularities in the pattern associated with positive and negative PRI changes—there is

Table 5 *SIPC Index Gains per Nation Associated with Positive, Negative, and No Changes in PRI* [a]

Energy Consumption Level and Type of Political Change	Mean SIPC Index Change per Nation Following Each PRI Change			Number of Nations	Net Number of Nations
Level I					
Positive	80	—	—	5	8
Negative	—	17	—	7	
No PRI change	—	—	92	13	13
Level II					
Positive	35	—	—	13	13
Negative	—	35	—	9	
No PRI change	—	—	75	2	2
Level III [b]					
Positive	47	—	—	10	11
Negative	—	23	—	8	
Level IV					
Positive	39	—	—	18	18
Negative	—	11	—	17 [c]	
No PRI change	—	—	40	1	1
Level V [b]					
Positive	7	—	—	10	10
Negative	—	—	—	4 [d]	

[a] Level of energy consumption controlled.

[b] Levels III and V had no nations without at least one PRI change between 1928 and 1960.

[c] Includes four cases from lowest level.

[d] Combined with negative group in Level IV.

not a perfectly steady decline in the size of the score from one energy-consumption level to the next.[12]

Regardless of the method used, the conclusion seems clear enough: Nations at very high levels of economic development are able to take advantage of stable government or positive political change, and they are likely to move toward completing the normal pattern of social-insurance programs. Social security growth is less likely to follow a negative PRI change than a positive change at *any* level of economic development. Again it is seen that nations with the lowest level of economic development are not introducing social insurance programs even when they have a positive PRI change. On the one hand, this reinforces the earlier conclusion that for these nations a rise in the level of the economy must precede the introduction of social-insurance programs. On the other hand, a positive change in political representativeness will tend to induce economically more-developed nations to introduce new social security programs.

DISCUSSION

An index (SIPE) measuring the general level of social security protection legislated or otherwise directed by the national government was developed. The SIPE index was closely related (.90) to the level of economic development, literacy (.83), and to a lesser extent (.58) urbanization. The .74 correlation of the SIPE index with the Political Representativeness Index (PRI) was found, after further analysis, to be related to variation in the SIPE index when the level of economic development was controlled.

The effect of different levels of political representativeness on the development of national social security programs varied with the level of economic development enjoyed by the nation. In nations with very low economic development, the push for social security development has, in most cases, yet to begin, despite the presence in this group of several different levels of political representativeness. This finding was interpreted in terms of the necessity of certain technological and bureaucratic prerequisites for successful introduction of social-insurance schemes. However, nations that have this capability (Levels I through IV) do not always exercise it. Within the mid-range of economic development (III and IV), the level of PRI was not powerfully related to SIPE. Nations

---

[12] An alternative method of computing SIPC change per political change rather than per nation provides a somewhat more consistent table when broken down in the same way as Table 5. At each level of energy consumption the average SIPC index change following each PRI positive change is larger than for negative PRI changes. The pattern of decline in SIPC change associated with decreasing energy consumption is also consistent for both positive and negative PRI change.

in the upper two economic-development strata not only had high SIPE scores but within each stratum SIPE was positively related to PRI. In general, the political condition that was most strongly related to low levels of social security development was colonial or quasicolonial status. With few exceptions (especially that of Iceland) little was done by occupying powers to institute social security programs. The difference between being politically dependent and being politically self-governing appears (Table 2) critical to the early development of social security programs. Once political independence is achieved, the degree to which the national government becomes more and more representative is also related to how rapidly the government acts to introduce national social security programs. This is most clearly demonstrated at the higher levels of economic development. In a separate analysis that controlled for the 1930 PRI level and ranked the 1930–60 PRI change against 1934–60 gains in SIPE, the size of PRI changes was positively related to SIPE gains.

A second index (SIPC) of government activity in the social security field was devised. A score was computed that measured the degree to which any new program instituted by a nation moved that nation closer to complete program coverage. Analysis of these scores revealed that social-insurance completion followed more upon positive political changes than upon negative political changes, whatever the level of economic development. Also, the few nations that enjoyed stable political structures had larger social security completion scores than did unstable nations.

If we are willing to speak of nations with the highest PRI scores as being democratic and of nations with lower scores as something less than democratic, we can engage the question of whether people living in a democracy enjoy levels of social security protection that are not provided to populations in other political systems. The analysis indicated that only a small difference could be found between nations at the very highest PRI level and a second group of nations above the mean on PRI. Further, at the upper levels of economic development even nations below the mean on PRI had SIPE scores close to those of the democratic nations.

The evidence presented in this paper supports the idea that national political, economic, and social systems are interdependent. Changes in the complexity of organization in one sphere are followed by changes in organization in other areas. The specific activities that engage the attention of national governments are not independent of the general level of development. Quite the contrary is true. In spite of very great differences among nations in ideological orientation as well as in type of political organization, we found that actual activities of government in the social security field were strongly related to the complexity of social organization in economic, social, and political institutions. Nations with high

levels of economic development but with less than "perfect" (i.e., democratic) political systems had government activities highly similar to those
undertaken by democratic governments. Further comparative studies of
government activities in other areas of social life will aid in understanding this conclusion. One might see the activities of government as intimately related to the problem of maintaining motivation and order in
societies as well as being a response to the democratically organized demands of the population. A government can act without being told what
to do. The scholar operating within a democratic context (and especially
that of the United States) may tend to view government activities as
being dependent upon the demands of secondary groups. A major but
tentative conclusion that can be drawn from this study of government
activity is that it need not await the petition of secondary groups. The
role (or even the existence) of politically relevant secondary groups in
guiding government decisions in many of the nations included in this
study is modest.

In many nations we would conclude that the introduction of social
security measures is a response by government to changes in the economic and social order that is not strongly affected by some degree of
departure from ideal democratic organizational forms. Similar levels of
social security coverage are found in nations whose governments are
thought to act in response to the popular will as occur in nations whose
governments are thought to act with less regard to public demands. It
appears that the level of social security in a nation is a response to deeper
strains affecting the organization of society. Governments may ignore
human needs, but there are rather tight limits on the extent to which they
may ignore organizational requirements.

APPENDIX A

Years of Social-Insurance Program Experience, 1934–1960, by Nation

Nation	Years	Nation	Years
Afghanistan	15	Cambodia	27
Albania	53	Canada	106
Argentina	75	Ceylon	52
Australia	118	Chile	129
Austria	121	China	37
Belgium	135	Colombia	46
Bolivia	54	Costa Rica	62
Brazil	101	Cuba	81
Bulgaria	100	Czechoslovakia	97
Burma	34	Denmark	117

Nation	Years	Nation	Years
Dominican Republic	55	Netherlands	130
Ecuador	86	New Zealand	131
Finland	96	Nicaragua	39
France	135	Norway	121
Germany	115	Pakistan	27
Great Britain	124	Panama	67
Greece	100	Paraguay	63
Guatemala	30	Peru	77
Haiti	10	Philippines	41
Honduras	9	Poland	95
Hungary	104	Portugal	100
Iceland	99	Romania	98
India	49	Russia	98
Indonesia	26	Salvador	39
Iran	40	Saudi Arabia	28
Iraq	40	South Korea	0
Ireland	125	Spain	131
Israel	45	Sweden	122
Italy	133	Switzerland	104
Japan	88	Syria	29
Jordan	6	Thailand	5
Laos	0	Turkey	44
Lebanon	36	United States	95
Luxembourg	122	Uruguay	92
Malaya	37	Venezuela	48
Mexico	65	Vietnam	31
Mongolia	0	Yemen	0
Nepal	0	Yugoslavia	115

APPENDIX B

The index used to measure differences among national political structures is computed according to a point system. Parliament and the executive branch of government are scored as follows.

A. Parliament Scoring

Two points if the largest party has less than 70 percent of the seats in
the lower or only chamber and achieved the seats through elections.

One and one-half points if the largest party has 70 percent or more
but the second party has at least 20 percent.

One point if the largest party has 70 percent or more and the second
party has less than 20 percent.

One-half point if the largest grouping in parliament is over 70 percent
with the second less than 20 *and* they do not represent parties selected

by election but are appointed to represent trade, commerce, ethnic, or other interests. Includes Fascist and Communist party systems.

No points if there is no parliament, if a former parliament is dissolved during the year by coup or revolt, if it is a "constituent assembly," or if the nation still has colonial status.

B. Executive Scoring

One and one-half points for each year under a chief executive who was selected by a party or parliament under conditions meeting the 70 and 20 percent rule.

One and one-half points if the chief executive is elected directly by the people in a competitive election held at the usual time, regardless of the 70–20 rule.

One point when the chief executive is selected by a party that is a sustaining force (has existed for 5 years as a party in parliament), but the party composition (is not a multiparty system) violates the 70–20 rule.

One point when the executive is selected by a party in a system that fails to observe the usual election time or goes outside the rules for having an election or has a non-competitive election or fails the 70 percent rule.

One-half point for junta, clique, non-party selection of leaders, or when existing leaders remain in power beyond the regular time.

No points to independent nations with hereditary rulers having chief executive power.

No points to nations with dependent colonial status or occupied by a foreign power.

In order to maintain a distinction between dependent and independent nations, one-half point was added to the over-all raw PRI score of each independent nation, while colonial or dependent nations received a score of zero.

It was possible for a nation to achieve from 0 to 4 points each year. A mean yearly PRI score was computed for each of the following four time periods: 1928–1934; 1935–1944; 1945–1954; 1955–1961, and a total of 304 scores (four for each of the seventy-six nations) was amassed and T-scored. The four distributions were T-scored separately as well. (A simple technique for computing the T-score is given in Allen E. Edwards, *Statistical Methods for the Behavioral Sciences* [New York: Holt, Rinehart & Winston, 1954]. For a single variable, T-scoring the raw data will yield a distribution with a mean of 50 and a standard deviation of 10.)

Part C

Beliefs and Values

HOW a given society develops its welfare system is not only a function of its level of industrialization, of its resources, of its elite, and of its political structure, but also of its *beliefs, values,* and *attitudes* about the needs of the population and the effects of attempting to meet those needs. We stress the role of beliefs and of cultural values because these are the cognitive and cultural components which help to determine both the recipients of service and the extent of service. For instance, if, in a given society, a subgroup is defined as being outside of the citizenry and as being undeserving of aid, then regardless of objective indices of the standard of living—such as the incidence of starvation—the society is unlikely to attempt to provide welfare services to that subgroup.

Cultural beliefs operate not only with reference to specific groups or programs but quite generally to limit the possibilities of collective action. If cultural tradition places a strong emphasis on individual responsibility and action, then collective solutions are likely to be resisted. On the other hand, a group can have values which stress the importance of collective action as a general rule and, consequently, welfare problems too will call forth a collective response. Similarly, if a society has a fatalistic belief system, placing responsibility for man's conduct on the large external forces of nature, collective action is less likely than if most people believe in the possibility of man's control of nature.

The two articles in this part illuminate the interplay of beliefs and values and welfare measures. The first selection, "A Comparative Study of the Role of Values in Social Action in Two Southwestern Communities," by Evon Z. Vogt and Thomas F. O'Dea, compares two communities located in relatively similar environments. One of the communities is "Mormon" and the other "Texan." Vogt and O'Dea stress that the historical value patterns held by these two groups have led to marked differences in their readiness to invest time and energy in community betterment projects. Although this article deals with communities, not total societies, the arguments would apply to larger social systems as well.

The article, "Hunger and Ideology," by Steven Marcus, is a review of a book on the Irish famine. Marcus stresses several facets of social structure and of belief that led to this great tragedy. First, since the British were essentially conquerors, they did not feel much responsibility and involvement with the people. Second, the ideas prevalent about the operation of the economy led to fears of intervention: if the British intervened and helped the starving, the supply of labor would be disrupted and they would be interfering with the natural order. Finally, they believed that poverty is a crime of the individual, and is his own responsibility.

A Comparative Study of the Role of Values

in Social Action in Two Southwestern

Communities

Evon Z. Vogt and Thomas F. O'Dea

It is one of the central hypotheses of the Values Study Project that value-orientations play an important part in the shaping of social institutions and in influencing the forms of observed social action. By value-orientations are understood those views of the world, often implicitly held, which define the meaning of human life or the "life situation of man" and thereby provide the context in which day-to-day problems are solved.[1] The present article is an outgrowth of one phase of the field research carried out in western New Mexico. It presents the record of two communities composed of people with a similar cultural background and living in the same general ecological setting.

The responses of these two communities to similar problems were found to be quite different. Since the physical setting of the two villages is remarkably similar, the explanation for the differences was sought in the manner in which each group viewed the situation and the kind of social relationships and legitimate expectations which each felt appropriate in meeting situational challenges. In this sphere of value-orienta-

[1] Clyde Kluckhohn, "Values and Value-Orientations in the Theory of Action: an Exploration in Definition and Classification," *Toward a General Theory of Action*, edited by Talcott Parsons and E. A. Shils, Cambridge: Harvard University Press, 1951, p. 410.

Evon Z. Vogt and Thomas F. O'Dea, "A Comparative Study of the Role of Values in Social Action in Two Southwestern Communities," *American Sociological Review*, 18, 1953, pp. 645–654. The authors are indebted to the Rockefeller Foundation (Social Science Division) for the financial support of the research reported in this paper as part of the Comparative Study of Values in Five Cultures Project of the Laboratory of Social Relations at Harvard University. We also wish to express our appreciation to Ethel M. Albert, Wilfrid C. Bailey, Clyde Kluckhohn, Anne Parsons, and John M. Roberts for criticisms and suggestions in the preparation of the paper.

tions a marked difference was found. Moreover, the differences in response to situation in the two cases were found to be related to the differences between the value-orientations central to these communities.

We do not deny the importance of situational factors. Nor do we intend to disparage the importance of historical convergenec of value-orientations with concrete situations in explaining the centrality of some values as against others and in leading to the deep internalization of the values we discuss. But the importance of value-orientations as an element in understanding the situation of action is inescapably clear. All the elements of what Parsons has called the action frame of reference—the actors, the means and conditions which comprise the situation, and the value-orientations of the actors enter into the act.[2] The primacy of any one in any individual case does not permit generalization. Yet the present study testifies to the great importance of the third element—the value-orientations—in shaping the final action which ensues.

FOCUS OF THE INQUIRY

The inquiry is focused upon a comparison of the Mormon community of *Rimrock*[3] with the Texan community of *Homestead*, both having populations of approximately 250 and both located (forty miles apart) on the southern portion of the Colorado Plateau in western New Mexico. The natural environmental setting is virtually the same for the two villages: the prevailing elevations stand at 7,000 feet; the landscapes are characterized by mesa and canyon country; the flora and fauna are typical of the Upper Sonoran Life Zone with stands of pinyon, juniper, sagebrush, and blue gramma grass and some intrusions of Ponderosa pine, Douglas fir, Englemann spruce and Gambel oak from a higher life zone; the region has a steppe climate with an average annual precipitation of 14 inches (which varies greatly from year to year) and with killing frosts occurring late in the spring and early in the autumn.[4] The single important environmental difference between the two communities is that Rimrock is located near the base of a mountain range which has elevations rising to 9,000 feet, and a storage reservoir (fed by melting snow packs from these higher elevations) has made irrigation agriculture pos-

---

[2] Talcott Parsons, *The Structure of Social Action*, Glencoe: Free Press, 1949, pp. 43–86; *Essays in Sociological Theory*, Glencoe: Free Press, 1949, pp. 32–40; *The Social System*, Glencoe: Free Press, 1951, pp. 3–24.

[3] "Rimrock" and "Homestead" are pseudonyms used to protect the anonymity of our informants.

[4] For additional ecological details on the region see Evon Z. Vogt, *Navaho Veterans: A Study of Changing Values*, Peabody Museum of Harvard University, Papers, Vol. XLI, No. 1, 1951, pp. 11–12; and John Landgraf, *Land-Use in the Rimrock Area of New Mexico: An Anthropological Approach to Areal Study*, Peabody Museum of Harvard University, Papers, forthcoming, 1953.

sible in Rimrock, while in Homestead there is only dry-land farming. Today both villages have subsistence patterns based upon combinations of farming (mainly irrigated crops of alfalfa and wheat in Rimrock, and dry-land crops of pinto beans in Homestead) and livestock raising (mainly Hereford beef cattle in both villages).

Rimrock was settled by Mormon missionaries in the 1870's as part of a larger project to plant settlements in the area of northern Arizona. Rimrock itself, unlike the Arizona sites, was established as a missionary outpost and the intention of the settlers was the conversion of the Indians, a task conceived in terms of the *Book of Mormon,* which defines the American Indian as "a remnant of Israel."

The early settlers were "called" by the Church, that is, they were selected and sent out by the Church authorities. The early years were exceedingly difficult and only the discipline of the Church and the loyalty of the settlers to its gospel kept them at the task. Drought, crop diseases, and the breaking of the earth and rock dam which they had constructed for the storage of irrigation water added to their difficulties, as did the fact that they had merely squatted on the land and were forced to purchase it at an exorbitant price to avoid eviction. The purchase money was given by the Church authorities in Salt Lake City, who also supplied 5,000 pounds of seed wheat in another period of dearth. The original settlers were largely from northern Utah although there were also some converts from the southern states who had been involved in unsuccessful Arizona settlements a few years earlier.

As the emphasis shifted from missionary activities to farming, Rimrock developed into a not unusual Mormon village, despite its peripheral position to the rest of Mormondom. Irrigation farming was supplemented by cattle raising on the open range. In the early 1930's the Mormons began to buy range land, and Rimrock's economy shifted to a focus upon cattle raising. Today villagers own a total of 149 sections of range land and about four sections of irrigated or irrigable land devoted to gardens and some irrigated pastures in the immediate vicinity of the village. The family farm is still the basic economic unit, although partnerships formed upon a kinship basis and devoted to cattle raising have been important in raising the economic level of the village as a whole. In recent years some of the villagers—also on the basis of a kinship partnership—purchased the local trading post which is engaged in trading with the Indians as well as local village business. In addition to 12 family partnerships which own 111 sections of land, there is a village cooperative which owns 38 sections. Privately-owned commercial facilities in the village include two stores, a boarding house, two garages, a saddle and leather shop, and a small restaurant. With this economic variety there is considerable difference in the distribution of wealth.

The Church is the central core of the village and its complex hierarchical structure, including the auxiliary organizations which activate women, youth, and young children, involves a large portion of the villagers in active participation. The church structure is backed up and impenetrated by the kinship structure. Moreover, church organization and kinship not only unify Rimrock into a social unit, they also integrate it into the larger structure of the Mormon Church and relate it by affinity and consanguinity to the rest of Mormondom.

Rimrock has been less affected by secularization than most Mormon villages in Utah and is less assimilated into generalized American patterns.[5] Its relative isolation has both kept such pressures from impinging upon it with full force and enhanced its formal and informal ties with the Church, preserving many of the characteristics of a Mormon village of a generation ago.

Homestead was settled by migrants from the South Plains area of western Texas and Oklahoma in the early 1930's. The migration represented a small aspect of that vast movement of people westward to California which was popularized in Steinbeck's *Grapes of Wrath* and which was the subject of investigation by many governmental agencies in the 1930's and 1940's.[6] Instead of going on to California, these homesteaders settled in a number of semi-arid farming areas in northern and western New Mexico and proceeded to develop an economy centered around the production of pinto beans. The migration coincided with the period of national depression and was due in part to severe economic conditions on the South Plains which forced families to leave their Texas and Oklahoma communities, in part to the attraction of land available for homesteading which held out the promise of family-owned farms for families who had previously owned little or no land or who had lost their land during the depression. The land base controlled by the homesteaders comprises approximately 100 sections. Each farm unit is operated by a nuclear family; there are no partnerships. Farms now average two sections in size and are scattered as far as twenty miles from the crossroads center of the community which contains the two stores, the school, the post office, two garages, a filling station, a small restaurant, a bean warehouse, a small bar, and two church buildings. Through the years, farming technology has shifted almost completely from horse-drawn implements to mechanized equipment.

With the hazardous farming conditions (periodic droughts and early killing frosts) out-migration from Homestead has been relatively high. A few of these families have gone on to California, but more of them

[5] Lowry Nelson, *The Mormon Village*. Salt Lake City: University of Utah Press, 1952, pp. 275–85.
[6] See especially the reports of the Tolan Committee, U.S. Congress, "House Committee to Investigate the Interstate Migration of Destitute Citizens," 76th Congress, 3rd Session, Volume 6, Part 6, 1940.

have moved to irrigated farms in the middle Rio Grande Valley and entered an agricultural situation which in its physical environmental aspects is similar to the situation in the Mormon community of Rimrock.

THE MORMON CASE

In broad perspective these two villages present local variations of generalized American culture. They share the common American value-orientations which emphasize the importance of achievement and success, progress and optimism, and rational mastery over nature. In the Mormon case, these were taken over from the 19th century American milieu in western New York where the Church was founded, and reinterpreted in terms of an elaborate theological conception of the universe as a dynamic process in which God and men are active collaborators in an eternal progression to greater power through increasing mastery.[7] The present life was and is conceived as a single episode in an infinity of work and mastery. The result was the heightening for the Mormons of convictions shared with most other Americans. Moreover, this conception was closely related to the belief in the reopening of divine revelation through the agency first of Joseph Smith, the original Mormon prophet, and later through the institutionalized channels of the Mormon Church. The Mormons conceived of themselves as a convenant people especially chosen for a divine task. This task was the building of the kingdom of God on earth and in this project—attempted four times unsuccessfully before the eventual migration to the west—much of the religious and secular social-ism of the early 19th century found a profound reflection. The Mormon prophet proposed the "Law of Consecration" in an attempt to reconcile private initiative with cooperative endeavor. Contention led to its aban-donment in 1838 after some five years of unsuccessful experiment. Yet this withdrawal did not limit, but indeed rather enhanced, its future influence in Mormon settlement. The "Law of Consecration" was no longer interpreted as a blueprint prescribing social institutions of a defi-nite sort, but its values lent a strong cooperative bias to much of later Mormon activity.[8] In the context of the notion of peculiarity and rein-forced by out-group antagonism and persecution, these values became

[7] The data from Rimrock are based upon seven months field experience in the com-munity during 1950–51. Additional data on this community will be provided in O'Dea's forthcoming monograph on *Mormon Values: The Significance of a Religious Outlook for Social Action.*
[8] The "Law of Consecration" became the basis of the Mormon pattern of cooperative activity also known as "The United Order of Enoch." Cf. Joseph A. Geddes, *The United Order Among the Mormons,* Salt Lake City: Deseret News Press, 1924; Edward J. Allen, *The Second United Order Among the Mormons,* New York: Columbia University Press, 1936.

deeply embedded in Mormon orientations. The preference for agriculture combined with an emphasis upon community and lay participation in church activities resulted in the formation of compact villages rather than isolated family farmsteads as the typical Mormon settlement pattern.[9]

While Rimrock and Homestead share most of the central value-orientations of general American culture, they differ significantly in the values governing social relationships. Rimrock, with a stress upon community cooperation, an ethnocentrism resulting from the notion of their own peculiarity, and a village pattern of settlement, is more like the other Mormon villages of the West than it is like Homestead.

The stress upon *community cooperation* in Rimrock contrasts markedly with the stress upon *individual independence* found in Homestead. This contrast is one of emphasis, for individual initiative is important in Rimrock, especially in family farming and cattle raising, whereas cooperative activity does occur in Homestead. In Rimrock, however, the expectations are such that one must show his fellows or at least convince himself that he has good cause for *not* committing his time and resources to community efforts while in Homestead cooperative action takes place *only* after certainty has been reached that the claims of other individuals upon one's time and resources are legitimate.

Rimrock was a cooperative venture from the start, and very early the irrigation company, a mutual non-profit corporation chartered under state law, emerged from the early water association informally developed around—and in a sense within—the Church. In all situations which transcend the capacities of individual families or family combinations, Rimrock Mormons have recourse to cooperative techniques. Let us examine four examples.

The "Tight" Land Situation

Rimrock Mormons, feeling themselves "gathered," dislike having to migrate to non-Mormon areas. However, after World War II the 32 returned veterans faced a choice between poverty and under-employment or leaving the community. This situation became the concern of the Church and was discussed in its upper lay priesthood bodies in the village. It was decided to buy land to enable the veterans to remain. The possibilities of land purchase in the area were almost nonexistent and it appeared that nothing could be done, when unexpectedly the opportunity to buy some 38 sections presented itself. At the time, the village did not have the needed 10,000 dollars for the down payment, so the sum was borrowed from the Cooperative Security Corporation, a Church Welfare Plan agency, and the land was purchased. The patterns revealed here—community concern over a community problem, and appeal to and reception of

---

9 Nelson, *op. cit.*, pp. 25–54.

aid from the general authorities of the Church—are typically Mormon. However, Mormon cooperation did not end here. Instead of breaking up the purchased land into plots to be individually owned and farmed, the parcel was kept as a unit, and a cooperative Rimrock Land and Cattle Company was formed. The company copied and adapted the form of the mutual irrigation company. Shares were sold in the village, each member being limited to two. A quota of cattle per share per year to be run on the land and a quota of bulls relative to cows were established. The cattle are privately owned, but the land is owned and managed cooperatively. The calves are the property of the owners of the cows. The project, which has not been limited to veterans, supplements other earnings sufficiently to keep most of the veterans in the village.

The Graveling of the Village Streets

The streets of Rimrock were in bad repair in the fall of 1950. That summer a construction company had brought much large equipment into the area to build and gravel a section of a state highway which runs through the village. Before this company left, taking its equipment with it, villagers, again acting through the Church organization, decided that the village should avail itself of the opportunity and have the town's streets graveled. This was discussed in the Sunday priesthood meeting and announced at the Sunday sacrament meeting. A meeting was called for Monday evening, and each household was asked to send a representative. The meeting was well attended, and although not every family had a member present, practically all were represented at least by proxy. There was considerable discussion, and it was finally decided to pay 800 dollars for the job which meant a 20 dollar donation from each family. The local trader paid a larger amount, and, within a few days after the meeting, the total amount was collected. Only one villager raised objections to the proceedings. Although he was a man of importance locally, he was soon silenced by a much poorer man who invoked Mormon values of progress and cooperation and pledged to give 25 dollars which was 5 dollars above the norm.

The Construction of a High School Gymnasium

In 1951 a plan for the construction of a high school gymnasium was presented to the Rimrock villagers. Funds for materials and for certain skilled labor would be provided from state school appropriations, providing that the local residents would contribute the labor for construction. The plan was discussed in a Sunday priesthood meeting in the church, and later meetings were held both in the church and in the schoolhouse. Under the leadership of the principal of the school (who is also a member of the higher priesthood), arrangements were made whereby each able-bodied man in the community would either contribute at least 50 hours of labor or 50 dollars (the latter to be used to hire outside laborers) toward the construction. The original blueprint was extended to include a row of classrooms for the high school around the large central gymnasium.

Work on the new building began in late 1951, continued through 1952, and is now (in 1953) nearing completion. The enterprise was not carried through without difficulties. A few families were sympathetic at first but failed to contribute full amounts of either labor or cash, and some were unsympathetic toward the operation from the start. The high school principal had to keep reminding the villagers about their pledges to support the enterprise. But in the end the project was successful, and it represented an important cooperative effort on the part of the majority.

The Community Dances

The Mormons have always considered dancing to be an important form of recreation—in fact a particularly Mormon form of recreation. Almost every Friday evening a dance is held in the village church house. These dances are family affairs and are opened and closed with prayer. They are part of the general Church recreation program and are paid for by what is called locally "the budget." The budget refers to the plan under which villagers pay 15 dollars per family per year to cover a large number of entertainments, all sponsored by the Church auxiliary organization for youth, the Young Men's Mutual Improvement Association, and the Young Women's Mutual Improvement Association. The budget payment admits all members of the family to such entertainments.

Observation of these dances over a six months period did not reveal any tension or fighting. Smoking and drinking are forbidden to loyal Mormons, and those who smoked did so outside and away from the building. At dances held in the local school there has been evidence of drinking, and at times fighting has resulted from the presence of non-villagers. But on the whole the Rimrock dances are peaceful family affairs.

Rimrock reveals itself responding to group problems *as a group*. The economic ethic set forth by Joseph Smith in the Law of Consecration is seen in the dual commitment to private individual initiative (family farms and family partnerships in business and agriculture) and to cooperative endeavor in larger communal problems (irrigation company, land and cattle company, graveling the streets, and construction of school gymnasium). For the Mormons, cooperation has become second nature. It has become part of the institutionalized structure of expectations, reinforced by religious conviction and social control.

THE HOMESTEADER CASE

The value-stress upon individual independence of action has deep roots in the history of the homesteader group.[10] The homesteaders were part of the westward migration from the hill country of the Southern Appalachians to the Panhandle country of Texas and Oklahoma and from there to the Southwest and California. Throughout their historical experience there has been an emphasis upon a rough and ready self-reliance and individualism, the Jacksonianism of the frontier West. The move to western New Mexico from the South Plains was made predominantly by isolated nuclear families, and Homestead became a community of scattered, individually-owned farmsteads—a geographical situation and a settlement pattern which reinforced the stress upon individualism.

Let us now examine the influence of this individualistic value-orientation upon a series of situations comparable to those that were described for Rimrock.

The "Tight" Land Situation

In 1934 the Federal Security Administration, working in conjunction with the Land Use Division of the Department of Agriculture, proposed a "unit re-organization plan." This plan would have enabled the homesteaders to acquire additional tracts of land and permit them to run more livestock and hence depend less upon the more hazardous economic pursuit of dry-land pinto bean farming. It called for the use of government funds to purchase large ranches near the Homestead area which would be managed cooperatively by a board of directors selected by the community. The scheme collapsed while it was still in the planning stages, because it was clear that each family expected to acquire its own private holdings on the range and that a cooperative would not work in Homestead.

The Graveling of the Village Streets

During the winter of 1949–1950 the construction company which was building the highway through Rimrock was also building a small section of highway north of Homestead. The construction company offered to gravel the streets of Homestead center if the residents who lived in the village would cooperatively contribute enough funds for the purpose. This community plan was rejected by the homesteaders, and an alternative plan was followed. Each of the operators of several of the service institu-

---

[10] The data from Homestead are based upon a year's field work in the community during 1949–50. Additional data on this community will be provided in Vogt's forthcoming monograph on *The Homesteaders: A Study of Values in a Frontier Community.* See also Vogt, "Water Witching: An Interpretation of a Ritual Pattern in a Rural American Community," *Scientific Monthly,* LXXV (September, 1952).

tions—including the two stores, the bar, and the post office—independently hired the construction company truck drivers to haul a few loads of gravel to be placed in front of his own place of business, which still left the rest of the village streets a sea of mud in rainy weather.

The Construction of a High School Gymnasium

In 1950 the same plan for the construction of a new gymnasium was presented to the homesteaders as was presented to the Mormon village of Rimrock. As noted above, this plan was accepted by the community of Rimrock, and the new building is now nearing completion. But the plan was rejected by the residents of Homestead at a meeting in the summer of 1950, and there were long speeches to the effect that "I've got to look after my own farm and my own family first; I can't be up here in town building a gymnasium." Later in the summer additional funds were provided for labor; and with these funds adobe bricks were made, the foundation was dug, and construction was started—the homesteaders being willing to work on the gymnasium on a purely business basis at a dollar an hour. But as soon as the funds were exhausted, construction stopped. Today a partially completed gymnasium, and stacks of some 10,000 adobe bricks disintegrating slowly with the rains, stand as monuments to the individualism of the homesteaders.

The Community Dances

As in Rimrock, the village dances in Homestead are important focal points for community activity. These affairs take place several times a year in the schoolhouse and are always well-attended. But while the dances in Rimrock are well-coordinated activities which carry through the evening, the dances in Homestead often end when tensions between rival families result in fist-fights. And there is always the expectation in Homestead that a dance (or other cooperative activity such as a picnic or rodeo) may end at any moment and the level of activity reduced to the component nuclear families which form the only solid core of social organization within the community.

The individualistic value-orientation of the homesteaders also has important functional relationships to the religious organization of the community. With the exception of two men who are professed atheists, all of the homesteaders define themselves as Christians. But denominationalism is rife, there being ten different denominations represented in the village: Baptist, Presbyterian, Methodist, Nazarene, Campbellite, Holiness, 7th Day Adventist, Mormon, Catholic, and Present Day Disciples.

In the most general terms, this religious differentiation in Homestead can be interpreted as a function of the individualistic and factionalizing tendencies in the social system. In a culture with a value-stress upon independent individual action combined with a "freedom of religion" ideology, adhering to one's own denomination becomes an important means of expressing individualism and of focusing factional disputes around a doctrine and a concrete institutional framework. In turn, the doctrinal differences promote additional factionalizing tendencies, with the result that competing churches become the battleground for a cumulative and circularly reinforcing struggle between rival small factions within the community.[11]

To sum up, we may say that the strong commitment to an individualistic value-orientation has resulted in a social system in which inter-personal relations are strongly colored by a kind of factionalism and in which persons and groups become related to one another in a competitive, feuding relationship. The homesteaders do not live on their widely separated farms and ignore one another, as it might be possible to do. On the other hand, they do not cooperate in community affairs as closely as does a hive of bees. They interact, but a constant feuding tone permeates the economic, social and religious structure of the community.

RELATIONSHIP BETWEEN THE TWO COMMUNITIES

Although there is some trading in livestock, feed, and other crops, the most important contacts between the two communities are not economic but are social and recreational. The village baseball teams have scheduled games with one another for the past two decades, and there is almost always joint participation in the community dances and in the summer rodeos in the two communities. Despite Mormon objections to close associations with "gentiles," there is also considerable inter-dating between the two communities among the teen-age groups, and three intermarriages have taken place.

In general, the homesteaders envy and admire the Mormons' economic organization, their irrigated land, and more promising prospects for good crops each year. On the other hand, they regard the Mormons as cliquish and unfriendly and fail completely to understand why anyone "wants to live all bunched up the way the Mormons do." They feel that the Mormons are inbred and think they should be glad to get "new blood" from intermarriages with homesteaders. They add, "That Mormon religion is something we can't understand at all." Finally, the homesteaders say that Mormons "used to have more than one wife, and some probably still do; they dance in the church, they're against liquor, coffee, and tobacco, and they always talk about Joseph Smith and the Book of Mormon."

[11] This relationship between churches and factionalizing tendencies has also been observed by Bailey in his unpublished study of a community in west Texas, in the heart of the ancestral home region of the present residents of Homestead. Cf. Wilfrid C. Bailey, "A Study of a Texas Panhandle Community; A Preliminary Report on Cotton Center, Texas," Values Study Files, Harvard University.

The Mormons consider their own way of life distinctly superior to that of the homesteaders in every way. Some will admit that the homesteaders have the virtue of being more friendly and of "mixing more with others," and their efforts in the face of farming hazards are admired, but Homestead is generally regarded as a rough and in some ways immoral community, especially because of the drinking, smoking, and fighting (particularly at dances) that takes place. They also feel that Homestead is disorganized and that the churches are not doing what they should for the community. For the past few years they have been making regular missionary trips to Homestead, but to date they have made no conversions.

COMPARISONS AND CONCLUSIONS

In the case of Rimrock and Homestead, we are dealing with two communities which are comparable in population, in ecological setting, and which are variants of the same general culture. The two outstanding differences are: (a) irrigation versus dry-land farming and associated differences in settlement pattern, compact village versus isolated farmstead type; [12] (b) a value stress upon cooperative community action versus a stress upon individual action. The important question here involves the relationship (if any) between these two sets of variables. Is the cooperation in Rimrock directly a function of an irrigation agriculture situation with a compact village settlement pattern, the rugged individualism in Homestead, a function of a dry-land farming situation with a scattered settlement pattern? Or did these value-orientations arise out of earlier historical experience in each case, influence the types of communities which were established in western New Mexico, and later persist in the face of changed economic situations? We shall attempt to demonstrate that the second proposition is more in accord with the historical facts as we now know them.

Nelson has recently shown that the general pattern of the Mormon village is neither a direct function (in its beginnings) of the requirements of irrigation agriculture, nor of the need for protection against Indians on the frontier. Rather, the basic pattern was a social invention of the Mormons, motivated by a sense of urgent need to prepare a dwelling place for the "Savior" at "His Second Coming." The "Plat of the City of Zion" was invented by Joseph Smith, Sidney Rigdon, and Frederick G. Williams in 1833 and has formed the basis for the laying out of most Mormon villages, even those established in the Middle West before the Mormons migrated to Utah.[13]

It is very clear that both the compact village pattern and the cooperative social arrangements centered around the church existed before the Mor-

[12] Cf. Nelson, *op. cit.*, p. 4.
[13] Nelson, *op. cit.*, pp. 28–38.

mons engaged in irrigation agriculture and had a strong influence upon the development of community structure not only in Utah but in the Mormon settlements like Rimrock on the periphery of the Mormon culture area. There is no objective reason in the Rimrock ecological and cultural setting (the local Navahos and Zunis did not pose a threat to pioneer settlements in the 1880's) why the Mormons could not have set up a community which conformed more to the isolated farmstead type with a greater stress upon individualistic social relations. Once the Mormon community was established, it is clear that the cooperation required by irrigation agriculture of the Mormon type and the general organization of the church strongly reinforced the value stress upon communal social action.

It is of further significance that as the population expanded and the Rimrock Mormons shifted from irrigation agricultural pursuits to dryland ranching in the region outside of the Rimrock valley, the earlier cooperative patterns modeled on the mutual irrigation company were applied to the solution of economic problems that are identical to those faced by the Homesteaders. Moreover, in midwestern and eastern cities to which Mormons have recently moved, church wards have purchased and cooperatively worked church welfare plan farms.

In Homestead, on the other hand, our evidence indicates that the first settlers were drawn from a westward-moving population which stressed a frontier-type of self-reliance and individualism. They were searching for a place where each man could "own his own farm and be his own boss." Each family settled on its isolated homestead claim, and there emerged from the beginning an isolated farmstead type of settlement pattern in which the nuclear family was the solidary unit. The service center which was built up later simply occupied lots that were sold to storekeepers, filling station operators, the bartender, and others, by the four families who owned the four sections which joined at a crossroads. Only two of these four family homes were located near the service center at the crossroads. The other two families continued to maintain their homes in other quarters of their sections and lived almost a mile from "town." In 1952 one of the former families built a new home located over a mile from the center of town, and commented that they had always looked forward to "getting out of town."

There is no objective reason in the Homestead ecological setting why there could not be more clustering of houses into a compact village and more community cooperation than actually exists. One would not expect those farmers whose farms are located 15 or 20 miles from the service center to live in "town" and travel out to work each day. But there is no reason why those families living within 2 or 3 miles of the village center could not live in town and work their fields from there. In typical Mormon villages a large percentage of the farms are located more than three miles from the farm homes. For example, in Rimrock over 31 percent, in Escalante over 38 percent, and in Ephriam over 30 percent of the farms are located from three to eight or more miles from the center of the villages.[14]

It is clear that the homesteaders were operating with a set of individualistic property arrangements (drawn, of course, from our generalized American culture) and that their strong stress upon individualism led to a quite different utilization of these property patterns (than was the case with the Mormons) and to the establishment of a highly scattered type of community. Once Homestead was established, the individualism permitted by the scattered dry-land farming pattern, and encouraged by the emphasis upon the small nuclear family unit and upon multi-denominationalism in church affiliation reacted on and strongly reinforced the value stress upon individual independence. It is evident that the homesteaders continue to prefer this way of life, as shown by their remarks concerning the "bunched up" character of a Mormon village and the fact that a number of families have recently moved "out of town" when they built new houses.

Of further interest is the fact that when homesteader families move to irrigated farms in the middle Rio Grande Valley, the stress upon individual action tends to persist strongly. They do not readily develop cooperative patterns to deal with this new setting which is similar to the situation in the irrigated valley of the Mormons at Rimrock. Indeed, one of the principal innovations they have been promoting in one region along the Rio Grande where they are replacing Spanish-Americans on the irrigated farming land is a system of meters on irrigation ditches. These meters will measure the water flowing into each individual farmer's ditches, and effectively eliminate the need for more highly organized cooperative arrangements for distributing the available supply of water.

In conclusion, we should like to reiterate that we are strongly cognizant of situational factors. If the Rimrock Mormons had not been able to settle in a valley which was watered by melting snow packs from a nearby mountain and which provided the possibilities for the construction of storage reservoir, they certainly could not have developed an irrigation agricultural system at all. In the case of Rimrock, however, the actual site of settlement was selected from among several possible sites in a larger situation. The selection was largely influenced by Mormon preconceptions of the type of village they wished to establish. In fact, Mormons chose the irrigable valleys throughout the inter-montane west. On the other hand, the physical environmental features for the development of irrigation were simply not present in the Homestead setting, and the people had no alternative to dry-land farming. There is no evidence to

---

[14] See Nelson, *op. cit.*, pp. 99 and 144 for data on Escalante and Ephriam.

suggest that had they found an irrigable valley, they would have developed it along Mormon lines. In fact, the homesteaders' activities in the Rio Grande Valley suggest just the opposite. It is clear that the situational facts did not *determine* in any simple sense the contrasting community structures which emerged. Rather, the situations set certain limits, but within these limits contrasting value-orientations influenced the development of two quite different community types. It would appear that solutions to problems of community settlement pattern and the type of concrete social action which ensues are set within a value framework which importantly influences the selections made with the range of possibilities existing within an objective situation.

Hunger and Ideology

Steven Marcus

Famine seems to be the last, the most dreadful resource of nature. . . . The vices of mankind are active and able ministers of depopulation. They are the precursors in the great army of destruction; and often finish the dreadful work themselves. But should they fail in this war of extermination, sickly seasons, epidemics, pestilence, and plague, advance in terrific array, and sweep off their thousands and ten thousands. Should success be still incomplete, gigantic inevitable famine stalks in the rear, and with one mighty blow, levels the population with the food of the world.

THOMAS MALTHUS

As every schoolboy knows, the Irish famine is one of the capital disasters of history. It broke upon a people who had been dominated by a foreign power for seven hundred years, and who lived in almost bestial servitude, poverty, misery, ignorance, and helplessness. The accounts of contemporary travelers uniformly attest to the extremity of Ireland's condition: one witness asserted that "no mode of life in Europe could seem pitiable after one had seen Ireland . . . the poorest among the Letts, the

Steven Marcus, "Hunger and Ideology," *Commentary*, November 1963, pp. 389–393.

Esthonians and the Finlanders, lead a life of comparative comfort";
another wrote that "the Negro in his chains" suffered less misery. Subsist-
ing under conditions of systematic exploitation and classic peonage, the
Irish peasants had been reduced to living off a single crop, the potato.
Indeed in certain back areas of Ireland "cooking any food other than the
potato had become a lost art." And yet, as if to demonstrate the ghastly
truth of Malthus's theory, the population of Ireland had been steadily
increasing. The calamity began with the blight of the potato crops in 1845
and 1846. A variety of public and private schemes for relief were undertaken, but such measures soon proved inadequate as the famine extended
through the following years and began to take cumulative effect. Hunger
was succeeded by disease, primarily by an epidemic of typhus, but bacil-
lary dysentery, hunger oedema, scurvy, and cholera were also general.
The vegetable blight was thus followed by human blight; the lightning-
like reproduction, spread, and infestation of the spores of the potato
fungus were equaled only by the rapidity with which typhus propagated
itself. "A brush in passing was enough to transfer the fever-transmitting
louse or its dustlike excrement to a new victim, and one fever-stricken
person could pass on infection to a hundred others in the course of a day."

Hunger and disease were followed by emigration, the third great agent
in the depopulation of Ireland, and "historically the most important event
of the famine." More than a million emigrants from Ireland left the unspeakable conditions of their homeland, journeyed under unspeakable
conditions across the Atlantic, and were treated unspeakably when they
arrived in North America. An even larger number crossed the Irish
channel to take up existence in Liverpool, Glasgow, and the ports of South
Wales. Ireland was more than decimated by the famine; according to the
best estimates—which are very rough—between 25 and 27 percent of its
population was in one way or another lost.

These are some of the gross facts of the famine, as they are retold in
Cecil Woodham-Smith's *The Great Hunger*,[1] a week by week account of
the long disaster and a work of unrelieved grimness and horror. Mrs.
Woodham-Smith goes in neither for picturesque detail nor comic-pathetic
diversions and almost never generalizes. Fact after relentless fact falls
on the mind, but they do not deaden perception. In Mrs. Woodham-
Smith's hands, abstract statistics come alive as human beings, as she
paradoxically undoes the usual effect of statistics, which is to imperson-
alize, average out, and distance our response to concrete experience. *The
Great Hunger* is a work of unusual distinction, informed at every point
by the knowledge that facts alone do not amount to history unless we
include among them the fact of consciousness.

As the historian G. M. Young once remarked, "the real, central theme

[1] Harper & Row, 418 pp., $6.95.

of History is not what happened, but what people felt about it when it was happening." The Irish famine itself occurred at a time in which consciousness was in the course of dramatically shifting. If we compare it, for example, with the Black Plague of 1348–1349, the differences are instructive. That earlier event is the worst catastrophe of this millennium of European history; modern authorities estimate that about one third of the population of the Continent perished. But how was the plague interpreted at the time of its occurrence? According to one scholar, Norman Cohn, it was regarded "in normal medieval fashion, as a divine chastisement for the transgressions of a sinful world." And the religious excesses, such as the flagellant processions, which then sprang up were "in part an attempt to divert the chastisement." After reading such accounts, the reader must conclude that these attitudes and practices were, to adapt a sociological term, "legitimate" responses to the situation—that is to say, they corresponded both to the means or resources then available for dealing with that situation, and to the furthest spiritual and intellectual stage of development to which society had then attained. At the time of the Irish famine, however, a similar attitude no longer elicits our assent. When Charles Edward Trevelyan, the Treasury official in charge of all the programs for Irish relief, gives voice to such sentiments, the reader detects in his pieties not only indifference and hard-heartedness but flummery as well. Mrs. Woodham-Smith dryly observes that, "The thought that famine was the will of God was a consolation to him, and he hoped that the Catholic priests were making this clear." And Trevelyan himself wrote: "It is hard upon the poor people that they should be deprived of knowing that they are suffering from an affliction of God's providence." A number of considerations converge to make this reference to Providence morally unacceptable. In the first place, means had been developed and were at hand to deal with and alleviate both famine and plague, but they were not fully employed. In the second, the religious argument or explanation is at this moment serving a classic ideological function—it is being used to screen other interests and motives, and as a partial extenuation of the British government's failure to provide adequate relief to the starving Irish. And third, at the time Trevelyan was writing, a humane consciousness had already come into existence which challenged the validity of his assumptions and the necessity of his conclusions.

The discrepancy between Trevelyan's attitude and what had become an authentic moral possibility at that moment in history leads us to note that death itself is relative and historical. Death as a fact is absolute, of course, but as civilization's control over nature advances, the number of morally legitimate or acceptable forms of death or dying steadily decreases. (In our culture today, for instance, death in a nuclear war seems on the verge of ceasing to exist as a moral possibility.) One of the things that makes the Irish famine an episode of large historical significance is that we can detect in it just such a shift in consciousness—it is in all likelihood the first disaster of its kind in history which was widely responded to, and continues to be thought of, as a moral outrage.

Still another kind of consciousness can be felt to exist in Mrs. Woodham-Smith's book. And this is the consciousness of our own time, of World War II, concentration camps, and race-murder. The charge has been brought against the British government that its treatment of the Irish people during the famine amounted to genocide, and it "has been accused, and not only by the Irish, of wishing to exterminate the Irish people . . . as Hitler wished to exterminate the Jews." As a historian, Mrs. Woodham-Smith is properly wary of such tempting analogies, and remarks that the 1840's must not be judged by today's standards; moreover, she adds, "whatever parsimony and callousness the British Government displayed towards Ireland, was paralleled seven years later by the treatment of their own soldiers which brought about the destruction of the British Army in the Crimea." Such disclaimers to the contrary notwithstanding, Mrs. Woodham-Smith's book was written in our time and could not have been written before it; the very form of the narrative, the choice of significant details, the emphases and shadings are all in some measure dictated by that fact. Just as in literature a classic work renews itself by impersonating a modern one, so also, as Philip Rahv once remarked, "the past retains its vitality in so far as it impersonates the present, either in its aversions or ideals." Indeed, on a strict definition, history can only be a study of the present, the past itself being merely one mode which the present takes. *The Great Hunger* would not be so interesting and important a work did it not offer this peculiar historical relevance, or if one were unable to feel that the past was being revealed in it as a genuine mode of the present.

It is in the scenes of mass horror and death that the impersonation of modernity can be felt most strongly. If the natural calamities of blight and plague were bad enough by themselves, the treatment of the Irish by their landlords and by the British government, that is to say by other human beings, was terrible in the extreme. The terror, of course, has to do with the fact that they weren't being regarded or treated as human beings, that their humanity was being denied. One of the first results of the blight, for example, was the mass eviction of Irish tenants from off the land. Troops and police would move in and demolish the tenants' houses on the spot. "The scene was frightful; women running wailing with pieces of their property, and clinging to door-posts from which they had to be forcibly torn; men cursing, children screaming with fright. That night the people slept in the ruins; next day they were driven out, the foundations of the houses were torn up and razed, and no neighbour was allowed to take them in." Homeless in their own homeland, alienated by official decree from their brothers, the evicted sought refuge "in what was called a 'scalp.' A hole was dug in the earth, two to three feet deep, roofed over with sticks and pieces of turf, and in this burrow a family existed." It is almost as if they were preparing graves for themselves beforehand; yet when these living dead were discovered in their holes in the ground, they were "remorselessly hunted out."

The scenes of mass starvation and death endlessly follow: of human beings dying alone, deserted, forgotten, abandoned by their very families; of bodies lying unburied and unknown along the roads and in ditches; of corpses of persons who died of starvation being eaten by cats and rats who were themselves skeletons. The island had become a vast death-camp, an emerald Golgotha, a green and pleasant pit of despair. Out of a multitude of such reports one will have to serve as representative of the rest. Here are the Irish children.

> The worst sufferers were the children; starving children were skeletons, many too far gone to be able to walk. The skin over the chest-bones and upper part of the stomach was stretched so tight that every curve of the breast-bone and ribs stood out in relief. . . . Starvation had affected the children's bones; the jaw-bone was so fragile and thin that a very slight pressure would force the tongue into the roof of the mouth. In Skibbereen, Elihu Burritt met children with jaws so distended that they could not speak; in Mayo the starving children had lost their voices. Many were in the stupor characteristic of death by starvation. Sidney Godolphin Osborne visited workhouses, infirmaries and hospitals and never heard a single child utter a cry or moan of pain—"in the very act of death still not a tear nor a cry. I have scarcely ever seen one try to change his or her position . . . two, three or four in a bed, there they lie and die, if suffering still ever silent, unmoved." . . . By April, 1847, children were looking like little old men and women of eighty years of age, wrinkled and bent . . . even the babies were "aged."
>
> A curious phenomenon was the growth of hair on starving children's faces. The hair on the head fell out and hair grew on the face. . . .

The descriptions of the Irish sufferings during the plague, of what they endured at the hands of the shipping agents and aboard the emigrant vessels, and of what further degradation awaited them on their arrival in Canada and the United States are more of the protracted same. Upon all of which direct comment is almost bound to prove inadequate. In *Past and Present*, an extraordinary book written in 1843, Thomas Carlyle addressed himself to the "condition of England"—which was bad enough. At one point he introduces the anecdote of a poor Irish widow in Edinburgh, who "went forth with her three children, bare of all resource, to solicit help from the Charitable Establishments of that City." She was refused by all, helped by none, until, exhausted, she sank down with typhus, died, and infected her lane with fever so that "seventeen other persons died of fever there in consequence." It is a very curious matter, Carlyle observes. "The forlorn Irish Widow applies to her fellow-creatures, as if saying, 'Behold I am sinking, bare of help: ye must help me!' They answer, 'No; impossible; thou art no sister of ours.' But she proves her sisterhood; her typhus-fever kills *them:* they actually were her brothers, though denying it! Had human creature ever to go lower for a proof?" It is a very impressive piece of writing, and yet one wants to ask if even this is adequate to the reality of the experience, or if anything could be.

One of the more striking implications of Mrs. Woodham-Smith's account has precisely to do with the consciousness of the witnesses of the famine, with the disparity that existed between what was happening and their understanding of what was happening, or between experience and their ability to respond to, much less master it. The constant refrain of those who observed the famine is, "It cannot be described." "The scenes which presented themselves were such as no tongue or pen can convey the slightest idea of. . . ." "It is impossible to go through the detail. . . ." "Believe me, my dear Sir, the reality in most cases far exceeded description. Indeed none can conceive what it was but those who were in it." The modern reference seems apposite again; the refrain recalls the statements made by witnesses when the concentration camps were opened at the end of the Second World War. Reality itself had grown so monstrous that human consciousness could scarcely conceive or apprehend it; reality overwhelmed the human capacity to respond coherently to it. The relations between reality and consciousness are, it goes without saying, inexhaustibly complex, but it may be said that some time during the middle of the 19th century the disparity I have been outlining began to be sensed or felt. One of the chief causes which brought about this development was the growth among the British middle classes of an awareness of what the life of the poor, of the urban and industrial working classes, was like.

If we turn to literature, that part of an age in which we expect consciousness to exist in its fullest and most precise reach, the disparity is even sharper. Dickens was the one novelist of the period who was anywhere near remotely strong enough to grasp directly and imaginatively this order of experience. Indeed he was regularly accused from various sides of "exaggerating" the facts of social distress. Yet if anything emerges clearly from a work like *The Great Hunger* (as it does from other similar documents of the age), it is, as Dickens himself often protested, that his art was a mild representation of what was actually happening. It was mild not by intention but because reality wholly outstripped the capacities of art, the capacities of consciousness, to encompass it. And it is during

the Victorian period that an important modern truth begins to emerge—
that however mad, wild, or grotesque art may seem to be, it can never
touch or approach the madness of reality.

But the statements of the observers that Mrs. Woodham-Smith cites,
or of men like Dickens and Carlyle, represented only one segment of
British opinion. Had more men been capable of such sentiments, the Irish
distress would not have been so enormous. But in fact the dominant
British consciousness at the time remained fixed at an opposite pole. This
attitude was compounded of several elements. To begin with, there was
a strain of sheer Podsnappery among the English; there were large and
frequent denials that any such thing as a famine was actually occurring,
or that the potato blight was anything but a false alarm and "the invention
of agitators." To profess a belief that the blight existed, wrote one reliable
contemporary, "was as sure a method of being branded as a radical as
to propose to destroy the Church." And if at last it ceased to be possible
to deny the blight and the famine, then the suffering of the Irish was
their own fault. Ireland was a disturbing thought to the English, Mrs.
Woodham-Smith writes, and "it was therefore a comfort to be able to
believe that the Irish were not starving or, if some of them were, the
depravity of the Irish was such that they deserved to starve; and to treat
Ireland's desperate appeals . . . as merely another whine from a professional beggar."

The belief in the economic theory of *laissez faire* was undoubtedly the
controlling influence in England's treatment of Ireland during the famine.
The ideas which combine to make this theory—such as the sacred rights
of property, complete liberty of enterprise, the laws of the market and of
supply and demand, and of government non-intervention in the economic
sphere—were held with fanatical, religious intensity by the largest majority of British politicians and authorities. Any plan for the relief of the
Irish was preconditioned by the requirement that private enterprise was
in no way to be interfered with. Most of the time this naturally led to no
relief. For example, during the first year of the famine, the British government bought certain small amounts of Indian corn with which it both
hoped to keep market prices on grain down and to feed a few of the Irish.
Since no trade in Indian corn existed in the United Kingdom, this was
not construed as an interference with private enterprise. But the scheme,
of course, failed: you cannot keep prices down in a market where food
does not exist because prices themselves cease to exist. Moreover, the
British might as well have purchased stones or rock salt for all the relief
the Indian corn provided. Corn was unknown as a food in Ireland; the
special facilities needed for milling it did not exist, and so the corn went
unground. Inspired with divine ignorance, the authorities then suggested
that the Irish eat it unground—in which state Indian corn is not merely
indigestible but downright dangerous. Luckily, however—if such an ex-

pression in this situation has any meaning—most of the corn remained in warehouses, since the British had, in addition, neglected to supply a way of distributing it to the people. The vaguely lunatic atmosphere of this episode recurs throughout the other operations of relief: from the recipes for soup, composed by Alexis Soyer "the famous French chef of the Reform Club," which "created a sensation in London," to the projects for public works which succeeded in ruining the roads of Ireland, it is all nightmare, impotence, and disaster.

The point is that the English did not really want to relieve the Irish; they did not believe it was morally right, and from the standpoint of economic theory it was unsound and "unnatural." One of the diagnostic attributes of any culture is its attitude toward poverty, and one can read the economic, social, and moral history of England in the history of its Poor Law. Confronted with eight million starving Irish, Charles Edward Trevelyan could write: "dependence on charity is not to be made an agreeable mode of life." Trevelyan was not simply unaware of the almost demented irony of this statement; in it he was expressing doctrines altogether typical of the British governing classes. On the one hand, poverty was an inevitable part of the economic system; the workings of this system were identified with laws of nature and so were not to be tampered with; on the other, poverty was the result of improvidence on the part of the poor for which they were not to be rewarded but punished. One of the results of such thinking is that by the 19th century in England poverty had come to be regarded as a kind of crime, and the poor were treated as criminals—if relief were made as "unattractive and difficult to obtain as possible," then the poor would presumably not be so willing to seek it. This more or less insane solution was applied wholesale to Ireland, but it too did not work. When it was proposed to allow destitute able-bodied men to receive relief by entering the workhouse, it was discovered that the workhouses had to be emptied first "of the aged and the infirm, of widows and children." Apart from producing still more suffering, this measure came to nothing since it proved difficult or impossible to carry out: in the immense workhouse at Tralee the inmates could not be turned out because they had "no clothes to put on and no shelter to which to return, for landlords customarily took advantage of destitute persons being forced to enter the workhouse to pull their cabins down." In the end nothing worked.

In the end nothing worked, and Ireland was left, according to Trevelyan's suggestion, to the "operation of natural causes"—which is to say that it was abandoned. These causes were not only the workings of supply and demand and providence but the causes enumerated in Malthus's theory as well, mass death from starvation and disease. Nassau Senior, the political economist and adviser on economic affairs to the British government, remarked that he "feared the famine of 1848 in Ireland would not kill more than a million people, and that would scarcely be enough to do much good." The Irish sickened, suffered, fled, and died in their millions; whether enough of them died to do much good is difficult to determine.

What becomes evident, then, is that the Irish people were as much the victim of ideas as they were of nature's indifference to humanity. They were the victims of intellectual error, and the Irish famine is an unsurpassable instance of the effects of ideology in its purest sense. For the doctrines of political economy and of Malthus were unadulterated ideology; they were laws of society pretending to be laws of nature—or as Marx was to phrase it, they represented the "bourgeois relations of production as eternal categories." And even though this ideological thinking worked to the material advantage of the British ruling classes, they too, we now can see, may be counted among its victims. For they were condemned to live in falsehood, and falsehood is always corrupting. Out of the intellectual falsehood in which the British ruling classes were steeped and the spiritual corruption which was its consequence sprang the enduring horror of the Irish famine—the unforgivable selfishness, indifference, and brutality with which the English permitted themselves to treat the Irish. That this treatment was sanctioned by what was then thought of as "scientific" and enlightened principles, and that the English administrators of this inhumanity were sincere in their beliefs and convinced of the advanced and even the benign nature of their views serves only to compound the desperate pathos of the event. But it serves as well to emphasize in that event what is exemplary in a modern way.

For these horrors were perpetrated by the most enlightened and civilized nation in the world during one of the greatest periods of its history. The Victorian period is universally and correctly thought of as the "age of reform"; during that time an unparalleled series of intellectual, scientific, social, and political advances took place in England. The spirit of humanity was abroad then as it has rarely been in human history; the literature of that period, the great novelists and the great Victorian critics, is in sum an incomparable contribution to our humanity and provides an incomparable humane heritage. To be sure, it was also a time of enormous social injustice; but what one usually feels in this regard is that during the Victorian period men had for the first time come into full possession of the consciousness of what social injustice is and means, that they were trying to do something about it, and that the reforming spirit, given enough time, would work successfully toward amelioration. And yet it is also a fact that Victorian England was directly and irretrievably responsible for the incomparable monstrousness of the Irish famine. The lessons for modernity to read in this are self-evident.

Whether these lessons will be read is something else again. For we, too, are by both temperament and tradition a reforming society confronted by problems whose solutions reform alone probably cannot bring about. And we, too, are an enlightened civilization bound in by ideology of which we are largely unaware and by contradictions with which we can scarcely cope. Whether we consider domestic problems—civil rights, unemployment, the farm problem—or international ones—the cold war, aid to underdeveloped areas—the difference between what might possibly be done and what will actually be done, is actually being done, is staggering. This difference, this gap between resources and performance, is in considerable measure a result of ideology, of thought which is socially determined yet unconscious of its determination. Since all political and historical knowledge, as Karl Mannheim has demonstrated, is ideological in the sense that it is inseparable from the particular values and position of a thinking subject and a social context, we cannot in such matters hope to attain some kind of absolute or transcendent truth. We can, however, enlarge our awareness of the truth that the ideas of all groups, including our own, are socially determined, that we as well as our adversaries think in ways or styles which are limited by our concrete social and historical situations. Only in this way can we reduce to a minimum the tendency toward self-apotheosis which is so characteristic of political and social ideas and so fatal in its consequences. The British in 1845–1849 were unable to do this, and the black record of the Irish famine was the result. If we today prove equally unable, the outcome is likely to be even worse.

Part D

Social Movements and Demands for Change

CHANGE is one of the hallmarks of an advanced industrial society. Although anthropologists may disagree as to the rates of change in small isolated societies, few serious observers deny the rapidity of change in modern society.

Social change impinges on welfare institutions in many ways. The definitions of welfare problems change as minimum standards are raised and as different categories of people are perceived as being worthy of aid and as being above or below the minimum standards. The organizational forms and policies for handling welfare problems change as professional groups, the broader public, and welfare organizations redefine the means of working on welfare problems. A full discussion of social change is beyond the scope of this volume. However, it is our purpose to look at several aspects of the processes by which change is introduced into social welfare institutions, and to discuss social movements as agents of change.

Social movements are collective attempts to achieve change. When there is dissatisfaction with the life situation of a group of people, the people may organize to attempt to change the society around them. Thus, social movements represent a crystalization of discontent. Many new welfare programs originate from social movements of varying degrees of strength and with differing social bases. (The articles by Robert Bremner and by Asa Briggs in Part A of this section referred to some of the historical social movements that have had an impact on welfare institutions.)

Obviously, not all social movements are successful. The first selection in this part, "Summary and Conclusions: Old Age and Political Behavior," by Frank Pinner, Philip Selznick, and Paul Jacobs, summarizes the results of a study of one social movement organization in California.

Even though problems of old age have been receiving greater publicity, Pinner and his associates determined that, in this case, the social movement organization was incapable of finding a way of linking itself to the broader community and to other interest groups in order to gain its ends.

The second selection, "Indigenous Social Movements," by Lloyd E. Ohlin, gives an analysis of the target structures and problems of social movements in local communities. Ohlin speaks of indigenous movements and organizations in contradistinction to those social movements that are national or supracommunity in scope. Ohlin's article represents a social engineering approach to social movements. That is, he raises the question of how social movements among the needy and dispossessed can be used quite rationally by professionals to help achieve welfare and community goals. This article resulted from Ohlin's participation in the Mobilization for Youth Program of New York, N.Y., and is discussed later in this volume by George Brager (Section III, Part E).

Summary and Conclusions:
Old Age and Political Behavior

Frank Pinner, Philip Selznick and Paul Jacobs

A number of central ideas have guided us in our study of the California Institute of Social Welfare, its leader, and its members. We have not regarded McLain's CISW as an isolated phenomenon without parallels in history. Rather, we have likened it to the organizations of other emerging and dependent social groups. Such groups have often been directed by leaders who were not representative of the constituency and who were not subject to membership control. It is apparent that the aged, newly emerging to a consciousness of distinct interests and problems, have difficulty in communicating with the institutions of the larger society. It is hard for them to develop effective leadership from within their own ranks. As a result, the aged tend to rely on outside sources of leadership.

FINDINGS

1. The CISW was organized by a political entrepreneur who has exercised exclusive personal control over the organization. This old-age pressure group was established in 1941 by a man who had made many attempts to find a political base. George McLain has dominated the organization and stamped it with his personality. This control has been markedly personal in character, summoning the direct loyalty and dependence of followers and staff. His leadership has been exclusive, reinforced by conscious efforts to forestall the emergence of strong secondary leaders who might stand between him and the members. The members' relation to McLain is not filtered through or modified by loyalties to intermediate groups and leaders.

2. Exclusive control has afforded the leader limited opportunities to use organizational resources for personal political advancement. In most

---

Frank Pinner, Philip Selznick, and Paul Jacobs, *Old Age and Political Behavior*, University of California Press, Berkeley, 1959, pp. 265–279.

organizations, officials enjoy enough discretion so that they may—if they
so desire—gain incidental personal advantages for themselves and their
friends. This is particularly true of organizations subject to one-man control. Of what advantage to McLain is his control over the CISW? His
gain is not primarily financial, for, despite the organization's large income, it does not appear that McLain has taken a significantly disproportionate share. On occasion he has attempted to use the movement to serve
his own political ambitions. In doing so, he was able to take advantage
of the power which society ordinarily attributes to one who has an apparently large following; and he was able to use the organizational machinery of the CISW, especially its funds, staff, and physical plant. The
single important instance of such an effort was McLain's bid for Congress
in 1952. These attempts have yielded no positive results; it is possible
that they are not to be repeated. At the same time, it is clear that the
members of the organization are not readily disposable for aims beyond
the narrow sphere of pension politics. They will work hard and give large
sums to further their direct interests by political means, and they will
sacrifice much to maintain the organiaztion, but they will not respond to
appeals for other objectives, including the political advancement of the
leader.

3. *The CISW is not an integrated part of the community; hence its
actions tend to be lacking in responsibility and effectiveness.* Members
of a functioning community are in many ways dependent on each other.
Because of this, each member must weigh the effect of his own conduct
on other members lest he find himself isolated and deprived of needed
coöperation. To be a member of a community is to accept its restrictions
as to aims that may be pursued and means that may be used. An isolated
group has greater freedom in its choice of activities, but by the same
token it cannot expect the sustained support of others. McLain and the
CISW have been isolated, not only from the general political community
but also from the community of welfare-oriented individuals and groups.
This isolation has made it easier for McLain to "go it alone" organizationally. He has paid a rather high price for this advantage, however.
At critical times he has been unable to win the support he needed from
like-minded persons, and, indeed, has alienated influential groups that
might have been on his side. Some of this alienation has resulted from
lack of insight into the likely responses of groups and their leaders, an
ignorance associated with isolation from the community. The isolation
of McLain personally and of the CISW as an organization does not mean
that individual members lack normal social contacts. The emphasis here
is on the relations among influential individuals and groups.

4. *The old-age assistance recipients we studied showed evidences of
status-anxiety.* Californians on the old-age assistance rolls, both members
and nonmembers of the McLain organization, are concerned about the

position they occupy in the social world. Being "on the pension" is a mixed blessing, for it suggests a loss of status in the eyes of others, a diminished claim upon the respect of the community. The pensioners are less concerned with improving their day-to-day personal relations with others, including their children, than they are with remedying this felt loss of status. Self-justification is important to them; they feel impelled to prove that they have lived thrifty, hard-working, respectable lives. Because of their anxiety over status, with its keynotes of respect and respectability, the pensioners are basically conservative. They are not radicals seeking to espouse new values, but people who want the means to live according to established social norms. McLain's members rate somewhat higher in status-anxiety than do non-member pensioners. This probably reflects a selective factor: strong feelings about loss of status stir resentments which make them more readily available for political participation. In addition, membership in the organization strengthens views about the pension, society, and self which show up as increased concern for social status.

5. *California's old-age security laws permit some pensioners to enjoy a "slightly privileged" status, and this group supplies a disproportionate share of CISW members.* Although all the recipients must satisfy a legal criterion of need, some are nevertheless better off than others. The slightly privileged include modest homeowners, people with spouses still living and therefore benefiting from combined grants, and those having allowable additional income. These distinct social and economic advantages facilitate political and social participation in community life. McLain's members tend to be among the slightly privileged; the more deeply involved the member, the more likely he is to share these advantages. Thus the membership is not a movement of the utterly dispossessed. This fact is consistent with our general knowledge that extreme poverty is more likely to be associated with apathetic withdrawal than with activist protest. The slightly privileged status of the McLain members is consistent with the related conclusion that this group shows a relatively greater amount of status-anxiety. Those who have some hold upon the material foundations of respectability are more likely to sustain the aspiration and resent the loss.

6. *Membership in the CISW does not offer new and satisfying personal ties.* There is little evidence that McLain members are drawn to the organization by the need for new friendships or a new community; nor do such relationships emerge. Some satisfactions probably do accrue from the sense of protection offered by McLain and from the sacrifices that membership entails. The dedication of many members is too great to be explained as normal interest-group participation. This high involvement does not mean, however, that the member has been deeply absorbed into a new, if isolated, community. The connections among the

members are too weak, and the group structure of the organization too attenuated. Rather this is an atomized "mass" group, marked by direct relations to a leader and weak relations among members.

7. *Participation in the CISW leads members to focus preëxisting negative feelings upon specific targets and increases their isolation from the community.* Among the old-age assistance recipients, the McLain members differ from nonmembers in degree rather than in kind. There is more resentment and distrust among members. And the more deeply involved members express the greatest sense of alienation from the community. Some of this negativism apparently results from the complexity of the welfare administration and the bewilderment it induces. As the pensioner's interest in the law rises, his awareness of its complexity also increases. A member is more likely to speak of the pension law as "full of red tape," "humiliating," "confused," and "tricky." This is probably related to status-anxiety, to resentment that the law does not do more to define and secure his position in society. Although participation in the CISW increases the pensioner's negative feelings toward some of the *institutions* of society, his negativism is not necessarily focused on *persons,* such as social workers.

Members are more prone than nonmembers to regard groups or individuals as enemies of the pensioners and other old people. Their negative attitudes clearly reflect McLain's propaganda targets. However, the "enemies" of the CISW members are not entirely of McLain's making. Nor does this negativism and distrust lead to unrestrained forms of hostility. The CISW is not, in this or any other sense, an extremist group.

8. *Communication within the organization runs from the energizing leader to the receptive, passive audience; but the members in turn communicate their dependency, admiration, and guilt.* McLain's members resemble customers, the more or less stable clientele of a product or service. Like television viewers and similar publics, they are held together by a public relations program carried on by an outside source for its own reasons. The members have no independent role, nor do they expect to have one. If they lost faith in the organization they would not think of intervening to change it, but would merely cease to support it, much as they might stop buying a product. This explains and perhaps justifies the fact that McLain acts as if he "owned" the organization. That it is "his" organization is generally accepted and understood. This organized audience is highly responsive, not to the CISW but to the leader as an individual. They send their money to him personally and shower him with expressions of gratitude and admiration, usually in letters which also show marked feelings of guilt when the contributions lag.

9. *There are wide variations in the degree of involvement of McLain followers; and the organization is sustained by a fluctuating core of devoted, self-sacrificing members.* From an organizational standpoint, one

of the most impressive features of McLain's movement is the substantial core of devoted followers he has been able to create. These include life members (who contribute at least $75), people paying installments on life memberships, club presidents, and other high contributors. The measure of involvement is chiefly financial. On the scale of slight privilege, the more involved members are better off than the rest of the members, just as the members as a whole have more advantages than nonmembers. In their attitudes toward pensions and pension politics, there is a similar gradation. Club presidents represent the organization's point of view most extremely; they are also the least sentimental and the most political-minded, being more willing than other core-group members to regard McLain as a political leader rather than as "good shepherd" or protector. As expected, the more involved members are most likely to be antagonistic toward those defined as enemies of the organization.

There is some evidence that increased participation as measured by activity rather than money contribution is accompanied by estrangement from McLain. The members who do the political work of collecting signatures are not necessarily uncritical of their leader. They are aware of the community's negative opinion and share it to some extent, but they feel that this lack of respectability is a necessary cost of political action, especially when no other channel is available.

10. *McLain has been readily able to mobilize the strength to place his initiative measures on the ballot, but his ability to influence the voters is low.* In a series of campaigns the members have provided the funds and the manpower to collect the necessary signatures for qualifying initiative measures. This response has been large enough to obviate the necessity of using paid petition circulators—a considerable achievement for a California organization. But the members are less readily mobilized for the campaign to pass the measure. McLain has not been able to create a political machine, that is, a network of effective local political clubs and precinct workers. It may well be that the members sense the importance of working to get a measure on the ballot but feel that the final outcome is beyond their power to affect. There is no evidence that McLain propaganda directed toward the general public has had any significant influence on the vote. Rather, it appears that the movement's partial success with the voters rests on widespread support for social welfare measures. The organization implicitly assumes that such support exists and that its main task is to present the issue for decision at the polls. The CISW's margin of victory or defeat depends more on the intensity of the campaign against a proposition than on its own campaign in favor of it.

11. *The McLain organization is basically unstable, dependent upon continuous exhortation by an indispensable leader.* Although it is based upon the pensioners' common interests, the CISW is not a securely established form of organization. It is highly dependent on the person of

McLain himself and would very likely disintegrate if he were no longer at its head. Moreover, the common economic interests of the aged are not so strongly felt as to lead easily to effective organization. Psychological appeals are important, and the task of organizing the pensioner constituency absorbs a very large part of the leader's energies and of the funds collected. Of course, most organizations dependent on voluntary contributions from members spend much time, money, and energy on internal mobilization; they have difficulty in showing a "profit" that can be spent on external activities. However, while no accurate comparison with other groups can be made, the internal orientation of McLain's propaganda seems especially great. Lacking a secure source of funds, the leader must have continuous access to his following and must unceasingly exhort them to remember their "true" interests by supporting the organization. This reinforces the leader's role as agitator and tends to force him into ways of speaking and acting that isolate him and his group from the larger political community. If we are correct in detecting a somewhat more conservative tendency in McLain's behavior, it may be because the agitational role is less urgently called for after the organization has achieved a certain continuity and stability. But it is safe to assume that the organizing of pensioners into a political pressure group will continue to be accompanied by agitational techniques and leadership.

12. *The McLain program does not involve basic opposition to the existing social and legal order.* The CISW is distinguished from earlier pension movements by an emphasis on specific changes within the existing framework of welfare legislation. McLain has not offered any general scheme for financing pensions or contributing to the national prosperity, with the exception of a plan to use surplus agricultural products for pensioners. The movement has no broad ideology or general critique of the social order. McLain's use of the initiative machinery, while constitutional, has tended to challenge the existing structure of power in the community. For that machinery permits political "assaults" which bypass established leaders and institutions and are not necessarily restrained by political accommodation. Yet even in this area McLain has met defeat by restricting goals in the direction of greater respectability. His lobbying activities, especially when transferred to the national scene, offer further opportunities for restraint, since lobbying demands a large measure of coöperation and compromise. To the extent that McLain increases his commitment to effective political action for short-run goals and gives up the search for independent political office, his program will probably become increasingly restrained and respectable.

ISOLATION, MARGINALITY, AND SOCIAL STATUS

In the introductory chapter, we asserted as a fact of experience that an isolated constituency, low in status, is likely to be organized by a marginal leader. The preceding findings reveal the mechanisms which, in the instance of the CISW, explain this relationship. These mechanisms involve a complex interplay between individual behavior and attitudes on the one hand and social and institutional arrangements on the other.

Isolation of the aged constituency is, first of all, a social fact; it consists in the relative dearth and superficiality of social contacts. It is, at the same time, a fact of individual behavior: the pensioners show low interest in personal relations, and little inclination to maintain or renew them. Isolation implies that the pensioners' position in society is inadequately defined in their own minds and in those of others—social workers, legislators, and the public at large. Such lack of definition produces disorientation and status-anxiety and makes it particularly difficult for the pensioner to conceive of his relations with others as reciprocal.

The leader, also, is isolated, although not in the same way as are the recipients. It is not primarily the dearth of contacts which separates the leader from relevant groups and individuals in the community, but the instability of those contacts. "Marginality"—the particular kind of isolation characteristic of the leader—manifests itself in his long, erratic career pattern and in his lack of firm relations with those groups in the community whose interests most closely resemble his own. Associated with marginality—either as a corollary or as a reflection of some personality trait—is a certain difficulty in maintaining and visualizing reciprocal relations with others; political setbacks thus are often a consequence of having misjudged the intentions and interests of other people. A counterpart of this lack of insight into the reciprocal nature of human relations is McLain's tendency to approach most personal and social questions as problems of status. This tendency well antedates his emergence as the leader of a pension movement; it has inspired his previous attempts at organizing those deprived of their rightful place in society—the unemployed and the "native sons" of his state; it also shows up in the slightly aristocratic overtones of his autobiographical notes and in his description of the traumatic effects upon him of his father's fall from social respectability.

It is consistent with McLain's behavior patterns and with his expressed ways of thinking that the organization he founds and leads should rely upon one-way communications as the main nexus between leader and members; the proprietary form of organization makes it particularly easy for the leader to develop and proclaim policies without membership participation. It is equally consistent with the behavior and attitudes of the pensioners that they should be attracted by an organization which does not call for intensive interaction. Similarly, it is natural for McLain to phrase the pensioners' problems in status terms, and equally natural for the pensioners to accept such phrasing.

The match between the isolated constituency and the marginal leader thus appears to result from similar social experiences of relative isolation and from the typical interpretation of such experiences. Where concrete personal relations between individuals are either absent or ill defined, status orientations are likely to be strong. Deprived of meaningful experiences with other people, the individual is unable to foretell the effects of his own behavior on others and of their behavior upon him; status orientations thus serve as substitutes for a more penetrating understanding of human situations.

The form of the Institute's organization thus is the "creation" of both leader and membership in the sense that it accommodates behavior patterns and orientations of both: preferences for one-way action and status definitions. How can we account for its durability?

Any organization which achieves a degree of permanence must contain some mechanisms insuring its continuance. Many an organization is able to endure by evolving a dense network of interpersonal relations which makes membership attractive; under such conditions, even shifts in program or in leadership do not necessarily result in large membership losses. The CISW, being unable to rely for its existence upon strong interpersonal ties, persists for different reasons. In order to maintain its membership and attract new recruits, it constantly helps to recreate the social conditions of its own existence. If status-anxiety is one of the conditions for the existence of the CISW, McLain's propaganda tends to maintain and nurture it. If another condition is personal isolation, the structure of the CISW does nothing to dispel it; for some of the members, increased negativism even appears to make sustained and constructive contacts more difficult. If a third condition of the Institute's emergence is the existence of a slightly privileged group, the program of the organization fosters the maintenance and perhaps even the enhancement of social and economic differentials among pensioners.

All this is not a matter of conscious design. It may well be argued, for instance, that McLain has made deliberate efforts to increase sociability within the organization and thus to make it more attractive to a more stable membership; if he did not succeed in this, the character of his membership is at least in part to blame. Similarly, the very conditions of his existence as a leader of pensioners seem to have frustrated McLain's attempts to escape from his marginal position in the political world: in trying to mobilize his membership he is under strong compulsion to employ the same propaganda devices and political tactics which set him apart from the common run of politicians and welfare-minded lobbyists.

This does not argue that the CISW cannot undergo change; nor does it preclude the possibility that the pensioners might achieve some other kind of political representation. We can only state that changes in the objectives and methods of the CISW are not likely to arise from tensions *internal* to the organization—given an unaltered social and political environment. For, such tensions as do exist within the Institute tend to maintain the organization in its present form rather than alter it. And changes observed in recent times—increased emphasis on systematic lobbying and greater service to members and constituents—have been chiefly responses to *external* conditions; among these have been the recurring defeats of the Institute's referendum campaigns and of McLain's personal quests for political office as well as changes in the political climate in California which has become more favorable to welfare programs.

The Institute's prospects for change would thus appear to hinge on the likelihood that altered orientations in the worlds of politics and social welfare will make for greater integration of the organization and of its constituency into a larger community. If the CISW and its aged constituents were in fact likely to subvert the democratic process, the chances of such integration would be slim.

ORGANIZATION AND POLITICAL CHANGE

The question whether the organization is capable of causing profound changes in the political world is one that originally motivated our research. What is the Institute's potential for effecting social change? This depends on an assessment of the nature of the organization. Is it a simple interest group or is it more nearly akin to some of the mass movements of recent times? To attempt answers to these questions, we must consider the elements of participation as they appear in different types of organizations.

There are three elements of participation: (1) *commitment*, the psychological importance to the individual of group membership and group goals; (2) *interpersonal experience*, the extent to which friendship and similar ties play an important role for the member; and (3) *rationality*, the extent to which the members take appropriate, cool-headed action to solve their problems. These elements combine in different ways in the interest group, the community, and the mass organization.

Elements of Participation in Organizations

Type	Commitment	Interpersonal Experience	Rationality
Interest groups	Low	Low	High
Community	High	High	High
Mass organization	High	Low	Low

In the interest group, commitment and interpersonal experience are usually low, while rationality is high. The organization is dedicated to the solution of practical problems and appears to its members as purely instrumental. A property-owners' association to protect the character of a neighborhood is one illustration. Commitment, entailing a willingness to act and sacrifice for the attainment of group goals, does not go beyond what is required by the task at hand. Interpersonal experience is low, since the members may rarely even meet; or, if they do meet, the contacts are strictly businesslike. Rationality here is high and consists in the search for the best means of attaining the single goal.

In the community, all three elements assume high values. Commitment is high because the community-type organization impinges upon the individual from many directions and binds him firmly into a network of social relations. Interpersonal experience is high because the community stimulates and builds upon friendships, informal groups, and family ties. Rationality is high, but differs from the singlemindedness of interest-group rationality in that the community participant must strike a balance among a number of goals and values. He is free, nevertheless, to make rational calculations according to his own interests.

The mass organization presents the paradox of high commitment combined with low interpersonal experience and low rationality. The members are highly responsive to directives issuing from the organization and its leaders, and they display great readiness to sacrifice for the organization. Sacrifice of economic self-interest is common. Personal relations tend to be dominated by manipulative political attitudes, and the members relate themselves directly to the leader rather than to each other. Rationality is seriously impaired by the members' inability to define their own needs and consequently to take appropriate steps for the satisfaction of such needs; the members tend to feel an inarticulate malaise which they hope the organization or its leader will relieve.

An observer of the CISW might easily conclude that this is simply an interest group. He would point to the organization's and the members' exclusive preoccupation with economic goals. And indeed, most of the political and propaganda activity is focused on obtaining larger pension payments and more liberal eligibility provisions. The observer might find additional support for the interest-group thesis in the small amount of interpersonal experience among members. Closer examination suggests, however, that mass participation is an important feature of the McLain movement. This conclusion is based on the fact that commitment to the organization is extraordinarily high among many members and on our doubts that participation is characterized by a high degree of rationality. Many members are clearly seeking psychic satisfactions through their sacrifices and their relation to the leader. While it is true that the members have a strong interest in economic betterment, their actions and attitudes betray vague, inarticulate aspirations reflecting deeper needs.

The struggle for economic goals may become the vehicle for other strivings and motivations, thus transforming the meaning of participation from interest-group membership to mass involvement. But there are no signs that such strivings have been transferred from the psychological level to that of social action. And the Institute's potential for social change, and the potential of its constituency, would therefore appear to be low.

Since it is uncertain whether the CISW can be expected to undergo profound changes, and unlikely that it will be able to alter its environment appreciably, the third possibility—that of integrative action originating in the community—must be explored. So long as poverty and dependency are corollaries of retirement, we should expect and accept political pressure on behalf of the aged. On broader grounds, separate organizations of the aged may well be undesirable, if only because they sharpen the isolation created by retirement from work and family life. Yet the problem of economic privation inevitably takes precedence and must find expression in the political arena.

The CISW's program is a narrow one, attempting only to better the pensioner's condition vis-à-vis the public-assistance programs. This one-sided insistence on monetary issues may give a distorted picture to the general public as well as to the pensioners. The pensioners need a sense of status and function in society; the public needs a greater awareness of the necessity for expanded resources to solve the complex problems of aging in an industrial society. Yet pressure-group activity, when nakedly pursued, appears to many as a raid upon the public treasury; and McLain's supporters can justify the program to themselves only by vague and defensive claims to respectability. A more constructive program should be so formulated as to give both the aged and the public an understanding of the underlying problems.

Separate organizations tend to increase the isolation of the aged by creating the image of a segregated and somewhat antagonistic group. Acrimonious political struggle sharpens this antagonism, crystallizes the opposition, neutralizes potential supporters, and creates irrelevant issues which stand in the way of proposals that would otherwise gain widespread community support. Granted that decisions of public policy regarding the aged will have to be reached eventually through the political process, an isolated pressure group can bring about a *premature* drawing of political lines.

Has the marginality of the CISW brought with it any serious threat to democratic political processes? Our general answer must be no. It is true that McLain's methods have not always been above reproach. It is true also that Myrtle Williams' accession to the office of state director of social welfare had something of the quality of a coup d'état. But democracy does not presume the unfailing virtue of all participants; nor should we damn a group for taking advantage of machinery that is too readily available or too easily abused.

Furthermore, there is no convincing evidence that McLain has been able to weld his followers into a solid phalanx of disgruntled individuals ready to act according to a leader's dictates. Many of the members have developed a deep and perhaps irrational loyalty to McLain. But it is clear that he cannot enlist them for causes alien to their special interests.

If there is concern about the political health of the community, it is arguable that the CISW gives less cause for it than do some of McLain's opponents. Some of the latter have endeavored to present the whole issue of old-age security as a feud between a "pension promoter" and the people of California. If the very real issues of old-age dependency are reduced to a discussion of individual morality, they cannot receive the public hearing they deserve.

The experience of the McLain movement does show, however, that community integration is an important clue to political responsibility. Isolation from the community has undoubtedly affected the organization's way of behaving, the nature of its leadership, and the response of the electorate. This suggests that political activity on behalf of the aged ought to become part of broader social welfare programs sponsored by groups that have a secure base in the organized community. If there is to be that kind of integration, however, there must also be a broad consensus regarding the propriety of political action to relieve old-age dependency.

Indigenous Social Movements

Lloyd E. Ohlin

Assuming that we can identify appropriate targets for action in the development of deprived urban areas, what role should indigenous persons play in meeting them? Today we rarely question whether we should urge members of local communities to undertake social action efforts in

Lloyd E. Ohlin "Urban Community Development" Paper presented at The Conference on Socially Handicapped Families, under the auspices of the French Commission for UNESCO at UNESCO, Paris, France, February 10–12, 1964, pp. 14–19.

their own behalf. We usually take the desirability of such involvement for granted as a fundamental tenet of a democratic creed. In recent years, we have had renewed emphasis on the necessity of such involvement to preserve a pluralistic society. Such ideological restatements rest on the premise that the health and growth of a democratic system require constant creation of new channels for the articulation, aggregation, and communication of the unrepresented interests of submerged segments of the population at those points of decision which materially affect their welfare.

Furthermore, mobilization of indigenous leadership and extensive resident participation in community affairs serves essential functions for the larger society. Since we often take such functions for granted our commitment to the development of indigenous social movements might be clarified briefly by enumerating a few of these functions more explicitly.

(1) Successful indigenous movements redistribute and broaden the basis of social power and the exercise of authority. By limiting the arbitrary use of power or the development of exploitative practices, they reduce pressures toward deviance.

(2) They heighten the personal investment of members in the established social order. In promoting personal satisfaction and a larger personal commitment and contribution, they enhance social stability, control and morale.

(3) They provide an arena for the training and recruitment of leaders for higher levels of organizational participation.

(4) They promote a more flexible fit of the rule systems of major social institutions to the distinctive life styles of the local community. By facilitating such accommodations, indigenous organizations protect the heterogeneity and cultural richness of the society and provide a broader base for cultural growth in many fields. By fostering the proliferation of subcultures or local styles of life, they furnish a buffer to the conformity demands of a mass society. By enlarging tolerance for certain forms of deviance, constructive channels are preserved for dissent.

Problems for Indigenous Action

The contribution of indigenous social movements will vary significantly with the problem that is selected as the target of community development efforts. This seems readily apparent when we consider such typical problems as medical care, housing renewal, racial conflict, assimilation of migrants, delinquency and crime, etc. Selection of the development problem significantly determines the activities the movement will engage in, the form of organization, the population segments involved, the sponsoring agents or groups, and the means employed to achieve goals.

However, it seems clear that certain types of problems are more readily

solved by indigenous effort than others. Unfortunately, we do not possess
an adequate classification of such problems. We need better criteria for
selecting those development problems most amenable to indigenous organizations with different levels of experience, scope, and competence.
Although such connections between particular social problems and organizational competence at different stages of community growth are
difficult to specify, it might be useful, nevertheless, to suggest some
tentative criteria now being used in the projects:

(1) What is the degree of indigenous awareness of the target problem?

(2) What is the level of intensity of indigenous concern about the
problem?

(3) What is the relative importance of the problem to residents in
relation to other problems which they may have?

(4) To what extent are remedial actions and appropriate organizational means either visible or accessible to interested indigenous persons
or groups?

(5) What do the indigenous members of the community perceive as
the probability of immediate or long-range solution?

Whatever the target problem selected, each community development
enterprise finds it necessary to address certain common issues in mobilizing indigenous participation. These issues may be stated as follows:

(1) What types of activities should an indigenous movement undertake?

(2) What forms of indigenous organization and relationship to other
organizations should be established?

(3) Who should take responsibility for initiating, supporting, and
promoting the indigenous organization?

(4) By what means should the indigenous movement be organized?

Activities of Indigenous Movements

The types of activity which indigenous movements should undertake
bear a direct relation to the problems on which they focus their attention.
The issue of what activities indigenous movements should sponsor must
thus be addressed in a specific context. What is deemed appropriate or
inappropriate reflects a variety of value judgments in addition to the
pragmatic appeal of successful consequences. Simply suggesting some of
the activities which are undertaken by indigenous social movements to
attack the problem of social alienation among community residents may
suggest typical issues that arise:

(1) Mobilize organizational resources for correcting deficiencies in
knowledge and skill in oneself and one's children to eliminate culturally
induced handicaps to competition.

(2) Institute processes of organizational change to alter the rules and decisions which now control access to existing opportunities. Identify the existing power structure in each area of active interest and mobilize critical alliances to bring change in institutionally controlled systems of opportunity. Unify, dramatize, and develop control over collective sanctions which members of the indigenous organization may invoke, as, for example, votes, public protests, purchasing power, etc.

(3) Develop liaison with persons and groups external to the local area who indicate a sympathetic willingness to bring pressures to bear on municipal and state-controlled centers of decision relating to the structure of opportunities within the local area. Work toward the achievement of some measure of local autonomy over the organization and operation of public and private institutions within the area which are administered from central locations outside the area.

(4) Develop financial resources; recruit and hire expert technical assistance for the guidance of indigenous social movements.

Although the relative merits or demerits of such activities may vary according to the immediate situation and the social values at work within it, they are being used for indigenous action under conditions of social alienation. In short, they enjoin members to educate themselves, dramatize problems, mobilize collective sanctions, and articulate and represent the neighborhood interests at appropriate levels of organizational decision bearing on the structure of opportunity systems within the area. They also suggest the difficulties inherent in deciding what are appropriate forms of activity under different conditions.

Form of Organization

The organization of the indigenous movement may take many forms, e.g., political movement, tenant association, consumer cooperative, educational alliance, parent-school association, social reform group, civic association, neighborhood or block council, fraternal or religious fellowship, etc. The type of organization must be closely related to the functions to be performed and the changes to be secured. However, we need much more information than we now have on the utility of different organizational patterns for achieving the types of objective which indigenous organizations usually set for themselves.

Sponsorship

Who should take responsibility for initiating, supporting, and promoting the development of indigenous social organizations? The problem of sponsorship is most difficult because indigenous social movements frequently produce effects which reorder or challenge the existing structure of power in the area of activity or decision that is the target of action.

To what extent can existing power structures in different areas of community activity be expected to stimulate or foster the articulation and expression of the interest of unorganized groups? This question deserves more extensive discussion than it has received, since there is a common tendency to ignore the way in which the articulation of these new interests inevitably result in some broader sharing of the existing distribution of power and control of opportunities. The question of sponsorship raises the problem of vested interests in its most acute form.

Whenever existing organizations are used to sponsor indigenous social movements the primary interests of the sponsoring organization tend to affect the selection of members, the form of the organization, the specification of objectives, and determination and control of the implementing activities. This apparently universal tendency raises a very basic issue: "What types of conditions can be developed so that restraints on the growth of new indigenous movements are minimized and the articulation of indigenous interests, rather than those of sponsoring organizations, are maximized?"

The solution is not easy to see. In several projects, a wide variety of sponsorships for different types of indigenous organizations seem to have a beneficial effect. This assures simultaneous action on a number of objectives and promotes the conditions for a competitive realization of indigenous interests. It may be possible to develop further a situation in which tenant associations, civic groups, block councils, political action movements, and the like, become engaged in competitive activity to win support among indigenous members of the community, as appropriate representatives of their interests in different types of decision areas. The dominance of sponsorship interests might then be held in check by the need to appeal competitively for membership support from indigenous groups. Whether the divisive effects of such competition would do more harm than good is difficult to determine as yet.

Means for Organizing Indigenous Movements

Considerable controversy has developed around the best means for initiating and developing indigenous movements. One approach to this problem relies heavily on the development of support from the most representative existing group in the project area as the core unit on which to build broader participation. It relies on conflict situations arising in the achievement of specific objectives of these indigenous members of the community as a device for mobilizing concern and recruiting new adherents to the central core of the movement. One of the difficulties in this approach lies again in the inherent restrictions imposed by the interests of the sponsoring group. Furthermore, these interests are likely to control the development of the new indigenous movement so as to shut off participation from community residents whose opposition to the sponsoring group had already been established. An alternative approach which relies on the unification of a broad range of existing groups within the area presents other difficulties. Such associations often represent little more than objectifications of the existing power structure in the area. It then becomes exceedingly difficult to secure representation for new indigenous interests in such associations.

Another major alternative lies in the development of a new movement to organize the unorganized without involving previously established organizations in the area. A serious obstacle (assuming the problem of sponsorship control has been appropriately solved) is the apathetic reception commonly encountered among residents to such new endeavors and the difficulty of making satisfactory initial demonstrations of collective power. The problem of apathy has recently received much discussion in the literature, particularly in relation to technical assistance projects in underdeveloped countries. A state of apathy among indigenous members of a community appears to arise when a discrepancy exists between the problem to be faced and the accessibility or feasibility of remedial actions. Residents feel apathetic when the problem appears to be beyond their control. They give up trying because of the difficulty of understanding the rules of the game or gaining access to the resources to exercise representative control over their own conditions of life.

One of the major tasks in the organization of indigenous social movements is the development of new understanding and techniques for combating apathy among community residents. Feelings of despair and powerlessness must be overcome before latent interests can be aroused and communicated. In many cases this may simply mean a program of training and education in which community residents come to perceive and appreciate the power of collective action. The approach that seems to promise most success involves a careful build-up of self-confidence in the possibilities of collective action by carefully setting initial action targets likely to produce relatively quick and successful outcomes. When the processes of collective action and its successful results are made highly visible to the residents, the possibility of building effective and enduring indigenous movements is greatly strengthened.

Part E

The Formation and Consequences of Policy

SOCIAL movements may influence welfare policy by creating pressures on people who are empowered to make decisions to change policy. But in order to understand how changes in policy come about, the whole structure and process of policy making must be understood. Furthermore, pressures for change come about within an existing structure of policy and organization; thus the direction of policy change is an outcome not only of pressures for change and of the structure of policy making but also of the forward-going nature of welfare institutions. Issues are defined in relation to what already exists.

The essay by Zbigniew Brzezinski and Samuel P. Huntington, "Policy Making in the U.S.A. and U.S.S.R.," compares the policy-making process and the dimensions of policy making in the United States and the Soviet Union. One major difference, of course, is that social-movement pressures are relatively subterranean in the U.S.S.R. Another and fundamental difference relates to the discussion of the elite structure, first broached in the selection by Clark Kerr and his co-authors in Part B of this section. The important point is that the structure of power in the United States is much more decentralized than in the Soviet Union. Brzezinski and Huntington point out that one of the costs of pluralism in decision making is a tendency for fractionation and inconsistency in program development.

The style of policy making that exists in the United States has been called "muddling through." In "The Science of 'Muddling Through,'" Charles E. Lindblom defends the procedure. Since Lindblom believes in incrementalism—in essentially ameliorative as opposed to revolutionary approaches to social change—he believes that "muddling through"— "successive limited comparison of alternatives" as opposed to "rational-comprehensive" planning—is the best process for policy formulation. His article is a provocative challenge to the planner who wishes to reshape the fabric of institutions.

Whether Richard Titmuss would agree with Lindblom is a difficult speculation. However, in "The Social Division of Welfare: Some Reflections on the Search for Equity," Titmuss shows how complex the development of welfare policy has been in Great Britain. His article attempts to isolate the various kinds of social-service policies and occupational benefits which affect the distribution of income in Britain. In modern times, some welfare policies have been thought of as a means of redistributing income from the rich to the poor. Titmuss tries to assess the extent to which some modern welfare policies work toward that goal, while others contradict it. Of course, redistribution from the rich to the poor is not the only, nor even a necessary, goal of welfare policy, but Titmuss explodes the easy assumption that current welfare policies actually do lead to such a redistribution.

Policy Making in the U.S.A. and U.S.S.R.

Zbigniew Brzezinski and Samuel P. Huntington

THE POLICY-MAKING PROCESS

While the essence of political leadership is the art of formulating and implementing policy, the character of the policy-making process differs from one political system to another. In the Soviet Union policy-making has two aspects. The political aspect pertains particularly to the relations among the top Party leaders, either in the struggle for power during a succession or in manipulation and/or accommodation during periods of stability. The operational aspect expresses the organizational vested interests of the ruling Party, including also its ideological purposes, in relation to the needs of the society as a whole. Thus while bureaucratic efficiency, economic productivity, and social well-being are high on the priority list of the Soviet policy-makers, they are not always the determining ends of policy-making. During periods of stability, operational considerations dominate; in crises, political ones do. In the United States, the pluralism of autonomous economic interests and the pluralism of political institutions participating in the policy-making process fuzzes the line between the operational and the political aspects of the process.

For purposes of analysis, the policy-making process can be divided into four phases. *Initiation* embodies the first response to a new need or problem and the first formulation of a proposal to deal with it. *Persuasion* involves efforts to build up support for the proposal among a larger number of groups. In this phase opposition develops, alternatives and amendments are suggested, and the original proposal is modified so as to win broader support. In the *decision* phase the modified proposal is either approved or vetoed by those who have the effective and legitimate authority to do so within the political system. The number of people who must approve the proposal so that it becomes "policy" or who can prevent it from becoming policy varies greatly from one political system to an-

Zbigniew Brzezinski and Samuel P. Huntington, "Policy Making in the U.S.A. and U.S.S.R.," *Political Power: USA/USSR*, The Viking Press, New York, 1964, pp. 202–232.

other and within any system often from one issue to another. Finally, in the *execution* phase, the policy which has now been blessed with legitimacy is presumably carried out. In actual fact, however, the policy-making process continues, and those groups which execute policy are able to remake it. In some instances they have to change it significantly to achieve the principal goals of the policy-deciders. In other instances, they may change it significantly to frustrate those goals.[1] This phase hence is often characterized by adaptation or distortion.

The processes of policy-making in the United States and the Soviet Union can be analyzed in terms of these phases. Similar groups (for example, military chiefs or party leaders) do not necessarily play similar roles in the processes in the two systems. Nor do the roles of groups in either system necessarily remain constant over a period of time. The processes change with changes in the issues of policy and the structure of power. In the American system, secular changes during this century have seen an increasing role for executive agencies in the initiation, persuasion, decision, and execution of military policy. Similarly, in the Soviet Union the very fact of the growth of Soviet industrial and military power enhanced the policy importance of managerial and military groups.

Initiation: Bubble Up and Trickle Down

Identifying precisely the sources of policy is a difficult task for the scholar in almost any political system. It is out of the question for the student of Soviet policy-making. It is possible, however, to attempt some comparative generalizations about the extent to which the top political leadership initiates policy, and the extent to which private groups, social forces, and lower-ranking governmental agencies share in initiating. A distinctive feature in the United States appears to be the extent to which the top political leadership does *not* play a major role in the generation of specific policy proposals. It is now a commonplace that, though Congress may approve, veto, amend, or postpone legislation, it rarely originates it. Much the same is true of the top leadership in the executive branch: the initiating role of the "Indians" or middle-level officials has become proverbial in Washington. A Cabinet officer, such as Defense Secretary Robert S. McNamara, who insists on playing an initiating role, is viewed as a strange phenomenon. In general, in the American system, initiation is a less important function for the top political leader than either decision or persuasion. To be sure, the position of the top leader gives him the "strategic opportunity" to initiate policy, but the option

[1] For helpful discussion of the phases of the policy-making process, see Harold D. Lasswell, *The Decision Process* (College Park, Md., 1956), and Paul H. Nitze, "Organization for National Policy Planning in the United States," Paper prepared for Annual Meeting, American Political Science Association, Sept. 10–12, 1959, Washington, D.C.

is rarely exercised.[2] The idea that "'policy' originates at the top and is passed down," Dean Acheson has said, is a misleading bit of folklore. It should be "clear to anyone with experience in government," he added, that "the springs of policy bubble up; they do not trickle down."[3]

This may well be clearer, however, to those with experience in American government than to those experienced in other governments. In NATO headquarters, for instance, American and continental styles of policy-making apparently differed markedly.[4] From what we know about the Soviet process, it would seem that their top leaders play an active role in policy generation. Undoubtedly ideas and proposals do drift up the party and governmental hierarchies. But the initiative in formulating most important policy measures probably rests with the Central Committee Secretaries and the departments of the central apparat. Each top leader must also have his own brain trust and personal staff which feeds ideas to him. Certainly the first formal proposal of a new policy is usually made by one of the top leaders. Policy may be initiated by an informal memorandum (*zapiska*) circulated by the First Secretary among his Presidium colleagues. Khrushchev, for instance, revealed in April 1963 that after visiting a number of major enterprises of the chemical industry he drafted a *zapiska* "concerning the further acceleration of the development of the chemical industry." This was subsequently discussed by the Presidium, and in December a Central Committee Plenum adopted a formal decision to launch a major development drive in the chemical industry.

In the post-Stalin period, policy-making on key issues in agriculture, industry, education, and other fields often followed similar patterns. Typically, the policy-making phase was preceded by a fairly prolonged period of difficulties and deficiencies, during which the problem to be dealt with became increasingly worse. During this period some public discussion might take place with respect to the problem and also some limited ad-hoc remedies might be initiated by the Party leadership. Much

[2] See: Dahl and Lindblom, *Politics, Economics, and Welfare*, p. 230. Alvin W. Gouldner, ed., *Studies in Leadership* (New York, 1950), p. 19.
[3] Dean Acheson, "Thoughts about Thought in High Places," *New York Times Magazine*, Oct. 11, 1959, pp. 20ff.
[4] American staff officers felt that "French and other European officers were too reluctant to conclude their studies with firm and precise proposals for action . . . and too quick to go to their superiors for advice on policy premises or on the way in which the problem should be formulated." French officers, on the other hand, regarded the American "bubble-up" procedure as rather peculiar. "Here one rarely receives higher guidance regarding the position to adopt," one French officer warned his successor. "Ideas do not circulate from top to bottom but from bottom to top." Laurence I. Radway, "Military Behavior in International Organization—NATO's Defense College," in Samuel P. Huntington, ed., *Changing Patterns of Military Politics* (New York, 1962), p. 109. Administratively speaking, the French staff officers apparently would be more at home at Warsaw Pact headquarters than in American-shaped SHAPE.

depends, however, on the political circumstances involved. During periods of stability there is an orderly development of the problem, with a certain measure of participation from below in the formulation of the new policy. During a succession struggle, the initiatives tend to come from above, abruptly, with an element of surprise, designed in part to put one's rivals on the defensive.

The problems of bureaucracy, waste, ministerial autarchy, over-centralization, and absence of machinery for regional planning plagued Soviet industry for many years prior to the industrial reorganization of 1957. But while the reorganization "followed upon a period, dating roughly from Stalin's death, of sustained and critical public discussion of shortcomings in the planning and direction of industry and their ill effects on industry's performance and its structural, locational, and technological evolution,"[5] Khrushchev's initiative to that end in February 1957 involved a sudden attempt to reverse remedies adopted only a few months earlier, in December 1956. At that time, the State Economic Commission (*Gosekonomkomissiia*) was endowed with new powers and staffed almost entirely with professional economic administrators; irrespective of its economic merits, this inherently weakened the relative position of the First Secretary. Similarly, his February attack on "ministerialism" and overcentralization, apart from its actual administrative justification, was bound to strengthen the political position of the head of the Party, since the Party would remain the only centralized political institution. Presumably both political and operational motives were also involved in Molotov's objections to the scheme, submitted by him in writing to members of the Presidium at three a.m. on the morning of the Central Committee session to which Khrushchev made his proposal, and in Malenkov's and Kaganovich's charges that the proposal would lead to anarchy.[6]

This first prolonged phase of "the development of the problem" thus ended with Khrushchev's open denunciation of the alleged evils and his proposals for drastic decentralization. The new policy was gestating but the struggle was far from over. At stake now was the power of the First Secretary. It is useful to compare this to the circumstances involved in the educational reform, launched by Khrushchev a year later, when his power had been more firmly consolidated. As in the case of the economy, from 1953 on the crisis in Soviet education steadily worsened as the ten-year schools turned out increasing numbers of graduates who were not prepared for productive labor and for whom there was no room in the higher educational institutions. The Party press repeatedly began to suggest that manual labor was as good as intellectual activity and the 20th

---

[5] A. Hoeffding, "The Soviet Industrial Reorganization of 1957," *American Economic Review, Papers and Proceedings,* May 1959, pp. 65ff.
[6] *Izvestia,* October 22, 1961. Also Bulganin's admissions to the CC Plenum of December 1958.

Party Congress stressed the importance of technical training. Finally, in April 1958 Khrushchev openly criticized the "existing separation of the school from life." As in the case with his February 1957 speech on economic administration, his criticism suggested possible remedies in only the vaguest terms, but in the case of the educational reform there was no sudden reversal of a recently instituted policy, nor were there any high political stakes. Khrushchev's speech, furthermore, was an outgrowth of earlier views.

Each speech, nonetheless, marked the beginning of the process of policy initiation. Each served notice on Soviet society that major overhauls were under consideration, and each stimulated a small amount of public debate concerning the existing evils and the ways in which they might be remedied. In each case, also, after an interval, the top leadership came forward with a formal policy proposal. The plans for industrial reorganization were embodied in Khrushchev's theses of March 30, 1957. The outlines of the educational reform were advanced in Khrushchev's memorandum of September 21, 1958, and in the theses jointly proposed by the Central Committee and the Council of Ministers on November 17, 1958. In this case Khrushchev apparently consulted with the regional Party secretaries and other officials about their dissatisfaction with the educational system. He then formulated his proposals for dealing with them. "The top decision-making leadership played the initiating role in the education reform, after having secured from the Party apparatus, as well as from government agencies, information concerning the problems of education." [7] In both instances the policy proposals of the top leaders embodied the basic ideas of the reforms which were eventually adopted. The pattern was thus: (1) several years of growing difficulties and discontent during which the specific groups directly involved presumably tried to make their complaints heard; (2) a formal denunciation of current evils by a top Party leader or leadership, with the timing and manner much influenced by the specific power relations within that leadership; (3) an interval of several weeks or months during which presumably the top leadership formulated and agreed to its basic proposals for dealing with the evils; and (4) the official announcement of these proposals in the form of a "memorandum" or "theses" from a top leader or top Party body. Clearly, in these and similar cases, policy initiation is the prerogative of the top leadership.

The exception to this pattern involves the relatively rare cases when the leader's initiative has been nipped in the bud, or at least delayed, by the combined opposition of most of the other top leaders and the most important policy groups in the country or simply by his own hesitations and ambivalence. Even as late as the mid-thirties Stalin failed to gain

[7] Thomas Bernstein, "Soviet Educational Reform" (MA Thesis, Columbia University, 1962), pp. 13–14.

the support of his colleagues for his proposal to arrest and try his former rivals. Obviously, the implications of this initiative were clear to the other Politburo members, the Party apparat, and the top officials of other bodies. Similarly, in 1961 Khrushchev did not succeed in reducing relatively the resources committed to heavy industry; a number of Presidium members, as well as the Army and the heavy-industry spokesmen were against it. Both leaders, however, were later able to return to their schemes.

The reasons behind the different patterns of leadership in policy initiation must involve differences between the United States on the one hand, and the Soviet Union and western Europe on the other. Four hypotheses suggest themselves.

First, society and politics in America are more egalitarian in character than those in Russia and Europe. This difference has been noted by European observers since Tocqueville. Presumably it affects policy-making even in hierarchical organizations. American social scientists have stressed the two-way flow of authority and influence in American governmental institutions.[8] One form which this egalitarianism may take is the limitation of the top leadership primarily to the decision function and domination of policy initiatives by lower-ranking groups in the power structure. In this way, a separation of functions contributes to a balance of power between various administrative levels.

A second explanation might derive from the legalistic flavor of American politics and the dominant role which lawyers play in both legislative and executive policy-making. This too distinguishes the American scene from Russia and western Europe. The "bubble-up" concept of policy generation implies an essentially judicial role for the political leader. Acheson, indeed, explicitly stressed what he termed "the judicial element in the function of headship." The chief of a government department, he argued, "must from time to time familiarize himself with the whole record; he must consider opposing views, put forward as ably as possible. He must examine proponents vigorously and convince them that he knows the record. . . ." These are lawyers' words, and the prominent role of lawyers in American politics may be responsible for the prevalence of this judicial definition of the role of the political leader. Certainly, this concept describes the way in which many congressmen define their job: viewing themselves as essentially judges or arbitrators who in semi-judicial hearings listen to the testimony of all sides and then attempt to formulate an equitable resolution of differences.

[8] See: Herbert Simon, *Models of Man: Social and Rational* (New York, 1957), pp. 66–68. Richard E. Neustadt, *Presidential Power* (New York, 1960). Dahl and Lindblom, op. cit., pp. 341–44. Richard F. Fenno, *The Presidential Cabinet* (Cambridge, 1959), Chap. 6. Samuel P. Huntington, *The Common Defense* (New York, 1961), pp. 146–166.

A third and related explanation may be differing attitudes *toward* government and political leaders. If the principal end of government is thought to be response to the felt needs of society, obviously policy proposals should originate with groups in society rather than with political leaders. The policy-initiation role of the leaders should be restricted not only vis-à-vis bureaucratic subordinates in the name of egalitarianism but also vis-à-vis private groups in the name of limited government. Generation of policy proposals by the political leaders presumably would mean the subordination of policy to power rather than vice versa. Certainly Soviet political leaders, particularly during the succession struggle of 1953–1957, did initiate policies as tactical maneuvers to advance their own positions. The policy-generating role of the top political leadership in America thus may be limited not only because the leadership is top but also because it is political. The traditions of continental Europe and of both czarist and Soviet Russia, on the other hand, certainly accord top governmental leadership a much more important role in generating policy proposals.

The fourth follows from the preceding and involves differing attitudes *of* government and political leaders. A leadership imbued with over-all goals derived from ideologically affected long-term perspectives has inherently a different conception of its role from that of a leadership that is guided by a tradition of pragmatic day-to-day reaction to events seen basically as part of a spontaneously unfolding reality. In the former case, to shape reality initiative must be monopolized by the leaders; in the latter case, initiative can impose itself on the leaders.

Persuasion: Consensus-Building and Mobilization

Persuasion is the development of support for a policy proposal beyond its original initiators. Generally it is necessary to obtain the support of a much larger number of groups in the United States than in the Soviet Union. As a result, there are significant differences in the processes of persuasion in the two systems. Persuasion in the United States can perhaps best be described as "consensus-building." [9] It is usually a competitive process between conflicting coalitions of interests, and many groups and institutions share in it. Persuasion, moreover, usually precedes decision. In the Soviet Union, on the other hand, persuasion can best be described as the "mobilization" of support. It is monopolized by the party, and it normally occurs not before but after the decision phase.

In the American system persuasion differs in domestic policy and in foreign policy. Important new domestic policies usually involve the passage of a bill through Congress and its approval by the President. The

[9] See Roger Hilsman, "Congressional-Executive Relations and the Foreign Policy Consensus," *American Political Science Review*, September 1958, pp. 725–44.

lead in the early stages of persuasion is taken by the leaders of the private group or governmental agency which has generated the policy proposal. They approach other groups and agencies who may have similar interests. They explore ideas with sympathetic senators and congressmen, and endeavor to enlist an active and committed core of congressmen, preferably situated in the relevant congressional committee. Throughout this process the broadening of the base of support for the proposal is accompanied by the modification of its contents as objections are met and concessions made. If the initiators of the proposal are astute they leave considerable leeway in their original proposal so that they can purchase the support of other groups without sacrificing their primary objectives. Frequently, and particularly with respect to major new policies, the supporters may organize an ad-hoc coordinating committee made up of representatives of continuing interest groups (labor, business, farm, veterans, and so on) who share a common interest in that particular piece of legislation.

While the proponents of the proposal are thus at work on a variety of fronts, the opposition is also usually stirring. Their job is easier. They have on their side not only inertia but also the structure of the legislative process. The proponents of the policy have to mobilize sufficient support to get their proposal past a number of possible "veto points." The opponents only have to hold the line at one of these. Like the defending forces in a military campaign they can concentrate their strength where the lay of the land is most favorable. Inevitably, both proponents and opponents are drawn into the competitive mobilization of political allies and into a struggle to shift the locus of decision to the most favorable arena. This latter involves questions of both timing—when to bring the issue to the fore—and institutional strategy—in which house of Congress, for instance, to bring it up first.

As the process of consensus-building broadens, the leadership in recommendation shifts to individuals and groups of greater prestige and authority. If the proponents are successful, key committee chairmen or other influential figures take the lead in recommending it within the legislature. Outside Congress, respected public figures—ex-Presidents, ex-generals, elder statesmen—are brought forward to appeal to wider and wider publics. From the executive branch, the Cabinet official primarily concerned usually takes over as the principal campaign manager for the proposal. At some point, the President himself comes to play an active role in the process of persuasion, usually toward the end rather than at the beginning of the process. Usually also, his hand is first felt behind the scenes— in the private persuasion, for instance, of other key figures—before it is shown openly. In many cases, the degree of presidential support determines the fate of the measure in Congress. Congress at times passes bills which the President does not want, but it rarely passes a major bill which he does want unless he demonstrates his concern by actively deploying and employing the prestige, powers, and persuasions of his office on behalf of the measure.

With respect to foreign-policy measures the process of persuasion is somewhat different. Here presumably the proposal is generated somewhere in the governmental bureaucracy. It is advanced within its originating department and circulated for comments and endorsement to other interested agencies. It may be taken up through the National Security Council or other inter-departmental committees, functioning, in effect, as small-scale executive legislatures. The leadership in recommendation continues to rest primarily with the officials of the originating department and eventually with the head of it. If serious opposition develops within the executive branch, it is up to those officials to mobilize the support necessary to persuade the President. At times, this search for support leads them outside the executive branch to Congress, sympathetic journalists, outside consultants, and what Paul Nitze has called "distinguished citizens' committees." On some issues of foreign and military policy, the presidential decision will be final. On other issues formal congressional approval is required, and the recommendation process here resembles the later stages in the process for domestic policy. On foreign-policy measures recommended to Congress, however, the President and his top subordinates are normally active at a much earlier stage in the process than they are on domestic issues. It is often in the President's interest to allow other groups to take the initiative in recommending a domestic measure to Congress. On foreign-policy measures, there are few other groups, and he must play an active role from the start in pushing the legislation through Congress.

In the Soviet Union the character of the persuasion phase is shaped by the close connection between policy initiation and policy decision. Most important policy proposals originate with the top leadership. This leadership also possesses the power of decision. Hence the step from generation to decision can be a very short one, certainly much shorter than it usually is in the United States. A Presidium member or Central Committee Secretary who advances a policy proposal has to win the support of only a dozen other men to secure its approval. In some cases he may have to win the support of only one other man. Where policies affect key policy groups—the military, economic planners, the agricultural bureaucracy—presumably the leaders of these groups are also consulted. In most instances, however, the institutional and other divisions which exist among the leaders of any particular policy group preclude their maintaining a united front against a proposal favored by the dominant faction in the top Party leadership. Thus, for much, if not most, of Soviet policy—and certainly for all foreign and military policy—only the leaders and those at the peaks of the relevant government bureaucracies become involved in the persuasion phase.

On some major issues, however, persuasion encompasses a much wider range of groups. Once the basic principles of a policy have been agreed upon, an intensive effort may be made to mobilize the interest and support of other groups outside the top leadership. The "theses" promulgated by the leaders may be discussed extensively in the press and in meetings throughout the country. In some instances these discussions (as with the 1961 discussion of the CPSU's draft program) may produce only minor modifications in detail. In other instances, however, they may produce some fairly significant changes. During the Stalinist period such discussions and mobilization efforts were relatively rare. Fear and coercion rather than persuasion made the policies adopted by the top leadership acceptable to other groups. Since Stalin's death, however, the leadership has found it desirable to stimulate, under appropriate conditions, discussion of its policy decisions and thereby to persuade the groups affected to accept them. Thereby, it can also discover where the shoe pinches and modify its policy or inaugurate new policies accordingly.

Debates of this sort occurred in connection with the pensions law of 1956, the educational reform and the abolition of the Machine Tractor Stations in 1958, and the Party program of 1961. In these cases, the predominant issues were operational, not power-political. The public debate over the educational reforms lasted about six weeks (November 17 to December 25, 1958). Representatives of many more or less formally organized specific interest groups participated: the Academy of Pedagogical Sciences, the Administration of Labor Reserves, secondary school administrators and principals, university officials, spokesmen for nationality groups (interested in preserving instruction in their language). The measure approved by the Supreme Soviet differed in many important respects from the proposals originally advanced by Khrushchev and the Central Committee. The idea of special schools for gifted children was dropped; the full-time secondary day schools were reinstated; the absolute requirement of full-time work before entering a higher educational institution was changed to "priority" for those with full-time work. All-in-all, important concessions were made to the academic experts, intelligentsia, and educational administrators who had urged the importance of academic education against that of productive labor.[10]

It is revealing to contrast the foregoing with the much more politically charged debate on the industrial reorganization proposed by Khrushchev in February 1957 and opposed by a Presidium group that subsequently attempted the unsuccessful "anti-Party" coup against Khrushchev in June

[10] See Bernstein, "Soviet Education Reform," pp. 106ff.

1957. Between the publication of Khrushchev's theses on March 30, 1957, and the approval by the Supreme Soviet on May 9 an extensive debate took place. Khrushchev and his supporters actively campaigned for the proposal, claiming that it would "strengthen the Leninist principle of democratic centralism" and taking oblique swipes at Molotov by suggesting that his Ministry of State Control must be "radically reconstructed." The opponents of the reform in the top leadership, who not accidentally were also Khrushchev's rivals—notably Molotov, Kaganovich, Bulganin, and the two top Party leaders specializing in economic affairs, Pervukhin and Saburov (both of whom had been active in adopting the December 1956 measures)—were ostentatiously silent. Nonetheless, *Pravda* and *Izvestia* published more than eight hundred letters commenting on the proposed reform, suggesting various adjustments. Some demanded even more decentralization and workers' control; some factory managers demanded more authority. In the process of developing support, Khrushchev made several significant changes. In order to win the approval of some key policy groups, the Ministry of Defense Industry, the Ministry of Aviation Industry, and six other important industrial ministries were exempted from the decentralization plan. Other groups were not as successful. Ten all-union ministries and fifteen union-republican ministries were abolished. The managers did not obtain more extensive freedoms for management; Khrushchev merely observed to the Supreme Soviet that "we must give serious thought to this matter so as to make the proper decisions." But subsequently no concessions were made in that area.[11] The reform restored the supremacy of the Party apparat, and its support for the reform was decisive.

The industrial reorganization and education discussions also indicated the limits within which public debate operates. In the reorganization debate, where Khrushchev was struggling against a majority of the Presidium, some factory managers did challenge the basic principle of substituting a territorial for a ministerial organization of industry. But the concessions that were made were a response not to the public debate but to the silent, *internal* bargaining within the system. In that bargaining, power was at stake, but it may be surmised from the scant evidence at hand that the pretense was maintained that only operational issues were involved. This inference is suggested by the nature of the objections voiced by Molotov or Malenkov, as well as by the type of arguments advanced by Khrushchev's rivals against his 1954 scheme to develop the virgin lands. Kaganovich, for instance, is said to have produced old czarist maps at a Presidium meeting to prove that Khrushchev was trying to develop a desert; Malenkov argued on technical grounds; others got the *Gosplan* (State Planning Commission) to state that there was no money

---

[11] Hoeffding, *American Economic Review* (May 1959), pp. 65ff.

for the scheme. In this manner, a direct political showdown was avoided, but the operational arguments served as a way of challenging the very foundations of the proposal and hence also the proponent's position. In the education debate, however, when Khrushchev was securely in power, the basic principle of combining education and labor was not challenged, while to a much greater extent the proposal was amended because of the openly voiced expert opinion of the specific interest groups involved. The discussion thus not only elicited helpful comments but also produced a virtually unanimous endorsement of the basic principles of the reform and, at the other extreme, specific criticisms of past inefficiencies.

Similarly, when Khrushchev proposed in late 1962 an even more sweeping reorganization of the entire state and Party machinery on the novel principle of two parallel industrial and agricultural hierarchies, no fundamental opposition during the recommendation phase was manifested and the scheme was adopted. Furthermore, with the Party's supremacy and Khrushchev's personal power firmly established, the same reform resulted in considerable recentralization of the economy, since considerations of economic efficiency, no longer complicated by political factors, dictated that course. As in the case of the education reform, these measures were presented for discussion to the interested groups involved. One device used quite effectively in recent years has been the calling of enlarged plenums of the Central Committee, including also hundreds of specialists as guests, to discuss the given proposal and to mobilize the acceptance of new policies by the affected groups. In the United States this process takes place before the basic decisions on those policies are made; in the Soviet Union it takes place afterward.

In a sense, this Soviet pattern of discussion and debate within the top leadership on the basic principles of a measure and then public debate on more limited questions parallels the legislative process in the British Parliament. There when a bill comes up for a second reading its basic principles are discussed. If these are approved, the bill is referred to committee, and subsequently at the report stage and third reading the details of administration and language are resolved. The Soviet two-stage recommendation process parallels this breakdown between generals and specifics, with, of course, the crucial difference that only a handful participate in the second reading while a huge segment of the population participates in the debate over specifics. In some respects, also, a parallel exists between the two-stage Soviet process and the pattern of decision on many American foreign-policy and military-policy issues where the final decision rests with the executive branch. In these instances, the distance between initiation of policy and decision on policy is short: typically from middle-level bureaucrats to the President. Apart from a few leading congressmen, non-executive groups are normally on the periphery of the process. Once the decision has been made and announced, however, these groups (stimulated by dissenters from within the executive branch) may provoke an extensive and far-reaching post-decision debate. Congressmen, journalists, and opposition party leaders may register vigorous protests and criticisms. Like the more tempered and cautious criticisms which may appear in the mobilization phase in the Soviet Union, these outspoken attacks in the United States can produce modifications of policy in practice. They certainly shape the Administration's anticipations of the reactions to its next decision in the same area and thereby also presumably affect the content of that decision. Anticipated reaction is thus a restraint in both the British and American cases; it is of much less significance in the Soviet Union, except during succession struggles.

Decision: Approval and Veto

In every political system there are formal loci of authoritative decision. In the Soviet Union the one crucial locus is the central apparat of the Party. By generating a policy proposal the Party leadership also approves and legitimizes it. On some issues this approval may be followed by considerable public debate of particular aspects of the proposal. At the close of this public debate the proposal, with some modifications, is then approved and legitimized again by the national legislature. This action by the Supreme Soviet, however, is only the culminating formal ratification of the policy-making process which has preceded it. By the time the Supreme Soviet considers a proposal all the key decisions have been made. Indeed, the two or three days' debate within the Supreme Soviet on such measures as industrial reorganization and education reform was stylized and empty compared to the relatively vigorous six weeks of public debate which had gone before. The effective decisions on what modifications to make in the original proposal as a result of the public debate were made by the Party leadership, not by the legislature.

In the American political system, decision is usually the result of consensus-building. The latter is the indispensable prerequisite to the former. The power of decision is dispersed among many different institutions in the United States. The diffusion of the power of decision compensates for the diffusion of the power to generate policy proposals. Ease of proposal is counterbalanced by ease of veto. In the American policy process, many are called but few are chosen. In the Soviet Union, few are called but all are chosen.

The mechanisms of decision reflect the sources of legitimacy. In the Soviet Union, the "correct" policy is that which is supported by the ideology. Authority to decide whether policy is in accord with ideology is monopolized by the central Party leadership. In the United States, on the other hand, policy is, in general, legitimate if it is widely approved— that is, if it rests on popular consent. That consent, however, can come only from the acquiescence of a number of governmental institutions reflecting various publics and interests. The road leads from a theory of popular government through the mechanism of multiple approvals to the harsh fact of minority veto. In addition, the process of decision is usually a continuing one through time. Approval takes place by accretion. In one sense, no single decision is ever final, and approval in one arena can be countered by disapproval in another. In the Soviet Union the decision phase—the authoritative legitimization of a proposal—is brief and unitary. In the United States it is time-consuming and segmented.

This does not mean that policy proposals in the Soviet Union do not require the approval of a number of people. But those who must approve are usually all part of a single, fairly small institutional complex: the Central Committee apparat. A policy proposal in any particular area of policy (e.g., agriculture, heavy industry, education) presumably benefits in the extent to which it receives, in reverse order of importance, the approval of: (1) the top officials of the government agency primarily concerned with the area; (2) the officials in the Central Committee department most directly concerned; (3) the Central Committee Secretary with primary responsibility for the area; (4) the Presidium member or members (if different from number 3) specializing in the area; (5) a majority of the Presidium; and (6) the top leader (Stalin, Khrushchev), if there is one. Depending upon the structure of power at the very top of the Soviet system, one or more of these six groups may be able to exercise a veto. By definition, the top leader always can. So also can a majority of the Presidium, although a political crisis would ensue if the top leader and a Presidium majority were irreconcilably opposed on an important issue. Vigorous disagreement with a policy proposal by any one of numbers 1 through 4, on the other hand, would presumably be handled by removing the dissenting official or officials. Obviously, a Presidium majority or top leader could not do this on every issue where a Cabinet minister or Central Committee secretary dissented. And hence on some measures undoubtedly the individuals primarily concerned can exercise an effective veto. Nonetheless, all those concerned are part of a single institutional hierarchy where, in the last analysis, control rests with the man or handful of men on top.

In the American system, one can also list the institutions whose approval is desirable for a policy. For a domestic policy proposal the list might encompass: (1) the top officials of the government agency primarily concerned; (2) the House committee specializing in the area; (3) the House Rules Committee; (4) the House; (5) the appropriate Senate Committee; (6) the Senate; (7) the President (or a two-thirds majority of both houses); and (8) the courts. This list dramatizes the contrast with the Soviet system. In the first place, the disapproval of any one of these institutions (except for number 1) is normally sufficient to kill a policy proposal. The means of circumventing any one of these institutions are relatively limited. Rarely does either house of Congress discharge its committee from consideration of a bill. Rarely do Congresses pass bills over presidential vetoes. Second, each institution is relatively independent of the others. Each acts on the proposal in terms of its own perspectives and interests and those of the groups with which it is affiliated (that is, "represents"). Consequently, the differences in viewpoint among these institutional deciders are likely to be much greater than they are among those concerned with policy in the Soviet Union. Third, the ability of one institution to influence another is limited. The President has resources which he can employ to persuade congressmen. The House and the Senate can exercise some control over their committees. The courts attach a presumption of validity to congressional enactments. Nonetheless, the costs of obstruction to any one institution are still relatively minor.

Multiple approval is also required for policies formulated within the American executive branch. It takes the form of "clearances" or "concurrences" from the agencies interested in or affected by the proposal. Approval is completed only when the proposal has been endorsed by the executive official with the appropriate legal and political authority. On policy of any consequence, this official is the President. On the other hand, the power to veto is not institutionalized to the same degree that it is in the congressional legislative process.[12] Within the executive branch, if seven out of eight agencies or top officials concerned with a policy approved it and one (other than the President) disapproved it, the probability of the proposal's becoming policy would still be very high.

Decision is always difficult, and in any political system it tends to be delayed. The process of recommendation with respect to congressional legislation usually lasts several years. A bill may be first introduced and advocated in one Congress; it may reach committee hearings in the next; and with luck it may be passed in a third. Time eventually produces the requisite support. In the executive branch similar tendencies to procrastinate are at work: policy proposals wind their way tediously through committees and conferences while political leaders strive to identify the formulas and phrases upon which all can agree. Often in both congressional and executive processes a stalemate develops, with the proponents of the proposal lacking the strength to push it through and the opponents lacking the ability to kill it off. The proposal drifts in limbo. In such circumstances eventual approval may depend upon a trigger event to alter the political balance of forces. In the United States the trigger event

---

[12] See, for example, the 1950 decision on rearmament, NSC 68, and the 1953 expansion of Continental defense, both of which were approved despite the opposition of officials directly responsible for them. Paul Y. Hammond, "NSC 68: Prologue to Rearmament," in Warner R. Schilling, Hammond, Glenn H. Snyder, *Strategy, Politics and Defense Budgets* (New York, 1962), pp. 267ff.; and Huntington, op. cit., pp. 47–53, 326ff.

is usually external to the political system. War, crisis, the development of new weapons by another state may prompt action on foreign policy and related issues. The Soviet sputniks were more or less directly responsible for legislation stimulating scientific research, aiding higher education, reorganizing the Pentagon, and increasing military expenditures. Similar dramatic events within American society are often necessary to break the log jam on domestic legislation. Revelation of the dangerous effects of thalidomide rapidly brought out of committee a drug-inspection bill which had languished in Congress for several years. Such stimuli produce a momentary crystallization of opinion which if expeditiously taken advantage of by the proponents of a measure can result in its formal approval.

Are trigger events equally necessary for decision in the Soviet system? Undoubtedly they do at times prompt decision on policy issues which have been hanging fire, both by stimulating them and offering a justification. For example, the conflicting pulls of armament, industrial development, and pressures for higher consumption has been felt by the top leadership for a number of years. Yet the June 1962 decision to announce suddenly, without public discussion, the drastic increase in food prices was made in the context of an aggravating international situation. This was also the case with the Soviet resumption of nuclear tests in September 1961. In addition, stimuli or triggers may also occur within the political system. Policy proposals and policy-making are closely related to the struggle for power. Hence, changes in the distribution of power are much more likely to stimulate policy proposals and decisions than they are in the United States. Zigzags in policy are often closely correlated with the changing fortunes of Party hierarchs. The whole strange pattern of the de-Stalinization campaign illustrates this: from its abrupt initiation in February 1956, through the subsequent partial "restoration" of Stalin in December 1956, through new attacks at the 21st and 22nd Party Congresses, and again a limited "rehabilitation" in late winter 1963. In each instance, new policies followed but in each the trigger was a shift in the internal power of the leader.

Execution: Amendment and Sabotage

Those who execute policy can also make it. They can do so by interpreting the words of the top decision-makers, by applying those words to unanticipated conditions, and by choosing which goals of the policy deciders will receive primary emphasis and which of conflicting goals will be given preference. The executors thus can amend policy to further the goals of the policy-makers, or can sabotage policy to frustrate them. The post-decision struggle over policy may be less visible than that which precedes decision, but it is no less real. In the long run, it is often more important.

In the American political system the execution phase in policy-making is delimited in time and in institutional responsibility. Formal approval of a policy proposal by President and Congress marks the beginning of the process of execution. The policy is passed into the hands of the appropriate administrators. Of crucial importance here is the role which these administrators have played in shaping the policy in the recommendation phase. If a new administrative agency is created to execute the new policy, it will probably be staffed initially by individuals who were its more ardent proponents before decision. Very possibly the attitudes of the administrators will more closely resemble those of the original generators of the proposal than they will the more moderate views of the coalition eventually responsible for its approval. At the other extreme, a policy may be assigned for execution to an existing agency which is already heavily committed to competing or even contradictory purposes. In this case the policy in execution may be even further removed from the goals of the generators than the one which was formally approved. Usually little leeway exists as to who must approve a proposal in order to give it authoritative sanction. There is greater leeway, however, as to who gets the responsibility for its execution.

In the Soviet Union initiation and decision are closely linked. So also are persuasion and execution. These functions are not assigned to different, specialized institutions in the same degree to which they are in the United States. Once a policy is approved in the United States the policy-deciding agencies often lose control over it. An act passed by Congress can be at the mercy of its administrators and the courts. A decade may pass before the courts have delimited its scope, defined its content, and removed all doubts concerning its constitutionality. The members of the relevant congressional committee and of the appropriations subcommittees can continue to play a major role in its execution, but groups not represented on these bodies can exercise little leverage. So also, the President can wield direct control over the execution of only a few policies at a time. Administrative agencies often administer a policy in their own way in the face of presidential indifference and even, at times, of presidential opposition. In the Soviet Union, on the other hand, the pressure on the executors to adapt or distort policy is greater, but so also are the means by which the policy deciders can limit the executors' independent action. The executors of policies are normally government agencies. The Party apparat, however, functions both as a generator of policy and as a supervisor of its execution. The apparat is continually available to the Party chiefs to check up on the execution of policy, to spur on government administrators, to stimulate one hierarchy through the competition of another. At times, policies may also, as in the case of the virgin-lands campaign of 1954, be directly administered through Party agencies as well as through governmental bureaus. Checking up on the execution of policy, insuring the proper "follow through" on top decisions, is a perennial problem in the American executive branch. American policy-deciders have tried to devise means (such as the legislative veto) to increase their control over the execution of policy. The Soviet system attempts to solve this problem by making the generator of policy the supervisor of its execution.

The Soviet policy-maker, however, faces a problem of scale that is qualitatively different from that faced by his American counterpart. The fact that all significant aspects of economic and social life in the Soviet Union are state-controlled creates a state bureaucracy with enormous problems of coordination. Soviet spokesmen themselves admit that the Soviet bureaucracy suffers from chronic inefficiency, poor organization, overplanning, and overstaffing. Conflicting instructions from the top, frequent plan changes (in one oblast the construction plan for 1962 was altered five hundred times! [13]), all affect the execution of policy. That is why so much effort is perennially put into the organization of effective control machinery, on both state and Party levels. The frequent changes in that organization suggest that the problem is far from being resolved.

Any policy involves both the definition of goals and the allocation of resources. The extent to which the top-level deciders of policy attempt to do either of these, however, may vary considerably. In general, where resources are scarce, leaders put more emphasis upon the definition of goals. The executors of policy then have to take responsibility for securing the resources to achieve those goals. Thus, in the Soviet Union economic production targets are set by the top agencies of the party and government. Theoretically, resources are also allocated by these agencies. But to achieve the goals of the economic plan individual factory administrators often may have to engage in semilegitimate or illegitimate practices. In a more affluent system such as the United States, top leadership decisions often take the form of an allocation of resources, and the definition of goals is more widely shared with policy-executing agencies than it is in the Soviet Union. In defining goals these agencies also generate new policy proposals which may eventually "bubble up" and be given official sanction.

The gap between the goals defined in Soviet policies and the resources which are allocated to achieve them gives rise to the phenomenon of "family circles." Local officials have a common interest in moderating goals, procuring resources, and collaborating with one another across governmental and party lines. The attempt to maintain a system of checks and balances in the execution of policy has the same effect in the Soviet system as in the formation of policy in the United States. Individuals and groups in theoretically competitive organizations get together to agree

[13] *Ekonomicheskaia gazeta,* November 17, 1962.

on the rules of peaceful coexistence. In the United States, bureaucrats, congressmen, and interest-group representatives collaborate to minimize the influence of the Administration and various outside groups in the policy-making process. In the Soviet system, lower-ranking bureaucrats in party and government collaborate to protect themselves against the spurs and prods of their superiors. From the communist viewpoint, the "family circles" which reduce competition and promote compromise in the execution of policy are just as evil as the "factions" which promote competition and disrupt harmony in the higher-level formulation of it. But they often have to be tolerated, since they may contribute to the execution of policy. With many goals set in an unrealistic manner at the top these informal circles stimulate a more effective distribution of limited resources on the working level. As a result, most prosecutions take place only when such circles fail in this informal function.

In the American system, the executors of a policy can expect to get considerable support from those groups primarily responsible for its official sanction during the first few years after it has been approved. After a while, however, the coalition of interests originally responsible for the policy dissolves. The number of groups directly concerned with it declines. The policy arena may come to be dominated by groups whose objectives differ considerably from those of the coalition responsible for the policy. The executive agency, as it is said, has "to come to terms" with the congressional committee responsible for its budget or the industry with which it has regular contact. This shift in objectives is particularly noticeable in the case of policies affecting powerful economic interests and administered by independent regulatory commissions. Gradually the goals of the commissions come to resemble those of the groups which they were created to regulate. In the Soviet Union, on the other hand, the Central Committee apparat always remains an important element in the constituency of an executive agency. While the pressures to modify a policy may be more diverse and immediate, the pressures to uphold its original conception are also more concrete and permanent.

THE DIMENSIONS OF POLICY MAKING

Three key questions are relevant to the analysis of any policy-making process. To what extent does the process produce clear-cut alternatives and facilitate choice between them? To what extent does the process facilitate the integration of policies in different areas of subject matter? To what extent does the process facilitate major innovations in policy?

These questions, it should be noted, are analytical, not evaluative. Analysis of a policy-making process may show that it fudges policy alternatives and obstructs major innovations. Whether these character-istics are good or bad, however, depends on whether one favors clear-cut choices and radical changes. An ardent reformer presumably would do just this; a defender of the status quo might well prefer very different characteristics.

Selection

For many years American scholars have debated how policy *ought* to be made. Should grand alternatives be formulated in sweeping, clear-cut fashion, and a decisive choice made between them? Or should policy develop through a series of small-scale adjustments to immediate needs? One scholar argues eloquently for "The Necessity for Choice"; another persuasively defends "The Science of 'Muddling Through.' " [14] However much they may disagree over how policy should be made, however, almost all agree on how it actually is made in the United States. Policy is the product of muddling through: it is the result of incremental, ad-hoc decisions, in which issues and values, ends and means are hopelessly confused. As a result, it lacks coherence, consistency, and rationality.

A pervasive characteristic of the American political system is the extent to which it frustrates choice between well-defined policy alternatives. American political parties are heterogeneous coalitions of interest groups and viewpoints. Both contain liberals and conservatives, isolationists and internationalists. Party heterogeneity also contributes to the fudging of issues in Congress. The process of recommendation in the national legislature results in moderation. Congressional procedures facilitate amendment in committee and on the floor. At times a bill may be so amended that its original proponents turn against it. The bill which emerges from Congress is usually a compound of many viewpoints and influences woven together through compromise and logrolling. Within the executive branch policy issues similarly tend to be compromised and obscured. Just as the compromise and fudging of issues in elections and in Congress stimulated demands for party responsibility and congressional reorganization, so also the same phenomena in the executive branch stimulated demands for drastic reforms there: abolition of committees, stronger presidential leadership, presentation of policy alternatives at the top levels of government.

Thus, in the American system, the structure of the parties often denies the voters a clear-cut choice in the electoral process; the complex and segmented character of congressional procedures often denies the congressmen a clear-cut choice in the legislative process; and the pressures for agreement among subordinate officials deny the President a clear-cut choice in the executive formulation of policy. The alternatives open to a policy-maker usually involve only marginal differences. The policy-maker himself, moreover, attempts to limit the consequences of his own choice; he tries to make the minimal choice so as to enhance his future

[14] Henry A. Kissinger, *The Necessity for Choice* (New York, 1960). Charles E. Lindblom, "The Science of 'Muddling Through,' " *Public Administration Review*, Spring 1959, pp. 79–88 (included in the present volume).

freedom of action; he wants "to decide without actually choosing." [15] The groups backing the policy may have opposing goals; agreement on means often exists without agreement on ends. The consensus underlying any one policy, moreover, usually differs from that underlying other policies. Majorities are transient. Enemies on one issue are allies on the next. The emphasis is on the short-run perspective, the pragmatic compromise. The grand choices are made more by accretion than by selection.

These characteristics of policy-making in American national government are also found in state and local governments, business corporations, and other institutions. They may well inhere in any complex policy-making process. The question here is: To what extent do they exist in the Soviet Union? If incremental, ad-hoc, short-range policy-making also prevails there, this would be fairly conclusive evidence that it is a universal characteristic of complex decision-making structures. If it is much less prevalent in the Soviet system, this would suggest that the ad-hoc method is typical of a particular type of political culture. On the whole, it can probably be said that Soviet history offers more examples of clear-cut selection, both domestically and in foreign policy. Both the Stalin period and the post-Stalin phase have been punctuated by dramatic new programs and reforms. The collectivization, the Stalin-Hitler pact, the Party-state reorganization of 1962, and the "peaceful coexistence" doctrine all involved sharp turns. It is, however, likely that gradually, with the Soviet Union becoming a more developed society, it will become more difficult for the leaders to change course abruptly, at least in domestic affairs, without causing major economic and social dislocations. While the lack of resources has in some important areas forced a piecemeal approach (this has been most evident in Soviet agriculture), it is also paradoxically a fact that the availability of resources inhibits their sudden concentration on a specific goal simply because more interests become involved in not suddenly altering the status quo. To the extent that the Soviet picture is a mixed one, the difference from the United States appears to be one of considerable degree but not of kind.

Integration

The modern state—communist or democratic—makes policy in many areas. Foreign affairs, military affairs, labor, industry, agriculture, finance, commerce, education, natural resources, welfare—all demand its attention to at least some degree. Each area of policy and policy-making is in part autonomous and in part interrelated with the other areas. The degree to which policy in one area is integrated with policy in another depends upon the power which the central policy-making institutions have vis-à-vis the specialized ones in each area.

[15] Warner R. Schilling, "The H-Bomb Decision: How to Decide without Actually Choosing," *Political Science Quarterly*, March 1961, pp. 24–46.

In the American system each policy area has a high degree of autonomy. American government, Ernest Griffith has said, is "government by whirlpools."[16] Congressmen, executives, bureaucrats, interest groups, local party leaders, technical experts, even newspapermen, tend to specialize in one or a few areas. The interaction among the specialists in an area tends to be much more frequent and intense than that among individuals in the same institution in different areas. To reverse an old truth: two congressmen, one of whom is an agricultural specialist, may have less in common than two agricultural specialists, one of whom is a congressman. In every whirlpool, of course, there are some individuals and institutions concerned with policy in other areas. But the ability of these general policy-making groups to influence policy in any one area is normally weak. Moreover, the connecting institutions themselves tend to fragment. Over the years many of Congress's policy-making activities have devolved to specialized committees, each concerned with one policy area and jealously guarding its prerogatives against invasion. The Appropriations Committee, which conceivably might play an integrating role, is divided into autonomous subcommittees, each responsible for one major supply bill. Among congressmen generally an informal specialization develops. Policy expertise is accorded deference and carries political weight. But the congressman who may be worth fifty or sixty votes on an antitrust measure is usually worth nothing on a foreign-policy issue. In most political systems the final power over policy is concentrated in the hands of less than a score of individuals, the cabinet in parliamentary democracies, the Presidium in the Soviet Union. The same is true of the United States, except that there are many cabinets and presidia. Except for the President, an individual in one is seldom found in another.

In the Soviet Union, on the other hand, the more explicit goals of the political leadership as well as greater scarcity of resources compel more conscious coordination of policy. In the United States little coordination is required between, for instance, agricultural and military policy. The individuals principally concerned with the formulation of the one are normally different (except for the President) from those concerned with the other. In the Soviet system, the two are directly related. Two major goals of the political leaders are increased agricultural production and strong military forces. The achievement of either requires large capital expenditures. Capital invested in one area is denied to another. As a result, the Presidium, the Secretariat, and the Central Committee have to maintain close control over both agricultural and military policy. In the United States, the absence of competition between the two areas enhances the power of the specialized interest groups and bureaucracies and reduces the control of the President in both fields. While American

[16] Ernest S. Griffith, *Impasse of Democracy* (New York, 1939), p. 182.

policy is made in many separate whirlpools, Soviet policy is boiled in a single caldron.

Both the instrumental American system and the ideological Soviet system contain certain biases in the distribution of power among different policy areas. In the Soviet Union, heavy industry has traditionally been in a favored position. The priority which the political leadership consciously gave it during the industrialization drive of the 1930s cannot now easily be removed by the political leadership—even in a totalitarian system. Time and again some Soviet leaders have spoken of the desirability of shifting resources into light industry, consumer goods, and agriculture. But in practice heavy industry has not suffered. In the Soviet Union, as well as in the United States, the redistribution of resources is easier by economic expansion than by conscious reallocation. Similarly, in the United States the political system is skewed in favor of private control of resources and the production of consumer goods. The difficulty which a Soviet leader faces in de-emphasizing heavy industry is comparable to the difficulty which an American leader faces in raising taxes.

The ability of the central institutions to coordinate policy also reflects differences in their nature. One of Khrushchev's charges against Stalin was that he reduced the importance of the Politburo by dividing it into committees concerned with particular policy areas. In effect, Stalin himself took over the function of integrating policy and compelled Politburo members to become primarily policy specialists. In the post-Stalin era, Presidium members have still specialized in particular areas, but apparently they have shared to a greater degree in the formulation of important policies. The integration of policy is one of their primary responsibilities as Presidium members. In the United States, on the other hand, only the President, with the aid of his staff, such as the White House assistants and the Budget Bureau, has the power and the right to coordinate. But inevitably his policy-integrating capacities are limited. Usually he must focus his attention on one or two key areas, such as foreign policy. Coordination in other areas is largely by default.

Innovation

A system incapable of innovation in the long run is incapable of survival. Policy innovation necessarily partakes of the general characteristics of the policy-formulation process. In the United States, the pressures for change tend to bubble up continually. At times there are periods of intense innovation as in domestic policy in the mid-1930s and in foreign policy in the late 1940s. But in general great leaps forward are rare. Change is slow and piecemeal. The growth of policy is similar to the growth of the common law. Once an innovation is made, however, it is seldom reversed. Congress rarely repeals a major statute; only slightly more frequently does the Supreme Court reverse itself on a major issue.

Policies are changed through the slow process of amendment, formal and informal, and are often supplemented by new policies with different and perhaps conflicting objectives. They may become outdated, but almost never are sufficient interests adversely affected by a major policy to procure its repeal. The price of innovation is high; but, once bought, change is permanent.

In the Soviet Union, in contrast, innovation tends to have a stop-and-start, trial-and-error quality. Major changes are initiated from the top. More of them take place when a new leader is attempting to consolidate his power. The first response to a new need often comes later than it would in the United States. Here, at least in part, the problem is rooted in the bureaucratic character of the Soviet leadership. "In the formally structured group, the idea man is doubly dangerous. He endangers the established distribution of power and status, and he is a competitive threat to his peers. Consequently, he tends to be suppressed." [17] While the same is true in the United States, as both Nelson Rockefeller and Chester Bowles might confirm, it is still possible for the "idea man" to generate support on the outside. In the Soviet Union he must do it inside the political system, and his task is doubly difficult because the Soviet bureaucracy is not only bureaucratically conservative, as most are, but also dogmatically conservative.

Innovation is easier in times of trouble and crisis. Success breeds its own conservatism, often represented by special interests and institutions. This is true of both the Soviet Union and the United States. In the United States recent years have seen a deepening chasm between the executive branch, representing more often the forces of change and innovation, and Congress, a conservative institution reflecting more frequently both the traditions and the interests of the past. In the Soviet Union the ability of the Soviet system to survive the difficult days of Stalinism and of the war created its own brand of conservatism, represented by the Party and state bureaucracy, permeated with individuals with a strong pro-industrial bias. The dramatic contrast between Kennedy calling for a New Frontier and for civil rights while Congress defended the old limits on federal power has had its counterpart in the Soviet Union, with Khrushchev seeking new welfare for the Soviet people while the apparat—out of both inertia and prejudice—quietly strove to reduce the impact of his proposals.

Once the top Soviet leadership determines that change is necessary, however, innovation can proceed expeditiously. All the energies of the regime are devoted to the recommendation and execution of the new policy. After Khrushchev obtained the approval of the Presidium for industrial reorganization in 1957, for instance, he insisted that this fundamental overhaul of Soviet industrial structure be carried out in two or three months. The gap between Khrushchev's first memorandum on ex-

[17] Victor A. Thompson, *Modern Organization* (New York, 1961), p. 91.

panding the chemical industry and the decision to rush headlong into a vast expansion program was similarly a matter of only a few months. This pattern reflects the concentration of the policy initiation and decision functions in the top leadership. It also may reflect the role of ideology, which may retard the initial decision to innovate but also may accelerate the innovation process once that decision is made. Innovation in the American system is often leisurely; in the Soviet system it is almost always undertaken in a spirit of crisis. Politically and psychologically, the Party seems to need and thrive upon crusades and crash programs. Its energies are mobilized and directed to the achievement first of one goal and then of another. This pattern appears to be typical of communist regimes generally. At times this seems to produce a trial-and-error approach to the solution of major policy problems. First one innovation is launched. If it does not solve the problem quickly, it is canceled, and another approach is tried. In areas of chronic trouble, such as agriculture, Soviet policy zigzags vigorously, first on one tack, then on another, and then off on a third. Such responses may be characteristic of any regime when it is faced with serious and continuing problems. Much of the atmosphere surrounding Soviet policy-making in an area like agriculture, for instance, seems similar to that of the New Deal in the early 1930s. "Bold, persistent experimentation" was Roosevelt's slogan; and like the Soviets the New Dealers did not hesitate to drop one policy if it did not work and to try another. Trial-and-error innovations thus appear on the American scene during periods of severe crisis, but they seem to be a permanent feature of the Soviet system. Hence policies once innovated are often reversed.

Whereas the slow process of piecemeal amendment typically alters major policies in the United States, in the Soviet Union policy reversals are often far-reaching, dramatic, and highly visible. They are caused by power struggles or critical shortages in resources. They usually involve a drastic decline in reputation of the sponsor of the original policy and the purging of his followers. Statements from the Party leaders abruptly terminate the ideological legitimacy of the old policy and hail the new one as the correct Marxist-Leninist solution.

In any political system centralized power makes innovation more possible although not necessarily more probable. During the last years of his rule Stalin created an atmosphere hostile to innovation. His successors, however, initiated rapid changes in many areas of Soviet policy. The diffusion of power in the American system, on the other hand, provides many channels through which changes may be initiated. If one channel is blocked, action may still be possible through another. During Reconstruction the initiative was with Congress; in the early twentieth century state governments took the lead in introducing female suffrage and welfare legislation; before World War II the President had the initiative in domestic policy and after the war he had it in foreign policy; the most important domestic-policy innovation of the 1950s, however, was made by the Supreme Court when it ordered the desegregation of the public schools.

In the years after World War II both the Soviet and the American political systems produced major innovations in policy. Their styles and methods, however, differed greatly. Whether these innovations were adequate is a question which cannot be answered here. At the least, it can be said that each system was able to make some major innovations in response to some major changes in its environment. Many political systems lack the capacity to innovate and to adjust to new challenges. Such was the case with neither the United States nor the Soviet Union. Neither lacked flexibility. Neither was frozen in *immobilisme*.

The Science of "Muddling Through"

Charles E. Lindblom

Suppose an administrator is given responsibility for formulating policy with respect to inflation. He might start by trying to list all related values in order of importance, e.g., full employment, reasonable business profit, protection of small savings, prevention of a stock market crash. Then all possible policy outcomes could be rated as more or less efficient in attaining a maximum of these values. This would of course require a prodigious inquiry into values held by members of society and an equally prodigious set of calculations on how much of each value is equal to how much of each other value. He could then proceed to outline all possible policy alternatives. In a third step, he would undertake systematic comparison of his multitude of alternatives to determine which attains the greatest amount of values.

In comparing policies, he would take advantage of any theory available that generalized about classes of policies. In considering inflation, for example, he would compare all policies in the light of the theory of prices. Since no alternatives are beyond his investigation, he would consider strict central control and the abolition of all prices and markets on the one hand and elimination of all public controls with reliance completely

Charles E. Lindblom, "The Science of 'Muddling Through,'" *Public Administration Review,* Spring, 1959.

on the free market on the other, both in the light of whatever theoretical generalizations he could find on such hypothetical economies.

Finally, he would try to make the choice that would in fact maximize his values.

An alternative line of attack would be to set as his principal objective, either explicitly or without conscious thought, the relatively simple goal of keeping prices level. This objective might be compromised or complicated by only a few other goals, such as full employment. He would in fact disregard most other social values as beyond his present interest, and he would for the moment not even attempt to rank the few values that he regarded as immediately relevant. Were he pressed, he would quickly admit that he was ignoring many related values and many possible important consequences of his policies.

As a second step, he would outline those relatively few policy alternatives that occurred to him. He would then compare them. In comparing his limited number of alternatives, most of them familiar from past controversies, he would not ordinarily find a body of theory precise enough to carry him through a comparison of their respective consequences. Instead he would rely heavily on the record of past experience with small policy steps to predict the consequences of similar steps extended into the future.

Moreover, he would find that the policy alternatives combined objectives or values in different ways. For example, one policy might offer price level stability at the cost of some risk of unemployment; another might offer less price stability but also less risk of unemployment. Hence, the next step in his approach—the final selection—would combine into one the choice among values and the choice among instruments for reaching values. It would not, as in the first method of policy-making, approximate a more mechanical process of choosing the means that best satisfied goals that were previously clarified and ranked. Because practitioners of the second approach expect to achieve their goals only partially, they would expect to repeat endlessly the sequence just described, as conditions and aspirations changed and as accuracy of prediction improved.

BY ROOT OR BY BRANCH

For complex problems, the first of these two approaches is of course impossible. Although such an approach can be described, it cannot be practiced except for relatively simple problems and even then only in a somewhat modified form. It assumes intellectual capacities and sources of information that men simply do not possess, and it is even more absurd as an approach to policy when the time and money that can be allocated to a policy problem is limited, as is always the case. Of particular importance to public administrators is the fact that public agencies are in effect usually instructed not to practice the first method. That is to say, their prescribed functions and constraints—the politically or legally possible—restrict their attention to relatively few values and relatively few alternative policies among the countless alternatives that might be imagined. It is the second method that is practiced.

Curiously, however, the literatures of decision-making, policy formulation, planning, and public administration formalize the first approach rather than the second, leaving public administrators who handle complex decisions in the position of practicing what few preach. For emphasis I run some risk of overstatement. True enough, the literature is well aware of limits on man's capacities and of the inevitability that policies will be approached in some such style as the second. But attempts to formalize rational policy formulation—to lay out explicitly the necessary steps in the process—usually describe the first approach and not the second.[1]

The common tendency to describe policy formulation even for complex problems as though it followed the first approach has been strengthened by the attention given to, and successes enjoyed by, operations research, statistical decision theory, and systems analysis. The hallmarks of these procedures, typical of the first approach, are clarity of objective, explicitness of evaluation, a high degree of comprehensiveness of overview, and, wherever possible, quantification of values for mathematical analysis. But these advanced procedures remain largely the appropriate techniques of relatively small-scale problem-solving where the total number of variables to be considered is small and value problems restricted. Charles Hitch, head of the Economics Division of RAND Corporation, one of the leading centers for application of these techniques, has written:

> I would make the empirical generalization from my experience at RAND and elsewhere that operations research is the art of sub-optimizing, i.e., of solving some lower-level problems, and that difficulties increase and our special competence diminishes by an order of magnitude with every level of decision making we attempt to ascend. The sort of simple explicit model which operations researchers are so proficient in using can certainly reflect most of the significant factors influencing traffic control on the George Washington Bridge, but the proportion of the relevant reality which we can represent by any such model or models in studying, say, a major foreign-policy decision, appears to be almost trivial.[2]

[1] James G. March and Herbert A. Simon similarly characterize the literature. They also take some important steps, as have Simon's recent articles, to describe a less heroic model of policy-making. See *Organizations* (John Wiley and Sons, 1958), p. 137.

[2] "Operations Research and National Planning—A Dissent," 5 *Operations Research* 718 (October, 1957). Hitch's dissent is from particular points made in the article to which his paper is a reply; his claim that operations research is for low-level problems is widely accepted. For examples of the kind of problems to which operations research is applied, see C. W. Churchman, R. L. Ackoff and E. L. Arnoff, *Introduction to Operations Research* (John Wiley and Sons, 1957); and J. F. McCloskey and J. M.

Accordingly, I propose in this paper to clarify and formalize the second method, much neglected in the literature. This might be described as the method of *successive limited comparisons*. I will contrast it with the first approach, which might be called the rational-comprehensive method.[3] More impressionistically and briefly—and therefore generally used in this article—they could be characterized as the branch method and root method, the former continually building out from the current situation, step-by-step and by small degrees; the latter starting from fundamentals anew each time, building on the past only as experience is embodied in a theory, and always prepared to start completely from the ground up.

Let us put the characteristics of the two methods side by side in simplest terms.

Rational-Comprehensive (Root)

Successive Limited Comparisons (Branch)

1a. Clarification of values or objectives distinct from and usually prerequisite to empirical analysis of alternative policies.

1b. Selection of value goals and empirical analysis of the needed action are not distinct from one another but are closely intertwined.

2a. Policy-formulation is therefore approached through means-end analysis: First the ends are isolated, then the means to achieve them are sought.

2b. Since means and ends are not distinct, means-end analysis is often inappropriate or limited.

3a. The test of a "good" policy is that it can be shown to be the most appropriate means to desired ends.

3b. The test of a "good" policy is typically that various analysts find themselves directly agreeing on a policy (without their agreeing that it is the most appropriate means to an agreed objective).

4a. Analysis is comprehensive; every important relevant factor is taken into account.

4b. Analysis is drastically limited:
  (i) Important possible outcomes are neglected.
  (ii) Important alternative potential policies are neglected.
  (iii) Important affected values are neglected.

5a. Theory is often heavily relied upon.

5b. A succession of comparisons greatly reduces or eliminates reliance on theory.

Coppinger (eds.), *Operations Research for Management*, Vol. II (The Johns Hopkins Press, 1956).

[3] I am assuming that administrators often make policy and advise in the making of policy and am treating decision-making and policy-making as synonymous for purposes of this paper.

Assuming that the root method is familiar and understandable, we proceed directly to clarification of its alternative by contrast. In explaining the second, we shall be describing how most administrators do in fact approach complex questions, for the root method, the "best" way as a blueprint or model, is in fact not workable for complex policy questions, and administrators are forced to use the method of successive limited comparisons.

INTERTWINING EVALUATION AND EMPIRICAL ANALYSIS (1B)

The quickest way to understand how values are handled in the method of successive limited comparisons is to see how the root method often breaks down in *its* handling of values or objectives. The idea that values should be clarified, and in advance of the examination of alternative policies, is appealing. But what happens when we attempt it for complex social problems? The first difficulty is that on many critical values or objectives, citizens disagree, congressmen disagree, and public administrators disagree. Even where a fairly specific objective is prescribed for the administrator, there remains considerable room for disagreement on sub-objectives. Consider, for example, the conflict with respect to locating public housing, described in Meyerson and Banfield's study of the Chicago Housing Authority [4]—disagreement which occurred despite the clear objective of providing a certain number of public housing units in the city. Similarly conflicting are objectives in highway location, traffic control, minimum wage administration, development of tourist facilities in national parks, or insect control.

Administrators cannot escape these conflicts by ascertaining the majority's preference, for preferences have not been registered on most issues; indeed, there often *are* no preferences in the absence of public discussion sufficient to bring an issue to the attention of the electorate. Furthermore, there is a question of whether intensity of feeling should be considered as well as the number of persons preferring each alternative. By the impossibility of doing otherwise, administrators often are reduced to deciding policy without clarifying objectives first.

Even when an administrator resolves to follow his own values as a criterion for decisions, he often will not know how to rank them when they conflict with one another, as they usually do. Suppose, for example, that an administrator must relocate tenants living in tenements scheduled for destruction. One objective is to empty the buildings fairly promptly, another is to find suitable accommodation for persons displaced, another is to avoid friction with residents in other areas in which a large influx

[4] Martin Meyerson and Edward C. Banfield, *Politics, Planning and the Public Interest* (The Free Press, 1955).

would be unwelcome, another is to deal with all concerned through persuasion if possible, and so on.

How does one state even to himself the relative importance of these partially conflicting values? A simple ranking of them is not enough; one needs ideally to know how much of one value is worth sacrificing for some of another value. The answer is that typically the administrator chooses—and must choose—directly among policies in which these values are combined in different ways. He cannot first clarify his values and then choose among policies.

A more subtle third point underlies both the first two. Social objectives do not always have the same relative values. One objective may be highly prized in one circumstance, another in another circumstance. If, for example, an administrator values highly both the dispatch with which his agency can carry through its projects *and* good public relations, it matters little which of the two possibly conflicting values he favors in some abstract or general sense. Policy questions arise in forms which put to administrators such a question as: Given the degree to which we are or are not already achieving the values of dispatch and the values of good public relations, is it worth sacrificing a little speed for a happier clientele, or is it better to risk offending the clientele so that we can get on with our work? The answer to such a question varies with circumstances.

The value problem is, as the example shows, always a problem of adjustments at a margin. But there is no practicable way to state marginal objectives or values except in terms of particular policies. That one value is preferred to another in one decision situation does not mean that it will be preferred in another decision situation in which it can be had only at great sacrifice of another value. Attempts to rank or order values in general and abstract terms so that they do not shift from decision to decision end up by ignoring the relevant marginal preferences. The significance of this third point thus goes very far. Even if all administrators had at hand an agreed set of values, objectives, and constraints, and an agreed ranking of these values, objectives, and constraints, their marginal values in actual choice situations would be impossible to formulate.

Unable consequently to formulate the relevant values first and then choose among policies to achieve them, administrators must choose directly among alternative policies that offer different marginal combinations of values. Somewhat paradoxically, the only practicable way to disclose one's relevant marginal values even to oneself is to describe the policy one chooses to achieve them. Except roughly and vaguely, I know of no way to describe—or even to understand—what my relative evaluations are for, say, freedom and security, speed and accuracy in governmental decisions, or low taxes and better schools than to describe my preferences among specific policy choices that might be made between the alternatives in each of the pairs.

In summary, two aspects of the process by which values are actually handled can be distinguished. The first is clear: evaluation and empirical analysis are intertwined; that is, one chooses among values and among policies at one and the same time. Put a little more elaborately, one simultaneously chooses a policy to attain certain objectives and chooses the objectives themselves. The second aspect is related but distinct: the administrator focuses his attention on marginal or incremental values. Whether he is aware of it or not, he does not find general formulations of objectives very helpful and in fact makes specific marginal or incremental comparisons. Two policies, X and Y, confront him. Both promise the same degree of attainment of objectives a, b, c, d, and e. But X promises him somewhat more of f than does Y, while Y promises him somewhat more of g than does X. In choosing between them, he is in fact offered the alternative of a marginal or incremental amount of f at the expense of a marginal or incremental amount of g. The only values that are relevant to his choice are these increments by which the two policies differ; and, when he finally chooses between the two marginal values, he does so by making a choice between policies.[5]

As to whether the attempt to clarify objectives in advance of policy selection is more or less rational than the close intertwining of marginal evaluation and empirical analysis, the principal difference established is that for complex problems the first is impossible and irrelevant, and the second is both possible and relevant. The second is possible because the administrator need not try to analyze any values except the values by which alternative policies differ and need not be concerned with them except as they differ marginally. His need for information on values or objectives is drastically reduced as compared with the root method; and his capacity for grasping, comprehending, and relating values to one another is not strained beyond the breaking point.

RELATIONS BETWEEN MEANS AND ENDS (2B)

Decision-making is ordinarily formalized as a means-ends relationship: means are conceived to be evaluated and chosen in the light of ends finally selected independently of and prior to the choice of means. This is the means-ends relationship of the root method. But it follows from all that has just been said that such a means-ends relationship is possible only to the extent that values are agreed upon, are reconcilable, and are stable at the margin. Typically, therefore, such a means-ends relationship is absent from the branch method, where means and ends are simultaneously chosen.

Yet any departure from the means-ends relationship of the root method

[5] The line of argument is, of course, an extension of the theory of market choice, especially the theory of consumer choice, to public policy choices.

will strike some readers as inconceivable. For it will appear to them that only in such a relationship is it possible to determine whether one policy choice is better or worse than another. How can an administrator know whether he has made a wise or foolish decision if he is without prior values or objectives by which to judge his decisions? The answer to this question calls up the third distinctive difference between root and branch methods: how to decide the best policy.

THE TEST OF "GOOD" POLICY (3B)

In the root method, a decision is "correct," "good," or "rational" if it can be shown to attain some specified objective, where the objective can be specified without simply describing the decision itself. Where objectives are defined only through the marginal or incremental approach to values described above, it is still sometimes possible to test whether a policy does in fact attain the desired objectives; but a precise statement of the objectives takes the form of a description of the policy chosen or some alternative to it. To show that a policy is mistaken one cannot offer an abstract argument that important objectives are not achieved; one must instead argue that another policy is more to be preferred.

So far, the departure from customary ways of looking at problem-solving is not troublesome, for many administrators will be quick to agree that the most effective discussion of the correctness of policy does take the form of comparison with other policies that might have been chosen. But what of the situation in which administrators cannot agree on values or objectives, either abstractly or in marginal terms? What then is the test of "good" policy? For the root method, there is no test. Agreement on objectives failing, there is no standard of "correctness." For the method of successive limited comparisons, the test is agreement on policy itself, which remains possible even when agreement on values is not.

It has been suggested that continuing agreement in Congress on the desirability of extending old age insurance stems from liberal desires to strengthen the welfare programs of the federal government and from conservative desires to reduce union demands for private pension plans. If so, this is an excellent demonstration of the ease with which individuals of different ideologies often can agree on concrete policy. Labor mediators report a similar phenomenon: the contestants cannot agree on criteria for settling their disputes but can agree on specific proposals. Similarly, when one administrator's objective turns out to be another's means, they often can agree on policy.

Agreement on policy thus becomes the only practicable test of the policy's correctness. And for one administrator to seek to win the other over to agreement on ends as well would accomplish nothing and create quite unnecessary controversy.

If agreement directly on policy as a test for "best" policy seems a poor substitute for testing the policy against its objectives, it ought to be remembered that objectives themselves have no ultimate validity other than they are agreed upon. Hence agreement is the test of "best" policy in both methods. But where the root method requires agreement on what elements in the decision constitute objectives and on which of these objectives should be sought, the branch method falls back on agreement wherever it can be found.

In an important sense, therefore, it is not irrational for an administrator to defend a policy as good without being able to specify what it is good for.

NONCOMPREHENSIVE ANALYSIS (4B)

Ideally, rational-comprehensive analysis leaves out nothing important. But it is impossible to take everything important into consideration unless "important" is so narrowly defined that analysis is in fact quite limited. Limits on human intellectual capacities and on available information set definite limits to man's capacity to be comprehensive. In actual fact, therefore, no one can practice the rational-comprehensive method for really complex problems, and every administrator faced with a sufficiently complex problem must find ways drastically to simplify.

An administrator assisting in the formulation of agricultural economic policy cannot in the first place be competent on all possible policies. He cannot even comprehend one policy entirely. In planning a soil bank program, he cannot successfully anticipate the impact of higher or lower farm income on, say, urbanization—the possible consequent loosening of family ties, possible consequent eventual need for revisions in social security and further implications for tax problems arising out of new federal responsibilities for social security and municipal responsibilities for urban services. Nor, to follow another line of repercussions, can he work through the soil bank program's effects on prices for agricultural products in foreign markets and consequent implications for foreign relations, including those arising out of economic rivalry between the United States and the U.S.S.R.

In the method of successive limited comparisons, simplification is systematically achieved in two principal ways. First, it is achieved through limitation of policy comparisons to those policies that differ in relatively small degree from policies presently in effect. Such a limitation immediately reduces the number of alternatives to be investigated and also drastically simplifies the character of the investigation of each. For it is not necessary to undertake fundamental inquiry into an alternative and its consequences; it is necessary only to study those respects in which the proposed alternative and its consequences differ from the status quo.

The empirical comparison of marginal differences among alternative policies that differ only marginally is, of course, a counterpart to the incremental or marginal comparison of values discussed above.[6]

Relevance as Well as Realism

It is a matter of common observation that in Western democracies public administrators and policy analysts in general do largely limit their analyses to incremental or marginal differences in policies that are chosen to differ only incrementally. They do not do so, however, solely because they desperately need some way to simplify their problems; they also do so in order to be relevant. Democracies change their policies almost entirely through incremental adjustments. Policy does not move in leaps and bounds.

The incremental character of political change in the United States has often been remarked. The two major political parties agree on fundamentals; they offer alternative policies to the voters only on relatively small points of difference. Both parties favor full employment, but they define it somewhat differently; both favor the development of water power resources, but in slightly different ways; and both favor unemployment compensation, but not the same level of benefits. Similarly, shifts of policy within a party take place largely through a series of relatively small changes, as can be seen in their only gradual acceptance of the idea of governmental responsibility for support of the unemployed, a change in party positions beginning in the early 30's and culminating in a sense in the Employment Act of 1946.

Party behavior is in turn rooted in public attitudes, and political theorists cannot conceive of democracy's surviving in the United States in the absence of fundamental agreement on potentially disruptive issues, with consequent limitation of policy debates to relatively small differences in policy.

Since the policies ignored by the administrator are politically impossible and so irrelevant, the simplification of analysis achieved by concentrating on policies that differ only incrementally is not a capricious kind of simplification. In addition, it can be argued that, given the limits on knowledge within which policy-makers are confined, simplifying by limiting the focus to small variations from present policy makes the most of available knowledge. Because policies being considered are like present and past policies, the administrator can obtain information and claim some insight. Non-incremental policy proposals are therefore typically not only politically irrelevant but also unpredictable in their consequences.

[6] A more precise definition of incremental policies and a discussion of whether a change that appears "small" to one observer might be seen differently by another is to be found in my "Policy Analysis," 48 *American Economic Review* 298 (June, 1958).

The second method of simplification of analysis is the practice of ignoring important possible consequences of possible policies, as well as the values attached to the neglected consequences. If this appears to disclose a shocking shortcoming of successive limited comparisons, it can be replied that, even if the exclusions are random, policies may nevertheless be more intelligently formulated than through futile attempts to achieve a comprehensiveness beyond human capacity. Actually, however, the exclusions, seeming arbitrary or random from one point of view, need be neither.

Achieving a Degree of Comprehensiveness

Suppose that each value neglected by one policy-making agency were a major concern of at least one other agency. In that case, a helpful division of labor would be achieved, and no agency need find its task beyond its capacities. The shortcomings of such a system would be that one agency might destroy a value either before another agency could be activated to safeguard it or in spite of another agency's efforts. But the possibility that important values may be lost is present in any form of organization, even where agencies attempt to comprehend in planning more than is humanly possible.

The virtue of such a hypothetical division of labor is that every important interest or value has its watchdog. And these watchdogs can protect the interests in their jurisdiction in two quite different ways: first, by redressing damages done by other agencies; and, second, by anticipating and heading off injury before it occurs.

In a society like that of the United States in which individuals are free to combine to pursue almost any possible common interest they might have and in which government agencies are sensitive to the pressures of these groups, the system described is approximated. Almost every interest has its watchdog. Without claiming that every interest has a sufficiently powerful watchdog, it can be argued that our system often can assure a more comprehensive regard for the values of the whole society than any attempt at intellectual comprehensiveness.

In the United States, for example, no part of government attempts a comprehensive overview of policy on income distribution. A policy nevertheless evolves, and one responding to a wide variety of interests. A process of mutual adjustment among farm groups, labor unions, municipalities and school boards, tax authorities, and government agencies with responsibilities in the fields of housing, health, highways, national parks, fire, and police accomplishes a distribution of income in which particular income problems neglected at one point in the decision processes become central at another point.

Mutual adjustment is more pervasive than the explicit forms it takes in negotiation between groups; it persists through the mutual impacts of groups upon each other even where they are not in communication. For all the imperfections and latent dangers in this ubiquitous process of mutual adjustment, it will often accomplish an adaptation of policies to a wider range of interests than could be done by one group centrally.

Note, too, how the incremental pattern of policy-making fits with the multiple pressure pattern. For when decisions are only incremental—closely related to known policies, it is easier for one group to anticipate the kind of moves another might make and easier too for it to make correction for injury already accomplished.[7]

Even partisanship and narrowness, to use pejorative terms, will sometimes be assets to rational decision-making, for they can doubly insure that what one agency neglects, another will not; they specialize personnel to distinct points of view. The claim is valid that effective rational coordination of the federal administration, if possible to achieve at all, would require an agreed set of values [8]—if "rational" is defined as the practice of the root method of decision-making. But a high degree of administrative coordination occurs as each agency adjusts its policies to the concerns of the other agencies in the process of fragmented decision-making I have just described.

For all the apparent shortcomings of the incremental approach to policy alternatives with its arbitrary exclusion coupled with fragmentation, when compared to the root method, the branch method often looks far superior. In the root method, the inevitable exclusion of factors is accidental, unsystematic, and not defensible by any argument so far developed, while in the branch method the exclusions are deliberate, systematic, and defensible. Ideally, of course, the root method does not exclude; in practice it must.

Nor does the branch method necessarily neglect long-run considerations and objectives. It is clear that important values must be omitted in considering policy, and sometimes the only way long-run objectives can be given adequate attention is through the neglect of short-run considerations. But the values omitted can be either long-run or short-run.

SUCCESSION OF COMPARISONS (5B)

The final distinctive element in the branch method is that the comparisons, together with the policy choice, proceed in a chronological series. Policy is not made once and for all; it is made and re-made endlessly. Policy-making is a process of successive approximation to some

---

[7] The link between the practice of the method of successive limited comparisons and mutual adjustment of interests in a highly fragmented decision-making process adds a new facet to pluralist theories of government and administration.

[8] Herbert Simon, Donald W. Smithburg, and Victor A. Thompson, *Public Administration* (Alfred A. Knopf, 1950), p. 434.

desired objectives in which what is desired itself continues to change under reconsideration.

Making policy is at best a very rough process. Neither social scientists, nor politicians, nor public administrators yet know enough about the social world to avoid repeated error in predicting the consequences of policy moves. A wise policy-maker consequently expects that his policies will achieve only part of what he hopes and at the same time will produce unanticipated consequences he would have preferred to avoid. If he proceeds through a *succession* of incremental changes, he avoids serious lasting mistakes in several ways.

In the first place, past sequences of policy steps have given him knowledge about the probable consequences of further similar steps. Second, he need not attempt big jumps toward his goals that would require predictions beyond his or anyone else's knowledge, because he never expects his policy to be a final resolution of a problem. His decision is only one step, one that if successful can quickly be followed by another. Third, he is in effect able to test his previous predictions as he moves on to each further step. Lastly, he often can remedy a past error fairly quickly— more quickly than if policy proceeded through more distinct steps widely spaced in time.

Compare this comparative analysis of incremental changes with the aspiration to employ theory in the root method. Man cannot think without classifying, without subsuming one experience under a more general category of experiences. The attempt to push categorization as far as possible and to find general propositions which can be applied to specific situations is what I refer to with the word "theory." Where root analysis often leans heavily on theory in this sense, the branch method does not.

The assumption of root analysts is that theory is the most systematic and economical way to bring relevant knowledge to bear on a specific problem. Granting the assumption, an unhappy fact is that we do not have adequate theory to apply to problems in any policy area, although theory is more adequate in some areas—monetary policy, for example— than in others. Comparative analysis, as in the branch method, is sometimes a systematic alternative to theory.

Suppose an administrator must choose among a small group of policies that differ only incrementally from each other and from present policy. He might aspire to "understand" each of the alternatives—for example, to know all the consequences of each aspect of each policy. If so, he would indeed require theory. In fact, however, he would usually decide that, *for policy-making purposes,* he need know, as explained above, only the consequences of each of those aspects of the policies in which they differed from one another. For this much more modest aspiration, he requires no theory (although it might be helpful, if available), for he can proceed to isolate probable differences by examining the differences in consequences associated with past differences in policies, a feasible program because he can take his observations from a long sequence of incremental changes.

For example, without a more comprehensive social theory about juvenile delinquency than scholars have yet produced, one cannot possibly understand the ways in which a variety of public policies—say on education, housing, recreation, employment, race relations, and policing—might encourage or discourage delinquency. And one needs such an understanding if he undertakes the comprehensive overview of the problem prescribed in the models of the root method. If, however, one merely wants to mobilize knowledge sufficient to assist in a choice among a small group of similar policies—alternative policies on juvenile court procedures, for example—he can do so by comparative analysis of the results of similar past policy moves.

THEORISTS AND PRACTITIONERS

This difference explains—in some cases at least—why the administrator often feels that the outside expert or academic problem-solver is sometimes not helpful and why they in turn often urge more theory on him. And it explains why an administrator often feels more confident when "flying by the seat of his pants" than when following the advice of theorists. Theorists often ask the administrator to go the long way round to the solution of his problems, in effect ask him to follow the best canons of the scientific method, when the administrator knows that the best available theory will work less well than more modest incremental comparisons. Theorists do not realize that the administrator is often in fact practicing a systematic method. It would be foolish to push this explanation too far, for sometimes practical decision-makers are pursuing neither a theoretical approach nor successive comparisons, nor any other systematic method.

It may be worth emphasizing that theory is sometimes of extremely limited helpfulness in policy-making for at least two rather different reasons. It is greedy for facts; it can be constructed only through a great collection of observations. And it is typically insufficiently precise for application to a policy process that moves through small changes. In contrast, the comparative method both economizes on the need for facts and directs the analyst's attention to just those facts that are relevant to the fine choices faced by the decision-maker.

With respect to precision of theory, economic theory serves as an example. It predicts that an economy without money or prices would in certain specified ways misallocate resources, but this finding pertains to an alternative far removed from the kind of policies on which administrators need help. On the other hand, it is not precise enough to predict the consequences of policies restricting business mergers, and this is the kind of issue on which the administrators need help. Only in relatively restricted areas does economic theory achieve sufficient precision to go far in resolving policy questions; its helpfulness in policy-making is always so limited that it requires supplementation through comparative analysis.

SUCCESSIVE COMPARISON AS A SYSTEM

Successive limited comparisons is, then, indeed a method or system; it is not a failure of method for which administrators ought to apologize. Nonetheless, its imperfections, which have not been explored in this paper, are many. For example, the method is without a built-in safeguard for all relevant values, and it also may lead the decision-maker to overlook excellent policies for no other reason than that they are not suggested by the chain of successive policy steps leading up to the present. Hence, it ought to be said that under this method, as well as under some of the most sophisticated variants of the root method—operations research, for example—policies will continue to be as foolish as they are wise.

Why then bother to describe the method in all the above detail? Because it is in fact a common method of policy formulation, and is, for complex problems, the principal reliance of administrators as well as of other policy analysts.[9] And because it will be superior to any other decision-making method available for complex problems in many circumstances, certainly superior to a futile attempt at superhuman comprehensiveness. The reaction of the public administrator to the exposition of method doubtless will be less a discovery of a new method than a better acquaintance with an old. But by becoming more conscious of their practice of this method, administrators might practice it with more skill and know when to extend or constrict its use. (That they sometimes practice it effectively and sometimes not may explain the extremes of opinion on "muddling through," which is both praised as a highly sophisticated

---

[9] Elsewhere I have explored this same method of policy formulation as practiced by academic analysts of policy ("Policy Analysis," 48 *American Economic Review* 298 [June, 1958]). Although it has been here presented as a method for public administrators, it is no less necessary to analysts more removed from immediate policy questions, despite their tendencies to describe their own analytical efforts as though they were the rational-comprehensive method with an especially heavy use of theory. Similarly, this same method is inevitably resorted to in personal problem-solving, where means and ends are sometimes impossible to separate, where aspirations or objectives undergo constant development, and where drastic simplification of the complexity of the real world is urgent if problems are to be solved in the time that can be given to them. To an economist accustomed to dealing with the marginal or incremental concept in market processes, the central idea in the method is that both evaluation and empirical analysis are incremental. Accordingly I have referred to the method elsewhere as "the incremental method."

form of problem-solving and denounced as no method at all. For I suspect that in so far as there is a system in what is known as "muddling
through," this method is it).

One of the noteworthy incidental consequences of clarification of the
method is the light it throws on the suspicion an administrator sometimes
entertains that a consultant or adviser is not speaking relevantly and re-
sponsibly when in fact by all ordinary objective evidence he is. The
trouble lies in the fact that most of us approach policy problems within
a framework given by our view of a chain of successive policy choices
made up to the present. One's thinking about appropriate policies with
respect, say, to urban traffic control is greatly influenced by one's knowledge of the incremental steps taken up to the present. An administrator
enjoys an intimate knowledge of his past sequences that "outsiders" do
not share, and his thinking and that of the "outsider" will consequently
be different in ways that may puzzle both. Both may appear to be talking
intelligently, yet each may find the other unsatisfactory. The relevance
of the policy chain of succession is even more clear when an American
tries to discuss, say, antitrust policy with a Swiss, for the chains of policy
in the two countries are strikingly different and the two individuals consequently have organized their knowledge in quite different ways.

If this phenomenon is a barrier to communication, an understanding
of it promises an enrichment of intellectual interaction in policy formulation. Once the source of difference is understood, it will sometimes be
stimulating for an administrator to seek out a policy analyst whose recent
experience is with a policy chain different from his own.

This raises again a question only briefly discussed above on the merits
of like-mindedness among government administrators. While much of
organization theory argues the virtues of common values and agreed
organizational objectives, for complex problems in which the root method
is inapplicable, agencies will want among their own personnel two types
of diversification: administrators whose thinking is organized by reference to policy chains other than those familiar to most members of the
organization and, even more commonly, administrators whose professional or personal values or interests create diversity of view (perhaps
coming from different specialties, social classes, geographical areas) so
that, even within a single agency, decision-making can be fragmented
and parts of the agency can serve as watchdogs for other parts.

The Social Division of Welfare:

Some Reflections on the Search for Equity

Richard Morris Titmuss

I

Some students of social policy see the development of "The Welfare State" in historical perspective as part of a broad, ascending road of social betterment provided for the working classes since the nineteenth century and achieving its goal in our time. This interpretation of change as a process of unilinear progression in collective benevolence for these classes led to the belief that in the year 1948 "The Welfare State" was established. Since then, successive Governments, Conservative and Labour, have busied themselves with the more effective operation of the various services, with extensions here and adjustments there and both parties, in and out of office, have claimed the maintenance of "The Welfare State" as an article of faith.

On this view it could be supposed that speaking generally, Britain is approaching the end of the road of social reform; the road down which Eleanor Rathbone and other reformers and rebels laboured with vision and effect. This would seem to be the principal implication of much public comment on the social services during the past few years, and one which has received endorsement in policy statements of the Conservative and Labour parties.[1] An analysis of the more important writings on the subject since 1948 lends support, for the dominant note, far from suggesting that social needs have been neglected, has been that "The Wel-

[1] See, for example, *One Nation*, Conservative Political Centre, 1950, and *The Welfare State*, Labour Party Political Discussion Pamphlet, 1952.

Richard Morris Titmuss, "The Social Division of Welfare: Some Reflections on the Search for Equity," in *Essays on the Welfare State*, London, George Allen & Unwin, 1959, pp. 34–59. The Sixth Eleanor Rathbone Memorial Lecture, given at the University of Birmingham on December 1, 1955, and published by Liverpool University Press in 1956.

fare State" was "established" too quickly and on too broad a scale. The consequences, it is argued, have been harmful to the economic health of the nation and its "moral fibre."

Against this background, compounded of uneasiness and complacency, criticism has mainly focused on the supposedly equalitarian aims or effects of the social services. It is said that the relief of poverty or the maintenance of a national minimum as an objective of social policy should not mean the pursuit of equality; "a fascinating and modern development" for the social services according to Hagenbuch.[2] The Beveridge "revolution" did not, it is argued, imply an equalitarian approach to the solution of social problems. The error of welfare state policies since 1948 has been, according to this diagnosis, to confuse ends and means, and to pursue equalitarian aims with the result that the "burden" of redistribution from rich to poor has been pushed too far and is now excessive. Thus, the upper and middle classes have been impoverished, in part a consequence of providing benefits for those workers who do not really need them. "Why," asks Macleod and Powell, "should any social service be provided *without* [their italics] test of need?" [3] Their conclusion, like that of Hagenbuch in his analysis of "The Rationale of the Social Services" [4] and other writers, is that there should be a closer relationship between what people pay in and what they take out. Social security should be based on "more genuine" actuarial principles, while the ultimate objective for other social services should be "self-liquidation" as more and more people are raised above a minimum standard of living to a position of freedom in which they may purchase whatever medical care, education, training and other services they require. The mass of the people would thus, in time, come to behave like, if they do not resemble, the middle classes (who at present are presumed to derive little benefit from the social services). Pursued to its logical conclusion then, "The Welfare State" would eventually be transformed into "The Middle Class State." Meanwhile, social legislation and its application should recognize much more clearly than it does at present that (as Macleod and Powell put it) "the social services only exist for a portion of the population," [5] namely, that portion which takes out more than it puts in.

These views were tersely summed up by *The Economist* in June 1954, when it affirmed, as a guiding principle for social policy, that "no one should live on the taxpayer unless he needs to." [6] Already, "the social well-being of the nation had been endangered by the redistribution of

[2] Hagenbuch, W., *Lloyds Bank Review*, July 1953, p. 5.
[3] Macleod, I. and Powell, J. E., *The Social Services—Needs and Means*, 1949.
[4] Hagenbuch, W., *op. cit.*
[5] Macleod, I. and Powell, J. F., *op. cit.*, p. 4.
[6] *The Economist*, June 5, 1954, p. 783.

wealth," [7] a phrase which, according to a variety of social theorists, embraced more deeply-felt anxieties than a simple material concern about economic and fiscal trends. De Jouvenel, for example, drew attention to the "sordid utilitarianism" of redistributionist social services; to a "precipitous decline" in voluntary, unrewarded services upon which culture and civilization depends, and to a "tremendous growth" in the power of the State as a consequence of the rising cost of the social services.[8] At the same time, two popular books by Lewis and Maude rounded out the picture of a decaying, overworked and anxious middle class.[9] Finally, we may note the specific counter-proposals of two other critics. Ffrangcon Roberts has entered a vigorous plea for State medicine to return a business profit, and for the benefits of the National Health Service to be reserved for economically productive workers.[10] Colin Clark, foreseeing a totalitarian threat in the continued existence of the social services, would "denationalize" them and entrust some remnant of their functions to the Churches, local friendly societies and voluntary organizations.[11]

II

Whatever their validity in fact or theory, these views have had an important influence in shaping opinion since 1948 about the future of the social services. They have helped, no doubt unwittingly, to produce in the public eye something akin to a stereotype or image of an all-pervasive Welfare State for the Working Classes. Such is the tyranny of stereotypes today that this idea of a welfare society, born as a reaction against the social discrimination of the poor law may, paradoxically, widen rather than narrow class relationships. As Gerth and Mills have pointed out ". . . if the upper classes monopolize the means of communication and fill the several mass media with the idea that all those at the bottom are there because they are lazy, unintelligent, and in general inferior, then these appraisals may be taken over by the poor and used in the building of an image of their selves." [12] That is one danger in the spread of the

[7] This statement, expressing a widely-held view of the effects of social policy, appeared in *One Nation*, published by the Conservative Political Centre in 1950.

[8] De Jouvenel, B., *The Ethics of Redistribution*, 1951.

[9] The authors illustrate their theme by describing how middle-class leisure has been drastically reduced while that enjoyed by the working-class has increased (*The English Middle Classes*, 1949, p. 214 and *Professional People*, 1952, Lewis, R. and Maude, A.). This apparently undesirable happening (if it has happened) is not peculiar to this country. In the United States "there is a tendency among social scientists today, not mitigated by Kinsey, to think that the lower classes have all the fun, the middle classes all the miseries and inhibitions" (Denney, R. and Riesman, D. in *Creating an Industrial Civilization*, Ed. Staley, E., 1952).

[10] Roberts, F., *The Cost of Health*, 1952, pp. 134–7.

[11] Clark, C., *Welfare and Taxation*, 1954.

[12] Gerth, H. and Mills, C. W., *Character and Social Structure*, 1953, pp. 88–9.

"Welfare State" stereotype. A second emanates from the vague but often powerful fears that calamity will follow the relaxation of discipline and the mitigation of hardship which, in the eyes of the beholders, seems implicit in this notion of collective benevolence. Such fears inevitably conjure up a demand for punishment and reprisal; the history of public opinion in recent years on the subject of juvenile delinquency (to take one example) is suggestive of the operation of what Flugel called the "Polycrates complex." [13]

These brief observations on contemporary thinking about social policy are essential to the argument that follows; they constitute the political frame of reference. Nevertheless, they are a poor substitute for a close and detailed analysis of the critical views so summarily mentioned. Such an analysis would require many more words than one essay allows and must, therefore, be deferred. However, having set the stage in this general way, it is now proper to state the main purposes of this paper: first, to examine certain assumptions underlying these views; second, to outline the development of three major categories of social welfare and, third, to relate these developments to trends in the division of labour and the search for social equity. At the end, in drawing together these different threads, it emerges that much of the criticism and all the complacency about "The Welfare State" is either irrelevant or unbalanced and that we need to reexamine, by returning to first principles, current notions of what constitutes a social service.

First, however, it is necessary to bring into view certain assumptions, seldom made explicit, which run through practically all the recent critical writings on social policy. It is assumed:

Firstly, that the intended or declared aims of social policy since the Beveridge Report of 1942 have been wholly or largely achieved in the translation of legislation into action. In other words, that the performance of welfare has more or less fulfilled the promise of welfare.

Secondly, that the aggregate redistributive effects of social service activity since 1948 have wholly or largely represented a transfer of resources from rich to poor.

Thirdly, that in the present inadequate state of knowledge about the working of social institutions it is possible to define what is a "social service" and to identify, in each sector of State intervention, who has benefited and who has paid.

Fourthly, that it is practicable, desirable and has any meaning in a complex society undergoing rapid and widespread change to abstract a "social service world" from the Greater Society, and to consider the functions and effects of the part without reference to the life of the whole.

The first and second assumptions call, I would suggest, for a detailed study of the "unintended consequences" of social policy over the past

[13] Flugel, J. C., *Man, Morals and Society*, especially chapters 11 and 18, 1945.

decade. This cannot be attempted here.[14] I must content myself with making explicit the nature of these assumptions. In the following section, however, I examine certain facts relevant to the third and fourth assumptions.

III

All collectively provided services are deliberately designed to meet certain socially recognized "needs"; they are manifestations, first, of society's will to survive as an organic whole and, secondly, of the expressed wish of all the people to assist the survival of some people. "Needs" may therefore be thought of as "social" and "individual" as interdependent, mutually related essentials for the continued existence of the parts and the whole. No complete division between the two is conceptually possible; the shading of one into the other changes with time over the life of all societies; it changes with time over the cycle of needs of the individual and the family; and it depends on prevailing notions of what constitutes a "need" and in what circumstances; and to what extent, if at all, such needs, when recognized, should be met in the interests of the individual and/or of society.

When we apply these formulations to modern society we note the importance of definition. What is a "need"? What is a "service"? What was yesterday's conception of "need" and "service"? Of one thing at least we can be certain when all else is uncertain; the situation in which different kinds of need arise and are recognized as "needs" has changed and will continue to do so. The Britain of the 1950's is a very different society from the Britain of the 1900's. Not only are the "needs" and "situations" different but they are differently seen. The social-individual equation of need is a different equation and, again, it is differently seen. Freud for one, in undermining our psychological innocence, and Marx for another, in opening our eyes to economic realities, contributed to changing our perception of the equation. So have the infinite and cumulative processes of social and technological change since the end of the nineteenth century.

It is this period I want to consider particularly, for it is this period of roughly fifty years—the era of rising expectations—that has witnessed the emergence and growth of those forms of state intervention which, by custom and common approval, have come to be called "the social serv-

---

[14] A critical examination of the primary data used by A. M. Cartter (to quote only one recent attempt to measure the redistributionist effects of the social services) would serve to show how tenuous are the conclusions, commonly drawn, about the fiscal consequences of "The Welfare State" (Cartter, A. M., *The Redistribution of Income in Post-war Britain*, 1955). Much the same could be said when individual social schemes are considered (see, for example, Ch. 3 on pensions and superannuation).

ices." The development of these services from the welfare revolution of 1905–1914 under a reformist Liberal Government, through the experience of two world wars and mass unemployment, to the Beveridge "insurance revolution" and its aftermath has been amply documented in legislative detail. At the same time as the services themselves developed in scope and range, the term "social service" has come to be applied to more and more areas of collective provision for certain "needs." It has indeed acquired a most elastic quality; its expanding frontiers, formerly enclosing little besides poor relief, sanitation and public nuisances, now embrace a multitude of heterogeneous activities. For example, Boer War pensions and disablement benefits were officially classified as social services in 1920; the Universities and public museums were added after the Second World War. And so on. No consistent principle seems to obtain in the definition of what is a "social service."

The following simple examples, taken from the present Treasury classification,[15] give some indication of the area of confusion concealed by the assumptions of the critics of social policy,[16] and warn us of the dangers in any conception of a self-contained social service system expressly designed for the transmission of benefits from one income group of the population to another.

1. Approved Schools and remand homes are social services. The probation service is not.

2. Further Education and Training for ex-members of the Defence Forces is a social service. The Youth Employment Service is not.

3. The training of doctors is a social service. Marriage guidance services are not.

4. Pensions and allowances attributable to the Boer War and First World War are social services. Industrial health services are not.

5. The family allowance is a social service. The child allowance as remission of tax is not.

6. The investigation of legal aid applications is a social service. Legal aid grants are not.

7. Village halls and playing fields are social services. Cheap tobacco for old age pensioners is not.

8. Technological training and further education is a social service. Subsidized housing for miners is not.

9. Compensation to doctors for loss of right to sell medical practices is a social service. Noncontributory pensions and superannuation under occupational pension schemes are not.

[15] This classification relates to "social service" expenditure. (*Monthly Digest of Statistics*, Central Statistical Office, May 1955).

[16] It should also be noted that all the definitions employed by the various authorities mentioned in this essay differ very substantially, namely, those used by *The Economist*, Macleod and Powell, Hagenbuch, Cartter, De Jouvenel and Clark.

10. University education is a social service. The training of domestic workers is not.

When so much confusion exists (and these examples are but a selection from a large body of data) it is difficult to know precisely what it is that the critics are criticizing. The assumptions concealed behind such vague generalities as "the social services" and "The Welfare State" thus seem to be largely irrelevant. This becomes clearer when it is understood that those acts of state intervention which have somehow or other acquired the connotation of "social" have developed alongside a much broader area of intervention not thought of in such terms but having in common similar objectives. It is this differential development I want to emphasize: the growth in the social division of welfare in response to changing situations and conceptions of "need."

Considered as a whole, all collective interventions to meet certain needs of the individual and/or to serve the wider interests of society may now be broadly grouped into three major categories of welfare: social welfare, fiscal welfare, and occupational welfare. When we examine them in turn, it emerges that this division is not based on any fundamental difference in the functions of the three systems (if they may be so described) or their declared aims. It arises from an organizational division of method, which, in the main, is related to the division of labour in complex, individuated societies. So far as the ultimate aims of these systems are concerned, it is argued that their similarities are more important than their dissimilarities. The definition, for most purposes, of what is a "social service" should take its stand on aims; not on the administrative methods and institutional devices employed to achieve them.

The development in this century of our first category of welfare—that which commonly goes by the term "social service"—has already been mentioned. A major factor in this development should now be noted, for it has played a similarly important role in the growth of our two other categories of welfare.

With the gradual break-up of the old poor law, more "states of dependency" have been defined and recognized as collective responsibilities, and more differential provision has been made in respect of them. These "states of dependency" arise for the vast majority of the population whenever they are not in a position to "earn life" for themselves and their families; they are then dependent people. In industrialized societies there are many causes of dependency; they may be "natural" dependencies as in childhood, extreme old age and child-bearing. They may be caused by physical and psychological ill-health and incapacity; in part, these are culturally determined dependencies. Or they may be wholly or predominantly determined by social and cultural factors. These, it may be said, are the "man-made" dependencies. Apart from injury, disease and innate incapacity, they now constitute the major source of instability in the satisfaction of basic needs. They include unemployment and under-employment, protective and preventive legislation, compulsory retire-ment from work, the delayed entry of young people into the labour market, and an infinite variety of subtle cultural factors ranging from the "right" trade union ticket to the possession of an assortment of status symbols. All may involve to some degree the destruction, curtailment, interruption or frustration of earning power in the individual, and more pronounced secondary dependencies when they further involve the wives, children and other relatives.

In general, many of these culturally determined dependencies have grown in range and significance over the past century, partly as a result of a process of cumulative survivorship, for those who experience such states of dependency do not now die as others did before the twentieth century. The total of current needs may be higher because of a propor-tionately higher representation of survivors of past dependency-creating experiences—wars, unemployments, injuries, enforced family separations and so forth. Apart, however, from the effects of this process, the domi-nating operative factor has been the increasing division of labour in society and, simultaneously, a great increase in labour specificity. This is perhaps one of the outstanding social characteristics of the twentieth century; the fact that more and more people consciously experience at one or more stages in their lives the process of selection and rejection; for education, for work, for vocational training, for professional status, for promotion, for opportunities of access to pension schemes, for collec-tive social benefits, for symbols of prestige and success, and in undergoing tests of mental and physical fitness, personality, skill and functional per-formance.[17] In some senses at least, the arbiters of opportunity and of dependency have become, in their effects, more directly personal, more culturally demanding, more psychologically threatening. There are more roles for the super-ego to play as one's appreciation of reality becomes more accurate.

We cannot, however, pursue here the deeper psychological implica-tions of this trend, implied but not described in detail by Durkheim when he observed that as man becomes more individual and more spe-cialized he becomes more socially dependent.[18] This is of primary im-portance in understanding the development of systems of welfare; this

[17] The assessment of specific labour skills now includes, in addition to the standard intelligence tests which attempt to measure verbal ability, visualization and numerical skill, such concepts as tone discrimination, accident proneness, taste sensitivity, colour blindness, digital dexterity, analogizing power, mechanical and clerical aptitude, and mental maturity. (See Caplow, T., The Sociology of Work, 1954.)
[18] Durkheim, E., The Division of Labour in Society, trans. G. Simpson, 1933, p. 131.

and the fact that, simultaneously, man becomes more aware of what has caused his dependency, and thus more exposed to uncertainty and conflict about the purposes and roles he himself is expected to fulfil. More self-knowledge of the "man-made" causes of dependency has been reflected in social policies through the greater recognition accorded to individual dependencies and their social origins and effects. It has also influenced the growth of our other categories of welfare.

I now turn, therefore, to consider these notions in relation to the development of fiscal welfare and occupational welfare.

IV

Under separately administered social security systems, like family allowances and retirement pensions, direct cash payments are made in discharging collective responsibilities for particular dependencies. In the relevant accounts, these are treated as "social service" expenditure since they represent flows of payments through the central government account. Allowances and reliefs from income tax, though providing similar benefits and expressing a similar social purpose in the recognition of dependent needs, are not, however, treated as social service expenditure. The first is a cash transaction; the second an accounting convenience. Despite this difference in administrative method, the tax saving that accrues to the individual is, in effect, a transfer payment.[19] In their primary objectives and their effects on individual purchasing power there are no differences in these two ways by which collective provision is made for dependencies.[20] Both are manifestations of social policies in

[19] As Cartter observed: "By reducing the tax liability of a person with dependents the State is sharing in the responsibility of caring for each taxpayer's family just as certainly as if it were paying cash allowances in each case." (Cartter, A. M., "Income-Tax Allowances and the Family in Great Britain," *Population Studies*, Vol. VI, No. 3, 1953, p. 219.) Other authorities also take the view that no distinction can be made between implicit and explicit transfer payments; see, for example, United Nations, *Economic Bulletin for Europe*, Vol. 4, No. 2, 1952; Haynes, A. T. and Kirton, R. J., "Income Tax in Relation to Social Security," *Journal of the Institute of Actuaries*, Vol. LXXII, Pt. 1, No. 333, 1944, pp. 83–5; and *Samordning Af De Nordiske Landes Statistik Vedrorende Den Sociale Lovgivning*, Copenhagen, 1955, reporting the agreement of the five Northern Countries that "tax deductions are quite analogous to . . . allowances in cash." Though the Royal Commission on the Taxation of Profits and Income did not address itself directly to this question there are innumerable references in the 612 pages of its Second and Final Reports which support this approach. Thus, in discussing relief for charities costing around £35m. a year, the Commission observes that this "does amount in effect to a grant of public moneys." (*Final Report*, Cmd 9474, 1955, p. 55; also *Second Report*, Cmd 9105, 1954.)

[20] Pigou recognized this in his *The Economics of Welfare* (4th ed. 1932, p. 98) when he wrote of tax relief for children as "deliberate and overt bounties" for large families. Curiously, however, the similarity of these reliefs to family allowances seems to have escaped Eleanor Rathbone.

favour of identified groups in the population and both reflect changes in public opinion in regard to the relationship between the State, the individual and the family.

Since the introduction of progressive taxation in 1907 there has been a remarkable development of social policy operating through the medium of the fiscal system. This has chiefly taken the form of increasing support for the family through the recognition of more types of dependencies and substantial additions to the value of the benefits provided. Another important aspect of this development is that, originally, these dependants' benefits were deliberately restricted to the lowest paid sections of the income tax population; in the course of time these restrictions have disappeared. The Royal Commission on Taxation now propose that such benefits should be allowed in the calculation of liability to surtax.[21]

A brief historical sketch of the main features of fiscal welfare shows the growth in public concern and responsibility for "states of dependency," family and kinship relationships, individual "self-improvement" and standards of "minimum subsistence" among income taxpayers. It shows too, as W. Friedmann has pointed out, the extent to which Taxation Acts are now regarded as social purpose Acts; [22] that taxation has more or less ceased to be regarded as an impertinent intrusion into the sacred rights of private property and that, for the purposes of social policy, it can no longer be thought of simply as a means of benefiting the poor at the expense of the rich.[23]

A child allowance of £10 for all children aged under 16 for those—as a "special consideration [24]—whose incomes were under £500 was introduced in 1909; thus ante-dating by thirty-seven years family allowances for second and subsequent children.[25] This has gradually risen (through thirteen changes to £100 in 1955.[26] The income qualification was raised in 1916, 1918 and 1919 and finally extended to all taxpayers in 1920. The allowance has been further developed to include children receiving full-time education at a university or other educational establishment for the reason that, in the words of the Royal Commission, "the child's immediate

---

[21] *Second Report,* Cmd 9105, 1954, p. 56.

[22] Friedmann, W., *Law and Social Change in Contemporary Britain,* 1954, p. 262.

[23] This would seem to be the implication of Professor Lewis' article "A Socialist Economic Policy," in *Socialist Commentary* (June, 1955, p. 171), and of Professor Robbins' criticisms of progressive taxation ("Notes on Public Finance," *Lloyds Bank Review,* October 1955).

[24] The Chancellor of the Exchequer in his Budget Speech, 1909, *Hansard,* Vol. IV, cols. 507–8.

[25] Thus, fiscal policy supports the first child in all circumstances; social welfare policy only does so when the parents are sick or unemployed.

[26] The 1909 benefit represented, at the maximum, an annual tax saving of 7s. 6d. per child. The corresponding figure for 1955 (earned income £2000) is approximately £48.

earning capacity has been foregone in order that he should qualify himself for work on a higher level in the future." [27] Social policy has thus been extended beyond the confines of support for childhood dependency to the support of individual "self-improvement." These allowances are given regardless of education and scholarship awards.[28] The Royal Commission now propose a further major development, namely, that the allowance should vary with the size of the taxpayer's income up to a limit of £160 for all income and surtax payers, and that such allowance should continue to the age of twenty-one for all "incapacitated" children.[29] The estimated cost of the existing allowances in 1955–1956 was £200 m.,[30] covering broadly about half the child population. We may illustrate these differences in social policy by considering the respective awards to two married men, one earning £2000 a year and one earning £400 a year. Both have two children aged under fifteen. The first father now receives an annual net bounty of £97; the second one of £28.[31] Over the lives of the two families the former will receive a total of £1455 and the latter a total of £422.[32] If the Royal Commission's proposal is adopted the bounty for the first father will rise to over £2200. The fact that already the child bounty rises steeply with increasing income appears to have been overlooked by Professor Robbins in his plea that, to "eliminate some of the injustices of progression," these allowances should be provided "in some measure proportionate to the expenses of the income group into which they are born." [33]

Equally fascinating to the sociologist is the story of when and why wives were recognized in this system of social welfare (significantly enough in 1918); aged, incapacitated and infirm kinship dependents;

[27] *Second Report,* p. 55. Or as Talcott Parsons puts it: "The development of adaptive socialized anxiety in middle-status life is all the more essential because the social and prestige rewards of this status must necessarily be postponed during the prolonged training of the child and adolescent for high skills and complex responsibilities." (Parsons, Talcott, cited in *The Sociology of Work,* Caplow, T., 1954.)

[28] The scale of assessing parents' contributions for state scholarships laid down by the Ministry of Education further increases the total benefit for taxpayers. It does so by allowing as deductions from income, superannuation contributions and life assurance payments up to a specified proportion of income. National insurance contributions are not allowable (see *Report of Working Party on Grants to Training College Students,* 1955, p. 21).

[29] Pp. 56–61.

[30] Information supplied by the Treasury (letter November 9, 1955).

[31] The basis of this calculation is a comparison, in both cases, with a married man without children. It assumes earned income, and takes account of family allowances, national insurance contributions (including tax treatment), earned income allowance and personal allowances. The rates used are for 1955–1956.

[32] If the first father happens to be a University don or eligible for an employer's child allowance scheme of £50 per child per year his total bounty is further increased.

[33] Robbins, L., "Notes on Public Finance," *Lloyds Bank Review,* October 1955, p. 12.

housekeepers according to particular situations of family need; widowed mothers; incapacitated wives; unmarried daughters assisting infirm taxpayers; "unmarried wives" and children of deceased members of the Forces; mourning costs (under Estate Duty); old age; professional "self-improvement"; [34] divorced wives,[35] unemployed taxpayers (loss of office compensation); married women at work (first introduced in 1920 in recognition of "extra household expenses"); [36] housekeepers for professional women on full-time work, and as a "special indulgence" for poorer taxpayers and those with precarious incomes finding it difficult to save for their dependents and for old age,[37] life assurance and superannuation allowances.[38] The latter benefit, though partly attributable to developments in fiscal policy, would seem to be more logically classified under "occupational welfare." It is, therefore, discussed under this head.

Underlying all these individual stories of the growth in fiscal welfare policies is a continuous search for a reasonable "subsistence minimum"

[34] Partly through benefits up to age 21; partly through relief for professional training expenses, and partly through the provision of "added years" in increased superannuation benefits. These "added years" are intended to cover years of professional training during which superannuation contributions were not paid (see, for example, *Local Government Superannuation (Benefits) Regulations*, 1954, Reg. 12).

[35] "A super-tax payer may and quite frequently nowadays does have a number of wives living at the same time since after divorce his ex-wives are not treated as one with him for tax purposes he can manage quite nicely since he is permitted to deduct all his wives' maintenance allowances from his gross income for tax purposes leaving his net income comparatively slightly affected." (Memorandum by Lord Justice Hodson to the Royal Commission on Marriage and Divorce, MDP/1952/-337.)

[36] *Second Report*, pp. 39–40. The allowance rose from a maximum of £45 in 1920 to, in effect, £172 in 1954. On grounds of social policy apparently the Royal Commission thought the present figure excessive.

[37] *Report of the Royal Commission on the Income Tax*, Cmd 615, 1920, para. 296.

[38] The conditions laid down for the right to these various fiscal benefits are mostly far more generous and pay more regard to the social realities of kinship relationships than those specified in the National Insurance Scheme. They merit an anthropological analysis. Under the former, for instance, widows can claim a housekeeper's benefit while, under the latter, elderly widows found by the Ministry to be "cohabiting" with elderly men have their pensions withdrawn. The fiscal benefit for adult dependents does not stipulate residence with the claimant; the corresponding National Insurance benefit does. Dependent relatives by marriage are covered for fiscal benefits; they are not prescribed under the Unemployment and Sickness Regulations (see also Section 24 of the National Insurance Act, 1946). There is no limit to the number of dependent relatives for whom fiscal benefits can be claimed; under the National Insurance scheme claimants are allowed only one dependent relative. If, however, payment is made for a dependent wife even one dependant relative is not admissible. The definition of a dependent relative for whom fiscal benefits can be claimed is wide enough to include almost any relative; for National Insurance purposes there is a narrowly prescribed list of kinship relationships. Moreover, male relatives must prove incapacity. This means that benefits can be claimed for a daughter at a University (though she must not earn more than 20s. a week in the vacations or at any other time) but not for a son.

for income tax payers.[39] It was needed as a basis for the various benefits, for fixing exemption limits and for determining the extent to which a taxpayer's kinship relationships and particular states of need should be recognized. This problem is, however, part of a much more fundamental one which has plagued the Royal Commissions after both world wars of reconciling, on the one hand, the imperious demands of preferential social policies with, on the other, "a general equitable principle" of fairness and progression in assessing individual taxable capacity.[40] This duality of roles is the major source of conflict and confusion. The more that the uniqueness of individual needs and dependencies is recognized and relieved in an occupational society based on individual rewards the more may principles of individual equity fall into disrepute. Since 1920, the concept of individualism in direct taxation has increasingly become more tenuous. For both Royal Commissions, the claims of social policy have overruled the claims of individual equity.[41] As a result, the cost of dependant's benefits has risen from a negligible figure in the early 1920's to over £425 m. today.[42] This compares with a total net cost to the Exchequer in 1954–1955 of £770 m. for all direct cash payments under national insurance, industrial injuries, family allowances, national assistance and noncontributory pensions.[43]

V

During the period that has witnessed these far-reaching developments in social and fiscal welfare benefits there has also occurred a great expansion in occupational welfare benefits in cash and in kind. They have now

[39] Not the least remarkable aspect of this search is the complete absence of any reference in all the relevant reports to the simultaneous search for a "subsistence minimum" as a basis for social welfare policies from 1920 to the Beveridge Report and subsequently. (See, for example, *Second Report*, p. 50 and Shehab, F., *Progressive Taxation*, 1953, especially pp. 260–6.)

[40] Cmd 9474, p. 21.

[41] The 1920 Commission concluded "that in all ranges of income some regard should be had to the taxpayer's marital and family responsibilities." (Pt. II, p. 29.) The 1954 Commission went further in their recommendations: ". . . their general tendency is to advocate that the tax scheme should recognize variations of individual circumstance more fully than it does at present." (*Second Report*, p. 25.) It therefore proposed, *inter alia*, a substantial disability benefit without test of means; an automatic infirmity benefit for all taxpayers at age seventy-five again without any test; a dependant relatives' allowance for deserted wives and mothers without proof of incapacity; an extension of the housekeeper allowance to cover non-resident child care services; universal superannuation benefits and so forth (p. 70).

[42] Including only child allowance, dependant relative allowance, age relief, housekeeper allowance, life assurance relief and wife's earned income relief. (Letter from Treasury, November 9, 1955).

[43] Central Statistical Office, *National Income and Expenditure*, 1955, table 37.

reached formidable and widespread proportions as the Final Report of the Royal Commission recognized.[44] Their ultimate cost falls in large measure on the Exchequer. They include pensions for employees, wives and dependants; child allowances; death benefits; health and welfare services; personal expenses for travel, entertainment, dress and equipment; meal vouchers; motor cars and season tickets; residential accommodation; holiday expenses; children's school fees; sickness benefits; medical expenses; education and training grants; cheap meals; unemployment benefit; medical bills [45] and an incalculable variety of benefits in kind ranging from "obvious forms of realizable goods to the most intangible forms of amenity." [46] The implications of this trend are cautiously noted by the Royal Commission: "Modern improvements in the conditions of employment and the recognition by employers of a wide range of obligations towards the health, comfort and amenities of their staff may well lead to a greater proportion of an employee's true remuneration being expressed in a form that is neither money nor convertible into money." [47]

A substantial part of all these multifarious benefits can be interpreted as the recognition of dependencies; the dependencies of old age, of sickness and incapacity, of childhood, widowhood and so forth. They are in effect, if not in administrative method, "social services," duplicating and overlapping social and fiscal welfare benefits. The rapidity of their growth in recent years has increasingly diminished the value and relevance of salary, wage and income statistics. Occupational pension schemes, to give one example of the present order of provision, may now cover one-half of the total male labour force (excluding agriculture).[48] Their cost to the Exchequer (including tax-free deferred salaries) already runs to £100 m. a year,[49] a figure substantially in excess of the present Exchequer cost of

[44] Pp. 67–75 and 410–2. In the 1955 Chance Memorial Lecture on "Welfare in Industry," Mr. H. V. Potter gave estimates of the total cost to industry in Britain of what he called "the social indirect services." These estimates, for twenty-two million employees, ranged from £550 m. to £880 m. a year (excluding national insurance contributions and statutory holiday payments). They also appear to exclude many of the items listed below involving individual benefits such as personal expenses, car allowances and so forth. (Potter, H. V., *Chemistry and Industry*, September, 1955, pp. 5–7.)

[45] To give evidence on one point: according to a statement in the *British Medical Journal*, 25 percent of all medical bills at one "leading nursing-home" are paid for their employees by firms. (*Journal Supplement*, October 8, 1955, p. 81.)

[46] P. 68.

[47] P. 72.

[48] For more details see Ch. 3. See also *Report of the Committee on the Economic and Financial Problems of the Provision for Old Age* (Cmd 9333, 1954) and Abel-Smith, B., and Townsend, P., *New Pensions for the Old*, 1955.

[49] In addition, life assurance relief was costing the Exchequer £35 m. in 1955–1956. (Letter from Treasury, November 9, 1955.)

national insurance pensions.[50] Contrary to the apparent intentions of the 1920 Royal Commission, which considered tax relief for such schemes appropriate for poorer taxpayers, the benefits have increasingly favoured wealthier taxpayers, through the medium of tax-free lump sums and other devices.[51] In this sense, they function as concealed multipliers of occupational success. Sick pay and other "social service" benefits have followed a similar upward trend. A recent official sample inquiry tentatively suggested that about half the claimants for national insurance sickness benefit were also covered by employer's sick pay schemes, the proportion ranging from one-third among manual workers to 90 percent for administrators.[52] Adding these benefits together, sickness is now a better financial proposition for many people than health.

No doubt many of these forms of occupational social services express the desire for "good human relations" in industry. Their provision is part of the model of the "good" employer.[53] But as they grow and multiply they come into conflict with the aims and unity of social policy; for in effect (whatever their aims may be) their whole tendency at present is to divide loyalties, to nourish privilege, and to narrow the social conscience as they have already done in the United States, in France and in Western Germany.[54] One fundamental question of equity that they raise (which is analogous to that raised by the dual roles of fiscal policy) is whether and to what extent social service dependency benefits should be proportionately related to occupational and income achievement. That is a question which, along with others, must be left unexamined in this paper.

VI

Three different systems of "social services" have been briefly surveyed in this paper. Considered as a whole, their development shows how narrowly conceived and unbalanced are the criticisms so frequently levelled

---

[50] See Ch. 3, p. 69.

[51] If the far-reaching proposals for extended benefits of the Millard Tucker Report are accepted—a State Paper which ranks in importance with the Beveridge Report—the cost of these benefits might well double in a few years, particularly as the Report insists that they "should not depend on a 'means test.'" (*Report of the Committee on the Taxation Treatment of Provisions for Retirement*, Cmd 9063, 1954, p. 101.)

[52] The great majority of these schemes were noncontributory. The inquiry was made by the Ministry of Pensions and National Insurance into a 5 percent sample of new claims for benefit in September, 1953. The results are probably subject to a substantial margin of error. (*Report of the National Insurance Advisory Committee on the Question of Benefit for Short Spells of Unemployment or Sickness*, 1955, paras. 73–5.)

[53] The Conservative Party advocates a wide extension in these schemes. (*The Industrial Charter. A Statement of Conservative Industrial Policy*, 1947, p. 30.)

[54] See United States Chamber of Commerce, *Fringe Benefits 1953*, and United Nations, *Economic Bulletin for Europe*, 1952, Vol. 4, No. 2.

at the one system traditionally known as "the social services" or, more recently and more ambiguously, as "The Welfare State." The latent assumptions which commonly underlie these criticisms can, therefore, have little relevance while they remain attached to a stereotype of social welfare which represents only the more visible part of the real world of welfare. The social history of our times inevitably becomes, in the process, sadly distorted.

At present, these three systems are seen to operate as virtually distinct stratified systems. What goes on within and as a result of one system is ignored by the others. They are appraised, criticized or applauded as abstracted, independent, entities.[55] Yet, despite this division, they all in varying degrees signify that man can no longer be regarded simply as a "unit of labour power"; they all reflect contemporary opinion that man is not wholly responsible for his dependency, and they all accept obligations for meeting certain dependent needs of the individual and the family. Nevertheless, despite these common social purposes, the search for equity between taxpayers—that like cases should be treated in like manner—proceeds regardless of the need for equity between citizens. The drive to "buy" good human relations in industry widens class and vocational divisions through the provision of differential welfare benefits based on occupational achievement. The lack of any precise thinking about what is and what is not a "social service" confuses and constrains the social conscience, and allows the development of distinctive social policies based on different principles for arbitrarily differentiated groups in the population.

Behind the facts of this development we can see the play of powerful economic and political forces; the strength and tenacity of privilege; the continuing search for equity in a rapidly changing society. Conceptions of "need" and "dependency" have simultaneously been profoundly affected by technological, industrial and social change—"the gales of creative destruction" to use Schumpeter's striking phrase.[56] The problems of equity in social policy have thus become more complex as a result of the accumulation of long-lived "disservices"; [57] the increasing division of labour; higher standards of labour specificity; the lengthening of the "natural"

---

[55] The Beveridge Report paid no particular regard to fiscal welfare benefits; the Reports of the Royal Commission on Taxation in discussing social policies virtually ignore the commonly termed "social services," and the Phillips Committee disregard fiscal benefits even to the extent of suggesting that the development of occupational pension schemes might reduce pension costs falling on the Exchequer (Cmd 9333, p. 64).

[56] Schumpeter, J. A., *Capitalism, Socialism and Democracy*, p. 84.

[57] Pigou developed systematically the notion of "uncharged disservices" and "uncompensated services" in his *The Economics of Welfare* (4th ed., 1932). For a discussion on trends and a more detailed treatment generally see Kapp, K. W., *The Social Costs of Private Enterprise*, 1950.

dependencies of childhood and old age; the diversification, creation and decay of functional skills and roles; and the growth of sectional solidarities which, in turn, have tended to enlarge the area and significance of social differentiation. More social differentiation—whether by age, class, education, personality, physical standards, intelligence quotient or professional qualification—may result, as G. Friedmann has observed, in more social inequalities.[58] Failure, ineffectiveness and social inferiority thus acquire a deeper significance. External inequalities—those which do not express natural inequalities—become "more insupportable as labour becomes more divided." [59] More insight into the complexities of human stress allied to the tendency of special groups to become more self-conscious leads to the search for sectional equalities. Insofar as they are achieved, the interests of society as a whole at one extreme, and of the "unattached" and dependent individual at the other, are subordinated to the interests of the group or class. The aims of equity, ostensibly set for society as a whole, become sectional aims, invariably rewarding the most favoured in proportion to the distribution of power and occupational success.

At the centre of this process of division based on the specialized content of individual occupational performance man becomes more dependent; he also becomes, in the pursuit of individual life goals, more aware of his dependency, more viable to failure, more exposed to pain.[60] The corollary for any society which invests more of its values and virtues in the promotion of the individual is individual failure and individual consciousness of failure.

Within this theoretical framework it becomes possible to interpret the development of these three systems of social service as separate and distinctive attempts to counter and to compensate for the growth of dependency in modern society. Yet, as at present organized, they are simultaneously enlarging and consolidating the area of social inequality. That is the paradox: the new division of equity which is arising from these separate responses to social change. And that, today, is the real challenge to social policy and to those who, mistakingly, still look to the past for a solution.

[58] Friedmann, G., "The Social Consequences of Technical Progress," *International Social Science Bulletin*, Vol. IV, No. 2, 1952, p. 254.
[59] Durkheim, *op. cit.*, pp. 384–5.
[60] For extended theoretical treatment, see Durkheim, E., *op. cit.*

Section II

Welfare Organizations in the Community

Part A

The Community Context of Welfare Organizations

THE growth of the so-called welfare state is, to a considerable extent, a history of the increased importance of federal legislation and of federally administered welfare programs. Nevertheless, considerable variation exists between communities in the structure and quality of welfare services. Most professionals in the welfare field, especially at the agency-executive level, are continually confronted with the problem of developing community support for their own agencies and support for broader welfare goals. The articles in this section develop the theme of the environmental limits and supports for welfare programs. The selections deal with the variation among communities in the provision of welfare services, with the bases of support that exist for different organizations within a community, and with the problems of interagency coordination and cooperation. The articles in this part on "The Community Context of Welfare Organizations," examine the implications for welfare of variations in community structure.

Because of the pluralism and even fragmentation of power in the United States and in our local communities, and because the welfare arena is always short of money, the agency executive who is going to promote his agency has to look to the larger community for support. If there is an elite group interested in his program he must use this group to build general community support. If there is no elite group interested in his program or, for that matter, interested in the community, he must create one! Norton Long's article, "The Local Community as an Ecology of Games," suggests the complexity and fragmentation of the local scene. Long uses the game analogy to suggest that in a community there are a number of different goals being sought by a wide range of players. Each organization and its supporting groups may be involved in several "moves" at the same time. That is, many welfare organizations are competing for resources and are trying to develop their own programs concurrently. Sometimes these games are mutually beneficial; but, at other times, one organization has to win and another has to lose.

The fact that there is a multiplicity of games going on in any medium-to-large city is readily determined. But does this multiplicity necessarily imply irrationality or lack of progress in achieving welfare goals? It may be that progress in the ecology of games is at a snail's pace. But only if the games, as played, retard implementation of welfare values are the games fully futile. Who wins the games is what counts.

In "A Typology for Comparative Local Government," Oliver Williams suggests that the results of welfare games depend on the structure of business and political elites in any community and on the ethos embodied by each of these groups. Williams is especially interested in the ethos, or guiding values, subscribed to by the dominant groups in a community. This ethos directs the activities of the elites and helps account for the variations in welfare services found in so many communities. Williams distinguishes four dominant types of ethos that he has observed in local communities: promotion of economic growth, providing life's amenities, maintaining traditional services, and arbitrating conflict. Each of these approaches leads to differences in community services.

Williams' analysis suggests that the socioeconomic and occupational composition of a community affects its welfare standards. In "Local Industrial Structures, Economic Power, and Community Welfare," Irving Fowler measures the extent to which differences in industrial base, in power structure, and in dominant political philosophy do, indeed, affect the level of living in a community. Fowler's definition of welfare is somewhat different from that employed in this volume (he focuses on the average level of living, not on the minimum standards). Nevertheless, he shows that the over-all level of living is related to the differences in the industrial and social structure of the community. Fowler explodes the notion that the presence of large absentee-owned businesses in a community is bad for the over-all welfare of the community (the presence of absentee-owned businesses may be bad for the funding of voluntary agencies).

Although the first three articles deal with the effect of community services on provision of welfare, the fourth article by Albert Rose, "The Social

Services in the Modern Metropolis," discusses the implications of urban change for welfare policy and organization. After summarizing the scope of ecological and demographic change that is taking place in large metropolises, Rose questions what these changes mean for the operation of welfare organizations. He proposes a number of modifications, designed to make welfare organizations more adaptive to the needs of the community.

The Local Community as an Ecology of Games

Norton E. Long

The local community whether viewed as a polity, an economy, or a society presents itself as an order in which expectations are met and functions performed. In some cases, as in a new, company-planned mining town, the order is the willed product of centralized control, but for the most part the order is the product of a history rather than the imposed effect of any central nervous system of the community. For historic reasons we readily conceive the massive task of feeding New York to be achieved through the unplanned, historically developed cooperation of thousands of actors largely unconscious of their collaboration to this individually unsought end. The efficiency of this system is attested to by the extraordinary difficulties of the War Production Board and Service of Supply in accomplishing similar logistical objectives through an explicit system of orders and directives. Insofar as conscious rationality plays a role, it is a function of the parts rather than the whole. Particular structures working for their own ends within the whole may provide their members with goals, strategies, and roles that support rational action. The results of the interaction of the rational strivings after particular ends are in part collectively functional if unplanned. All this is the well-worn doctrine of Adam Smith, though one need accept no more of the doctrine of beneficence than that an unplanned economy can function.

While such a view is accepted for the economy, it is generally rejected for the polity. Without a sovereign, Leviathan is generally supposed to disintegrate and fall apart. Even if Locke's more hopeful view of the naturalness of the social order is taken, the polity seems more of a contrived artifact than the economy. Furthermore, there is both the hangover of Austinian sovereignty and the Greek view of ethical primacy to make political institutions seems different in kind and ultimately inclusive in purpose and for this reason to give them an over-all social directive end.

Norton E. Long, "The Local Community as an Ecology of Games," *American Journal of Sociology*, LXIV, 1958, pp. 251–261. This paper is largely based on a year of field study in the Boston Metropolitan area made possible by grants from the Stern Family Foundation and the Social Science Research Council. The opinions and conclusions expressed are those of the author alone.

To see political institutions as the same kind of thing as other institutions in society rather than as different, superior, and inclusive (both in the sense of being sovereign and ethically more significant) is a form of relativistic pluralism that is difficult to entertain. At the local level, however, it is easier to look at the municipal government, its departments, and the agencies of state and national government as so many institutions, resembling banks, newspapers, trade unions, chambers of commerce, churches, etc., occupying a territorial field and interacting with one another. This interaction can be conceptualized as a system without reducing the interacting institutions and individuals to membership in any single comprehensive group. It is psychologically tempting to envision the local territorial system as a group with a governing "they." This is certainly an existential possibility and one to be investigated. However, frequently, it seems likely, systems are confused with groups, and our primitive need to explain thunder with a theology or a demonology results in the hypostatizing of an angelic or demonic hierarchy. The executive committee of the bourgeoisie and the power elite make the world more comfortable for modern social scientists as the Olympians did for the ancients. At least the latter-day hypothesis, being terrestrial, is in principle researchable, though in practice its metaphysical statement may render it equally immune to mundane inquiry.

Observation of certain local communities makes it appear that inclusive over-all organization for many general purposes is weak or non-existent. Much of what occurs seems to just happen with accidental trends becoming cumulative over time and producing results intended by nobody. A great deal of the communities' activities consist of undirected co-operation of particular social structures, each seeking particular goals and, in doing so, meshing with others. While much of this might be explained in Adam Smith's terms, much of it could not be explained with a rational, atomistic model of calculating individuals. For certain purposes the individual is a useful way of looking at people; for many others the role-playing member of a particular group is more helpful. Here we deal with the essence of predictability in social affairs. If we know the game being played is baseball and that X is a third baseman, by knowing his position and the game being played we can tell more about X's activities on the field than we could if we examined X as a psychologist or a psychiatrist. If such were not the case, X would belong in the mental ward rather than in a ball park. The behavior of X is not some disembodied rationality but, rather, behavior within an organized group activity that has goals, norms strategies, and roles that give the very field and ground for rationality. Baseball structures the situation.

It is the contention of this paper that the structured group activities that coexist in a particular territorial system can be looked at as games. These games provide the players with a set of goals that give them a sense of success or failure. They provide them determinate roles and calculable strategies and tactics. In addition, they provide the players with an elite and general public that is in varying degrees able to tell the score. There is a good deal of evidence to be found in common parlance that many participants in contemporary group structures regard their occupations as at least analogous to games. And, at least in the American culture, and not only since Eisenhower, the conception of being on a "team" has been fairly widespread.

Unfortunately, the effectiveness of the term "game" for the purposes of this paper is vitiated by, first, the general sense that games are trivial occupations and, second, by the pre-emption of the term for the application of a calculus of probability to choice or decision in a determinate game situation. Far from regarding games as trivial, the writer's position would be that man is both a game-playing and a game-creating animal, that his capacity to create and play games and take them deadly seriously is of the essence, and that it is through games or activities analogous to game-playing that he achieves a satisfactory sense of significance and a meaningful role.

While the calculability of the game situation is important, of equal or greater importance is the capacity of the game to provide a sense of purpose and a role. The organizations of society and polity produce satisfactions with both their products and their processes. The two are not unrelated, but, while the production of the product may in the larger sense enable players and onlookers to keep score, the satisfaction in the process is the satisfaction of playing the game and the sense in which any activity can be grasped as a game.

Looked at this way, in the territorial system there is a political game, a banking game, a contracting game, a newspaper game, a civic organization game, an ecclesiastical game, and many others. Within each game there is a well-established set of goals whose achievement indicates success or failure for the participants, a set of socialized roles making participant behavior highly predictable, a set of strategies and tactics handed down through experience and occasionally subject to improvement and change, an elite public whose approbation is appreciated, and, finally, a general public which has some appreciation for the standing of the players. Within the game the players can be rational in the varying degrees that the structure permits. At the very least, they know how to behave, and they know the score.

Individuals may play in a number of games, but, for the most part, their major preoccupation is with one, and their sense of major achievement is through success in one. Transfer from one game to another is, of course, possible, and the simultaneous playing of roles in two or more games is an important manner of linking separate games.

Sharing a common territorial field and collaborating for different and particular ends in the achievement of over-all social functions, the players in one game make use of the players in another and are, in turn, made use of by them. Thus the banker makes use of the newspaperman, the politician, the contractor, the ecclesiastic, the labor leader, the civic leader —all to further his success in the banking game—but, reciprocally, he is used to further the others' success in the newspaper, political, contracting, ecclesiastical, labor, and civic games. Each is a piece in the chess game of the other, sometimes a willing piece, but, to the extent that the games are different, with a different end in view.

Thus a particular highway grid may be the result of a bureaucratic department of public works game in which are combined, though separate, a professional highway engineer game with its purposes and critical elite onlookers; a departmental bureaucracy; a set of contending politicians seeking to use the highways for political capital, patronage, and the like; a banking game concerned with bonds, taxes, and the effect of the highways on real estate; newspapermen interested in headlines, scoops, and the effect of highways on the papers' circulation; contractors eager to make money by building roads; ecclesiastics concerned with the effect of highways on their parishes and on the fortunes of the contractors who support their churchly ambitions; labor leaders interested in union contracts and their status as community influentials with a right to be consulted; and civic leaders who must justify the contributions of their bureaus of municipal research or chambers of commerce to the social activity. Each game is in play in the complicated pulling and hauling of siting and constructing the highway grid. A wide variety of purposes is subserved by the activity, and no single over-all directive authority controls it. However, the interrelation of the groups in constructing a highway has been developed over time, and there are general expectations as to the interaction. There are also generalized expectations as to how politicians, contractors, newspapermen, bankers, and the like will utilize the highway situation in playing their particular games. In fact, the knowledge that a banker will play like a banker and a newspaperman like a newspaperman is an important part of what makes the situation calculable and permits the players to estimate its possibilities for their own action in their particular game.

While it might seem that the engineers of the department of public works were the appropriate protagonists for the highway grid, as a general activity it presents opportunities and threats to a wide range of other players who see in the situation consequences and possibilities undreamed of by the engineers. Some general public expectation of the limits of the conduct of the players and of a desirable outcome does provide bounds to the scramble. This public expectation is, of course, made active through the interested solicitation of newspapers, politicians, civic leaders, and others who see in it material for accomplishing their particular purposes and whose structured roles in fact require the mobilization of broad publics. In a sense the group struggle that Arthur Bentley described in his *Process of Government* is a drama that local publics have been taught to view with a not uncritical taste. The instruction of this taste has been the vocation and business of some of the contending parties. The existence of some kind of over-all public puts general restraints on gamesmanship beyond the norms of the particular games. However, for the players these are to all intents as much a part of the "facts of life" of the game as the sun and the wind.

It is perhaps the existence of some kind of a general public, however rudimentary, that most clearly differentiates the local territorial system from a natural ecology. The five-acre woodlot in which the owls and the field mice, the oaks and the acorns, and other flora and fauna have evolved a balanced system has no public opinion, however rudimentary. The co-operation is an unconscious affair. For much of what goes on in the local territorial system co-operation is equally unconscious and perhaps, but for the occasional social scientist, unnoticed. This unconscious co-operation, however, like that of the five-acre woodlot, produces results. The ecology of games in the local territorial system accomplishes unplanned but largely functional results. The games and their players mesh in their particular pursuits to bring about over-all results; the territorial system is fed and ordered. Its inhabitants are rational within limited areas and, pursuing the ends of these areas, accomplish socially functional ends.

While the historical development of largely unconscious co-operation between the special games in the territorial system gets certain routine, over-all functions performed, the problem of novelty and breakdown must be dealt with. Here it would seem that, as in the natural ecology, random adjustment and piecemeal innovation are the normal methods of response. The need or cramp in the system presents itself to the players of the games as an opportunity for them to exploit or a menace to be overcome. Thus a transportation crisis in, say, the threatened abandonment of commuter trains by a railroad will bring forth the players of a wide range of games who will see in the situation opportunity for gain or loss in the outcome. While over-all considerations will appear in the discussion, the frame of reference and the interpretation of the event will be largely determined by the game the interested parties are principally involved in. Thus a telephone executive who is president of the local chamber of commerce will be playing a civic association, general business game with concern for the principal dues-payers of the chamber but with a constant awareness of how his handling of this crisis will advance him in his particular league. The politicians, who might be expected to be protagonists of the general interest, may indeed be so, but the sphere of their activity and the glasses through which they see the problem will be determined in great part by the way they see the issue affecting their political game. The generality of this game is to a great extent that of the politician's calculus of votes and interests important to his and his side's success. To be sure, some of what Walter Lippmann has called "the public philosophy" affects both politicians and other game-players. This indicates the existence of roles and norms of a larger, vaguer game with a relevant audience that has some sense of cricket. This potentially mobilizable audience is not utterly without importance, but it provides no sure or adequate basis for support in the particular game that the politician or anyone else is playing. Instead of a set of norms to structure enduring role-playing, this audience provides a cross-pressure for momentary aberrancy from gamesmanship or constitutes just another hazard to be calculated in one's play.

In many cases the territorial system is impressive in the degree of intensity of its particular games, its banks, its newspapers, its downtown stores, its manufacturing companies, its contractors, its churches, its politicians, and its other differentiated, structured, goal-oriented activities. Games go on within the territory, occasionally extending beyond it, though centered in it. But, while the particular games show clarity of goals and intensity, few, if any, treat the territory as their proper object. The protagonists of things in particular are well organized and know what they are about; the protagonists of things in general are few, vague, and weak. Immense staff work will go into the development of a Lincoln Square project, but the twenty-two countries of metropolitan New York have few spokesmen for their over-all common interest and not enough staff work to give these spokesmen more substance than that required for a "do-gooding" newspaper editorial. The Port of New York Authority exhibits a disciplined self-interest and a vigorous drive along the lines of its developed historic role. However, the attitude of the Port Authority toward the general problems of the metropolitan area is scarcely different than that of any private corporation. It confines its corporate good citizenship to the contribution of funds for surveys and studies and avoids acceptance of broader responsibility. In fact, spokesmen for the Port vigorously reject the need for any superior level of structured representation of metropolitan interests. The common interest, if such there be, is to be realized through institutional interactions rather than through the self-conscious rationality of a determinate group charged with its formulation and attainment. Apart from the newspaper editorial, the occasional politician, and a few civic leaders the general business of the metropolitan area is scarcely anybody's business, and, except for a few, those who concern themselves with the general problems are pursuing hobbies and causes rather than their own business.

The lack of over-all institutions in the territorial system and the weakness of those that exist insure that co-ordination is largely ecological rather than a matter of conscious rational contriving. In the metropolitan area in most cases there are no over-all economic or social institutions. People are playing particular games, and their playgrounds are less or more than the metropolitan area. But even in a city where the municipal corporation provides an apparent over-all government, the appearance is deceptive. The politicians who hold the offices do not regard themselves as governors of the municipal territory but largely as mediators or players in a particular game that makes use of the other inhabitants. Their roles, as they conceive them, do not approach those of the directors of a TVA developing a territory. The ideology of local government is a highly limited affair in which the office-holders respond to demands and mediate conflicts. They play politics, and politics is vastly different from government if the latter is conceived as the rational, responsible ordering of the community. In part, this is due to the general belief that little government is necessary or that government is a congery of services only different from others because it is paid for by taxes and provided for by civil servants. In part, the separation of economics from politics eviscerates the formal theory of government of most of the substance of social action. Intervention in the really important economic order is by way of piecemeal exception and in deviation from the supposed norm of the separation of politics and economics. This ideal of separation has blocked the development of a theory of significant government action and reduced the politician to the role of registerer of pressure rather than responsible governor of a local political economy. The politics of the community becomes a different affair from its government, and its government is so structured as to provide the effective actors in it neither a sense of general responsibility nor the roles calling for such behavior.

The community vaguely senses that there ought to be a government. This is evidenced in the nomination by newspapers and others of particular individuals as members of a top leadership, a "they" who are periodically called upon to solve community problems and meet community crises. Significantly, the "they" usually are made up of people holding private, not public, office. The pluralism of the society has separated political, ecclesiastical, economic, and social hierarchies from one another so that the ancient union of lords spiritual and temporal is disrupted. In consequence, there is a marked distinction between the status of the holders of political office and the status of the "they" of the newspapers and the power elite of a C. Wright Mills or a Floyd Hunter. The politicians have the formal governmental office that might give them responsible governing roles. However, their lack of status makes it both absurd and presumptuous that they should take themselves so seriously. Who are they to act as lords of creation? Public expectation neither empowers nor demands that they should assume any such confident pose as top community leaders. The latter position is reserved for a rather varying group (in some communities well defined and clear-cut, in others vague and amorphous) of holders for the most part of positions of private power, economic, social, and ecclesiastical. This group, regarded as the top leadership of the community, and analogous to the top management of a corporation, provides both a sense that there are gods in the heavens whose will, if they exercise it, will take care of the community's problems and a set of demons whose misrule accounts for the evil in the world. The "they" fill an office left vacant by the dethronement of absolutism and aristocracy. Unlike the politicians in that "they" are only partially visible and of untested powers, the top leadership provides a convenient rationale for explaining what goes on or does not go on in the community. It is comforting to think that the executive committee of the bourgoisie is exploiting the community or that the beneficent social and economic leaders are wearying themselves and their digestions with civic luncheons in order to bring parking to a congested city.

Usually the question is raised as to whether *de facto* there is a set of informal power-holders running things. A related question is whether community folklore holds that there is, that there should be, and what these informal power-holders should do. Certainly, most newspapermen and other professional "inside dopesters" hold that there is a "they." In fact, these people operate largely as court chroniclers of the doings of the "they." The "they," because they are "they," are newsworthy and fit into a ready-made theory of social causation that is vulgarized widely. However, the same newspaperman who could knowingly open his "bird book" and give you a run-down on the local "Who's Who" would probably with equal and blasphemous candor tell you that "they" were not doing a thing about the city and that "they" were greatly to be blamed for sitting around talking instead of getting things done. Thus, as with most primitive tribes, the idols are both worshiped and beaten, at least verbally. Public and reporters alike are relieved to believe both that there is a "they" to make civic life explicable and also to be held responsible for what occurs. This belief in part creates the role of top leadership and demands that it somehow be filled. It seems likely that there is a social-psychological table of organization of a community that must be filled in order to remove anxieties. Gordon Childe has remarked that man seems to need as much to adjust to an unseen, socially created spiritual environment as to the matter-of-fact world of the senses.

The community needs to believe that there are spiritual fathers, bad or good, who can deal with the dark: in the Middle Ages the peasants combated a plague of locusts by a high Mass and a procession of the clergy who damned the grasshoppers with bell, book, and candle. The Hopi Indians do a rain dance to overcome a drought. The harassed citizens of the American city mobilize their influentials at a civic luncheon to perform the equivalent and exorcise slums, smog, or unemployment. We smile at the medievals and the Hopi, but our own practices may be equally magical. It is interesting to ask under what circumstances one resorts to DDT and irrigation and why. To some extent it is clear that the ancient and modern practice of civic magic ritual is functional—functional in the same sense as the medicinal placebo. Much of human illness is benign; if the sufferer will bide his time, it will pass. Much of civic ills also cure themselves if only people can be kept from tearing each other apart in the stress of their anxieties. The locusts and the drought will pass. They almost always have.

While ritual activities are tranquilizing anxieties, the process of experimentation and adaptation in the social ecology goes on. The piecemeal responses of the players and the games to the challenges presented by crises provide the social counterpart to the process of evolution and natural selection. However, unlike the random mutation of the animal kingdom, much of the behavior of the players responding within the perspectives of their games is self-conscious and rational, given their ends in view, It is from the over-all perspective of the unintended contribution of their actions to the forming of a new or the restoration of the old ecological balance of the social system that their actions appear almost as random and lacking in purposive plan as the adaptive behavior of the natural ecology.

Within the general area of unplanned, unconscious social process technological areas emerge that are so structured as to promote rational, goal-oriented behavior and meaningful experience rather than mere happenstance. In these areas group activity may result in cumulative knowledge and self-corrective behavior. Thus problem-solving in the field of public health and sanitation may be at a stage far removed from the older dependence on piecemeal adjustment and random functional innovation. In this sense there are areas in which society, as Julian Huxley suggests in his *The Meaning of Evolution,* has gone beyond evolution. However, these are as yet isolated areas in a world still swayed by magic and, for the most part, carried forward by the logic of unplanned, undirected historical process.

It is not surprising that the members of the "top leadership" of the territorial system should seem to be largely confined to ritual and ceremonial roles. "Top leadership" is usually conceived in terms of status position rather than specifiable roles in social action. The role of a top leader is ill defined and to a large degree unstructured. It is in most cases a secondary role derived from a primary role as corporation executive, wealthy man, powerful ecclesiastic, holder of high social position, and the like. The top-leadership role is derivative from the other and is in most cases a result rather than a cause of status. The primary job is bank president, or president of Standard Oil; as such, one is naturally picked, nominated, and recognized as a member of the top leadership. One seldom forgets that one's primary role, obligation, and source of rational conduct is in terms of one's business. In fact, while one is on the whole pleased at the recognition that membership in the top leadership implies—much as one's wife would be pleased to be included among the ten best-dressed women—he is somewhat concerned about just what the role requires in the expenditure of time and funds. Furthermore, one has a suspicion that he may not know how to dance and could make a fool of himself before known elite and unknown, more general publics. All things considered, however, it is probably a good thing for the business, the contacts are important, and the recognition will be helpful back home, in both senses. In any event, if one's committee service or whatever concrete activity "top leadership" implies proves wearing or unsatisfactory, or if it interferes with business, one can always withdraw.

A fair gauge of the significance of top-leadership roles is the time put into them by the players and the institutionalized support represented by staff. Again and again the interviewer is told that the president of such-and-such an organization is doing a terrific job and literally knocking himself out for such-and-such a program. On investigation a "terrific job" turns out to be a few telephone calls and, possibly, three luncheons a month. The standard of "terrific job" obviously varies widely from what would be required in the business role.

In the matter of staffing, while the corporation, the church, and the government are often equipped in depth, the top-leadership job of port promotion may have little more than a secretary and an agile newspaper-man equipped to ghost-write speeches for the boss. While there are cases where people in top-leadership positions make use of staff from their own businesses and from the legal mill with which they do business, this seems largely confined to those top-leadership undertakings that have a direct connection with their business. In general, top-leadership roles seem to involve minor investments of time, staff, and money by territorial elites. The absence of staff and the emphasis on publicity limit the capacity of top leadership for sustained rational action.

Where top leaderships have become well staffed, the process seems as much or more the result of external pressures than of its own volition. Of all the functions of top leadership, that of welfare is best staffed. Much of this is the result of the pressure of the professional social worker to organize a concentration of economic and social power sufficient to permit him to do a job. It is true, of course, that the price of organizing top leadership and making it manageable by the social workers facilitated a reverse control of themselves—a control of whose galling nature Hunter gives evidence. An amusing sidelight on the organization of the "executive committee of the bourgeoisie" is the case of the Cleveland Fifty Club. This club, supposedly, is made up of the fifty most important men in Cleveland. Most middling and even upper executives long for the prestige recognition that membership confers. Reputedly, the Fifty Club was organized by Brooks Emery, while he was director of the Cleveland Council on World Affairs, to facilitate the taxation of business to support that organization. The lead time required to get the august members of the Fifty Club together and their incohesiveness have severely limited its possibilities as a power elite. Members who have tried to turn it to such a purpose report fairly consistent failure.

The example of the Cleveland Fifty Club, while somewhat extreme, points to the need on the part of certain activities in the territorial system for a top leadership under whose auspices they can function. A wide variety of civic undertakings need to organize top prestige support both to finance and to legitimate their activities. The staff man of a bureau of municipal research or the Red Feather Agency cannot proceed on his own; he must have the legitimatizing sponsorship of top influentials. His task may be self-assigned, his perception of the problem and its solution may be his own, but he cannot gain acceptance without mobilizing the influentials. For the success of his game he must assist in creating the game of top leadership. The staff man in the civic field is the typical protagonist of things in general—a kind of entrepreneur of ideas. He fulfils the same role in his area as the stock promoter of the twenties or the Zeckendorfs of urban redevelopment. Lacking both status and a confining organizational basis, he has a socially valuable mobility between the specialized games and hierarchies in the territorial system. His success in the negotiation of a port authority not only provides a plus for his taxpayers federation or his world trade council but may provide a secure and lucrative job for himself.

Civic staff men, ranging from chamber of commerce personnel to college professors and newspapermen, are in varying degrees interchangeable and provide an important network of communication. The staff men in the civic agencies play similar roles to the Cohens and Corcorans in Washington. In each case a set of telephone numbers provides special information and an effective lower-echelon interaction. Consensus among interested professionals at the lower level can result in action programs from below that are bucked up to the prestige level of legitimitization. As the Cohens and Corcorans played perhaps the most general and inclusive game in the Washington bureaucracy, so their counterparts in the local territorial system are engaged in the most general action game in their area. Just as the Cohens and Corcorans had to mobilize an effective concentration of top brass to move a program into the action stage, so their counterparts have to mobilize concentrations of power sufficient for their purposes on the local scene.

In this connection it is interesting to note that foundation grants are being used to hire displaced New Deal bureaucrats and college professors in an attempt to organize the influentials of metropolitan areas into self-

conscious governing groups. Professional chamber of commerce executives, immobilized by their orthodox ideology, are aghast to see their
members study under the planners and heretics from the dogmas of free-
enterprise fundamentalism. The attempt to transform the metropolitan
appearance of disorder into a tidy territory is a built-in predisposition
for the self-constituted staff of the embryonic top metropolitan management. The major disorder that has to be overcome before all others is the
lack of order and organization among the "power elite." As in the case of
the social workers, there is a thrust from below to organize a "power
elite" as a necessary instrument to accomplish the purposes of civic staff
men. This is in many ways nothing but a part of the general groping after
a territorial government capable of dealing with a range of problems that
the existing feudal disintegration of power cannot. The nomination of a
top leadership by newspapers and public and the attempt to create such
a leadership in fact by civic technicians are due to a recognition that there
is a need for a leadership with the status, capacity, and role to attend
to the general problems of the territory and give substance to a public
philosophy. This involves major changes in the script of the top-leadership
game and the self-image of its participants. In fact, the insecurity and
the situational limitations of their positions in corporations or other institutions that provide the primary roles for top leaders make it difficult to
give more substance to what has been a secondary role. Many members
of present top leaderships are genuinely reluctant, fearful, and even
morally shocked at their positions' becoming that of a recognized territorial government. While there is a general supposition that power is
almost instinctively craved, there seems considerable evidence that at
least in many of our territorial cultures responsibility is not. Machiavellian
virtu is an even scarcer commodity among the merchant princes of the
present than among their Renaissance predecessors. In addition, the educational systems of school and business do not provide top leaders with
the inspiration or the know-how to do more than raise funds and man
committees. Politics is frequently regarded with the same disgust as
military service by the ancient educated Chinese.

It is possible to translate a check pretty directly into effective power
in a chamber of commerce or a welfare agency. However, to translate
economic power into more general social or political power, there must
be an organized purchasable structure. Where such structures exist, they
may be controlled or, as in the case of *condottieri*, gangsters, and politicians, their hire may be uncertain, and the hired force retains its independence. Where businessmen are unwilling or unable to organize their
own political machines, they must pay those who do. Sometimes the pay-
master rules; at other times he bargains with equals or superiors.

A major protagonist of things in general in the territorial system is the
newspaper. Along with the welfare worker, museum director, civic tech-

nician, etc., the newspaper has an interest in terms of its broad reading public in agitating general issues and projects. As the chronicler of the great, both in its general news columns and in its special features devoted to society and business, it provides an organizing medium for elites in the territory and provides them with most of their information about things in general and not a little of inside tidbits about how individual elite members are doing. In a sense, the newspaper is the prime mover in setting the territorial agenda. It has a great part in determining what most people will be talking about, what most people will think the facts are, and what most people will regard as the way problems are to be dealt with. While the conventions of how a newspaper is to be run, and the compelling force of some events limit the complete freedom of a paper to select what events and what people its public will attend to, it has great leeway. However, the newspaper is a business and a specialized game even when its reporters are idealists and its publisher rejoices in the title "Mr. Cleveland." The paper does not accept the responsibility of a governing role in its territory. It is a power but only a partially responsible one. The span of attention of its audience and the conventions of what constitute a story give it a crusading role at most for particular projects. Nonetheless, to a large extent it sets the civic agenda.

The story is told of the mayor of a large eastern metropolis who, having visited the three capital cities of his constituents—Rome, Dublin, and Tel Aviv—had proceeded home via Paris and Le Havre. Since his staff had neglected to meet the boat before the press, he was badgered by reporters to say what he had learned on his trip. The unfortunate mayor could not say that he had been on a junket for a good time. Luckily, he remembered that in Paris they had been having an antinoise campaign. Off the hook at last, he told the press that he thought this campaign was a good thing. This gave the newsmen something to write about. The mayor hoped this was the end of it. But a major paper felt in need of a crusade to sponsor and began to harass the mayor about the start of the local antinoise campaign. Other newspapers took up the cry, and the mayor told his staff they were for it—there had to be an antinoise campaign. In short order, businessmen's committees, psychiatrists, and college professors were mobilized to press forward on a broad front the suppression of needless noise. In vindication of administrative rationality it appeared that an antinoise campaign was on a staff list of possibilities for the mayor's agenda but had been discarded by him as politically unfeasible.

The civic technicians and the newspapers have somewhat the same relationship as congressional committee staff and the press. Many members of congressional committee staffs complain bitterly that their professional consciences are seared by the insistent pressure to seek publicity. But they contend that their committee sponsors are only impressed with research that is newsworthy. Congressional committee members point out that committees that do not get publicity are likely to go out of business or funds. The civic agency head all too frequently communicates most effectively with his board through his success in getting newspaper publicity. Many a civic ghost-writer has found his top leader converted to the cause by reading the ghosted speech he delivered at the civic luncheon reported with photographs and editorials in the press. This is even the case where the story appears in the top leader's own paper. The need of the reporters for news and of the civic technicians for publicity brings the participants of these two games together. As in the case of the congressional committee, there is a tendency to equate accomplishment with publicity. For top influentials on civic boards the news clips are an important way of keeping score. This symbiotic relation of newsmen and civic staff helps explain the heavy emphasis on ritual luncheons, committees, and news releases. The nature of the newspapers' concern with a story about people and the working of marvels and miracles puts a heavy pressure for the kind of story that the press likes to carry. It is not surprising that civic staff men should begin to equate accomplishment with their score measured in newspaper victories or that they should succumb to the temptation to impress their sponsors with publicity, salting it to their taste by flattering newspaper tributes to the sponsors themselves. Despite the built-in incapacity of newspapers to exercise a serious governing responsibility in their territories, they are for the most part the only institutions with a long-term general territorial interest. In default of a territorial political party or other institution that accepts responsibility for the formulation of a general civic agenda the newspaper is the one game that by virtue of its public and its conventions partly fills the vacuum.

A final game that does in a significant way integrate all the games in the territorial system is the social game. Success in each of the games can in varying degrees be cashed in for social acceptance. The custodians of the symbols of top social standing provide goals that in a sense give all the individual games some common denominator of achievement. While the holders of top social prestige do not necessarily hold either top political or economic power, they do provide meaningful goals for the rest. One of the most serious criticisms of a Yankee aristocracy made by a Catholic bishop was that, in losing faith in their own social values, they were undermining the faith in the whole system of final clubs. It would be a cruel joke if, just as the hard-working upwardly mobile had worked their way to entrance, the progeny of the founders lost interest. The decay of the Union League Club in *By Love Possessed* is a tragedy for more than its members. A common game shared even by the excluded spectators gave a purpose that was functional in its time and must be replaced— hopefully, by a better one. A major motivation for seeking membership in and playing the top-leadership game is the value of the status it confers as a counter in the social game.

Neither the civic leadership game nor the social game makes the territorial ecology over into a structured government. They do, however, provide important ways of linking the individual games and make possible co-operative action on projects. Finally, the social game, in Ruth Benedict's sense, in a general way patterns the culture of the territorial ecology and gives all the players a set of vaguely shared aspirations and common goals.

A Typology for Comparative Local Government

Oliver P. Williams

Accelerated urbanization in the United States has stimulated a renewed interest in the area of local government. Part of this interest promises to express itself in the form of comparative studies, producing a need for standards by which to guide research. Without adequate guides there is the danger that we shall produce a series of seriatim descriptions which will answer few general questions. This paper, which outlines a typology of the roles of local government, is addressed to this problem.

The study of comparative government begins with the knowledge that different political regimes make different responses to widely experienced but similar problems. Explanation or analysis of the differences between these policy responses is the primary objective of comparative research. In comparative studies dealing with the policies of nations, differences are usually written quite large and consequently the objectives of research are clear. In local government, because of the number of units and their superficial similarity, the initial objectives become obscured.

Community differences have been described in terms of ecology, demography, social stratification, power structures, governmental structures,

Oliver P. Williams, "A Typology for Comparative Local Government," *Midwest Journal of Politics*, 1961, pp. 150–164. This paper was developed in conjunction with a study of four communities, a project sponsored by the Institute for Community Development, Michigan State University. The larger study is being undertaken in collaboration with Charles R. Adrian, who also contributed most helpful counsel and advice in developing the ideas for this article. Norton Long in his article "Aristotle and Local Government," *Social Research*, 24 (Autumn, 1957), 287–310, furnished the germinal idea through his restatement of the Aristotelian concept "ethical constitutions."

and political processes. But these findings are meaningless unless they are related to policy differences among communities. Lacking such a relationship, the sum total of data on communities generally represent an inchoate and unmanageable mass of knowledge from the standpoint of political science.

The policy framework developed in this paper pertains to the roles of local government. The concept "role of government" may be given at least two interpretations. It may refer to *images of the proper* role of government or to the *actual* role of government. A typology of roles based on the first interpretation will be outlined initially. Conversion of the typology for the second usage will be discussed subsequently.

The typology characterizes four different roles for local government: (1) promoting economic growth; (2) providing or securing life's amenities; (3) maintaining (only) traditional services; (4) arbitrating among conflicting interests. The development of the typology will proceed thusly: first, each role will be described, followed by a discussion of the relationship between the roles and forms of governmental structure; second, the convertibility of the typology for different uses will be considered; finally, the operational character of the typology and criteria for its application will be discussed.

The images of the role of local governments, embodied in the typology elaborated below, are analytical constructs. They are not based directly on any documentary evidence of group attitudes, samplings of public opinion or other specific sets of data. However, the germinal ideas for each role were found generally in the literature of case studies on community decision making as well as in this author's research designed to conduct a comparative study of politics in four cities. The utility of the typology as an economical summary of prevailing views regarding the proper role of local government must still be verified through repeated applications to concrete situations.

The first type characterizes the role of government as *the promotion of economic growth*. The object of government is to see that the community grows in population and/or total wealth. Born of speculative hopes, nurtured by the recall of frontier competition for survival, augmented by the American pride in bigness, the idea that the good, "thriving" community is one which continues to grow has been and still remains a widely held assumption in urban political thinking. It is essentially an economic conception drawing an analogy between municipal and business corporations. Just as the first must grow to prosper, so must the city increase in population, industry, and total wealth. But the parallel is not simply an analogy, for according to this view the ultimate vocation of government is to serve the producer.

Although this image is endorsed most vigorously by those specific economic interests which have a stake in growth, its appeal is much broader. The drama of a growing city infects the inhabitants with a certain pride and gives them a feeling of being a part of progress—an essential ingredient of our national aspirations. The flocking of people to "our" city is something like the coming of the immigrants to our national shores. It is a tangible demonstration of the superiority of our way of life in that others have voluntarily chosen to join us. Growth also symbolizes opportunity, not only economically, but also socially and culturally. Large cities have more to offer in this respect than smaller ones.

There are certain groups which have such concrete stakes in growth that they are likely to be the active promoters of this image, while others in the city may give only tacit consent. The merchant, the supplier, the banker, the editor, and the city bureaucrats see each new citizen as a potential customer, taxpayer or contributor to the enlargement of his enterprise, and they form the first rank of the civic boosters.

The specific policy implications of this image of the role of government are varied. Historically, local government was deeply embroiled in the politics of railroad location, land development, and utility expansion. But today city government is more handicapped than it was in the nineteenth century as an active recruiter of industry, for the vagaries of industrial location are determined more by economic market considerations than by the character of locally provided services. Although there are a number of ways in which economic growth may be served, producer oriented political activity often expresses itself negatively; that is, nothing should be done which might hinder the community's growth. The city should have "a good reputation." Politics should be conducted in a low key. The image of stability and regularity in city finances must be assured. Friendliness toward business in general should be the prevailing attitude of city officials.

But to some, growth itself is not a desirable goal for a community. Indeed, it is the very thing to be avoided. Growth breeds complexities which, in turn, deny the possibilities of certain styles of life. For some the role of local government is *providing and securing life's amenities.* "Amenities" is used here to distinguish between policies designed to achieve the comforts and the necessities of life as opposed to only the latter. Obviously both comfort and necessity are culturally defined attributes of living standards; nevertheless, the distinction is useful. Most communities recognize the demand for amenities in some fashion, but only an occasional community makes this the dominant object of collective political action. Many cities have their noise and smoke abatement ordinances, but the idea of creating a quiet and peaceful environment for the home is hardly the central purpose of government.

The policies designed to provide amenities are expressed by accent on the home environment rather than on the working environment—the citizen as consumer rather than producer. The demands of the residential environment are safety, slowness, quiet, beauty, convenience, and restfulness. The rights of pedestrians and children take precedence over the claims of commerce. Growth, far from being attractive, is often objectionable. That growth which is permitted must be controlled and directed, both in terms of the type of people who will be admitted and the nature of physical changes. It is essentially a design for a community with a homogeneous population, for civic amenities are usually an expression of a common style of living. Furthermore, because amenities are costly, the population must have an above average income. All expenditures for welfare are unwanted diversions of resources. Those asking for public welfare assistance are seeking necessities which other citizens provide for themselves privately. Consequently, this image finds expression chiefly in the middle to upper income residential suburbs.

However, as we descend the scale from larger to smaller cities, middle-class consumers are not necessarily isolated in a self-imposed suburban exile, and their demands may become channeled toward the core city itself. In other places, a fortunately located large industrial facility may allow a city of persons with modest means to enjoy costly amenities. The Ford Motor Company's tax base supplies Dearborn, Michigan, with sidewalk snow removal and a summer resort. There are villages with iron mines within their limits, located in the Upper Peninsula of Michigan, which have free bowling alleys in the city hall and other rarely found city services.

Amenities are also likely to become a dominant concern of local government in the traditional small town which is threatened by engulfment from a nearby major urban complex. Such a town will not be characterized by the homogeneity of the suburb, nor will its particular kind of amenities require costly expenditures, for the amenities being secured are simply those which are a function of small town life. Because growth of the town was slow, the necessary capital investments for urban life were amortized over a very long time. A sudden population influx threatens both the style of life and the cost of maintaining that style. However, all small-town civic policies can hardly be characterized as the desire to preserve amenities, for conditions in many small towns make a mockery of that term.

This leads us to our third image of the role of local government—that of *maintaining traditional services* or *"caretaker government."* Extreme conservative views toward the proper role of government can be more effectively realized at the local than at any other level. The expansion of governmental functions often can be successfully opposed here by the expedient of shunting problems to higher levels. Such evasions of difficult problems give the appearance of successful resistance to the extension of government and thus reinforce the plausibility of maintaining a caretaker local-governmental policy.[1]

"Freedom" and "self-reliance of the individual" are the values stressed by this view. Private decisions regarding the allocation of personal resources are lauded over governmental allocation through taxation. Tax increases are never justified except to maintain the traditional nature of the community. This substitution of individual for public decisions emphasizes a pluralistic conception of the "good." The analogy to *laissez faire* economics is unmistakable. It is not surprising that the caretaker image is associated with a policy of opposition to zoning, planning, and other regulations of the use of real property. These sentiments are peculiarly common to the traditional small town.

Among the individuals most likely to be attracted by this view, especially in its extreme form, are retired middle-class persons who are homeowners living on a very modest fixed income. Squeezed by inflation and rising taxes, it is not surprising if they fail to see the need for innovation, especially when it means to them an absolute reduction in living standards. The marginal homeowners, the persons who can just barely afford the home they are buying, whatever its price, are also likely to find the caretaker image attractive. They must justify a low-tax policy.

Finally, the fourth image sees the purpose of local government as *arbitrating between conflicting interests*. Emphasis is placed upon the process rather than the substance of governmental action. Although the possibility of a "community good" may be formally recognized, actually all such claims are reduced to the level of interests. The view is realistic in the popular sense in that it assumes "what's good for someone always hurts someone else." Given this assumption, government must provide a continuous arbitration system under which public policy is never regarded as being in final equilibrium. The formal structure of government must not be subordinated to a specific substantive purpose; rather, the structure must be such that most interests may be at least considered by the decision makers.

That the proper role of government is to serve as an arbiter is held most logically by interest groups that fall short of complete political control, including, especially, the more self-conscious minorities. The numerical or psychic majority does not have to settle for a process, but can act directly in terms of substantive conceptions of the community good. The minority can only hope for access.

The most conspicuous interests that self-consciously espouse an arbiter function for government are neighborhood and welfare-oriented groups. Ethnic blocs reaching for a higher rung on the political ladder, and home-

[1] Arthur J. Vidich and Joseph Bensman, *Small Town in Mass Society* (Princeton: Princeton University Press, 1958), Chs. V, VII; esp. pp. 113–114.

owners and businessmen with stakes in a particular neighborhood, especially one threatened by undesired changes, make claims for special representation. The psychological minorities—persons low on the socio-economic scale—also stress the need for personal access. In the four-city study mentioned above it was found that welfare matters were high among the subjects about which city councilmen were personally contacted. This was true even though welfare was entirely a county function. Welfare is a highly personal problem, at least from the viewpoint of the person in need. Perhaps personal access is desired because it seems more legitimate to obtain welfare in exchange for political support than to obtain it by merely qualifying under bureaucratically defined standards.

Government-as-arbiter does not mean a neutral agency (government) balancing diverse pressures with mathematical precision. The accommodation envisioned is not one which operates according to a fixed standard of equity or political weighing. Rather it is a government of men, each with weaknesses, preferences, and partialities. It is just this human element in government which opens up the possibility that the imbalance between the weight of the majority and the minorities may become redressed.

The four types of images may be classified into two groups—those implying a unitary conception of the public "good" and those implying a pluralistic conception. The unitary conceptions are stated in substantive terms; i.e., "promoting economic growth" and "providing or securing life's amenities." The types which incorporate a pluralistic notion of the "good" stress a procedural role for government. "Arbitration among conflicting interests" clearly denotes this procedural emphasis.

The third type, "maintaining traditional services," presents a special problem with respect to the unitary-pluralistic dichotomy. A policy favoring a limited role for government seems to constitute a unitary conception of the good; however, the premise of this view is that the public good is achieved by maximizing the opportunity for individuals to pursue their private goals. The role of government is held in check so that a greater range of choices may be retained by individuals. Hence, this third type is essentially pluralistic in its objectives.

This unitary-pluralistic distinction is important to an understanding of the relationship between attitudes towards governmental structure and those towards the proper role of government. The formal structure which is most consistent with arbiter and caretaker government is one which includes a plural executive, ward elections for councilmen, and other decentralizing devices. These arrangements provide multiple access to policy makers and, by decentralizing leadership, make programmatic political action more difficult.

Centralization and professionalization of the bureaucracy are attractive to those who can control and desire to exploit control to achieve specific substantive goals. Though it is true that the early advocates of civic reform acted in the name of economy, most successful reforms have been followed by action programs. Promotion of economic growth or increased amenities have formed the inarticulate premise of most of these efforts, even though the more neutral language of procedural adjustments has often been employed. Through strengthening the office of mayor, the appointment of city managers, and the institution of at-large elections, centralization usually leads to a reduction in the political strength of certain particularistic interest groups or minorities. Professionalization of the personnel in a city bureau may achieve some economies, but it also creates a political force pressing for the extension of the services performed by that bureau. Thus the reform devices are most consistent with the two types of unitary views of the community good.

It should be stressed at this point that the prime concern here is with the development of the typology and not with the implicit hypotheses regarding the groups which support each type. The foregoing references to group interests are used only to suggest the plausibility of the types by citing the relationships among them and familiar forces within communities.

II

The typology has been elaborated in terms of images of the proper role of local government. The necessary data for verification of the types would include some kind of opinion sampling. However, the typology may be used for other purposes and differing kinds of data. It may be converted into a typology of *actual* roles of government or even of prevailing norms among all community policy-making institutions.

Let us consider the typology's utility in the second sense—as a classification for the actual roles of government. For this purpose the emphasis in data collection should pertain to prevailing policies. As a policy typology, the fourth category—arbitration between conflicting interests—poses a problem. Arbitration is not, strictly speaking, a policy in the same sense as promoting economic growth, providing and securing life's amenities or maintaining traditional services. However, in classifying prevailing governmental policies this fourth type may act as a useful category for characterizing cities in which the policy complexes embodied in the other three types are continuously compromised and no one or even pair of the other policy types epitomizes civic actions over any substantial period. (Under such a usage a more appropriate title than "arbitration" might be chosen.) However, in some cities the arbiter type, as first defined, will be useful as a completely parallel policy category. This will be where the process of adjusting claims among various and disparate interests becomes the all pervasive preoccupation of officials and the norm for policy determination generally.

In the literature of case studies in community decision making there are illustrations of each of the four types. Springdale Village described by Vidich and Bensman is nearly a complete prototype of caretaker government.[2] Whyte reports the preoccupation with amenities in the politics of Park Forest.[3] The government of Middletown as described by the Lynds was primarily concerned with the interests of the producer.[4] Perhaps the best illustration of arbiter government is found in Meyerson and Banfield's study of public housing site choices in Chicago;[5] their study pertains to only one governmental policy, and is, therefore, not an accurate characterization of Chicago government generally. But with regard to policy formation in this one area, Meyerson and Banfield stress the way in which the political party, working through the city government, acted as an arbiter compromising the aims of all claimants in the political struggle.

III

These four illustrations have only limited value, however, in demonstrating that the types may be made operational, for the application has been made *post factum*. Consequently, it may be more meaningful to use our four city study, where the typology was self-consciously employed to delineate the policy orientations of a panel of cities. The original inquiry into these four communities was designed to furnish a basis for generalizations regarding the function of the size of a city in influencing its political process. For control purposes four cities were chosen which were similar in many respects. All were core cities of small metropolitan areas with a population of approximately 50,000, were independent manufacturing centers outside of the immediate economic orbit of larger metropolitan centers, were located in the same state, and thus were subject to the same constitutional and legal limitations. All had home rule charters, city managers, and the non-partisan ballot. These governmental features had been in use in all four cities for approximately thirty years.

Policies of the cities were studied over a ten-year period. The problems which the cities faced were very similar. However, the responses were so dissimilar that explanation of the differences proved a more absorbing

[2] *Ibid.*

[3] William H. Whyte, Jr., *The Organization Man* (New York: Simon & Schuster, 1956).

[4] Robert S. and Helen Merrell Lynd, *Middletown in Transition* (New York: Harcourt, Brace, 1937).

[5] Martin Meyerson and Edward C. Banfield, *Politics, Planning, and the Public Interest* (Glencoe, Ill.: The Free Press, 1955).

subject than summarizing constant behavior. The typology was developed in order to handle the data on these disparate responses.

Criteria were established to judge the policies of each city according to the four types. The criteria were used in a comparative fashion, rather than through the application of an ideal type; consequently, the cities were simply ranked according to the degree of emphasis that was placed on a particular type of policy. The following standards, stated in abbreviated terms, were used. (The standards employed in the study were somewhat more elaborate, but still the need for further refinements remained apparent.) A city's willingness to provide and secure amenities was assessed first in terms of expenditures for selected consumer-oriented services. Secondly, panels of experts in relevant service areas were asked to rate the four cities according to the standards of their own profession. (The assumption was made that the professional experts generally favored increased service levels within their specialties and consequently that cities which were rated high by the panels gave greater stress to amenities.) The standard for caretaker government was resistance to innovations and opposition to tax increases. The data were based upon general council policies, referendum proposals, and referendum results. A commitment to government by arbitration was gauged by the prevailing customs of representation, the availability of access for minorities and interests, attitudes of the councilmen toward their representative function, and, most importantly, the extent of preoccupation with parochial claims in the total policy making process.

In developing a criterion for the economic growth type, it was necessary to distinguish between a policy of catering to business interests generally and one aimed at general economic prosperity for a community. In every city there are specific economic interests which have a stake in city policies: the enfranchised taxicab companies oppose enfranchisement of additional companies; merchants want municipal parking lots to be located near their stores; realtors work for zoning changes to facilitate a particular sale. This type of activity is universal in city politics. Such interests will dominate city policy if broader interests do not. But if the clashing claims of these various and routine economic interests dominate city government, the government-as-arbiter role would describe the situation. A policy of promoting economic growth is not compatible with all business interests. At the time of the study all four cities were core cities of small metropolitan areas; consequently, there were limited opportunities for unilateral expressions of civic boosterism through the core city governments alone. The competitive position of these cities vis-à-vis other cities could be improved by central business district renovation, improved transportation facilities, and some urban renewal projects. However, the clearest expression of a policy of economic growth had to be made through metropolitan programs. Thus the criteria for

Table 1   *A Typological Profile of Four Cities*

	Low	———→Medium	————→High	
Economic growth	Delta		Beta	Alpha
			Gamma	
Amenities	Delta	Beta	Gamma	Alpha
Caretaker	Alpha	Gamma	Beta	Delta
Arbiter	Alpha		Gamma	Beta	Delta

this type were based on the stress which cities placed on aiding the competitive position of core city retailers and on metropolitan policies designed to facilitate industrial and commercial recruitment.

Table 1 represents a typological profile of the four cities—for convenience called Alpha, Beta, Gamma and Delta—showing their comparative rating according to the above criteria. There is no pretence that mathematical rigor has been employed in the scaling process. Assuming that the distinctions are meaningful, how may the typological profile be employed in comparative research?

As stated above, the four cities were quite similar in certain gross respects. In policy behavior, Alpha and Delta were at opposite extremes within this four city universe. What were the factors that distinguished them from each other and from the other two? An economic profile of the four cities revealed that Alpha was in many respects unique. Economic differences appeared particularly important in explaining the strong emphasis on amenities in Alpha.

Alpha was roughly comparable to the other three in its long-term economic growth pattern. Wages were lower than in some of the other cities, but so was unemployment. Perhaps more important, there was a very high percentage of locally owned industry. In the other cities most of the original local industries had been sold to national concerns, while in Alpha the sons and grandsons of the original proprietors retained ownership and were very active in community affairs. Lastly, the Alpha city boundaries had been expanded to include the upper income suburbs. In the other cities, the highest income groups lived in suburbs outside the city boundaries, and these suburbanites often disparaged the grubby politics of the core city dwellers.

A study of referendum votes revealed that in all four cities the strongest support for increases in services, and hence tax increases, came from the highest income groups. The lower income groups were nearly always the most intransigent opponents of increased services. This is not to say the very lowest income groups were in this class, for this sector was largely self-disfranchised in local politics. The consumer preferences of the upper income groups were channeled into the core city politics in

Alpha, whereas they were expended in the suburbs around the other three cities. The upper income groups in Alpha had developed a formidable political organization which had controlled the city government for generations. This act of proprietorship almost certainly stemmed in part from the local industrial ownership pattern. However, it cannot be inferred that there is a simple correlation between economic stability and home-owned industries on the one hand and preference for amenities on the other. The economic variable only illustrates one line of inquiry.

A second, and in many ways more revealing, element in the political life of these four cities lay in the recruiting process for elected officials. This is not to say that the city councils were powerful political bodies or that city council positions were avidly sought. Quite the contrary; the council leadership role was often minimal. But in the low-key style of politics of these cities, the composition of the council could mean the difference between doing something and doing nothing. The council's function of providing legitimation, encouragement, specialized access or vetoes set the tempo of the political process.

In Alpha recruitment was dominated by wealthy businessmen through an informal clique which was self-perpetuated. It was a combination of the Lynds' X family, since the core was built around old families, and Hunter's crowds. The clique recruited candidates both from its own membership and from professionals or minor businessmen it trusted. It was not unusual for the chairman of a multimillion dollar corporation to be councilman or mayor of this city. Again, the industrial ownership pattern may have influenced this behavior. The councilmen endeavored to act like members of the board of directors of a corporation, though often they learned that there were certain discrepancies between the model and the public body. But the model was real in certain ways. For instance, a highly regarded group of professional administrators was recruited to which most details of running the city were delegated. The primary result was a strong emphasis on civic amenities. Moreover, the council showed great willingness to take on rather ambitious projects (often related to community growth), especially when compared to the other cities.

Beta also had a recruiting group, but it was a public body with open membership, comprised mainly of businessmen who were lesser luminaries than those in Alpha. According to the city charter, nominations were made by wards, which produced a decided handicap for this group's recruitment activities. Its candidates were usually small entrepreneurs, lesser professionals, and second- and third-level executives. Once in office, these men received no organized sustenance from the recruiting organization. Beta's council was subjected to all the pressures of neighbors, friends, clients, and associations in a most exposed fashion. As a result, the council gave the public impression of great vacillation. However, its general policy was, in fact, conservative. A safe course was followed of protecting the taxpayer's dollar, getting along for less, occasionally undercutting the professionals, tolerating lagging salaries for city employees, and procrastinating on difficult decisions. Unlike in Alpha, members of this body rarely, if ever, performed any leadership function on city projects. Leadership passed to the associations of which the most vocal was an anti-tax front group for the local real estate association. Thus Beta was ruled by a government of brokers (arbiters) alternately yielding to the caretaker sentiments of the formidable real estate group and the designs of the civic boosters hoping for economic expansion.

Gamma was in many ways a hybrid of Alpha and Beta. The at-large elections provided a more satisfactory recruiting milieu for the upper income groups. The banks, the chamber of commerce, and the manufacturers associations sponsored a number of candidates who were subsequently elected. However, the control was never complete, and a political dialogue developed on the council between those who acted essentially as aldermanic ambassadors and those who claimed to think in terms of the "whole community." Depending on the year, the policies emanating from this council would resemble those of either Alpha or Beta.

Delta had an old fashioned political organization built around the city employees' union and fed by patronage. Drawing support from the lower-income areas of the city, a sector which was usually politically inert in the other cities, this group was in political ascendancy throughout the ten years studied. It was a strange alliance of patronage seekers and low-tax supporters which produced its own peculiar variety of local politics. Wages were not particularly high for city employees, for this was too obvious a drain of tax dollars. However, the union controlled work rules, and professionalism was largely undercut by patronage promotions and appointments. The result was a fairly high tax rate in fact, and an elaborate system of access which enabled small requests to be expeditiously handled, while services were poor when measured in professional terms. Thus Delta resembled Beta in some respects. It differed in ignoring policies directed toward economic growth. Both the interests of most local businessmen and the consumer interests of upper-middle-class areas were largely frustrated. Thus by relating prevailing community values to the recruitment process, stress was placed on at least one pattern of political behavior which might have been overlooked had no typology been used. The clearest expressions of prevailing policies (in Alpha and Delta) were the products of organized politics. The more formless politics of Beta and Gamma reflected the lack of strong political organization.

Let us pursue the subject of interest groups as a third illustration of the utility of the typology. In tracing down the goals of various groups in city politics, it was discovered that similar groups with ostensibly the same objectives behaved differently in different cities. The boards of realty may be used as an example. A popular national image of realty interests characterizes them as dedicated to keeping the property tax low. This describes very accurately the realty organization in Beta, a city which stressed the caretaker role for government. Not only did the realtors adhere to this policy but they invested great resources to influence city policies. But in Alpha, the realtors were publicly on record supporting nearly every proposed civic improvement designed to increase the city's amenities or potential for economic growth. In Gamma, the realtors' official policy was very similar to that in Beta, but the organization did not pursue these objectives with equal vigor. In Delta, a city in which business groups had little influence at city hall, the realtors, as an organized group, had no political program. Thus in the four cities, it appeared that the activities of the realtors followed the prevailing community values rather than their own narrow economic interests. It may be objected that their narrow economic interests were indeed served by conforming to community mores. But this merely points anew to the necessity for revealing and characterizing the dominant values of a community as a guide for understanding the political behavior of particular groups.

IV

A final word of caution should be added on the use and abuse of this or similar typologies. The typology should not be applied with the idea that every action of a city government can be neatly tagged under one of the categories. Furthermore, prototype cities are probably rare, and most cities have a complex typological profile. Similarly most citizens harbor a sympathy for more than one of these roles for local government. Many individuals or organizations active in city politics publicly support all four roles for local government and stoutly maintain they are compatible. But pushed far enough each of the roles is incompatible with all of the others. This is the fault line where alliances are breached and the previous consensus in a community erupts into open antagonisms. The object, then, is not to seek too simple a characterization of communities. But differences are real and these differences must be first conceptualized so that other forms of comparative analysis may take on meaning and significance. Then questions can be raised which ask whether the crucial differences explaining various types of governmental roles lie in political organization, legal structure, organizational life, size of place, regional heritage or economic conditions.

Local Industrial Structures, Economic Power, and Community Welfare

Irving A. Fowler

An old ideological conflict over who should control economic activity and to what ends reappeared in postwar America. Most conservatives were alarmed by the growth of economic and political power of farmers, organized workers, and centralized federal agencies. Most liberals, on the other hand, were equally alarmed by the persistent presence of vast concentrations of private economic power, despite fifty years of vigorous anti-trust agitation. Both political camps were apprehensive over the American economy's stability. The continuous inflationary spiral and its generation of acrimonious strife between labor and management inflamed the ideological clash further.

The deepest root of this ideological conflict rests in the cultural ideology of liberal capitalism, a system of beliefs about what the structure, control, and performance of the economy should be like. Shorn of considerable detail, the ideology prescribes an economic structure composed of many small, locally-centered economic units, controlled primarily by open and freely competitive market forces. The presumed result is a maximum of economic welfare and a social environment responsive to the "needs of the people." The opposite structure, composed of a few large, absentee-centered economic units, administering prices in monopolistic markets, is proscribed, because it is presumed to result in a minimum of welfare and in a social environment exploitative of the people. The ideology also contends, implicitly or explicitly, that social and political pluralism will result, that this pluralism is a valuable corollary of economic competition, and that the competition of men for political power will somehow serve the society in the same way as compe-

Irving A. Fowler, "Local Industrial Structures, Economic Power, and Community Welfare," *Social Problems*, VI, 1, 1958, pp. 41–51. A major portion of this paper was presented at the Eastern Sociological Society meetings in New York City, April 14, 1957. Acknowledgements are gratefully made to Robert Hardt for his critical review of an earlier draft of this paper. This paper won the Fourth Annual Helen L. DeRoy award of the Society for the Study of Social Problems.

tition does in the economic sphere. More detailed examinations of the ideology are available in Galbraith (9, pp. 11–34), Moore (16, pp. 417–454), Williams (27, pp. 138–140), and Sutton (24, entire volume).*

Ten years ago, Mills and Ulmer published a study of small-business versus big-business cities (15) confirming the ideological "theory." Their study tentatively concluded that big-business tends to depress while small business tends to raise the level of local "civic" welfare, as measured by the Thorndike G score. Their more detailed findings were that small business cities had more "balanced" economies with larger proportions of independent entrepreneurs who showed greater concern for local civic affairs.

Publication of this and another study by the Senate Small Business Committee (10) created a furor over the respective contributions of small –versus big-business to societal and to local community well-being. The furor was another indication that the ideological issues were still very much alive in the behavior of many Americans.

Some social scientists are still as much victims of the ideology as other Americans. The ideology's prescriptions are implicit in the work of some community organization people. A few sociology texts still quote the Mills-Ulmer findings uncritically (3, 5). Some economists continue to exhort public policy-makers to legislate the ideology's prescriptions into law (11, 17, 21). With so many Americans, lay and scientific, still basing their behavior on the cultural biases of the ideology of liberal capitalism, it is little wonder that empirical analysis of all types of social power have been impeded for so long.

The fact that the current American economy differs widely from that prescribed by the ideological "theory" needs little documentation here. Many studies show conclusively that oligopolistic markets are typical (2, 9, 23). Big business managers share much economic control over these markets with leaders of large farm, labor, retail, and governmental organizations. Yet there is no evidence that the ubiquitous private "concentration of economic power" has had adverse effects on the *entire society's* social welfare (4, 13, 25). A review of evidence on small–versus big-business dominanance *in industrial cities* discloses, upon careful examination, highly variable effects (8). The question of the differential effects of diverse kinds of local industrial structures and local power structures on local well-being remained problematical enough to suggest that continuous study is required.

PURPOSE OF PAPER

This paper presents the results of a recent empirical test of three hypotheses involving the relationship between the characteristics of local

* A bibliography appears at the end of this article.

economies, local power structures, and community welfare (8). The first
hypothesis, derived from the ideology's implications and from one of the
Mills-Ulmer study conclusions, asserts that:

> Small-business industrial structures will produce higher levels of welfare
> than big-business structures, other relevant factors remaining relatively
> constant.

The second hypothesis, again derived from the ideology and from Mills
and Ulmer's interpretation of their other findings, asserts that:

> Local pluralistic power structures will produce higher levels of welfare
> than local monolithic power structures.

The third hypothesis asserts that:

> The "type of industry" variable has an equal, if not greater, effect on
> welfare as do other industrial structure variables, other relevant factors
> remaining constant.

Although Mills and Ulmer were unable to include "type of industry"
in their classification of structures, a review of the evidence suggested
that such an inclusion would be essential for more adequate classifications of local industrial structures. The factors to be held constant in the
tests of the first and third hypotheses were geographical location, similarity of terrain, climate, size, and character of population. No factors were
held constant in the test of the second hypothesis.

METHOD

The hypothetical tests were accomplished through partial * replication
and extension of the Mills-Ulmer design: the *ex post facto* experiment.
Thirty small New York State cities (10,000 to 80,000 in size in 1946) were
selected in a fashion following the Mills-Ulmer procedure. Their general
economic and demographic structures were analyzed prior to classifying
their industrial and power structures for hypothetical tests. Small—versus
big-business industrial structures were operationally defined in terms of
the following two criteria and data:

(a) *The degree of concentration of employment,* based on percent of
total industrial employment employed by large establishments, defined

---

* Partially replicatory for two reasons: (a) limited research resources confined city
selection to one state and to smaller size cities; and (b) the latter necessitated the
creation of a new index of welfare, since the Thorndike G score was available for
cities of 25,000 or over only.

as those with 500 or more wage earners, arbitrarily defined at the 30 city median of 62.2 percent, 1950.

(b) *The degree of local—versus absentee-ownership,* based on percent of total industrial employment employed by absentee-owned establishments, arbitrarily dichotomized at the 30 city median of 65.1 percent, 1950.

Since institutionalized power relations inevitably involve the evaluation of the worth and distribution of goods and services (economic values), the prestige of others (stratification values), and the control of others' behavior in a territorial area (political power values), pluralistic versus monolithic local power structures were operationally defined in terms of the following five criteria and data:

(a) *The degree of concentration of employment,* described above.

(b) *The degree of industrial unionism,* based on the estimated percent of all industrial workers organized in all types of legitimate industrial unions, arbitrarily dichotomized at the 30 city median of 80 percent, 1947–1949.

(c) *The degree of presence of the "old" middle class,* based on the percent of total employed civilian labor force "self-employed," arbitrarily dichotomized at the 30 city median of 10.0 percent, 1947.

(d) *The degree of conformity to the social characteristics (nativity, ethnicity, and religion) of the American society's majority,* based on the estimated percent of the total population native-born, white, Protestant, arbitrarily dichotomized at the 30 city estimated median, 1940.

(e) *The degree of political conservatism,* based on the percent of total party enrollment registered in the Republican party, arbitrarily dichotomized at the 30 city median of 59.6 percent, 1947.

The hypothesis assumes that a "pluralistic" power structure exists when (a) there are diverse sources of social power, (b) exercised by numerous persons over smaller numbers of others, (c) in many separated spheres of social life. Contrariwise, a "monolithic" power structure exists when a small group of persons, deriving power from a few sources, hold power over numerous others in many spheres of their social life.

The light-dispersed versus heavy-concentrated industrial structures were operationally defined in terms of the following two criteria and data:

(a) *The degree of concentration of employment,* described above.

(b) *The degree of light—versus heavy-industry,* based on annual average value-added by manufacturing per industrial wage earner, arbitrarily dichotomized at the 30 city median of 52.24 per cent, 1947.

Local welfare was also operationally defined and measured in terms of a new composite index called the General Social Welfare (GSW) score, replacing the Thorndike G score used by Mills and Ulmer.* The GSW score was derived from a total of 48 individual variables,† ranked in terms of whether more or less of the item would be regarded as indicative of "high" welfare and the rank "one" always designated the "highest" value. These 48 ranking were combined into the following eleven major welfare subcomposites:

1. Income
2. Income security
3. Consumer purchasing power
4. Home ownership
5. Housing adequacy
6. Health needs
7. Health facilities
8. Literacy
9. Adequacy of educational provision
10. Political expression
11. Municipal wealth and service

Mean ranks of these subcomposites were re-ranked and then totalled to derive the GSW scores. Lower values of the GSW scores denoted higher welfare levels. Arithmetically, the thirty cities' GSW scores could range from 11 to 330; the actual scores ranged from 89 to 277.

Controlled comparisons of cities were made with relevant variables held constant except the presumed independent variable: the prescribed and proscribed types of industrial structures.

A combination of two methods was used to equate the sample pairs of cities; *frequency distribution control* and *precision control*. The presumed dependent variables, the various levels of local welfare, were then compared to see if they confirmed or denied the predictions of the specific hypotheses.

RESULTS

Table 1 presents seven pairs of cities for evidence to test the first hypothesis. The first five pairs compare well on five control variables (metropolitan status, population size, percent foreign-born white, percent non-white, and degree of dependence on manufacturing); the last two

---

* Thorndike G scores were available for only 17 of the 30 selected cities. Despite dissimilarity in data, time period, and weighting, a rank order correlation of the 17 G scores with their corresponding GSW scores produced a coefficient of 0.69, significant at the 0.01 level. This finding supported the assumption that local welfare levels were fairly stable functions of underlying socio-economic structures.
† A complete list of these 48 items will be provided upon request.

Table 1   *Small versus Big-Business City Industrial Structures Contrasted in Ownership and Employment, by GSW Scores; 1930–1948 (the Top City in Each Pair is Small-Business)*

| Paired Cities | Control Variables [a] | | | Independent Variables [c] | | Dependent Variable |
	Population 1940	Manufacturing Ratio [b] 1940	Percent Absentee Establish- ments 1950	Employed by Large Establish- ments 1950	GSW Scores [d] 1930–1948
SB	28,589	48	47.2	14.7	203.5
BB	21,506	46	72.9	65.9	124.5
SB	18,836	47	38.4	41.1	94.5
BB	15,555	54	65.1	62.4	110.5
SB	23,329	71	15.5	0.0	167.5
BB	24,379	68	75.0	65.4	94.5
SB	12,572	74	48.8	21.9	173.5
BB	17,713	71	85.0	87.4	228.0
SB	10,666	78	3.5	0.0	204.0
BB	11,328	58	95.6	95.6	198.7
SB	42,638	62	13.2	47.0	150.5
BB	34,214	68	78.1	81.0	209.0
SB	10,291	42	29.4	0.0	139.5
BB	45,106	48	66.0	79.6	136.5

[a] All cities have independent metropolitan status. Two control variables, per cent foreign born white and non-white, have been excluded for lack of table space.

[b] The higher the ratio, the higher the degree of dependence on manufacturing. This ratio is based on the percent of employees employed in industry, computed as a per-cent of "aggregate employment" in four types of economic activity: industry, retail trade, wholesale trade, and service trade.

[c] The data for these indices was gathered in personal surveys of the selected cities. "Large" establishments were defined as those with 500 or more industrial employees.

[d] The lower the GSW score, the higher the local community welfare.

pairs compare well on three or four of these control variables. In each case of pairs, the top city is small-business with the least concentration of employment and the least absentee-ownership; the bottom city is big-business with the greatest concentration of employment and the most absentee-ownership.

The table shows that in only three out of seven pairs of cities are the results consistent with ideological predictions, that is, small-business structures having higher levels of general social welfare than big-business structures. In a series of less rigorous hypotheses tests, the same inconclusive results were found.

Table 2 *Thirty Local Power Structures, by Degree of Pluralism and by Mean GSW Scores (each Criterion Dichotomized into High and Low Values and Equally Weighted)*

No. of Criteria on which Cities Are High [a]	Each Type		Combine Types	
	No. Cities	Mean GSW Scores [b]	No. Cities	Mean GSW Scores
Pluralistic Pole:				
A. Five highs [d]	1	237.0	8	212.2 [c]
B. Four highs	7	208.7		
C. Three highs	7	158.2	15	164.2
D. Two highs	8	169.4		
E. One high	5	130.6	7	119.5
F. No highs [e]	2	91.9		
Monolithic Pole:				
No. of cities	30		30	

[a] The following cities fall into the listed types: (A) Hudson; (B) Cohoes, Gloversville, Little Falls, Middletown, Oswego, Rome, Troy; (C) Amsterdam, Auburn, Geneva, Glens Falls, Johnstown, Massena, Poughkeepsie; (D) Beacon, Cortland, Dunkirk, Kingston, Olean, Oneida, Watertown, Watervliet; (E) Binghamton, Corning, Elmira, Endicott, Jamestown, and (F) Johnson City and Lockport.

[b] The lower the GSW scores, the higher the local community welfare.

[c] The differences between these mean scores are statistically significant. An H equal to 12.84 was computed with a probability of 0.01 being due to chance.

[d] Low concentration of employment, high industrial unionism, large "old" middleclass, high social heterogeneity of population, and high political liberalism.

[e] High concentration of employment, low industrial unionism, small "old" middleclass, high social homogeneity of population, and high political conservativism.

Table 2 presents a typology of local power structures based on dichotomized values of five of the listed criteria: degree of concentration of employment, industrial unionism, "old" middle-class, social heterogeneity, and political conservatism. On the assumption that each indexed criterion is of equal weight, there are six possible combinations of highs and lows, ranging from five highs and no lows (the most pluralistic end of the continuum) to five lows and no highs (the monolithic, or least pluralistic end of the continuum).

The findings from Table 2 are sharply opposite to the ideological expectations. Local pluralistic power structures in greatest conformity with the five attributes prescribed by the ideology were negatively associated with high levels of welfare. The monolithic (or least pluralistic) power structures, in which there existed the greatest likelihood of coalesced social, economic, and political elites, and the least likelihood of social challenge to these cities from diverse socio-economic groups with their own socio-economic interests to pursue, were positively associated with higher levels of welfare. Equally interesting is the apparent linearity of the negative association in this sample of thirty cities—the higher the degree of local pluralism (socially, economically, and politically), the lower the local welfare score.

The third hypothesis asserted that the exclusion of the "type of industry" variable or criterion from any classification of industrial structures makes the latter inadequate. To make this test, structures with light industry and dispersed employment were compared with structures having heavy-industry and concentrated employment. Table 3 presents five pairs of contrasted cities with appropriate data on the control, independent, and dependent variables.

Table 3   *Light-Dispersed Employment versus Heavy-Concentrated City Industrial Structures by GSW Scores: 1930–1948 (the Top City is Light-Industry with Dispersed Employment)*

Paired Cities	Control [a] Population 1940	Manu- facturing Ratio 1940	Independent An Average Value Added by Manufac- turer per Wage Earner: 1946	Percent Employment by Large Establish- ments 1950	Dependent GSW Scores 1930– 1948 [b]
A	10,666	78	$3858	0.0	204.0 [c]
B	11,328	58	9512	95.6	198.7
C	23,329	71	4037	0.0	167.5
D	24,379	68	6612	65.4	94.5
E	22,062	55	4944	32.2	223.0
F	21,506	46	7249	65.9	124.5
G	12,572	74	4624	21.9	173.5
H	15,881	66	6009	62.5	145.5
I	28,589	48	3745	14.7	203.5
J	45,106	48	5530	79.6	136.5

[a] See footnotes in Table 1.

[b] The lower the GSW score, the higher the local community welfare.

[c] Applying the H test, and H = 260.8 results with a P less than 0.001.

Analysis shows that in five out of five cases one type of structure is consistently and positively associated with higher welfare levels. The hypothesis that "type of industry" has an important determinant effect on welfare can thus be accepted as tenable. In the paired cases studied, a specific general "type of industry" (heavy, producer goods industry, coupled with concentration of employment) had a consistently positive association with higher welfare levels.

The major findings of the study this paper reports were therefore as follows:

(a) Local "concentrations of economic power" *do not* have invariant "adverse" effects on local welfare levels.

(b) The *type of industry* found in a local industrial structure has an important determinant effect on local welfare levels.

(c) In the 30 cities studied, the industrial structures in *least* conformity with the ideological model (those with higher absentee-ownership, higher concentrations of employment, more heavy industry) tended to have slightly higher welfare levels than structures with the opposite characteristics.

(d) In the 30 cities studied, the local power structures in *least* conformity with the ideological model (those with higher concentrations of employment, low degrees of industrial unionism, low proportion of the "old" middle-class, low degrees of political liberalism, and low degree of social heterogeneity) tended to have substantially higher welfare levels than the structures with the opposite characteristics.

INTERPRETATION

The findings were obviously at sharp variance with the Mills-Ulmer study and ideological implications. The discordance of this study's finding with past evidence, which partially confirmed the ideology, requires a complex interpretation of related levels of socio-economic phenomena. But because the evidence is confined to just one level (local), this paper's interpretation can only suggest connections between the empirical findings and the conditions and processes in the larger economy.

The sample cities with big-business structures tended to have higher welfare levels for four reasons related to the technically advanced nature of modern industry. First, their more advanced technical mode of production demands larger numbers of more highly skilled and higher paid personnel. Being part of large national industrial organizations, with a greater degree of control over particular markets, such local establishments can more readily absorb such higher personnel costs. Second, their local establishment, usually the result of careful site selection and a long-range capital commitment, increases the local assessed valuation of industrial, and, indirectly, personal property, thus making more tax revenue potentially available for public services for longer periods of time.

Third, this relatively long-range commitment to site, this attraction of higher skilled personnel, plus the demand for specific supply relations, stimulates the growth of ancillary industries with similar characteristics. Finally, local consumers, like all consumers, benefit from the big-business establishment's contribution to the firm's and industry's constant increments to technically advanced productive methods and products. Thus, these and numerous other factors intimately related to the nature of the industry,* whether intensely competitive or monopolistically competitive, have as determinant an effect on community welfare as the nature of industrial organization of either.

All the above local benefits were contingent, however, on the specific industry's stage of development in the locality or region, and on deeper market forces in the entire economy. If the industrial units were newly located or in earlier developmental stages, these welfare benefits would be observable locally for some time, precluding of course, severe deflationary conditions. If, on the other hand, the local units were obsolescent and the entire industry's geographical center was shifting, such benefits could be subject to dramatic reversals. Thus, the expansion of new industries and the contraction of old has entailed highly dynamic geographical shifts of local centers of production. And, while the entire economy may benefit from locational as well as technological competition, these benefits will not and cannot fall evenly on the local populations involved (14).

With the implication that local economic and political elites were coalesced, why did not the more monolithic local power structures depress local welfare in the manner that Mills and Ulmer described? (See ref. 15, pp. 22–31.) The answer is simply that in both studies the coalesced power of big-business structures was more apparent than real. Mills and Ulmer abstracted from their data only that which permitted the construction of the malevolent picture that adherents of the ideology would be expected to present.

Such a picture could not take into consideration the following types of socio-economic phenomena: (a) the immensely complex, historical growth pattern of modern industries and how their periodic "abuse" of economic power has provoked defensive-protective reactions of specific buyers and sellers; and (b) how these developing bargaining relations intersected in different structural locations (9). All of which shows how historically in Western democracies the exercise of coalesced economic and political power and its consequences have been highly limited *to specific issues, groups or organizations, or areas.* Nor does their picture

* A large number of diverse variables were found associated with city welfare levels, the most important of which were: (a) the extent and availability of raw resources, (b) costs of assembling materials, and (c) costs of marketing finished products.

indicate how frequently big-business executives are disinclined to "exploit" local social elements. Angell, for instance, reports that big-business executives were either disinterested in local affairs, or, if involved, had a baneful influence on local affairs, not because of any abuse of power, but because they were inept and unrepresentative leaders (1, p. 105).

Most evidence presented here would suggest that the actions of local economic and political elites were determined by larger forces over which neither they nor those exposed to their power have much control. Furthermore, little sociological attention is given to the local community dependence on extra-community organization and to the frequent relinquishing of local authority to the broader social structure as Sjoberg points out (22).

Important factors in the modern situation would thus seem to have made it increasingly difficult to "abuse" economic power in the local community. Among such factors, the following appear to be highly significant: (a) the growth pattern of modern industry and defensive-protective adjustments of related economic groups and organizations; (b) the growth of public power to protect "public welfare"; (c) the growth of personal resistance to unlimited exercise of all types of social power; (d) the changing occupational structure, with its "professionalization" of labor (7); and (e) the solvent of increasing wealth. In short, the paradoxical finding that *local* monolithic power was not abusive economically can only be explained by the growing restraints upon it coming from the increasingly pluralistic power in the general social structure.

SOCIAL PROBLEM IMPLICATIONS

It appears obvious that these findings provide no calm harbor for those who hope ideological conflict over the respective contributions of small versus big-business to local welfare will evaporate. So long as the "insecurity of illusion" (9) of the cultural ideology of liberal capitalism persists, tensions between important economic and political actors in the American scene will continue.

The tensions will provide fertile soil for the continuance of still other types of social problems, only a few of which can be mentioned here. There is some evidence, for instance, that irresponsible scape-goating of big-business executives had turned modern management's attentions to the labyrinths of "human relations" to such an extent that it has lost sight of its primary economic role: production (6, 26). A frequent problem is the mass manipulation of ideological symbols to obscure issues in the political struggle for control of governments (State and Federal) and their power to intervene in private economic affairs in the name of "public welfare." Less frequently cited, but widespread, is the following type of abuse by *inaction of locally centered* private economic and political power holders: powerful local proponents of the ideology blaming extra-local forces or persons for their own inability to act constructively on the local scene, despite the availability of numerous "enabling" resources provided by extra-local organizations in the health, welfare, civil rights problem areas. Both of the latter are so frequently observable that they require no documentation here.

Social scientists have only recently begun to contribute solutions to those problems by systematic conceptual clarification and empirical analysis of significant power problem areas. Galbraith's differentiation between "original" and "countervailing" economic power and their dynamic development (9), Parson's clarification of economic and political power (13, p. 121), William's analysis of the interpenetration of American economic and political institutions (27), Rosenberg's application of Reisman's concept of "veto" groups to the desegregation issue (20, 19), and Sutton's detailed examination of the social functions of the American Business Creed (24) herald a significant "break-through" the cultural biases against investigating power problems. A sociology of knowledge inquiry into the sources, supports, and consequences of these cultural biases would be a worthy additional contribution, and provide, at the same time, a greater historical understanding of past and future power struggles in democratic societies. At any rate, sociologists and economists appear ready to produce something like Lasswell's and Kaplan's treatise on power (12) in the field of the sociology of economic organizations and institutions.

SUMMARY

This paper presented the results of an empirical test of three hypotheses derived from ideology of liberal capitalism and from a previous study of the presumed effects of small–versus big-business on local "welfare."

Small-business cities were found to have no higher levels of welfare than big-business cities; to the contrary, small-business cities tended to have lower levels of welfare. The "type of industry" was found to be an important criterion for more adequate classification of industrial structures. In the cases studied, heavier durable-goods industry and concentrated employment were associated with higher welfare levels. The major conclusion was, therefore, that "concentrations of economic power" *do not have invariably adverse* effects on community welfare.

In a less rigorous test of the local power structure hypothesis, similar results were found. The least pluralistic power structures (concentrated employment, low industrial unionism, small "old" middle-class, low political "liberalism," and low population heterogeneity) were associated with higher welfare levels.

These findings were obviously at sharp variance with the Mills-Ulmer study and with ideological expectations. A complex interpretation of related levels of socio-economic phenomena, tying the empirical findings of this paper to other observations on conditions and processes in the larger political economy, was required.

In the cases studied, big-business cities had higher welfare for reasons related to its monopolistically competitive and technically advanced nature. They paid higher wages, enhanced local property and tax revenues, stimulated the growth of ancillary industries, and, being forced to bargain with massive retail organizations, contributed indirectly to greater consumer satisfaction. All of these benefits, however, were dependent on whether the general economy was stable or deflationary.

Interpretation of the findings is facilitated, if conceptual distinctions are made between "original" and "countervailing" economic power, between "economic" and "political" power, and between intra-local and extra-local levels of organization. It is furthermore suggested that certain social problems will persist unless these distinctions are broadly disseminated among the people.

American social scientists have only recently broken through these biases. It would not be remiss to say that the American people and their democratic values would benefit immensely, if this "break-through" is consolidated by further intensive study.

REFERENCES

1. Angell, Robert C., "The Moral Integration of American Cities," Supplement to the *American Journal of Sociology*, 57 (July, 1951).
2. Blair, John M., *et al.*, *Economic Concentration and World War II*, Report of the Smaller War Plant Corporation to the Special Committee to Study Problems of American Small Business, U.S. Senate, 79th Cong., 2nd Sess., Doc. No. 206 (Wash.: USGOP, 1946).
3. Broom, Leonard, and Philip Selznick, *Sociology* (Evanston, Ill.: Row, Peterson and Co., 1955), pp. 420–424.
4. Clark, Colin, *The Conditions of Economic Progress* (London: Macmillan Co., 1940), pp. 148–149.
5. Cuber, John F., *Sociology: A Synopsis of Principles* (New York: Appleton-Century-Crofts, Inc., 1955 edit.), pp. 413–418.
6. Drucher, Peter F., *The New Society* (New York: Harper and Bros., 1950).
7. Foote, Nelson N., and Paul K. Hatt, "Social Mobility and Economic Advancement," *American Economic Review*, 43 (May, 1953), 364–378.
8. Fowler, Irving A., *Local Industrial Structures, Economic Power, and Community Welfare: Thirty Small New York State Cities 1930–1950* (unpublished Ph.D. dissertation, Cornell University, September, 1954).
9. Galbraith, John K., *American Capitalism: The Concept of Countervailing Power* (New York: Houghton, Mifflin Co., 1952).
10. Goldschmid, Walter R., *Small Business and the Community: A Study in Central Valley of California on Effects of Scale of Farm Operations*, Report of the Special Committee to Study Problems of American Small Business, U.S. Senate, 79th Cong., 2nd Sess., No. 13 (Wash.: USGOP, 1946).

11. Hayek, Frederick A., *The Road to Serfdom* (Chicago: The University of Chicago Press, 1944).
12. Lasswell, Harold D., and A. D. H. Kaplan, *Power and Society: A Framework for Political Inquiry* (New Haven: Yale Univ. Press, 1950).
13. Leven, Maurice, Harold G. Moulton, and Clark Warburton, *America's Capacity to Consume* (Washington: Brookings Institution, 1934).
14. McLaughlin, Glenn E., *Growth of American Manufacturing Areas* (Pittsburgh: Bureau of Business Research, University of Pittsburgh, 1938).
15. Mills, C. Wright, and Melville J. Ulmer, *Small Business and Civic Welfare*, Report of the Special Committee to Study Problems of American Small Business, U.S. Senate, 79th Cong., 2nd Sess., No. 135 (Wash.: USGOP, 1946).
16. Moore, Wilbert E., *Industrial Relations and the Social Order* (New York: Macmillan Co., revised edit., 1951), pp. 417–454.
17. Mund, Vernon A., *Government and Business* (New York: Harper and Bros., 1956).
18. Parsons, Talcott, *The Social System* (Glencoe: The Free Press, 1951).
19. Riesman, David, *The Lonely Crowd* (New Haven: Yale Univ. Press, 1950).
20. Rosenburg, Morris, "Power and Desegregation," *Social Problems*, 3 (April, 1956), 215–223.
21. Simons, Henry, *Economic Policy for a Free Society* (Chicago: University of Chicago Press, 1948).
22. Sjoberg, Gideon, "Urban Community Theory and Research: A Partial Evaluation," *American Journal of Economics and Sociology*, 14 (Jan., 1955), 199–206.
23. Stocking, George W., and Myron W. Watkins, *Monopoly and Free Enterprise* (New York: The Twentieth Century Fund, 1951).
24. Sutton, Francis X., *et al.*, *The American Business Creed* (Cambridge: Harvard University Press, 1956).
25. Woytinsky, *et al.*, *Employment and Wages in the United States* (New York: Twentieth Century Fund, 1953), pp. 49–53.
26. Williams, Robin M., Jr., *American Society: A Sociological Interpretation* (New York: Alfred A. Knopf, Inc., 1951).

The Social Services in the Modern Metropolis

Albert Rose

The ancient Greek linguists who put together the words *mētēr* (mother) and *polis* (city) clearly intended the resultant *metropolis* to describe "the mother or parent city or state of a colony" of Greek cities or states. In Late

Albert Rose, "The Social Services in the Modern Metropolis," *Social Service Review*, 1963, Vol. XXXVII, No. 4, pp. 375–389.

Latin the metropolis designated the chief or capital city of a country, state, or region. Early "metropolitans" would no doubt be startled by our description of the modern metropolis and the relationship between the hard-pressed central city (the mother) and her ungrateful and difficult offspring (the suburbs).

A more modern definition would run as follows: A metropolitan area is a group of urban municipalities linked closely—physically, economically, and socially—so that in many ways they may be considered a single community. Almost always there is one large city as the center of economic and social life in a metropolis.

Metropolitan communities grow primarily from the inside outwards rather than chiefly through the process of settlement by new people on the outskirts of the existing city. Residents of the central city, together with some new people, move beyond its boundaries. There they are governed by established rural or semirural governments, or they group together to found new governments of their own. These people are replaced in the more densely populated central regions by new populations whose influx may even have played a part in the outward movement of older residents.[1]

This expanded definition is a part of the traditional twentieth-century exposition of the phenomenon of urban growth into metropolitan status. Thirty years ago one of the more pleasant definitions of a metropolitan area was that it was like a vast pancake, "what is poured into the center gradually oozing to the extremities." If this description were apt in the past it surely is no longer a very good metaphor to describe the present situation in most United States and Canadian settings.

The social services, the first of the two concepts in the title of this paper, may be defined as those socially provided community services designed to assist individuals and families to maintain themselves physically and socially when threatened by such common risks as relatively low income, unemployment, physical and mental illness, disability, widowhood, old age, and death. Services also deal specifically with the inability or incapacity of many persons to live with and/or relate to each other as husband and wife, as parents and children, as neighbor to neighbor, as person to person. The definition implies that the social services attempt to meet the "needs" of people and that these needs of individuals and families have been socially determined and accepted through a process of collective or community judgment. The organizations created by the community to help people meet their needs are normally described as the welfare, health, and recreation services.

These services may be provided by a public authority, whether munici-

---

[1] Committee on Metropolitan Problems, Civic Advisory Council of Toronto, *First Report*, § 1, November, 1949, pp. 1–2. The writer served as director of research for the committee and as editor of its three reports.

pal, state or provincial, or federal; or they may be provided by a voluntary organization. A voluntary organization is defined as one whose governors or directors are not appointed by, or the services controlled or totally financed by, government, and which depends on volunteer services and volunteer responsibility for policy, administration, and stewardship.

One further specification is essential with respect to the geographical locus of the analysis. The argument will be more or less relevant to the North American scene, more specifically to the United States and Canada. It will have much less relevance to conditions in the United Kingdom or in western Europe, and almost no relevance elsewhere in the world.

THE SOCIETY OF THE METROPOLITAN ERA

The modern metropolis is a manifestation of the rapid development of Western urbanized and industrialized society. In turn, the metropolis is becoming the focal point of a rapidly emerging late-twentieth-century urban society and its culture. In order to understand and appreciate the problems with which the social services must deal, the major elements in this rapidly changing society and its structure must be clearly delineated.

1. We Live in a Society of Substantial Population Growth, in Both Absolute and Relative Terms

During the last thirty years the population of the United States increased by some 50 million persons and the population of Canada rose from little more than 10 million to 18.5 million, a much larger relative increase. This has been the consequence, in the case of Canada, of one of the highest birth rates and lowest death rates in the world and a tremendous immigration from Europe, from the United Kingdom, from the United States, and to a lesser extent from many other countries. This immigration, since 1946, when the nation had 11.5 million persons, has amounted to nearly 2.5 million. The earlier postwar immigrants have in addition done their share in producing vast numbers of children. Nevertheless, the Dominion Bureau of Statistics has judged the influence of natural increase at 75 percent and immigration at 25 percent during the 1950's.

2. We Live in a Society which Is Increasingly Urban and Metropolitan in Nature

In the United States, total population increased by 18.5 percent from 1950 to 1960; but the increase in 212 Standard Metropolitan Statistical Areas was 26.4 percent. In 1960, about 63 percent of the people in the United States lived in these metropolitan areas.

For Canada, the increase in total population from 1951 to 1961 was 30.2 percent; but the increase in 17 Census Metropolitan Areas was more than 54 percent. In 1961, about 45 percent of the Canadian population lived in these metropolitan areas. If we apply the United States definition of a metropolitan statistical area, which is more flexible than the Canadian, this proportion rises to 49 percent.

It has been predicted that over the next two decades population in the United States will increase by some 65–80 million and that all of this increase will take place in metropolitan areas. The Royal Commission on Canada's Economic Prospects, 1955–1980, reported in 1957 that Canada's population will reach 27 million in 1980, that 79 percent will be urban, and that two-thirds of the people will live in metropolitan areas.

During the 1950's, when the residents of metropolitan areas in the United States increased in number by 26.4 percent, the population of the central cities rose merely by 10.7 percent, while outside the central cities the increase in the vast suburbs was 48.6 percent. Our urbanization, therefore, has been for the most part a suburbanization, and many of the most notable central cities in the nation have lost population. These include Baltimore, Boston, Buffalo, Chicago, Cincinnati, Cleveland, Minneapolis, Nashville, New York, Newark, Philadelphia, Pittsburgh, the two Portlands, Richmond, Rochester, St. Louis, San Francisco and Oakland, Syracuse, Trenton, and Washington. In fact, out of 130 cities with 100,000 or more persons, 43 (one-third) lost population between 1950 and 1960. This trend is less noticeable in Canada, where the younger cities still have some vacant land, but Toronto's population has been declining slowly throughout the postwar period.

3. We Live in a Society in which Age Distribution and the Dependence-Independence Balance Have Changed Radically

The 1951 census of Canada revealed that there were fewer people in the age groups 10–14 and 15–19 than in 1941. This was a startling consequence of the low birth rate of the "threadbare thirties." The impact of this shortage upon the need for skilled entrants into the labor force and upon the need for aspirants to professional careers in human-service professions, particularly teaching, nursing, and social work, can scarcely be underestimated.

Within the past twelve years there has been a substantial change in the picture. By the mid-1950's in both countries, for the first time those under the age of 15 comprised almost one-third of the entire population; the 15–19 age group made up an additional 6–7 percent. At the same time, the opportunities for relatively high earnings by young persons who left school in the late 1940's and early 1950's are disappearing in response to technological change, with their counterparts in the 1960's destined for a lifetime of unemployment.

We have come to realize as well that our population over the age of

60 accounts for about 12.5 percent of the total. In fact, in Canada, while one in every eight persons is over the age of 60, one in every twelve persons is over 65, and one in every twenty persons is 70 years or over. The proportions in the United States in 1960 are slightly more impressive —one in eleven persons over 65 and one in seventeen persons over 70.

These figures give a rough indication of the requirement that somewhat less than half our people must produce goods and services to support the dependent majority. Yet our economic system does not appear to be growing rapidly enough to provide employment for the "productive" group, which will increase substantially in numbers, if not in proportion, during the next twenty years at least. These facts about population distribution by age are of tremendous importance for the social services.

4. We Live in a Society of Great Population Mobility

In both countries individuals and families are constantly on the move. Some of these movements represent traditional voluntary migration from Europe and other continents to North America, from Puerto Rico to New York; additional migration occurs from the underdeveloped areas in our nations to the industrialized areas, from Nova Scotia to Ontario, from the southern United States to the northern and far western cities. Some of the mobility is the consequence of the deployment of executives and employees within and between states, and on an international scale. Some of the movement is intra-urban, from the central city to the suburbs and vice versa, from one house to another (on the average about every four years) within or between local municipal units.

Mobility and migration have been primarily responsible for fundamental change in the racial, ethnic, religious, and age distributions within the metropolis. It is now commonly understood that a great many young families with children have left the central cities and/or settled directly in the suburbs, leaving behind several overlapping groups of people in disproportionate numbers; namely, the elderly, the poor, the racial or ethnic minorities. There is no doubt that by 1980 the proportion of non-white persons in the central cities of several eastern United States metropolitan areas will far exceed one-half.

One important difference between the United States and the Canadian metropolis must be illustrated. In Canada, the minority groups are most commonly described as "ethnic" rather than "racial." In part this is not because Canadians are less concerned about discriminatory practices in employment and housing but because there are, for example, only some seven thousand Negroes in Metropolitan Toronto in a total population of more than 1.8 million persons. Moreover, questions concerning nationality or ethnic origin and religion have remained in the Canadian Census to date. Although it would be naïve to suggest that strong barriers to free settlement do not exist, none is as strong as the formidable constraint which forestalls the movement of Negroes into the suburbs of the cities in the United States.

5. We Live in a Society Described as "Affluent"

It is not difficult to demonstrate that our two nations are affluent if a comparison is drawn between the present and the past centuries, between the present decade and that of the 1930's or the wartime decade of the 1940's. After all, we are not attempting to measure happiness or well-being or cultural attainment from an individual or national point of view. We look primarily at Gross National Product, average per capita and family incomes, and the statistics of production.

In Canada, for example, GNP reached $6 billion in 1929, fell to $3.5 billion in the depth of the depression, yet had not returned to the 1929 level when World War II broke out. GNP in 1962 reached $40 billion, seven times that of 1939, while population had risen by some 65 percent. Per capita personal income had increased nearly four times, from about $400 to $1,600 in 1961. Even with a rise in the price level of some 250 percent, per capita purchasing power had perhaps doubled.

In the United States, GNP exceeded $104 billion in 1929, fell to $56 billion in 1933, yet by 1940 had not returned to the 1929 level. GNP in 1961 reached $520 billion, more than five times that of 1940, while population had risen by less than 40 percent. Per capita personal income was $595 in 1940, and more than $2,200 in 1960 at current prices. Once again per capita purchasing power had probably doubled. These averages, of course, hide the considerable variation in income between the under-developed or economically depressed areas and the highly industrialized or prosperous areas and between the central cities and the higher-income suburbs in the metropolis.

Our respective nations are affluent, as well, in that our people already possess or may purchase the greatest number and variety of durable and other consumer goods available anywhere in the world or in the history of mankind. We are glutted with goods, not merely cars and appliances, but also food and clothing. Yet we have been unable to discover a method of distributing these goods more equitably, and we have not been able to provide "decent, safe, and sanitary" housing for a substantial proportion of our people. We maintain and tolerate gross deprivation in the midst of plenty.

The fact is that Professor Galbraith's concept of the affluent society has been greatly misunderstood during the past five years. Many people apparently assumed that Galbraith believed that poverty had been eliminated and that we were all wealthy. No such notion was intended. Rather, his thesis was simply that, while this was the first time in history that virtually everyone was *not* in poverty, our economic system required a vast investment of social capital to insure economic growth and employment for a rapidly expanding population.[2]

In the United States today, as Michael Harrington has emphasized in *The Other America*,[3] somewhere between 20 and 25 percent of the people are, by any definition, poor. They have inadequate housing, food, medical care, and opportunity. They number between 40 and 50 million persons. The numbers really do not matter in the final analysis, but no study I have examined, depending upon its definition of low income, has set the figure at less than 30 millions in poverty. In Canada some years ago, I worked out the proportion of population in dire poverty, defined as complete dependence upon public funds, at one in sixteen persons. This excluded low-income, so-called self-supporting families.[4]

While there are rural persons in poverty, the greatest proportion of families in the lowest two-fifths of the income scale are living in or moving to the central cities of metropolitan areas. There they are in the process of developing a new and modern urban culture of poverty which the social services on the current pattern seem helpless to confront.

6. We Live in a Society of Gross Economic and Social Anomalies

Poverty in the midst of plenty is merely the all-inclusive consideration. Perhaps there is less poverty in the midst of greater plenty than prevailed a half-century ago. The specific tendencies within the over-all situation are even more disturbing. For at least seven years we have witnessed increasing total employment and increasing unemployment simultaneously; we note higher prices or inflation together with increased unemployment. We note vast public expenditures and very substantial deficits in our governmental balance sheets and yet a slowness and retardation of economic growth such that vast numbers of new entrants to the labor force cannot secure full-time or consistent employment, and more established members of the labor force can only with difficulty secure new jobs, once they become unemployed. We have a great increase in the number of older persons, yet it is increasingly difficult for a person over 35 years of age to secure re-employment.

In Canada there are 100,000 new young entrants to the labor force each year compared with 5,000 a year when World War II began. Many jobs are available in industry, business, and the professions for which there are few candidates because the level of training or skill required is well beyond the typical attainment of most members of the labor force.

[2] John K. Galbraith, *The Affluent Society* (Boston: Houghton Mifflin Co., 1958), pp. 322–33.
[3] New York: Macmillan Co., 1962, *passim* and Appendix.
[4] Albert Rose, "Housing the Poor and the Aged" (lecture delivered before the Staff Course on Urban Renewal, Central Mortgage and Housing Corporation, Ottawa, Canada, March, 1958), pp. 6–9.

We are fond of insisting that ours is a child-centered society. Surely, never was so much read and said by so many parents concerning so many children. Yet the social services in our metropolises must not only attempt to help a larger number of unmarried mothers, mentally ill and/or grossly neglected children, and juvenile delinquents, but, in many communities, must deal with higher rates of these facets of social breakdown than prevailed in the postwar years.

Although we insist that ours is a child-centered society, the proportion of wives in the labor force in the United States has increased from 15 percent in 1940 to 30 percent in 1957. In Canada, one in every four persons in the labor force is a woman, and half of these persons, some 800,000 are married women. We are not certain what the proportion of working mothers is, but we know that it is substantial. We know, as well, that the family in the affluent society can often attain a home, a car, and all the rest of the so-called laborsaving devices only when both parents are employed.

This brief analysis of some of the major social and economic tendencies in our late-twentieth-century society leads me to the conclusion that the social services, as we know them in the metropolis, are ill-equipped indeed to deal with the consequences of industrialization, urbanization, and metropolitan growth. The social and economic life these forces have spawned has changed drastically, while the patterns of service have remained rigid and unyielding.

PRESENT PATTERNS OF THE SOCIAL SERVICES
IN THE METROPOLIS

A résumé of the evolution of the social services is not to be considered typical of any specific metropolitan area in North America, yet to some extent it will identify characteristic developments. In general it will be more truly descriptive of cities in the United States from St. Louis and Chicago to the East, and of cities in Ontario and the Atlantic Provinces in Canada.

As the 1920's began, most of the essential features of the present patterns of voluntary welfare, health, and recreation services had been clearly established. Family, child welfare, visiting nursing, and certain institutional services for elderly people and children were being provided under denominational auspices. Federations of Jewish, Roman Catholic, and so-called nonsectarian community services, which included many agencies clearly Protestant in denomination, had been organized. The first welfare federation encompassing all three groups appeared in Cleveland before 1914, and the community chest movement spread rapidly during the 1920's.

Admittedly, there were privately sponsored or voluntary agencies which had their roots in the early part of the nineteenth century, but these were exceptions to the general rule. The settlement house, like the Charity Organization Society, was imported from England during the last third of the century and reached its full flowering in serving the vast numbers of immigrants from Europe who crowded into eastern United States and Canadian cities and typically as far west as Chicago and Winnipeg from the 1880's until World War I.

Public welfare departments as a function of municipal government did not develop in many cities until the early 1930's and then only in response to the most serious economic depression in our history. In Canada the local municipality has traditionally been responsible for the dispensing of "poor relief," but the voluntary agencies (and the Catholic church in Quebec) played a major role through and beyond World War II. The far western provinces, however, as in the United States, developed relatively more adequate public welfare programs and relied upon a wider administrative unit, the county or the provincial/state department of welfare.

One or two major voluntary services—typically the Family Service Association, to use a generic title—began to branch out within the central city during the two decades 1919–1939. For the most part, however, the characteristic pattern of service was one based upon a central office in the downtown area to which clients came and from which workers traveled to the residences of individuals and families who required counseling, health services, and often financial assistance. New agencies which came into being either before or after World War I fitted easily into the prevailing patterns, the dominant characteristics of which were, and are today in many metropolitan areas, centralization, a denominational basis, and the provision of a specialized service as a unitary function.

In the early postwar years the first rumblings of discontent from outside the central cities were clearly heard. The early denominational federations had come together in a community chest or experimental wartime federation, and these structures were converted into United Community Funds in the late 1940's or early 1950's. Fund-raising for a large proportion of the local welfare and health services had become centralized in what was visualized as a permanent federation. However, only a very few of the participating agencies in the early postwar campaigns were located in and serving the suburban areas.

Nevertheless, the campaign organization had every right to expect to secure volunteer workers and voluntary contributions from residents beyond the borders of the central city. First the canvassers, then the campaign directors, then the social planning councils, in that order, were asked and were hard put to answer one of the more difficult questions in fund-raising: "What and where are the voluntary services which are intended to meet the needs of local residents?" The pressure of population movement and the unrewarding efforts to tap the increasing individual and family incomes of suburban dwellers led a few agencies to locate branches beyond the city and others to offer services more widely. Most agencies attempted to serve suburban residents in one way or another from their downtown locations.

In retrospect it seems to have dawned upon us in the early 1950's that the familiar view of the suburban dweller as "problem-free" or relatively independent in problem-solving, versus the downtown city dweller as "needful" and relatively dependent upon external help, was not entirely accurate. The tricky questions of the fund-raising drives were based upon individual or community expressions of concern about meeting clearly identified but unmet needs. There was not, however, a widespread disposition in the suburban areas to encourage the downtown agencies to offer familiar services to individuals and families merely by locating branches in various locations. There was a strong feeling that the staff members and board members in the city did not truly understand the needs of local communities in the suburbs.

This analysis is not intended to imply in any way that the services provided in the central city have been or are adequate. The new problems simply do not respond to the traditional methods. As well, the old dream of clearing out the downtown slums and rehousing the poor and the problem-ridden families in decent housing was soon to become a nightmare. Slum clearance and rehousing proved not to be the panacea hoped for. Many displaced families refused the opportunity of moving into public housing and became the residents of the "untreated" slums across the way. Many families who were rehoused did not undergo miraculous change in their living habits and health conditions (although a good proportion did improve their lives significantly) and moved out to be slowly swallowed up in the overcrowded urban core. The failure of public housing has been a great blow to the social services in the metropolis. There was never enough housing provided, and its administration as real estate, rather than as a social institution, helped to confound its objectives.

The development of the newer and more sophisticated concept of urban renewal, which included rehabilitation and conservation of neighborhoods as well as clearance and urban redevelopment, posed new and equally difficult problems for the social services. The new authorities began to develop plans for the neighborhood or the entire community and programs rightly and roundly criticized by health and welfare professional staff. When, however, the physical planners asked for the social plans of the agencies or their suggestions for improvement, there was little or no response. Moreover, the urban renewal programs, in themselves, created vast dislocation for the residents of traditional neighborhoods, productive of sufficient pressure upon the social services that they have been fully occupied in dealing with current catastrophe, let alone the design of the future.

Robert C. Weaver, administrator of the Housing and Home Finance Agency, told the National Conference on Social Welfare in 1961:

> What is more disturbing to me is the opportunity missed by communities to seize this moment of relocation to bring about the social rehabilitation of the family. For it is just at the moment that a family has been uprooted, has been provided through relocation assistance with the means of establishing a new home, and has been brought into contact with the social agencies of the community, that miracles can be accomplished.
>
> It is no surprise that communities have swept their human tragedies into slums and forgotten them. But having embarked upon a program to tear up the slums, and having turned these tragedies up to the light, should the community *then* so blithely forget them? [5]

Let us admit that in the voluntary or privately provided sector of the social services there is not enough of anything to do an adequate job with present boundaries, let alone throughout the metropolitan area. There is not enough money; there is not enough staff—trained or untrained; there are not enough facilities, from physical space to automobiles. At the same time, there is not enough planning; there is not enough consideration of the demands of the future; there is not enough vision.

This summation applies equally as well to the publicly provided or tax-supported services in the community. Human need has never "recognized" local or municipal or county boundaries, and the history of the social services since the sixteenth century in England indicates the futility of man's attempt to provide services on such a basis. Nevertheless, in the modern metropolis, whether a person lives in one municipality or another makes a real difference to him and his family. The anachronism of residence requirements has persisted in an area which is a single community. The standards of service differ sharply from one locality to another, and differences range all the way from a situation of almost "no service" to one of "quite adequate service." It makes a very real difference where you live in the metropolis and surely this fact, in itself, is an anachronism.

FUNDAMENTAL ISSUES IN PLANNING
THE SOCIAL SERVICES

Four basic issues must be debated and resolved if progress is to be made toward the attainment of the over-all objective of providing services adequate in quantity and quality for every resident of the metropolis. These issues are: (1) decentralization versus centralization; (2) amalga-

[5] *Social Welfare Forum, 1961,* p. 34.

mation versus federation (denominational services versus universal services; services for ethnic groups); (3) specialized services versus multifunctional services; and (4) radical new patterns of organization and administration versus traditional old patterns. This formulation by no means exhausts all of the issues, but it will suffice. It is recognized that these propositions are not entirely mutually exclusive.

Decentralization versus Centralization

The question of decentralization versus centralization is not merely a matter of geographical location (although there is a clear geographical component) but involves, as well, questions of philosophy and administration. In what manner should the opportunity of securing help be offered to people? A bedside nursing service obviously must be offered at the bedside. A homemaker service involves visiting the home and perhaps living within it for some time. When it comes to the counseling services, however, we arrive at one of the "gray areas." In one view, the person who seeks help is in some way demonstrating a resolve to be helped by traveling to an office. Perhaps this is so. We talk about "starting where the client is" but he may have to travel ten or fifteen miles before we discover "where he is."

This argument is in no way intended to depreciate the past efforts of certain agencies to decentralize their operations by creating district offices or in other ways offering help in a manner convenient to their clients. This process could have been continued in the 1950's and 1960's throughout the metropolitan area, but the sectarian or denominational basis of many agencies would have made it necessary for several counseling services—whether described as family service, child welfare, youth counseling, or whatever—to duplicate the process. The picture of all or many agencies spreading their tentacles along the major arterial roads of the metropolis is difficult to visualize with equanimity, nor could it be justified from an economic or administrative point of view.

Decentralization thus involves a further major question. This concept can be understood not merely as the creation of new, properly located branches of long-established services but also as the creation of new organizations to provide familiar and entirely unfamiliar services in appropriate locations under new auspices, perhaps public auspices. Which of these patterns should be encouraged in rapidly expanding urban areas? Which pattern is most likely to encourage the interest and participation of members of local communities?

Amalgamation versus Federation

One of the most significant consequences of the historical evolution of social welfare and health agencies under voluntary auspices has been the development of somewhat similar services offering help to various groups differentiated on the basis of age, sex, nature of disability, or some other criterion. Thus we find a Big Brother Movement and a Big Sister Association; a John Howard Society and an Elizabeth Fry Society; a YMCA and a YWCA; a Jewish Vocational Service and a Youth Counseling Service; an Arthritis and Rheumatism Society and a community rehabilitation center.

Is there a case for the amalgamation of certain pairs or groups of organizations? What values are to be gained and what values are to be lost if such amalgamations were to occur? Of more importance, how could such amalgamations be brought about in a society of multiple associations in which there appears to be strong support—at least for a time—for that which is new and apparently provides for an unmet need, and less support for the long-established organizations?

If there is a case for amalgamation but no real prospect of attaining voluntary or forced mergers, perhaps there is some middle ground between the present situation and the concept of amalgamation, namely, the notion of federation. It may not be conceivable that some of the pairs of agencies cited previously as examples would develop close relationships within their respective jurisdictions throughout the metropolis. It is entirely conceivable—in fact, imperative—that such federations develop in the form of partnerships to provide services in community renewal areas within the central city and in health and welfare centers in the rapidly growing areas outside the city.

Denominational Services versus Universal Services

This issue is considered as a portion of the larger question of amalgamation versus federation since it poses a special problem within the over-all framework. A good deal of social planning by the Jewish and Roman Catholic federations, respectively, is also involved in this pattern.

It is sufficient to emphasize that certain groups in the community hold firmly to the view that the values inherent in the provision of services to people on a denominational basis are sufficiently important that a certain amount or degree of overlapping and even, perhaps, waste in the midst of inadequacy must be tolerated. Nevertheless, it seems to be a fact that neither of the two major denominational family service agencies has been able to adjust, with any degree of flexibility, to the changing demands of its constituency.

In the one case, the Jewish community in many metropolitan areas has moved en masse to relatively new locations within the past decade, while improving its social and economic position. Decentralization, additional staff, new programs are all required and have not been possible in sufficient measure. In the other case, the Roman Catholic community has increased as a proportion of total population and substantially in absolute terms. Decentralization, vast numbers of additional staff, new programs—

for example, programs designed to meet the needs of ethnic enclaves in
Canadian cities—are urgently required. If these adjustments have been
possible, they have escaped public notice.

In practical terms, the question is whether a continuation of the present
pattern is essential throughout the entire metropolitan area, or whether
some method may be developed whereby the essential values are retained without spotting denominational services throughout the entire
urban area.

Services for Ethnic Groups

In Canadian metropolitan areas we have been so concerned since the
late 1940's to make it clear to newcomers that they are human beings like
any other residents, that we have in fact treated them just like anyone
else—that is, they have a better than even chance of not receiving the
help they require. There is, of course, so much more to the situation that
mere sarcasm will not nearly suffice. Newcomers arrive with a different
orientation to the prevailing notions of the respective responsibilities of
voluntary and public services. Many do not speak, read, or understand
the language. Each ethnic group is in a different stage of development
as far as its own internal or voluntary assumption of responsibility is
concerned.

The consequence is that we have witnessed the creation of barriers to
communication and real, if not brick or stone, walls surrounding major
ethnic enclaves. We talk about "them" and "us," about "their" customs
and "ours." We suspect that there are real barriers to the use of the social
services by newcomers, but we do not really know what these barriers
are or why they are barriers. We do know that no Italian or German or
Polish or whatever family or child welfare or other major service has
been created. There is sometimes grumbling about the pre-eminence of
Catholic or Jewish services for newcomers, for family service, vocational
counseling, and the like.

Once more the question is how best to provide services available to
all residents of the metropolis without reference to ethnic origin or religion. If I add the word "race" I shall clearly include the American
dilemma. The established agencies have apparently not been sufficiently
flexible to meet the challenge of diversity and heterogeneity. Can they
be made more flexible and, if so, how?

Specialized Services versus Multifunctional Services

Specialization has emerged in the social welfare and health services
on many bases: the marital or family status of the people to be served;
the age or sex of the potential client; the nature of the service to be provided; the denomination of those to be served; the means of arrival in the

country, by birth or immigration; the nature of the apparent problems of those to be served; client income by size and source—to name the most important of the many possibilities.

Fortunately, few people seem to be happy with the results of the attempt to offer a specialized service. Many agencies have indicated that they are inevitably drawn well beyond the apparent limits of their specialized function. Family service agencies become involved with children, naturally; child welfare services become involved with the entire family; family service agencies become involved with elderly persons; services for the elderly become involved with families, that is, the children of their clients; family and child welfare services become involved with the problem of counseling youthful persons; youth counseling services are involved with the family; visiting nursing services become involved with family budgets; health services become involved with the family; rehabilitation agencies become involved with the services of general and mental hospitals; hospitals become involved with the entire family of the sick person. The situation, as Alice might have said, has become "a very involved one."

The fundamental issue is whether we should, and how we can, encourage the emergence of multifunctional services through the process of federation or amalgamation. If we cannot accomplish this objective in the older settled areas, can we start afresh in the newer urban areas—and in the community renewal areas—with a "total service" rather than by the provision of several specialized splinters? The simple problem of transportation for the client in the metropolis, if he must make many visits to specialized services located all over the map, is appalling. This does not rule out, of course, the possibility of a unification of location for several specialized services.

Radical New Patterns of Organization and Administration versus Traditional Old Patterns

The propositions and questions raised in this paper lead inevitably to this one overarching issue of prime importance. Will it be possible to provide satisfactory social welfare, health, and recreational services in the rapidly expanding metropolis through a continuation of the present patterns of service, albeit with appropriate refinements, modifications, and improvements? Or will it be necessary to consider entirely new approaches if the social services are to meet the challenges posed in the society of the metropolis? It seems to me that there is little doubt about the resolution of this issue, at least in theoretical terms.

One of the most provocative and potentially rewarding suggestions is the proposal that "health and welfare centers" be developed in appropriate locations throughout the metropolitan area. In addition to the matter of location, the concept of a "health and welfare center" implies a number of fascinating possibilities ranging over an entire spectrum of combinations.

At the broader end of the distribution the implications include decentralization of services; a unified location for many services; a combination of publicly and voluntarily provided services; a combination of welfare and health services; a multifunctional approach without regard to age, marital or family status, ethnic origin, or denominational qualification; and a potentially high level of interservice referral and co-operation. The sponsorship of such a center could be a public authority, but it is not inconceivable that a social planning council might fulfil this role. It would require a board of directors drawn from the local community and a professional director who would not be identified with any specific service but would be charged with administrative responsibility.

The essence of the proposition is to make available to any person as much and as many of the services as he is likely to require, in one location, accessible, decentralized, in both the public and private spheres of influence, in both the welfare and the health field. As a member of what has been described sometimes as "a special interest group," the citizen may elect to be counseled by a professional worker of his own denomination. This is the only major concession the writer would care to make.

It is freely and frankly admitted that the difficulties involved in implementing the changes suggested in this discussion of "fundamental issues in planning" are enormous. There is, however, increasing recognition in the field of social planning of the probable consequences, particularly for the privately provided services, if we continue to drift or cling tenaciously to present patterns.

One might be inclined to insist, at this point in the argument, that these are not the really vital issues at all. The most important problems involve, rather, such terribly difficult tasks as the following: How do we develop new methods of education for children from low-income and culturally deprived homes, so as to reduce functional illiteracy, school drop-outs, and learning disabilities? How do we reduce unemployment by new forms of job training among the young, by the retraining of adults, and by the creation of new jobs? How do we encourage self-help among individuals and groups in the neighborhood? How do we extend the amount and quality of social services to the "hard-to-reach" and the multiproblem family in the low-income population? One can only agree that these are among the most essential tasks. Yet the issues which have been considered in this discussion must be resolved if the social services in the metropolis are to play a significant role.

The social services have not been sufficiently flexible to meet the challenges of the past fifteen years—rapid growth in population, the incorporation of vast numbers of newcomers into the community, increasing emphasis on service for the whole family and the whole person within the family, improved techniques in treating mental illness and in the field of physical, vocational, and social rehabilitation.

It is not a secret that there is widespread dissatisfaction with the agencies and with the social-planning apparatus in the metropolis. It is not a secret that the major foundations are tending to bypass the social services in their sponsorship of experimental programs to meet critical human needs in the central cities. It is not a secret that the traditional community welfare councils are facing the greatest challenge in their history.[6]

The Social Planning Council of Metropolitan Toronto has recently released the first Interim Report of its 1962 Needs and Resources Study. The report states:

> Unless public funds become available for some of the voluntary agencies there will be serious curtailment of services at a time when needs are expanding rapidly. When funds are short the tendency is to allocate the funds available to remedial, custodial, and, to a lesser extent, rehabilitation services at the expense of services which prevent personal and family breakdown or are designed to improve family life and develop individual self reliance, self respect and character.
>
> It is now clear to the Committee that the present level of voluntary support and the present system of municipal grants are not meeting the financial problem of the voluntary agencies and the indications are that the gap between needs and resources is widening.

There is little evidence that the social services are sufficiently flexible to meet the challenges of the next two decades—continued population growth toward a metropolis twice the present size, a rapidly expanding urbanization requiring an effective partnership between social planners and physical planners,[7] a replanning of the urban core to make it a viable community for human beings as well as for automobiles and computers, and a probable continuation of chronic unemployment at a high level as untrained and uneducated young people swell the ranks of the mass of "blue-collar" workers whose jobs will disappear forever in the

---

[6] Robert H. MacRae, "The Challenge of Change to Community Welfare Councils" (address to the "Million and Over Club," Chicago, September 29, 1962), p. 6.

[7] It is encouraging to note a developing interest in this relationship between physical and social planning and the respective planners. Clearly, an improvement in the nature and techniques of social planning will not be sufficient to insure the provision of services, adequate in quality and quantity, to the residents of the metropolis. The work of Herbert Gans and Robert Morris should be mentioned in this context. See, particularly, Herbert J. Gans, "Social and Physical Planning for the Elimination of Urban Poverty," *Washington University Law Quarterly*, February, 1963, pp. 2–18.

age of automation. The political, the economic, the cultural, and the social patterns have all changed radically and will continue to change. The architects of these changes are for the most part aware of the potential role and responsibilities of the social services. They are beseeching the social planners for new models to be copied, for new designs from which to work. Let us hope that these are forthcoming—and fairly soon.

Part B

Support Bases for Welfare Organizations

ALTHOUGH the United States has been called an affluent society, few people deny the reality of the scarcity of monies for welfare programs. A welfare organization must somehow make claim to monies for public and collective purposes which otherwise would be spent on private wants. Since the clientele rarely, if ever, pays the full cost of welfare programs, welfare organizations must mobilize resources from the community, either through taxes collected by the government or through voluntary donations. (In many instances, because of social pressure, seemingly voluntary donations are voluntary in form only.) Because the clientele does not fully pay for services, the market supports and controls of welfare organizations are less operative than those for business organizations. Instead, the welfare organization is supported and controlled through either the governmental machinery or through various fund-granting agencies and/or such community representatives as boards of directors.

The processes of organizational support and control are closely interlinked, since the ability of people to sanction welfare programs by withholding various kinds of resources—legitimacy, money, volunteer time, and prestige—represents a fundamental control over the lines of action which organizations take. We discuss the control of organizations more explicitly in Part A of Section III. In the present part, the selections deal with aspects of the support bases for agencies.

In the United States, even though there has been a great rise in the extent of federal welfare programs since the beginning of the New Deal, organizations conducted under voluntary auspices have continued to receive a great deal of support and prestige. The article by Ray Elling and

Sandor Halebsky, "Support for Public and Private Services," discusses community support for public and voluntary hospitals in the state of New York. After introducing the notion of an environmental support base for organizations, the article documents many of the consequences of differential support bases for organizational operation. A hospital that has the stronger external support base is more likely to be able to operate effectively. The article also clarifies the importance of the auspices of the organization for the quality of welfare services. That is, welfare organizations must be linked to various control groups in the society and community. The ability of the organization to gain continuing support depends upon the groups to which the organization is linked.

The article by Charles Perrow, "Organizational Prestige: Some Functions and Dysfunctions," deals with the attempt of organizations to gain autonomy in the community by manipulating their prestige. Perrow discusses two kinds of prestige indices—those that are intrinsic to the goals of the organization and those that are extrinsic. He suggests that the reliance on extrinsic prestige for validating the worth of an organization may lead to certain bureaucratic pathologies, which actually hinder the attainment of the intrinsic purpose of the organization. His analysis, although based initially on his observation of a hospital, is applicable to all kinds of organizations, including state welfare departments, family service agencies, and mental hospitals.

The last article of this part deals with the problems of gaining the support and commitment of volunteers. This article, "Philanthropic Activity and the Business Career," by Aileen Ross, develops the theme that the participation of business executives in fund-raising drives is closely linked to the success of the executives' careers. Aileen Ross also points to a change in the support base of voluntary agencies: whereas, at one time, philanthropic activity was the province of the old and wealthy families of a community, the center of philanthropic activity, at least for men, has passed to the business community and the large corporation because of the importance of the modern business corporation in fund-raising drives.

Support for Public and Private Services

Ray H. Elling and Sandor Halebsky

In 1958, of the twenty-one million admissions to nonfederal short-term general hospitals in the United States, almost one-fifth—approximately four million—were to city or county hospitals.[1] Codes of medical ethics as well as general values of our society lead us to expect that patients handled in these hospitals will have in general as good treatment and facilities as those cared for in other institutions. Yet if a hospital does not receive adequate support, it is not as likely to achieve its goals as the well-supported hospital. Thus patients in such a hospital would be handicapped because of social elements not directly related to their illness.[2]

It is interesting but hardly accidental that social science research has only very recently developed an interest in the problem of hospital support.[3] Medical care expenditures in general and expenditures for hospital care in particular have risen significantly in recent years both in this country[4] and abroad.[5] Added to these personal expenditures have been the large outlays for hospital plant and facilities which in turn require

[1] Estimate made from *Hospitals*, 33 (guide issue; Aug. 1, 1959), Part 2.

[2] Differential treatment according to social characteristics rather than diagnosis has been documented elsewhere. Cf. A. B. Hollingshead and F. C. Redlich, *Social Class and Mental Illness* (New York, 1958).

[3] Sol Levine and Paul E. White, Exchange as a Conceptual Framework for the Study of Interorganizational Relationships, *Administrative Science Quarterly*, 5 (1961), 583–601. A study of hospital-community relations has begun at the University of Michigan. A study in Mississippi used judges to rate community relations of hospitals in general, but did not consider explicitly the receipt of support. See J. V. D. Saunders and J. H. Bruening, Hospital-Community Relations in Mississippi, *Rural Sociology*, 24 (1959), 48–51.

[4] Health Information Foundation, Our Increased Spending for Health, *Progress in Health Service*, 9 (Feb. 1960).

[5] T. E. Chester, Health and Hospital Services in the United States, A Comparative Analysis, *The Hospital*, 56 (Sept.–Oct., 1960), 15.

Ray H. Elling and Sandor Halebsky, "Organizational Differentiation and Support: A Conceptual Framework," *Administrative Science Quarterly*, 6, 1961, pp. 185–210. This research is supported by N.I.H. Grant W-127. The authors gratefully acknowledge the assistance they have received from others associated with the project, particularly Professors Milton I. Roemer, Rodney F. White, and Vaughn Blankenship.

large sums for maintenance once they are established. Increased spending for health services and facilities has occurred for a number of reasons —increased specialization of medicine, rapid change in technology and need for hospital improvements, increasing costs of equipment, rising staffing ratios, higher salaries, and so on.[6] In capital expenditures alone, with population expansion, rising demand for hospital care, and costs per hospital bed ranging around twenty thousand dollars, the investment of almost ten billion dollars between 1945 and 1959 for new hospitals has been insufficient to keep up with the needs.[7]

But increasing expenditures, though important, are not the only reason for current concern with the problem of hospital support. Over the last century, the hospital has changed from a segmental institution, serving only those who could not provide adequate facilities at home, to a community institution used and valued by almost all segments of the community. Coupled with this development of greater contact between hospital and community, however, has been a gradual depersonalization of treatment relationships attendant upon increased specialization and complexity. Thus while the hospital is more recognized and valued for its potentialities, it may incur resentment because of its cost and impersonality. Public criticism is reflected in numerous popular articles and opinion polls.[8] It has become a practical question of some import, then, to discover the types of hospitals and kinds of settings which have been associated with the hospital's receiving support under our relatively unregulated system of hospital care.

Many factors may affect the ability of an organization to achieve its goals. Internally there may be a lack of harmony; members of the institution [9] may be unclear as to goals; there may be conflicts between goals; or there may be other internal factors familiar to students of organizational theory.[10] On the other hand, environmental conditions may also

[6] Henry N. Pratt, Factors Affecting Hospital Costs, *New York State Journal of Medicine*, 60 (1960), 369 ff.

[7] *Principles for Planning the Future Hospital System* (U.S. Department of Health, Education and Welfare, Public Health Service Publication No. 721; Washington, D.C.: U.S. Government Printing Office), Table 3, p. 216; Edward T. Chase, Revolution in Hospitals, *Architectural Forum*, 111 (Aug., 1959), 127 ff.

[8] For example, see special supplement, The Crisis in American Medicine, *Harpers*, 221 (October, 1960), 121–168; and E. L. Koos, " 'Metropolis'—What City People Think of Their Medical Services," in E. G. Jaco, ed., *Patients, Physicians and Illness* (Glencoe, 1958), pp. 113–119.

[9] The terms "institution" and "organization" are used interchangeably here to mean a group of persons organized in a division of labor into a hierarchy of social roles to achieve certain purposes and having at their disposal shared vocabulary and some physical setting and materials. See Everett C. Hughes, The Study of Institutions, *Social Forces*, 20 (1942), 307–311, for the distinction between the use of the word "institution" in this sense and its use in the sense of a practice such as "marriage" or "property."

[10] James G. March and Herbert A. Simon, *Organizations* (New York, 1958).

influence effectiveness. Competition with other organizations,[11] changing societal definitions of goals,[12] shifts in the legitimacy granted to an institution,[13] and general economic and cultural conditions [14] can influence the organization's attainment of objectives directly [15] or through their influence on support.

In view of the importance of relations between an organization and its environment, it is curious that social scientists have been preoccupied in their empirical researches with human relations within organizations.[16] There are a number of exceptions,[17] but, generally, external relations and

[11] Walter B. Miller, Inter-Institutional Conflict as a Major Impediment to Delinquency Prevention, *Human Organization*, 17 (1958), 20–23; also, Marshall E. Dimock, "Expanding Jurisdictions: A Case Study in Bureaucratic Conflict," in R. K. Merton, et al., eds., *Reader in Bureaucracy* (Glencoe, 1952).

[12] James D. Thompson and William McEwen, Organizational Goals and Environment: Goal Setting as an Interaction Process, *American Sociological Review*, 20 (1955), 206–210; Burton R. Clark, Organizational Adaptation and Precarious Values, *American Sociological Review*, 21 (1956), 327–336.

[13] Clark, *op. cit.;* Christopher Sower et al., "The Death of the Health Council," in *Community Involvement* (Glencoe, 1957), ch. xi.

[14] Sheldon L. Messinger, Organizational Transformation: A Case Study of a Declining Social Movement, *American Sociological Review*, 20 (1955), 3–10. The organization facing a new cultural environment may have to incorporate a new role, that of the intermediary; see John Adair, The Indian Health Worker in the Cornell-Navaho Project, *Human Organization*, 19 (1960), 59–63.

[15] A comparative study revealed that good patient care is achieved in Swedish hospitals with fewer personnel per patient than in American hospitals. There is evidence that more than one of the conditions we have mentioned may be operating directly on goal attainment. For example, the author suggests that efficiency may be greater because of the presence of full-time physicians, thereby avoiding the duplication and likely confusion. On the other hand, a general cultural emphasis on hard work and co-operation may help explain the findings. Cf. Paul A. Lembcke, Hospital Efficiency—A Lesson from Sweden, *Hospitals*, 33 (1959), 34–38.

[16] William F. Whyte, *Man and Organization* (Homewood, Ill., 1959), Part I; Amitai Etzioni New Directions in the Study of Organizations and Society, *Social Research*, 27 (1960), 223–228.

[17] Philip Selznick, *TVA and the Grass Roots* (Berkeley, 1949), and those works already noted. Also, William R. Dill, Environment as an Influence on Managerial Autonomy, *Administrative Science Quarterly*, 2 (1958), 409–443; Amitai Etzioni, Interpersonal and Structural Factors in the Study of Mental Hospitals, *Psychiatry: Journal for the Study of Interpersonal Processes*, 23 (Feb., 1960), 13–22; John M. Gaus, *Public Administration and the U.S. Department of Agriculture* (Chicago, 1949); Neal Gross, Some Contributions of Sociology to the Field of Education, *Harvard Educational Review*, 29 (1959), 275–287; Morris Janowitz et al., *Public Administration and the Public* (Ann Arbor, 1958); Charles Perrow, Organizational Prestige: Some Functions and Disfunctions, *American Journal of Sociology*, 66 (1961), 335–391; Robert V. Presthus, Social Bases of Bureaucratic Organization, *Social Forces*, 38 (1959), 103–109; Robert Somer, The Mental Hospital in the Small Community, *Mental Hygiene*, 42 (1958), 487–496; James D. Thompson et al., eds., *Comparative Studies in Administration* (Pittsburgh, 1959). For earlier works with implications for the study of organization and environment, see O. D. Duncan, Urbanization and Retail Specialization, *Social Forces*, 30 (1951), 267–271; A. B.

particularly problems of gaining support have been underemphasized.[18]

Some attention has been given to support, in the minimal sense of elements necessary for group existence and maintenance. Georg Simmel, for example, gave attention to such essential elements as a name, banner, or other identifying symbols. He also pointed up the importance of numbers of individuals both in the formation of certain types of groups and in lending continuity to groups.[19] Malinowsky has clarified other essential elements of an institution—a system of social roles reflecting a division of labor, material facilities, and a statement of purpose.[20] Only recently, however, has support, beyond conditions of mere group existence and maintenance, come into focus.[21]

This research set out to discover the aspect of the hospital and its environment that are related to the hospital receiving some of the elements it needs in order to give good patient care.[22] We suggest a framework to study the relations between internal and external variables or attributes

Hollingshead, *Elmtown's Youth* (New York, 1949); Everett C. Hughes, The Ecological Aspect of Institutions, *American Sociological Review*, 1 (1936), 180–188. Many studies of the operation of political parties in different settings are also relevant, of course. For a work that treats the environment as the major motive force in human development, consult H. T. Buckle, *History of Civilization in England* (New York, 1913), especially Vol. I, pt. I.

[18] Generally, when an organization's relationship to its environment is studied, it is primarily in terms of its attempts to maximize its power or influence. Thus there is consideration of the activities of interest groups in general, as in David Truman's *The Governmental Process* (New York, 1951); or of particular interest groups, as for example Wesley McCune's *The Farm Bloc* (New York, 1943); Grant McConnell's work on the American Farm Bureau Federation, *The Decline of Agrarian Democracy* (Los Angeles, 1953); or Oliver Garceau's study of the American Medical Association, *The Political Life of the American Medical Association* (Cambridge, Mass., 1941). There is little direct attention given, however, to an institution's external relationships as these center upon the particular problem of its obtaining support from the environment.

[19] *The Sociology of Georg Simmel*, Kurt H. Wolff, trans. and ed. (Glencoe, 1950).

[20] *A Scientific Theory of Culture* (Chapel Hill, 1944). He uses the notion of the charter to exemplify the goal statement of an institution. This implies an excessively formal and explicit statement, however, which is inappropriate for the study of many informal organizations.

[21] Levine and White, *op. cit.* This paper conceptualizes exchanges between health organizations. The definition given to exchange admits of negative interactions such as insults, impediments, or more serious signs of conflict, but the authors' development of this concept seems to include only positive interactions between organizations, that is, those which would aid in the attainment of goals. Thus the use of exchange by these investigators is equivalent to our notion of support.

[22] An early statement of the research plan and suggestions from exploratory studies is given in Milton I. Roemer and Rodney F. White, Community Attitudes toward the Hospital, *Hospital Management*, 89 (Jan.–Feb., 1960). A research note on variation in types of support appears in Ray H. Elling, What Do We Mean by Hospital Sup port?, *Modern Hospital*, 96 (Jan., 1961), 84.

of an organization and the support it receives from its environment. This paper will report our findings with respect to one internal attribute, namely sponsorship.[23] As used in this framework, support refers to an institution receiving from its environment those elements it needs to achieve its goals. Without support an organization cannot be effective. As used here, support is held to be both an independent variable determining various internal aspects of hospital effectiveness and also a dependent variable determined by various internal aspects of the hospital and by external characteristics of the hospital community. In the study reported here, the external characteristic of particular importance is the stratification system. It is held that the research findings support the interpretation that hospital sponsorship is important in determining the elements in the community stratification system with which the hospital will be associated. Different sponsorship leads to different associations. This in turn influences the degree of support forthcoming from the community to the hospital.

Many comparisons of extreme differences in support might be made from those examined. To take one, there is the county hospital in an urban center which closed its doors just as the study was starting. It was a short-term general hospital like all the others in the study. The community, according to a Community Chest report, needed more beds, but this hospital was located in a converted jail and its facilities had not been renovated. This example might be compared with two voluntary hospitals in the same city which merged and obtained enough money from a fund drive and Hill-Burton (federal) aid to build a new plant. The county hospital had lost in its relative proportion of admissions over the years and the other two had gained. The county hospital had an insignificant staff of volunteer workers associated with it while the other two, especially after their merger and the construction of the new building, had a very active staff of volunteers. These women not only worked in the hospital but made articles in their homes for the hospital gift center and sought subscriptions for new equipment, art works for the lobby, and contributions for patient-library facilities. The new hospital, as compared to the county hospital, had considerably more funds, patients, and volunteers.

These are important elements of support but they are not the only ones. A hospital also needs a qualified and devoted staff, active board members, a generally favorable climate of attitudes, and other help as well.

[23] The term sponsorship designates the nature of the controlling and administrative body legally responsible for a hospital. Four types of sponsorship are common: a voluntary, nondenominational corporation; a governmental body—either city, county, state, or federal; a religious organization; or a private individual or corporation. In this paper, local governmental (city and county) hospitals are compared with voluntary, nondenominational hospitals.

The elements of support required for any particular type of institution depend upon its needs with respect to achieving its goals. In the case of a friendship group, support may be determined simply by conditions affecting the frequency of members' interaction and the extent of their identification with the group. In the case of a complex organization like an industrial concern or a hospital, the elements of support will be manifold.

We could compare the county hospital with the merged voluntary hospital in many respects. As Talcott Parsons points out, any system may be regarded in its "internal" and "external" aspects.[24] We might point up differences in size, qualifications of medical staff, equipment, number of services, socioeconomic characteristics of patients, death rates, and other "internal" characteristics. On the other hand, we could also discuss differences between these hospitals in their relations to the environment. Although the hospitals discussed here are in the same community and therefore differences in the over-all environment cannot operate to influence support, as they might in the case of a cross-community comparison, it is clear that there may be differential ties to the community which help to explain the differences we noted in support. Doctors of the merged voluntary hospitals may tend to belong to *the* country club while doctors in the county hospital may be general practitioners with relatively low incomes who play golf at the municipal golf links. The patients may come from different social-class levels and living areas. The board members of the voluntary hospitals may come from top prestige and influential levels while the county hospital may have mainly the less influential lawyers or businessmen on its board.

The community stratification system within which the hospital must function and seek support is an external feature to which it has to adjust. Any given system of vertical stratification tends to order the institutions, associations, individuals, behaviors and ideologies in a community into a hierarchy of prestige groups with certain associated values. Of particular importance for this research is the fact that institutions may become identified with given elements of the stratification system. Such identifi-

---

[24] General Theory in Sociology, in R. K. Merton *et al.*, eds., *Sociology Today* (New York, 1959), p. 5. Parsons' treatment of "external" and "internal" follows Homans' development of these concepts. This approach treats the external elements of an organization as those which mediate between the particular organization and its environment, whereas internal elements are those relationships which are concerned with the integration of the elements which compose the organization. While our research employs these distinctions, we also use these terms to distinguish between characteristics or components of the hospital (for example, number of personnel per patient) and those of its surrounding community environment (for example, per capita expendible income). Thus our use of "external" may refer to external relations as well as characteristics of the context.

cation may be in part a matter of intent and in part a matter of latent operation of the stratification system.

The hospitals within a community may be regarded as players in a game who seek to differentiate themselves, as would members of any social system, both with respect to their internal characteristics and with respect to their ties to the environment.[25] This may be a conscious process, as when the administrator of one hospital tries to establish ties to a medical school before administrators in other hospitals are able to do so. Much of this differentiation seems to occur in a latent way with little deliberate action or awareness of how the system operates. The importance of institutional differentiation for our problem is that it may influence a hospital's relative ability to draw support from its environment.

The sponsorship of the hospital was one of the internal characteristics which we felt would be related to environmental support. From the point of view of the surrounding community, knowledge of the controlling body of an organization is essential in determining whom the institution represents. Within a system of stratification, in other words, the nature of the sponsoring group is important in differentiating an institution from others in terms of its class character and consequently, it was felt, might result in the organization's being associated with different sources having varying amounts of support to offer.

METHODS AND PROCEDURES

The data-gathering procedures of this research were carried out in two phases. The first, from which the findings of this paper are taken, consisted essentially of gathering from a number of sources data on support, internal characteristics, and community characteristics for all (136) upstate New York short-term general nonproprietary hospitals. Of this group, 90 were voluntary and nondenominational; 23 were local governmental hospitals. This phase of the study was intended (1) to permit a check on hypothesized relationships between internal and environmental characteristics and community support by securing information on enough cases to allow cross tabulations to be made and (2) to permit the selection of high-low support pairs for detailed comparison during the field-study phase of the research. In this second phase, two hospitals of similar size and sponsorship in single-hospital towns provided one comparison. Other comparisons were made between two well-supported hospitals and two poorly supported hospitals in the same urban center. One objective of the field study was to gather data on internal hospital

[25] Everett C. Hughes, in a personal communication regarding an earlier draft of this paper, has reminded us of this important point. See further Norton Long, The Local Community as an Ecology of Games, *American Journal of Sociology*, 64 (1958), 251–261.

characteristics. Visits were made to each, using observation, interviewing, and questionnaire techniques. Another purpose of the field study was to examine the relationships between the selected hospitals and their communities. Consequently, data on these relationships and the social organization of the communities were gathered through interviews with key informants and through interviews and questionnaires administered to three categories of persons—community leaders, practicing physicians, and the general public. This data should contribute significantly toward further clarifying the relationship suggested here between sponsorship, social stratification, and support. Analysis of data from the field-study phase is in process. The present paper is based on the first phase in which data were collected from the census of hospitals.

Like any other type of organization one might study, the hospital shades off into other institutions. There are, for example, nursing homes and sanatoriums, which one would hesitate to exclude from the category of hospitals. On the other hand, there are some organizations called hospitals which hardly fit the usual pattern. Thus it was decided somewhat arbitrarily to include only those institutions listed in the 1959 American Hospital Association's annual guide issue of *Hospitals*. This resulted in the exclusion of eleven institutions that have the word "hospital" in their names but are not listed in the guide because they do not meet certain minimal criteria. The study sample further excluded proprietary hospitals, long-term hospitals (those with an average length of stay of 30 days or more), special hospitals (those treating one disease such as tuberculosis or mental illness), and those in or near the New York metropolitan area. It was thought that the remaining 136 could be regarded as relatively homogeneous with respect to goals,[26] disease range, and length of

[26] As Levine and White indicate, *op. cit.*, the objectives of an organization are important determinants of what it receives from and sends to other organizations. There is variation among the hospitals in our sample as to their emphasis on teaching and research. There is also variation in the diseases treated, since some may receive a higher proportion of serious cases or more cases of a particular type such as maternity or operative. These are ways in which hospitals are differentiated from one another and may influence the support received by the institution. Some variation in these respects is desired, however, in order that their effects can, be examined. But it is felt that relative homogeneity as to goals exists. The goal of profit has been more or less excluded by omitting proprietary hospitals. And it is probably true that almost all hospitals mix teaching and research in some degree with patient care. In any case, it is relatively safe to assume that good patient care is the dominant goal in all our hospitals, for it is the goal by which the hospital gains legitimacy and it is the rallying point around which disputes as to hospital organization are usually settled. In this connection, see the exchange between a medical administrator and a representative of the American Board of Radiology: Albert W. Snoke, Financial Relationships between Radiologists and Hospitals, *Hospitals*, 34 (Jan. 16, and Feb. 1, 1960), 38–42, 43–45 ff.; also Paul R. Hawley, Responsibility of the Hospital to the Community, *Hospital Progress*, 37 (May, 1957), 86–88 ff.

stay, but would still allow variation in important internal and external characteristics without involving the complexities of the metropolitan environment.

Since it would be difficult to study the degree to which a complex institution receives every element it needs to fulfill its goals, we limited our examination to three important types of support which could be measured relatively easily.

Feeling that a hospital needs sufficient funds for expansion to meet the increasing utilization of hospitals and for improvements to adjust to a rapidly changing technology, we constructed a monetary support index from information about donations, fund drives, increase in permanent endowment, bond issues, Hill-Burton aid, and other governmental appropriations. Income from patients was excluded sinec there is considerable evidence that hospitals in our system need and desire as much external income as they can obtain, even to balance their budget in current operations, to say nothing of making capital improvements.[27] Dollar amounts were obtained for a ten-year period, 1949–1958, from several sources [28] and were totaled. Results were expressed in terms of dollars per 100 beds in order to control for size of hospital. Since great reliance could not be placed on the exact dollar amount obtained by totaling figures from several sources, it was decided to place the distribution into broad categories of high, medium, and low.

Aside from the financial support it gains from patients, the hospital obviously must have patients in order to fulfill its goals. Also, if a hospital gains significantly in admissions, the administrator is able to make a good case that it should expand. The guide issue from 1949 to 1958 of *Hospitals* provided information on admissions which served as an index of patient channeling.[29]

[27] The chronic difficulties, however, which many (administrators) even among the bigger American hospitals experience, their uncertain recourse to flag days, charities and community chests for making up existing deficits are a wholesale reminder that perhaps we (in Britain) have made some progress since the war!" Chester, *op. cit.*, p. 13.

[28] The New York State Joint Hospital Survey and Planning Commission provided information on Hill-Burton funds. Information on money received from fund drives, bond issues, and other governmental funds was obtained from a mail questionnaire. Annual reports made by all hospitals to the New York State Department of Social Welfare yielded data on donations from community chests and other sources for current operations and gave information on increases in permanent endowment funds; these reports also yielded information for validating monetary support since we were able to calculate increase in plant value.

[29] An attempt to use rate of occupancy as the index of patient channeling failed because it can increase as a result of decreasing the number of beds and reporting habits were found to vary considerably. The term "patient channeling" is used instead of "patient choice" in recognition of the factors other than patient election (such as doctor's preference) that determine which hospital a patient goes to. A

The third type of support examined was community participation in the hospital. Measures of volunteer activity and personnel turnover were used to reflect this type of support.[30]

In order to facilitate some aspects of the analysis, a general index of support was constructed on the basis of each hospital's position with respect to funds, patients, and community participation.[31] It should be noted that while we refer to this as a "general index" it is not an index of *general support*, which would have to include many more types of support.

Information was obtained from numerous sources on internal hospital characteristics such as number of physicians on the staff, range of services, personnel-patient ratio, death rate, characteristics of the administrator, and other aspects. Information on various characteristics of the hospital's locality [32] were obtained through the census or similar sources.[33] Data for these localities include an estimate of population increase, industrial composition, effective buying income per capita, educational level, and other aspects of the hospital's environment.

One source of primary data employed in the first phase of the research was a 14-page questionnaire which was mailed to the administrators of all the hospitals included in our study. Relatively complete returns were received from 126 (92 percent). This was very encouraging in view of the numerous questionnaires which administrators receive. In part, the result was attributed to follow-up with letters, phone calls, and in numer-

---

hospital's relative position on patient channeling was determined by (1) the gain or loss it showed in its proportion of admissions to all hospitals in the study over the ten-year period, 1949–1958, and (2) the percentage gain or loss it showed in its own admissions between 1949 and 1958.

[30] A mail questionnaire sent to administrators yielded the data to calculate number of volunteers per 100 beds and number of volunteer hours per 100 beds in 1957 and 1958. Personnel turnover was determined by information on the number of employees leaving during these years and information from *Hospitals*, guide issues, for these years on number of employees. Each hospital was assigned to a high- or low-community-participation position on the basis of its position relative to other hospitals on the distributions above. Equal weight was given to each measure. Since there are two measures of volunteer activity and only one of personnel turnover, the former contribute most to the index of community participation.

[31] Detailed information on the procedures followed in the construction of this index as well as other indices used in the study will be supplied on request.

[32] The named place in which a hospital is located served to determine the boundary of its community. The problem of delineating a hospital's community by any other means (such as its service area) seems to be an insurmountable one if a number of hospitals are to be compared and data obtained on the characteristics of the surrounding areas thus determined.

[33] *Sales Management*, 83 (July, 1959), current survey of industrial buying power; U.S. Bureau of the Census, *Census of Population: 1950*, Vol. 2, Part 32 (Washington, D.C., 1952); State of New York, Department of Commerce, *Business Fact Book* (Albany, 1957).

ous cases personal visits. It is probable that the investigators' association with Cornell and the Sloan Institute of Hospital Administration also contributed to this good response.

In this paper, we give major emphasis to the hospital's sponsorship. Sponsorship classifications indicated in *Hospitals*, guide issue, 1959, were used. The support received by city and county hospitals sponsored by local government is compared with the support received by hospitals sponsored by voluntary, nondenominational organizations. The position of church-sponsored hospitals will be discussed in future publications. Since we are dealing with the census of hospitals in the upstate area, no significance tests are applied in the tables which follow.

RESULTS

The local government hospitals studied received considerably less monetary support in general than did the voluntary, nondenominational hospitals. Table 1 shows that whereas 40 percent of the voluntary hospitals were in the top category in the monetary index, only 14 percent of governmental hospitals were in this category. In the lowest category, we find 57 percent of the governmental and only 25 percent of the voluntary hospitals.

This finding is valid with respect to particular kinds of monetary support, such as money received from fund drives and contributions. One might object that this is to be expected, for even though there is no prohibition against their receiving money in this way, local governmental hospitals generally obtain additional funds through bond issues or governmental grants. While the governmental hospitals in our study show some gain through these channels, it is not enough to make up for the greater amount received by voluntary hospitals from legacies, donations, and fund drives. Even with respect to Hill-Burton aid, which is presum-

Table 1 *Sponsorship and Monetary Support*

	Monetary Support							
	Low		Medium		High		Total	
Sponsorship	No.	%	No.	%	No.	%	No.	%
Voluntary	22	(25)	31	(35)	35	(40)	88	(100) [a]
Governmental	12	(57)	6	(29)	3	(14)	12	(100) [a]

[a] Information was insufficient on two voluntary and two governmental hospitals.

ably open to all hospitals in areas with demonstrated needs and is administered by a quasi-governmental state agency, Table 2 shows that
whereas slightly more than half (51 percent) of the voluntary hospitals
received this support, little more than one-third (35 percent) of the governmental hospitals received this support.

This tendency for the governmental hospital to receive less monetary
and material support is true with respect to a general measure of plant
growth, that is, increase in plant value.[34] Local governmental hospitals
have more often declined in value or but slightly increased while voluntary hospital plants have more often greatly increased in value. Impressions gained from visits to most of the localities in our sample suggest
that city and county hospitals are more often in old, inadequate buildings,
while most voluntary hospitals are not.

Turning to patient channeling as a measure of support, we find the
trend less sharp but still in the same direction. Whereas about three-fifths
(61 percent) of the voluntary hospitals in the study were in the "high"
category of our index of patient channeling, only about half (52 percent)
of the governmental hospitals were in this position. When we examine
only those hospitals within localities where two or more hospitals exist,
the relationship is thrown into high relief. In Table 3 we see that in
centers with more than one hospital, nearly three-fifths (59 percent) of
voluntary hospitals showed moderate to high gains while only one of
seven governmental hospitals in these settings (14 percent) escaped the
"low" category. Noting the trend toward lower occupancy figures in
municipal hospitals, one investigator attributed the change in the use of
the hospital to health insurance.[35] While insurance may play a role in

Table 2 *Sponsorship and Hill-Burton Aid*

	Hill-Burton Aid					
	None		Some		Total	
Sponsorship	No.	%	No.	%	No.	%
Voluntary	44	(49)	46	(51)	90	(100)
Governmental	15	(65)	8	(35)	23	(100)

[34] Information on this item was obtained from annual reports to the New York State
Department of Social Welfare. It seemed useful to check our results on the monetary
index by examining increases in plant value because on occasion hospitals receive
gifts of buildings and land rather than money and this item could be expected to
reflect over-all plant growth. Since information for a number of hospitals was missing
on this item, it can only be used as a partial validation of our results on funds.
[35] E. Ginsberg, *A Pattern for Hospital Care, Final Report of the New York State
Hospital Study* (New York, 1947), pp. 149–170.

Table 3 *Sponsorship and Gain in Patient Admissions over a Ten-Year Period (in Localities Having More than One Hospital)*

| | Gain in Admissions | | | | | |
| | Low | | Medium-High | | Total | |
Sponsorship	No.	%	No.	%	No.	%
Voluntary	13	(41)	19	(59)	32	(100) a
Governmental	6	(86)	1	(14)	7	(100)

a Two voluntary hospitals are new since 1949 and are not included here.

patient channeling, there is generally no formal arrangement which prevents the insured patient from using the local governmental hospital. Yet they have tended to go to voluntary hospitals, and this movement, as we shall see, is consonant with the generally lower support received by governmental hospitals.

With respect to community participation in the hospital, the distinction between voluntary and governmental sponsorship is least clear. Local governmental hospitals seem to do almost as well as voluntary hospitals in obtaining volunteers, and there is only a slight tendency for governmental hospitals to have a higher rate of personnel turnover. Still, when we examine the number of hours contributed by volunteers per 100 beds, we find that of those providing complete information [36] 53 percent of the voluntary hospitals in contrast to 37 percent of the governmental hospitals were above the median on this measure. While the governmental hospital may be at some disadvantage in the area of community participation, it is apparently not quite as handicapped with respect to this type of support as it is in other areas. It would be interesting to compare the composition of the volunteer groups associated with governmental and voluntary hospitals in terms of social class and other variables. Unfortunately, our study does not include this information.

When the indices for funds, patients, and community participation are combined in a general index of support which gives equal weight to each type of support, the picture of differences between voluntary and governmental hospitals is considerably sharpened. Table 4 indicates that only around a third (33 percent) of the voluntary hospitals fell in the low-support category while approximately three fifths (59 percent) of the governmental cases received low support.

[36] Fourteen voluntary and four governmental hospitals did not return questionnaires or gave incomplete responses on this point.

Table 4 *Sponsorship and Position on a General Index of Support*

| | Support | | | | | | | |
| | Low | | Medium | | High | | Total | |
Sponsorship	No.	%	No.	%	No.	%	No.	%
Voluntary	29	(33)	36	(40)	24	(27)	89	(100) [a]
Governmental	13	(59)	4	(18)	5	(23)	22	(100) [a]

[a] Included here are all cases for which information was available on at least two of the three areas—funds, patients, and community participation. Therefore the totals in this table are larger than in some of the previous ones. A blank in one area of support simply meant that it was not counted in arriving at an average score. There was insufficient information on one voluntary and one governmental hospital.

This general position of local governmental hospitals is exemplified in the following quotation from a local newspaper concerning recent efforts of a poorly supported city hospital to improve its position:

> (Hospital Switchboard): "Good morning. General Hospital."
> (Caller): "Oh, I'm sorry. I must have the wrong number."
> (Switchboard): "No, this is City Hospital, but the name has been officially changed to General Hospital."
> (Caller): "Oh, sure, I DID read something about that . . ."
>
> With a flourish of his pen, Gov. Nelson A. Rockefeller last Friday signed a bill changing the name, but the actual transformation of a practical public image and elimination of the "City Hospital" reflex will take a bit more doing.
> Wonder why anyone would go to such trouble to change the name of a hospital? The hospital's board of managers felt the name "City Hospital" tended to stigmatize the institution as one primarily interested in serving welfare patients, as is the case with some municipally operated hospitals elsewhere. City . . . oops, General . . . Hospital, however, counts only 15 to 20 per cent of its patients as welfare recipients.[37]

Perhaps other factors explain the relationship we have found between sponsorship and support. The news story suggests that a hospital is stigmatized by having a high proportion of welfare patients. It is true that the local governmental hospitals in our study tend to have a higher pro-

[37] The source is not cited here for reasons of identity. Actually, the figure given for the proportion of welfare patients places this hospital in the upper 13 percent of the distribution of all hospitals in our study on this characteristic. The median for welfare patients was between 7.5 percent and 9.0 percent.

portion of welfare patients. When this factor is controlled,[38] however, it does not significantly alter the tendency for the governmental hospitals to receive less support. When there is a low proportion of welfare patients, the governmental hospital tends to receive about the same support as the voluntary hospital. When there is a medium or high proportion of welfare patients, however, the voluntary hospital receives more support than the governmental hospital.

Perhaps when other internal factors are held constant the relationship disappears. Perhaps there would be no relationship between sponsorship and support if we held constant (one at a time) the following factors: size of the hospital, range of services offered, number of house and paid staff per 100 patients, number of active and associate physicians on the staff, number of other personnel per 100 patients, interest in research as indicated by number of papers published by the medical staff, affiliation with a medical school, presence of an outpatient department, length of time administrator has been in the field, occupational composition of the board, or the death ratio. While some of these variables appear to weaken the relationship between sponsorship and support when they are held constant, the tendency for cases to fall in the expected direction remains.

The same holds true for the external variables which we examined. Whether one holds constant the estimated percentage change in population between 1950 and 1958, the size of the locality in terms of estimated population in 1958, the number of firms employing 500 or more persons, the effective buying income per capita, educational level, or other characteristics of the locality on which we have data, the relationship between sponsorship and support does not disappear. Again by controlling variables, the relationship becomes less marked, but the tendency remains. As an example of this type of analysis, if we hold the number of hospitals in the locality constant, we find, as indicated in Table 5, that the general index of support remains related to sponsorship whether we examine the relationship within localities having a single hospital or several hospitals. A close inspection of Table 5, however, suggests that the relationship is clearer in localities with more than one hospital. In other words, the governmental hospital tends to receive more support when it is the only hospital than it does when there are other hospitals in the community.

While it appears that the relationship between sponsorship and support stands in spite of controlling other variables on which we have data, holding sponsorship constant does not destroy the relationship of certain

[38] Controls were applied in terms of broad categories such as high, medium, and low. Thus within the group of hospitals having a high proportion of welfare patients, the voluntary hospitals tend to receive more support than do the governmental cases. It should be noted, however, that when such controls are applied the number of expected cases in any category becomes so small that these findings can only be taken as suggestive.

Table 5 *Sponsorship and General Index of Support by Number of Hospitals in the Locality*

Number of hospitals: Sponsorship	Support					
	Low		High		Total	
	No.	%	No.	%	No.	%
One:						
Voluntary	15	(27)	41	(73)	56	(100)
Governmental	7	(47)	8	(53)	15	(100) [a]
More than one:						
Voluntary	14	(42)	19	(58)	33	(100) [a]
Governmental	6	(86)	1	(14)	7	(100)

[a] Information is lacking from one voluntary and one governmental hospital on more than one of the three components of this index—i.e., funds, patients, and community participation.

other variables to support. These are not discussed here since the object of this paper is not to explore exhaustively the factors influencing the support received by an institution, but rather to present a framework and employ it in an empirical example.

DISCUSSION

Two questions arise here. First, what are the implications of our findings with respect to sponsorship for a theory of support? And second, how is local governmental sponsorship as compared to voluntary sponsorship related to support? These are interrelated questions. By examining the second, we may also arrive at some answer to the first.

Although the relative position of governmental as compared to voluntary institutions in the health field is of great interest, the position of governmental institutions in our society is a much broader problem. The whole civil service movement may be regarded as an effort to upgrade the quality and prestige of persons employed in governmental organizations. The pioneering studies of Leonard D. White [39] determined that the public's attitudes toward public employment were not as favorable as those held toward corresponding private positions. He also reported that the lowest prestige was attached to employment by a municipality. And

[39] The Prestige Value of Public Employment, *American Political Science Review*, 26 (1932), 910–914, and *The Prestige Value of Municipal Employment in Chicago* (Chicago, 1929).

although state and national employees carried more prestige, they did not attain the level of prestige accorded employees of private enterprise. A more recent study by Janowitz, Wright, and Delany suggests that there has been an improvement in the prestige level of governmental as compared to private employment in recent years. But this investigation still reports that 53 percent of the respondents would grant greater prestige to a doctor on the staff of a voluntary hospital while only 25 percent would attribute greater prestige to the doctor attached to a city hospital.[40] Furthermore, these investigators found that contrary to the general tendency of persons to rate the prestige of their own positions above the level granted them by others, governmental employees and their families tended to rate governmental employment lower than others did. The lack of respect for government regulations and the feeling that the government is somehow a thing apart from the community are often encountered. Pedestrian, dirty tasks like sewage disposal and street cleaning are left to government while various voluntary citizens' groups of "middle-class" and "upper-middle-class" character undertake the glamorous, challenging endeavors of public service.

Does our study of support offer any explanation of the position of governmental hospitals and perhaps shed some light on the position of governmental institutions in our society?

It does not seem entirely adequate to explain the low support of local governmental hospitals solely in terms of their serving a higher proportion of welfare and other low-prestige patients, although this undoubtedly is a factor. Such patients have been shown to receive less adequate care in other settings.[41] An example is given by a physician in one of the communities studied who pointed up the use of the county hospital as a medical "dumping ground," when he asked, "When they close the county hospital, where will I send my crocks?" But as we have seen, controlling the factor of proportion of welfare patients does not destroy the relationship between sponsorship and support. Furthermore, the problem of low support remains in any case, since one may go beyond the association between welfare patients and other low-prestige patients and governmental hospitals to ask, "Why should these patients be channeled to these hospitals?" Perhaps part of the explanation of low support is circular. The fact that local governmental hospitals tend to be in less adequate buildings and in some ways receive less acceptable personnel [42] may deter

---

[40] M. Janowitz et al., Public Administration and the Public—Perspectives toward Government in a Metropolitan Community (Michigan Governmental Studies No. 36; Ann Arbor, 1958), p. 64. It should be noted, however, that since a particular city hospital was named in their questions, this result may be influenced by other characteristics of the institution.

[41] Hollingshead and Redlich, op. cit.

[42] The Hospital Council of Greater New York, Foreign-Trained Interns and Residents in New York City Hospitals, The Bulletin, 14 (1959), 1–6.

patients and doctors from using them and work against interest and support. Again, these explanations only point up the problem.

The city or county general hospital is similar in most respects to the voluntary general hospital. Medically, it is similar in offering a wide range of services—emergency, medical, surgical, maternity, pediatric, and so on. Organizationally, it has board, staff, and administrative relationships similar to those of the voluntary hospital. There is a pronounced *social* difference, however. Until the modern hospital movement developed in the latter part of the nineteenth century with the advent and practice of bacteriology and aseptic surgery, all hospitals, as Edward D. Churchill points out, were institutions providing last comforts to the sick poor.[43] There was no problem of various strata of society associating with one another in the same institution. But with improved medical technology, hospitals became places to go for cure rather than places to die. "The best" in medical care moved from the home and the doctor's office into the hospital. As the hospital became a treatment center positively valued by all classes, but especially the "middle" and "upper" classes, a certain amount of specialization in type of patient developed and preserved thereby the stratification of the community. Voluntary hospitals have drawn business, industrial and society leaders to their boards and have not left any channel of formal control open to the broader public. City and county hospitals, on the other hand, while they may have similar persons on their boards,[44] have remained "the people's" hospitals in the sense that popular control and identification has been partially retained through the election of local governmental officials.

It is suggested that as a consequence of the class character of their control, voluntary and governmental hospitals experience differentials in support consistent with the general differential distribution of rewards in society according to class position. Perhaps the relatively higher support received by the governmental hospital when it is the sole community hospital is due to there being less of a division of labor along social-class lines in such a setting than there is when the community's support must be divided among several hospitals.

While other investigators have offered evidence for the low position of

[43] The Development of the Hospital, in N. Faxon, ed., *The Hospital in Contemporary Life* (Cambridge, Mass., 1949), p. 33–34.

[44] While local governmental hospitals may have some of the same types of business and industrial leaders on their boards, the findings of our study suggest that the proportions differ. Information on occupations of board members was gathered and classified with high reliability according to categories which included one for "top economic and production people." Whereas 28 percent of voluntary hospitals had more than 30 percent of the board members in this category, none of the governmental hospitals had more than 30 percent of their boards composed of this type of person. See further C. Covert, No "Common Man" on Hospital Boards, *Syracuse Herald-Journal*, Oct. 20, 1959.

governmental institutions, the comparison of local governmental hospitals with voluntary hospitals suggests an explanation. The political system is the major means of control of governmental institutions. In a democratic society, the political system, far from being the power instrument of the capitalist ruling class, as Marx maintained, has often been a major means of control and representation available to ordinary citizens. As changes in medical technology have encouraged the use of the hospital by all elements of society, "upper" elements have preserved the class structure of the community by organizing their own facilities outside of control of the masses and to some extent beyond their participation. As Peter H. Rossi states:

> Historically, the development of voluntary civic associations may be interpreted as the reaction to the loss of political power on the local scene by high status groups who built a set of community organizations which they could control, being out of reach of the mass vote of lower class groups.[45]

To us it appears that it is the role played by governmental institutions in our society in general which has led to the low support of governmental hospitals. We are not employing the usual argument of the popular critic of government that it is inherently bad or incapable. Our findings are, rather, a comment on the position of governmental organizations in American society in general. It should be noted, however, that our findings may be limited to local governmental institutions. Perhaps at the state and national levels, control of government is distant enough from the ordinary person to minimize class differences between private and governmental spheres.

Our study raises the question of the social-class role of government. What is this role at the local, state, and national levels within our own society? What relationship has government had to different classes in different societies and different historical periods? For example, could the exercise of power in the political sphere have been regarded as "dirty" or crude when the king and his court ruled and "the public" had less control than is the case in a democracy?

Sponsorship has theoretical significance from two points of view. To the administrator and other role-players in the organization, it indicates the segment of the community with which the institution is associated both in terms of control and in terms of support. And to the community and the wider society, it appears to serve as one way of differentiating institutions and dividing resources among them. The processes involved in the governmental organization receiving less support and other factors

---

[45] "A Theory of Community Structure," paper delivered at the annual meeting of the American Sociological Association, Chicago, Sept. 4, 1959.

important in these processes remain as questions for further exploration. There is a further point of theoretical interest. Even though we have examined the relationship between an "internal" characteristic of an organization and the support it receives, we had to discover the meaning of the internal factor in the broader social environment before we could understand its implications for support. This is the case since support must come from the environment. Internal factors will only have significance for support insofar as they have meaning in the social environment of an organization.

SUMMARY

By way of exemplifying a framework and its use in an empirical investigation, the problem of support was examined in 136 upstate New York short-term general hospitals. The literature relative to the problem of support was discussed. Support was defined as the receipt by an organization of the elements it needs in order to achieve its goals. Voluntary, nondenominational hospitals were compared as to their receipt of funds, patients, and community participation. Although differences were not great as to receipt of patients, volunteers, and turnover, they were marked in the area of funds. A combined index of support clearly indicated the disadvantaged position of governmental hospitals. While certain other variables included in the study weakened this relationship when they were held constant, the small number of cases available for such analysis tend to fall in the expected direction in spite of applying such controls. This result is interpreted in terms of the social-class role of governmental institutions in our society, and it is suggested that sponsorship differentiates between organizations so as to associate them with elements of the community which have varying ability to channel support to the organization.

Organizational Prestige: Some Functions and Dysfunctions

Charles Perrow

This paper calls attention to the image the public holds of an organization and to some of its consequences upon the organization's internal dynamics. The importance of the public image and the consequences of the attempt to shape it became evident during the study of the goals and authority structure of a 300-bed voluntary general hospital, from which many of the illustrations here are drawn.[1] Other illustrations from a variety of organizations are offered to suggest the widespread applicability of the analysis.

An organization is dependent upon the environment for many things, such as the charter to operate, personnel, operating revenue, and funds for expansion and development, but dependency entails some loss of autonomy. Reducing dependency upon the environment is one way of increasing autonomy, but most organizations cannot minimize input if they are to expand or maintain a competitive position. Autonomy can also be increased, however, by controlling dependency, thus making it possible to expand and increase organizational power while cultivating new publics.

One of the many ways of controlling dependency is to create and maintain a favorable image of the organization in the salient publics.[2]

[1] Charles Perrow, "Authority, Goals and Prestige in a General Hospital" (unpublished Ph.D. dissertation, University of California, Berkeley, 1960). Elaboration and documentation of points made in this paper will be found in Part III of that study.

[2] Some other ways: co-optation of outsiders into the policy-determining structure of the organization (see Philip Selznick, *TVA and the Grass Roots* [Berkeley: University of California Press, 1949]); anticipating consumer wants and similar strategies of

Charles Perrow, "Organizational Prestige: Some Functions and Dysfunctions," *American Journal of Sociology*, 66, 1961, pp. 854–866. Revision of a paper read at the August, 1959, annual meeting of the American Sociological Society. The research was supported in part by a Predoctoral Research Fellowship, National Institute of Mental Health, United States Department of Health, Education, and Welfare. I am indebted to Philip Selznick and Sheldon Messinger for helpful suggestions.

If an organization and its product are well regarded, it may more easily attract personnel, influence relevant legislation, wield informal power in the community, and insure adequate numbers of clients, customers, donors, or investors. Organizations may be placed along a continuum from unfavorable to favorable public images. A predominantly favorable image we shall call "prestige," and it may range from low to high.

INTRINSIC AND EXTRINSIC REFERENTS

Prestige may rest upon the quality of the goods or services produced by the organization, as judged by those capable of evaluating the product. However, the image of the product, irrespective of its own essential quality, may be determined by association with some value-laden symbol or with characteristics of the organization that bear no necessary relation to the quality of the product, such as the physical appearance of the unit where the product is made or distributed or the organization's labor policies, political leanings, charitable donations, and so forth.

While an analytical typology may be derived from such considerations as these, in this preliminary analysis only a crude distinction will be made—that between prestige based on intrinsic or extrinsic characteristics of the goods or services. Intrinsic characteristics are fundamental to official purposes of the organization and are regarded by the organization as essential to maintaining standards of production set forth in official goals. Extrinsic characteristics are not essential to maintaining production standards, though they may be vital in insuring acceptance and resources.

Since official goals may be ambiguous and difficult to determine, and since the essentialness of a contribution may be disputed, it is sometimes difficult to distinguish between what is intrinsic and what is extrinsic. An example of intrinsic characteristics is the durability and efficiency of an automobile, relative to its price. Extrinsic characteristics would be the entertainment programs on television that the company sponsors, association with status symbols in its advertising, and the elegance of showrooms and techniques of salesmen. Styling might be either intrinsic or extrinsic, depending upon the organization's goals and the perspective of the person who interprets them.[3]

The term "ethical drug house" conveys an image that relies on an

---

controlling dependencies (see Peter F. Drucker, *The Practice of Management* [New York: Harper & Bros., 1959], pp. 52–67). See also the suggestive discussion of bargaining, co-optation, and coalition in James D. Thompson and William J. McEwen, "Organizational Goals and Environment: Goal-setting as an Interaction Process," *American Sociological Review*, XXIII (February, 1958), 23–31.

[3] Thus, styling in the "Jeep" is not an intrinsic matter as concerns prestige, but in most popular automobiles styling has become intrinsic, at least from the point of view of sales personnel.

intrinsic referent: of a firm with a reputation for producing drugs of exact specifications and making no unwarranted claims. This is intrinsic to the operation of the organization and is governed by professional and technical standards. But the organization may also build up prestige through "institutional advertising," sales techniques and packaging: these would be extrinsic characteristics. The presumption is that the image based on extrinsic referents will promote public favor and even be a substitute for an image based on intrinsic referents among those unable to evaluate the quality of the product. In some cases it may even replace an unfavorable image: if the quality of a highly publicized drug, such as a vaccine, is found wanting, prestige may be recouped through an intensification of efforts to exploit extrinsic characteristics.

It is the nature and the value of extrinsic characteristics that the group to be influenced—the "target group"—can judge them directly and form an appropriate image.[4] This is not always the case with intrinsic qualities; the target group may not be qualified to evaluate them. In this case the indorsement, through use or certification, of the product by another group capable of judging its essential quality can be used to validate the prestige claim made by the organization; or indirect indexes may be used which attest to intrinsic quality without directly measuring it. It is rarely necessary to use these two strategies to promote prestige based on extrinsic characteristics; the strategies require considerable effort and are utilized primarily for maximizing prestige based on intrinsic qualities.

DIRECT MARKETING OF INTRINSIC REFERENTS

Providing the product can stand scrutiny, intrinsic rather than extrinsic characteristics are preferred as the basis for prestige. If the organization's goods or services are consumed by a specific group capable of judging its essential quality unaided, problems of prestige are simplified. The marketing of products entails the marketing of intrinsic referents upon which prestige is based. This would be the case with specialized toolmakers, custom clothiers, or any organization producing goods or services for another organization under contractual specifications. Some emphasis upon extrinsic characteristics is to be expected; it almost always helps but is not crucial.

In the hospital that was studied—let us call it "Valley Hospital"—research in cancer chemotherapy provides an example of simplified production and marketing. The target group, an organization supporting cancer research, can easily judge the effectiveness of the results, and all

---

[4] Sheldon Messinger, in a personal communication, points out that it is also "the *danger* of extrinsic prestige that it may be directly judged by the public and has no necessary connection to the goods or services. Consider the fate of a competent actor after a scandal."

the researchers need to do to control their dependence upon the agency for grants is to test chemicals according to established methods. But, by and large, there are few occasions when the official goals of the hospital—promoting the health of the community through care of patients, teaching and research of high quality—can be properly evaluated by the clients, or donors. To promote prestige based on intrinsic quality, "validating groups" and indirect indexes are useful.

VALIDATING GROUPS

Organizations regularly make claims for the intrinsic quality of their products, but with increasingly complex and specialized goods and services many potential consumers cannot adequately evaluate these claims. Claims to quality, and thus prestige, may be validated by another group or organization with appropriate experience and resources if it uses or tests the product. This service has become so important that special organizations using standardized testing methods have been established. The presumed approval of competent groups must be publicized in order to validate claims. But the prestige of validating groups themselves may be endangered if indiscreet or excessive use is made of their evaluations. They may restrict the marketing of their evaluations or even forbid marketing, as do the consumer research organizations. The more difficult it is to establish intrinsic quality, the more the organization will need other groups for validation of claims, but the more these other groups will tend to limit the marketing of their presumed indorsement. Attempts to evade limitations may bring the organization into conflict with the validating group, as occurs when drug companies attempt to use articles in medical journals for validation of prestige claims or associate their products with symbols of the medical profession.

In Valley Hospital the claim to provide exemplary care of the patient is validated when, for example, an organization for crippled children contracts with it to provide care for its clients. Such validations are discreetly publicized. Research grants from well-reputed agencies are another example. However, some agencies disapprove of publicity, and, as much as it may wish to, the hospital is unable to market their much-desired approval.

INDIRECT INDEXES

If the goods or services produced for specialized consumers are so highly technical or experimental that no evaluation is possible, the organization tends to rely upon indirect indexes of intrinsic quality, that is, upon publicizing characteristics of the organization which are thought to insure quality. The reputation of the personnel, the specialized equipment, the number of research projects in operation—all these are familiar indexes used for this purpose in the hospital and other research organizations. Indexes of promoting the health of the community are, for instance, statistics on the amount of free and partly paid care given patients. The teaching program attests to contributing to medical education and suggests a high quality of care for all patients. However, statistics on the amount of free care do not necessarily mean good care, nor does the number of medical students necessarily indicate their quality, the teaching they receive, or the care they give. Indeed, some persons claim that the hospital's standards in these matters are low and that in part this is due precisely to the emphasis upon serving a large number of free patients and attracting a large number of interns and residents. Similarly, a social agency, in an effort to increase the support of its donors, may increase the number of clients served while quality of service deteriorates. Reliance upon indirect indexes of intrinsic prestige may thus subvert quality, since the indexes become more important and valuable to the organization than the quality they are supposed to suggest.[5]

THE NEED FOR EXTRINSIC REFERENTS

When competition presents the client, consumer, or donor with a choice of organizations to support, it may be necessary to supplement indexes of intrinsic quality with extrinsic indexes. Indeed, the use of extrinsic referents is essential in the case of mass-produced products of equal quality. Marginal differentiation makes the product distinctive, even though it does not contribute to quality, and the differences can easily be publicized and promoted. Marginal differentiation is sought not only in the

---

[5] While indirect indexes are usually used because direct validation is impossible, indirect indexes may also be used when the organization does not have dependable direct ones. Subversion of intrinsic quality is similar to "displacement of goals" as described by Merton and others (Robert K. Merton, *Social Theory and Social Structure* [Glencoe, Ill.: Free Press, 1949], p. 155), where, however, the example is the bureaucrat's emphasis upon rules for their own sake. Our example is the organization's emphasis upon indexes for the sake of prestige. Peter M. Blau provides examples of displacement dictated by organizational needs in *The Dynamics of Bureaucracy* (Chicago: University of Chicago Press, 1955). Sheldon Messinger discusses the attempt to maintain the "core-identity" of the Townsend organization in "Organizational Transformation: A Case Study of a Declining Social Movement," *American Sociological Review*, XX (January, 1955), 3–13. Closer still to our own example is the analysis of dependency upon students and the criteria of legislators and professionals (Burton R. Clark, *Adult Education in Transition: A Study of Institutional Insecurity* [Berkeley: University of California Press, 1956]). What Clark calls the "marginality" of adult education we would speak of as a condition of high dependency which is uncontrolled. The defense of "precarious values," in Clark's sense, is difficult without the autonomy afforded by control over dependency, that is, without, in part, prestige (*ibid.*, chaps. ii, vi).

product but in other aspects of the organization, such as plant design, packaging, contacts with target groups, and, of course, in advertising.[6] Since extrinsic characteristics, by definition, are unrelated to the essential quality of the product, their virtually unlimited varieties are assiduously explored by organizations conducting "motivation" or marketing research.

The production and marketing of extrinsic characteristics conferring prestige are developed to a high degree in all mass-produced consumer goods. Attempts to promote images of intrinsic quality are still very common, however, as instanced by the cigarette industry's tests of filters, aging of tobaccos, and the approval of "men who know tobacco best." Extrinsic themes are not limited to competitive industries. Monopolies also are dependent upon the public and seek to influence the public's image by, for example, appeals to the way they support free enterprise or by association with cultural refinement, as found in "institutional advertising." Apparently, the more successful the organization, the more irrelevant may be the themes and the closer they may draw toward values of the society as a whole, thus implying an even stronger claim for support. An example is an advertisement containing only a brief statement of a democratic ideal symbolized by a painting.

EXTRINSIC REFERENTS IN THE HOSPITAL

The hospital, in its dependence upon donors, physicians, and patients, is subject to competitive pressures. Local donors will respond better to intrinsic qualities or indirect indexes of them, and the hospital prefers this method of control. However, reliance upon extrinsic referents is sometimes necessary: for example, Valley Hospital has a policy restricting the use of human-interest stories—an extrinsic item. Direct competition with another hospital for donations forced Valley Hospital to abandon the policy and, instead, to send human-interest stories to a local paper as the other hospital had been doing.

Physicians will bring patients to the hospital available to them that offers the best facilities. But when similarly equipped hospitals compete for doctors, the enterprising hospital will emphasize extrinsic details which insure the physician's comfort, convenience, and deference. A new administrator at Valley Hospital increased the percentage of occupied beds from the lowest in the city to the highest for comparable hospitals in part through such devices.

Patients are incompetent to judge the care they receive from the hospital: they are unable to gain the information required to make a judgment,

[6] Many extrinsic characteristics are easily produced, marketed without effort, and culturally prescribed, and these are not characteristics of any particular organization. However, we are concerned with concerted, conscious strategies for influencing the image of the target group.

and they lack the knowledge to interpret correctly what they do experience. They may, however, judge many superficial aspects of the professional care and especially the "hotel" aspects of hospital care. The hospital has placed great emphasis upon producing extrinsic items which patients are able to evaluate, and a public relations department promotes them assiduously. In a four-year period an average of over eight news items a year appeared in the mass media covering such subjects as wine with meals and a beauty salon for maternity patients. Emphasis upon these hotel-like services has helped increase occupancy and kept the name of the hospital before the public. Other patient-oriented features include extended visiting hours and circulating coffee carts for visitors, television sets for patients, snacks and special cookery, elaborate devices to suppress noise, and meticulous housekeeping.

The creation of a public relations department (headed by a former newspaperwoman) coincided with a concerted attempt to increase occupancy, donations, and prestige in general. The department both stimulates and publicizes innovations. Its success, while bringing the hospital awards from the American Hospital Association, engendered criticism from within and without. However, most other hospitals in the city subsequently created their own departments, perhaps, considering the publicity Valley Hospital was receiving, in self-defense.

Shaping the image held by external groups is the explicit task of public relations departments. However, the work may be carried on by other groups or individuals in organizations. The administrator of Valley Hospital was looked upon by some of his staff as an "outside man," more active in dealing with the public than with internal affairs. Current research in correctional institutions suggests that the division of labor, commonly found at the apex of large organizations between an "outside" man and an "inside" man, is effective.[7] While an implicit or explicit assignment of public relations functions to individuals or groups does not necessarily signify the production and marketing of extrinsic characteristics, concerted efforts to shape images suggests that the product cannot "speak for itself" and that prestige based on these referents is also desired. Of course, personnel who deal with external groups are also involved in bargaining and in political functions that have only a remote relationship to organizational prestige.

[7] Mayer Zald, "Multiple Goals and Staff Structure: A Comparative Study of Correctional Institutions for Juvenile Delinquents" (unpublished Ph.D. dissertation, University of Michigan, 1960), chap. v. An administrative reorganization to make this division explicit seems to have occurred recently in General Motors Corporation (*Fortune*, November, 1958, pp. 123 ff.). Wilensky has analyzed the role of lawyers as publicists in labor unions and the dependency they seek to control (Harold L. Wilensky, *Intellectuals in Labor Unions* [Glencoe, Ill.: Free Press, 1956], chap. v, esp. pp. 74–79).

DEFLECTION OF RESOURCES

Emphasis upon extrinsic details conferring prestige is likely to create internal problems for the organization. The personnel, because of training habit or professional standards, may complain that resources are diverted from essential to peripheral activities. At Valley Hospital they complained of the importance given to hotel-like innovations and concessions to physicians. Some administrative personnel felt that the creative energies and talents of the administrator were expended upon publicity-producing "frills" or physicians' conveniences while serious administrative matters were neglected, eventually to the patients' detriment. Nurses complained that requests by private patients for coffee or other services described in brochures took time from the care required by free and part-paying patients. Interns and residents complained that patients were unwilling to interrupt their telephone conversations or snacks for necessary examination and treatment. Physicians found that allowing unlimited visiting hours interfered with their work. The hospital may unwittingly be encouraging the selection of a clientele that demands more and more of these services. But it cannot afford to redress what personnel see as the proper balance between services and care without finding some other way to attract patients. Such complaints are probably common in organizations.

MULTIPLE DEPENDENCIES

Problems associated with prestige also stem from dependence upon a number of groups, each of which responds to a given type of prestige. At Valley Hospital, for example, local donors are needed to support expansion, new facilities, research, and teaching. Since donors are themselves unable to judge the intrinsic virtues of most goods or services, the hospital relies upon validation of its claims by other groups and indirect indexes. At the same time, however, it is also dependent upon support from agencies that are capable of making intrinsic judgments—particularly those that operate nationally. These agencies may regard the publicized indexes as extrinsic and irrelevant and may feel that their support is being exploited. Finally, a group within the hospital may seek to promote an image which conflicts with the image the organization seeks to promote.

Much ill will, for example, was created by attempts of trustees and the administrator to exploit the dramatic and unique nature of new facilities for a highly specialized type of surgery. On two occasions the administrator argued that the community gave $100,000 for the facilities, that the donors would be pleased most by publicity in national magazines, and "that was what they gave the money for." However, the staff of the specialized unit argued that publicity in this form would endanger grants from the national agencies supporting the research, whose representatives would view it as irrelevant to the project, that it would expose the staff to ridicule from other physicians since facilities rather than research results were being publicized, and that publicity would increase the demand for services on behalf of those patients who were not good research material, thus impeding the research program. The facilities were evidence of intrinsic quality to local target groups but were judged extrinsic to official goals by the researchers and agencies supporting the current research.

Physicians as a whole have relationships which conflict with those of the hospital: they are dependent upon outside colleagues and the profession as a whole for validation of individual claims for prestige, for validation of the claims of the profession itself, and for maintaining professional contacts. A basic tenet of the profession, occasioned by competitive practice as much as anything, is the avoidance of publicity. While they may seek it individually, collectively the medical staff must oppose publicity in most cases. The hospital, on the other hand, finds that use of physicians' names or pictures serves to give authenticity to news releases and creates interest in the hospital. This, in part, has led to a long series of disputes between the respective public relations committees of the medical staff and the hospital, restricting the ability of the hospital to publicize legitimate prestige items.

PRESTIGE AND GOALS

We have identified three general sources of organizational strain and possible subversion of goals stemming from efforts to control dependencies through promoting organizational prestige. The production of indirect indexes of intrinsic quality may take precedence over maintaining the quality of goods and services. Resources may be diverted from activities supporting official goals to those which produce and market extrinsic characteristics. Finally, multiple dependencies may interfere with the marketing of either intrinsic or extrinsic referents and may create conflicts within the organization or between the organization and its target groups.

Decisions regarding indirect indexes of prestige, the allocation of resources, and marketing methods may shape the character of an organization through establishing precedents and long-range commitments. An unacknowledged priority of goals based upon an expedient calculus of gain may emerge. There was tentative evidence of this possibility at Valley Hospital. The key targets of efforts to create prestige were potential patients and local donors. Maximal organizational resources were devoted to activities which furthered prestige in their eyes, while minimal resources were received by some of those activities which had little or no relevance to prestige, even though they were essential for achieving official goals.

Thus, while preventive medicine was a goal of the hospital, little was done to support it. The authorities were indifferent to the ineffectiveness and disorganization of one small, unglamorous, but potentially valuable diagnostic program, which, in untrained hands, threatened to do more harm than good. However, a proposal to build and maintain a museum of medicine on the premises which would be open to community and the schools was actively considered, despite the expense and effort involved. Though of less value than the diagnostic program, it could be billed as a part of the program of preventive medicine, while substantially contributing to prestige.

More striking was the fate of one service essential to the major goal of providing patient care of high quality. This was a goal far from achieved in the case of free and part-paying patients in the outpatient department, largely because good care there does not at present bring prestige. The department was denied funds for remedying even the grossest physical deterioration and obsolescence; attendance and performance of the staff was undisciplined, and efforts to reform the department were, for several years, not backed by the authorities in the organization. On the other hand, while the outpatient department was in a state of physical deterioration and professional neglect, funds, much energy, and inventiveness went into constructing and publicizing an elaborate, highly specialized surgical suite, even though its contribution to official goals was relatively peripheral.

Striking a balance between the conflicting demands for goal achievement and increasing inputs in the form of donations and patient revenue is difficult. Without prestige, whether based on intrinsic or extrinsic qualities, resources may be inadequate to achieve goals or provide for expansion and development. But, without proper use of resources for avoidance of intra- and interorganizational conflicts and achievement of all goals for which responsibility is acknowledged and assumed, control of dependencies may be a hollow accomplishment.

Philanthropic Activity and the Business Career

Aileen D. Ross

This article attempts to set forth the various ways in which participation in philanthropic activity influences the career of the businessman. It is the contention of this study that philanthropy, most particularly the organization of financial campaigns, is a substantial activity of the successful businessman. Moreover such activity not only facilitates business careers in ways well recognized by the fraternity of successful businessmen, but also enters as a substantial ingredient in the public relations programs of modern corporations.

The analysis of the material on which the study is based falls under three main headings: A) business position and the demands of financial campaigns; B) major facets of the philanthropic career; and C) some background characteristics of men who have held important positions in campaigns.

BUSINESS POSITION AND THE DEMANDS
OF FINANCIAL CAMPAIGNS

As money-raising campaigns for charitable purposes have increased in number and scope on the North American continent, it is now essential for most businessmen to take part in them. In fact, it is very difficult for

Aileen D. Ross, "Philanthropic Activity and the Business Career," *Social Forces*, 32, No. 3, 1954, pp. 274–280. This paper was read at the meeting of the Eastern Sociological Society, Harvard University, March 28, 1953. I am indebted to professor Everett C. Hughes for stimulating discussions on this topic, and to Mrs. Nancy Brooks for assistance in gathering and analyzing data. The materials of the paper were drawn in part from interviews with 70 men who had held prominent positions in the large city-wide money-raising campaigns of Wellsville, an Eastern Canadian city. Supplementary data on their careers were accumulated from a variety of sources including: complete records for 13 city-wide campaigns held in Wellsville from 1909–1922; records for Community Chest campaigns from 1930–1951; and all published volumes of *Who's Who in Canada, The Canadian Who's Who, Canadiana,* and *The Directory of Directors*. Additional material was taken from the back and current files of the two leading newspapers in Wellsville and from records of many other Wellsville campaigns.

a man to avoid canvassing once he is well started in his business career.[1] The individual usually begins as a door-to-door canvasser, and from there advances in the campaign hierarchy to team captain, then to divisional captain, and then to a low position on an executive committee. From this position he moves up to vice-chairman and is finally made chairman of a campaign. After that he will be put on the Special Names committee,[2] and eventually may become chairman of that committee, which is the pinnacle of campaign positions.[3]

As many of the important businessmen of Wellsville have moved up to important executive positions in campaigns in some such manner, we can now talk of "philanthropic careers" as well as "business careers." However, a career in philanthropy is dependent *on* the business career, for a man must be high up in the business world before he is in a position of sufficient influence to take over the top philanthropic positions.

So much publicity is necessarily attached to the large city-wide money-raising campaigns that the success or failure of a canvasser is clearly visible, and he may therefore become a marked man in the business world. Success will mean that other positions of importance in the community will open out to him, such as membership in important clubs, executive positions on welfare agencies, hospitals or universities, as well as further advancement in business. This relationship between advancement in business and philanthropy is outlined in the following interviews:

> PUBLIC RELATIONS HEAD OF LARGE RETAIL FIRM. If you study the lists of campaign workers, you will find an amazing parallel between the level a man holds in his place of business and the level he holds in the campaign. Thus, if you are working at the bottom part of some business organization you will be ringing doorbells. You can't possibly head a campaign and deal with people who are the heads of large corporations. As you go up in the business world you go up in philanthropy. If you are at the top in a business or financial corporation you will appear at the top of the campaign.

> PRESIDENT OF FIRM. You will find that when a man first gets into this game he will be given some sort of minor campaign position depending on his business position. My own men have taken these positions, but as they have progressed with the firm so they have taken on more responsi-

---

[1] Throughout this article the term "canvassing" will be used to describe time given to any kind of campaign activity.

[2] Since the Special Names committee is responsible for canvassing the largest individual and corporation subscribers, it is composed solely of influential businessmen.

[3] This advancement does not necessarily take place in one particular campaign. The individual may take part in a number of different important city-wide campaigns such as the Community Chest, Red Cross, Salvation Army, Y.M.C.A., hospital or university campaigns, during his philanthropic career. Smaller campaigns are not important to his career.

bility in these campaigns. Furthermore they are helping themselves since I am watching them to see how they get along. They are ambitious, which is all to the good. They realize that we want them to do this work, and they will do a good job when we set them to it.

It is these minor executives, whom it is important to bring into the campaigns, because they will later on become important men if they are any good.

I think other businessmen try to do the same thing with their own men. They see to it that they take over these campaign responsibilities and if they do a good job they keep them in mind for the future. I think these young men realize this, and now they are trying to get into the campaigns without anyone asking them. Now I have a letter here from a young lawyer who has only been out in the field for about five years, but already he is into all these campaigns. That young fellow is going to make a name for himself!

Another point to be noted is that as a man advances in the campaign hierarchy he becomes better trained for its higher positions, and also comes more and more into contact with men who are influential in business.

LAWYER. The top leaders have participated from year to year in the campaigns. They become part of it, and each year they become more and more experienced. They are just moved up to the vacancy above. Of course there is a sort of screening process which takes into account the respectability of the person and the type of occupation that will permit him to hold the position. The whole organization of philanthropic activity is arranged like a ladder. Once you start in the system you slowly climb up—and if you have real and vital interest you reach the top rungs.

Through coming to know these men, both as friends and as business associates, he becomes still more powerful in the philanthropic structure. For it is only influential men who can elicit the large individual and corporation subscriptions essential for the success of any large campaign.

Occasionally a man of exceptional qualifications will be put into a top philanthropic position without working his way up in the structure, but as participation in philanthropy has become more and more an essential part of the business career, this is the exception rather than the rule.

The few businessmen who refused to take part in the Wellsville campaigns were criticized by interviewees who thought that such behavior would eventually react on their careers.

GENERAL MANAGER, BANK Y. It's *very* important for a man to take part in campaigns. Just as important for a lawyer or an accountant as for a businessman. It's important for their firms too. A man who won't take his share is thought a lot less of—and probably it affects his business.

Hence, although it was impossible to find a direct correlation between the business careers and the philanthropic careers of all the men studied, records and interviews showed that there is a decided relationship between the rise of a man to the top executive positions in charitable campaigns, and his rise in the business hierarchy.

MAJOR FACETS OF THE PHILANTHROPIC CAREER

The Importance of Sponsorship

Since business institutions have gradually taken over the control of the collection of money for all large city-wide campaigns,[4] an "inner circle" of important businessmen has gradually come to control the top executive positions in these campaigns. This inner circle chooses either one of its own members for important campaign positions or a man whom they wish to see advance in the business world.[5]

> HEAD OF PUBLISHING FIRM. Stewart Black was the logical man to choose to head the Z Campaign. He was a man well known in the city, he had done a lot of this sort of thing over the years, and he had a good family name. But perhaps most important of all he was *au fait* with the important people around here. He travelled in the same circle with them, and could talk to them in their own language. He didn't have to get to know the important people in Wellsville—he was one of them. By choosing him, the organizers knew what they were doing; they were choosing a good sponsor, someone whom the important people would accept without hesitation. I don't think this campaign system could continue without this sort of thing. The only way to get the important people behind you is to have someone leading the campaign who is one of them.

This sponsorship of participants in philanthropy can be seen as a way in which the inner circle manages to perpetuate itself. For, through their ability to control the incumbents of the top positions, they are able to pass on the control of philanthropy to a group which will carry it on in the way in which they would approve.

The choice of executives for the large campaigns is taken very seriously by the inner circle, and a careful selection of candidates is made. Interviewees said that they often sat "for hours" to be sure that they got the "right" person. Not only must they perpetuate their own group, but they

---

[4] Aileen D. Ross, "Organized Philanthropy in an Urban Community," *Canadian Journal of Economics and Political Science*, XVIII (November 1952), 482–485.

[5] Four aspects of the inner circle are of importance when considering its implication for philanthropy: its importance in sponsoring campaigns; its control of philanthropy; its importance as a vehicle for careers; its importance as sponsoring individuals for campaign positions. It is this last function of the inner circle that will be dealt with **here.**

must be sure that their man will be able to make a success of the campaign.

Sponsorship of the inner circle is in fact so important that a man cannot possibly attain a top position by volunteering his services. Rather, he must wait until he is approached by one or more of the inner circle and asked to take the position.

GENERAL MANAGER, TRUST COMPANY. You don't just volunteer for these positions—it isn't done; you wait until you are asked. In fact, I don't know what would happen if you *did* volunteer! When asked, you are expected to say "Yes," but it is considered bad to show any eagerness. I am sure that if someone volunteered to be chairman of the next campaign he would be turned down.

Reasons for Participating

The pressures that can be exerted on people to participate in philanthropy coming from friends, business associates, and members of the inner circle have been described in another article.[6] Pressures also come through family and religious training, which may instill a sense of duty and responsibility to the community. This training may exert great influence on men whose families have been engaged in philanthropy for several generations.

Pressures to participate also come from one's business firm, for philanthropic activity is now such an important part of the public relations of business concerns that in most cases a man is automatically expected to canvass when he reaches a certain business position.

GENERAL MANAGER, RETAIL FIRM D. My interest in philanthropy arose because I was at the head of a large firm. In this position it is just part of your job. I suppose that there are families who have a tradition along these lines, but I think that most of us are active in philanthropy because we are doing the particular jobs that we are.

Hence, at certain levels of business, active participation is expected of the *business position*, regardless of who the incumbent may be.

Indeed, participation has become so essential that many business enterprises now include "training" for these community responsibilities as part of the regular training of their staff.

GENERAL MANAGER, BANK Y. Training for philanthropy is a very important part of the training in our bank. It's our policy to drill into our men from the very beginning that they *must* take an interest in the community they're working in. Even if they're just a manager in a small town they

---

[6] Aileen D. Ross, "Social Control in Philanthropy," *American Journal of Sociology,* LVIII (March 1953), 451.

must take an interest in the new hospital, or school, or whatever it is. We get reports each year on every clerk in every branch, and this shows whether they take an interest in their community affairs or not. They're reprimanded if they don't show this community interest. Stress right through is on this. And it's all for public relations. We *have* to do it—the competitions between banks is so great. So we are all trained to take community responsibility. We expect to see the result of it somewhere in our balance sheet!

There is also a growing realization on the part of ambitious young men that participation is important to their careers, so directly or indirectly they may seek these positions.

PROFESSIONAL ORGANIZER B. G. told someone in his firm to get on with the job of canvassing, and he did it because he thought he was pleasing the boss, and that it might mean something for him if he did a good job. That's the way it works.

DEPARTMENT HEAD, RETAIL FIRM D. Each person along the line resents being asked to canvass, but on the other hand is glad that he is singled out. He knows that his name will appear on a sheet in the main office, meaning that his name comes to the attention of top management.

Many, too, recognize that through participation they are able to meet people and make contacts which may eventually be of business or "social" use.

PROFESSIONAL ORGANIZER A. Even the ordinary volunteer canvassers get to know people whom they would not ordinarily meet. I can give you an example of this. There was a cocktail party at a particular home here in Wellsville a few days ago for the various team captains and vice-chairmen. Many of these men would never have gone to that house for a cocktail party, and they probably never will again. But the campaign gave them a chance to see the inside of the house and meet other people whom they would not usually meet. That sort of thing goes on a lot. People know they will rub elbows with a lot of important people. They will make friends and contacts. A man makes acquaintances in his work and maybe at his club, but these campaigns are an opportunity for him to meet a lot of other people, and make a lot of friends. That's the way it works. You can see the friendships being made all around you.

These contacts are of particular importance for the broker, lawyer, insurance agent, or others whose success in business depends on personal contacts.

LAWYER. A man in the selling field has much to gain from philanthropic work. Each contact that he makes in this group will widen his clientele.

A great many sellers probably depend a great deal on this activity for their business careers.

Finally, some corporations feel that philanthropy can serve as an important training in salesmanship, so they urge their men to take part.

The reasons for participation are therefore complex, and include pressures which the individual cannot escape, rewards and the hope of reward, and training which will improve the man's business position.

Testing the Individual

It has been pointed out that philanthropic activity is an exceptionally good way in which to test a man's ability, as the success of any canvasser is clearly marked in terms of dollars and cents. Many corporations realize this, and consciously use campaign activity to test a promising young man.[7]

> PROFESSIONAL ORGANIZER E. He is the center of all publicity. The spotlight is on him for a long time and he is placed before people's eyes. It certainly helps him in his business or profession.

Hence, a man's success or failure will receive a great deal of publicity in the business world, particularly if he is in a high position in an important campaign. This means that some men may try to avoid high positions because they feel that the risk of failure is too great and would be detrimental to their careers.

> PRESIDENT OF FIRM. If you are given a job in a campaign you simply *cannot* fail. It would be a reflection on your business and organizational ability. It is taken for granted that you will succeed. And people are apt to remember you because your name has been prominent. But no one is sure that their name will not be remembered equally well as a person who has done a poor job.

So important is success that the head of a campaign may try to arrange the objective of the campaign for an amount of money which he is reasonably sure that he can collect.

> PROFESSIONAL ORGANIZER F. I don't think that the chairman of the last Q. Campaign wanted an objective that was too high. It's a feather in his cap if he can make it. . . . It helps him a lot and people take note of him. Once a person heads a campaign that goes over, he is a marked man. He will be asked to do it again and again.

[7] Norman Miller, "The Jewish Leadership of Lakeport" in Alvin W. Gouldner (ed.), *Studies in Leadership* (New York: Harper and Brothers, 1950): "Functionally the [campaign] organization serves for the prestige-candidate as a stage from which he can make a regular and conspicuous show of his efforts" (p. 213).

Failure to achieve the campaign objective is felt to be such a stigma on the executive of a campaign that some of the smaller campaigns may not publish their failures.

> PROFESSIONAL ORGANIZER G. Mr. X (professional organizer) says that for some reason a number of campaigns don't make their objective, but say they do. He knows positively of several that didn't this year, and yet wouldn't admit it. Mr. X thinks that perhaps they think that it will be a stigma against them if they don't make it.

Another fear comes from the angle of personal competition. A man may not wish to take over a high executive position for fear that he will not be able to come up to the standard set by a personal or business rival in another campaign.

> PRESIDENT, BANK Y. The Z. Campaign was a terrible strain right up to the end because we really didn't think we'd make it. They hadn't made their objective for a number of years. But I was *bound* that I would! I nearly killed myself doing it! You always want to do better than the other fellows! John Brown (member of a rival firm) is chairman this year. I bet he'll try to outdo me!

Hence, philanthropic activity can now serve as a testing-ground on which corporations can judge the abilities of participants. Failure may entail so much harmful publicity that some men are loath to take over the executive positions.

BACKGROUND CHARACTERISTICS OF MEN
IN IMPORTANT POSITIONS IN CAMPAIGNS

The first two sections have shown that a relationship exists between participation in business and participation in philanthropy. This section extends this analysis to show the relationship of family background, positions in other philanthropic agencies, and club membership to campaign participation and economic success.[8] This information was obtained for a random sample of 67 men who had held high executive positions in the annual Community Chest Campaigns of Wellsville. All of these men had

---

[8] Everett C. Hughes, "The Institutional Office and the Person," *American Journal of Sociology*, XLIII (November 1937): "The interlocking of the directorships of educational, charitable and other philanthropic agencies is due . . . to the very fact that they are philanthropic. Philanthropy, as we know it, implies economic success; it comes late in a career. It may come only in the second generation of success. But when it does come, it is quite as much a matter of assuming certain prerogatives and responsibilities in the control of philanthropic institutions as of giving money. The prerogatives and responsibilities form part of the successful man's conception of himself, and part of the world's expectation of him" (p. 411).

held high positions in business or the professions, and many directorships of corporations. By type of business affiliation, the 67 men were distributed as follows: finance, 23; industry, 15; professions, 8; transportation and communication, 7; insurance, 3; merchandising, 3; publishing, 3; wholesale, 2; real estate, 1; machinery repair, 1; and capitalist, 1. The positions in business held by these 67 men included: chairman of board, 3; president, 17; vice-president, 11; general manager, 8; assistant general manager, 1; manager, 3; assistant manager, 2; associate treasurer, 1; secretary, 1; proprietor, 1; partner, 13; general counsel, 1; and unknown, 5.[9]

Family Background

As the ethnic composition of the top social classes of Wellsville is largely of English and Scottish origin, it is not surprising to find that the tradition of *noblesse oblige* is still strong among the old wealthy families. Many of these families were early community benefactors through their donations of hospital or university buildings. The names of their descendants are still identified with the prestige attached to these concrete symbols of benevolence. If descendants of these families hold high executive positions in business and especially if the business concern still bears the family name, then these men are "naturals" for high executive positions in philanthropy.

> PRESIDENT OF LARGE WHOLESALE FIRM. Jim Reid was the natural person to head the last hospital campaign. The Reids have been interested in the hospital for generations. Jim's father was Chairman for years. Then the Reids are one of the great Wellsville families. And Jim is popular and has lots of friends whom he could get to help. And he has energy and lots of time because he works in a firm that could allow him time to do it.[10]

However, as philanthropic activity has changed from the control of the religious institutions and upper classes to the control of business it was not unexpected to find that family position is not now as important in obtaining high positions in philanthropy. Today it is more essential to have a business organization behind the incumbent of a top executive position, for his business firm can assist him by looking after his work during the campaign and loaning additional staff, and as their representa-

[9] The random sample was drawn from the Campaign Chairmen, and men on the Special Names Committee of the Community Chest Campaigns from 1930–1951. The information given here and in Table 1 was obtained from the sources outlined in footnote 1. The figures cannot claim to be accurate; they only represent the positions found in the available sources. It is therefore highly probable that the men represented in the sample have held many more directorships in corporations and executive positions in social agencies, hospitals and universities than Table 1 indicates.

[10] Jim Reid is in the firm which still bears the family name. It should be noted that there is a double pressure to engage in philanthropy for such men, coming from both their business and family positions.

tive he can use their name as a lever to get subscriptions and personnel.

Hence, although high family position still serves an important function for philanthropic activity through inculcating ideas of responsibility to the community, and family names can act as symbols of prestige in the campaign, they are only additional assets for acquiring high positions. It is now more essential for the incumbent to have an important business position in a firm which will back him in his money-raising efforts.

> PRESIDENT, BANK Y. No, I don't agree that your family background is all important, because anyone that runs a campaign *must* have an organization behind him who can help. For example, when I took over the chairmanship of the Q Campaign I wrote to each of our branch bank managers. I told them that I didn't insist at all that they should work in the campaign, but that I would be very glad for any assistance that they could give me. And everyone of them worked terribly hard to help. But families are important in giving a sense of responsibility. It's born into some families—like the L family. Of course the first L was one of the biggest crooks, but he managed to pass on a sense of responsibility to others to his children.

Social Agencies

Executive positions on boards of social agencies have traditionally been the prerogative of the top social classes.[11] These positions identify the incumbents with the leisured class, and are another important media for gaining community recognition. It was not possible to get completely accurate information for board memberships for the sample of 67 men. However, data found for 46 of the 67 men show that they had held positions on 146 boards of charitable agencies (see Table 1).

While universities and hospitals are not usually included in the category of "social agencies," they are so dependent on private financial support in Wellsville that, for the purpose of this paper, they can in fact be placed in this category. Executive positions on the boards of these two institutions are the pinnacle of the prestige positions in Wellsville. Table 1 shows that of the 67 men included in the sample, 12 had been Governors or Chancellors of universities, and 41 had held executive positions on the boards of local hospitals.

These figures indicate that executive positions in social agencies are another important adjunct to the business career. Moreover, these positions mark the incumbent as a person ready—and fit—for further philanthropic responsibilities and higher business positions.

[11] Everett C. Hughes, "The Institutional Office and the Person," *loc. cit.*, p. 411. Professor Hughes quotes a survey in New York City that showed that the governing boards of settlement houses in that city were made up of people with prestige in business and professional life. This pattern has also been traced in Warner's studies of Yankee City; see W. L. Warner and P. S. Lunt, *The Social Life of a Modern Community* (New Haven: Yale University Press, 1941).

Table 1 *Executive Positions Held in Business, Hospitals, Universities, and Social Agencies, and Club Membership for Businessmen Who Have Held High Executive Positions in Campaigns*

		Total
Business enterprises	Directorships [a]	458
Hospitals	Executive positions	41
Universities	Governors and chancellors	12
Social agencies [b]	Executive positions	146
Club memberships [c]	Highest-ranking club (38 memberships)	38
	Second-ranking clubs:	
	2 Social clubs (58 memberships)	58
	6 Recreational clubs [d] (128 memberships)	128
	Third-ranking clubs:	
	3 Social clubs (43 memberships)	43
	7 Recreational clubs (61 memberships)	61
	Total number of club memberships	328
	Total number of clubs	19
Total number of men		67

[a] No record of directorships found for 4 men.
[b] No record of executive positions in social agencies found for 21 men.
[c] No record of club membership found for 7 men.
[d] Recreational clubs include golf, badminton, racket, tennis, skating, curling, yachting, and hunt clubs.

Club Membership

Many studies have shown the growing importance of club membership as a distinctive mark of social class position. In this study records and interviews showed a relationship between the individual's rise in the business hierarchy and his rise in the "club hierarchy." That is, many of the men studied were able to join the top-ranking clubs in Wellsville only after they had obtained certain positions in business.

Interviewees claimed that clubs have a distinct relationship to philanthropy for they "provide meeting-places to discuss strategy." In other words, as one of the important functions of clubs is to provide a locale for cliques, many of the informal decisions about personnel and subscriptions are carried out in their milieu, and friends are recruited.

PARTNER, ACCOUNTING FIRM. Bill drew a lot of clubmen into the F Campaign when he became Chairman of the Special Names Committee.

It is perhaps as difficult for the club member to resist the pressures to participate in philanthropy coming from fellow clubmen as it is for businessmen to resist the pressure coming from business associates. If this is so, it follows that participation in campaigns is expected of certain "club memberships" as such, in much the same way that it is expected of certain business positions.

Table 1 shows that the sample of 67 men had held 38 club memberships in *the* top-ranking club of Wellsville, 186 memberships in second-ranking clubs, and 104 memberships in third-ranking clubs. As no record of club membership could be found for 7 men, this means that the 60 men included in the sample had held 328 memberships in Wellsville's top 19 clubs. Club membership can thus be said to have a distinct relationship to a man's philanthropic career as well as to his business career.

CONCLUSIONS

Two important results have ensued from the gradual monopolization of money-raising campaigns by the business world.

On the one hand, philanthropic activity now serves as a means by which the modern businessman can strengthen his position in a highly competitive world by taking over as many philanthropic positions as possible. On the other hand, business firms must now engage in philanthropic activity in order to compete with rival firms and in order to enhance their relations with the public. This means that ambitious men will recognize the importance of philanthropic participation for their careers, and business enterprises will see that their men participate in order that they may benefit from the reflected publicity.

Before the development of organized philanthropy in Wellsville, church membership and activity in church work were important adjuncts to the businessman's career. Now, however, it is much more important for the businessman to identify himself with philanthropic activity. This is largely due to the fact that the competitive nature of the campaigns displays the skills of the participants, and the publicity given the campaigns places the participant visibly before the public. In fact, participation in the large city-wide campaigns now gives a man and his firm more publicity than many of the usual advertising channels.

This paper has tried to show the relationship that now exists between business, philanthropy, and other community prestige-positions. It can be summed up in the words of an interviewee:

> MANAGER OF TRUST COMPANY. There is a definite way up the business ladder in Wellsville. The bottom rung is to be Chairman of the G (lunch) Club. The top rung is to be Chairman of the Chamber of Commerce. In between you are on the executive of the Community Chest Campaigns, and join the A (top-ranking) Club. I've seen it happen again and again! If you make the Chairmanship of the G Club, you're made! Then "THEY" will see that you get to the top. But you *have* to be good or "THEY" won't back you!

Part C

Interdependence and Coordination among Welfare Organizations

WELFARE organizations must be able to coordinate their activities with other organizations whose goals and clientele are similar or, at least, interdependent. The police department and the local settlement house share a clientele and, to some extent, have common goals. All organizations have at least two kinds of external relations: they must gain support from the environment, and they must coordinate or come to terms with both competitive and/or potentially cooperating agencies.

But coordination has its costs—it takes time, money, and personnel. One of the repeated laments of people who have attempted to work with welfare agencies is that it is difficult to get the agencies to coordinate. Not only does coordination require time, money, and personnel, but also it may be inappropriate for some kinds of agencies.

The first two selections in this part deal with the difficulties of coordination and the conditions under which organizations should or should not attempt to coordinate. The first article, "Interagency Coordination in Delinquency Prevention and Control," by William Reid, uses an "exchange theory" of coordination to distinguish three levels of coordination: (1) *ad-hoc case coordination* costs the least, and does not require great organizational commitment or exchange; (2) *service integration* occurs when agencies have a general policy of working together for certain types of cases, and have established rules for handling these cases; and (3) *program integration* occurs when two or more agencies set up special programs, jointly coordinated and jointly managed, to accomplish goals that both agencies have in common. Reid finds that organizations with similar goals have little desire to coordinate at the program-integration level. He is essentially pessimistic about the chances of highly developed coordination in cases where organizations are given a constant supply of money and personnel.

In "Goals, Structures, and Strategies for Community Change," by Martin Rein and Robert Morris, the authors interpret the efficacy of an organization's coordination attempts as being a function of the essential goals of the organization. In broad terms, agencies that try to change the society have less to gain from strategies of coordination than agencies that have "integrative goals"—that is, goals of gaining conformity to accepted values. For instance, a community welfare council is less concerned with changing the society than with making sure that all of the welfare agencies implement previously agreed-upon values. On the other hand, the NAACP is more interested in attempting to change the value consensus. The very success of the Welfare Council is dependent on "getting along" with the various organizations in the community, but the NAACP must pursue change, no matter what course the other organizations take (this does not rule out the fact that there are some kinds of coordinating strategies for organizations such as the NAACP). Rein and Morris relate the strategies of achieving goals to the structure of organizations. Both the Rein and Morris article and the one by Reid represent areas of sociological analysis that have become prominent only in the last few years.

The selection by J. H. Robb, "Family Structure and Agency Coordination: Decentralisation and the Citizen," examines the problem of coordination from a somewhat different perspective. Robb raises the question of how the many branches of the New Zealand Public Service impinge on the loosely knit family. He argues that because, so often, the different branches have narrow definitions of their tasks, and because the family in modern society is loosely knit, there is a tremendous wasted effort involved in the relationships between families and agencies. Often there may even be contradictory efforts by the different branch representatives. Robb concludes with suggestions for alternative modes of organizing the Public Service.

Interagency Coordination

in Delinquency Prevention and Control

William Reid

The low level of coordination among social welfare agencies has long been considered a major problem for community organization. The terms "duplicating," "overlapping," and "fragmentary" have become, in fact, pejorative cliches to describe the state of the social services. Despite efforts by community organizers and others, the "coordination gap" has persisted and, in the eyes of some, has worsened. Kahn, for example, states that "coordination of services and programs [in child welfare] is urgent because the United States is experiencing an urban child care crisis of very considerable size." [1] In a report to Congress, the Children's Bureau observed: "Existing services which could contribute to treatment control and prevention are poorly coordinated, so that an integrated attack on the problem [juvenile delinquency] is not possible." [2] Such statements exist for most areas of social welfare organization.

This chronic problem raises some acute questions. What is really involved in coordination? What accounts for its relative absence? Why does it occur under some circumstances but not under others? Answers to these and other questions are necessary if there is to be a knowledge base for effective action. Ideally, such knowledge should be organized

[1] Alfred Kahn, " 'A Coordinated Pattern of Service'—Shibboleth or Feasible Goal?" in *Basic Issues in Coordinating Family and Child Welfare Programs*, eds. Charles P. Cella, Jr., and Rodney P. Lane (Philadelphia: University of Pennsylvania Press, 1964), p. 7.
[2] National Institute for Mental Health, *Report to the Congress on Juvenile Delinquency* (Washington, D.C.: Government Printing Office, 1957), p. 9.

William Reid, "Interagency Coordination in Delinquency Prevention and Control," *Social Service Review*, December 1964. This paper was prepared as a part of the Community Organization Curriculum Development Project of the School of Social Service Administration of the University of Chicago. The project is supported by a grant from the President's Committee on Juvenile Delinquency and Youth Development.

into a systematic body of concepts and hypotheses—that is, into a theory of coordination.

This paper presents a set of formulations that may contribute to theory development. These formulations will be limited to one type of interagency coordination, which may be called "unmediated" coordination, that is, coordination between two or more agencies through their own devices without mediation of another agency, such as a welfare council. Agencies of their own accord can develop referral agreements, sponsor joint programs, and so on. A theory of how and why such interaction occurs is prehaps a preliminary step toward understanding the role of the coordinating agency.

The current analysis will be further restricted to social welfare organizations offering direct services to individuals and families with the goal of juvenile delinquency prevention and control. As this broad field of activity includes most major types of social agencies, whatever theory is developed here may have relevance for the general social agency system. Specifically, however, analysis is focused on the direct-service agencies in corrections, family service, public welfare, child welfare, mental health, and youth services. To these are added the schools and youth divisions of police departments. As both the police and schools may assume "service" roles in relation to delinquency control, for purposes of this paper they will be considered as social agencies. The terms "agency" and "organization," as used generically in the paper, refer for the most part to the foregoing group of community agencies.

COORDINATION AS A SYSTEM
OF INTERAGENCY EXCHANGE

The first task in developing a theory of interagency coordination is to specify the essential dimensions of this type of agency interaction. How can coordination be most fruitfully defined and described? What are its key components?

A particularly useful framework for viewing coordination has been developed by Levine and White.[3] These writers suggest that co-operative arrangements among agencies can be viewed as a system of exchanges. In order to achieve their objectives organizations must possess or control certain resources—personnel, services, funds, etc. Since most agencies do not possess all the resources needed to achieve their goals, they frequently turn to one another to obtain them. In more general terms Levine and White define organizational exchange as "any voluntary activity

[3] Sol Levine and Paul E. White, "Exchange as a Conceptual Framework for the Study of Interorganizational Relationships," *Administrative Science Quarterly*, V (March, 1961), 583–601.

between two organizations which has consequences, actual or anticipated, for the realization of their respective goals or objectives." [4]

It is legitimate to ask in relation to any new concept: How is it useful?
What does it contribute? Any new addition to already overcrowded conceptual highways should facilitate the flow of traffic and not jam it
further.

First, the exchange formulation draws attention to the importance of
agency goals. Organizational activity, including coordination, can be
seen as directed toward achieving goals of concern to the organization,
however the organization defines them. Viewing coordination as an exchange through which agencies attempt to achieve their goals forces
consideration of what these goals actually are. In this type of analysis
one need not assume that the most important agency goals lie in furthering the welfare of the community or that agencies in a community are
bound together in a closely knit system in which each seeks similar goals
through different means. Much of the prescriptive writing on coordination assumes that agencies have or should have common goals. It is
another matter, however, to examine agency goals for what they are,
without prior assumptions or illusions. Only in this way can the subject
of interagency coordination be dealt with analytically.

Second, the concept of exchange calls attention to the fact that any
coordinating activity involves agency resources—defined here as any
elements the agency needs to achieve its goals. It then becomes possible
to describe any coordinating activity in terms of the kinds of resources
included in the transaction. Funds, facilities, personnel, services, information, and clients (or other recipients of service) comprise the major
resources most agencies need to achieve their goals. Lacking such needed
resources, agencies may seek exchanges. Thus, agencies earlier in our
history found themselves in need of information about clients' contacts
with other agencies. Their solution was to develop a system of exchang-
ing one resource—information about clients—through an organization appropriately called the Social Service Exchange. Other types of coordinating activities can be specified in similar terms. Contracted service
arrangements are exchanges of funds for personnel and services. Referrals involve exchanges of clients. Joint programs may involve exchanges of facilities. Agencies may also exchange services. For example,
a family service agency provides counseling services to clients referred
by a welfare department. In exchange, the welfare department adjusts
its concrete services to these clients in line with recommendations of the
family agency. An exchange need not involve a transfer of resources from
one agency to another. As in the above example, it may be carried out by
using resources in special ways for the benefit of one another. In effect,

[4] Ibid., p. 588.

however, agencies still derive from each other resources needed to further their own objectives.

By considering the extensiveness of the exchange in terms of the quantity and value of resources one can distinguish various types and levels of coordination.

The first or lowest level may be called "*ad hoc* case coordination." At this level, coordinated activity is generated by individual practitioners to meet the needs of particular clients. Decisions about what and when to coordinate are left to the practitioner. Formal interagency agreements are not usually involved. Specific exchanges include chiefly information, referral and, to a lesser degree, service. Perhaps the bulk of coordination takes place at this level.

A second level is "systematic case coordination" or, to use Kahn's terminology, "service integration." [5] Here, coordinated activity is still on the case level, with the goal of meshing services from different agencies in relation to the particular case. This level of coordination, however, is carried on in accordance with specific rules and procedures developed by the agencies. Interagency agreements may cover referrals or allocations of responsibility relating to types of cases. Special interagency coordinating devices, such as case-conference committees, may be set up. At this level interagency exchanges are systematic and extensive. Exchanges of information and referrals are routine. There is emphasis on planned exchanges of services. For example, agencies may be accorded major service and coordinating responsibility for all cases in which they have made first contact, or agencies may be given responsibility for providing specific types of service.

A third level may be described as "program coordination." [6] Here, coordination is centered not on individual cases but on agency programs. This level of coordination includes development of joint agency programs, mutual assistance in development or extension of programs, or mutual modification of programs to bring about more rational alignment of agency functions. Two agencies may develop a joint street-club program; an agency may send detached personnel to another to perform specialized counseling services; two child-care agencies with duplicating functions may decide to divide responsibilities, with one concentrating on homemaker service and the other on foster placement. Interagency exchanges at this level may be extensive and complex.

Within these three types and levels of coordination there is then a rough progression in terms of the extent and value of agency resources exchanged. *Ad hoc* case coordination draws minimally upon these resources, whereas program coordination may encompass a much larger

[5] Alfred J. Kahn, *Planning Community Services for Children in Trouble* (New York: Columbia University Press, 1963), p. 110.
[6] Ibid., p. 112.

portion of the agency's resources. With increasingly greater agency investment there may be progressive increase in agency caution about engaging in coordinating ventures. This may account particularly for the relative scarcity of coordination at the second and third levels.

DETERMINANTS OF COORDINATION

A second major task in creating a theory of coordination involves specification of the conditions that determine whether coordination will take place. It may be generally hypothesized that at least three conditions must be present before coordination can occur in any substance. Agencies must have (1) shared goals, (2) complementary resources, and (3) efficient mechanisms for controlling whatever exchanges are involved. These three conditions will be discussed in some detail.

Shared Goals

When agencies are seeking similar or identical goals, a major force for coordination is brought into play. Each agency has a stake in the goal attainment of the other, and both therefore may become willing to enter into exchanges to further mutual objectives. Moreover, sharing of goals leads to logical divisions of responsibility and labor which can reduce the burdens of each. The importance of this condition has been stressed by at least two studies of interagency relationships.[7]

Agencies, of course, have multiple goals that vary in degrees of explicitness, breadth, and vitality. General goals stated in official declarations of purpose often bear little relation to the operational goals that guide agency activities.

The operational goals of the agency determine decisions and actions. Though often difficult to locate and define, these goals are crucial in coordination. Two organizations may nominally share a broad, formal goal of "reducing juvenile delinquency." One organization—a police department—may view this goal primarily in terms of vigorous law enforcement. The other organization—a family agency—may interpret it as alleviating psychological problems of disturbed youngsters. The operational goals of the organizations may then be quite divergent and may offer little basis for coordination.

Most of the agencies of concern here acknowledge and, in a sense, share broad, formal goals relating to delinquency control and prevention. At the level of operational goals, much of this apparent consensus seems to dissolve. If not working at cross purposes, agencies seem often to be

[7] M. M. Ahla Annikki, *Referred by Visiting Nurse* (Cleveland: The Press of Western Reserve University, 1950); Sol Levine, Paul E. White, and Benjamin D. Paul, "Community Interorganizational Problems in Providing Medical Care and Social Services," *American Journal of Public Health*, LIII (August, 1963), 1183–1195.

working at different purposes. Somehow the objectives shared on paper become reduced in practice to goals that are limited and discrepant. An examination of how this process of goal reduction operates will add to our understanding of why operational goals so often are not shared and why coordination so often fails to occur.

First, the operational goals of an agency may be determined by the resources at its disposal. Etzioni has remarked that ". . . one of the most important observations of students of organizations is that the 'tools' in part determine the goals to which they are applied."[8] For example, an agency may select from a range of permissible goals those goals that can be most effectively achieved through the services it has to offer. Family agencies and mental health clinics, for example, have such general objectives as promoting family welfare or mental health. Such objectives would nominally cover the population and problems of interest in delinquency control. These agencies are free, however, to define within this goal framework the specific clientele and problems to be treated.

It is notoriously difficult to treat delinquent adolescents through the conventional casework and psychotherapeutic methods these agencies regard as their prime resources. Such treatment normally requires considerable professional time, not only with the youngster, but with family members and community agencies. The success rate is low. These agencies may therefore decide to expend their limited resources on clients who will yield maximal goal achievement with minimum strain. The goals of such agencies then become concentrated upon a selected clientele— individuals or families with problems, capacity, and motivation that fit the agency's definition of service. Delinquent youth may be regarded by these agencies as a marginal, second-best clientele. To a considerable extent they may be "defined out" of the agency's actual goals relating to kind of clients served or kind of problems treated.

In other cases, a scarcity of resources may force agencies to cut back goals to their essentials, as the agencies define them. An understaffed youth center in a congested urban area, seeing its actual goals in terms of "keeping the kids off the streets," may forego any serious aspirations to a program of delinquency prevention. An underbudgeted and overcrowded school may give up its concerns for the "whole" child and settle for imparting whatever classroom learning it can. In a social welfare system in which demands for service far exceed resources, agencies may be forced to settle for minimum objectives.

Organizational goals may also be tied to various procedural and administrative concerns—the well-known bureaucratic dysfunction of "goal displacement": meeting deadlines, getting reports out, processing cases may assume the status of major agency goals. In emphasizing administra-

[8] Amitai Etzioni, *Complex Organizations* (New York: Holt, Rinehart & Winston, 1961), p. 143.

tive routines the agency often loses sight of its larger objectives. One observer, for example, remarked that a certain parole department was "procedure-bound." Though charged with the objective of rehabilitating youthful offenders, its energies actually were directed at completion of social studies. Rather than serving as a tool in the rehabilitation process, studies became ends in themselves. It was difficult for staff members to raise their sights above the immediate task and to see how their own organization related to others.

Limited agency goals must finally be seen in the context of the historical development of the social service system. Social agencies were created to meet specific social needs as they become manifest in the community. Limited goals relating to these original conceptions of function have usually continued. In some cases broader goals have been added as a way of rationalizing the agency's existence in relation to prevailing social welfare values rather than as serious aims. Thus, public welfare departments in many cases operate in terms of such hoary and circumscribed objectives as maintaining the sanctity of the means test, despite official goals of rehabilitation and the like. As Mencher writes:

> The organization of social services frequently suggests that of an automobile plant in which a number of specialized centers manufacture parts according to their own unique specifications; then, after the processing of the parts has been completed, a group of experts are called in to see whether or not the parts can be assembled into a car.[9]

The more limited agency goals become, the less chance there is for sharing of goals to occur. Areas of common purpose are reduced as each agency seeks to discharge highly specific and narrowly defined functions. Often agencies formally concerned with delinquency control operate in terms of very limited objectives. The police department seeks to investigate criminal activities and arrest offenders; the probation department endeavors to gather information to enable the court to make a disposition; the parole department attempts to keep youngsters from being reinstitutionalized; individual treatment agencies see their function with delinquent youngsters as one of diagnosis and referral; youth-serving agencies have limited recreational goals; schools define their functions in terms of achieving specific learning objectives. These organizations may have "on their books" or acknowledge in one way or another common goals relating to a community-wide program of delinquency prevention or total rehabilitation of disturbed adolescents. Such goals may not be translated, however, into operational goals that guide day-to-day activities. If they are not, a base for exchange is lacking.

[9] Samuel Mencher, "Principles of Social Work Organization," *Social Casework*, XLIV (May, 1963), 265.

The "shared-goal" formulation can be used to examine a well-known precipitant of coordinated activity—the community crisis. It is fairly well established that community crises may promote solidarity, cohesion, and coordinated effort.[10] Groups within the community react by pulling together and taking joint action to ward off the common threat. Most large communities have experienced juvenile delinquency crises of one sort or another. These usually consist of a widely publicized wave of youthful violence or criminal activity—gang fights, stabbings, murders. Important citizens, community groups, and social agencies become alarmed. Pressure for remedial action mounts. Meetings of agency representatives are held. Decisions are made about who can do what. Joint programs of action are developed. Many, if not most, demonstration projects involving coordinated agency efforts in this field have their origins in this kind of community crisis.

In terms of the current formulation the crisis can be seen as first expanding and activating individual agency goals relating to reduction of delinquency. Temporarily, at least, serving the delinquent population is accorded high priority in the agency's array of goals. Since the same phenomenon is occurring simultaneously in a number of agencies, shared goals emerge. Agencies then become willing to exchange resources as a means of achieving these superordinate goals.

This crisis-provoked coordination, as we know, may prove quite evanescent. When the crisis dies down, so does the coordinated activity. In some instances patterns of coordination built up in crisis situations are preserved through specific structures and programs. Without such developments, however, coordinative arrangements tend to dissipate as agencies return to their precrisis modes of operation. Many crisis-based demonstration projects have met this fate. One carefully planned and well-executed project, for example, succeeded in developing an unusual degree of coordination among previously unrelated neighborhood agencies. With the project and crisis over, coordination quickly receded to its previous levels.

When the crisis serves to expand and activate goals relating to delinquency reduction, diminution of the crisis produces the opposite effect. As delinquency problems become of less concern, or at least less visible, agencies withdraw priorities attached to antidelinquency goals and return them to other objectives. The shared goal of delinquency prevention and control becomes dissolved in the process, or at least loses force.

Complementary Resources

A sharing of goals may be a necessary condition for interagency exchange. It is not, however, a sufficient condition. For exchange to occur,

10 William H. Form and Sigmund Nosow, *Community in Disaster* (New York: Harper & Bros., 1958), p. 236.

each agency must be able to provide the other with resources it needs to achieve its goals. In other words, there must be complementary resources. For example, a police department and a youth-serving agency share the common goal of prevention of gang fighting. Neither organization is able to achieve its goals without assistance from the other. The police need the on-the-spot intervention that skilled gang workers from the youth-serving agency are able to provide. That agency in turn needs help from police in spotting incipient flare-ups or in applying legal sanctions. Exchanges of information, clients, personnel, and services logically take place.

Complementary resources may be lacking for various reasons. The fact that agencies may have goals uniquely shaped to their resources, as noted above, may lead to insular self-sufficiency. To some extent this state of affairs characterizes many agencies specializing in psychological treatment. The goals of two agencies may be to provide the particular kind of casework that the agencies are in fact able to provide. Though goals may be similar, each agency has the resources to achieve these goals as they define them, and significant exchanges are not likely to occur. An agency ready to coordinate is perhaps one whose goals exceed its resources.

Another form of agency self-sufficiency merits examination. This may occur in large organizations in which specialized personnel or departments provide the needed spectrum of resources. A school system in a large city is a common example. The school system may share with various agencies the goal of better adjustment of children. Because of its size, the school system may find it more efficient to develop its own resources to cope with the adjustment problems of its children. Adjustment teachers, counselors, school psychologists, social workers, guidance departments, or special schools may be brought into the system for this purpose. Referrals within the system may reduce exchanges with outside organizations that may also be able to supply similar resources. In a study of voluntary health organizations Levine and White found large corporate agencies engaging in fewer exchanges than small agencies organized in a federated structure.[11]

Such developments often lead to duplication of services within the community. The school system may develop its own child guidance facilities despite the existence of community child guidance agencies serving the school population. Nevertheless, the school may decide that it would be more efficient to have its own child guidance resources, and may not necessarily be concerned with problems of duplication.

Agencies may share goals, but may have insufficient resources to achieve them. Attempts at exchange may prove futile as agencies become disillusioned with one another's ineffectiveness. Thus, a public employment service and a parole department share the objective of developing

[11] Levine and White, *op. cit.*, 592.

an effective job location program for delinquent youth. An exchange involving personnel for facilities is worked out. An employment counselor is attached to the parole department. His mission is to work closely with parole officers toward setting up such a program. The obstacles, however —such as finding employers who will hire referred parolees—prove too great and the program fails to develop.

Such instances of resource inadequacy are often used to support the thesis that agencies need more resources and not more coordination. It is certainly true that coordination cannot take place in a resource vacuum; on the other hand, an increase in agency resources may stimulate coordination—as the agency then has more of value to exchange.

Coordination Control and Costs

It has been suggested that shared goals and complementary resources are essential prerequisites for interagency coordination. These in fact are often sufficient conditions for simple types of coordination—such as the *ad hoc* case variety. For more elaborate forms, however, some means of control must be established. For systematic case coordination such control mechanisms may take the form of interagency agreements, of regularly scheduled case conferences between staff members of different agencies, or interagency committees. Program coordination may require such mechanisms as formal agreements, accountability procedures, interagency conferences, and allocations of coordinating responsibilities to specific staff members.

These control devices require an investment of agency resources apart from resources involved in the actual exchange. Staff time is the resource most heavily drawn upon to insure adequate regulation. This resource, however, is perhaps the most precious and costly for most agencies.

In a study of interagency relationships, Johns and Demarche found that agency staff members ranked "lack of time" first in a series of possible obstacles to coordination.[12] Time is often dismissed as a trivial factor in such considerations, particularly by those who do not have to expend it. Community organizers in the above study rated "lack of time" extremely low as a reason for lack of coordination. Time, however, becomes important when it is seen as an expenditure of resources—a cost. "Lack of time" may then be a way of saying that the values received from coordinating activities do not merit the costs of maintaining them.

These costs tend to increase as exchanges become more complex. Litwak and Hylton have made the point that activities that can be standardized can be coordinated the most easily.[13] Interagency exchanges of

[12] Ray Johns and David F. Demarche, *Community Organization and Agency Responsibility* (New York: Association Press, 1951).
[13] Eugene Litwak and Lydia Hylton, "Interorganizational Analysis: A Hypothesis on Coordinating Agencies," *Administrative Science Quarterly*, VI (March, 1962), 412.

information about cases can often be standardized on forms and handled by clerical personnel. Systematic coordination of the efforts of a number of practitioners in relation to a particular case, however, involves activities that are diffuse, complicated, and impossible to standardize. Consequently, the costs in staff time to engineer such coordinated efforts may be large.

Regulation of practitioner activities is difficult, not only because of their inherently diffuse nature, but also because they may reflect basic policies of the participating agencies. Often policies run counter to the goals of whatever coordinated efforts are being attempted. If coordination control is at the practitioner or even supervisory level, policy issues cannot be resolved. The control operation must then be expanded to include agency administrators at various levels. Much the same may be said about program coordination. Not only are the activities likely to be highly complex and difficult to routinize, but control devices must often be expanded to involve total staff. Executives, for example, may make certain agreements about a coordinated program, but these may remain only on paper unless there is careful regulation of activities at the practitioner level—a time-consuming and costly business.

Such problems may be compounded when the agencies are large and heavily bureaucratic. Here coordination control must deal not only with an imposing agency array of department heads and specialists but also with the agency's own internal organizational problems.

Difficulties in coordination between a family service agency and a large school system offer a case in point. The family agency and the school system had worked out a number of apparently simple arrangements for referrals of children and families and case conferences after referrals had been completed. Agency contacts with the school were complicated, however, in each case, because it was necessary to deal with so many of the school personnel—teachers, assistant principals, guidance counselors, psychologists, nurses, and so on. Usually no one of these school personnel possessed either sufficient information about the child or sufficient responsibility for him to serve as the sole contact point with the family agency. Moreover, the school specialists often did not act in concert. A referral might be made to the family agency by the assistant principal before receipt of psychological test results necessary for the agency to make a case decision. To obtain case data or to engage in case planning, family agency staff often found themselves in the position of coordinating activities of the school staff. Under the weight of these bureaucratic complexities, the arrangements frequently broke down. Repair and maintenance needless to say, proved costly for both school and agency.

In sum, control of complex interagency coordination is both costly and difficult to achieve. The difficulty and the cost are directly related. Agencies may be unwilling to pay dearly for a questionable product. Thus they are often reluctant to devote expensive staff time and other resources to less than adequate regulation of complex exchanges. Unless commitment to shared goals and need of complementary resources provide sufficient force, agencies may decide that coordination is not worth the price.

SUMMARY AND IMPLICATIONS

Coordination in the field of delinquency prevention and control has been viewed as an exchange of resources among organizations. Different types of coordination have been distinguished and related to different levels of exchange. Three conditions for coordination have been set forth. For substantial interagency coordination to occur there must at least be sharing of goals, a complementarity of resources, and an efficient system of control whose cost is commensurate with values received. Various reasons for the scarcity of coordination have been examined in the light of these conditions.

The emphasis placed upon obstacles may leave the reader with the impression that unmediated coordination is very difficult to achieve and may even be an enterprise of dubious value. That is quite the impression we wished to convey.

The idea that coordination is difficult to achieve is, of course, not new. It has been repeated in endless ways throughout fifty years of community organization literature. What may be new—at least to some—is the notion that coordination may not necessarily be advantageous to the agencies involved, as they define their goals and functions. We have often tended to view coordination in terms of what is desirable or functional for the community. From the community's point of view, coordination of services is a cherished objective. Agencies may also desire this objective in the abstract, or for other agencies, but may not be committed to improving their own levels of coordination. What may be functional for the community may not be functional for the agency.

The view of the welfare community as a tight system of interdependent agencies may confuse wish with reality. In the ecology of the community, agencies perhaps may be viewed more realistically as relatively autonomous units, each seeking to achieve its own rather than common goals through use of resources that are difficult and costly to coordinate. In such an ecology, unmediated coordination of any substance and duration may be a relatively rare event. This at least seems to be the fact.

The view that coordination may be disadvantageous to individual agencies does not necessarily mean that it is undesirable from the community's point of view. This could mean, however, that means of achieving desired coordination may have to be altered. To accomplish coordination much more may be needed than bringing agencies together, developing channels of communication between them, or providing mediation.

These faciliative approaches are always useful but are sufficient only when agencies really want to cooperate and are waiting for the community organizer to help them to do this. If we do not make this assumption, then we may need stronger medicine—for example, the deployment of economic and political resources as a means of bringing about fundamental changes in agency goals. This view also means that greater coordination of services may not in many instances be worth the efforts to achieve it, and that community organization resources may often be better allocated to other objectives.

Goals, Structures, and Strategies
for Community Change

Martin Rein and Robert Morris

The attempt to develop a systematic theory which describes and analyzes social work practice is gathering momentum. The effort in community organization is no exception. Valuable insights have been contributed by a score of writers, drawing upon their unique experiences.[1] The National Association of Social Workers and the Council of Social Work Education are endeavoring to define the foundations or boundaries of practice.[2] However, efforts to date have not yet reconciled in one scheme the variety of practices encompassed by the term "community organization." Concepts drawn solely from practice descriptions must deal with welfare planning councils, governmental commissions and interdepartmental committees, united funds, neighborhood councils, specialized planning bodies such as mental health associations or health councils, and the organizing

---

[1] Carter, Kahn, Hunter, Wilensky and Lebeaux, Schwartz, Gurin, Seeley, *et al.*
[2] See, for example, "Identifying Fields of Practice in Social Work," by the Subcommittee on Fields of Practice, National Association of Social Workers Commission on Social Work Practice, *Social Work*, VII, No. 2 (1962), 7–14.

Martin Rein and Robert Morris, "Goals, Structures, and Strategies for Community Change," *Social Work Practice 1962*, National Conference on Social Welfare, Columbia University Press, New York, pp. 127–145. The authors wish to express their grateful appreciation to Robert S. Weiss for his many helpful suggestions.

activities of national agencies as diverse as the Family Service Association of America (FSAA) and the National Foundation, to say nothing of community development.

This diversity in practice does not easily submit to an encompassing theoretical framework, except at the most general level. This paper seeks to avoid global theories, and to understand the diversity by asking: "How do the goals, structures, and strategies (in behavior) of organizations affect each other? It is our initial thesis that success in achieving a goal in community organization depends upon the use of a structure and a strategy appropriate to that goal; conversely, no method, however well implemented is effective in all circumstances. Use of this simple guide depends upon a more penetrating analysis of each term: What goals do we mean? What alternative structures are available? What strategies can be drawn upon?

We do not lack broad goals for our social work efforts, but a great gap exists between the aim of all welfare, let us say, "a healthy society," and the more limited aims of a single voluntary family service or child-serving agency or department of public welfare. True, each of these agencies favors a good life for all, strong family and interpersonal relations, and a community with adequate resources to meet individual and group needs; but closer to everyday practice the goals of each are quite different in their operational aims, the types of problems the community calls upon them to handle, and the methods they use to achieve these aims.

Attempts to classify agencies in regard to either aims, functions, or methods may be found in the growing social work literature which is concerned with social problems and planned change. We shall consider the problem of organizational goals from still another perspective—the extent to which goals may be described as primarily committed to change in the sense of achieving predetermined objectives or integration in the sense of conforming to common values.

This polarization has utility for describing the direct-service agency and its individual clients as well as those agencies engaged in community activities. To illustrate, goals of change have been equated with a belief that many acceptable solutions to perceived problems are possible for the individual; and integration has been equated with conformance to accepted solutions by the individual. An agency or society committed to change must necessarily hold as its norm the pluralism of many solutions in the sense that an open arena exists where many agencies pursue their independent aims; one committed to integration necessarily singles out a narrow band of homogeneous standards which it urges its members to conform to and which are considered socially desirable goals.

Social work in the large is committed both to pluralistic norms, captured in such concepts as self-determination, and to promotion of the acceptance of certain widely held social goals. Individual agencies, however, are more concerned with one or the other. Their methods and strategies are determined in part by such differences. Perhaps this explains the persistent differences in method and program between, let us say, a child-protective agency which encourages its clients to conform to child-rearing patterns which they do not accept and a family agency which attempts to help its clients realize the goals they do believe in; similar differences can be seen between a settlement house and the YMCA or Boy Scouts.

One type of agency, for example, encourages immigrants to adapt their cultures to the American way of life while retaining their cultural diversity or pluralism; another type stresses the melting pot and the integration of previous cultures into a single homogeneous culture.

Can the same concepts be fruitfully used to describe the field of community organization or community planning? Think of a variety of community organization agencies: welfare councils, mental health associations, a state interdepartmental planning committee in aging, the American National Red Cross, or the FSAA. Each one of these is a miniature welfare system, made up of many subunits called agencies, or chapters, or departments. Among such organizations it is possible to distinguish at least two basic aims, one dealing with pluralism or change and the other with integration or homogeneity. These goals are, in turn, associated with different organizational arrangements and require the use of sharply different strategies or means. The simultaneous pursuit of both integration and change leads to conflict. Decision as to which aim is primary is required or we run the risk of forsaking both.

In community organization, we deal with the relationship of relatively autonomous agencies (or subunits) to each other and to a larger welfare system. Community organization has been concerned chiefly with the evolution of acceptable common standards to which these agencies can conform—the general community need or interest, good practice, and so forth. For some agencies, adherence to these norms is primary. However, other agencies have only a secondary interest in such conformity; they are mainly interested in achieving their own self-established ends. The former are committed to homogeneous goals and integration; the latter, to heterogeneity and pluralism.

A welfare council must start with the relation of service agencies to each other and assume that there is an overriding community interest to which individual agency acts must or should conform. The FSAA depends on the local family agencies' acceptance of certain standards. The Department of Health, Education, and Welfare's interdepartmental committee on aging operates on the premise that the Department's aims can be stated and that bureaus and agencies should subordinate their acts to these more general ends. In each case, the organization seeks integration between its general, homogeneous, conforming ends and the acts of its subunits. Promoting cooperation and coordination between these frequently diverse units is the measure of the achievement of integration. The encouragement of better working relationships between these subunits within the sponsoring organization is taken as prima-facie evidence that a greater welfare integration has been achieved and social goals reinforced. This agency integration, in fact, is seen as symbolic of community integration.

For this class of organization (or system of agencies), achievement of specific goals is, of course, desired (such as less juvenile delinquency, more casework, and so on); but this is secondary to, and dependent upon, the integration within. Such agencies usually express their goals in broad and diffuse terms. Such statements seem best to serve their integration aims, since they avoid the specificity which may breed conflict.

By contrast, the goals of other types of agencies are concerned with change and not integration; they emphasize their own specialized predetermined interest. They are committed to specific, limited, and concrete goals. They are less concerned with the impact of the achievement of their goals on other organizations. They are convinced of the singular importance of their selected goals, and the action they take to achieve them accounts for the greater expenditure of the organizations' resources.

Change-oriented organizations have the quality of a social cause. Within the health and welfare context we find such organizations as the Planned Parenthood Federation of America, Inc., committed to birth control, the National Association for Advancement of Colored People (NAACP) to racial integration, the Children's Bureau to the rights of children.

The specialized health drives found in any local community offer perhaps the most dramatic example of action taken by cause-oriented organizations, the validity of whose aims is considered self-evident and the vigorous pursuit of activities that will contribute to their achievement as natural and desirable.

Such agencies attempt to use their structure and personnel to reach these goals. In contrast, organizations concerned with integrative goals use their structure and personnel first to resolve differences or to coordinate various efforts.

To maximize the accomplishment of either of these goals appropriate organizational structure and strategy are required. Our major premise is that certain strategies and structures are more appropriate for goals of change and other structures and strategies are more consistent with goals of integration.

We need next to identify what we mean by "strategy," which is defined here as a settled course of action. The pattern which it selects from among a field of alternatives is employed by an organization in the belief that the chosen action will contribute most to achieve its ends. A strategy involves a set of basic assumptions about a style of action judged most appropriate to accomplish specific aims. It involves the broad directives, not the specifics nor the details which may better be described as "tactics." Strategy and tactics are instrumental, means-oriented approaches to achieve specified organizational goals.

In the relationship among various welfare organizations, it is possible to specify two different strategies which we term "cooperative rationality" and "individual rationality."

COOPERATIVE RATIONALITY

This strategy comprises the following characteristics: consensus; legitimacy; rationalism; avoidance of controversy; and a fusion of ends and means. Each facet is interrelated; ideally, all the essentials of the strategy are present.

In the cooperative rationality strategy there is a search for unity in the interests of diverse groups; a search for common values with a tacit understanding based on implicit rules that nonshared ends, which can embarrass the participants or cause conflict, are assiduously avoided. One point upon which all groups of social welfare organizations can agree is the need to expand all welfare service, but they are in disagreement as to which services are more vital than others. They prefer not to set goals which commit them to the expansion of one program while others are sacrificed. Setting a common goal of providing more resources for everyone avoids the necessity of making specific choices. When choice is required, as unhappily it must be, then other strategies, such as compromise, competition, and bargaining, must be pursued. Cooperative rationality seeks to set goals about which all, or nearly all, participants are in agreement.

An essential component of the strategy is the art of arriving at interorganizational consensus. The health and welfare community, as we have said, is characterized by differences in goals and norms. This segmented character of social welfare organizations makes the search for consensus most difficult. Genevieve Carter, a close observer of social welfare planning, notes these diverse and partially conflicting values and comments on the problems they pose:

> This complexity, inherent in the planning council organization, becomes most apparent when you attempt to specify sub-objectives or goals of a planning council. We must keep these goals highly generalized, at least for interpretation purposes, because the more we specify the more we

must reconcile the conflict of values within the organization. . . . searching analysis is likely to upset our ideals which we need to keep intact in order to carry on with today's operations.[3]

Thus, an endemic problem limiting the effective use of this strategy is how to arrive at group decisions without becoming enmeshed in conflicts that will destroy the organization. A major task of this strategy becomes the achievement of internal integration. The completion of this task and the survival of the organization are, at least in part, testaments to the achievement of integration aims; failure to survive is evidence of non-integration, rupture, and schism.

To facilitate reaching conclusions based on common aims and to avoid failure, a great deal of emphasis is placed on the use of process. This is a procedure for involving, in various ways, persons who have a stake in the decision outcome. Those who follow a cooperative rationality strategy accord the process of involvement a high degree of sacredness. In this view, involvement is equated with democracy; it is the foundation on which the strategy rests. The social work literature which supports this view cites the central role of open communication. The chief mechanism or vehicle to secure involvement, to permit open communication, and to reach agreement is the committee. The professional is seen as the enabler, the catalyst, the facilitator of the involvement process, an expert trained in the art of preserving democracy. Rossi refers to this professional as the engineer of consent.[4]

In practice, however, involvement seldom takes this turn. Agreement is usually reached by the selective and discriminative use of communication. A more realistic description of how consensus is achieved suggests that it is often necessary to make decisions on important issues outside the committee, not in order to undermine the democratic process, but to facilitate the process without destroying the committee through schism. These sessions provide settings for homogeneous subgroups, each of which meets to accommodate to internal differences among its own members. This harmonious climate permits a closing of ranks after alternative positions have been explored. At the committee meeting itself, a unified position is presented on behalf of each subgroup. Often there is an informal exchange among these subgroups prior to the committee meeting. Further, to achieve consensus, a selective agenda is developed to cover matters on which there is known agreement. Also, reports and studies are

[3] Genevieve W. Carter, "The Content of the Community Welfare Council Research Job," in *Issues in Community Welfare Research,* Proceedings of the National Workshop on Community Welfare Research Personnel (Indianapolis: United Community Funds and Councils of America, Inc., 1958), p. 43.

[4] Peter H. Rossi, "What Makes Communities Tick?" *Public Health Reports,* LXXVII (1962), 117–24.

secured which focus on areas of agreement; taking votes is avoided till near unanimity is assured. Thus, in this view, the committee is not seen as a working group but as a platform from which a public reaffirms and thereby legitimizes decisions arrived at in private, and "in this essentially ceremonious and harmony-creating capacity the committee system serves a useful purpose." [5]

An integral part of the search for shared goals and the use of democratic procedures is legitimation by the community. This is achieved in part by the requirement that the set goals must favor no special interest, must be noncontroversial, and must be in the community's best interest; that is, they must contribute to increasing community solidarity and to reducing community conflict and strain. Thus, the goals emanate from a now legitimate source—the community itself, further buttressed by the use of democratic process so important in our culture. Characteristic of this strategy is the indefiniteness with which the term "community" is used. The term is meant to cover all persons and interests, but it is not defined. Nor are mechanisms available which permit us to reach such an ideal community, so that it remains vague and general.

Several related tactics grow out of this key plank in the cooperative rationality strategy, namely, the use of community notables and appeal to grass roots opinion. In fact, the participation of community leaders is essential to legitimating the effort. In addition, citizen participation may also facilitate implementation of decisions. Participation by both segments of the community is considered tangible evidence of support, approval, and legitimation.

Fact-finding, study, and research are other essential dimensions of this strategy, since these scientific procedures are believed to offer objective approaches to identifying means of achieving the goals sought. Since the rightness of the goals is unquestioned, once revealed, the facts are believed to speak for themselves, and once known, will invariably lead to the action that they indicate.

INDIVIDUAL RATIONALITY

Individual rationality, by contrast, starts with predetermined, specialized, vested interests. This strategy is less responsive to the needs and wishes of other local community organizations; instead, its chief commitment is to the pursuit of its own interests. Whereas cooperative rationality appeals to one view of democratic principles, which asserts that legitimate values are those all hold in common, individual rationality places greater stress on pluralistic values and on the inherent legitimacy of each unique and special objective. Proponents of this strategy focus on a

[5] Arthur Vidich, "Government Philanthropy and Private Philanthropy" (mimeographed).

rationality of "realism"; it is rooted in a tough-mindedness which tries
to respond to the world in terms of how it does function rather than how
it *ought* to function. True, the aims are believed to be in the community
interest and the aims are made legitimate by the support of various leaders, but this similarity to a cooperative strategy cannot obscure the fact
that the interests are premised upon a prior belief in the correctness of
each objective.

Starting with firm, specific goals, the sponsors ask, what is the most
rational means of accomplishing their aims? Writers who have tried to
develop decision theory state the problem in terms of the action that
should be taken by an organization in order to maximize its stated value
position, or, more bluntly, its stake.

A first premise in this strategy is that a group knows what it wants,
or favors a particular decision among many possibilities. It selects one
decision because it believes that this would contribute to achievement
of its short- or long-term goals, enhancement or maintenance of the organization's ideology, control of resources, or stability of position. Thus,
the organization may be said to have a stake in that decision. An organization seeks to get a decision implemented in a way that has most "payoff" for this stake. "Payoff" in this sense is the potential reward which
accrues from a favorable decision.

In order to maximize its stake, an organization attempts to influence
those who can control the decisions. This may involve going directly to
the power or center of control, but more frequently health and welfare
organizations employ a circuitous route. Intermediaries (as Banfield calls
them) who are usually civic leaders act as allies or "fronts" for the organization which is anxious that a particular decision be made.[6] The key to
the process is to convince or influence others that it is in their best interest
to favor the decision that the organization supports and to act in concert
with the agency to arrive at a favorable decision. Results are achieved
by persuasion, coercion, or by any suitable means. The method used is,
in part, contingent on available resources and the extent to which sanctions can be imposed (the distribution of rewards or deprivations in
terms of prestige or economic gain). Depending upon what it can offer
in a trade or an alliance, the organization will enter into coalitions.
These coalitions are usually temporary, unstable, means-oriented alliances
among groups with varying goals. There is a limited range of consensus
among them.[7]

---

[6] Edward C. Banfield, *Political Influence* (New York: Free Press of Glencoe, 1961).
[7] A public strategy follows a similar process. This approach is often used when an
agency has limited resources at its disposal and therefore limited capacity to develop
coalitions. In this situation the organization reaches out to the public in the hope of
winning support for its position. The major difference between an individual and a
public strategy is similar to C. P. Snow's distinction between closed- and open-door

Briefly, then, we can relate goals to strategies. A strategy of individual rationality is best suited for goals of change, for new ideas where diversity or pluralism should be encouraged. Cooperative rationality is suited to conformity, when groups are asked to accept common goals and standards.

Action and decisions arrived at through an individual rationality generally are based on "compromises patched up among competing parochial interests."[8] By contrast, action sought by, or in, a cooperative rationality approach attempts to arrive at decisions which are based on common values held by participating groups.

The structure of an organization is another factor in bringing about community change. We have singled out for analysis two types, defined in terms of the degree of homogeneity of their members. Specifically, there is the federated and the simple organization. The federated structure is an association of agencies or autonomous substructures, such as members of a local welfare council or chapters of national organizations. Each of these agencies is a self-directing unit, neither wholly dependent upon, nor responsible to, the federated structure of which it is a part. They participate in the work of the federated body through representatives who link up the autonomous work of their organizations and the federation in which they participate. Subunits belong to the federation on a voluntary basis. They may withdraw at will, particularly if they feel that further participation may hinder rather than help their home agency. These organizations are primarily accountable to themselves and only secondarily to the federation. Participating units view any action taken by the federation in relation to its consequence for themselves.

The second type, the simple structure, is composed of a homogeneous group of like-minded individuals or organizations which share common goals and values. Its members are primarily responsible to themselves. The old Townsend Clubs, an organization of older people run by older people for the benefit of older people, provide an example of the simple structure. The National Foundation, the Association for Mental Retardation, and the NAACP are still other examples of organizations in which sponsor and client are closely interrelated. In this sense, the members are customers of the services they seek to promote. These groups have in common the fact that each one is concerned with furthering a particular program. They are also similar in that they draw their membership from persons who have a primary commitment to that specific aim.

This contrasts with the federated structure whose members try to incorporate loyalty to the federated body while maintaining a primary

---

politics. A public strategy is pursued by weak organizations which try to bring issues into the open because they feel that they can maximize their stake most in an open arena. A full development of this position can be found in Elmer Eric Schattschneider, *The Semisovereign People* (New York: Holt, Rinehart & Winston, Inc., 1960).

[8] Banfield, *op. cit.*, p. 324.

allegiance to their base organization. Frequently, the simple organizations take on the character of their cause. A single relatively homogeneous group of persons is responsible for setting the policy of the organization. They have similar ideological beliefs, a likemindedness of purpose in their commitment to the principles and goals of the interest which they are trying to further.

These two organizational structures, the federated and the simple, are in a sense ideal types and are seldom found in their pure form. In practice, a federated organization may be dominated by a single group which controls its economic resources. For example, business elements control some united funds. The nature of the participation of constituent autonomous groups is largely influenced by the strength of this control. On the other hand, simple organizations frequently make every effort to include representatives of other groups within the community, in order to give the organization community sanction and dull the sharp edge of partisanship. The more such persons are included in the structure of a simple organization, the more it takes on the character of a federated structure; and similarly, the more the federated structure is controlled by a single group, the more it resembles a simple structure. Simple or federated structures form a continuum, and only at the extremes are they most clear-cut.

A useful way of distinguishing one type of organization from another is to recognize their primary goal orientations, of which two fundamental ones are change and integration. The utility of drawing this distinction between basic organizational commitments rests on the assumption that they are not compatible and that of necessity a choice must be made between them. What follows rests upon the validity of this distinction, which has been made in other contexts by other authors.[9]

An organization's structure and the major type of strategy it employs may be seen as critical to the realization of its goals. When structure and strategy are consistent with goals, the organization operates at maximum efficiency and has the greatest opportunity of achieving these goals. Inconsistency between structure, strategy, and goals may lead to ineffectiveness, dilution, and displacement of goals.

[9] Parsons distinguishes between expressive (integrational) and instrumental (change) roles within social systems, while Gordon and Babchuk separate voluntary associations along the same dimension. Warren's classification of horizontal and vertical structures within a community utilizes the differences in these two value positions. Here, we express the primary distinction between integration and change in terms of organizational goals. See Talcott Parsons, *The Social System* (Glencoe, Ill.: Free Press, 1951); C. Wayne Gordon and Nicholas Babchuk, "A Typology of Voluntary Associations," *American Sociological Review*, XXIV (1959), 22–29; Roland L. Warren, "Toward a Reformulation of Community Theory," *Human Organization*, XV, No. 2 (1956), 8–11.

Table 1   *Relationship between Goals, Structures, and Strategies*

	FEDERATED	SIMPLE
	1	2
Cooperative rationality	Integration	Ritualism
Individual rationality	Survival	Change
	3	4

Cells 1 and 4 on the diagonal represent goals, while cells 2 and 3 on the diagonal involve potential goal displacements and will be considered later.

Table 1 illustrates the ways in which structures, strategies, and goals interlock. It shows that a federated structure and a cooperative rationality strategy are most consistent with goals of integration. On the other hand, a simple structure coupled with an individual rationality is most congruent with achievement goals of change. We shall discuss the nature of this congruence, the consequences which follow from a "poor fit" between organizational structures, strategies, and goals, and some of the difficulties that reality imposes upon realizing these ideal types.[10]

CELL 1: THE INTEGRATIVE SYNDROME

In our highly complicated, industrial society, social welfare organizations are fragmented according to the specializations they are best qualified to offer. Along with varying technical competencies, these independent organizations hold different values, some of which are in partial conflict with each other. These organizations compete for scarce community funds or staff. It is difficult yet necessary to integrate these organizations in order to have a rational organized community welfare system. The central task of an integrative organization is to locate homogeneous values which may serve as the basis for united action.

The federated structure, a prototype of which is a community council, is an appropriate structure for goals of integration since it assures representation from all the important segments of the community. However, while it lays the groundwork for integration, it simultaneously carries the seeds of conflict. Each member represents not only a differing value position, but has primary allegiance to his home organization. The degree of accountability to the home agency will affect the representative's ability to function independently of it, and will partly determine his receptiveness to the federated structure's goals. Similarly, his willingness to reach

[10] This analysis is limited to an organization's internal machinery. We recognize, of course, that goal achievement is related to conditions outside the organization as well.

consensus with other representatives will depend upon the extent to which his values (the values of his subgroup) are strengthened by concerted action of the federated organization. As a result, it is rare for a council to press for specific priorities which will reduce support from important members, or to take social action not approved by nearly all of its important agencies.

Given this diversity of interests and allegiances, a cooperative rationality is ideally suited to reducing tension and strain and arriving at agreement. It is able to do this by avoiding predetermined objectives, involving all parties in the decision-making process, and engaging in a search for common values. Ideally, allegiance to member organizations and particularistic values will be minimized in the effort to pull together for the common good. To the extent to which home organizations represent different religious, economic, and political subgroup interests, the ability of the federated body to remain intact and to function harmoniously, at least symbolically, indicates that the corresponding subgroups in the community are also able to work together.

In this situation where the structure of an organization comprises conflicting interests the only action possible is action that derives from common values. Integration is, therefore, not only a necessary precursor of united action, but in itself becomes a goal of the organization. Thus, a federated structure and a cooperative rationality become essential for aims of integration, and structure, strategy, and goals reinforce each other.

To maximize the likelihood that consensus will emerge, integrative organizations limit their membership to agencies which subscribe to values and employ means that will promote harmony rather than discord. Thus integrative organizations shun the Planned Parenthood Federation in some Northeastern communities, or the NAACP in some Southern Communities. Despite their own strong desire to be accepted by the integrating agency, these organizations are excluded because they embody values and aims not easily reconcilable with those of other member organizations. Exclusion of these agencies from the federated structure permits the pursuit of integration, for at least a limited group of agencies.

CELL 2: THE PROBLEM OF RITUALISM

When organizations employ inappropriate structures, or inappropriate strategies, or both, they are in danger of displacing or diluting their goals. Displacement of goals may take the direction of ritualism (going through acceptable motions but with limited or no results) as the table suggests. In the case of achievement-oriented organizations, this occurs in one of two ways. The action agency may develop a cooperative rationality or a federated structure or both. When both are present, the degree of ritualism will be greater.

An organization which is committed to achievement of action goals may become concerned with securing the aid of other community agencies, and in so doing it focuses on winning cooperation rather than accomplishing its aims. An ideology develops which suggests that cooperation has some inherent value. Slowly, goals change to adapt to cooperative means. Cooperation becomes an end in itself, and original aims are displaced or lost sight of.

Some affiliates of the Planned Parenthood Federation are examples of this process. They sometimes become overly concerned with interagency cooperation, a course which affords little instrumental value for this organization. To achieve cooperation, their goals have shifted from birth control to child spacing to premarital counseling. In this process of goal succession, which is more complex than we can describe here, cooperative rationality displaced action ends, and the agency is in danger of going through motions which end in inaction.[11]

On the other hand, ritualism may develop when a change-oriented agency shifts its structure from a simple to a federated type. This happens when its membership is recruited from different community subgroups (often in the name of being democratic) who have only minimal commitment to the objective. While these subgroup representatives may not be held formally accountable by their Community subgroups, their very presence forces the change-oriented organization to consider the implications of action in terms of its effect upon these subgroups. And the potential for action is thereby reduced. If our formulation is valid, we would expect an organization like the Urban League to be most susceptible to the problem of ritual because it is comprised of representatives of both the white and the Negro communities. Fear of offending either subgroup can lead to inaction and avoidance of aggressively pursuing its aims.

An integration-oriented organization may also be prone to ritualism when it abandons its federated structuer for a simple one in order to maintain harmony and to avoid internal conflict. When agencies of this type of organization are too disparate in their views to allow for easy common agreement, those that prevent consensus may not be permitted in in order to facilitate consensus. To illustrate, if a recreation or group work council excludes the Police Athletic League, church recreation centers, public playground agencies, and so on, because they lack professional social work staffs, the very purpose of the council is lost. A few councils are still dominated by a few agencies. When the very groups that must be integrated are excluded in order to reduce conflict, to the point that members are not truly representative of diverse community

---

11 Martin Rein, "An Analysis of a National Agency's Local Affiliation in Their Community Contexts: a Study of the Planned Parenthood Federation" (New York: Planned Parenthood Federation of America, Inc., 1961; mimeographed), p. 117.

factions, and the organization begins to resemble the group of like-minded individuals that comprise the simple structure, the integrative aims are displaced. Litwak notes that "from this point of view the elimination of conflict is a deviant instance and likely to lead to the disruption of inter-organizational relations." [12] We consider this to be ritualism since the organization is unable to fulfill its integrative aims yet cannot act as a change agency due to its overstress on cooperation and the avoidance of conflict.

The minimal role that public welfare agencies play in many community councils is perhaps the most striking example of the exclusion of an appropriate agency. A major organization that provides health and wel-fare services to the bulk of the clients in the community may belong and yet not participate deeply, while a number of minor organizations at-tempt to coordinate each other's work. This should not be taken as a blanket criticism of welfare councils, which are often criticized for the wrong reason—that they are not action-oriented. Integration is important in our society, and becoming more so as we become more specialized. We are suggesting that council actions are ritualistic when they try to avoid integration, which is their task, by excluding groups which must be brought together.

CELL 3: THE PROBLEM OF SURVIVAL

When, at the cost of its constituent agencies, an integrative organiza-tion exerts its primary energies in the direction of maintaining and en-hancing itself we have goal displacement in the direction of survival. While the federated structure is retained, the interests of its affiliated members are overlooked. The integrative organization forsakes its co-operative rationality, at least for the moment, and pursues instead an individual rationality. It coerces, offers preferential treatment, or in other ways tries to induce selected organizations to affiliate with it. For ex-ample, organizations like Catholic Charities and the Salvation Army are permitted to join the United Fund with the unofficial understanding that they will be allowed to continue their independent fund-raising efforts. Or, the Red Cross is admitted and its budget allotment is determined largely by its previous fund-raising efforts. Bargaining power, rather than community need, or consensus, arrived at through interaction with mem-ber agencies, becomes the negotiable currency. The potential contribution of the Red Cross, or other national voluntary health organizations, to strengthening the United Fund is the primary criterion employed in making concessions to these organizations. On the other hand, organi-zations like the Cystic Fibrosis National Research Foundation and the

[12] Eugene Litwak and Lydia F. Hylton, "Interorganizational Analysis," *Administrative Science Quarterly*, VI (1962), 397.

Multiple Sclerosis National Society, which may be sorely in need of integration, are overlooked and disregarded because they have little financial support to contribute, and because they present little threat to the integrative organization. Community need is overlooked or minimized as the search for resources replaces the search for common values.

CELL 4: THE CHANGE SYNDROME

In a changing society, it is often necessary for some organizations to address themselves primarily to innovation. The very nature of innovation or planned change produces resistance in some quarters. To overcome such opposition, organizations must be willing to engage in controversy.

To do this, an organization must accept diverse and pluralistic value schemes as a given in reality. While it is not averse to common values, it starts with predetermined objectives which are believed to have special value. Success is measured by the degree to which these objectives are achieved. Unlike the integration orientation, which is concerned primarily with global values, goals arrived at through consensus and cooperation among members, a focus on achievement imbues an organization with concern for specific, clearly defined, and limited aims. These aims are often infused with a causelike quality, and their accomplishment becomes urgent and worthy of sacrifices.

To further these specific and urgent aims, a simple structure of like-minded individuals is most effective. Ideally, members owe sole or primary allegiance to this organization and are not in conflict with each other over goals, nor do they have divided loyalties to their other commitments.[13] The unity from within is essential to engaging in controversy with forces outside the organization. The aim here is not to represent community subgroups with differing interests, but to push for the agency's objectives in relative disregard for these groupings.

Since the very nature of the organization's goals may lead to controversy, an individual rationality is employed. The strategy of doing away with opposition by a search for a common denominator inherent in a cooperative rationality is replaced by recognition of conflict as inevitable and possibly desirable. Persuasion, use of sanctions, and any means compatible with democratic values are condoned. Both its simple structure, which permits accord on predetermined goals, and its individual rationality allow the organization to pursue its aims aggressively and without fear of internal disharmony. That such action-oriented agencies become embattled in bitter community conflict is well-documented in the *Fortune*

---

[13] Sills's classic study of the volunteers of the former Polio Foundation explores the reasons for the unusual ability of one national voluntary health organization to get individuals to make such commitments. See David L. Sills, The Volunteers (Glencoe, Ill.: Free Press, 1957).

article which describes Pittsburgh's attempt to develop a united fund.[14]

Thus we are able to see the necessity for change goals to be housed in a simple organization composed of like-minded individuals, operating within a framework which permits conflict with other community forces, and able to resist community sanctions and pressures which press the organization to identify with common values.

This has been a limited attempt to piece together a fragment of theory for community organization, drawing upon limited studies, logical analysis, and observation. Its validity and utility need to be tested in many situations. Two can be suggested: the attempt of welfare councils to move from coordination to active planning for urban renewal; and the efforts of the President's Committee on Juvenile Delinquency to extend resources and coordinate service while attempting to promote the "opportunity" theory.[15] As community health and welfare organizations become less concerned with integrative goals and more concerned with community planning, there emerges a growing need to adopt a different organizational structure and different strategy successfully to pursue these new goals. Our efforts are likely to succeed more rapidly if we can evolve practical theories to guide our actions rather than relying upon trial-and-error testing of methods.

[14] Donald S. Connery, "Business and Charity: the Pittsburgh Skirmish," *Fortune,* April, 1957, pp. 144–46, 250–57.

[15] This theory holds that delinquency is engendered because opportunity for conformity to social and economic aspirations is limited. See Richard A. Cloward and Lloyd E. Ohlin, *Delinquency and Opportunity: a Theory of Delinquent Gangs* (Glencoe, Ill.: Free Press, 1960).

Family Structure and Agency Coordination:
Decentralisation and the Citizen

J. H. Robb

INTRODUCTION

As I am not a student or practitioner of public administration, I have not been concerned primarily with public administration as such. My intention has been to offer a sociologist's comments on certain aspects of New Zealand society, most particularly the structural relationships between the Public Service and the community in general.

Naturally enough, administrators tend to study an administrative system from the inside, to be concerned primarily with its internal workings; by contrast, I have taken what Fesler [1] has called "the worm's eye view" of the administrative process, looking at it rather from the position of those who are administered. Though there are many points from which one might begin such a description, one could, in theory, because of the interrelations of all parts of society, pursue the analysis from point to point until all aspects of the society had been brought under review. [2] In the brief compass of this paper I can attempt no such feat, even though many of my statements must necessarily be rather sweeping and lacking in detail. I hope, however, to illustrate this interdependence sufficiently to indicate its relevance to my theme.

In his description of the "worm's eye view" Fesler "starts with the individual citizen as the point from which to gain sound perspective. It is on him that all governmental activities converge. Unless they make sense at the point of convergence, no mechanical harmony at each of

---

[1] J. W. Fesler, *Area and Administration* (University of Alabama Press, 1949), p. 9.
[2] This point is elaborated by M. J. Levy, *The Structure of Society* (Princeton University Press, 1952).

J. H. Robb, "Family Structure and Agency Coordination: Decentralisation and the Citizen" in *Decentralisation in New Zealand Government Administration*, Oxford University Press, New York, 1961, pp. 35–55.

the governmental centres from which these impulses originate can be accepted as an index of sound stagecraft." [3] While I agree with this statement in general, I think we can usefully begin at a slightly different point. The individual citizen is, in important respects, an abstraction, a mythical Robinson Crusoe-like creature. All of us, most of the time, are influenced powerfully in our behaviour and attitudes by those with whom we are closely associated. It therefore makes more sense to consider our citizen not as an individual, but as a member of some group of close associates. Of the various groups which one might choose for this purpose, I have chosen the family. I might equally as well have chosen the work group, or the neighbourhood, or some other unit, and a full analysis which starts with the family would lead on to these, as it would also lead from them back to the family, had I chosen to start from one of these other points.

My intention is first to describe certain significant features of family structure in New Zealand, and to consider the way in which these influence the impact of governmental administrative processes, and modify the responses of citizens. From there I will turn to the Public Service, viewing it not as an administrative process, but as a social system, and I will attempt to describe, first, the relations of this system to the citizen-in-his-family, and, secondly, the way in which certain aspects of the structure of this system affect its operation as perceived by the citizen. Finally, I will outline some changes which seem to be necessary if the system is to be efficient, not only in its internal workings, but also in its relationship to the community.

FAMILY AND COMMUNITY IN NEW ZEALAND

The relationship of families to the rest of the community usually takes the form of a network, that is to say, except in the smallest and simplest of communities, it is unusual to find a situation in which the families in an area form an organised group with social relationships existing between each family and every other family in the group.

> For example, supposing that a family, X, maintains relationships with friends, neighbours, and relatives who may be designated as A, B, C, D, E, F . . . N, one will find that some but not all of these external persons know one another . . . B might know A and C but none of the others; D might know F without knowing A, B or E. Furthermore, all of these persons will have friends, neighbours and relatives of their own not known to family X. In a network the component external units do not make up a larger social whole; they are not surrounded by a common boundary.[4]

[3] *Op. cit.*, p. 10.
[4] Elizabeth Bott, *Family and Social Network* (London: Tavistock Publications, 1957), pp. 58–59.

Although this state of affairs is more or less universal in western societies, there are very wide variations in the degree of connectedness in these networks. In some situations the number of individuals who interact with family, and who also interact with each other, will be quite high. The network is then said to be closely knit. In other situations there will be little or no interaction among the various families and individuals which interact with the family. In this case the network is loosely-knit. Any family network can be placed on a scale running from the extreme of closely knit to the extreme of loosely-knit. Closely-knit networks tend to be found in small, stable communities where most of the adults were born and brought up in the neighbourhood where they have, as adults, established their own families. A changing, mobile society is characterised by loosely-knit networks.

This is not just an exercise in theoretical classification. The type of network which characterises a particular society has extremely important practical implications for the working of that society. For example, it seems that the looser the networks the closer and more important become relationships *within* the family group. If we consider how this situation applies in New Zealand, we find that New Zealanders are a highly mobile people. Only a minority of our adults live in the cities or towns in which they were born; fewer still live in the same neighbourhood. It is possible that a majority of New Zealanders move at least twice during their adult lives.[5] These high rates of mobility are particularly common in the cities and larger towns, where a majority of the population lives. They are one of the influences producing in New Zealand a system of extremely loosely knit networks.[6]

It is characteristic of a community with loosely connected networks that influences from outside the family tend to impinge upon it from different parts of the network and via different members of the family in a somewhat disconnected, unrelated and even contradictory fashion. It then becomes the task of the family to evolve a pattern of living which will permit these varied external influences to be handled in such a way that adequate harmony and consistency is maintained within the family group. This demands a high level of communication and cooperation within the family, particularly between husband and wife. If the task is completed reasonably successfully, as it is in most families, it makes for

[5] For more detailed information on the mobility of New Zealanders, see Athol A. Congalton (ed.), *Hawera—A Social Survey* (Hawera Star Publishing, 1954); J. H. Robb and Anthony Somerset, *Report to Masterton*, Masterton Printing Co., 1957; and mimeographed reports by J. R. McCreary, School of Social Science, Victoria University of Wellington, on social surveys of the older people of New Zealand. Other unpublished data from research carried out at the School of Social Science, Victoria University of Wellington, points in the same direction.
[6] These statements refer to pakeha families only. In Maori communities closely-knit networks are more common.

a very solid and well-integrated family group, but if the marriage is in some ways unsatisfactory it can throw a considerable additional strain upon it. These facts undoubtedly have an association with such phenomena as the rather high rates of marriage breakdown in many Western countries and some of the social problems of new housing areas.

This condition of affairs has some important consequences for the present subject. Many state services, especially welfare services, have as one of their main functions, that of supplying, on a formal basis, supports and services which are informally made available in a closely-knit network. The families which fail to integrate the influences which come to them through the loosely-knit network are those most in need of these services, but if the services are offered in a piece-meal uncoordinated fashion they will also need to be integrated within the family and will, in the very process of bringing help, place an additional strain on the family at the point where it is already weakest.

In the case of the families which have successfully adapted to the loosely knit external network by developing a closely-knit internal structure, the effects are rather different. Officials who administer the services will often appear to be in contact with a single member of the family. This individual's responses may often seem to be unpredictable and illogical, because the official commonly judges them as though they were the responses of a single independent person, and not, as would be proper, as the responses of a whole family group which is subject to many and diverse pressures quite outside the knowledge of the official.

This type of analysis could be pursued further, but I hope I have taken it far enough to indicate that the citizen is not affected by, and does not respond to, the actions of administrators merely as an independent individual. The actual nature of his perception of, and responses to, the administrative process will be considerably affected by the structure of the family group to which he belongs. The family is not, of course, the only group to which he belongs. The family is not, of course, the only group which affects his perception and actions in this way, but usually it is the most important.

Membership of a work-group is usually important also; in some settings more important than the family. Each member of the family will belong to groups which affect his behaviour in various ways, including his responses to the requirements and the services of the State and its officials. It is a characteristic of the loosely-knit network that each member of the family will typically belong to groups to which the other members of the family do not belong.

There is one other feature which is characteristic of our society at the level of the individual and his membership groups. This is an aspect of our culture which is commonly referred to by some such term as "a democratic way of life," but I want to avoid this expression as I am referring to something wider and more pervasive than a particular political ideology, though the practice of democratic political forms considerably accentuates the conditions I am about to describe.

A modern industrial society demands rather high levels of education and technical skill. Many occupations involve frequent actions based on the judgment of the individual worker who must take responsibility for these judgments, and as the proportion of skilled workers rises, this situation becomes more and more usual. All citizens are expected to know, understand and obey a rather elaborate set of laws and regulations. In voting at elections, they are asked to judge between technically complicated courses of action in relation to a wide variety of matters. In the majority of cases the judgments may not be made very competently, but the citizen is assured that he is expected to make them. In a whole variety of ways, through his trade union, in the activities of voluntary associations and through participation in such organisations as Parent-Teacher Associations, he is encouraged to involve himself in discussions relating to specialist and technical matters, and to make his opinions known. Officially sponsored advertisements, broadcast talks by the "Radio Doctor," official and semi-official publications like *Health* and *Family Doctor*, have the effect of assuring him that he can, and should, take an actively intelligent and responsible interest in his own and his family's health. Officially approved educational techniques encourage independent thought, willing expression of opinion and active participation in the life of the community.

However imperfectly any of these influences may operate, there can be no doubt that their combined effect is very considerable in tending to produce citizens who are ready to ask for what they require, object vigorously to what they dislike, and demand explanations and justifications for the activities of specialists and experts in all fields. It is important to note that these attitudes very readily become generalised, and that the process cannot be halted sharply at a particular point. Resistance by officials or specialists of any kind to demands for information and consultation is likely to produce fairly marked reactions, as these resistances run counter to one of the main influences of our society.

THE PUBLIC SERVANT AND THE FAMILY

The New Zealand Public Service, more than most such services, is a highly centralised organisation. Many duties and responsibilities which in other countries are delegated to local authorities are, in New Zealand, retained by the central Government and administered by the Public Service. In my discussion of these matters, I refer chiefly to the welfare departments, since these have the most obvious and direct impact on the family, but I am sure that a similar analysis could be made of the relationship between other agencies and, for example, business firms and local authorities.

Obviously, no administrative system as large as the New Zealand Public Service can be completely centralised, and it is, therefore, important for us to look at this term in more detail in order to see exactly what it means in this context. Normally, decentralisation can be on the basis of area or function, or more usually, some combination of the two.[7] In the New Zealand Public Service the functional aspect is by far the more important. So far as decentralisation by area is concerned, many departments have district offices in the main towns and cities but the amount of responsibility and discretion delegated in these district offices seems usually to be small. There is some delegation in welfare fields of function to local bodies such as hospital and education boards, always under very strict control from the centre. This control has, in recent years, tended to increase rather than diminish. Delegation to non-governmental agencies such as the Plunket Society, or organisations providing services for old people, is practised only to a very slight extent. In short, such centrifugal tendencies as do exist involve, for the most part, the dispersal of services rather than of responsibility, and in most cases the delegation is of a specific function with strict control from the centre. There are some examples of genuine decentralisation, notably the city, borough and country councils, but, even here, a small range of functions is involved, decreased still further by the proliferation of local *ad hoc* bodies such as harbour boards, electricity boards, drainage boards, rabbit boards, and so on.

The main vertical subdivisions within the Public Service are functional. New Zealand has an unusually large number of departments,[8] especially for so small a country, which means that the functional divisions are very narrow. This is exaggerated by the fact that many departments are further subdivided into divisions which often have a fairly high degree of autonomy in spite of an inevitable overlap in the fields of their responsibilities.[9] A further complication enters into the picture because the functional division of "portfolios" amongst Cabinet Ministers is made on a somewhat different basis to the division among Departments, with the result that the overlapping occurs in a different way at the top political and top administrative levels.

Because real life, and the problems of families, are no respecters of administrative functional distinctions, and because each functionally differentiated department makes its own arrangements about area bound-

[7] Fesler, *op. cit.*, pp. 16–18.

[8] R. J. Polaschek, *Government Administration in New Zealand*, Wellington (New Zealand Institute of Public Administration, 1958), p. 76.

[9] Cf. The overlapping responsibilities of Hospitals, Nursing and Maternity Services Divisions with respect to the operation of maternity wards in general hospitals.

aries, it is not uncommon for persons, particularly in the smaller centres, to be involved in problems which require them to deal with two departments on the same matter, only to discover that this means communicating with officials from two different centres, perhaps a hundred miles apart, and even on different islands.

The combination of narrow functional differentiation with extreme centralisation and hierarchical organisation has important consequences for lines of communication which run almost exclusively to and from the centre and hardly at all laterally, a fact which is officially recognised and enforced by the rule that public servants may not comment officially on the work of other departments. The result is that a citizen confronted by a problem which crosses a public service boundary, whether functional or geographical, has the greatest difficulty in seeing it whole because there are inadequate lines of communication between the various officials with whom he must deal. Any official who knows himself to be uninformed about some aspect of the problem which is partly the responsibility of another department, will naturally commit himself as little as possible on the subject, and the result is what one author has referred to as the "discourtesies of silence" [10] which frequently leave the citizen anxious and angry. Unlike the citizen, the official has no "family group" which acts as a communications centre and, in many cases, he can only pass on to the citizen the fragmentary information which he has, leaving the family with the task of fitting the pieces together, sometimes unaware that they are not in possession of some quite important item.

There are some other features of the Public Service which accentuate these problems of communication.[11] In New Zealand, unlike most other countries, it is usual for a departmental head to be professionally qualified in the field which is his department's chief concern. This means, inevitably, that, unless he is a superman, his professional loyalties and prejudices become involved in his administrative work, while differences in professional background add to his difficulties of communication with other departmental heads.[12]

The narrowly functional definition of departmental responsibilities is associated with a tendency to appoint in each department a very narrow range of professional staff, yet many of the situations in which the citizen is brought into contact with the Public Service require the knowledge

[10] R. M. Titmuss, *Essays on the Welfare State* (London: Allen and Unwin, 1958), p. 125.

[11] I have discussed these and other related matters elsewhere from a slightly different point of view. See "The Role of Voluntary Welfare Organisations," *Political Science*, March 1960, Vol. 12, Number 1, pp. 11–27.

[12] A former director of the Division of Nursing, Department of Health, has said: "Professional officers are apt to consider their point of view as preeminent." Mary Lambie, *My Story: Memoirs of a New Zealand Nurse* (Christchurch: N. M. Peryer Ltd., 1956), p. 174.

and services of more than one profession. There are two possible "solutions" to this dilemma. Either different aspects of the problems will be referred to different departments, with all the consequent difficulties of poor communication, especially if, as sometimes happens, the conclusions reached by the two departments are contradictory; or one department will succumb to the temptation to deal with the whole problem, even in the absence of appropriate specialists, and require some of its employees to cover a much wider range of duties than is really warranted by their particular qualifications, with an inevitable lowering of standards and a tendency to obscure the need for the specialist services.

Examples of the first "solution" occur rather frequently in the case of problems associated with physically or mentally handicapped children, when both the medical and educational services (including one or more of the specialist Divisions of the two Departments concerned) are involved. The end result is sometimes that of a family, already burdened by a difficult problem, faced with the additional task of attempting to reconcile apparently conflicting decisions on the part of two organisations whose only channel of communication seems to be through the family with the problem. The family may or may not genuinely understand either or both of the, often quite complicated, decisions.

Examples of the second type of "solution" are the use of Public Health Nurses as all-purpose social workers, in spite of the fact that their training is in nursing and public health work, and only at the most elementary level, in social work; and the use in several departments and divisions of psychologists and social workers to undertake work which would be more appropriately carried out by psychiatrists, or at any rate under psychiatric supervision.

The existence of problems of this type was recognised by the Consultative Committee on Infant and Pre-School Health Services and their recommendations, including the setting up of a Child Health Council, were intended to overcome them.[13] For reasons which are discussed more fully below, I cannot share the Committee's optimism over the effects of their recommendations.

It thus appears that the relation of the Public Service to the family is a most uncomfortable one. The family, linked to the loosely-knit community network by a series of contacts through individual members of the family, will be faced with increased difficulties if these links are not joined to other well-integrated and effective centres of communication. Contacts with the Public Service are certainly not usually of this type. One might take as a concrete example the likely experience of a family which includes a partially deaf child. At first, this is the relatively simple

---

[13] *Report of the Consultative Committee on Infant and Pre-School Health Services* (Wellington: Government Printer, 1960), pp. 33–34.

problem of the relationships of one total individual to other total individuals within the family group. When the child goes to school, the deafness becomes an important practical problem within this particular sphere, but involving only the child directly. The loosely-knit network has come into operation. With admirably worthy and humane intent, the State has provided a range of services for such children. If these services were effectively coordinated by the child's teacher (whether in an ordinary or special class) or in some other way, they would be wholly admirable in effect, but this is not what happens. The child will be examined by the school doctor and referred for specialist examination, perhaps at the local hospital. A parent (usually the mother) will be given some information, including instructions on any hearing aid fitted, but normally no report will be passed to the teacher. She may obtain some information from the mother, the accuracy of which will depend on the mother's understanding and the clarity of the doctor's or nurse's explanation. From time to time, as with other children, the child will be seen by the school doctor and nurse, who may discuss the situation with the mother and give any advice they feel to be appropriate.

In the meantime, the child's teacher will be attempting to make sure that the child learns as well as others in the class. It may be that, during a period prior to the diagnosis of deafness, the child was thought to be backward, and the headmaster may request an examination by the educational psychologist. The results of this will be communicated to the school, but, unless the psychologist makes a special effort to see that this is done, it is unlikely that the medical authorities will know anything about the results of this examination when they advise the mother on her treatment of the child. The psychologist will discuss his results with the parents. If the teacher is still worried, she may call on the services of the Visiting Teacher. This may mean no more than consultations between these two teachers, but the Visiting Teacher may call to see the mother, who is in any case likely to discuss the child with the class teacher at Parent-Teacher Association meetings or at specially arranged interviews. The views she hears and the advice she receives which, like the other views and advice, she tries to pass on to her husband, may not conflict with those she has heard from the doctor and psychologist, but they will be from a different point of view, directed at different aspects of the child's situation, and expressed in different terms. She may well find them quite incompatible. If, as is often the case, the child has a speech defect due to his failure to hear clearly, he is likely to be referred to a speech clinic. Communication between speech therapists and schools is normally quite good, but, even so, the picture is still more complicated as far as the family is concerned and another apparently disconnected person brought in.

I want to emphasize that I have not described an exaggerated or abnormal case. I have assumed that the child is physically healthy, intellectually and emotionally normal, and not delinquent; that all records have been accurately kept and all official forms filled in and forwarded to the proper authorities; that the child has not experienced frequent changes of teachers, that the teacher is of at least average competence and that the home is of at least average standards. With less satisfactory conditions it is possible for up to seven officials to be in active contact with a family in connection with a single child, and for there to be almost no communication between some of them. It is important to remember that all these complications refer to something which, however important, is only one aspect of this child's situation and experience, and is additional to all the usual problems faced by parents in keeping in touch with the important influences affecting their child.

APPLICATIONS

These brief descriptions of the two units that I am concerned with, the Public Service on the one hand, and the citizen-in-his-family on the other, should at the very least have indicated that words like "centralisation" and "decentralisation" are not very suitable as battle cries. One of the most basic requirements of a really satisfactory battle cry is that it should present a simple issue in simple terms, but the matters to which these words refer are anything but simple. Not only is decentralisation a matter of degree and not an absolute condition, but it is also a condition which varies considerably in its effects according to other conditions which are associated with it.

For a whole variety of reasons which are well known and which relate, among other things, to questions of administrative efficiency, economic planning and national unity, decentralisation in the sense of complete delegation of authority to an organisation controlling all aspects of affairs in a particular locality, is simply not feasible in a modern, complex, industrial society. As stated earlier, an alternative form is the division of authority on a functional basis, but, just as it is possible to subdivide a geographical area in many different ways, so a variety of bases can be chosen for functional differentiation. For example, the occupational classification of persons employed by the administrative authority (doctors, teachers, engineers, etc.), the type of problem dealt with (economic, communications, welfare, etc.), or the categories of persons served (children, business men, the under-privileged, etc.), may all be used singly or in combination as bases for a functional division of the total administrative task. It may be that the most appropriate method of differentiation varies from one area of administration to another, but for the moment all we need to note is that there is considerable variation among these methods so far as consequences are concerned.

As soon as a total system is subdivided, communication becomes a problem, and this problem is particularly marked when functional differentiation is combined with a high degree of centralisation in the organisation responsible for each function (e.g. in each public service department) and a considerable sub-division of each functional organisation on a geographical basis without any real delegation of authority (e.g. a series of strictly controlled district offices). This produces poor communication at a local level without any real decentralisation. This situation, which one author has called "dispersal," [14] is described by him as the "inherent weakness" of administration in an industrial type society. "The critical political and administrative problem" of such a system, according to Riggs, is "the coordination of functions," or "systematisation," designed to overcome the weakening effects of dispersal. Although, in one sense of the term, New Zealand is hardly an industrial society, it is certainly of this general type, and it appears to me that its administrative system is "dispersed" in an extreme degree.

If we examine the problem of communication in this setting and with special reference to the New Zealand departmental structure, we find two contrasting situations. Within each functional grouping (e.g. a department or a division), and especially where this has a narrow occupational base, there is an extremely high degree of efficient communication based on professional loyalties, common technical vocabularies, shared interests and attitudes towards special problems. Between the functional groupings, however, communication is at a minimum because the very things that facilitate it *within* the group act as barriers to it *between* groups and, except at the very highest levels, there are few formal arrangements to overcome these barriers. If, therefore, one looks at what goes on *within* the groups, one often gets an impression of a high level of efficiency; the smooth and rapid working of well-oiled machinery.

If one looks at the consequences of this on problems which overlap or fall between two functional areas, one often gets an impression of a very low level of efficiency, like an imperfectly adjusted lathe which cuts out only part of the total pattern. It is all rather too reminiscent of the famous hospital bulletin, "The operation was completely successful, but, unfortunately the patient died."

It seems probable, that to the extent that effective end results are achieved, this is largely due to efficient communication altogether outside the administrative system; in the particular instance already described, within the family. We are faced by a fundamental question which can be regarded as an administrative, political, or moral problem, accord-

14 Fred W. Riggs, "Agraria and Industria" in *Toward the Comparative Study of Public Administration*, edited by W. J. Siffin (Bloomington: Indiana University Press, 1959), pp. 93–94.

ing to your own preference. Who ought to be given the task of providing
for effective communication, the public service or the public, the administrators or the administered? At the moment, I am interested in this as
an administrative problem, and I suggest that the answer then depends
on whether you define efficiency chiefly in terms of the smoothly running
machinery, or the effectiveness of the contribution which that machinery
makes to the satisfactory completion of a total task.

This last concept, that of a completed total task, is I think an important
one, well-recognised in the field of industrial management as a basis for
worker satisfaction.[15] In the type of situation I am considering here, the
matter becomes more complicated because the task does not involve the
manipulation of inanimate objects, but is concerned with the activities
and problems of human beings, and, therefore, the sense of wholeness
and completion needs to develop in two groups of people simultaneously,
the public servants, and the members of the public. If this is not achieved,
there will be dissatisfaction on one side or the other. The public servants,
like any other worker, if he is to gain real satisfaction from his work,
must experience the sense of achievement that comes from being involved, either as an individual or as a member of a "team," in the completion of a "whole" task. The citizen, as we have already seen, will experience considerable strain and dissatisfaction unless his problem, which
he perceives as a whole, is dealt with as a whole. We have also noted the
lack of formally organised lateral communication which prevents such
problems from being handled as a whole.

But it is striking that there is also a very small number of informal
lines of communication in the New Zealand Public Service, though it is
well established that these can, under some circumstances, be more
effective than those which have been formally arranged. There is, I think,
a powerful reason acting against any such development. If an official,
involved in a task of the type I have been describing, develops informal
relationships with a colleague in another department who is engaged on
other aspects of the same task, one of the first consequences will be his
discovery that he is not involved in a "whole" task. This would not matter
if he could then develop an informal "team" relationship so that he could
come to perceive himself as an integral member of a group confronting
the "whole" task. This is unlikely to happen. The complexity of the situation, the number of people involved, the weight of public service tradition, and the frequency with which the officials involved change because
of transfers, all operate to prevent this. Informal relationships are, therefore, likely to be unsatisfactory, to reduce job satisfaction without providing any workable alternative. Avoiding communication, therefore,
becomes an important protective device. It is only insofar as such contact

[15] A. K. Rice, *Productivity and Social Organisation* (London: Tavistock Publications,
1958), p. 34.

can be avoided that the sense of completing a "whole" task can be retained and some real satisfaction experienced in the job.

A somewhat different aspect of this problem can be seen in the reluctance of some officials to request either the development of formal relationships with specialists in other departments, or the appointment in their own department of a specialist in some related field. This reluctance can sometimes be traced to a fear that the official's superiors will regard such requests as confessions of failure, an inability to do the job properly. This is also shown by the fact that some officials who have developed informal relationships conceal this fact from their superiors, again because they fear that it will cause them to be judged as incapable of doing their jobs properly,[16] and therefore having to call in outside assistance.

It is important to note that these difficulties are not a consequence of inadequacies or weaknesses on the part of the officials concerned. They are built into the structure of the system and nothing but a radical alteration of the system can get rid of them. If we accept Riggs' contention that "dispersal" is a condition of weakness, and my contention that the New Zealand Public Service is extremely dispersed, we are faced with the question as to possible remedies; alternative forms of organisation which, again in Riggs' terms, will systematise the Service, by coordinating the functions which have become so divided. It would be a magnificent understatement to say that such a question is not easy to answer, and perhaps an impertinence for anyone, even vastly better informed than myself, to attempt an answer here. I can, therefore, do no more than raise some points which seem to me to be important in this connection.

The high degree of centralisation involved in each of the separated functional units tends to result in a very great amount of standardisation, which can be maintained only by close inspection from the centre, with very little delegation of real responsibility down the line. This is a state of affairs which, whatever the intention, implies a lack of confidence in the staff controlled. It also has a very restricting effect on those in contact with the public, and increases their tendency to uncommunicativeness. An official who reveals by his behaviour that he is under strict surveillance is unlikely to engender confidence in the public or develop in himself the feeling that he is doing a really worthwhile job. I suspect that this situation plays a considerable part in the failure of the Public Service to retain so many of its best men in its middle and upper-middle ranks. If these points are correct they imply a considerable argument in favour of decentralisation in the sense of increased delegation of responsibility, including a reduction in detailed inspection and control from the centre.

The dispersed nature of the organisation of the Public Service has a

---

[16] A similar resistance by "line" managers to the appointment of specialists because of a feeling that this implies failure on their own part is discussed by Rice, *op. cit.*, p. 247.

further important consequence from the point of view of the general public. When responsibility for a problem which is seen by the public as a unit is divided up among departments, it becomes difficult for citizens to exercise any control over public affairs. Attempts to have policy changed through pressure from public opinion are frustrated by the fact that no person or department has effective control over the matter in question, and any change at one point must await change at some other point, and so on round a seemingly endless circle. This situation, a policy of *divide et impera* in reverse, probably has the effect of forcing an undue number of relatively trivial decisions to Cabinet level, as it is only here that the necessary over-riding authority can be obtained. At the same time, it tends to make the ordinary citizen feel rather helpless and resentful in the face of what he feels to be overwhelmingly and improperly powerful public service.[17] This feature, along with others already discussed in relation to the problem of dispersal, seems to point to a need for greater integration of functions.

In the light of the discussion so far, it seems to be clear that mere decentralisation in the conventional sense will not, of itself, solve the problems posed. I believe there are advantages to be gained from delegating increased powers and responsibilities to local bodies. But, while so many of these bodies, such as hospital boards and education boards, have the same narrow functional basis as the departments from which the powers are delegated, not much impression is made on the problem of dispersal. The inability of the citizen to make effective contact with the administrative system remains.

One well-known means by which an organisation may broaden its functional basis is by involving other bodies, with related interests, in its work. Selznick,[18] in an extremely interesting analysis of this process which he labels "co-optation," points out that it may involve the sharing of actual power, or merely a sharing of the burdens of power, and that it may be on a formal or an informal basis. In general, according to Selznick, the informal process is more likely to involve an actual sharing or transfer of power, while formal arrangements more often provide a public "front" which chiefly has the purpose of "legitimising" the co-opting organisation in the eyes of the public. It is reasons of this kind which make me very dubious of the effectiveness of, for example, bodies, such as the Child Health Council envisaged by the consultative Committee already referred

[17] For a discussion of similar situations in a different setting, see Elaine and John Cumming, "The Locus of Power in a Large Mental Hospital," *Psychiatry*, November 1956, Vol. 19, No. 4, pp. 361–369, and Merton J. Kahne, "Bureaucratic Structure and Impersonal Experience in Mental Hospitals," *Psychiatry*, November 1959, Vol. 22, No. 4, pp. 363–375.

[18] P. Selznick, *T.V.A. and the Grass Roots* (Los Angeles: University of California Press, 1953), pp. 359 ff.

to, in overcoming the problems of dispersal. This is not to argue that such a Council would have no value, but simply that it would be ineffective in overcoming this basic problem, in spite of the fact that this was one of the main reasons given for proposing its establishment.

Processes of planned and organised change within an organisation can be exceedingly uncomfortable for its members. Rice [19] discusses the need for "protection" of personnel from the stresses associated with changes of this kind. The Public Service seems to me to be particularly vulnerable in this sense. The fact that it is a "public" organisation under political control, makes it peculiarly susceptible to outside comment and attempted interference. At the same time, its lack of internal communication prevents any effective attempts to reorganise and reform quietly from within. As long as this situation lasts, I can see no possibilities of development in the Public Service, except through politically imposed, rather abrupt and sweeping reforms at irregular intervals, following periods of mounting public dissatisfaction. This is surely an uncomfortable prospect for all concerned, public and public servant alike.

Given freer internal communication, it should be possible for the Public Service to build into its organisation some kind of research and development function (which might not necessarily be in continuous operation, and might not be staffed necessarily, or entirely, by public servants) which would permit the Service to keep itself more effectively geared to the needs of the community by a steady series of relatively small, internally organised changes. This should afford the Service a much greater degree of protection against external criticism, not by erecting barriers against it, but by creating conditions in which it is less likely to appear.

The central requirement seems to me to be a major reorganisation of the way in which the various functions of the Public Service are allocated to the various departments. This reorganisation in my view would involve three features. First, a very considerable reduction in the number of departments, which means a considerable amount of amalgamation.[20] Second, a good deal of alteration in the bases on which functional differentiation is made within these larger departments, and, third, a complete abandonment of the practice of appointing professionals as heads of various specialist departments and divisions.

The aim behind these procedures is twofold. First, to improve communications, and, second, to produce, as far as possible, a correspondence between the "whole" tasks which derive from departmental organisation, and the "whole" problems which confront the families, neighbourhoods,

---

[19] Rice, *op. cit.*, pp. 248–250.
[20] This is not, of course, a new idea. It is put forward, for example, by Leslie Lipson (*The Politics of Equality*, University of Chicago Press, 1947, pp. 365–420), but I have argued for it on somewhat different grounds.

local bodies, business firms and other organisations which have dealings with the Public Service. Unless these two objectives are achieved, decentralisation can be little more than an empty, formal gesture.

An example may be the simplest way of indicating the kind of thing I have in mind. There is, I believe, a strong case for the establishment of a welfare department which would include as a minimum the present Departments of Social Security and Health, large sections and perhaps the whole of the Department of Education, the Penal Division of the Department of Justice and the Welfare Division of Maori Affairs. Within this new department, functional differentiation between divisions should be largely on the basis of the type of person with whom a division is concerned. Maori welfare would remain the function of a separate division, but a new children's division would take over most of the functions of the present Education Department (including child welfare), and also the Child Hygiene Division of the Health Department and the School Medical and Dental Services. The Penal Division could probably remain as at present. The administration of medical benefits should certainly be associated with the administration of sickness and invalidity benefits and probably with the administration of hospitals and clinical services. I can see no good reason for severing the present Welfare Division of the Health Department from the administration of age benefits and Universal Superannuation.

I must stress that these suggestions are intended to be illustrative of a general principle, and not a plan which I visualise as hard and fast in all its details. It will be impossible to obtain an arrangement that can be relied upon under all circumstances to produce an exact correspondence between the requirements of administrative efficiency and the convenience of citizens. The important point is to aim as nearly as possible at such an ideal. There may well be more than one arrangement which would approximate reasonably to the ideal. Almost any kind of amalgamation would be preferable to the present situation.

With an organisation of the type described, there would be no justification whatever for the appointment of professional specialists as departmental and divisional heads, as each of such organisations would be concerned with bringing a number of professional specialisms to bear on a given range of problems. At the same time, of course, the need for professional knowledge and advice would be undiminished and an essential part of such a scheme would be the employment of professionals as advisors and specialist workers, with arrangements whereby they could obtain promotion to senior ranks, without having to abandon the practice of their special skills by changing to purely administrative duties. The professionals could then be genuine specialists, employed for their special qualifications and promoted on the basis of their competence in their own special fields.

Given this degree of integration at the centre, the problem of arranging for adequate communication and unification of services on a more local level should cease to be insuperable, and some genuine decentralisation would become possible, on the basis of greater delegation of power and responsibility, either to district offices or to local bodies. Even if something approximating to the present education and hospital boards were retained, the unification at the centre should sharply reduce the degree of dispersal at the local level. For example, there should be no difficulty under these circumstances in having the school Medical and Dental Services administered at the local level by education boards.

I hope that, if I have done nothing else, I have at least illustrated something of the complexities involved in the decentralisation of the public services; complexities which arise from the inter-relationships of the social systems affected by the situation. As a result concepts like "efficiency" which are inevitably involved in this problem are far from simple. One must, I think, continually ask such questions as "Efficient for whom?", "Efficient for what purpose?", remembering that, as I have pointed out earlier, two sets of people (public and public servants) are necessarily affected and that both of them will pass judgment on this matter of efficiency, often using different criteria.[21] The problem which needs solution is not that of choosing between these two points of view but that of finding a form of organisation which will, to a reasonable degree, meet the needs of both. I do not think myself that this is impossible.

[21] The situation is, of course, complicated by the fact that public servants are also members of the public, a fact which is especially obvious in relation to the work of other Departments than their own.

Section III

Goals, Internal Organization,
and Client Relations

Part A

Goal Setting and Organizational Requirements

THE articles in this section analyze the operation of welfare organizations and welfare programs. Up to now we have been concerned mostly with the societal and community context of welfare programs, but here we focus on the structure of welfare organization per se by dealing with the goal-setting process, the internal structure of organizations, and the relationship of organizations to their clientele. Four main topics are treated: in Part A we discuss the determinants of organizational goal setting; in Part B the treatment turns to the internal structures of organizations; in Part C we concentrate on the nature of professions and the relationships of professionals to bureaucracies; and in Parts D and E the selections are concerned with organization-client relations.

The articles in Part A cover a central topic in organizational theory: the processes shaping the missions of organizations. Welfare organizations, like other formal organizations, are characterized by having specific goals. Formal organizations must produce a product or service which is evaluated by significant groups in the society or community. Failure to produce a satisfactory service leads either to a change in goals or a decline of support. However, the goals or service of many welfare organizations are different in several respects from those of other large-scale organizations. First, there is often a relatively low consensus in the society about the value of the services of welfare organizations. While some groups argue that the organizations are not doing enough about a particular welfare problem, other groups contend that the organizations are doing too much—in fact, these groups completely deny the importance of the service. Second, welfare organizations often have means and ends which are not clearly linked—at least, it is not always clear how the stated ends should be achieved. For instance, although the programs necessary for income maintenance are clear enough, the goals and means of rehabilitation programs are subject to conflicting criteria of evaluation and to conflicting philosophies of treatment. In the absence of empirical criteria of effectiveness, different philosophies contend with each other.

Third, many welfare organizations differ from private profit-making organizations in the process by which goals are established. Similar to governmental agencies and schools, the market of buyers do not establish directions for the organization as much as do controlling interest groups. In any organization the chief executive and his staff must make decisions about directions; but where, in business, the executive must respond to the market, in welfare organizations the response is to relevant control and professional groups.

In the first article in Part A, "Organizational Goals and Environment: Goal-Setting as an Interaction Process," James D. Thompson and William J. McEwen examine the dynamic process by which goals are set. These authors suggest that organizational goals are developed through an interaction process with other organizations and groups. Thompson and McEwen argue that interaction with other organizations can range from competition to bargaining, cooptation, and coalition. Each of these types of interaction suggests somewhat different processes of goal setting. Of course, to the extent that an organization offers a service upon which other groups are heavily dependent, it gains control over its goal-setting process.

The topic of goal setting and, by implication, the control of goal setting is extended by James Senor in "Another Look at the Executive-Board Relationship." Boards of directors in voluntary agencies may serve dual functions: they can represent the organization to the community, essentially promoting the organization, and they can serve as agents of community control, reflecting the value preferences and goals of the community or groups from which they come. Senor is largely concerned with the control function, and he develops several propositions regarding the conditions under which executives become autonomous in relation to their boards.

Although the first two articles deal with the problem of goal setting and control in very general terms, the selection by Gresham Sykes, "The Regime of the Custodians," gives an analysis of the goal-setting problem in a concrete case: the case of a maximum security prison. The prison and correctional system may exemplify, better than any other organization, the problems that occur because of the contradictory goals of an organization. On the one hand, the prison represents an instrument of social control as much, or more, than an instrument of social welfare. If its goals were only to keep criminals out of society, we would not consider the prison as a part of the social welfare system. But, since prisons are often supposed to reform criminals, they can also be considered as a part of the welfare system. Sykes points out that the prison must not only attempt to control and reform prisoners but must also, because of resource shortages, maintain itself financially. Sykes discusses how these potentially conflicting tasks are brought into working harmony.

The goals and goal choices considered in this section do not, by any means, exhaust the range of variation for welfare organizations. Any sociological analysis of specific programs or organizations begins with an analysis of goals and the goal-setting process. These processes are involved at several points throughout this section.

Organizational Goals and Environment:

Goal-Setting as an Interaction Process

James D. Thompson and William J. McEwen

In the analysis of complex organizations the definition of organizational goals is commonly utilized as a standard for appraising organizational performance. In many such analyses the goals of the organization are often viewed as a constant. Thus a wide variety of data, such as official documents, work activity records, organizational output, or statements by organizational spokesmen, may provide the basis for the definition of goals. Once this definition has been accomplished, interest in goals as a dynamic aspect of organizational activity frequently ends.

It is possible, however, to view the setting of goals (i.e., major organizational purposes) not as a static element but as a necessary and recurring problem facing any organization, whether it is governmental, military, business, educational, medical, religious, or other type.

This perspective appears appropriate in developing the two major lines of the present analysis. The first of these is to emphasize the interdependence of complex organizations within the larger society and the consequences this has for organizational goal-setting. The second is to emphasize the similarities of goal-setting *processes* in organizations with manifestly different goals. The present analysis is offered to supplement recent studies of organizational operations.[1]

It is postulated that goal-setting behavior is *purposive* but not necessarily *rational;* we assume that goals may be determined by accident, i.e., by blundering of members of the organization and, contrariwise, that

---

[1] Among recent materials that treat organizational goal-setting are Kenneth E. Boulding, *The Organizational Revolution,* New York: Harper and Brothers, 1953; Robert A. Dahl and Charles E. Lindblom, *Politics, Economics, and Welfare,* New York: Harper and Brothers, 1953; and John K. Galbraith, *American Capitalism: The Concept of Countervailing Power,* Boston: Houghton Mifflin, 1952.

James D. Thompson and William J. McEwen, "Organizational Goals and Environment: Goal-Setting as an Interaction Process," *American Sociological Review,* February, 1958, Vol. 23, 1, pp. 23–31.

the most calculated and careful determination of goals may be negated by developments outside the control of organization members. The goal-setting problem as discussed here is essentially determining a relationship of the organization to the larger society, which in turn becomes a question of what the society (or elements within it) wants done or can be persuaded to support.

GOALS AS DYNAMIC VARIABLES

Because the setting of goals is essentially a problem of defining desired relationships between an organization and its environment, change in either requires review and perhaps alteration of goals. Even where the most abstract statement of goals remains constant, application requires redefinition or interpretation as changes occur in the organization, the environment, or both.

The corporation, for example, faces changing markets and develops staff specialists with responsibility for continuous study and projection of market changes and product appeal. The governmental agency, its legislative mandate notwithstanding, has need to reformulate or reinterpret its goals as other agencies are created and dissolved, as the population changes, or as non-governmental organizations appear to do the same job or to compete. The school and the university may have unchanging abstract goals but the clientele, the needs of pupils or students, and the techniques of teaching change and bring with them redefinition and reinterpretation of those objectives. The hospital has been faced with problems requiring an expansion of goals to include consideration of preventive medicine, public health practices, and the degree to which the hospital should extend its activities out into the community. The mental hospital and the prison are changing their objectives from primary emphasis on custody to a stress on therapy. Even the church alters its pragmatic objectives as changes in the society call for new forms of social ethics, and as government and organized philanthropy take over some of the activities formerly left to organized religion.[2]

[2] For pertinent studies of various organizational types see Burton R. Clark, *Adult Education in Transition*, Berkeley and Los Angeles: University of California Press, 1956; Temple Burling, Edith M. Lentz, and Robert N. Wilson, *The Give and Take in Hospitals*, New York: G. P. Putnam's Sons, 1956, especially pp. 3–10; Lloyd E. Ohlin, *Sociology and the Field of Corrections*, New York: Russell Sage Foundation, 1956, pp. 13–18; Liston Pope, *Millhands and Preachers*, New Haven: Yale University Press, 1942; Charles Y. Glock and Benjamin B. Ringer, "Church Policy and the Attitudes of Ministers and Parishioners on Social Issues," *American Sociological Review*, 21 (April, 1956), pp. 148–156. For a similar analysis in the field of philanthropy, see J. R. Seeley, B. H. Junker, R. W. Jones, Jr., and others, *Community Chest: A Case Study in Philanthropy*, Toronto: University of Toronto Press, 1957, especially Chapters 2 and 5.

Reappraisal of goals thus appears to be a recurrent problem for large organization, albeit a more constant problem in an unstable environment than in a stable one. Reappraisal of goals likewise appears to be more difficult as the "product" of the enterprise becomes less tangible and more difficult to measure objectively. The manufacturing firm has a relatively ready index of the acceptability of its product in sales figures; while poor sales may indicate inferior quality rather than public distaste for the commodity itself, sales totals frequently are supplemented by trade association statistics indicating the firm's "share of the market." Thus within a matter of weeks, a manufacturing firm may be able to reappraise its decision to enter the "widget" market and may therefore begin deciding how it can get out of that market with the least cost.

The governmental enterprise may have similar indicators of the acceptability of its goals if it is involved in producing an item such as electricity, but where its activity is oriented to a less tangible purpose such as maintaining favorable relations with foreign nations, the indices of effective operation are likely to be less precise and the vagaries more numerous. The degree to which a government satisfies its clientele may be reflected periodically in elections, but despite the claims of party officials, it seldom is clear just what the mandate of the people is with reference to any particular governmental enterprise. In addition, the public is not always steadfast in its mandate.

The university perhaps has even greater difficulties in evaluating its environmental situation through response to its output. Its range of "products" is enormous, extending from astronomers to zoologists. The test of a competent specialist is not always standardized and may be changing, and the university's success in turning out "educated" people is judged by many and often conflicting standards. The university's product is in process for four or more years and when it is placed on the "market" it can be only imperfectly judged. Vocational placement statistics may give some indication of the university's success in its objectives, but initial placement is no guarantee of performance at a later date. Furthermore, performance in an occupation is only one of several abilities that the university is supposed to produce in its students. Finally, any particular department of the university may find that its reputation lags far behind its performance. A "good" department may work for years before its reputation becomes "good" and a downhill department may coast for several years before the fact is realized by the professional world.

In sum, the goals of an organization, which determine the kinds of goods or services it produces and offers to the environment, often are subject to peculiar difficulties of reappraisal. Where the purpose calls for an easily identified, readily measured product, reappraisal and readjustment of goals may be accomplished rapidly. But as goals call for increasingly intangible, difficult-to-measure products, society finds it more difficult to determine and reflect its acceptability of that product, and the signals that indicate unacceptable goals are less effective and perhaps longer in coming.

ENVIRONMENTAL CONTROLS OVER GOALS

A continuing situation of necessary interaction between an organization and its environment introduces an element of environmental control into the organization. While the motives of personnel, including goal-setting officers, may be profits, prestige, votes, or the salvation of souls, their efforts must produce something useful or acceptable to at least a part of the organizational environment to win continued support.[3]

In the simpler society social control over productive activities may be exercised rather informally and directly through such means as gossip and ridicule. As a society becomes more complex and its productive activities more deliberately organized, social controls are increasingly exercised through such formal devices as contracts, legal codes, and governmental regulations. The stability of expectations provided by these devices is arrived at through interaction, and often through the exercise of power in interaction.

It is possible to conceive of a continuum of organizational power in environmental relations, ranging from the organization that dominates its environmental relations to one completely dominated by its environment. Few organizations approach either extreme. Certain gigantic industrial enterprises, such as the *Zaibatsu* in Japan or the old Standard Oil Trust in America, have approached the dominance-over-environment position at one time, but this position eventually brought about "countervailing powers." [4] Perhaps the nearest approximation to the completely powerless organization is the commuter transit system, which may be unable to cover its costs but nevertheless is regarded as a necessary utility and cannot get permission to quit business. Most complex organizations, falling somewhere between the extremes of the power continuum, must adopt strategies for coming to terms with their environments. This is not to imply that such strategies are necessarily chosen by rational or deliberate processes. An organization can survive so long as it adjusts to its situation; whether the process of adjustment is awkward or nimble becomes important in determining the organization's degree of prosperity.

---

[3] This statement would seem to exclude antisocial organizations, such as crime syndicates. A detailed analysis of such organizations would be useful for many purposes; meanwhile it would appear necessary for them to acquire a clientele, suppliers, and others, in spite of the fact that their methods at times may be somewhat unique.

[4] For the *Zaibatsu* case see Japan Council, *The Control of Industry in Japan*, Tokyo: Institute of Political and Economic Research, 1953; and Edwin O. Reischauer, *The United States and Japan*, Cambridge: Harvard University Press, 1954, pp. 87–97.

However arrived at, strategies for dealing with the organizational environment may be broadly classified as either *competitive* or *co-operative*. Both appear to be important in a complex society—of the "free enterprise" type or other.[5] Both provide a measure of environmental control over organizations by providing for "outsiders" to enter into or limit organizational decision process.

The decision process may be viewed as a series of activities, conscious or not, culminating in a choice among alternatives. For purposes of this paper we view the decision-making process as consisting of the following activities:

1. Recognizing an occasion for decision, i.e., a need or an opportunity.
2. Analysis of the existing situation.
3. Identification of alternative courses of action.
4. Assessment of the probable consequences of each alternative.
5. Choice from among alternatives.[6]

The following discussion suggests that the potential power of an outsider increases the earlier he enters into the decision process,[7] and that competition and three sub-types of co-operative strategy—*bargaining, co-optation,* and *coalition*—differ in this respect. It is therefore possible to order these forms of interaction in terms of the degree to which they provide for environmental control over organizational goal-setting decisions.

Competition

The term competition implies an element of rivalry. For present purposes competition refers to that form of rivalry between two or more organizations which is mediated by a third party. In the case of the manufacturing firm the third party may be the customer, the supplier, the potential or present member of the labor force, or others. In the case of the governmental bureau, the third party through whom competition takes place may be the legislative committee, the budget bureau, or the chief

[5] For evidence on Russia see David Granick, *Management of the Industrial Firm in the U.S.S.R.,* New York: Columbia University Press, 1954; and Joseph S. Berliner, "Informal Organization of the Soviet Firm," *Quarterly Journal of Economics,* 66 (August, 1952), pp. 353–365.

[6] This particular breakdown is taken from Edward H. Litchfield, "Notes on a General Theory of Administration," *Administrative Science Quarterly,* 1 (June, 1956), pp. 3–29. We are also indebted to Robert Tannenbaum and Fred Massarik who, by breaking the decision-making process into three steps, show that subordinates can take part in the "manager's decision" even when the manager makes the final choice. See "Participation by Subordinates in the Managerial Decision-Making Process," *Canadian Journal of Economics and Political Science,* 16 (August, 1949), pp. 410–418.

[7] Robert K. Merton makes a similar point regarding the role of the intellectual in public bureaucracy. See his *Social Theory and Social Structure,* Glencoe: The Free Press, 1949, Chapter VI.

executive, as well as potential clientele and potential members of the bureau.

The complexity of competition in a heterogeneous society is much greater than customary usage (with economic overtones) often suggests. Society judges the enterprise not only by the finished product but also in terms of the desirability of applying resources to that purpose. Even the organization that enjoys a product monopoly must compete for society's support. From the society it must obtain resources—personnel, finances, and materials—as well as customers or clientele. In the business sphere of a "free enterprise" economy this competition for resources and customers usually takes place in the market, but in times of crisis the society may exercise more direct controls, such as rationing or the establishment of priorities during a war. The monopoly competes with enterprises having different purposes or goals but using similar raw materials; it competes with many other enterprises, for human skills and loyalties, and it competes with many other activities for support in the money markets.

The university, customarily a non-profit organization, competes as eagerly as any business firm, although perhaps more subtly.[8] Virtually every university seeks, if not more students, better-qualified students. Publicly supported universities compete at annual budget sessions with other governmental enterprises for shares in tax revenues. Endowed universities must compete for gifts and bequests, not only with other universities but also with museums, charities, zoos, and similar non-profit enterprises. The American university is only one of many organizations competing for foundation support, and it competes with other universities and with other types of organizations for faculty.

The public school system, perhaps one of our most pervasive forms of near-monopoly, not only competes with other governmental units for funds and with different types of organizations for teachers, but current programs espoused by professional educators often compete in a very real way with a public conception of the nature of education, e.g., as the three R's, devoid of "frills."

The hospital may compete with the midwife, the faith-healer, the "quack" and the patent-medicine manufacturer, as well as with neighboring hospitals, despite the fact that general hospitals do not "advertise" and are not usually recognized as competitive.

Competition is thus a complicated network of relationships. It includes scrambling for resources as well as for customers or clients, and in a complex society it includes rivalry for potential members and their loyal-

[8] See Logan Wilson, *The Academic Man*, New York: Oxford University Press, 1942, especially Chapter IX. Also see Warren G. Bennis, "The Effect on Academic Goods of Their Market," *American Journal of Sociology*, 62 (July, 1956), pp. 28–33.

ties. In each case a third party makes a choice among alternatives, two or more organizations attempt to influence that choice through some type of "appeal" or offering, and choice by the third party is a "vote" of support for one of the competing organizations and a denial of support to the others involved.

Competition, then, is one process whereby the organization's choice of goals is partially controlled by the environment. It tends to prevent unilateral or arbitrary choice of organizational goals, or to correct such a choice if one is made. Competition for society's support is an important means of eliminating not only inefficient organizations but also those that seek to provide goods or services the environment is not willing to accept.

Bargaining

The term bargaining, as used here, refers to the negotiation of an agreement for the exchange of goods or services between two or more organizations. Even where fairly stable and dependable expectations have been built up with important elements of the organizational environment —with suppliers, distributors, legislators, workers and so on—the organization cannot assume that these relationships will continue. Periodic review of these relationships must be accomplished, and an important means for this is bargaining, whereby each organization, through negotiation, arrives at a decision about future behavior satisfactory to the others involved.

The need for periodic adjustment of relationships is demonstrated most dramatically in collective bargaining between labor and industrial management, in which the bases for continued support by organization members are reviewed.[9] But bargaining occurs in other important, if less dramatic, areas of organizational endeavor. The business firm must bargain with its agents or distributors, and while this may appear at times to be one-sided and hence not much of a bargain, still even a long-standing agency agreement may be severed by competitive offers unless the agent's level of satisfaction is maintained through periodic review.[10] Where suppliers are required to install new equipment to handle the peculiar demands of an organization, bargaining between the two is not unusual.

The university likewise must bargain.[11] It may compete for free or unrestricted funds, but often it must compromise that ideal by bargaining away the name of a building or of a library collection, or by the conferring of an honorary degree. Graduate students and faculty members may be

[9] For an account of this on a daily basis see Melville Dalton, "Unofficial Union-Management Relations," American Sociological Review, 15 (October, 1950), pp. 611–619.
[10] See Valentine F. Ridgway, "Administration of Manufacturer-Dealer Systems," Administrative Science Quarterly, 1 (March, 1957), pp. 464–483.
[11] Wilson, op. cit., Chapters VII and VIII.

given financial or other concessions through bargaining, in order to prevent their loss to other institutions.

The governmental organization may also find bargaining expedient.[12] The police department, for example, may overlook certain violations of statutes in order to gain the support of minor violators who have channels of information not otherwise open to department members. Concessions to those who "turn state's evidence" are not unusual. Similarly a department of state may forego or postpone recognition of a foreign power in order to gain support for other aspects of its policy, and a governmental agency may relinquish certain activities in order to gain budget bureau approval of more important goals.

While bargaining may focus on resources rather than explicitly on goals, the fact remains that it is improbable that a goal can be effective unless it is at least partially implemented. To the extent that bargaining sets limits on the amount of resources available or the ways they may be employed, it effectively sets limits on choice of goals. Hence bargaining, like competition, results in environmental control over organizational goals and reduces the probability of arbitrary, unilateral goal-setting.

Unlike competition, however, bargaining involves direct interaction with other organizations in the environment, rather than with a third party. Bargaining appears, therefore, to invade the actual decision process. To the extent that the second party's support is necessary he is in a position to exercise a veto over final choice of alternative goals, and hence takes part in the decision.

Co-optation

Co-optation has been defined as the process of absorbing new elements into the leadership or policy-determining structure of an organization as a means of averting threats to its stability or existence.[13] Co-optation makes still further inroads on the process of deciding goals; not only must the final choice be acceptable to the co-opted party or organization, but to the extent that co-optation is effective it places the representative of an "outsider" in a position to determine the occasion for a goal decision, to participate in analyzing the existing situation, to suggest alternatives, and to take part in the deliberation of consequences.

The term co-optation has only recently been given currency in this country, but the phenomenon it describes is neither new nor unimportant. The acceptance on a corporation's board of directors of representatives of banks or other financial institutions is a time-honored custom among

---

[12] For an interesting study of governmental bargaining see William J. Gore, "Administrative Decision-Making in Federal Field Offices," *Public Administration Review,* 16 (Autumn, 1956), pp. 281–291.

[13] Philip Selznick, *TVA and the Grass Roots,* Berkeley and Los Angeles: University of California Press, 1949.

firms that have large financial obligations or that may in the future want access to financial resources. The state university may find it expedient (if not mandatory) to place legislators on its board of trustees, and the endowed college may find that whereas the honorary degree brings forth a token gift, membership on the board may result in a more substantial bequest. The local medical society often plays a decisive role in hospital goal-setting, since the support of professional medical practitioners is urgently necessary for the hospital.

From the standpoint of society, however, co-optation is more than an expediency. By giving a potential supporter a position of power and often of responsibility in the organization, the organization gains his awareness and understanding of the problems it faces. A business advisory council may be an effective educational device for a government, and a White House conference on education may mobilize "grass roots" support in a thousand localities, both by focussing attention on the problem area and by giving key people a sense of participation in goal deliberation.

Moreover, by providing overlapping memberships, co-optation is an important social device for increasing the likelihood that organizations related to one another in complicated ways will in fact find compatible goals. By thus reducing the possibilities of antithetical actions by two or more organizations, co-optation aids in the integration of the heterogeneous parts of a complex society. By the same token, co-optation further limits the opportunity for one organization to choose its goals arbitrarily or unilaterally.

Coalition

As used here, the term coalition refers, to a combination of two or more organizations for a common purpose. Coalition appears to be the ultimate or extreme form of environmental conditioning of organizational goals.[14] A coalition may be unstable, but to the extent that it is operative, two or more organizations act as one with respect to certain goals. Coalition is a means widely used when two or more enterprises wish to pursue a goal calling for more support, especially for more resources, than any one of them is able to marshall unaided. American business firms frequently resort to coalition for purposes of research or product promotion and for the construction of such gigantic facilities as dams or atomic reactors.[15]

[14] Coalition may involve joint action toward only limited aspects of the goals of each member. It may involve the complete commitment of each member for a specific period of time or indefinitely. In either case the ultimate power to withdraw is retained by the members. We thus distinguish coalition from merger, in which two or more organizations are fused permanently. In merger one or all of the original parts may lose their identity. Goal-setting in such a situation, of course, is no longer subject to inter-organizational constraints among the components.

[15] See "The Joint Venture Is an Effective Approach to Major Engineering Projects," *New York Times,* July 14, 1957, Section 3, p. 1 F.

Coalition is not uncommon among educational organizations. Universities have established joint operations in such areas as nuclear research, archaeological research, and even social science research. Many smaller colleges have banded together for fund-raising purposes. The consolidation of public school districts is another form of coalition (if not merger), and the fact that it does represent a sharing or "invasion" of goal-setting power is reflected in some of the bitter resistance to consolidation in tradition-oriented localities.

Coalition requires a commitment for joint decision of future activities and thus places limits on unilateral or arbitrary decisions. Furthermore, inability of an organization to find partners in a coalition venture automatically prevents pursuit of that objective, and is therefore also a form of social control. If the collective judgment is that a proposal is unworkable, a possible disaster may be escaped and unproductive allocation of resources avoided.

DEVELOPMENT OF ENVIRONMENTAL SUPPORT

Environmental control is not a one-way process limited to consequences for the organization of action in its environment. Those subject to control are also part of the larger society and hence are also agents of social control. The enterprise that competes is not only influenced in its goal-setting by what the competitor and the third party may do, but also exerts influence over both. Bargaining likewise is a form of mutual, two-way influence; co-optation affects the co-opted as well as the co-opting party; and coalition clearly sets limits on both parties.

Goals appear to grow out of interaction, both within the organization and between the organization and its environment. While every enterprise must find sufficient support for its goals, it may wield initiative in this. The difference between effective and ineffective organizations may well lie in the initiative exercised by those in the organization who are responsible for goal-setting.

The ability of an administrator to win support for an objective may be as vital as his ability to foresee the utility of a new idea. And his role as a "seller" of ideas may be as important to society as to his organization, for as society becomes increasingly specialized and heterogeneous, the importance of new objectives may be more readily seen by specialized segments than by the general society. It was not public clamor that originated revisions in public school curricula and training methods; the impetus came largely from professional specialists in or on the periphery of education.[16] The shift in focus from custody to therapy in mental hospitals derives largely from the urgings of professionals, and the same

[16] See Robert S. and Helen Merrell Lynd, *Middletown in Transition,* New York: Harcourt, Brace, 1937, Chapter VI.

can be said of our prisons.[17] In both cases the public anger, aroused by crusaders and muck-rakers, might have been soothed by more humane methods of custody. Current attempts to revitalize the liberal arts curricula of our colleges, universities, and technical institutes have developed more in response to the activities of professional specialists than from public urging.[18] Commercial aviation, likewise, was "sold" the hard way, with support being based on subsidy for a considerable period before the importance of such transportation was apparent to the larger public.[19]

In each of these examples the goal-setters saw their ideas become widely accepted only after strenuous efforts to win support through education of important elements of the environment. Present currents in some medical quarters to shift emphasis from treatment of the sick to maintenance of health through preventive medicine and public health programs likewise have to be "sold" to a society schooled in an older concept.[20]

The activities involved in winning support for organizational goals thus are not confined to communication within the organization, however important this is. The need to justify organization goals, to explain the social functions of the organization, is seen daily in all types of "public relations" activities, ranging from luncheon club speeches to house organs. It is part of an educational requirement in a complicated society where devious interdependence hides many of the functions of organized, specialized activities.

GOAL-SETTING AND STRATEGY

We have suggested that it is improbable that an organization can continue indefinitely if its goals are formulated arbitrarily, without cognizance of its relations to the environment. One of the requirements for survival appears to be ability to learn about the environment accurately enough and quickly enough to permit organizational adjustments in time to avoid extinction. In a more positive vein, it becomes important for an organization to judge the amount and sources of support that can be mobilized for a goal, and to arrive at a strategy for their mobilization.

[17] Milton Greenblatt, Richard H. York, and Esther Lucille Brown, *From Custodial to Therapeutic Patient Care in Mental Hospitals*, New York: Russell Sage Foundation, 1955, Chapter 1, and Ohlin, *loc. cit.*

[18] For one example, see the Report of the Harvard Committee, *General Education in a Free Society*, Cambridge: Harvard University Press, 1945.

[19] America's civil air transport industry began in 1926 and eight years later carried 500,000 passengers. Yet it was testified in 1934 that half of the $120 million invested in airlines had been lost in spite of subsidies. See Jerome C. Hunsaker, *Aeronautics at the Mid-Century*, New Haven: Yale University Press, 1952, pp. 37–38. The case of Billy Mitchell was, of course, the landmark in the selling of military aviation.

[20] Ray E. Trussell, *Hunterdon Medical Center*, Cambridge: Harvard University Press (for the Commonwealth Fund), 1956, Chapter 3.

Competition, bargaining, co-optation, and coalition constitute procedures for gaining support from the organizational environment; the selection of one or more of these is a strategic problem. It is here that the element of rationality appears to become exceedingly important, for in the order treated above, these relational processes represent increasingly "costly" methods of gaining support in terms of decision-making power. The organization that adopts a strategy of competition when co-optation is called for may lose all opportunity to realize its goals, or may finally turn to co-optation or coalition at a higher "cost" than would have been necessary originally. On the other hand, an organization may lose part of its integrity, and therefore some of its potentiality, if it unnecessarily shares power in exchange for support. Hence the establishment *in the appropriate form* of interaction with the many relevant parts of its environment can be a major organizational consideration in a complex society.

This means, in effect, that the organization must be able to estimate the position of other relevant organizations and their willingness to enter into or alter relationships. Often, too, these matters must be determined or estimated without revealing one's own weaknesses, or even one's ultimate strength. It is necessary or advantageous, in other words, to have the consent or acquiescence of the other party, if a new relationship is to be established or an existing relationship altered. For this purpose organizational administrators often engage in what might be termed a *sounding out process.*[21]

The sounding out process can be illustrated by the problem of the boss with amorous designs on his secretary in an organization that taboos such relations. He must find some means of determining her willingness to alter the relationship, but he must do so without risking rebuff, for a showdown might come at the cost of his dignity or his office reputation, at the cost of losing her secretarial services, or in the extreme case at the cost of losing his own position. The "sophisticated" procedure is to create an ambiguous situation in which the secretary is forced to respond in one of two ways: (1) to ignore or tactfully counter, thereby clearly channeling the relationship back into an already existing pattern, or (2) to respond in a similarly ambiguous vein (if not in a positive one) indicating a receptiveness to further advances. It is important in the sounding out process that the situation be ambiguous for two reasons: (1) the secretary must not be able to "pin down" the boss with evidence if she rejects the idea, and (2) the situation must be far enough removed from normal to be noticeable to the secretary. The ambiguity of sounding out has the

---

[21] This section on the sounding out process is a modified version of a paper by James D. Thompson, William J. McEwen, and Frederick L. Bates, "Sounding Out as a Relating Process," read at the annual meeting of the Eastern Sociological Society, April, 1957.

further advantage to the participants that neither party alone is clearly responsible for initiating the change.

The situation described above illustrates a process that seems to explain many organizational as well as personal inter-action situations. In moving from one relationship to another between two or more organizations it is often necessary to leave a well defined situation and proceed through a period of deliberate ambiguity, to arrive at a new clear-cut relationship. In interaction over goal-setting problems, sounding out sometimes is done through a form of double-talk, wherein the parties refer to "hypothetical" enterprises and "hypothetical" situations, or in "diplomatic" language, which often serves the same purpose. In other cases, and perhaps more frequently, sounding out is done through the good offices of a third party. This occurs, apparently, where there has been no relationship in the past, or at the stage of negotiations where the parties have indicated intentions but are not willing to state their positions frankly. Here it becomes useful at times to find a discrete go-between who can be trusted with full information and who will seek an arrangement suitable to both parties.

CONCLUSION

In the complex modern society desired goals often require complex organizations. At the same time the desirability of goals and the appropriate division of labor among large organizations is less self-evident than in simpler, more homogeneous society. Purpose becomes a question to be decided rather than an obvious matter.

To the extent that behavior of organization members is oriented to questions of goals or purposes, a science of organization must attempt to understand and explain that behavior. We have suggested one classification scheme, based on decision-making, as potentially useful in analyzing organizational-environmental interaction with respect to goal-setting and we have attempted to illustrate some aspects of its utility. It is hoped that the suggested scheme encompasses questions of rationality or irrationality without presuming either.

Argument by example, however, is at best only a starting point for scientific understanding and for the collection of evidence. Two factors make organizational goal-setting in a complex society a "big" research topic: the multiplicity of large organizations of diverse type and the necessity of studying them in diachronic perspective. We hope that our discussion will encourage critical thinking and the sharing of observations about the subject.

Another Look at the

Executive-Board Relationship

James M. Senor

This paper seeks to examine a particular aspect of the relationship between boards of directors and executive directors of private social work
agencies. It notes the popular view in social work literature that regards
the relationship as a partnership, but suggests that this view is not valid,
that it is contradicted by the reality as well as the organizational theory
of the managerial level—the executive being subordinate to the higher
level control, the board of directors. While holding that the relation is not
one of partners, the author nonetheless submits several propositions descriptive of situations that permit the executive to maximize his power at
the expense of the board.

The literature dealing with the relationship between the board and
executive of private social work agencies describes it as a partnership in
administration, each—the executive and the board—bringing unique skills,
experience, and knowledge into the arena of administrative responsibility.
Typical of these descriptions is that of Ray Johns, who defines the relationship as one of co-equals in a common enterprise. "It is that of equal
partners. . . . It is not that of superior and subordinate; neither lay
nor professional workers are . . . superior to each other." [1] Hertel also
stresses that "modern social agency administration has come to mean
partnership." [2]

It is here suggested that, these descriptions notwithstanding, the rela-

---

[1] Ray Johns, *Executive Responsibility* (New York: Association Press, 1954), p. 221.
[2] Frank J. Hertel, "Administration Defined" in Florence Hollis, ed., *Some Dynamics
of Social Agency Administration* (New York: Family Service Association of America,
1945), p. 1. It is interesting to note that Hertel includes membership and staff as well
as executive and board in the partnership scheme (p. 5).

James M. Senor, "Another Look at the Executive-Board Relationship," *Social Work*,
8, April 1963, pp. 19–25. James M. Senor, M.S.S.A., is a doctoral candidate at the
Graduate School of Social Work, University of Pittsburgh. This is the summary of a
paper presented at a seminar at the University of Pittsburgh in November 1961.

tionship is not a partnership—how can it be? The board hires the executive and can fire him at any time. He has no corresponding authority over the board as a group or over any single one of its members, or even over those persons on echelons lower than the board such as, for example, members of committees and subcommittees. It is the board that adopts policy for the agency. However much or little the executive may participate in discussions on a policy, it is the board that finally must decide what it shall be.[3] And having been determined, it becomes the executive's obligation to carry the policy out. Whether he approves of it or not, he must put policy into practice and pass it on to the rest of the staff. His recourse, if his feelings are sufficiently strong, is to resign. Partnership implies equality; this is hardly a relationship of equals!

WHEN THE EXECUTIVE IS SUPERORDINATE

Even though the relationship is not one of equals, and even though the board by definition and function is dominant over the executive, there arise many situations when the reverse is true, when the executive is superordinate. The author is not here evaluating whether this is wise or foolish or good or bad for agency operation, or arguing against the view that there are times when effective practice requires the executive to be in ascendance. Whether the executive "ought" to be more in a power position with respect to the board does not enter into this consideration.

Personality factors of the administrator are also ruled out. It would not be unexpected for an agency head with a domineering personality to be more apt to move into the board's province, to become involved in "considerable usurpation of functions,"[4] to respond to his inner personal drives for power and prestige. But the propositions stated here do not examine the personality make-up of the executive. All that is intended is to explore variables that cause this increase of power[5] of the executive

[3] Talcott Parsons, *Structure and Process in Modern Society* (Glencoe, Ill.: The Free Press, 1960), p. 64. Parsons used the term "control mechanism" in describing a board of directors of a "typical private non-profit organization." He sees it as controlling the managerial level (executive director), while mediating the needs of the latter with those of the outside environment.

[4] Johns, *op. cit.*, p. 220. He acknowledges this development, but explains it as due to a *growth* of competence and expansion of the conception of the role of some professionals. This explanation is too kind. The writer of this article feels that growth of professional competence would exert the opposite effect, that is, a restraint by the executive not to violate the jurisdiction of the board. Furthermore, usurpation can be traced to, among other causes, personality dominance coupled with *lack* of professional discipline and competence, as well as to causes offered elsewhere in this paper.

[5] "Power" is described as possessing or exercising authority or influence. Terms such as "dominance," "superior," "superordinate," "ascendancy," and "control" are used interchangeably and as synonyms of power. They describe the position of the executive. Opposite descriptions such as "submissive," "subordinate," and "losing control" indicate the board's position in relation to the executive.

at the expense of the board. Stated as an inquiry, the problem is: What are some characteristics of the agency and of the board of directors that increase the power of the executive director at the expense of the board?

The propositions can be categorized as those based on (A) characteristics of the agency, and (B) characteristics of the board.

A. Those propositions classified by characteristics of the agency are:

1. The more "total" the institution, the more powerful the executive.

2. When the board loses physical, social, and verbal contact with the agency, and thus when its knowledge is based primarily on what the executive communicates, it becomes weaker with respect to the executive.

3. The more an agency staff supports the executive, the stronger he is with respect to the board.

4. The more an agency program requires a highly technical staff for implementation, the more dominant is the executive.

B. Those propositions classified by characteristics of the board are:

1. The greater the latent role conflict among board members, the easier it is for the executive to increase his power.

2. The more the board members seek or expect allocations from the agency or the community in terms of individual awards, honorary titles, and other acts of distinction creation, the more the executive holds a pivotal position of power.

THE ISOLATED BOARD

The more total the institution, the more powerful the executive. A total institution has been described as having four central features:

> *First,* all aspects of life are conducted in the same place and under the same single authority. *Second,* each phase of the member's daily activity will be carried out in the immediate company of a large batch of others, all of whom are treated alike and required to do the same thing together. *Third,* all phases of the day's activities are tightly scheduled . . . [and] imposed from above through a system of explicit formal rulings. . . . *Finally,* the contents of the various enforced activities are brought together as parts of a single over-all rational plan purportedly designed to fulfill the official aims of the institution.[6]

Among private "total" institutions are TB sanatoria, homes for the blind, and rehabilitation centers for disturbed and delinquent juveniles. Other examples are prisons and mental hospitals.

[6] Erving Goffman, "The Characteristics of Total Institutions," in Amitai Etzioni, ed., *Complex Organizations: A Sociological Reader* (New York: Holt, Rinehart and Winston, 1961), pp. 313–314.

The features quoted above have pertinent consequences for members of the board of directors in at least three ways. First, because of the nature of activities and the fact that all aspects of living occur in the same place, the total institution is physically isolated from its environment; this isolation is not only from that part of the environment which provides the wherewithal the agency needs to operate—staff, funds, clients, and so on—but also from the portion that determines its policies and is ultimately responsible for its administration and operation—the board of directors.

Second, because of the nature of the activities, aims, and functions of the institution, it is highly unlikely that a board member or someone in his family would become an inmate; for the same reasons it is improbable that inmates would be of the same social circle as the board member. Being out of physical and social contact, not having a friend or relative in the agency, not likely himself to be a client—these situations forced on the board member by the features of the total institution stand in sharp contrast to the situation of the board member in nontotal agencies. In many of the latter members of the board are participating members of the program. The health clubs, hobby groups, and art classes of YMCA's, Jewish community centers, adult education organizations, and other group work, recreation, and informal education agencies attract a high percentage of board members. Their children often participate in scout movements and in agency summer camps.[7]

It is not unusual for social acquaintances of board members to seek services in family counseling, child adoption, planned parenthood, and similar organizations. Thus, through direct participation, firsthand contact by visits to the programs, and reports of family and friends, the board member can know what is going on in the agency, what its operational problems are, how recipients of services (or their families) feel about them, how policy affects practice, whether administration is efficient or inefficient. Furthermore, since the executive knows the board member is informed or can find out about these matters, he tends to be more solicitous of the board member's approval and is sensitive to his reactions and evaluations. Thus, he reports often to the board members, officially and informally, so that his interpretation of events in and affairs of the organization will be known to them.

Isolated from and out of contact with a total institution, the board of directors leaves the operation more completely in the hands of the executive. Board members stay away, take a "hands off" attitude. Information

---

[7] In a large community center for which the author worked nearly every person serving on the agency's branch operating committee or a member of his family took part in center activities. The same was true for over half the members of the central board of directors. This is not uncommon, especially in group service agencies serving the upper-lower, middle, and lower-upper economic classes.

regarding what goes on in the total institution comes to them via reports by the executive. They know only what he tells them. He controls channels of communication and they do not have the other sources of information so common in nontotal agencies.

Should a board member pay a visit to the total institution, hoping to obtain a firsthand account, he would find it difficult to do so. This is the third result of the consequences of the characteristics as described by Goffman. The schedule is rigid, "with one activity leading at a pre-arranged time into the next, the whole circle of activities being imposed from above through a system of . . . formal rulings." [8] The way of life of the residents would be so routinized and foreign to him that the board member could not obtain a real "feel" of the place, know what it is like to be a client, or be aware of the agency's operational problems.

Hence, because of the consequences of the characteristics of the total institution, the board members are on the "outside," out of touch and uninformed, and the executive is in control. Even matters of policy interpretation tend to be more in the hands of the executive here than they are in a nontotal organization. It is more difficult to contact or call board members together for an interpretation and, besides, the executive is far more familiar with the agency's problems.

A corollary proposition regarding nontotal institutions can be drawn from the above discussion. Situations arise in which members of the board lose physical, social, and verbal contact with the agency, do not or cannot participate in the program, and are not aware of what is taking place. Their knowledge of the agency is based on what the executive tells them. This state of affairs can develop through lack of interest by the members of the board, absentee board membership, deterioration to low status by the agency, or a variety of other reasons. Whatever the reasons may be, however, the proposition submitted is that, when such a situation develops, *when the board loses physical, social, and verbal contact with the agency, and thus when its knowledge is based primarily on what the executive communicates, it becomes weaker with respect to the executive.*

EXECUTIVE-STAFF SOLIDARITY

The more an agency staff supports the executive, the stronger he is with respect to the board. In an agency in which the staff is in sympathy with and behind the executive, the latter is in a strategic position in his relations with the board members. He can more easily resist their changes and innovations and thwart policy decisions. Opposition probably would not be open. An executive could appear to comply, but could "pass the word along" to staff that he does not favor the change or the new policy.

[8] Goffman, *op. cit.*, p. 314.

With their co-operation through covert resistance, implementation of the Board's decision could be delayed or defeated altogether.[9]

Executive and staff solidarity against the board may strengthen the executive in yet another manner, namely, by his being able to defend his special interests and keep his mistakes or weaknesses from coming to the attention of the board. Commentators on bureaucracy have observed the effect of staff protecting each other, "covering up," and presenting a united front against outside forces (clients, policy-making group, public). In discussing bureaucracy, Merton noted the tendency of bureaucrats to stick together and the consequences therefrom.

> Functionaries have a sense of common destiny for all those who work together. They share the same interests, especially since there is relatively little competition. . . . In-group aggression is minimized. . . . The *esprit de corps* and informal social organization which typically develops in such situations often leads the personnel to defend their entrenched interests rather than to assist their clientele and elected higher officials.[10]

While Merton and Lowell were referring to a public bureaucracy, the elected officials of such are usually the policy-making group, and would correspond to the board of directors of a private agency. The same situation can exist in a private agency; the proposition is therefore submitted that the more an agency's staff supports the executive, the stronger he is with respect to the board.

CONTROLLING COMMUNICATION

The more an agency's program requires a highly technical staff for implementation, the more dominant is the executive. Increased control by the executive comes about (1) through his almost complete control of the channels of communication between board and staff and (2) through his being part of a particular profession and affiliated with a professional association.

Board members have negligible contact with the program or staff of an agency whose service is highly technical and whose staff must be

---

[9] Lawrence Lowell, in *The Government of England*, Vol. 1 (New York: The Macmillan Co., 1910), p. 179, noted how the staff and permanent undersecretary (administrator) of a ministry can control the incoming elected minister (who represents the policy-making group). By withholding information, putting blocks in his way, and frightening him with predictions of embarrassing developments arising from contemplated action, the staff and undersecretary were able to thwart plans for change.

[10] Robert K. Merton, *Social Theory and Social Structure* (Glencoe, Ill.: The Free Press, 1957), p. 201.

professionally trained in a highly specialized field. Unless a member of the board is also trained in this technical discipline, he cannot comprehend the day-to-day functioning of the organization. With regard to agency business, he probably does not speak the language of the practitioner and has no occasion to communicate with him as he would in the types of nontotal institutions referred to earlier. Even if the board member is competent in this or an allied discipline, professional ethics would keep him aloof. For example, a medical man on the board of a psychiatric or rehabilitative organization would remain distant from the program and refrain from discussing matters with the staff (unless he were called explicitly on a consultative basis). Doctors, and other professionals as well, have an unwritten rule not to get involved in cases in which the patient is not theirs.

Communication of staff to board and board to staff is controlled by the executive. Each can speak to the other only through him. The situation is akin to an hourglass, with the executive controlling the waist.

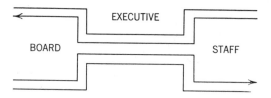

This point, and the power possibilities it holds for the administrator, has been well illustrated by Hawkes in his description of executive-staff-board relationships in a psychiatric hospital. In discussing the role of the administrator, he says:

> . . . the fact that this role is linked by implicit contract to both sections also creates the possibility of increased power and control. The mental hospital administrator is able to exert control over each of the two important groups, because to each he is the only representative and main spokesman of the other one.[11]

Putting it inversely, Hawkes adds:

> It is safe to generalize that to the extent that the administrator allows or encourages communication between the two groups to that extent he loses power and control both inside and outside the hospital organization.[12]

[11] Robert W. Hawkes, "Role of the Psychiatric Administrator," *Administrative Science Quarterly*, Vol. 6, No. 1 (June 1961), p. 101.
[12] *Ibid.*, p. 104.

Superiority based on technical knowledge has been described also in the field of education.

> The principal comes to the board meeting as a technical expert and as the day-to-day administrator of board policies. As the day-to-day administrator of policy and as an expert, he enjoys a tactical advantage over the board members who are concerned with education only once a month.[13]

Identification of the executive with the particular profession tied into the agency's services also tends to bear out this proposition. If, as is often the case, the executive is trained in the same professional discipline as the staff, his dominance over them (as a professional colleague) becomes greater and the board's sway over the staff more remote. This comes about through the influence of the professional standards on which the executive is knowledgeable. In both these areas the board members, being laymen, are on the outside.

Thompson and Bates, in their discussion of technology and administration, have observed that technological development "is accompanied by the proliferation of professional and technical societies and associations, each with its unique values and codes of ethics," which can command the allegiance of the professional. They further note that in a highly technical organization there is

> . . . greater opportunity for the demands of the organization to conflict with those of the profession, and at the same time a greater opportunity for the individual employee to enforce demands on the organization by invoking sanctions from the profession.[14]

This observation has pertinence for the above proposition. An executive (also an employee of the board) who is a professionally trained technician working in a specialized social work agency can use the power of ethics and values of the profession and the authority of standards of the professional association against the board should there be conflict over technical matters. For example, a board could hardly deny the request of an administrator of a psychiatric agency that a section of a building be razed, expensive equipment purchased, or major routines of long standing changed if these were recommended in the name of "adequate health and safety standards."

[13] Arthur J. Vidich and Joseph Bensman, *Small Town in Mass Society* (Princeton, N.J.: Princeton University Press, 1958), p. 192.
[14] James D. Thompson and F. Bates, "Technology, Organization and Administration," in James D. Thompson *et al.*, eds., *Comparative Studies in Administration* (Pittsburgh, Pa.: University of Pittsburgh Press, 1959), p. 180.

In short, the character of an agency whose program requires a highly trained staff for implementation has "built-in" elements that can permit increased exercise of power by the executive over the board of directors.

ROLE OF BOARD MEMBERS

The greater the latent role conflict among board members, the easier it is for the executive to increase his power. As pointed out by Thompson, latent role conflict is present in various types of organizations; people carry to their jobs beliefs, attitudes, and values irrelevant to the task or purpose that brings about their association with an organization.[15] Individuals differ in politics, ancestry, social habits, economic class, ethnic identification, religious affiliation, and many other characteristics. Although Thompson was discussing these roles with regard to members of ideological organizations or technicians in industry, the army, and the like, the author submits that they exist as well at the board level. And just as latent role distinctions can "spill over" into official roles in technologies, they can become manifest among board members and result in conflict. When this happens, the board becomes divided and it is not unexpected when the competing elements seek the support of the executive. Hence, his power is heightened at the board's expense.[16]

The more the board members seek or expect allocations from the agency or community in terms of individual awards, honorary titles, and other acts of distinction creation, the more the executive holds a pivotal position of power. Honorary titles are bestowed by many agencies, usually to senior board members with many years of voluntary service. Other occasions exist in agency affairs when granting an award is in order. The completion of a fund-raising campaign, the end of a term of office by a president, dedicating a new part of a building made possible by a generous donation, the anniversary of election to the board of an older member are illustrations of such occasions.

Shall an award be made, a title bestowed, a gift given? If so, to whom and of what nature? If the allocations are not customary, these questions must be answered, and the view of the administrator is crucial. He is considered neutral and is invariably consulted. His opinions, direct or

[15] James D. Thompson, "Organizational Management of Conflict," *Administrative Science Quarterly,* Vol. 4, No. 4 (March 1960), p. 393.
[16] The author worked in and lived through such a situation. Latent role conflicts smoldered, then burst out over internal board differences on the purposes, program, and posture of a community organization social work agency. Conflict was so intense that it carried into activities outside the organization. Friendships were affected and life in other organizations to which competing board members belonged was disrupted. As a noncommitted neutral, the executive was "sought" by both sides, was a rallying and consolidation point, and had power and influence not ordinarily possessed in situations when latent role conflict had not erupted.

indirect, as to whether someone should receive a title, award, or the like carry much weight. Moreover, it is not unusual for the executive to be the initiator of such sought-after agency allocations.[17] For these reasons and others, board members seek to remain in his "good graces." Consciously or not, they realize his power to influence the granting or withholding of acts of distinction creation, and this tends to increase his influence in other areas of their relationship with him.

SUMMARY

Several characteristics of private social work agencies and their boards have been examined in terms of how they tend to increase the power and influence of the executive director over the board of directors in the hope of focusing attention on factors that shape the relationship between them. These do not exhaust the list of agency and board characteristics, nor do they touch on characteristics of other segments of the agency—staff, the executive himself, clientele, community—that tend to emphasize this trend of dominance, nor have qualities been scrutinized that bring about the opposite effect—overdominance of the board with respect to the executive.

Since the partnership theory does not seem to be realistic, it appears that identifying and examining the many characteristics of agency board, staff, executive, and so on, as well as focusing on the nature of power and organizational variables in our society, generally would bring to light more sharply what the executive-board relationship is, what the consequences of various types of relationships are, and what the respective parties need to do and be aware of to approach the preferred relationship. In view of this, further studies of characteristics and their effects would seem to be in order.

[17] Harleigh B. Trecker, *New Understandings of Administration* (New York: Association Press, 1950), p. 173. As Trecker has pointed out, "The executive has a role in board and committee formulation and composition." This includes suggesting persons for nomination and renomination to the board and for appointment to chairmanship and membership positions on committees. Further, the administrator is a status source and object in most social agencies, and status accrues from being associated with him within and outside agency activities.

The Regime of the Custodians

Gresham M. Sykes

To say that man is a social animal is also to say that man never lives in a world completely of his own choosing. He is always confronted with the fact that there are others who attempt to make him conform to rules and procedures and he must somehow come to grips with these external demands. He may accept them in whole or in part, turning them into demands which he places on himself, or he may reject them and try to avoid the consequences; yet he can never completely ignore them.

Our concern now is with the social order which the custodians of the New Jersey State Prison attempt to impose on their captives—the massive body of regulations which is erected as a blueprint for behavior within the prison and to which the inmate must respond. This social order (not yet a reality but a statement of what should be) represents a means, a method of achieving certain goals or accomplishing certain tasks; and, as we have pointed out before, the nature of this social order becomes clear only when we understand the ends it is supposed to serve. We will find, however, that the relationships between means and ends in prison are far from simple.

We have indicated that the prison is an instrument of the State, an organization designed to accomplish the desires of society with respect to the convicted criminal. But such a statement is, after all, only an analogy and we must not view the prison as a machine which simply and automatically translates the dictates of society into action. The tasks assigned to the prison must be given priorities; general social objectives must be transformed into specific organizational aims; assumptions must be made about the nature of the criminal and his reactions to confinement; and the limitations placed by society on what the prison can do in pursuit of its mission must be taken into account. In short, the regime which the custodians struggle to impose on the inmate population may indeed be a

---

Gresham M. Sykes, "The Regime of the Custodians," *The Society of Captives,* Princeton University Press, Princeton, 1958, pp. 13–40.

means of fulfilling the objectives allotted by the larger social order and only becomes explicable in light of these objectives. But the rules and routines of the prison officials represent a choice among alternative means and we must examine the basis of this choice as well as the objectives themselves.

II

It is true that keeping criminals confined can be agreed on as a necessary measure, whether retribution, deterrence, or reform is taken as the only proper aim of imprisonment. Being held in custody can, as I have indicated, be viewed as a means of paying back the offender, a method of discouraging the actual or potential criminal, or a device for maintaining access to the patient. Beyond this point, however, the translation of general social tasks into specific organizational procedures runs into difficulties.

First, there is the question of precisely what steps must be taken to insure custody. The difficulties of holding men against their will are commonly recognized, it is true, and as James V. Bennett, Director of the Federal Bureau of Prisons, has pointed out:

> When one takes into consideration the antiquity of most prisons, the flimsiness of some prison structures, the Rube Goldberg character of the locking devices, the hit or miss standards used in selecting men for "trusty" assignments, the extent of overcrowding, personnel shortages, and the increasingly more desperate character of the offender, there are few enough escapes.[1]

But there are many critics who believe that far too great an emphasis is placed on custody and that the many measures used to prevent escapes constitute a backward, irrational ritual. Those who stress custody are, from this point of view, typical examples of the "bureaucratic personality," individuals who have elevated a means to the status of an end,[2] and custodial routines are simply the residue of a punitive orientation toward the criminal, the contaminated man. The endless precautions, the constant counting of the inmate population, the myriad regulations, the institutionalized suspicion of the periodic searches—these, it is held, are the expression of groundless fears and hatreds rather than reason. Criticism is not actually directed against custody per se but against precautions to prevent escapes which are carried too far; and in solving this problem,

[1] James V. Bennett, "Evaluating a Prison," *The Annals of the American Academy of Political and Social Science,* Vol. 293, May 1954, p. 11.
[2] Robert K. Merton, "Bureaucratic Structure and Personality," in *Social Theory and Social Structure,* Glencoe, Ill.: The Free Press, 1949.

prison officials responsible for the security of the institution may find themselves cast willy-nilly into the role of offering bullheaded opposition to progress in penal methods.[3]

Second, there is the question of the standard of living which is to be accorded the prisoner. Those who hold that retribution or deterrence should be the primary task of the prison are inclined to believe that the mere loss of liberty is insufficiently painful to accomplish these ends. The inmate must be made to suffer within the walls, not through the use of the thumbscrew, the rack, or the starvation diet which have been barred as forms of cruel and unusual punishment since the 18th Century, but by a series of deprivations which will clearly demonstrate the advantages of remaining within the law or which will underline the condemnation of criminal behavior. Those, however, who hold that reformation is the major aim of imprisonment—who feel that if the custodial institution fails to reform it fails altogether—are apt to argue that such additional penalties present an insuperable barrier to therapy. Repression within the prison simply breeds new antagonisms, creating a situation which is almost completely antithetical to modern concepts of psychiatric care. This viewpoint receives additional support from those who would make life in prison less painful or frustrating on humanitarian grounds alone, regardless of whether or not a more "permissive" and "supportive" atmosphere advances or hinders the work of rehabilitation.

Third, men in the maximum security prison must somehow be supported and the traditional solution has been that inmates should support themselves as far as possible. Yet this raises a number of difficult issues, for the solution has been an uneasy one: The State views the labor of prisoners with deep ambivalence. The criminal in the custodial institution is in a position somewhat like that of a wayward son who is forced to work by a stern father. The troublesome youth may not earn his keep, but at least he is to be employed at honest labor; and if his earnings make up only a portion of his expenses, that is better than nothing at all. It should not surprise us if the parent in our simile is motivated by a curious blend of economic self-interest, faith in the efficacy of work as a means of spiritual salvation, and a basic, hostile feeling that no man should escape the burden of supporting himself by the sweat of his brow. Similar forces are perhaps at work when society demands that the custodial institution take on the appearance of a self-sustaining community. The organization of the inmate population into a labor force capable of supporting itself may, however, create serious custodial problems—in addition to

---

[3] The argument is often intensified by the fact that in the prison those charged with the duty of custody and those given the duty of reforming the criminal are frequently drawn from widely different social, economic and intellectual backgrounds and possess disparate degrees of experience in custodial institutions.

eliciting cries of outrage from private enterprise in the free community.[4] Strict concern for custody or a view of work as part of the criminal's punishment can destroy a program of efficient production. And using work as a means of resocializing the adult offender may be diametrically opposed to both economic and custodial considerations.

A fourth problem in accommodating the multiple tasks assigned the prison revolves around the issue of internal order. If a prisoner in solitary confinement smashes his head against the wall, it is an individual madness; if he refuses to eat or bathe himself, his rebellion stops short with the limits of his cell. In the maximum security prison, however, the maintenance of order is far more complex than the restraint of self-destructive impulses or isolated gestures of protest. The freedom of the prisoner, whether it is granted in the name of humanity, economic efficiency, or reformation, and limited though it may be, creates a situation in which crimes among inmates are possible. Theft, murder, fraud, sodomy—all exist as possible acts of deviance within the prison and the custodians have the duty of preventing them from being converted into realities. As in the case of custody, however, difficulties arise at two points. First there is the question of the specific measures which must be taken to insure the maintenance of order; and second there is the question of the value or priority to be attached to the maintenance of order as opposed to possibly competing objectives. If extensive regulations, constant surveillance, and swift reprisals are used, prison officials are likely to run headlong into the supporters of reform who argue that such procedures are basically inimical to the doctor-patient relationship which should serve as the model for therapy.

Finally, there is the question of just what should be done to reform the captive criminal. Of all the tasks which the prison is called upon to perform, none is more ambiguous than the task of changing criminals into noncriminals. The goal itself is far from clear and even when agreement can be reached on this point, as we have mentioned before, the means to achieve it remain uncertain.

The administrator of the maximum security prison, then, finds himself confronted with a set of social expectations which pose numerous dilemmas when an attempt is made to translate them into a concrete, rational policy. Somehow he must resolve the claims that the prison should exact vengeance, erect a specter to terrify the actual or potential deviant, isolate the known offender from the free community, and effect a change in the personality of his captives so that they gladly follow the dictates of the law—and in addition maintain order within his society of prisoners and see that they are employed at useful labor. If the policy of the prison

[4] For an illuminating discussion of prison labor, see Edwin H. Sutherland, *Principles of Criminology* (revised by Donald R. Cressey), New York: J. B. Lippincott Company, 1955, Chapter Twenty-Five.

sometimes seems to exhibit a certain inconsistency, we might do well to look at the inconsistency of the philosophical setting in which the prison rests. In any event, let us examine the resolution of these problems as they are expressed in the regime which the officials of the New Jersey State Maximum Security Prison attempt to impose on their captives.

III

THE TASK OF CUSTODY

There seems little doubt that the task of custody looms largest in the eyes of the officials of the New Jersey State Prison and in this they differ but little from most if not all of the administrators who are charged with the responsibility for maximum security institutions in the United States. The prison exists as a dramatic symbol of society's desire to segregate the criminal, whatever reasons may lie behind that desire; and the prison wall, that line between the pure and impure, has all the emotional over-tones of a woman's maidenhead. One escape from the maximum security prison is sufficient to arouse public opinion to a fever pitch and an or-ganization which stands or falls on a single case moves with under-standable caution. The officials, in short, know on which side their bread is buttered. Their continued employment is tied up with the successful performance of custody and if society is not sure of the priority to be attached to the tasks assigned the prison, the overriding importance of custody is perfectly clear to the officials.

If the wall and its guards were sufficient to prevent escapes, the task of custody in the New Jersey State Prison would be made relatively simple. In fact, however, these barriers are effective only because of a wide variety of security measures which must be carried out deep within the prison itself. The 20-foot climb and the pointing guns are hazards, but they are not insurmountable if the prisoner can effect a happy juxta-position of materials, time, place, and events. A ladder constructed of dental floss which can be hidden in the palm of one hand; a fight in another part of the prison to serve as a momentary diversion; the prisoner waiting in the exercise yard for the welcome cover of darkness; a prison uniform stripped of its distinguishing marks to serve as civilian dress— these are the preparations for escape which must be detected long before the final dash for freedom occurs. To the prison officials, then, the guards on the wall form the last line of the institution's defenses, not the first, and they fight their battle at the center of their position rather than at its perimeter.

But are the custodians and their captives really locked in such combat? Is there a touch of something akin to paranoia in the ceaseless precau-tions of the officials? Certainly there is no convincing proof that the majority of the imprisoned criminals are bent on flight. In fact, the prison officials are convinced that only a few restraints are needed to persuade many of their prisoners from attempting to escape. The officials are aware that there are psychological walls surrounding their community—such as the threat of being a hunted man or the imminence of parole—which are more powerful than those of stone for many men. Nearly 55 percent of the inmates in the institution can look forward to being released within two years after their arrival and 85 percent will be discharged within four years; a precarious freedom won by a dangerous escape may make the game seem hardly worth the candle. Yet at the same time the officials of the prison are convinced that *some* inmates—an unknown number—will seize the slightest opportunity to break out of the institution and that in dealing with these men a moment's inattention is an invitation to disaster. Since hardly a year goes by without the detection of an attempted escape, the suspicions of the officials are far from groundless. The plan may be discovered in its earlier phase—as when a half-finished tunnel was found under the floor of an industrial shop—or aborted only at the last moment—as when a prisoner was killed by the guards on top of the laundry after he had escaped from the death house where he awaited his execution in the electric chair. But whether uncovered soon or late, the attempts to escape occur with sufficient frequency to persuade the officials that their security measures are not the foolish gestures of an old woman looking under the bed for the thief who is never there.

Unfortunately, the prison officials can predict only in the grossest fashion *which* of their captives will try to elude them, however certain they may be that some will do so. It is true that there are a few prisoners who can clearly be labelled "security risks"—men so intransigent in their dislike of imprisonment that no plot is too daring, no risk too great, if the goal is freedom. These are the *escape artists* in the argot of the inmates and in another social situation (a prisoner-of-war camp for example) such men often serve as symbols of indomitable courage. But the guards of New Jersey State Prison can rarely allow themselves the luxury of abstracting personal qualities from the context in which they are exhibited. The few criminals who will certainly try to escape are simply viewed as the identifiable nucleus of a larger, ill-defined body of rash prisoners who might attempt to escape under favorable circumstances. The custodians, then, face a population of prisoners requiring various degrees of surveillance and control, ranging from the utmost vigilance to perhaps none at all. Their difficulty is that with the exception of a handful of *escape artists* they have no dependable way of distinguishing the requirements of one man from another. In the light of the public uproar which follows close on the heels of an escape from prison, it is not surprising that the prison officials have chosen the course of treating all inmates as if they were equally serious threats to the task of custody; stringent security measures are imposed on the entire inmate population with the full realization that much of the effort may be unnecessary.

Searching cells for contraband material; repeatedly counting all inmates to insure that each man is in his appointed place; censoring mail for evidence of escape plans; inspecting bars, windows, gratings, and other possible escape routes—all are obvious precautions. The custodians, however, do not stop with these, for they have found to their bitter knowledge that in a maximum security prison the most innocent-appearing activity may be a symptom of a major breach in the institution's defenses. Pepper stolen from the mess-hall may be used as a weapon, to be thrown in the eyes of a guard during a bid for freedom. A prisoner growing a moustache may be acquiring a disguise to help him elude the police once he has gotten on the other side of the wall. Extra electrical fixtures in a cell can cause a blown fuse in a moment of crisis. A fresh coat of paint in a cell may be used by an industrious prisoner to cover up his handiwork when he has cut the bars and replaced the filings with putty.

All of these seemingly innocent acts and many more like them are prohibited, therefore, by the regulations of the prison. If it is argued that such security measures are based on relatively rare events, the officials can only agree. They will add, however, that prisoners are ingenious in devising ways to escape and it is the duty of the officials to prevent escapes from occurring. If it is argued that the elaborate system of regulations which is established in the name of custody must prove irksome to the prisoner who has never contemplated escape—well, the Army has a classic expression for such situations.

THE TASK OF INTERNAL ORDER

If custody is elevated to the first rank in the list of tasks to be accomplished by the prison, the objective of maintaining internal order is a close second. And it must be admitted that under the best of circumstances the maintenance of order among a group of men such as those who are confined in the New Jersey State Prison would present formidable problems. A committee appointed by Governor Alfred E. Driscoll in 1952 to investigate the prison noted that the institution has long served as a dumping ground or catch basin for the state's entire correctional system; and in their report the committee stated that

> . . . the inmate population of Trenton Prison included, in addition to the "ordinary" prisoners who constitute the majority of the population, insane and near-insane, mental defectives, unstable psychopaths, some

of them highly assaultive, prisoners convicted as sexual psychopaths, passive homosexuals, aggressive "wolves" with long records of fights and stabbings, escape artists, agitators, and "incorrigibles" of all ages.[5]

Whatever may be the personal traits possessed by these men which helped bring them to the institution, it is certain that the conditions of prison life itself create strong pressures pointed toward behavior defined as criminal in the free community. Subjected to prolonged material deprivation, lacking heterosexual relationships, and rubbed raw by the irritants of life under compression, the inmate population is pushed in the direction of deviation from, rather than adherence to, the legal norms. The nature and the consequences of the deprivations and frustrations of existence in the custodial institution will be a major concern in later chapters; at this point it is enough to point out that the custodians' task of maintaining order within the prison is acerbated by the conditions of life which it is their duty to impose on their captives. The prison official, then, is caught up in a vicious circle where he must suppress the very activity that he helps cause. It is not surprising that he should overlook his part in the process, that he should tend to view the prisoner as innately vicious or depraved. The conduct of the inmate is used to justify further repressive measures and the antagonisms between the guard and his prisoner spiral upward.

In addition to their responsibility for enforcing the laws of the free community (such as the prohibitions against murder, assault, theft, homosexuality, etc.), the custodians demand, obedience to an extensive body of regulations peculiar to the prison alone. Many of these rules are theoretically intended to curb behavior which might endanger custody, but there remains a set of regulations intended to promote "quiet," "peaceful," or "orderly" relationships within the New Jersey State Prison, according to the custodians. When we examine these rules we cannot help but be struck by their apparent pettiness and perhaps a few illustrations will make my point clear. The following are taken from the *Handbook for Inmates*, issued to each prisoner on his arrival:

> When the bell rings for meals, work, or other assignment, turn out your light, see that your water is turned off, and step out of your cell promptly.

> Form by twos when passing through the Center. Keep your place in line unless you are ordered to step out.

> When walking in line maintain a good posture. Face forward and keep your hands out of your pockets.

[5] New Jersey Committee to Examine and Investigate the Prison and Parole Systems of New Jersey, *Report*, November 21, 1952.

On returning to your Wing, go directly to your cell, open the door, step in, and close the door without slamming it.

Gambling in any form is not allowed.

Do not speak or make any gestures to persons who are visiting the institution.

Such regimentation has long been a focus of attack for the critics of penal institutions and a number of writers would argue, along with the authors of a recent textbook on criminology, that "many such asinine injunctions could be eliminated immediately." [6] Certainly a regime which involves such detailed regulations is distasteful from the viewpoint of democratic values, but before we condemn the prison officials as oppressors, who allow rules to grow through sheer stupidity or a willful disregard for man's dignity, let us examine their position.

First, there is the question of the nature and extent of the disorder which would arise within the prison if the custodians did not exercise strict supervision and control over the activities of the inmates. There are few who will claim that in the complete absence of supervision and control the inmate population would live harmoniously within the walls of their prison. Rather, criticism has been directed against the apparent triviality of many regulations which seem to have no other purpose than the domination of the prisoner for the sake of domination alone. Why, for example, must inmates pass two by two through the Center? Why must inmates go directly to their cells on returning to the Wing? The answer of the custodians is plain: They are few and the inmates are many. A moment's escape from surveillance provides the prisoner with an opportunity to perform a variety of serious illegal acts. What is innocent now may prove dangerous later—as when a route of exchange for cigarettes becomes a route of exchange for weapons. Gambling may lead to unpaid debts, unpaid debts may lead to a knifing. In brief, say the custodians, the maximum security prison is not a Boy Scout camp and do not ask us to treat it as if it were. We are dealing with men inured to violence and other forms of anti-social behavior and order can be maintained only if we establish rules which eliminate the situations in which such behavior can arise.

Second, there is the question of the value of order within the prison as opposed to the value of the individual's freedom from rigid supervision and control. In this matter the New Jersey State Prison differs sharply from the free community which rarely prohibits acts that *may* lead to harmful consequences. Outside the walls a certain amount of harmful or illegal behavior is taken as the inevitable and, in a sense, acceptable

[6] Harry Elmer Barnes and Negley K. Teeters, *New Horizons in Criminology*, New York: Prentice-Hall, Inc., 1952, pp. 438–439.

consequence of individual freedom. The social cost of eliminating deviance or reducing deviance to a minimum is held to be greater than the social cost of the deviance itself. In the prison, however, a different calculation is at work —the assurance of order is regarded as worth the price paid in terms of the inmate's subjugation to detailed regulations. The reason for this critical reversal of values is much the same as in the case of custody: Public reactions to "disturbances" within the prison make it abundantly clear that such events are to be avoided at all costs.

It is quite possible that the custodians overestimate the amount of disorder which would occur in the absence of rigid controls reaching far into what seem to be irrelevant areas of life. And, possibly, the price paid for eliminating disorder is far too high. One is a question of fact and the other is a question of value, but the prison official is neither a scientist free to experiment nor a philosopher. In the regime of the custodians of the New Jersey State Maximum Security Prison, the dilemma between a permissive social atmosphere and internal order has been resolved in favor of the latter.

THE TASK OF SELF-MAINTENANCE

In giving precedence to the tasks of custody and the maintenance of order, the officials of the New Jersey State Prison move in the direction of ever greater control of their captives. The prisoner is, in a sense, sacrificed to these objectives and the prevention of escapes and disturbances within the walls is purchased by means of the inmate's autonomy. There are only a few to mourn his loss and if the prisoner himself complains, he is apt to be ignored on the grounds that a man who has committed a crime has given up the rights of the free individual. He is, after all, it is said, a man who is supposed to be undergoing punishment and it is argued that a permissive or supportive atmosphere for the prisoner—demanded on the grounds of reformation or humanitarianism—must be forfeited for more important concerns. When it comes to the isue of penal labor, however, the custodians face a knottier problem. The efficient use of inmate labor in the production of goods and services also requires a more permissive or supportive atmosphere for the prisoner, if only in the sense that some attention must be paid to the opinions, attitudes, and desires of the inmate in order to motivate him to work. And the efficient use of inmate labor is not thrust aside without serious repercussions.

Now it is true that the New Jersey State Prison does not produce goods or services for the market which are equal in value to the cost of the institution's operation; a variety of social and economic interests prohibit the products of prison labor from entering into direct competition with those of private enterprise.[7] And although the prison does manufac-

[7] See footnote 4.

ture articles (such as automobile license tags, clothing, office furniture, etc.) for the use of other institutions and agencies of the state, the value of these products is far less than the sum required to support the prison. None the less, the production of goods for use by the state in these so-called State-Use industries is an important gesture in the direction of a self-sustaining community in terms of labor: Approximately one half of the inmates are thus employed. In addition, the inmate population is required to perform the many details of institutional housekeeping, as we have mentioned before. As in every society, there are some men who cannot work and some men for whom no work can be found, together comprising a group—known as the Idle Men—approximately 300 in number. But the great majority of prisoners are employed in a variety of occupations in an enforced mimicry of the free community. The following presents a typical picture of work assignments in the New Jersey State Prison:

Work Assignment	Number of Inmates
Bakers	16
Band	18
Barbers	11
Center runners	3
Photographers	2
Commissary department	66
Engineer department	1
Garage	6
Hospital department	34
Ice plant	3
Industrial office	6
Industrial store room	4
Inmates' store	3
Laundry	19
Prison store room	21
Receiving gate	2
Repair department	52
Runners and helpers	66
School and library	6
Shipping platform	4
Print shop	23
Shoe shop	41
Machine shop	15
Tailor shop	108
Tag shop	60
Woodworking shop	25
Utility gang	12
Outside store room	3
Trucks	3

Work Assignment	Number of Inmates
Officers' personal service	11
Yard gang	22
Swill platform	3
Inside sanitary detail	3
Front house cleaners	4
Upholstery shop	27
Not capable of working	40
Unemployed	203
In quarantine	55
Sick in hospital	25

Whether prisoners labor as a duty, a privilege, an economic necessity, or as a cure, the fact that custodians and inmates are caught up in the complex of work has profound implications for the nature of imprisonment. In the first place, if inmates work they must have some freedom of movement and this provides an opportunity for interaction which would otherwise be lacking. In the second place, tools and materials must be provided, thus greatly broadening the resource base of this society of captives, if somehow the stream of goods flowing into the prison can be deflected from its legitimate channel. Unlike a community living in a harsh physical environment where no effort can overcome the stinginess of nature, the prisoners live in an environment made harsh by man-made decrees and only officialdom stands interposed between the inmates and many of the amenities of life as represented by institutional supplies. In the third place (and this is perhaps the most important of all) the fact that prisoners work carries with it the implication that the prison produces, that there is some result for the thousands of man-hours expended each day. To a large extent the prison officials are held responsible for the output of the inmate sand thus the custodians are drawn willy-nilly into the problems of an economic enterprise. The custodians cannot remain simply custodians, content to search a cell for contraband or to censor the mail; now they must manage men as well.[8]

To get prisoners to work is, however, a far different matter from preventing escapes or maintaining internal order. It is true that if prisoners refuse to work they can be placed in solitary confinement or deprived of a variety of privileges. And since an inmate's sentence is reduced by one day for each five days that he works, a refusal to work can lead to a loss of this so-called Work Time.[9] These threats in the background appear

[8] The task of organizing the labor of prisoners is shared with the officials in charge of State-Use Industries but the custodians must still be viewed as deeply enmeshed in a managerial role.

[9] The law of New Jersey stipulates that each prisoner may reduce the sentence he receives from the court by (a) earning one day per week for performing work assign-

to be sufficient to convince most of the inmate population that an out-right refusal to work is unwise, but at the same time they appear to be incapable of preventing more subtle forms of rebellion. Apathy, sabotage, and the show of effort rather than the substance—the traditional answers of the slave—rise in the prison to plague the custodian-manager and his limited means of coercion cannot prevent them from occurring.[10]

The inability of the prison officials to elicit *conscientious* performance from their captives is not due simply to the fact that theirs is an involuntary labor force, a group of men who have been recruited unwillingly and in whom a residual hostility remains. Of equal or greater importance is the fact that incentives for the prisoner are almost completely lacking within the context of captivity. The wages of the inmate are fixed by the State Board of Control within a range of 10 cents to 35 cents per day, depending on his assignment, and this munificence is hardly calculated to stir the inmate to heights of effort. The monotonous, unskilled nature of most jobs in the prison provides little intrinsic work satisfaction and the incentive of Work Time, like retirement benefits and other distant rewards of the free community, presents many drawbacks as a motivating force for here and now. There exists no hierarchy of power and responsibilities in the inmate labor force, since guards or civilian work supervisors exercise all supervision and control, thus eliminating the bait of promotion. Praise and recognition from the custodians for work well done have little value for the criminal in prison and the zealous prisoner must face the gibes and aggression of his fellow captives.

In attempting, then, to organize the inmate population into an efficient or conscientious working force—as opposed let us say, to a group of men who appear on the job and go through the motions—the custodians of the maximum security prison are confronted with a set of relatively unique administrative problems. The custodians, it is true, can push their prisoners into the semblance of work but beyond this point they move with difficulty. Unlike the masters of a concentration camp, the prison officials are barred from using extreme penalties, such as brute force or starvation, to extract high levels of effort. Unlike the managers of an industrial

---

ments conscientiously (Work Time); and (b) earning commutation of his sentence, up to 60 days during the first year of imprisonment and in increasing amounts for subsequent years, for orderly deportment and manifest efforts at self-control and improvement (Good Time). Cf. New Jersey Department of Institutions and Agencies, Research Bulletin No. 18 "Two Thousand State Prisoners in New Jersey," Trenton, New Jersey, May 1954.

[10] The prison officials are prohibited by law from physically forcing an inmate to work. In order to prevent inmates from refusing to work one day and agreeing to work the next (which might lead to serious disruptions in the scheduling of work activities) the officials have established a rule which asserts that any inmate who refuses to work must remain among the Idle Men for six months. Thus a refusal to work does not win a day of leisure to be traded for a fractional extension of one's sentence; rather, it entails a serious loss of Work Time and a prolonged period of enforced inactivity.

enterprise in the free community, they are denied the use of the common rewards of work incentives, such as meaningful monetary rewards or symbolic forms of recognition. The result tends to be a minimum of effort on the part of the prisoner—a form of inefficiency which is economically feasible only because the production of goods and services in the prison is but loosely linked to the discipline of the open market. Prisoners must be provided for, regardless of whether or not their own efforts are sufficient to win the means of subsistence. If the value of their work is small, they will be little affected, as long as they do not openly rebel. If the value of their work is large, they have no reason to look forward to increased benefits. The custodians, however, do not enjoy such a tolerance and they must pay attention to the output of the prison even if the prisoners do not; it is true that the prison will not go out of business, but the custodians may very well find themselves replaced.

In short, the officials of the New Jersey State Prison find themselves in the uncomfortable position of needing the labor of their captives far more than do the captives themselves; and at the same time the officials prohibit (and are prohibited from) the use of effective rewards and punishments to secure conscientious performance. When we add the burdens of security and internal order which make the simplest job cumbersome, through the need for surveillance and control, it is not surprising that the custodians find the task of making the prison an approximation of a self-sustaining community both difficult and discouraging.[11] With too many men for too few jobs, ham-strung by worn-out and outmoded machinery, lacking an adequate budget, under pressure from economic interests in the free community, and hampered by their own commitment to competing objectives, the officials of the New Jersey State Prison are in an unenviable position. It is in this light that we must interpret the scene encountered so often in the prison—a group of five or six inmates conversing or sleeping in the corner of an industrial shop or in a storeroom, unmolested by their guard. If the scene is a parody of the stereotype of penal servitude, it is the prisoners and not the custodians who find the situation humorous.

THE TASK OF PUNISHMENT

It is sometimes said that criminals are placed in prison not *for* punishment but *as* punishment;[12] presumably, stress is being placed on the

---

[11] The tasks of preventing escapes and maintaining internal order pose many problems for the efficient organization of work beyond those encountered on the job itself. The classification committee—which gives out work assignments within the prison—cannot afford to fill vacant jobs on the basis of the skills and experience of prisoners. Instead, they must pay primary attention to the opportunities offered by a particular job for "getting into trouble" and an inmate's record for violence, homosexuality, alcoholism, etc.

[12] See Sanford Bates, *Prisons and Beyond*, New York: The Macmillan Company, 1936.

idea that the officials of the custodial institution are determined not to hurt their captives either physically or mentally beyond the pain involved in confinement itself. And, in a certain sense, it would certainly appear to be true that the administrators of the New Jersey State Prison have no great interest in inflicting punishments on their prisoners for the crimes which they committed in the free community, as paradoxical as it may seem. There is no indication in the day-to-day operation of the prison that the officials have any desire to act as avenging angels; nor do the officials exhibit much attachment to the idea that a painful period of imprisonment is likely to deter the criminal who has been confined—the reappearance of discharged prisoners has made them grow cynical on that score.

It is true that punishing physical conditions are still inflicted on the prisoners to some extent, for as late as 1952 the committee to investigate the New Jersey State Prison could report that:

> . . . the prison buildings are in the bad condition that one would expect from their age. . . . Proper sanitary standards are difficult to maintain. Among the prisoner's complaints were that rats infest the buidings of the prison, that sewer gas escapes from the service tunnel between the cells . . . and that sanitary conditions are generally bad.[13]

And it is true that isolated acts of brutality on the part of the guards still occur. But the gross sadism and systematic neglect which aroused the anger of John Howard and similar critics of prisons have largely disappeared in the United States today with a few notable exceptions; and the New Jersey State Prison follows not the exceptions but the general rule.

Yet if the custodians are not motivated by a desire to inflict punishments, how are the many deprivations imposed on the inmates to be explained? Why, for example, are prisoners permitted to spend only twenty-five dollars each month at the inmate store for items such as tobacco, candy, soap, and so on? Why is so-called hobby work sharply curtailed? Why is the number of visits and letters from the outside world which are allowed the prisoner so small? These, indeed, are the questions raised by the inmates themselves and they believe they know the true answer: The officials wish to punish the prisoner but they cannot openly admit it. The claim of the officials that the many restrictions, the many punishing features of prison life, are inflicted in the name of custody and internal order is simply viewed as a rationalization. The "basic" motive of the officials, according to many inmates (and to many critics of the penal system as well), is hatred of the confined criminal and it is this which determines the nature of the custodians' regime.)

[13] New Jersey Committee to Examine and Investigate the Prison and Parole Systems of New Jersey, *Report,* November 21, 1952.

Now we have argued before that a punitive orientation toward the criminal does exist in society and that this orientation is reflected in the conditions of prison life. And it is certainly true that many prison officials believe that, in general, criminals should be punished. But to say that a desire for retribution is the basic or primary motive of the officials as they go about their daily routines is quite another thing. In fact, it would appear to be at least equally valid to claim that the maintenance of a quiet, orderly, peaceful institution is the dominant desire of the custodians and that the past criminality of the prisoner serves as a justification for the stringent controls which are imposed to achieve this end. The objective of eliminating incidents is not a rationalization for inflicting deprivations on the criminal within the walls; *rather, the reverse is true and the prior deviance of the prisoner is a rationalization for using such extreme measures to avoid any events which would excite public indignation.*

In any case, the officials of the New Jersey State Prison rarely turn to the behavior of the captive before he entered the institution as something for which atonement must be secured. In reality, much of the officials' activity is defined not as punishing but as providing adequate food, housing, medical care, etc., for the society of captives which is their responsibility. Of course, it could be argued that these and similar measures to maintain a decent standard of living or adequate standard of care are merely additional weapons for the custodians in their task of maintaining an orderly institution. The threat of reducing the standard— of placing a man in solitary confinement, restricting his diet, or withdrawing recreational and visiting privileges—can be viewed merely as a mechanism of control in dealing with men who are already being punished near the limits set by society. There is undoubtedly some truth in this, as we shall see shortly, and it is certainly not a simple fondness for the prisoner which drives the custodians of the New Jersey State Prison to take such an interest in his well-being. At the same time to view provisions for the inmate's welfare as nothing more than a manipulative attempt to grant privileges which can later be taken away is to ignore a fundamental link which exists between the captors and their captives. Guards and prisoners are drawn from the same culture and they hold many of the same values and beliefs. They share a common language and a common historical experience. They may stand opposed across the chasm which separates the convicted felon and the law-abiding citizen or the perhaps even greater chasm which divides the ruler and the ruled. But the criminal in the maximum security prison today is not defined as an individual who has been stripped of his humanity and it is this fact which does much to temper the totalitarian power system of the prison.

THE TASK OF REFORM

If the officials of the New Jersey State Prison are relatively indifferent when it comes to punishing their prisoners for their past sins, so also are they relatively indifferent when it comes to saving their prisoners from sins in the future. It is true that there is frequent mention of "individualization of treatment," "correction," "self-discipline," "a favorable change in attitudes," and so on, by the Department of Institutions and Agencies.[14] And it is true that within the prison itself a number of counsellors, a chaplain, a psychologist, and several teachers for the inmate school have the duty of somehow implanting that inner conviction in the offender which will keep him from the path of crime when he is released. But allegiance to the goal of rehabilitation tends to remain at the verbal level, an expression of hope for public consumption rather than a coherent program with an integrated, professional staff.

There are some writers, of course, who claim that any attempts to rehabilitate the offender in prison are futile. Some argue that the causes of criminal behavior do not lie within the individual himself, but in the social environment, in the form of slums, poverty, underworld associates, etc. Since the prison experience does not and cannot touch these, imprisonment is a waste of time as far as reformation is concerned; and to place an individual in custody for breaking the law is as foolish as locking up a dollar bill because it has lost its purchasing power. Others argue that the causes of crime are to be found deep in the individual's unconscious mind. Prison officials are not equipped by either training or experience to eradicate these causes and in any case the authoritarian, custodian-prisoner relationship is enough to warp the soul of the innocent, let alone the guilty. The officials of the New Jersey State Prison do not, in general, accept such pessimistic arguments, but at the same time they are far from sanguine about their ability to rehabilitate the offender. In fact, in so far as reform of the prisoner is seriously considered as a basis for the formation of administrative policy, the officials tend to take a position which is a complex mixture of faith and cynicism: Imprisonment is very likely to be defined as a success if only it does not make the offender worse. If progress is impossible, then one should at least fight against retreat.

In many of the custodial institutions in the United States today, this view of the task of reform as a holding action finds expression as an attempt to avoid the more corrosive abnormalities of prison existence. Provisions for medical care, recreation, schooling, library facilities, visiting privileges—all, it is held, make the prison less of a prison, and imita-

[14] See, for example, New Jersey Department of Institutions and Agencies Research Bulletin No. 111, November 1953.

tion of the free community may be justified not only on humanitarian grounds but also on the grounds of its possible effects on the criminal's behavior after he has left the prison. Since there is no valid test of the individual's criminal proclivities, no one can say with assurance that a given custodial regime has led a prisoner backward, forward, or left him untouched; and prison officials are free to pursue their hope that imitation of the free community at least does no harm and perhaps may do some good.

However, under the rule of the Warden of the New Jersey State Prison at the time of this study, the idea that the confined criminal can at least be prevented from deteriorating, if he cannot be cured, has taken a somewhat different turn. With wide experience in the administration of penal institutions and with professional training in the social sciences, the Warden has hammered out a philosophy of custody in which the prevention of deviant behavior among inmates while in prison is the most potent device for preparing the prisoner to follow the dictates of society when he is released. Education, recreation, counselling, and other measures designed to lessen the oppressiveness of prison life assume a relatively minor position compared to a system of control which attempts to make the prisoner learn compliance to duly constituted authority. It is important to examine his views at some length, for the maximum security prison, like every organization, bears the mark of the particular men in power. The following statement appears in the Warden's report on the operations of the New Jersey State Prison for the year 1953–1954:

> Custody is frequently dismissed as a rather sordid and punitive operation, consisting chiefly of keeping inmates perpetually locked, counted, and controlled. Almost as if in opposition to this, treatment and welfare are described as attempts to introduce freedom and dignity into custody's restrictive, punitive context by the provision of recreation, education, and counselling. This traditional contrast, disfigured by bias and half-truth, misses the central reality of the inmate's life in prison.
>
> The reality is simply this: The welfare of the individual inmate, to say nothing of his psychological freedom and dignity, does not importantly depend on how much education, recreation, and consultation he receives but rather depends on how he manages to live and relate with other inmates who constitute his crucial and only meaningful world. It is what he experiences in this world; how he attains satisfactions from it, how he avoids its pernicious effects—how, in a word, he survives in it that determines his adjustment and decides whether he will emerge from prison with an intact or shattered integrity. The significant impact of institutional officials is therefore not in terms of their relations with the inmate alone, but in terms of a total effect on the social world in which he is inextricably enmeshed. In these terms, an evaluation of the institution's contribution to the welfare of its inmates may not realistically be made with the typical institutional platitudes and statistics about hours

of recreation, treatment, and education. The evaluation must rather be made in terms of how the prison authorities are affecting the total social climate, how successful they are in enabling the less hostile persons to advance themselves, how successfully they are protecting these people from intimidation or exploitation by the more antisocial inmates, how effectively they curb and frustrate the lying, swindling, and covert violence which is always under the surface of the inmate social world.

The efficient custodian now emerges from the role of restrictor and becomes the one who safeguards inmate welfare. Most inmates will admit and even require the keepers to assume this function. They understand that the metal detector which uncovers a file intended for an escape attempt will also detect a knife intended for the unsuspecting back of a friend. Inmates will privately express their relief at the construction of a segregation wing which protects them from the depredations of men who are outlaws even in the prison world. Much as they complain of the disciplinary court which punishes them for their infractions, they are grateful for the swift and stern justice meted out to inmates who loot their cells. In short, these men realize, sometimes dimly, sometimes keenly, that a control system which is lax enough to permit thievery and intimidation must eventually result in a deterioration and vicious circle.

I have suggested previously that such an argument might be viewed simply as a rationalization for the totalitarian regime of the custodians.[15] It might be claimed that this argument is at best a guess, since we do not have definite proof that securing compliance with the regulations of the prison increases the individual's readiness to conform to the general normative demands of society when he is released. And it might be asserted that the argument is a valid one, not because of hypothetical consequences for reform, but because strict control is necessary to create tolerable living conditions among hundreds of inmates confined in a small space. At this point, however, it is not the validity of the argument that is relevant for our analysis but its implications for the regime of the custodians. By viewing the enforcement of prison regulations as being more important for the rehabilitation of the criminal than education, recreation, consultation, etc., the Warden has reinforced the traditional low priority attached to the efforts of those charged with the task of reform. Whatever value might be attached to such a system of priorities, its meaning for the social structure of the prison is clear: It is the control of the prisoner's behavior which is stressed rather than the control of the prisoner's mind, on the grounds that if the individual's actions are forced to match normative demands, the mind will follow after. And in this respect the prison differs markedly from a number of systems of totalitarian power which seek to capture the emotional and intellectual allegiance of

[15] It should be noted that this report was written shortly after a number of serious riots when there was a pressing need to clarify the position of the custodial force and to bolster its morale.

those who are ruled as well as their overt obedience. In the eyes of the officials of the New Jersey State Prison, the task of reform does not consist primarily of an ideological or psychological struggle in which an attempt is made to change the inmates' beliefs, attitudes, and goals. Instead, it consists largely of a battle for compliance. The officials of the prison, then, are indifferent to the task of reform, not in the sense that they reject reform out of hand as a legitimate organizational objective, but in the sense that rehabilitation tends to be seen as a theoretical, distant, and somewhat irrelevant by-product of successful performance at the tasks of custody and internal order. A released prisoner may or may not commit another crime in the free community, but that crude test of the prison's accomplishments in the area of reform lies far away. Within the walls, in the clearcut scope of the custodian's responsibilities, the occurrence of escapes and disorders is a weightier concern.

IV

Emile Durkheim, Thurmond Arnold, Sir James Stephen, and many others have pointed out that the legal process serves as a highly dramatic method of affirming collective sentiments concerning the wrongness of criminal behavior. Norms, once implanted, do not thrive without replenishment and the punishment of the offender symbolizes anew the immorality of the deviant act.

Yet in a modern, complex society, the punishment of the offender has grown complex and we are no longer satisfied to stone the individual for his crime. We have created a social organization—the prison—which stands interposed between the law-abiding community and the offender. We have created new demands concerning how the offender should be handled and we have continually changed the limits within which the demands should be fulfilled. The result has been something of a jerry-built social structure, pieced together over the years and appealing to few. The custodians, however, can find little comfort in the conflicts and ambiguities of the free community's directives concerning the proper aims of imprisonment. They must somehow take these demands and these limited means and construct a regime—a social order—to which they hope they can make their captives conform. If the regime is a totalitarian one, it does not necessarily mean that the custodians believe that a society in which crime is checked by imposing rigid controls and deprivations is preferable to a society in which crime is checked by other means. Rather, it expresses in part our own lack of knowledge about how to better proceed; and, in part, it reflects the fact that when all else is said and done, society is still apt to attach the greatest importance to the prevention of escapes and disorders regardless of the cost.

The officials of the New Jersey State Maximum Security Prison, then, have designed a social order which should—in theory at least—minimize the possibility of escapes and disturbances within the walls. Self-maintenance and exacting retribution appear much farther down on the list of objectives and the task of reform is perhaps the lowest of all—unless, of course, securing adherence to prison regulations is in fact the best road to rehabilitation. But as we pointed out in the beginning of this chapter, this social order is not a reality but a statement of what *should* be. We must now examine what occurs in actuality.

Part B

Organizational Structure

THE process of industrialization leads not only to increased institutional differentiation but to a growth in the scale of society and to a change in the size of organizational units. More and more, people work in large-scale organizations and, more and more, clients and customers deal with large organizations. Welfare organizations, too, have grown in scale and complexity, although many of them—especially the voluntary agencies—are relatively small and simple in their structure. The purpose of the articles in this part is to introduce some of the key terms necessary for the analysis of the internal structure and problems of welfare organizations.

The selection chosen from my own writings, "Organizational Control Structures in Five Correctional Institutions," discusses the distribution and channels of influence in complex organizations. I analyze the differences in the balance of power and the level of departmentalization found in five institutions for juvenile delinquents. A control structure of an organization refers to the distribution of power and the channels for utilizing power that are found in that organization. This article also relates the structure of the organization to its basic goals.

The article by John Cumming and Elaine Cumming, "Social Equilibrium and Social Change in the Large Mental Hospital," demonstrates the use of theoretical analysis of large-scale organization for changing the effectiveness of a mental hospital. The full range of concepts of complex organization—formal and informal structure, authority patterns, communication channels, coordinating mechanisms, and the like—were imaginatively employed as tools of analysis to plan a drastic restructuring of a mental hospital's day-to-day operating format.

Finally, the article by Edwin J. Thomas, "Role Conceptions and Organizational Size," raises the question of how role conceptions are related to organizational size, structure, and setting. Thomas shows that even though the many branches of a state welfare agency had similar goals, the fact that the branches varied in size, were located in different kinds of communities, and varied in their internal hierarchical structure affected the concept of the workers' role, the ethical commitment, and the relationship of workers with clients.

Organizational Control Structures
in Five Correctional Institutions

Mayer N. Zald

Like universities and mental hospitals, most correctional institutions are organizations that have multiple goals. One can characterize the goals of any given correctional institution in terms of the relative importance of custodial or treatment purposes; some institutions have almost purely custodial goals, some have "mixed goals," and some have almost purely treatment goals.

Custodial goals are operative when an organization devotes a large part of its energies and resources to the control and containment of inmates; treatment goals are operative when a large part of organizational resources and energies are devoted to the rehabilitation and positive social change of inmates.

Organizational goals are conceptualized as the analytic independent variable; action necessary to implement custodial or treatment goals leads to, or requires, differences in organizational control structures.

Two institutions whose goals are approximately the same might differ sharply in structure and practice, however, if they employ different methods. A mental hospital, for example, which utilizes mainly electro-convulsive and other neurological therapies has different staff-patient relationships and practices than one using primarily psychotherapy. In treatment institutions for delinquents there are important differences in structure required by individual treatment (psychotherapy, casework, or counseling) as contrasted with milieu treatment (interpreting behavior and changing the individual through his relationship with others).

This paper concentrates on the relationship between custodial and treatment goals and aspects of organizational control structures—the pat-

Mayer N. Zald, "Organizational Control Structures in Five Correctional Institutions," *American Journal of Sociology*, Vol. LXVIII, No. 3, 1962, pp. 335–345. This study was done as part of a larger study of institutions for juvenile delinquents directed by Robert D. Vinter and Morris Janowitz under a grant from the National Institute of Mental Health (M-2104), United States Public Health Service.

tern of departmentalization and the distribution and balance of power among executives and employees of five institutions for delinquents.[1] My central assumption is that implementation of custodial or treatment goals requires different relationships between institutions and the local community, between various groups of employees, and between employees and inmates. These differences directly affect the control structure of the institution.[2]

The control structure of an organization can be described in terms of the distribution of power and the channels for utilizing power.[3] The pattern and amount of departmentalization and interdepartmental relationships are part of the structure of control because they reflect the way in which responsibility (and control) is delegated. The balance of power among executive and staff groups reflects both the formal delegation of control and the informal seizure of control by some executives and groups. My general thesis is that institutions with dominant treatment goals differ in their control structure from those with dominant custodial goals; the more complex departmental structure and tasks require a wider distribution of power among the executives and a different allocation of power among both executives and staff groups.

Two major hypotheses are examined:

Hypothesis 1: *In mixed-goal and treatment institutions power is distributed among executives; whereas in more custodial institutions power*

[1] There have been few studies from a sociological point of view of institutions for delinquents. For a case study see Robert D. Vinter and Roger Lind, *Staff Relationships and Attitudes in a Juvenile Correctional Institution* (Ann Arbor: School of Social Work, The University of Michigan, 1958). For current approaches to the study of prisons and mental hospitals, see George Grosser (ed.), *Theoretical Studies in Social Organization of the Prison* ("SSRC" Pamphlet, No. 15 [New York: Social Science Research Council, 1960]); Donald Cressey (ed.), *The Prison: Studies in Institutional Organization and Change* (New York: Holt, Rinehart & Winston, 1961); and Milton Greenblatt, Daniel J. Levinson, and Richard H. Williams (eds.), *The Patient and the Mental Hospital* (Glencoe, Ill.: Free Press, 1957).

[2] Goals also have more indirect consequences for the attitudes of employees toward inmates, the amount and pattern of conflict, and the role problems of employees. On the patterns of conflict in correctional institutions see my "Power Balance and Organizational Conflict in Correctional Institutions for Delinquents," *Administrative Science Quarterly*, VII (June, 1962), 22–49. On the role problems of employees see Cressey, "Contradictory Directives in Complex Organizations: The Case of the Prisons," *Administrative Science Quarterly*, IV (June, 1959), 1–19.

[3] The concept of organizational control structure used here is more inclusive than that used by Arnold Tannenbaum and his associates. They include only the distribution of influence among groups in their definition of the control structure, in effect assuming or ignoring the patterned channels through which influence is utilized. See Arnold S. Tannenbaum and Robert L. Kahn, "Organizational Control Structure: A General Descriptive Technique as Applied to Four Local Unions," *Human Relations*, X (May, 1957), 127–40; and Tannenbaum and Basil Georgopoulos, "The Distribution of Control in Formal Organizations," *Social Forces*, XXXVIII (October, 1957), 44–50.

is not distributed, only the superintendent possesses power. Internal practices required in treatment institutions are more complex, less routinized, and more individualized than those in custodial institutions. Similarly, because he must obtain a larger amount of resources per inmate than his counterpart in custodial institutions, and because he must defend the relatively open quality of his program, the superintendent of an institution with treatment goals must concern himself more with external affairs than his counterpart in a custodial institution.

Differences in the relative dominance of custodial and treatment goals among institutions lead to differences in the substantive bases of decisions and imply differences in the importance attached to various activities (e.g., containment, counseling, etc.). Therefore, aside from the extent to which executive power is shared, difference in goals between institutions leads to the allocation of power to executives who differ in their values and goal commitments, that is, to a difference in the balance of power. In a mixed-goal institution, the executive responsible for internal activities is likely to pursue custodial goals and the executive concerned with external affairs ostensibly will pursue treatment goals. Such an arrangement placates the demands of specialized publics for a rehabilitative program at the same time that it insures attainment of basic custodial goals. In a treatment institution, however, the executive responsible for internal control must be fully committed to treatment goals.

Differences in the basic goals of the institution lead not only to differences in the criteria on which decisions are based but also to differences in the amount of power held by various groups within the institution, because custodial and treatment goals require different staff groups to be in control of decisions about discipline and activities for inmates.

Hypothesis 2: *In custodial institutions the influence and authority of the cottage parent is likely to be relatively high and that of a social service worker relatively low. The reverse will tend to hold true in individual treatment institutions; since milieu treatment attempts to involve more of the staff in the decision-making process, a "team" concept results and a general sharing of power is likely. In all institutions teachers are relatively isolated from the major operating problems of the organization and are likely to have little influence.*

Although social service workers have power in both the individual- and milieu-treatment institutions, they differ in their relationship to the other staff members. In a milieu institution the social service staff can make its influence felt only through other staff members; in individual-treatment institutions social service workers may function relatively independently of the rest of the staff. I shall explore both the power of staff groups and the kinds of relationships existing among staff groups.

Before the data pertaining to these hypotheses are presented, the sample institutions must be briefly described.

THE SAMPLE INSTITUTIONS

From a large number of institutions whose goals were known on a reputational basis by experts,[4] five were selected for intensive study.[5] In Table 1 the goals, number of inmates and employees, and type of control (public or private) of each institution are shown.

Each of these institutions, particularly those with treatment goals, had been subject to processes of change and conflict in recent times. All of them formally stressed some form of rehabilitation goals (as has been true historically for institutions for delinquents). But institutions with such older or traditional concepts of rehabilitation as "training" also stressed custodial aims. The description of each institution which follows locates the goals with reference to the relative dominance of custody and treatment and highlights important features of each institution's operation.

Dick Industrial School [6] stressed discipline, training, and containment in its goal statements. Operating its own farm, Dick was an isolated, custodial institution.

[4] One representative of the United States Children's Bureau and a professor of social work interested in correctional institutions helped to pick the initial sample. They were asked to name a wide variety of institutions with specific reputations for emphasis on custodial or treatment programs. The reputations of institutions are obviously composites of their goals and their operating procedures. The use of reputations as an index of goals would make my argument circular because I would be using a consequence of structure analytically as a determinant of structure. Institutional goals were independently and directly measured by using data obtained from official statements of goals, interviews with executives, and staff responses to questionnaire items. These measurements indicated that my judgments of goals based on reputations were largely supported (see "Multiple Goals . . . ," *op. cit.*, pp. 64–114). Furthermore, if one uses as a measure of treatment goals the input of treatment personnel, it is clear that our most custodial institution had the lowest ratio of social service workers to inmates, 1 to 125, whereas our most treatment-oriented institution had a ratio of 1 to 12. The underlying model is a rational and unfolding one; persons in authority have responsibility for implementing goals and take action to pursue those goals, including hiring appropriate personnel. Personnel in interaction then help to change definitions of goals.

[5] The selection of institutions met four requirements: (1) an array of institutions among the custodial-treatment dimension; (2) institutions of different sizes as a control measure; (3) both public and private institutions; and (4) institutional goals related to the action program of the organization.

I did not attempt to select a representative sample but aimed instead at maximizing comparison of the effects of goals. Comparison of the five institutions to the universe of institutions in the United States indicates that, in fact, they are not representative of the universe of institutions. Institutions with low inmate-staff ratios and high per capita costs are overrepresented, indicating most likely an overrepresentation of treatment institutions (*ibid.*, pp. 51–54). But the institutions selected do fulfil the requirements of my comparative design.

[6] The institutions have been given false names to preserve guaranteed anonymity. The first two or three letters of each name serve as a mnemonic device for some salient aspect of the institutional program.

Table 1   *Five Sample Institutions, by Goals, Size, and Control, Public or Private*

	Size	
Goals	Small	Large
Custodial		Dick Industrial School 260 Inmates 65 Staff members Public
Mixed	Regis Home 56 Inmates 13 Staff members Private	Mixter Training School 400 Inmates 177 Staff members Public
Treatment	Inland School 60 inmates 40 Staff members Private	Milton School for Boys 200 Inmates 117 Staff members Public

Regis Home, the smallest institution in the study, was run by a Catholic religious order. Although some boys received individual counseling, Regis aimed primarily at educating and training the boys. The Home was located in an urban community and sent its boys to twenty schools in the community.[7] Discipline was firm, although less punitive than at Dick, and all counseling, especially in regard to sexual practices, had to conform to the tenets of the governing religious order.

*Mix*ter, a *mix*ed-goal institution, was the largest in the study. Mixter represents a benign custodial type which minimizes repressive sanctions while not fully developing a treatment program.

*Mil*ton, which stressed a *mil*ieu approach, and *In*land, which stressed *in*dividual treatment, were the two institutions in the sample with relatively dominant treatment goals. They differed from each other in that Milton was a large public institution while Inland was a small private

[7] Since there was no attempt to contain delinquents at Regis, its inclusion in the study might be questioned. To fill the required cells of the design of my study a small institution emphasizing containment was sought. Since none was available, excluding Regis would have left an important gap in the comparisons. Its small size permits comparisons with Inland School, and its emphasis on education and respect reflects a parallel with older concepts of rehabilitation.

institution. Milton had changed to a milieu approach after a decade and a half of growth and conflict. Its milieu approach was intended to eliminate tensions between professional and lay personnel by having them consult often with each other as well as to implement treatment philosophy.

Because Milton was a public institution and had to accept all delinquents sent to it, it was not able to dispense with custodial goals as completely as Inland. Inland defined itself as a "residential treatment center" and its personnel placed a great deal of stress on the delinquent's progress in counseling.

To summarize, I consider Dick to have had the most custodial goals of the institutions in the sample, followed by Regis and Mixter. Although Inland was able to dispense with custodial emphases to a greater extent than Milton, both Milton and Inland were clearly institutions with dominant treatment goals. With this array of institutions it is possible to compare smaller institutions with larger; public institutions with private; and institutions with custodial, mixed, and treatment goals.[8]

DEPARTMENTAL STRUCTURE AND ADMINISTRATIVE POWER BALANCE

The hypothesis that power is more widely distributed among executives in treatment institutions than in custodial ones rests on the greater complexity of organization tasks and on the greater external demands on the superintendent in the former. Without delegating authority, the superintendent would have an overextended span of control. Formal delegation of authority often takes place through the creation of departmental structures, and institutions with different basic goals and methods set up different types of departmental patterns. Since departmental structures also affect the relations among staff groups, before presenting data which bears directly on the first hypothesis, I will discuss the departmental structures of the five institutions as they relate to correctional institutions in general.

Such custodial institutions as Dick and, to a lesser extent, Regis operate on a routine and repetitive basis and require little departmentalization.[9] When containment and control of inmates are achieved, organizational goals are fulfilled. Thus, the co-ordination of the staff is required primarily

[8] The absence from the sample of large private or small public institutions means that comparisons for the variables of size and control are confounded. My primary comparisons, however, deal with the custodial-treatment dimension, and I believe these missing data do not seriously affect the basic analysis of the effects of custodial and treatment goals.

[9] A department is defined as a relatively self-contained subsystem of an organization. A group of workers can be considered members of a department when there is a designated liaison or responsible supervisor for the group. Workers performing similar tasks but relating individually to the superintendent, assistant superintendent, or another executive are not considered members of a department.

for physical movement of inmates and for rotation of personnel shifts. The executive can easily maintain an extended span of control.

Both Dick and Regis had simple formal structures. Of course, Regis' small size as well as its basically routine operation accounted for its lack of departmentalization. Dick was partially departmentalized; only the academic school and the farm had effective departmental heads. Even though each of the five cottages had a nominal leader, all cottage parents often reported directly to the superintendent. No attempt was made to delegate control of the cottages to a department head, and there was little supervision of cottage parent activity. Furthermore, the departmentalization of the farm did not stem from a desire to implement more complex programs for the boys or to control employee relations with inmates; it occurred only after Dick's farm production was criticized by a citizen's committee and was an attempt to insure an adequate variety of food. Although Dick was larger than Inland, it had less departmentalization, suggesting that size alone does not account for the degree of departmentalization. Moreover, the superintendent and assistant superintendent at Dick had little difficulty in meeting role demands, indicating that under prevailing conditions further departmentalization was not required.

In contrast to custodial institutions, such mixed-goal and treatment institutions as Mixter, Milton, and Inland cannot operate as routinely, and more complex combinations of personnel must be co-ordinated. Both Mixter and Inland had multiple department structures, a form which is most likely to occur when each of the diverse tasks of the institution is relatively autonomous. In an institution with mixed goals, for instance, cottage life, education, treatment, recreation, and maintenance might each be in a separate and unintegrated department. Such an institution as Inland, operating under individual treatment philosophy, also allows departments to function independently, since the relevance of activity in the school or cottage to the rehabilitative process is not stressed, and high integration of departments thus is not required.

Although the larger size of Mixter resulted in more subsystem divisions than at Inland, the basic structure in both institutions was similar. Social service, training and education, cottage life, and business and maintenance each comprised separate departments, no one of which had control over the others. At Mixter the superintendent took responsibility for integrating the activities of the various departments, while at Inland the assistant director performed this function.

The departmental structure at Mixter permitted the superintendent to have a reasonable span of control, while at Inland the assistant superintendent was not so fortunate. The emphasis on individual relations to inmates, inmate voluntarism, and non-routinized programs, as well as his role as chief disciplinarian, overextended the range of control of the assistant superintendent. Although Inland had less than one-fourth the number of employees of Mixter and two-thirds as many as Dick, and although its over-all departmental structure was similar to that of Mixter's, the lack of a highly routinized program led to continuous operating pressures on the assistant superintendent.

Milieu-treatment institutions operate on criteria that are more consistently applied throughout the institution than in either mixed-goal or individual-treatment institutions, in this respect resembling custodial institutions. But the milieu institution differs from the custodial institution in its attempt to rationalize greater areas of organizational activity, in the complex combination of personnel, and in the substantive bases of the decisions it makes.

Milton was divided into two major divisions, the business and maintenance division and the clinical division. Under the direction of a psychiatrist, the clinical division had responsibility for all activity with the inmates. The social service staff, which in multiple departmental structures usually gives direct service to clients but only consultant service to the rest of the staff, assumed responsibility for the supervision of the cottage staff. The social service staff and the cottage parents worked together on cottage committees to make decisions about the boys. The basic therapeutic role was not defined as a one-to-one relationship between a clinical staff member and a delinquent but was, theoretically, the relationship between the boy and all staff members with whom he had contact. But, although the school and vocational training areas were under the direction of the clinical director, they were not as fully incorporated into the unitary authority structure as the cottage area. The "dual-division" structure that operated at Milton permitted to a greater extent than a multiple-department structure the centralized control over all activity in which inmates are involved. Personnel dealing with treatment were placed directly in control of the day-to-day operating staff of the institution.[10]

These patterns of departmentalization establish the official range of hierarchical positions in an institution, but they do not reveal the actual amount of power or influence that a group or individual may exercise. My first proposition deals with the distribution of power among executives.

In my analysis I was able to compare the staff members' perceptions of the distribution of power among executives within an institution as well as to compare the power of executives in similar positions in different institutions.[11] Employees of the institutions were asked to rate the amount

[10] In "The Reduction of Role Conflict in Institutional Staff," *Children*, V (1958), 65–69, Lloyd Ohlin has described a similar structural development in a girls' training institution; caseworkers were given administrative responsibility for the management of the cottages. One result of such a change is to partially shift conflict from an interrole to an intrarole level.

[11] Several kinds of data were collected in all five institutions. (1) Historical records and institutional publications were examined. (2) Loosely structured observations of

Table 2 *Distribution of Perceived Executive Power: Staff Perception of High Influence of Various Members of Executive Core*

Executives Rated	Percent of High Influence [a]				
	Dick	Regis	Mixter	Milton	Inland
Superintendent	79	100	59	52	62
Assistant director	34	11	23	65	81
Head of social service	11	0	19	12 [b]	19
Head of cottage parents	10 [c]	[d]	52	26	3
Principal of school	15	[d]	8	7	5
Total number	(62)	(9)	(155)	(108)	(37)

[a] Percentages are given for the highest point of a five-point scale ("A great deal of say").

[b] Business manager substituted for head of social service at *Milton*.

[c] Farm manager substituted for head of cottage parents at *Dick*.

[d] No head of cottage parents or school principal at *Regis*.

of influence possessed by each of the members of the executive core.[12] Table 2 presents the proportion of staff attributing "high influence" to each of them.[13]

In Dick and Regis, the more custodial institutions, a large proportion of the staff thought only the superintendent had "a great deal of say," while in Mixter, Milton, and Inland, the staff believed that the superin-

organizational practices and conferences were carried out over a two-week period in each institution. (3) Extended interviews with members of the executive core (the superintendent, assistant superintendent, and heads of major departments) were conducted. (4) Questionnaires were distributed to all staff members, yielding a response rate of 85 percent or more in each of the institutions. The interrelationship of measures and observations is stressed. In no case was a datum accepted as veridical when it did not jibe with other data.

[12] Respondents were asked: "In general, how much say or influence in the way——is run would you say each of the following individuals or groups has? (Put one check on each line.)" Respondents checked a five-point scale.

[13] To the extent that "real power" is overtly expressed, employee ratings of the power of executives is a legitimate reflection of the amount of power wielded. To the extent that power relations are masked or indirect, we would expect employee perception of power to be based on the actual amount of influence of the executive core, and power to be conceived of as a "whole"—as a general attribute. Herbert Simon ("Introduction to the Theory and Measurement of Influence," *American Political Science Review*, XLIX [1955], 431–51) and Nelson Polsby ("Community Power: Three Problems," *American Sociological Review*, XXIV [1959], 796–803) have both argued that a general influence rating may conceal the differentiated power wielded in different contexts. Nevertheless, a general measure of attributed power has some validity and has the merit of methodological simplicity.

tendent and at least one other member of the executive core had a great deal of influence. In fact, the data in Table 2 indicate that at Inland and Milton a larger proportion of the staff regarded the assistant superintendent rather than the superintendent as having "a great deal of influence." These data add credibility to our first hypothesis. It may be noted that both the school principals and social service directors were consistently perceived as having little power.

One might ask, however, if these findings necessarily related to the goals and departmental structures of these institutions or were merely accidentally associated in these institutions. The personalities of the superintendents, the size of the institutions, and—in the case of Regis—the structure of the religious order were variables which might have contributed to the great amount of power attributed to superintendents at Dick and Regis and to the smaller amount of power attributed to them at Mixter, Milton, and Inland.

In accounting for the magnitude of difference between the treatment and custodial superintendents one cannot ignore these factors. The small size of Regis minimized the need for delegation and decentralization of decision-making, while the particular personality of the superintendent at Dick contributed to the staff perception of his role as highly concentrated in power.

While the personality attributes of the superintendents of custodial institutions contributed to the image of their high power, the converse seemed to be true in the treatment institutions. The superintendent at Milton felt that his training did not qualify him to make decisions about the treatment of children, leading him to defer often in judgment to the professionals on his staff. On the other hand, although Inland's director had training that might be considered appropriate, his interpersonal relations were characteristically very tense, and the assistant director instead gained the allegiance and loyalty of the staff.

To say that such factors minimize the magnitude of the difference in patterns of power between custodial and treatment institutions is not to vitiate the over-all pattern. The creation of more than one office with authority in treatment institutions necessitates a wider distribution of power. To act effectively each department must have the right to make some decisions, and professional treatment personnel in particular must be given more power. Furthermore, the superintendents may have to spend a good deal of time on matters not directly concerned with the internal operation of the institution, such as the relationship of the institution to the community, etc.

If executive power is shared in mixed-goal or treatment institutions, among whom is it shared? The clinical director and assistant director at Milton and Inland, respectively, were attributed high power by the staff, while at Mixter the head of the cottage-life department was perceived as the second in command. The attribution of high power to the clinical director at Milton and to the assistant director at Inland was in line with their official status, and both attempted to implement treatment goals. But the division of power between the superintendent and the head of cottage life at Mixter did not correspond to their official status, and might appear to have indicated a bifurcation of power between rehabilitational and custodial goals, the superintendent representing rehabilitative programs and the head of cottage life custodial programs. But this separation was more apparent than real: although the superintendent claimed to be committed to rehabilitational goals, in practice he concentrated his attention on benign custodial aims. Moreover, the head of cottage life, though custodially oriented, was opposed to using means which he considered overly repressive. In fact, there was little conflict between the superintendent and the head of cottage life; the superintendent felt that the head of cottage life was doing a much better job than two social workers who had previously held the position and "couldn't stand the pressure." Contrary to my expectations, the two men's approaches were not so far apart—I underestimated the pressures for consensus among major executives.

The attribution of high power to the head of cottage life at Mixter was due to his official position inasmuch as the training director was officially the second in command (52 percent attributed "a great deal of say" to the head of cottage life, whereas only 23 percent attributed "a great deal of say" to the training director). Power was given to the head of cottage life because he guaranteed control and containment in a situation in which repressive sanctions were banned. The head of cottage life and his assistants acted as roving police, backing up the cottage parents in their decisions and controlling situations beyond the scope of cottage parent power. Of course, the director of cottage life also had to co-ordinate a staff of approximately seventy men. But the problems of co-ordination were relatively routine and were partly delegated to the assistant cottage-life supervisors. By itself, the role of co-ordinator would not have called for granting a high degree of power to the head of cottage life.

I have argued that the clinical director at Milton, the assistant director at Inland, and the head of cottage life at Mixter were in particularly central positions for organizational control; but except for discussing the position of the training director at Mixter, I have not analyzed why other executives were not attributed high power. In all of the institutions the school principal and the director of social service influenced the over-all operation of the institution only by their consultant relationship to the superintendent or assistant superintendent. Although they could influence considerably the operation of their own departments, their influence on the rest of the institution was indirect.

It would be a mistake, however, to conclude that the principals or the social service directors were powerless or that their positions did not vary somewhat from institution to institution. Approximately 50 percent of the staff at Mixter and Inland perceived the heads of social service to have "a great deal of say" or "considerable say," the highest two categories in our list of alternatives. Field observations indicated that the assistant director at Inland relied on the head of social service for many clinical decisions, while the superintendent at Mixter consulted more with the head of social service than he did with the training director. The influence of the social service director, especially at Inland, was related to the importance of his position for pursuing treatment aims.

THE BALANCE OF POWER OF STAFF GROUPS

The balance of power among cottage parents, social service workers, and teachers, like the balance of power among executives, is a function of the goals of the organization. I hypothesized that the influence of social service personnel is likely to be higher in treatment institutions than in custodial institutions, while the power of cottage parents is likely to be higher in custodial than in individual treatment institutions. Since the milieu institution requires a team organization, a more general sharing of power is likely.

To measure the power of the various groups in making decisions about clients, I asked the staff of each institution to judge the amount of influence cottage parents, social service workers, and teachers had in making judgments about how the boys should be handled (Table 3).[14]

The statistical differences clearly indicate that a larger proportion of the staff attributes high influence to social service workers in treatment institutions than in custodial institutions. The smallest proportion attributes high influence to social service workers at Dick and Regis, a larger proportion attributes high influence to them at Mixter, and the largest proportion attributes high influence to social service workers at Inland and Milton. Cottage parent power tends to decline as we move from custodial to individual-treatment institutions; however, the cottage-committee structure at Milton, where cottage parents shared in decision-making, led to the cottage parents there being thought of as having high influence by a larger proportion of the staff than at any of the other institutions.

On the other hand, teachers were attributed a relatively low amount of influence in all the institutions. Data in Table 2 indicate that the school principals also were seen as having little influence in the institutions, suggesting that the academic schools had little over-all authority or control

---

[14] Respondents were asked: "How much influence do each of the following groups have in making decisions about *how the boys should be handled?*" Respondents checked a four-point scale.

Table 3 *Distribution of Perceived Group Power: Staff Perception of High Influence of Social Service Workers, Cottage Parents, and Teachers*

	Percent of High Influence				
Groups Rated	Dick	Regis	Mixter	Milton	Inland
Social service	39	22	49	76	76
Cottage parents	50	33	34	70	8
Teachers	23	a	11	17	19
Total number	(62)	(9)	(155)	(108)	(37)

a No teachers at Regis.

in operating the institutions. The school personnel were not central to the definition of institutional philosophy and were restricted to an unproblematic area of institutional operation.

It was originally anticipated that within custodial institutions a larger proportion of the total staff would believe the cottage parents have high influence. This was not so perceived by the social service staff. As it turned out, only 11 percent more of the staff at Dick perceived the cottage parents to have "a great deal of influence," while at Mixter 15 percent attributed more power to social service than to cottage parents. Two factors may account for my incorrect prediction. First, as low-paid, low-status staff at the bottom of the administrative hierarchy, the cottage parents tended to make decisions within the bounds of discretion set by the administrators. Although cottage parents in custodial institutions had more discretion about discipline and more influence on the discharge of inmates, they did not formulate basic rules and procedures. On the other hand, even in the custodial institutions the higher salaried and more educated social service staff members, although they did not make decisions about individual boys, were able to influence the executives in the formulation of policy.

Second, although in the more custodial institutions cottage parents had high discretion to discipline and grade the boys, this power was shared with other staff members who worked with the boys. At Dick, any person who worked with the boys was allowed to paddle or punish them. At Mixter, while the cottage parent gave each boy 50 percent of his monthly grade (which was the basis on which he was discharged), teachers and detail supervisors made up the rest of the grade. By contrast, at Milton the cottage committee meted out serious discipline, and the cottage parent on duty had a range of possible sanctions not available to teachers or supervisors.

Table 4   *Percentage of Total Staff and of Cottage Parents at Milton and Inland Perceiving High Degree of "Helpfulness" of Social Service Advice*

Group	Milton	Inland
Total staff:		
Total number	108	37
Percent	61	43
Cottage parents:		
Total number	35	7
Percent	71	29

It is interesting to note that the over-all amount of power attributed to all staff groups was higher at Milton than at any other institution, and lowest at Dick and Regis. (The question permitted all groups to be ranked high, under the assumption that more or less power may be mobilized, depending on both the number of decisions and the number of people involved in decisions in an organization.) This may indicate that milieu treatment requires more decisions and involves more people than custodial institutions, leading to a higher actualization of potential power within the organization.

The data in Table 3 quite clearly indicate the power of social service workers in treatment institutions. Role definitions, however, vary in different institutions so that power expresses itself or is used in very different ways. In the individual-treatment institution the authority of social service is based to a large extent on the staff perception of the prevailing treatment philosophy and on the social service workers' control over decisions made about individual clients. In the milieu institution, although social service workers can make many decisions, they also are required to work through and with other staff members.

In Table 4 are given the proportions of (*a*) all staff and (*b*) cottage parents alone at Milton and Inland who viewed social service advice as helpful.[15] The data clearly indicate the utility of social service to other personnel at Milton. The entente that existed between cottage parents and social service workers in the milieu institution was especially strong; over twice the percentage of cottage parents at Milton as compared with cottage parents at Inland found social service guidance to be of help. Although the ratio of clinical personnel to other personnel was approximately the same at Milton and Inland, the constant attempt of clinical personnel at Milton to accomplish their aims through the milieu program led them to be useful resources for others.

[15] Respondents were asked: "How much help are the people in social service in advising how to work with the boys?" Three alternatives were used.

Through a comparative study of five institutions for delinquents I have explored the effects of goals and related methods on organizational control structures. After describing the five sample institutions and their departmental structures my analysis based on questionnaire and field data has supported two propositions. (1) As organizational complexity increases and organization-community relations lead to greater external commitments by the superintendent, the chief executive must share power. In a mixed-goal institution it is likely that power is shared with a person with basically custodial aims, while in institutions with dominant treatment goals power must be given to a person concerned with treatment goals. (2) The balance of power among groups is also a function of organizational goals: social service personnel acquire great influence in treatment institutions, while cottage parent influence is less, except when the major focus of the institution is on the group-living situation, as in the milieu institution.

This analysis has assumed that the structure of control evolves to solve problems of goal implementation; without an organizational structure to support and control staff behavior, organizational objectives are not met. My analysis has been primarily static, comparing institutions at one point in time. A study of any one institution would show that goals are often in flux as forces internal and external to the organization press for redefinitions or extensions of emphasis. Moreover, in correctional institutions movement toward greater treatment or custodial emphasis brings about opposite pressures from groups with divergent perspectives. Even though the basic pattern of departmentalization may be relatively stable, an ebb and flow of power among groups and among executives is likely to occur as compensating policies and mechanisms are introduced.

Social Equilibrium and Social Change
in the Large Mental Hospital

John Cumming and Elaine Cumming

EQUILIBRIUM

The years following the introduction of insulin coma therapy in 1935 have been marked by increasing optimism about the initial active treatment of the mentally ill. However, there has been an almost equal pessimism about the fate of the patient who fails to respond to these treatments during his first months in hospital. This pessimism is part of the process which imparts to the large, publicly supported mental hospital its uniquely depressing quality. On the whole, these public institutions are unmanageably large; they are economically depressed, running on a fraction of the cost of general hospitals, schools or jails; they are chronically understaffed; and they are usually cut off from the mainstream of professional life. We attempt here to describe what in our experience is the most common type of large, traditional mental hospital. It should be pointed out, however, that other types exist and merit further analysis.

John Cumming and Elaine Cumming, "Social Equilibrium and Social Change in the Large Mental Hospital," *The Patient and the Mental Hospital*, M. Greenblatt, ed., The Free Press, Glencoe, Ill., 1957, pp. 49–72. The empirical materials presented here are based on the authors' experiences in a state-supported mental hospital caring for some 2,000 patients. The organizational and planning change reported took place between June, 1954 and September, 1955, at which time the authors left the hospital. The data concerning the hospital population subsequent to that date were provided by Dr. I. L. W. Clancey, who sponsored and collaborated in the original work. We believe that the persistence of the program is an indication of the soundness of the conceptual basis as well as a tribute to Dr. Clancey's continued inspiration and effort. Portions of this material have been utilized in recent articles by J. Cumming and Elaine Cumming (1956), Elaine Cumming and J. Cumming (1956), and Elaine Cumming, I. L. W. Clancey, and J. Cumming (1956). We gratefully acknowledge the permission of the editors of *Psychiatry* to use the material in its present form.

General Patterns

Most of these massive hospitals can be looked upon as reasonably permanent social systems. When they are located in geographically remote places, far from cities, their "total community" quality is even more striking. It is true that they have the *formal* structure of a modern bureaucracy in which promotion is based upon laid-down standards of qualification and performance; jobs are described in specific terms and have specific functions, and authority lines are clearcut. But much of this is on paper only. Informally, the large hospital has many features of a paternalistic, traditional society rather than a democratic, rational one. There are cliques of *elite* who exercise power that goes far beyond their legitimate authority; this they can do because others abrogate their authority through ignorance, error, or a desire to be relieved of it. Once such authority is abrogated, the general institutional inertia prevents its return to the legitimate holders. The legitimate authority holders, such as doctors, are often not the people with the longest tenure in the hospital. Informal power gained through seniority tends to prevent the exercise of power by those who rightfully have it. The importance of informal groupings is expressed in such phrases as "so-and-so *really* runs this place." Characteristically, no one knows how this comes to be; it is vaguely attributed to "political influence" or to nepotism.

With this pattern of traditionalism there is a devaluation of new ways and a compensating ideology that "this is the best hospital in this part of the country." Obviously, innovations are not needed in a society which is already so satisfactory. Furthermore, a great deal of the daily round is governed by tradition, and in such a situation change is seldom welcomed. In the higher reaches of the hierarchy, few regulations are committed to paper. Rules, guiding principles, and even the personal records of the ward personnel are filed in the memories of the senior staff members. This lore is passed along by word of mouth. Rumors are the life blood of the institution because they are often the only way of communicating vital information.

There is seldom more than one doctor for every two hundred patients in the large mental hospital. This means that the doctor's influence on the condition of patients is carried out largely through the nursing staff. But the doctor is often much less acquainted with the hospital and its lore than are the nursing staff. Furthermore, large mental hospitals have caste-like hierarchies (Lemert, 1951; Rowland, 1939) and there is little inter-action across caste lines. It thus becomes important to "know the ropes"; seniority is valuable and "going through the mill" is a virtue. Young doctors attempting to make changes are discouraged by the repeated "when you've been here as long as I have, Doctor. . . ." which they hear from senior ward staff. Traditional and static, the mental hospital is hard to change, especially for the doctor who is always outnumbered and usually outmaneuvered.

These are not the only reasons that the mental hospital is hard to change. Just as important is the low level of integration at which it operates. Few goals are shared by the various hospital departments; only the safe custody of patients comes readily to mind. For the most part, the various departments pursue their own aims—the farm producing food, the electrician maintaining the electrical equipment in working order, and the ward staff keeping the patients docile and tractable. Interaction between the ward staff and the farm staff, for example, is limited to the ritualistic handing over of docile patients at the beginning and at the end of the working day.

Interaction is important because out of it rules develop informally and a workable code of social behavior is established. It is in interaction that behavior is tried out and modified or rejected, that thoughts are verbalized and made to have connection with the ongoing social life of the environment (Cameron, 1943). In daily exchanges, culture is accrued, a distinctive group structure develops, and sanctions are applied. The scanty interaction among the various groups and the lack of coordination or common supervision practically guarantee departmental autonomy. This is often most striking in the gap between the "male side" and the "female side" where there may be radically different policies.

Autonomy of purpose is very noticeable between ward staff and ancillary staffs. As there are seldom opportunities for professional interaction between departments, there are few exchanges of ideas, clashes of opinions, and developments of new norms and goals. Complete autonomy is of course impossible, but such integration as exists in the mental hospital is brought about high in the hierarchy. At the ward level no decisions are made which might affect general policy; thus a minimum is done, for nothing can be done without decisions (Barnard, 1938).

The traditional mental hospital is a granulated social system; it is crosscut horizontally by caste lines and crosscut vertically by the functional autonomy of the parts. This means that when the task of changing its operation is undertaken, the task of raising the level of integration of the system must be simultaneously undertaken. Bringing about changes in each one of these social granules is beyond the power of any individual or team, and therefore, without integration and communication, any change is restricted to the granule in which it began.

The Nursing Staff and Its Norms

In large hospitals most of the nursing function is performed by aides. These are the crucial members of the hospital staff because they have the most contact with the patients. Through them therapeutic intentions must be mediated. However, they are responsible to, interact with, and so learn their values from, the ward supervisors who are likely to be senior members of the ward staff. The supervisors have usually been in the hospital a long time and have learned their orientation to patients from the most senior of the nursing hierarchy, the administrative officers.

The administrative officers usually have long tenure and "know the ropes." They are in positions of authority in the hospital and they are rarely forced to communicate information; indeed, they can increase their own power by withholding information. It is not surprising that they are vitally concerned with maintaining the *status quo*. Their natural enemy is the young and enthusiastic doctor with new ideas and a desire to promote change. His program carries the implied suggestion that the senior nursing officers are inadequate for duties based on newer concepts; they can therefore be counted upon to resist change persistently, over long periods of time, and usually successfully. This is not to say that they have no valuable skills or that they are incapable of changing. However, special methods must be devised if their belief and value systems are to be changed.

Many hospitals are organized along the following lines. There are two separate nursing hierarchies, one for the male side and one for the female. Each is headed by a Chief Nursing Officer with a Deputy and a small staff of administrative officers. The Chiefs will probably be responsible to the Clinical Director or even to the Superintendent, and the whole nursing staff will be responsible to the Chief Nursing Officer. Two important features of the social position of the Chief's staff give them considerable power beyond the authority formally vested in their position. First, their ability to withhold information from newcomers makes the latter very dependent upon their good will; and second, their usual position of independence from the ward doctor enables them to go over his head to a higher medical authority in order to state their case. As the ward doctor is often of very short tenure in the hospital, he has no firm informal bonds with the senior medical staff. Moreover, unlike the senior nursing personnel, he may not share with the senior medical staff a body of common beliefs regarding how a mental hospital should be run. If he stays long enough he usually sees the light.

Thus, the nursing hierarchy is one of the points of maximum stability in the hospital. Beneath the administrative nursing hierarchy comes the ward supervisor, and it is from his echelon that the recruits for the administrative office are chosen. On the whole, the supervisor reflects the norms of the hierarchy, and he in turn passes them on through daily interaction to the aides and attendants under his control. The content of the most carefully thought out training program for aides can be radically undermined by what is called the "ward culture," which is the system of norms developed over time in the process of interaction between staff members working together on the wards.

⟋ As a rule, the culture on chronic wards includes such beliefs as: "schizophrenia is incurable"; "there is little use in sending a patient out if he is going to come back shortly"; "the conditions under which the patient lives are the only possible conditions for this type of patient." These beliefs are reflected in such remarks as "if you gave them nice things they would just destroy them," "this is the dirty type of patient," etc. In short, the nursing staff as a whole, under the socializing influence of those with highest rank and longest tenure, believe that their jobs are hard and often unpleasant, but that they are doing them as well as possible under the circumstances. ⟋

The Business Office

Large mental hospitals operate on an extremely small per capita budget, and diet, equipment, facilities, etc., show the signs of this deprivation. This leads to some of the most characteristic stigmata of the large hospital. It is crucially important that hospital personnel often work under conditions much less adequate than they would have in any other job or than they have at home. This means that they develop a double standard of what is "enough"; but it also produces a strain toward "getting more" in the hospital setting if only because of the invidious comparison of working conditions between hospital and home.

The people who can relieve this strain will tend to have power out of proportion to their formal position; plumbers, painters, carpenters and electricians, all of those needed to keep a small community operating, can exercise the power of withholding. Although this power is not very great in any one person's hands, it can be passed upward. There may be an informal understanding between these people and their chiefs about who shall receive things and who shall be denied them; in the army this would be the division between those able and those not able to "scrounge." At the top of this hierarchy is the Business Office, which is thus in an excellent position to accumulate power from below.

The result of the accumulation of power by the Business Office is frustration for the medical and nursing staff when they try to "get things." The nursing staff may also have the feeling that the business staff and service tradesmen are valued more highly than themselves (Elaine Cumming and J. Cumming, 1956). There is always potential strain between these two groups in the large hospital because the legitimate purpose of the Business Office is to balance the books, while that of the medical staff is to treat patients whatever the cost. In the worst hospitals the strain is minimal because the senior medical staff have accepted the norms of the business hierarchy; in the best hospitals the strain is minimal because the power of the business hierarchy is largely broken up and reallocated in medical hands. In most hospitals there is considerable strain, and this represents one good place to begin changes.

The Physicians

In his relationship to the chronic wards of the large hospital, the physician has a very difficult role. In the active treatment of new cases, he is on familiar ground although even there his role is unlike the one he learned during his years of training. The medical man is trained almost exclusively in dealing with the individual patient, and the training of the psychiatrist is even more oriented to the two-person relationship. He does not think readily in terms of large groups of patients and the therapeutic environment he may create for them. Furthermore, his authority often seems held in question. In a typical, small, non-teaching, general hospital, the doctor stands outside of the line authority in the role of consultant. His right to give orders to nurses is, in the limiting case, gained solely by the consent of the nursing hierarchy. The nurses for their part grant him this consent because of the technical training which uniquely qualifies him to make certain decisions. In short, his academic and professional qualifications *alone* legitimate his authority. He is not formally responsible to anyone in the hospital, and neither is anyone responsible to him. This has also been the pattern for many of the large mental hospitals, but there are very important differences between the two situations. In most mental hospitals, unlike general hospitals, the doctor must act out his entire professional role within the hospital. He does not use the hospital as one of alternate specific instruments for a part of his work. If a general practitioner does not believe the nursing service of a hospital is adequate, he has several choices; he can leave the hospital staff, or remonstrate with the head nurse, or appeal to the Clinical Director or the Medical Superintendent (whichever is above him in the line authority) and many of the features of the hospital discussed above make this a procedure unlikely to yield success.

A young ward doctor, newly arrived in the hospital, may want to change many features of the wards he works on. It is then that a fundamental difference between the general hospital and the mental hospital appears. The doctor finds that he has no administrative control of the ward and that the standards of ward personnel are quite different from his own. He must decide whether to assume administrative responsibility for the stock of soap on the ward or to accept the existing standards of "enough soap." The frustration he meets at this point is that his professional qualifications no longer legitimate his authority. He finds, in the limiting case, that his only authoritative decisions are those unequivocally concerned with "life and death." By the same token, it is in the limiting case only where the danger of death is perceived that the doctor has free access to the commodities he wants. If he tries to legitimate his right to demand more soap by his medical degree, he finds himself up against a morass of reasons—with which he cannot argue because he doesn't know enough—why there is a scarcity of soap. He must get into the line authority and run his wards if he is to give his patients the best chance for recovery.

By virtue of his training and experience the psychiatrist feels that it should be enough that he become aware of maltherapeutic situations and call them to the attention of those whose duty it is to rectify them. He soon discovers that it does not work this way. His decisions concerning ward situations have no "legitimacy" because the nursing hierarchy believes that he knows nothing about mental hospitals. Only by being willing to incorporate into his role not only the authority but also the *responsibility* for the ward will he be able to influence his patients' environment.

Many doctors will not accept administrative responsibility; it offends their image of themselves as therapists. They do not see the relationship between running a ward and doing therapy. This is partly because they have no formal training in administration and no expectation of having to administer, and partly because the administrative needs of a large "back ward" are so grossly primitive, e.g., for soap, clothing, dishes (Deutsch, 1949). Often the doctor prefers to abrogate his potential authority rather than to worry himself about such details. He grumbles because of the deprivation, but he feels that he is not a suitable person to attack the problem. Thus, by default, someone else administers it for him; the nursing hierarchy and the business office take over the soap problem and the doctor has started to learn the ropes.

After this initiation, the medical doctor has three paths open to him: (a) he can resign, and a great many do; (b) he can learn the wisdom of doing things the old way and yield to the hospital culture (he will probably refer to the limitations imposed by "red tape" and "bureaucracy" if he discusses why his original ardor cooled); (c) he can accept a certain degree of administrative responsibility for his wards. If he looks upon this duty as "administrative therapy" and sees the added therapeutic leverage he gains by assuming it, he will find it extremely rewarding (Stanton and Schwartz, 1954). (For further discussion of these issues, see the papers in this volume by Hamburg, by Kennard, and by Sharaf and Levinson.)

The Patients and the Wards

The numbers of patients in state-supported hospitals vary from under 100 to ten thousand or more. The hospital in which most of our own researches were carried out was probably close to the average with nearly two thousand patients. Most of the people in such hospitals at any given time are "chronic" and have long hospital lives, some as high as fifty or sixty years. In our hospital the average stay was about twelve years and the average age was about fifty years.

The patient population contains two distinct groups because the hospital acts on its incoming patients like a centrifuge. One half or more of those admitted to hospitals with even meagre treatment facilities stay a short period, undergo a remission of the disease process, and return to society. A small group fail to respond to treatment and are transferred to the "continued treatment" or chronic wards. At any given moment the great majority of the population is made up of these slowly accumulated chronic patients who have failed to leave hospital. Often their psychotic process has undergone a process of attrition; but hospital life with its meagre facilities and low level of social interaction has taken its toll, and they are listless, silent, uncomplaining, and inert. These patients form the precipitate that the centrifuge has separated from the incoming mass.

The centre of the chronic patient's life is the ward. It is usually over-crowded and bare but clean and tidy. One of the firmly held values of older nursing staff is that a good supervisor has a clean and tidy ward. Many wards contain large numbers of patients, usually inactive for a large part of the day. Interaction among patients is low on chronic wards, and lower still between patients and nursing staff. If the nursing staff is entrenched, they will have a recognizable sub-culture, high morale, and firm resistance to change. Thus the wards may often be deprived and drab, but the nursing staff have shared beliefs about the patients which allow them to accept this situation comfortably.

Many patients work in the hospital industries, e.g., the laundry, the farm, the upholsterer's shop. Without this patient labor, the hospital could not operate on its tiny outlay per patient. The patient who is getting better is put to work; if he continues to improve, his work is valuable, and there is then set up a complicated strain toward keeping him in the hospital, cured of his psychosis, but soon too desocialized to go home. Here again business and therapeutic goals clash. How can the business office perform its duties if the best workers are always being discharged? But how can a doctor be expected to remain interested and alert when his best therapeutic results are constantly being sabotaged?

THE GOALS AND METHODS OF CHANGE

We are interested primarily in the goals of change for the *chronic* service of the hospital. We shall focus here upon one aspect of the prevention of chronicity: the breaking up of the traditional, static quality of the chronic wards so that they may become genuinely "continued treatment" wards.

Our general goal is to reorientate all hospital personnel away from the idea that most mental illness becomes chronic, and towards the idea that most mental illness is, like physical illnesses such as arthritis, chronic and recurrent, but with long periods of remission during which the patient is relatively normal. The belief that many patients are better off in hospital must, in our opinion, be replaced by the belief that the patient is—except for the period of acute illness and treatment—almost always better off at home. To paraphrase the late Fiorello La Guardia: the worst home is better than the best mental hospital.

In the hospital in which we have done our major work, our primary specific goals were: (a) to reduce the chronic population by rehabilitation and discharge; (b) to improve conditions for those refractory to such rehabilitation; and (c) to remotivate the nursing and attendant staff toward handling future patients so as to assure them a hospitalization of minimum length under conditions of maximum therapy.

In order to accomplish these primary goals we had secondary and still more specific goals: to reorganize the nursing and business hierarchies so as to allow rational, therapeutic (rather than traditional "custodial") motivation to be acted out; and to reorganize the care of our long-stay patients so as to allow the rehabilitation of as many as possible.

Methods for changing a large mental hospital must be closer to methods used for increasing production in a factory than to those of increasing the efficiency of medical techniques. We developed methods for bringing about change in our hospital by studying: (a) the techniques used in industry to promote new output norms; (b) the needs and goals of the hospital and its members; (c) the reports of "total push" programs attempted elsewhere; (d) and most important, the previous attempts to change our hospital.

Previous Attempts at Change

There had been two outstanding attempts to change the nature of our hospital, and from them we learned a great deal. The first of these, a new nursing training program (described by McKerracher, 1949) had been designed to introduce to newly recruited aides and attendants a modern, humane, therapeutic approach to the mentally ill. After several years it was judged an academic and professional success but a failure inasmuch as it had not changed the "ward culture." Equipped with hindsight, we were able to discover important reasons for failure. First, the designers of the program had not introduced structural changes in the hospital hierarchy so as to raise the level of integration and communication in the hospital. There was not enough opportunity for the carriers of the new program to interact with people at all points in the structure. In a granulated system with a low interaction rate, one must either raise the level of integration and communication and hence of interaction, or else seek to change each semi-autonomous granule separately.

The training program personnel were able to interact intensively only with newly inducted trainees, a low prestige group; they were quite unable to reach the stable, culture-bearing group of senior nurses and aides. Furthermore, their opportunity for interaction even with the trainees was confined to the classroom; attempts to teach on the ward were abandoned in the face of repeated resistance from the nursing hierarchy.

The designers of the training program had not recognized the importance of seniority in the static hospital society, and they had promoted two capable but junior staff members to high-ranking training positions on the basis of their attitudes and orientations. In doing so, they induced great anxiety and hostility among the old-line staff who by continuing non-cooperation defended themselves against this implied label of inadequacy. The architects of the new program overlooked the principle that the most popular people are usually the norm-bearers; the two men promoted from the nursing ranks could not be norm-bearers because they were the least traditional men in a traditional subculture. It is not surprising that they were sabotaged. We knew that we had to start our re-education with those whose opinions were the most valued by the staff—the old-line supervisors.

We learned also from the work of an energetic team of two doctors. They had demonstrated on a treatment ward that deteriorated and incontinent schizophrenic patients would show social improvement if they were placed in an improved social environment, whether they had physical treatment or not (Miller and Clancy, 1952). However, as soon as the tremendous energy of the two doctors had been removed, the old situation reappeared upon the (culturally unchanged) ward.

Probably the most difficult ward pattern to modify is one in which staff-to-staff interactions are high, norms are correspondingly strong and articulate, and the patients are "deteriorated." The patients are expected to be dependent and passive; they are excluded from the culture-making process of the staff and they have none of their own. We have known really degraded wards where the staff never tried to communicate with the patients, who were in turn mute and incontinent, but where the ward itself was tidy and staff morale was high. A supervisor on such a ward says, "These patients are what we call dirty patients and they are incurable; we can't expect anything of them at all, but we can keep the ward clean." Upon such wards develop the myth that "this is the best mental hospital in the West."

Although our predecessors were unable to interact with enough staff members to change the culture of the total nursing group, they had overcome the immense hurdle of convincing many of them that something could be done.

Structural Changes

Our first task was to raise the level of communication in the hospital. Over many years our hospital had achieved a stable equilibrium, impervious to most attempts at change.[1] The nursing service had been run without interference by the Chief's Office and the Head Nurse's Office in a tacit collaboration with the medical administrators and the Business Office. The last office had complete control over all spending; no department had its own budget. The relationship of the rank and file of the nursing service to the business hierarchy was not amiable. The tradesmen who maintained the hospital's equipment thought the nursing and medical staff irrationally demanding, and the latter considered the former to be arbitrarily withholding in their approach to ward needs. Elaborate scrounging relationships existed between senior nurses and tradesmen.

The medical men were responsible to the Clinical Director, but no one was responsible to them. Ward staff had, of course, to obey medical orders from the doctors, but in all other matters the aides' final authority was the Chief's Office or the Head Nurse's Office. Differences of opinion between doctors and the Chief's Office were resolved by the Medical Superintendent, usually in favor of the Chief's Office. Doctors were expendable but the good-will of the nursing hierarchy was not. The doctors themselves, furthermore, did not wish the ward responsibility that authority over the staff would entail.

One of the outstanding aspects of the structure of our nursing service was the small size of its executive echelon. Considering that there were nearly two thousand patients and a nursing staff of about 350, its two Chiefs, two Deputies, and five Assistants to cover three shifts were enough for only the most routine daily administrative duties. Together with an almost total absence of staff meetings and a lack of formal job specification, this poverty of decision-making roles practically guaranteed that the minimum would be done and that communication and integration would be low.

Our first move, therefore, was to create a set of new "coördinating" roles in the nursing hierarchy. Two of these were at the Deputy Chief level, six at the Assistant Chief level. These officers were to have a double function: to increase the efficiency and quality of the nursing service, and to integrate ward activities. The number was intended to be suitable for intensive interaction with the medical doctors in discussions and meetings. There were, furthermore, enough of them to meet with the ward staffs often enough to have an appreciable effect upon their attitudes and

[1] This is not literally true. There had been over the years a slow drop in the use of camisoles and cuffs. This was spoken of with considerable nostalgia by members of the chief's office. The fact that once "everyone in the disturbed ward was in a jacket" was used by the old-line staff as evidence that they were progressive.

beliefs. In this way a new therapeutic approach could be spread fan-wise through the hospital.

It is sometimes assumed that interaction among staff members is less therapeutic in potential than is interaction between staff members and patients, but in our experience a staff that is engrossed in planning programs for patients exercises great leverage upon chronic wards. New standards of patient welfare and patient therapy can become institutionalized in the course of such planning. We doubt that integrated therapeutic ward programs are possible without a high level of staff-to-staff interaction.

The coördinating group were charged with the job of planning the reconstruction of ward life. This included "getting things" and "getting things done." Hitherto the nursing hierarchy had been too weakly staffed at the executive level—and too weakly motivated—to spend sufficient time at the kinds of activity necessary in a large bureaucracy for procuring equipment and material needed for ward programs. The new roles were also meant to provide a more efficient, integrated, and therapeutic nursing service through which the medical staff could introduce their own attitudes and ideas at the ward level.

As in many hospitals, the Chief's Office and the Head Nurse's Office had been the fulcrum of the medical service, and through entrenched informal groupings these administrative officers had tended to control the flow of communications. They often received information directly when it should have come through ward supervisors, and they often withheld information that should have been distributed to ward staffs. This had greatly enhanced their power, as control over communication must always do. We laid down firm lines of communication and announced that for the time being protocol would in all cases be observed. We did not want the old patterns of informal communication that would short-circuit some of the new role-holders to survive in the new structure. We were prepared for some informal channels to develop, but we hoped that this would happen only after the proper channels were well enough known so that when a person used an informal channel, he would be well aware of doing so. In a changed pattern of communication, vital information must never be withheld or misdirected without formal sanction; if it is, the new pattern cannot become institutionalized.

At the same time, a change was made in the authority position of the Nursing Training Office. It had stood outside the nursing hierarchy since the training program mentioned above. This pattern is no doubt preferable where administrative goals coincide with training goals. However, in our case the old-line nurses in the Chief's Office had no power to discipline the training staff who in turn had no power to force their program upon the nursing hierarchy; the result was stalemate and encapsulation.

Nursing training was therefore restored to the Nursing Service under a well-qualified Nursing Officer.

Finally, the Deputy Nursing Officers in charge of coördinating therapeutic activities were made responsible in these activities to the medical staff rather than to the Chief's Office. In administrative matters these Nursing Officers were still responsible to the Superintendent of Nursing. Therefore, formal regulations regarding reporting and communication with the Nursing Office were introduced, in order to avoid overlapping of authority (Henry, 1954). Until their responsibilities to the Nursing Office were institutionalized, these Deputies were tempted to communicate solely with the medical staff who were in charge of the more interesting of the activities required by their roles.

Getting the hospital to operate as one coördinated institution was a formidable undertaking. It had run along for years without much contact between the male and female sides. The first step was the physical removal of the Chief's Office and the Head Nurse's Office, together with all the new appointees and the Training Office Staff, to new common quarters. Previously they had been separately housed on their own sides. Now they were together on neutral ground with an opportunity for informal communication.

The choice of people to fill the new positions was very important to hospital integration. We took advantage of the waiting period (while the new positions were being formally secured) to conduct a campaign of anticipation. The following examples of the preliminary efforts are taken from notes made during the work done with male attendants.

A meeting of all the male ward supervisors was called. The new jobs were described to them and they were asked to complete sociometric ballots indicating which male staff members should be promoted to these new positions. Although the voting did not follow rigid seniority lines, the eight men who received almost all of the votes were among the fifteen most senior male staff members in the hospital. This list of highly chosen men coincided exactly with our own list of the senior men most able to do a good job. Although we know there were some exceptionally good young men of less seniority, we decided that the following three principles were too important to violate: (a) norm-bearers are highly chosen. New programs are better introduced by norm-bearers than by deviants; (b) in a stable system, when all else is equal, seniority is the fairest criterion for promotion; (c) very few roles in any society should be structured so that exceptional people must hold them, because most people are unexceptional (Linton, 1936).

The next step in the anticipatory socialization of these men was orienting them to the type of problem with which they would be dealing. Committees studied ward procedures e.g., the condemning of old clothing and requisitioning of new, in order to recommend changes that would promote patient welfare. A comittee drafted a plan for the reorganization of the geriatrics ward. A key man was assigned to prepare a weekly bulletin keeping all branches of the hospital informed of any news which might otherwise circulate only by rumor.

At this stage considerable enthusiasm began to appear. Many evening hours were spent at planning activities, although this was never required. We did not, at this stage, do any formal teaching of special attitudes but rather expected the men to orientate themselves to the welfare of the patient in the activities in which they were engaged. We hoped a common involvement in therapeutic goals would emerge. Knowing a good deal about "ward culture" we could anticipate which of our planned changes would be acceptable and which intolerable to this group of men.

A great deal of our effort was spent in persuading the old guard that things *could* be done. They found it hard to accept the idea that a routine could be changed without dire consequences. Besides this traditionalism, the poverty of the environment and the poor communication system had frustrated them so often in the past that their skepticism was profound. They considered it impossible that each patient have his own clothes when the lockers were broken; the lockers could not be fixed because the tinsmith [2] had refused once before to fix them. At this juncture it was vital for us to ensure that the tinsmith fix the lockers and, in general, to exercise leadership having a shade of "charisma," in order to overcome the inertia of the staff.

During this period, new roles of Superintendent of Nursing and Deputy Superintendent of Nursing were created to replace the Chief Attendant and Head Nurse. It was stipulated that if the Superintendent was a woman the Deputy must be a man, and *vice versa*. These two role-holders were charged with the duty of unifying the nursing services across the hospital. This they were to do by such steps as centralizing the booking procedures. Booking of nurses to wards became uniform across the hospital, and one person only was needed to handle the task. Steps of this nature were designed to increase communication, to widen the scope of action of the executive officers, and to generate new standards of administrative procedure.

We broke sharply with tradition by offering the Ward Supervisors' posts, made vacant by promotions to the new positions, to men or women without regard to whether the ward were on the male or the female side of the hospital. This interchangeability of senior staff was a major step toward integration of the two sides of the hospital.

A series of minor structural changes followed these major shifts. For example, two large male wards were consolidated for the purpose of

[2] Our apologies to the tinsmith for referring to him in this fictitious but typical example.

administration. One supervisor administered the wards and two supervised the therapeutic program. This division of labor forced communication and coördination across these two wards, with a rise in efficiency of both. Furthermore, the role of ward administrator became an important safety-valve for certain staff members whose rigid and traditional approach to hospital procedures made them uncomfortable in the new therapeutic situation.

To improve the relationship between the business side and the nursing and medical service, weekly meetings were held between the Business Manager and the senior medical staff. Much that had never been communicated before came under review, and plans for more rational budgeting procedures were set up. These meetings were often marked by sharp conflict between business and therapeutic interests, but they did much to bring the business office into better accord with therapeutic goals.

At the same time a determined attempt was made to reorientate the tradesmen toward the goals of the nursing service. The Superintendent of Maintenance was invited to planning conferences concerning even minor changes in the physical arrangements. The old practice of requisitioning minor repairs was modified to increase contact between the two services. This was one of our most fruitful maneuvers and won the support of the people controlling vital equipment and commodities. We made no effort to "teach" them; rather, we solicited their technical and special skills in problem solving.

We have not discussed the full extent of the changes made, nor were the changes made the only ones possible. In general, the goal of raising the integration and communication level may be achieved in a number of ways. Our use of nursing staff may be excessive for some hospitals.

Changing from Traditional to Rational Norms

If a large state-supported mental hospital is to have an effective therapeutic program, it must be carried out by the nurses and aides. We shall attempt here to describe our initial steps in using aides in new therapeutic roles, and the difficulties we and they encountered.

As soon as the new Nursing Officers were formally appointed, we began a daily training program. For six weeks we met as a group each morning for an hour, and for the next six months we met three mornings a week. Ultimately these meetings were modified to short business discussions, but in the beginning the staff discussed numerous problems. We used each problem to delineate certain principles of ward management. We discussed the sociology of small groups, some principles of formal organization, and some of the practical findings from industrial sociology where these were applicable to the ward situation. Repeatedly we emphasized the importance of communication and the use of proper channels in maintaining morale in the hospital.

Individual psychodynamic psychiatry was not emphasized in the discussion sessions. However, the Nursing Officers requested some training in this field; we then gave a set of general orientation lectures in psychopathology and subsequently taught them to take routine psychiatric histories from new patients. They enjoyed this variation from the group work which was their chief responsibility, and because they were closer to the patients in cultural background than were the doctors they established rapport more easily. Shortly after the program began, the Nursing Officers were formed into a group and taught group therapy techniques. During their training experience, each was assigned to one group of chronic patients and one group of active patients so that they could develop practical skills at the same time that they were learning the method.

Each Nursing Officer scheduled regular meetings with ward supervisors and staff members. In these meetings he acted as intermediary between ward staff and medical doctors on the one hand, and between ward staff and nursing hierarchy on the other. A great many useful suggestions for patient care and management emerged from these meetings, as did a great many objections and resistances. The latter was almost as useful as the former; for the first time there was a place in which such formal expressions of belief were appropriate, and once expressed they were available for examination and modification by their peers and the Nursing Officers.

We were fortunate in obtaining funds to send four Nursing Officers on a tour of hospitals where active rehabilitation programs had been under way for some time. Their contact with the Nursing personnel in these places considerably strengthened their motivation and understanding.

Changing Long-Stay Patients

Though we aimed at improvement for all patients, limitations of resources, personnel, and sometimes the patients' illnesses, caused some unevenness in the program. Our older patients probably benefited the least. We had obtained governmental support in the physical rehabilitation of the wards, something that permitted marked improvement in the standard of physical care of the aged. However, we did not embark on any determined program of social rehabilitation with this group. Fortunately, we discovered that bedside care of the aged by the recovering younger schizophrenics seemed beneficial to both groups. A small group of such patients were therefore employed at spoon-feeding the older patients, tidying and cleaning the ward, and so on. We found that when formal tasks were done, they then played checkers or chatted with their bed-ridden patients. As Jones (1954) points out, the use of patients as therapists is a largely unexplored area.

We started with the premise that no patient in any mental hospital should be mute or incontinent, and that hospital practice alone was responsible for this deplorable condition. We felt, moreover, that the strongest sanctions against such anti-social behavior would be the interpersonal sanctions of a primary group. Consequently, with the incontinent group as with others we concentrated primarily upon the promotion of group interaction. At first we yielded to the demands of nursing staff and doctors for the use of intensive Electro-Convulsive Therapy to "get them back in touch." But as the Nursing Officers acquired experience with group processes, the use of E.C.T. fell off spontaneously, not only on this ward, but throughout the hospital. However, we found chlorpromazine of continuing value in altering the forms of social interaction.

Actively psychotic patients probably benefited most from the program, and in turn were the most rewarding to work with. Here, emphasis was placed on intensive group interaction: In work, in recreation, and in formal group psychotherapy. Our goal was to recapture these people in the web of social interaction which controls behavior and promotes participation. To his amazement, one Nursing Officer was able to give five of his first eight patients either pre-discharge parole or recreation leaves within six months after starting a formal therapy group on a chronically disturbed ward. We attempted to keep the groups intact and to move patients as a group when their condition warranted it. The recognized exception to this rule was that a patient was discharged as soon as his condition had improved enough to warrant it.

The "workers" and "trusties" proved a harder group to deal with than the more actively psychotic patients. They had found in the hospital security and a measure of secondary gain. They were also involved in a social system of some strength, and their way of life was legitimated daily through their successful adjustment to hospital life. Our main effort was to reorient them through discussion of the rewards outside the hospital. In reality terms, too, a good deal of time had to be spent on this group, assessing their chances for rehabilitation outside the hospital. Our progress here was inhibited by the fact that the hospital could ill accept a wholesale loss of patient-workers. This will be discussed below.

PROBLEMS OF CHANGE

Some of our problems were created by our own errors; other problems were built into the tradition of neglect and isolation and deprivation which is the heritage of the large, state-supported hospital.

Problems with Nurses

No staff welcomes programs of general change which they have not themselves initiated. Such programs carry an implicit criticism of the *status quo* and a suggestion that the staff may not be adequate to perform new duties. Members of the entrenched administrative branch of the nursing service were quite bitterly opposed to our plan, which threatened their power by introducing into the hierarchy a number of clinically oriented roles coördinate with their own. They tried to discourage the more popular ward supervisors from applying for the new positions. They played upon the supervisors' anxieties by announcing that the program would not last, that the positions would not be permanent, and that policy changes would leave the appointees without jobs and without their present security of union membership. Although these matters were discussed and straightened out in a general meeting of the potential candidates, there was, for some time, an underlying fear of loss of prestige which they felt might accompany identification with a new and perhaps impermanent program.

With this conflict-ridden beginning, it is not surprising that our Nursing Officers met difficulties when they took over their new tasks. They were sometimes greeted on the wards with hostile and derisive remarks concerning their new positions. They had only recently been peers of the supervisors and could not overnight command the degree of respect accorded the older and more deeply entrenched administrative officers of the same rank. Fortunately, this reaction from the supervisors had been anticipated and discussed. The Officers set about to win the ward supervisors over to their side. They became, with medical backing, the people who "got things" and arranged services that made the wards easier to operate. Eventually they seemed to be accepted, if occasionally somewhat grudgingly, by most of the staff.

In the appointment of the Male Nursing Officers an error was made. One man was much less senior than the other four; he had been chosen, contrary to our own expressed principle, on merit alone, and he did not succeed in gaining acceptance from the ward staff. It is doubtful that the staff considered him unsuitable for the position, but they seemed to resent not having had a chance to pass on his suitability as they had with the previous four.

A second problem was related to the fact that not all of the most senior supervisors had been equally suitable candidates for promotion to the clinical positions. Two very senior ward supervisors who had received no choices in the sociometric rating and who had not applied for appointment were firmly resistant to the new program. These two men had for years run the type of ward on which the staff members read magazines, got the patients to polish their shoes now and then, played pool with one another, and seldom talked with the patients. They had never organized patient activities of even the simplest sort. It had always been thought that a certain amount of teasing and sadism took place on these idle wards and that it was permitted as long as no one got caught. However, neither supervisor would support a staff member who had been caught red-handed abusing a patient. Their wards were marked by very low morale.

Assignment of these supervisors to problem-solving tasks was a failure. Finally, a formal reprimand was delivered to one of them and, according to regulation, was placed on his file. This rather drastic punishment had a salutary effect at least for the time being. However, among staff members who firmly believed that the old ways of handling patients were the best, solidarity strengthened during the change. The supervisors who were sociometric isolates when viewed as part of the supervising group were in fact members of small sub-groups of highly interactive minorities. It is difficult to shift norms in these groups because their morale is high, especially under attack. Over a long period of time, in carefully structured working groups, these persons might learn a less fatalistic and hopeless approach to mental illness, but this seems doubtful. Formal sanctions or discharge seem to be the only short-run solution to the problem they create. Perhaps the most useful concept for dealing with these people would be that of personality; but we had neither the time nor the resources to work with these people in terms of manipulation of personality, and they probably would not have coöperated.

One problem we might have avoided was anxiety among the Nursing Officers over the lack of a clear-cut role.[3] This problem was exacerbated by the ward supervisors who demanded to know just what the new positions did encompass. Our inability to be specific in laying down the functions of the new Nursing Officers had risen from the lack of precedent in giving ward staff diffuse responsibility. We simply did not know how much they could assume. We feel now that we could have been more specific in our demands upon these people. Milieu therapy implies that the role is a diffuse one, that the incumbent takes responsibility for the total environment of the patient. This means that the Nursing Officer should have been prepared to act as both a task leader and an integrative leader (Bales, 1953). In order to exercise instrumental leadership, the Officers should have had specific knowledge of the proper lines of communication with the hospital's resources. Furthermore, we could have made certain that each purveyor of "things" and services clearly recognized his right to communicate regarding them. As an integrative leader, the Nursing Officer must work to modify the norms of ward staff without allowing tensions to develop to disrupting levels. He should have had specific instructions to hold frequent meetings with staffs on the wards.

The problem of internalization is always present when an incumbent learns a new rule. Internalization was difficult for our Nursing Officers because they shared in two worlds and had two reference groups, the

[3] This material was obtained from the Nursing Officers in a series of recorded group discussions about eight months after their appointment.

doctors and the nursing staff. However, as a non-commissioned officer does, they learned to live with this difficult but not impossible role.

Problems with Doctors

In order to do their job, our Nursing Officers had to have an authority among the nursing staff at least equal to that traditionally enjoyed in mental hospitals by the administrative nursing hierarchy. Often in state-supported institutions the authority necessary for carrying out a clinical program has been usurped by non-clinical people or abrogated by the medical staff (Elaine Cumming and J. Cumming, 1956). If such a process has taken place, there may be a struggle before authority can be invested in the Nursing Officer role. We were fortunate in having the support and backing of the Medical Superintendent and Clinical Director in this process, but we faced a serious problem of the authority relationship between the Officers and the ward doctors.

As we noted earlier, the training of psychiatrists makes it difficult for them to understand a social-psychological approach to hospital problems. In our experience, the doctors trained in traditional and descriptive psychiatry had the most difficulty in accepting the program while those with no psychiatric training coöperated well. One doctor trained in Public Health as well as in Psychiatry was a constant source of strength to the Nursing Officers. Two doctors with a Kraepelinian orientation, although extremely efficient in the areas in which they had been trained, were convinced that the therapeutic management of wards was futile.

Specific problems with doctors emerged during the training of the Nursing Officers. We found that on each ward we had developed two, unstable, overlapping three-man groups. One consisted of the Doctor, the Nursing Officer, and the Senior Psychiatrist. The other consisted of the Doctor, the Nursing Officer, and the Ward Supervisor. Conflict soon developed between doctors and Nursing Officers; the doctors were, in some cases, almost eager to assist the ward supervisors in resistive manipulation of the Nursing Officer. An unsympathetic physician in charge of a ward run by one of the old-line, unreconstructed supervisors described above, could effectively block almost any change. For example: A Nursing Officer establishes a therapy group on a chronic disturbed ward; in a short time a patient shows striking improvement and the ward supervisor calls this to the attention of the doctor, neglecting to mention that the patient is a member of a therapy group. The doctor transfers him to a better ward which effectively isolates him from his group and removes him from therapy. When the Nursing Officer complains to the Senior Psychiatrist, the doctor says that he did not know who was on group therapy—the ward supervisor has not told him, and he cannot find the time for ward meetings—and that he considers it inhumane to keep a man on a disturbed ward when he is no longer disturbed. The doctor states that membership in a therapy group is less important than residence on a "better" ward. Moreover, the doctor objects to the impractical and routine disrupting proposal of moving groups of patients off the disturbed ward at one time. Either the doctor must be ordered to comply or the therapy group must be given up—dismal alternatives from the point of view of morale.

In the above example, the doctor and the ward supervisor aligned themselves against the Nursing Officer. Other disruptive alignments also took place. If the supervisor supported the new program and orientated himself to the Nursing Officer, the doctor was left in a position of impotence which he sometimes tried to resolve by winning the supervisor over to opposition to the program. Alternatively, the doctor might become cynical and apathetic, or resign from the staff.

Our panacea for the difficulty was—reluctantly—to remove the dissenting doctors from the line authority. They were made consultants to the Clinical Director on the admissions wards where they worked with incoming patients. Meanwhile the chronic wards were administered by the Nursing Officers under the medical supervision of the Senior Psychiatrist and the coöperative physicians. Although this solved our problem, it is an inadequate general plan. Ultimately, physicians in mental hospitals will have to take administrative responsibility if hospital care is to improve.

Unexpected Problems, Solvable and Unsolvable

We shall give two examples of unexpected problems, one solved, the other unsolved. During the reorganization of the nursing hierarchy, the small group of men from the old "chief's office" began to show signs of status anxiety. Their complaints centered on "increased work" although there was no evidence for this. However, closer study showed that they had inadvertently been required to work more evening and night shifts than they had done before the reorganization. Not having to do shift work is an important sign of status in any organization, and these men were comparing themselves to the new Nursing Officers who had no shift obligations. In spite of the fact that they were the responsible officials in the hospital on the evening and night shifts, they still felt deprived in comparison to the new men. This problem of demoralization was easily solved.

A more difficult problem related to the isolation of the hospital. As long as our nursing staff had little emotional investment in their work, they were satisfied with the location of the hospital because they had enduring personal ties in the community. Once they had visited other hospitals and had experienced the comradeship of other persons facing similar problems, they felt isolated in their work for the first time. This problem is repeated for medical doctors, psychologists, auxiliary therapists, and others. The more skilled they become, the more need they have for professional interchange with others occupying similar roles, and the more frustrating the isolation is to them. This problem was unsolvable in our case except by planning as many trips, discussions with visitors, institutes, etc. as we could, but it is no doubt generally recognized that the practice of building hospitals in remote places serves chiefly to lower the level of service given.

Problems with the Public

Probably our most crucial unresolved problem involved the status of the patient-workers. We were never able to reconcile fully the needs of therapy and the needs of the hospital community in the placement of patients. It seems inevitable that as long as patient labor is integral to the running of these hospitals, many patients will have to pay the price of chronicity. We can only hope that active programs, aimed at reducing the numbers of chronic patients, will impress legislators sufficiently to encourage them to provide funds sufficient to ensure that a patient is employed only during a necessary, transitional period in his rehabilitation, not because patient labor is necessary to keep the hospital going.

SERENDIPITIES

A number of unexpected insights have provided happy landmarks in our hospital work. One of these occurred while we were analysing the types of staff and patient interactions on certain wards. We recalled that some hospitals are well-staffed and have small wards, but they have very little staff-to-staff interaction because only one or two people are on duty at any one time. Such wards may have active programs and high recovery rates. However, the individual qualities of staff members tend to assume undue importance when the ward program is a one-man affair. With a larger staff group, even mediocre personnel can be given sufficient guidance and interaction with their peers in the work situation so as to develop highly therapeutic norms which they would not acquire working alone or nearly alone on wards. Thus the small ward, the goal of many institutions, may have a latent drawback: The norm-creating process cannot be exploited when there is no true work group.

A second serendipity occurred at about the ninth month of our rehabilitation program. We had been gratified by a drop of nearly ten percent in the total hospital census during this period although at the same time the admission rate had been rising. We first interpreted this to mean that the hospital had been in equilibrium population-wise and that the work we had applied to it had shifted this equilibrium downward. The drop had enabled us to close the worst ward on the male side of the hospital and convert it into recreation space by distributing the few remaining patients through the other wards. A sister hospital lacking an intensive program had not had a drop in census.

However, we then observed that the total census of the hospital had remained remarkably stable from 1950 until 1953 (prior to any concerted program of change), while the admission rate had been rising by fifty percent (Table 1). We needed to explain why the population had not in the past increased by the number of surplus admissions each year. This lag between increase in intake and increase in census is caused by what administrators know as "statistical pressure," and as thinking of this process led to our unexpected insight, we shall explain how it operates.

It is well recognized that the decision to discharge a patient is related to the question of how badly his bed is needed. Since most hospitals are somewhat crowded, what constitutes sufficient overcrowding to exert a "statistical pressure" toward discharge? Overcrowding in a mental hospital is a term without absolute meaning. If it is referred to a standard such as that established by the American Psychiatric Association, it will have fairly precise meaning to hospital administrators. But overcrowding to nursing staff is compounded of many things: Absolute density of bodies for sleeping space, the number of patients who have occupied this particular space in the past, the activities prescribed for patients, and the number of patients in other wards. A further ingredient is the value judgment of how much crowding is humane and decent. In our hospital a ward had been reduced suddenly in size from 220 to 135 patients. Then, for a time it was thought not to be overcrowded, but during the course of years it had slowly been redefined as overcrowded once again, as indeed it was.

For the nursing staff, overcrowding is a normative matter, and the norms can be changed. Let us consider a ward upon which the following norms are firmly institutionalized: (a) the ward is defined as overcrowded; (b) it is considered possible (though not likely) for a patient to be discharged from this ward; (c) patients should not be sent from

Table 1

	December 31 1950	December 31 1951	December 31 1952	December 31 1953	December 31 1954	December 31 1955
Admissions for the previous year	362	407	550	538	525	683 [a]
Balance in hospital	1915	1942	1959	1952	1881	1809

[a] This sudden rise in rate is partly accounted for by the increased rate of turnover of patients. Using a "bouncing ball" model, patients are discharged even when there is some expectation of their return. Nevertheless, they create pressure on the hospital's facilities whether they are admissions or readmissions.

this ward to an inferior one, for these patients do not deteriorate. This set of conditions can easily be met on a custodial ward with high standards of care. If this ward is also relatively uncrowded so that better wards object to receiving its patients, then as the population rises there will be a strain leading to a higher rate of discharge.

However, this is not a simple process of taking the most nearly well patient and disposing of him; it is a more subtle and probably more efficient process. Interaction on all mental hospital wards delineates the difference between the role of patient and the role of nurse. On chronic wards this difference is exaggerated to a caste-like extent, and the relationship between staff member and patient tends toward that of benign planter and slave in the Old South. It is assumed that the patient will neither leave the hospital nor be eligible for an equalitarian relationship with the staff member. When under the conditions of overcrowding outlined above, a promising candidate is sought for discharge, the stable caste relationship on the ward is interrupted and a new type of relationship emerges. If a patient is considered for discharge, an implicit hypothesis about him is formed among the staff members: "This person is able to carry on an acceptable social life in the outside world." One way of testing this hypothesis is to interact with this person as if he were a normal individual and to notice how he responds. It is rather similar to inviting applicants for an executive post to dinner, to see if they are socially competent.

What starts as an experiment has unintended consequences. The staff member's initiation of normal social interaction brings into play a whole network of expectations which often bring the patient into closer conformity with socially acceptable conduct. For a patient with an acute psychosis, these cues and sanctions may be insufficient, but for a patient whose psychosis has undergone some spontaneous attrition, they will tend to have a resocializing effect.

Even when we had reduced our population by nearly ten percent, the process continued. We realized in retrospect that not only had we had the pressure of a high admissions rate, but we had created an artificial pressure by redistributing among the wards the remaining patients from the ward we had been able to close, as well as the total population of a temporarily closed geriatrics ward.

Numerous fruitful experiments in manipulating norms of overcrowding might be undertaken, thus turning to useful account the latent consequences of this manifestly bad aspect of large hospitals. For example: Ward populations have a statistical variation over any period of time; each ward has some empty beds most of the time. One can determine the prevalent norms about how many empty beds there should be. If four beds are thought to be the proper number to have empty on a ward, ten could be taken down and stored at some point when through chance there were sixteen empty beds. The space might be used for easy chairs or for on-ward occupational therapy equipment. A new norm of "enough" will develop in perhaps two to three weeks on a ward with a high staff-to-staff interaction.

RESULTS OF CHANGE

We cannot hope to recognize, let alone describe in full, the total result of our efforts in a static, traditional, mental hospital. However, certain results have been mentioned as we have told our story, and certain indices which are very revealing can be examined. Results in our hospital may differ markedly from those in other hospitals where such programs emphasize somewhat different goals and where conditions differ markedly to start with.

In our hospital, total population has dropped remarkably (see Table 1 above). Furthermore, the handling of patients has changed dramatically. Table 2 below shows the reduction in the amount of restraint, seclusion, and shock now used for controlling patients. The use made of these techniques of control is one of the most sensitive indicators of the level of care a hospital offers.

Other signs of positive change are available. We expected a temporary recession of morale as a result of the dislocation of old patterns, but from the start, sickness and absenteeism rates as well as staff resignations gave no sign of lowered morale. We were encouraged to believe that not only did we achieve the coöperation of the old-line staff, but we aroused in them latent therapeutic attitudes which in turn provided sufficient satisfaction to compensate for the temporary dislocation of accepted patterns. This impression is strengthened by a spontaneous revolt among members of the nursing staff against the tradition-honored practice of using male ward personnel to relieve shortages in the cleaning and servicing depart-

Table 2

	January 18–31, 1955	January 18–31, 1956
Restraint	78 Patients for a total of 4170 hours	7 Patients for a total of 90½ hours
Seclusions	19 Patients, hours unrecorded	4 Patients, hours unrecorded
Male Seclusions		
Female Seclusions	31 Patients for 2160 hours	36 Patients for 572 hours
E.C.T. to control behavior (female only)	58 Patients receiving a total of 149 E.C.T.	9 Patients receiving 26 E.C.T.

ments. The male ward staff complained that they were being hampered in their nursing efforts by routine jobs of cleaning, sanitation, and maintenance which could in no way be considered therapeutic.

There is evidence of increased coöperation between departments. For example: A spokesman for the maintenance staff suggested that some of the patient laborers should be placed under the supervision of nursing staff during working hours in order that they might be employed to therapeutic as well as service ends.

Increased patient activity is evident both in occupations and in recreation. The numbers of chronic patients occupied has risen sharply and to a large extent the increased activity goes on in groups. Admission ward patients are offered increased group activity and take more responsibility for their own programming. This raised level of activity comes from the planning and initiative of the nursing staff; we have thus succeeded in some measure in creating a hospital organization where much less hinges upon the initiative of doctors and much more on the continued performance of nurses in therapeutic roles. In our case this was essential because medical staff turnover is so high. In other hospitals medical leadership may play a somewhat greater role, although there will probably never be sufficient psychiatrists to assume the main burden of initiative in most hospitals.

An encouraging evidenc of change is the improved appearance and condition of the wards. The very worst male ward has been closed and the space converted to recreation. Incontinence has been drastically reduced. As a result, the laundry can keep a better supply of work clothes available and the patients can be cleaner on all of the chronic wards.

Countless subjective evidences of change are available. Ward staff members speak freely of a renewed interest in their work, and doctors speak of the unexpected skills and abilities among the nursing staff.

Just as there are unintended problems which arise during the manipulation of a social structure, so are there unanticipated rewards. For example, although we expected to gain a great deal from the nurses' vast knowledge of the hospital, we had not anticipated the advantage of bringing directly into the process of handling patients a group of men having the same background as the patients. In most large hospitals, especially those far from urban centers, medical staff and patients differ greatly in cultural background. We found that case histories assumed a new vigor when the remarks of the patients were interpreted by the Nursing Officers who knew their home district; relatives were happier when they had talked to someone who understood their problems more closely; the nurses could offer solutions to problems of rehabilitation which would not have occurred to anyone in less close touch with the local culture. The Nursing Officers' judgment of when patients would prove acceptable in their homes was much superior to our own. This latent gain was made possible by increased use of the ward staff in responsible roles; their "know-how" probably reduced by considerable time the stay of many patients in our hospital and contributed to the decline in population.

SUMMARY

We selected norm-bearing, highly chosen ward staff in a large public hospital and trained them for positions of clear-cut authority as Nursing Officers. Their efforts in the new roles led to their being defined by ward personnel as useful through their ability to perform adaptive tasks. The Nursing Officers then became accepted and respected on the wards. Having achieved both the desire and the ability to set up therapeutic ward activity programs, they were able in interaction to influence the work norms of the total ward staff. The appropriateness of the new programs was remarkably well recognized and the programs themselves accepted at all levels. We were able to establish a system of ramifying interaction patterns throughout the social structure of the hospital. The resulting norms regarding patient care were more nearly in accord with modern psychiatric thought; their goal is the expulsion of the patient rather than his indefinite retention in the hospital. Many of the problems encountered during the program have been described above.

Because of the fundamental nature of culture formation and the normative control of individual behavior, we believe that our methods have general relevance. It is our thesis that improved methods of patient care must be based on social, cultural, and psychological considerations in addition to those derived from medical practice.

REFERENCES

Bales, R. F. The equilibrium problem in small groups. In Parsons, T., and Bales, R. F. *Working Papers in the Theory of Action*. The Free Press of Glencoe, Illinois, 1953.

Barnard, C. I. *The function of the executive*. Cambridge, Harvard University Press, 1938.

Cameron, N. The paranoid pseudo-community. *Amer. J. Sociol.*, 1943, 49, 32–38.

Cumming, Elaine and Cumming, J. The locus of power in the large mental hospital. *Psychiatry*, 1956, 19, 361–369.

Cumming, Elaine, Clancey, I. L. W., & Cumming, J. Improving patient care through organizational changes in the mental hospital. *Psychiatry*, 1956, 19, 249–261.

Cumming, J. and Cumming, Elaine. Affective symbolism, social norms, and mental illness. *Psychiatry*, 1956, 19, 77–85.

Deutsch, A. *The mentally ill in America*. (2nd Ed.) New York, Columbia Univer. Press, 1949.

Henry, J. The formal social structure of a psychiatric hospital. *Psychiatry*, 1954, 17, 139–151.

Jones, M. *The therapeutic community*. New York, Basic Books, 1954.

Lemert, E. M. *Social Pathology*. New York: McGraw-Hill, 1951.

Linton, R. Status and role. In *The study of man*. New York: D. Appleton Century, 1936.

McKerracher, D. G. A new program in the training and employment of ward personnel. *Amer. J. Psychiatry*, 1949, 106, 259–264.

Miller, D. H. and Clancy, J. An approach to the social rehabilitation of chronic psychotic patients. *Psychiatry*, 1952, 15, 435–443.

Rowland, H. Friendship patterns in the state mental hospital. *Psychiatry*, 1939, 3, 363–373.

Stanton, A., and Schwartz, M. *The mental hospital*. Illinois, Basic Books, 1954.

Role Conceptions and Organizational Size

Edwin J. Thomas

The growth of organizations from modest-sized structures, often housed under one roof, to bureaucratic giants has brought a proliferation of administrative units and their dispersion over wide geographical areas. Although the units of these bureaucracies are generally part of the same organizational structure and are committed to achieving common objectives by means of uniformly applied operating procedures, the physical separation of bureaus and offices allows differences among them to germinate and grow. An important source of such differences is the number of persons in the local administrative units. These different sized units are a promising site for research on large-scale organizations because some of the characteristics that would normally vary freely in unrelated organizations are held equal.

Much still remains to be learned about the relations between the size

Edwin J. Thomas, "Role Conceptions and Organizational Size," *American Sociological Review*, 24, 1959, pp. 30–37. The findings reported here are based upon data collected in one phase of a research project financed by funds from the State of Michigan for research and service in the utilization of human resources. The project was located in the University of Michigan School of Social Work. The author is indebted to W. J. Maxey, Lynn Kellogg, and Willis Oosterhof of the Department for the consultation and cooperation given in the study; to Mrs. Donna McLeod of the research staff for assistance in collecting data and in statistical analyses; and to Morris Janowitz, Leo Meltzer, Henry J. Meyer, and Robert Vinter for critically reading an early draft of this paper.

of an organization and the behavior of its members.[1] A central question of practical and theoretical significance is the extent to which an organization's size facilitates or impedes efforts to attain its formally stated objectives. To answer this question research must be focused upon two related problems: delineation of the differences in behavior of members in organizations varying in size; and consideration of how these behavioral correlates of size affect the organization's capacity to achieve its goals. Such research should add to the further understanding of those non-formal characteristics of large organizations that affect organizational behavior.

This study compares the role conceptions, the degree of role consensus, and the quality of work of welfare workers in different sized organizational units of a state welfare department. The objectives of the welfare program and the formal requirements for the performance of roles were the same throughout the organization. In comparing small and large units in the department many formal characteristics of the welfare bureaus were thus held constant. Of course, not all of the possibly influential variables were controlled because of differences in history and location of the bureaus.

Attention in the presentation of findings is given to the relationship of the variables to organizational size and, in the discussion of results, to interpretation of why the variables were associated with size and to the relationship of the size of the welfare bureau and their effectiveness in the attainment of one of the organizational goals.

THE ORGANIZATION

The Michigan State Department of Social Welfare administers a program of public assistance through bureaus located in 83 counties. Bureaus range in size from those of one person, who makes investigations and serves as bureau supervisor, to one with hundreds of employees. If suf-

---

[1] One of the few empirical studies of the size of organizations is Frederic W. Terrien and Donald L. Mills, "The Effect of Changing Size Upon the Internal Structure of Organizations," *American Sociological Review*, 20 (February, 1955), pp. 11–14. Discussions of organizational size are found in Theodore Caplow, "Organizational Size," *Administrative Science Quarterly*, 1 (March, 1957), pp. 485–491; and Kenneth E. Boulding, *The Organizational Revolution*, New York: Harper, 1953.

The importance of size as a variable was noted long ago by Spencer, Durkheim, and Simmel, whose observations are well-known on this subject. Examples of recent laboratory work include: Robert F. Bales, "Some Uniformities of Behavior in Small Social Systems," in G. Swanson, T. M. Newcomb, and E. Hartley, editors, *Readings in Social Psychology*, New York: Holt, 1952, pp. 146–159; Robert F. Bales and Edgar F. Borgatta, "Size of Group as a Factor in the Interaction Profile," in A. Paul Hare, Edgar F. Borgatta, and R. F. Bales, editors, *Small Groups: Studies in Social Interaction*, New York: Knopf, 1955, pp. 396–413; A. Paul Hare, "Interaction and Consensus in Different Sized Groups," in D. Cartwright and A. Zander, editors, *Group Dynamics: Research and Theory*, Evanston, Ill.: Row, Peterson, 1953, pp. 483–492.

ficiently large, a bureau includes public assistance workers who investigate applications for financial assistance, case and bureau supervisors, and clerical personnel. Within a bureau the chain of authority runs from bureau supervisor to case supervisor and from case supervisor to public assistance worker, with each case supervisor generally supervising six to seven workers.

As noted earlier, the formal requirements of the role of public assistance worker are uniform throughout the organization. All workers have met the same minimal requirements for the job, all perform the same types of functions, and all follow the same rules and procedures as set forth in the manual of operation for the investigation of applications for assistance. At the same time, however, the role can be conceived and performed in different ways because of certain ambiguities in how it is defined (apart from other reasons). Consider, for example, the role of workers who handle cases in the Aid to Dependent Children program (these are the workers studied in this investigation). The federal laws define the ADC task too generally to be of much help in determining many concrete decisions.[2] In contrast, the manual of operation, while very specific with respect to conditions of eligibility for financial assistance, does not cover numerous service problems met by the worker. Thus there is latitude for individual variability in performance and for different conceptions of the role.

PROCEDURE AND FINDINGS

The sample of 109 public assistance workers who handled ADC cases consisted largely of females, and most were married. A majority had worked in public assistance for less than four years, 22 percent for less than a year. While three-quarters of the workers had college degrees, only nine percent had specialized in social work and none had obtained a Master's degree in social work.

The sample was drawn from small, medium, and large administrative units. The "small" bureaus were those in which there were at least two but no more than five workers, and no more than a two-level hierarchy. A random sample of six small bureaus was drawn containing a total of 18 workers, all of whom participated in the study. The "medium-sized" bureaus were those that had six or more workers or a three-level hierarchy,

---

[2] The ADC program was set up to enable needy children who are deprived of a parent to receive financial assistance so that a homemaker can remain in the home to care for them. More recent legislation expands the purpose, adding that it should "help maintain and strengthen family life," and help families "attain the maximum self-support and personal independence consistent with the maintenance of continuing parental care and protection. . . ." From "Social Security Amendment of 1956," Section 312.

but no more than three such levels. Five medium-sized bureaus were selected on a non-random basis, contributing 59 workers who handled ADC cases. The offices ranged in size from six to 22 workers and tended to be located in the more highly industrialized, urban counties. There was only one large bureau, Wayne County; it had a five-level hierarchy, with the positions of ADC division head and director above the level of case supervisor and below the level of bureau director. Thirty-two workers were selected from a pool of 96 ADC workers assigned to two different divisions by choosing four supervisory units at random. The mean number of workers in the small offices was 3.8; comparable figures for medium and large size were 17.4 and 45.5, respectively.

There was a direct relationship between the size of the bureaus and the number of hierarchically ordered strata, since bureaus in the sample were selected by criteria of size and number of strata. For the 83 bureaus in the state there was also a marked positive relationship between the number of employees and the number of strata.[3]

The amount of specialization of function for the worker increased with size. Specialization for three of the four categories of cases was found in the largest bureau in the sample. In the two next largest ones, only a few of the workers had caseloads made up exclusively of ADC recipients, and for the remaining bureaus specialization by type of case was not found.

Characteristics of the workers in the units also differed by size. In the smaller administrative units there were found more older workers, more workers without college degrees, more who had married, more having children, and more workers with long experience in public assistance. The workers in the smaller units, as compared with the larger ones, moreover, lived in a more rural environment.

The personal characteristics of the workers were the only correlates that could be controlled statistically in the analysis of results reported below. There was no satisfactory way to separate the effects of specialization, degree of stratification, and population setting from those of the numbers of workers. Hence, even when the effects of personal characteristics were controlled, there was no way to determine whether it was the number of workers or some other factor that produced the effects. The results presented below were analyzed first without controls for variables operating concomitantly with size and, subsequently, with controls for the personal attributes of the workers. The different sized bureaus are labeled "small" or "large" as a matter of convenience; it should be understood that not merely the number of workers differentiates the offices.

Questionnaires were administered to the participating workers and to their case supervisors in the 12 administrative units. The questions referred

[3] Relationships between the number of vertical strata and the mean number of workers and clerical personnel were as follows: for one stratum, 2.0 employees; for two strata, 5.6 employees; for three strata, 18.5 employees; and for five strata, 213.0 employees.

to a wide range of variables. One of these, termed *role consensus*, is indicated by the degree of agreement between the public assistance worker and his supervisor about the importance of functions performed by workers. The amount of agreement was assumed to reflect the degree to which workers and supervisors shared a frame of reference regarding the importance of workers' functions. Eleven areas of knowledge and skill (for example, determining financial eligibility, job mechanics, and casework methods) relevant to performance of the role of the public assistance worker were rated for importance on a seven-point scale by workers and supervisors and discrepancy scores were computed.

Another variable, termed *breadth of role conception*, refers to the number of activities or functions conceived as part of the role. In the questionnaire the workers were presented with nine activities (for example, budgeting and referral for vocational counselling) and were asked to indicate for each function whether they "always," "sometimes," or "never" performed it in cases for which that activity, as a type of service, *was needed*. Numerical values were assigned to responses and total scores were computed. The higher the score, the more broadly the role is conceived.

Another aspect of role, often implicit rather than formally defined, is the ethical commitment that it requires of individuals. In public welfare, as well as in other service fields, those responsible for giving the services are guided by ethical precepts. A test of *ethical commitment* was devised to measure some of these, more exactly termed a test of commitment to the ethics of professional social work, since it consists of items relating to seven ethical areas highly endorsed by a sample of 75 professionally trained social workers.[4] The content of the items, given in Table 1, may be clustered into two categories: (a) how the worker should behave with a client, and (b) who should receive the benefits of social work services and under what conditions. To complete the validation, the responses of the professionally trained social workers were compared with those of the sample of public assistance supervisors and workers drawn in this study. In contrast to the professionally trained group, the majority of whom had obtained Master's degrees in social work, the public assistance workers generally had little such specialized training. Table 1 shows that the "correct" alternatives are most highly endorsed by the professional group

---

[4] This group consisted largely of members of the local chapter of the National Association of Social Workers. Almost every respondent had received the degree of Master of Social Work. The questions of the test took the same form for each ethical area. First a problem was presented followed by two opposing alternatives for action a worker might take in such a situation. The assumption underlying the instrument was that each course of action implied a different ethical justification. It is not assumed that all ethical guidelines directing the efforts of workers were sampled in the test, although the ones specified are assumed to be important.

Table 1 *Percentages of Workers, Supervisors, and Members of Professional Association Selecting "Correct" Alternatives for Items of the Test of Commitment to the Ethics of Professional Social Work*

		Group		
Content of Item [a]	Inferred Underlying Value [b]	Workers (N = 109)	Supervisors (N = 26)	Members of Professional Group (N = 75)
1. In interviewing, sacrifice directness *versus* ask direct questions	Humanitarian *versus* utilitarian	49	54	63
2. Motivate by offering information *versus* urge directly	Noncoercive *versus* coercive	72	88	97
3. When client is upset, discuss feelings *versus* ignore them	Concern *versus* nonconcern for client's feelings	83	88	92
4. When client makes you angry, analyze your anger *versus* ignore it	Awareness *versus* nonawareness of self as an instrument of change	72	92	97
5. Financial aid given to all *versus* to those who use it wisely	Help universally *versus* help selectively	38	68	69
6. Illegitimacy demands focus on helping individual adjust *versus* changing individual	Acceptance *versus* nonacceptance of deviance	28	38	74
7. Client making curtains in messy house, compliment *versus* mention housecleaning	Positive *versus* negative methods to motivate	60	75	96

[a] The first of the alternatives for each item is the "correct" one.

[b] The first of the polarities of underlying values is the one matched to the "correct" alternative for its corresponding item.

and least highly endorsed by the workers, with the supervisors' responses falling between these extremes.

A final set of measures is related to the quality of the worker's performance on the job. It was possible to learn about the cognitive aspect of performance through indications of the analytic skill of workers as indicated by their ability, first, to identify the problems of families and, second, to propose appropriate treatment plans. To measure the first item, the workers were asked to describe the problems they noted for the members of a family depicted in a case vignette; responses were transformed into a numerical score of diagnostic acuity.[5] To measure the second aspect of analytic skill, the workers were asked to describe what they would do for the individuals described in the case if they had the required time; responses were coded and scores were obtained for *appropriateness of treatment plans.*[6] A motivational aspect of performance was inferred from responses to a question about how much the worker would like to work on the case described in the vignette.[7]

RESULTS

Workers' conceptions of their roles differed according to the size of the welfare office. In the smaller bureaus there was found to be greater *role consensus* between the worker and his supervisor about the importance of functions that workers perform (Table 2), greater *breadth of role conception* (Table 3), and higher *ethical commitment* (Table 4).

Quality of Performance

The size of the administrative unit was found to be associated with all indicators of the quality of the worker's performance. Those workers scoring high on the three measures are much more likely to be in the small bureaus than in the larger ones (Table 5).

[5] Responses were coded into the following categories: non-existent problems (scored -2), superficially conceived problems (-1), problems manifest in the case ($+1$), and appropriately inferred underlying problems ($+2$). Scores were the algebraic sum. Kendall's *tau* is $+.74$ for the scores of two coders ($N = 20$).

[6] Responses were coded into plans inappropriate to the case (scored -2), plans to aid with manifest problems ($+1$), and plans to help with appropriately inferred underlying problems ($+2$). Scores were the algebraic sum. Kendall's *tau* is $+.80$ for the scores of two coders ($N = 20$).

[7] For the most part, the interrelationships among these variables are positive. Scores on diagnostic acumen are directly related to scores on appropriateness of treatment plans ($X^2 = 18.25$, $p < .001$) and on ethical commitment ($X^2 = 9.31$, $p < .01$); they bear no relationship, however, to motivation to help recipients. Scores on appropriateness of treatment plan are not related to those on ethical commitment, but are related to those of motivation to help recipients ($X^2 = 6.85$, $p < .01$). Scores on ethical commitment are positively associated with those on motivation to help recipients ($X^2 = 4.11$, $p < .05$).

Table 2 *Number of Workers Having Large and Small Discrepancy Scores in* Role Con- sensus, *by Size of Administrative Unit*

Size of Administrative Unit	Discrepancy Score	
	Small (0–1)	Large (2–3)
Small	14	0
Medium	54	4
Large	21	11
	$X^2 = 15.00, p < .01$	

Table 3 *Number of Workers Conceiving Their Roles Narrowly and Broadly, by Size of Administrative Unit*

Size of Administrative Unit	Breadth of Role Conception	
	Narrow (0–4)	Broad (5–8)
Small	4	14
Medium	20	37
Large	18	14
	$X^2 = 6.48, p < .05$	

Table 4 *Number of Workers Scoring High and Low on* Ethical Commitment, *by Size of Administrative Unit*

	Scores on Ethical Commitment	
Size of Administrative Unit	Low (1–4)	High (5–7)
Small	3	15
Medium	35	23
Large	26	6
	$X^2 = 20.04, p < .001$	

Table 5 *Number of Workers Scoring High and Low on Measures of the Quality of Performance, by Size of Administrative Unit*

Size of Administrative Unit	Scores on Diagnostic Acuity		Scores on Appropriateness of Treatment Plan		Motivation to Help Recipients	
	High (4–8)	Low (0–3)	High (5–7)	Low (0–4)	High (3–7)	Low (1, 2)
Small	13	5	14	4	15	3
Medium	23	36	21	38	21	38
Large	6	25	10	20	12	19
	$X^2 = 13.46, p < .01$		$X^2 = 11.26, p < .01$		$X^2 = 13.30, p < .01$	

The Effects of Personal Background Factors

Analyses were made with controls for age, education, experience on the job, marital status, and number of children. This procedure involved the relationship between organizational size and a dependent variable, holding constant the control factor whenever it was found that the control characteristic was associated with the dependent variable. The .05 level of significance was used as a choice point.

Using this technique, age is the only control factor related both to the size of bureaus and the magnitude of discrepancy of *role consensus*. Although the smaller bureaus had more older workers and more workers with small discrepancy scores, the effects of size remained with age held constant.[8]

Two of the control factors are closely associated with the *breadth of role conception*. Broadly conceived roles were found more often for older workers and for those with lengthy experience in public assistance; the first relationship yields a X^2 of 17.73, the second a X^2 of 16.21, both giving p values of less than .001. When age and experience are controlled, size is no longer related to the *breadth of role conception*. Since there were more older workers and workers with longer experience in the smaller units, age and experience, and not other factors associated with size, account for the breadth of conception of roles.

Both the education and experience of workers are related to scores of *ethical commitment*. The less well educated and those with longer experience on the job most frequently show high as opposed to low scores on ethical commitment; the X^2 is 8.51 for the former ($p < .01$) and 4.05 for the latter ($p < .05$). The effects of size remain, however, when education and experience are each held constant.[9]

The only control variable found to be related to any of the three indicators of the quality of the worker's performance was the number of children the workers had; those workers having children had higher scores on motivation to help recipients than did those having no children

---

[8] The percentages of workers under 39 years of age with low discrepancy scores for the small, medium, and large bureaus are 100, 84, and 69, respectively; for workers 40 years or older the comparable percentages are 100, 100, and 40. The Ns are too small to compute statistical tests.

[9] The percentages of workers with bachelor's or higher degrees having high scores for the small, medium, and large bureaus were respectively 60, 32, and 13 ($X^2 = 5.31$, $p < .06$); for workers having attained less than a bachelor's degree, the percentages for small, medium, and large bureaus were 91, 47, and 37 ($X^2 = 8.24$, $p < .02$). The percentages of workers with less than four years' experience having high scores for the small, medium, and large bureaus were respectively 50, 31, and 17 ($X^2 = 10.56$, $p < .01$); for workers with more than four years of experience, the percentages for the small, medium, and large bureaus were 78, 48, 16 ($X^2 = 9.92$, $p < .01$).

($X^2 = 5.40$, $p < .05$). The effects of size remained for workers with or without children.[10]

DISCUSSION AND CONCLUSIONS

Why should the variables examined here be associated with organizational size? Like many others, size is not a "pure" variable—a single unitary phenomenon. Size is more like an index because of its relationship to a complement of variables associated with the number of persons in the organization. The findings of this study provide suggestions about these variables, but offer few clues about *why* they are associated with size or about their interrelationships. We now turn to these questions.

Most of our results may be accounted for plausibly in terms of the population and the community setting of the county in which the welfare bureau was located. The size of the bureau itself depends largely upon the population size of a county, since the more populous counties are likely to contain more individuals in need of welfare assistance. Although organizational size bears no necessary relationship to the population of the area in which the organization is located, one may be an index of the other to the extent that (a) the organizational unit serves a portion of the population, as does a welfare bureau, and (b) the unit is located by such arbitrary geographical criteria as county, state, or region.

The association of the workers' personal characteristics with the size of welfare bureaus probably indicates that the pool of potential employees in the counties with large populations differs from those with small populations. Available information indicates that some of the contrasts between workers in the smaller and the larger bureaus parallel those between rural residents and residents of cities.[11] This study provides no information about whether or not there is also selective retention of workers as a consequence of bureau size.

Roles were found to be more broadly conceived by workers in the smaller bureaus. The control analysis shows that age and experience account for the breadth of conception of roles. Welfare workers in rural areas change jobs less often than their urban counterparts, partly because there are fewer occupational alternatives and fewer welfare jobs from which to choose that pay as well or better than public assistance.[12] Rural

---

[10] The percentages of childless workers having high scores in the small, medium, and large bureaus are, respectively, 71, 22, and 33 ($X^2 = 5.80$, $p < .06$); for those workers with one or more children, the percentages in the small, medium, and large bureaus are 91, 44, and 57 ($X^2 = 7.39$, $p < .05$).

[11] Persons residing in rural areas are less well educated, more often married, generally more fertile, and less mobile occupationally than urbanites. See Noel P. Gist and L. A. Halbert, *Urban Society* (Fourth Edition), New York: Crowell, 1956.

[12] This conclusion is supported by information provided by the Michigan State Department of Social Welfare.

welfare workers therefore would be expected to be older and more experienced than urban ones. Furthermore, rural areas contain fewer specialized social services, making it necessary for the welfare worker in the rural area to take over informally more functions as part of her role than her urban colleagues.

Another correlate of organizational size is the ethical commitment of workers. Differences in ethical commitment can not be attributed to variations of professionalization, for none of the workers had had professional training in social work. The community setting of the welfare offices and the rural background of the workers account for the workers' ethical orientation most adequately. High scores on the test indicate a generally more positive approach to recipients—an approach probably growing out of a more intimate relationship with recipients in the smaller communities. The writer has been told by experienced welfare workers of the differences between working in the smaller and the larger urban communities. In the small community they note that there is more frequent community contact with recipients; perception of recipients as individuals more often than as "clients"; less social distance between worker and recipient, due in part to similarity of ethnic background; and greater need to attend to more of the recipients' problems. Consequently, the worker in the small bureau is more likely to be willing to assume greater personal responsibility for the recipient and to have more compassion for the recipient as a person than the worker in an urban bureau.

The attitude of helpfulness toward others and the "positive" approach to recipients engendered by the small community probably explain why workers in the small bureaus evidenced performance of higher quality than those in the larger ones. The measures of quality of performance were skill in analyzing problems of recipients, appropriateness of treatment plans, and motivation to help recipients—all of which reflect the extent of the worker's willingness to do a complete and adequate job of helping recipients. That the rural workers are more willing than those in urban settings to help recipients and to put forth the extra effort needed to analyze thoroughly the recipients' problems and to propose suitable treatment is consistent with the earlier observations about the small community.

The community setting of the bureaus does not readily explain why size is related to role consensus. Past theoretical and empirical work indicates that consensus is likely to be greater in small than in large groups.[13] In this

---

[13] See Emile Durkheim, *The Division of Labor in Society*, Glencoe, Ill.: Free Press, 1949, pp. 80–131; and A. Paul Hare, *op. cit.*, pp. 507–518. It may be noted the small group provides conditions well-suited to the development of consensus: there is likely to be a relatively rapid rate of interaction and a relatively smaller divergence of opinion and behavior, due to a smaller range of opinion and behavior than in large groups.

study, size alone is probably not the only organizational characteristic contributing to role consensus.

Another correlate of organizational size is the extent to which there was vertical and horizontal differentiation. Size enables differentiation to occur by providing a larger number of persons over whom functions may be distributed and by increasing the range of individual skill and ability needed to give feasibly different assignments to persons. In the organizational units studied here, differentiation in the larger bureaus was further facilitated by administrative policy stipulating the proportion of supervisory personnel required for a given number of workers and by the belief that specialized handling of cases is efficient only in the largest bureaus.

This discussion of the correlates of organizational size suggests that the number of workers may be a less potent variable in affecting the behavior of members than the community setting of the organizational unit. Studies of organizational units of an extended bureaucracy differing in size should be undertaken where it is possible to differentiate them in terms of the population size and type of community in which the units are located.

From another viewpoint, some of the variables used in this study can be said to reflect organizatioanl effectiveness in providing services to families. These variables include the measures of the quality of work, ethical commitment, and breadth of role conception signified by the number of different services workers would perform for families were they needed. These three indications of service are negatively associated with the size of the organizational unit: the smaller bureaus show greater commitment to the ethics of professional social work, greater breadth of role conception, and better quality of work. To the extent that these variables reflect differences in performance of workers, the results indicate that the organizational goal of providing services to recipients was more effectively attained in the smaller welfare bureaus.

The findings of the study do not help to answer the question of how effectively the bureaus attained the organizational goal of determining eligibility for financial assistance.

Why were the small bureaus better able than the larger ones to provide services to families? If the interpretations of the findings presented above are correct, it is largely because the influences of the small community encourage a service orientation toward recipients. The impact of community setting thus may be viewed as reaffirming the significance of the secondary organizational goal, that of providing services, through orienting workers more toward the service aspects of their roles. The part played by the actual size of the welfare bureau is probably minimal, except in so far as it serves to mediate, through primary relationships, the service goal. The fact that role consensus was greater in the smaller bureaus may indicate greater cohesion of the primary groups and readier acceptance of the goal to provide service.

Part C

Professions and Organizations

THE growth of professions is as endemic to modern society as is the growth of large-scale organizations. Many of the early workers in the social welfare field were without specialized training. Often, involvement in social welfare activities was motivated by a general commitment or feeling that something had to be done about a welfare problem. Not only did the early workers have little training but there was scant recognition that specialized training was needed. However, the growth of modern social welfare institutions has been accompanied by the growth of social welfare professions.

Professions are, in some ways, organized on principles that are contradictory to those of large-scale organizations. Where large-scale organizations are typically hierarchical and locality-based, professions are collegial associations that are cross-community in their linkages. In many ways, there is a built-in potential for conflict between professionals and large-scale organizations because professions develop ideal standards of operation while agencies must grapple with their environments and develop operating standards that often depart from those that the professions consider as ideal.

The first article, "Attributes of a Profession," by Ernest Greenwood, attempts to define the basic nature of all professions. An occupation is considered a profession when it is based on a systematic body of theory, when its practitioners have authority over its work rules and recommendations, and have the sanction of the community for operating over its distinct occupational sphere. It also has a respected code of ethics and a professional culture.

Being a member of a profession gives an employee a set of standards for evaluating the organization and his own performance apart from the requirements of the specific agency. On the one hand, if professionals control the agency they can partially impose professional standards on it. On the other hand, professional standards almost always give the professional a base from which to criticize or praise the operation of any agency. But most agencies will never be able to live up to full professional standards—operating requirements and goals assigned to the organization by the larger society make the meeting of professional standards difficult. Furthermore, because professions are based on evolving fields of knowledge, new standards develop. The article by Lloyd Ohlin, Herman Piven, and Donnell Pappenfort, "Major Dilemmas of the Social Worker in Probation and Parole," deals with the relation of professionals to agency structure. These authors analyze the role dilemmas and conflicts of the social worker who is confronted with conflicting role expectations from clients, the agency, and the community—role expectations that his profession only partially equips him to handle. The concept of role dilemmas and conflicts utilized by Ohlin and his co-workers is a central part of the sociological theory of roles.

The final selection of this part, "Professions in Process," by Rue Bucher and Anselm Strauss, examines the process by which professions differentiate, develop subgroups with collective identities, and begin to resemble social movements. Although Bucher and Strauss look at the process among medical doctors, the same process can be seen in the social-work profession where group workers, community organizers, and caseworkers contend over the proper definition of social work and the relative emphasis to be given to different specialties and styles of work. The significance of this article is that it highlights an important part of the process of social change through which professions develop new ideologies and technologies, and fight for a different allocation of resources for solving welfare problems.

Attributes of a Profession

Ernest Greenwood

The professions occupy a position of great importance on the American scene.[1] In a society such as ours, characterized by minute division of labor based upon technical specialization, many important features of social organization are dependent upon professional functions. Professional activity is coming to play a predominant role in the life patterns of increasing numbers of individuals of both sexes, occupying much of their waking moments, providing life goals, determining behavior, and shaping personality. It is no wonder, therefore, that the phenomenon of professionalism has become an object of observation by sociologists.[2] The sociological approach to professionalism is one that views a profession as an organized group which is constantly interacting with the society that forms its matrix, which performs its social functions through a network of formal and informal relationships, and which creates its own subculture requiring adjustments to it as a prerequisite for career success.[3]

Within the professional category of its occupational classification the United States Census Bureau includes, among others, the following: accountant, architect, artist, attorney, clergyman, college professor, dentist, engineer, journalist, judge, librarian, natural scientist, optometrist, phar-

[1] Talcott Parsons, "The Professions and Social Structure," *Social Forces*, Vol. 17 (May 1939), pp. 457–467.

[2] Theodore Caplow, *The Sociology of Work* (Minneapolis: University of Minnesota Press, 1954).

[3] Oswald Hall, "The Stages of a Medical Career," *American Journal of Sociology*, Vol. 53 (March 1948), pp. 327–336; "Types of Medical Careers," *American Journal of Sociology*, Vol. 55 (November 1949), pp. 243–253; "Sociological Research in the Field of Medicine: Progress and Prospects," *American Sociological Review*, Vol. 16 (October 1951), pp. 639–644.

Ernest Greenwood, "Attributes of a Profession," *Social Work*, II, July 1957, pp. 45–55. Ernest Greenwood, Ph.D., is associate professor in the School of Social Welfare, University of California, Berkeley. The writer is indebted to Dr. William A. Kornhauser, Sociology Department of the university, for his constructive criticisms during the preparation of this paper.

macist, physician, social scientist, social worker, surgeon, and teacher.[4] What common attributes do these professional occupations possess which distinguish them from the nonprofessional ones? After a careful canvass of the sociological literature on occupations, this writer has been able to distill five elements, upon which there appears to be consensus among the students of the subject, as constituting the distinguishing attributes of a profession.[5] Succinctly put, all professions seem to possess: (1) systematic theory, (2) authority, (3) community sanction, (4) ethical codes, and (5) a culture. The purpose of this article is to describe fully these attributes.

Before launching into our description, a preliminary word of caution is due. With respect to each of the above attributes, the true difference between a professional and a nonprofessional occupation is not a qualitative but a quantitative one. Strictly speaking, these attributes are not the exclusive monopoly of the professions; nonprofessional occupations also possess them, but to a lesser degree. As is true of most social phenomena, the phenomenon of professionalism cannot be structured in terms of clear-cut classes. Rather, we must think of the occupations in a society as distributing themselves along a continuum.[6] At one end of this continuum are bunched the well-recognized and undisputed professions (e.g., physician, attorney, professor, scientist); at the opposite end are bunched the least skilled and least attractive occupations (e.g., watchman, truckloader, farm laborer, scrubwoman, bus boy). The remaining occupations, less skilled and less prestigeful than the former, but more so than the latter, are distributed between these two poles. The occupations bunched at the professional pole of the continuum possess to a maximum degree the attributes about to be described. As we move away from this pole, the occupations possess these attributes to a decreasing degree. Thus, in the less developed professions, social work among them, these attributes appear in moderate degree. When we reach the mid-region of the continuum, among the clerical, sales, and crafts occupations, they occur in still lesser degree; while at the unskilled end of the continuum the occupa-

---

[4] U.S. Bureau of the Census, *1950 Census of Population: Classified Index of Occupations and Industries* (Washington, D.C.: Government Printing Office, 1950).

[5] The writer acknowledges his debt to his former students at the School of Social Welfare, University of California, Berkeley, who, as members of his research seminars, assisted him in identifying and abstracting the sociological literature on occupations. Their conscientious assistance made possible the formulation presented in this paper.

[6] The occupational classification employed by the U.S. Census Bureau is precisely such a continuum. The categories of this classification are: (a) professionals and semiprofessional technical workers; (b) proprietors and managers, both farm and nonfarm, and officials; (c) clerical, sales, and kindred workers; (d) craftsmen, skilled workers, and foremen; (e) operatives and semiskilled workers; and (f) laborers, unskilled, service, and domestic workers (U.S. Bureau of the Census, *op. cit.*).

tions possess these attributes so minimally that they are virtually non-existent. If the reader keeps this concept of the continuum in mind, the presentation will less likely appear as a distortion of reality.

SYSTEMATIC BODY OF THEORY [7]

It is often contended that the chief difference between a professional and a nonprofessioanl occupation lies in the element of superior skill. The performance of a professional service presumably involves a series of unusually complicated operations, mastery of which requires lengthy training. The models referred to in this connection are the performances of a surgeon, a concert pianist, or a research physicist. However, some nonprofessional occupations actually involve a higher order of skill than many professional ones. For example, tool-and-die making, diamond-cutting, monument-engraving, or cabinet-making involve more intricate operations than schoolteaching, nursing, or social work. Therefore, to focus on the element of skill per se in describing the professions is to miss the kernel of their uniqueness.

The crucial distinction is this: the skills that characterize a profession flow from and are supported by a fund of knowledge that has been organized into an internally consistent system, called a *body of theory.* A profession's underlying body of theory is a system of abstract propositions that describe in general terms the classes of phenomena comprising the profession's focus of interest. Theory serves as a basc in terms of which the professional rationalizes his operations in concrete situations. Acquisition of the professional skill requires a prior or simultaneous mastery of the theory underlying that skill. Preparation for a profession, therefore, involves considerable preoccupation with systematic theory, a feature virtually absent in the training of the nonprofessional. And so treatises are written on legal theory, musical theory, social work theory, the theory of the drama, and so on; but no books appear on the theory of punch-pressing or pipe-fitting or brick-laying.

Because understanding of theory is so important to professional skill, preparation for a profession must be an intellectual as well as a practical experience. On-the-job training through apprenticeship, which suffices for a nonprofessional occupation, becomes inadequate for a profession. Orientation in theory can be achieved best through formal education in an academic setting. Hence the appearance of the professional school, more often than not university affiliated, wherein the milieu is a contrast to that of the trade school. Theoretical knowledge is more difficult to master than operational procedures; it is easier to learn to repair an

[7] The sequence in which the five attributes are discussed in this paper does not reflect upon their relative importance. The order selected has been dictated by logical considerations.

automobile than to learn the principles of the internal combustion engine. There are, of course, a number of free-lance professional pursuits (e.g., acting, painting, writing, composing, and the like) wherein academic preparation is not mandatory. Nevertheless, even in these fields various "schools" and "institutes" are appearing, although they may not be run along traditional academic lines. We can generalize that as an occupation moves toward professional status, apprenticeship training yields to formalized education, because the function of theory as a groundwork for practice acquires increasing importance.

The importance of theory precipitates a form of activity normally not encountered in a nonprofessional occupation, viz., theory construction via systematic research. To generate valid theory that will provide a solid base for professional techniques requires the application of the scientific method to the service-related problems of the profession. Continued employment of the scientific method is nurtured by and in turn reinforces the element of *rationality*.[8] As an orientation, rationality is the antithesis of traditionalism. The spirit of rationality in a profession encourages a critical, as opposed to a reverential, attitude toward the theoretical system. It implies a perpetual readiness to discard any portion of that system, no matter how time honored it may be, with a formulation demonstrated to be more valid. The spirit of rationality generates group self-criticism and theoretical controversy. Professional members convene regularly in their associations to learn and to evaluate innovations in theory. This produces an intellectually stimulating milieu that is in marked contrast to the milieu of a nonprofessional occupation.

In the evolution of every profession there emerges the researcher-theoretician whose role is that of scientific investigation and theoretical systematization. In technological professions [9] a division of labor thereby evolves, that between the theory-oriented and the practice-oriented person. Witness the physician who prefers to attach himself to a medical research center rather than to enter private practice. This division may also yield to cleavages with repercussions upon intraprofessional relationships. However, if properly integrated, the division of labor produces an accelerated expansion of the body of theory and a sprouting of theoretical branches around which specialties nucleate. The net effect of such developments is to lengthen the preparation deemed desirable for entry into the profession. This accounts for the rise of graduate professional training on top of a basic college education.

[8] Parsons, *op. cit.*

[9] A technology is a profession whose aim is to achieve controlled changes in natural relationships. Convention makes a distinction between technologists who shape non-human materials and those who deal with human beings. The former are called engineers; the latter practitioners.

PROFESSIONAL AUTHORITY

Extensive education in the systematic theory of his discipline imparts to the professional a type of knowledge that highlights the layman's comparative ignorance. This fact is the basis for the professional's authority, which has some interesting features.

A nonprofessional occupation has customers; a professional occupation has clients. What is the difference? A customer determines what services and/or commodities he wants, and he shops around until he finds them. His freedom of decision rests upon the premise that he has the capacity to appraise his own needs and to judge the potential of the service or of the commodity to satisfy them. The infallibility of his decisions is epitomized in the slogan: "The customer is always right!" In a professional relationship, however, the professional dictates what is good or evil for the client, who has no choice but to accede to professional judgment. Here the premise is that, because he lacks the requisite theoretical background, the client cannot diagnose his own needs or discriminate among the range of possibilities for meeting them. Nor is the client considered able to evaluate the caliber of the professional service he receives. In a nonprofessional occupation the customer can criticize the quality of the commodity he has purchased, and even demand a refund. The client lacks this same prerogative, having surrendered it to professional authority. This element of authority is one, although not the sole, reason why a profession frowns on advertising. If a profession were to advertise, it would, in effect, impute to the potential client the discriminating capacity to select from competing forms of service. The client's subordination to professional authority invests the professional with a monopoly of judgment. When an occupation strives toward professionalization, one of its aspirations is to acquire this monopoly.

The client derives a sense of security from the professional's assumption of authority. The authoritative air of the professional is a principal source of the client's faith that the relationship he is about to enter contains the potentials for meeting his needs. The professional's authority, however, is not limitless; its function is confined to those specific spheres within which the professional has been educated. This quality in professional authority Parsons calls *functional specificity*.[10] Functional specificity carries the following implications for the client-professional relationship.

The professional cannot prescribe guides for facets of the client's life where his theoretical competence does not apply. To venture such prescriptions is to invade a province wherein he himself is a layman, and, hence, to violate the authority of another professional group. The professional must not use his position of authority to exploit the client for

---

[10] Parsons, *op. cit.*

purposes of personal gratification. In any association of superordination-subordination, of which the professional-client relationship is a perfect specimen, the subordinate member—here, the client—can be maneuvered into a dependent role. The psychological advantage which thereby accrues to the professional could constitute a temptation for him. The professional must inhibit his impulses to use the professional relationship for the satisfaction of the sexual need, the need to manipulate others, or the need to live vicariously. In the case of the therapeutic professions it is ideally preferred that client-professional intercourse not overflow the professional setting. Extraprofessional intercourse could be used by both client and professional in a manner such as to impair professional authority, with a consequent diminution of the professional's effectiveness.

Thus far we have discussed that phase of professional authority which expresses itself in the client-professional relationship. Professional authority, however, has professional-community ramifications. To these we now turn.

SANCTION OF THE COMMUNITY

Every profession strives to persuade the community to sanction its authority within certain spheres by conferring upon the profession a series of powers and privileges. Community approval of these powers and privileges may be either informal or formal; formal approval is that reinforced by the community's police power.

Among its powers is the profession's control over its training centers. This is achieved through an accrediting process exercised by one of the associations within the profession. By granting or withholding accreditation, a profession can, ideally, regulate its schools as to their number, location, curriculum content, and caliber of instruction. Comparable control is not to be found in a nonprofessional occupation.[11] The profession also acquires control over admission into the profession. This is achieved via two routes. First, the profession convinces the community that no one should be allowed to wear a professional title who has not been conferred it by an accredited professional school. Anyone can call himself a carpenter, locksmith, or metal-plater if he feels so qualified. But a person who assumes the title of physician or attorney without having earned it conventionally becomes an impostor. Secondly, the profession persuades the community to institute in its behalf a licensing system for screening those qualified to practice the professional skill. A *sine qua non* for the receipt of the license is, of course, a duly granted professional title. Another prerequisite may be an examination before a board of inquiry

---

[11] To set up and run a school for floral decorating requires no approval from the national florists' association, but no school of social work could operate long without approval of the Council on Social Work Education.

whose personnel have been drawn from the ranks of the profession. Police power enforces the licensing system; persons practicing the professional skill without a license are liable to punishment by public authority.[12]

Among the professional privileges, one of the most important is that of confidentiality. To facilitate efficient performance, the professional encourages the client to volunteer information he otherwise would not divulge. The community regards this as privileged communication, shared solely between client and professional, and protects the latter legally from encroachments upon such confidentiality. To be sure, only a select few of the professions, notably medicine and law, enjoy this immunity. Its very rarity makes it the ultimate in professionalization. Another one of the professional privileges is a relative immunity from community judgment on technical matters. Standards for professional performance are reached by consensus within the profession and are based on the existing body of theory. The lay community is presumed incapable of comprehending these standards and, hence, of using them to identify malpractice. It is generally conceded that a professional's performance can be evaluated only by his peers.

The powers and privileges described above constitute a monopoly granted by the community to the professional group. Therefore, when an occupation strives toward professional status, one of its prime objectives is to acquire this monopoly. But this is difficult to achieve, because counter forces within the community resist strongly the profession's claims to authority. Through its associations the profession wages an organized campaign to persuade the community that it will benefit greatly by granting the monopoly. Specifically the profession seeks to prove: that the performance of the occupational skill requires specialized education; that those who possess this education, in contrast to those who do not, deliver a superior service; and that the human need being served is of sufficient social importance to justify the superior performance.

REGULATIVE CODE OF ETHICS

The monopoly enjoyed by a profession vis-à-vis clients and community is fraught with hazards. A monopoly can be abused; powers and privileges can be used to protect vested interests against the public weal.[13] The pro-

[12] Many nonprofessional occupations have also succeeded in obtaining licensing legislation in their behalf. Witness the plumbers, radio operators, and barbers, to mention a few. However, the sanctions applied against a person practicing a nonprofessional occupation are much less severe than is the case when a professional occupation is similarly involved.

[13] Abraham Flexner, "Is Social Work a Profession?" in *Proceedings of the National Conference of Charities and Corrections* (Chicago: 1915), pp. 576–590.

Robert K. Merton, "Bureaucratic Structure and Personality," in Alvin Gouldner, ed., *Studies in Leadership* (New York: Harper & Brothers, 1950), pp. 67–79.

fessional group could peg the price of its services at an unreasonably high level; it could restrict the numbers entering the occupation to create a scarcity of personnel; it could dilute the caliber of its performance without community awareness; and it could frustrate forces within the occupation pushing for socially beneficial changes in practices.[14] Were such abuses to become conspicuous, widespread, and permanent, the community would, of course, revoke the profession's monopoly. This extreme measure is normally unnecessary, because every profession has a built-in regulative code which compels ethical behavior on the part of its members.

The profession's ethical code is part formal and part informal. The formal is the written code to which the professional usually swears upon being admitted to practice; this is best exemplified by the Hippocratic Oath of the medical profession. The informal is the unwritten code, which nonetheless carries the weight of formal prescriptions. Through its ethical code the profession's commitment to the social welfare becomes a matter of public record, thereby insuring for itself the continued confidence of the community. Without such confidence the profession could not retain its monopoly. To be sure, self-regulative codes are characteristic of all occupations, nonprofessional as well as professional. However, a professional code is perhaps more explicit, systematic, and binding; it certainly possesses more altruistic overtones and is more public service-oriented.[15] These account for the frequent synonymous use of the terms "professional" and "ethical" when applied to occupational behavior.

While the specifics of their ethical codes vary among the professions, the essentials are uniform. These may be described in terms of client-professional and colleague-colleague relations.

Toward the client the professional must assume an emotional neutrality. He must provide service to whoever requests it, irrespective of the requesting client's age, income, kinship, politics, race, religion, sex, and social status. A nonprofessional may withhold his services on such grounds without, or with minor, censure; a professional cannot. Parsons calls this element in professional conduct *universalism*. In other words, only in his extraoccupational contacts can the professional relate to others on particularistic terms, i.e., as particular individuals with concrete personalities attractive or unattractive to him. In his client contacts particularistic considerations are out of place. Parsons also calls attention to the element of *disinterestedness* in the professional-client relationship.[16] In contrast to the nonprofessional, the professional is motivated less by self-interest and more by the impulse to perform maximally. The behavior corollaries of this service orientation are many. For one, the professional

[14] Merton, *op. cit.*
[15] Flexner, *op. cit.* Parsons, *op. cit.*
[16] Parsons, *op. cit.*

must, under all circumstances, give maximum caliber service. The non-professional can dilute the quality of his commodity or service to fit the size of the client's fee; not so the professional. Again, the professional must be prepared to render his services upon request, even at the sacrifice of personal convenience.

The ethics governing colleague relationships demand behavior that is co-operative, equalitarian, and supportive. Members of a profession share technical knowledge with each other. Any advance in theory and practice made by one professional is quickly disseminated to colleagues through the professional associations.[17] The proprietary and quasi-secretive attitudes toward discovery and invention prevalent in the industrial and commercial world are out of place in the professional. Also out of place is the blatant competition for clients which is the norm in so many non-professional pursuits. This is not to gainsay the existence of intraprofessional competition; but it is a highly regulated competition, diluted with co-operative ingredients which impart to it its characteristically restrained quality. Colleague relations must be equalitarian; intraprofessional recognition should ideally be based solely upon performance in practice and/or contribution to theory.[18] Here, too, particularistic considerations must not be allowed to operate. Finally, professional colleagues must support each other vis-à-vis clientele and community. The professional must refrain from acts which jeopardize the authority of colleagues, and must sustain those whose authority is threatened.[19]

The ways and means whereby a profession enforces the observance of its ethical code constitute a case study in social control. Self-discipline is achieved informally and formally.

Informal discipline consists of the subtle and the not-so-subtle pressures that colleagues exert upon one another. An example in this connection is the phenomenon of consultation and referral.[20] Consultation is the practice of inviting a colleague to participate in the appraisal of the client's need and/or in the planning of the service to be rendered. Referral is the practice of affording colleagues access to a client or an appointment. Thus, one colleague may refer his client to another, because lack of time or skill prevents his rendering the needed service; or he may recommend another for appointment by a prospective employer. Since professional ethics precludes aggressive competition and advertising, consultation and referral constitute the principal source of work to a professional. The consultation-referral custom involves professional col-

---

[17] Arlien Johnson, "Professional Standards and How They Are Attained," *Journal of American Dental Association*, Vol. 31 (September 1944), pp. 1181–1189.

[18] Flexner, *op. cit.*

[19] This partly explains why physicians do not testify against each other in malpractice suits.

[20] Hall, *op. cit.*

leagues in a system of reciprocity which fosters mutual interdependence. Interdependence facilitates social control; chronic violation of professional etiquette arouses colleague resentment, resulting in the cessation of consultation requests and referrals.

A more formal discipline is exercised by the professional associations, which possess the power to criticize or to censure, and in extreme cases to bar recalcitrants. Since membership in good standing in the professional associations is a *sine qua non* of professional success, the prospect of formal disciplinary action operates as a potent force toward conformity.

THE PROFESSIONAL CULTURE

Every profession operates through a network of formal and informal groups. Among the formal groups, first there are the organizations through which the profession performs its services; these provide the institutionalized setting where professional and client meet. Examples of such organizations are hospital, clinic, university, law office, engineering firm, or social agency. Secondly, there are the organizations whose functions are to replenish the profession's supply of talent and to expand its fund of knowledge. These include the educational and the research centers. Third among the formal groups are the organizations which emerge as an expression of the growing consciousness-of-kind on the part of the profession's members, and which promote so-called group interests and aims. These are the professional associations. Within and around these formal organizations extends a filigree of informal groupings: the multitude of small, closely knit clusters of colleagues. Membership in these cliques is based on a variety of affinities: specialties within the profession; affiliations with select professional societies; residential and work propinquity; family, religious, or ethnic background; and personality attractions.

The interactions of social roles required by these formal and informal groups generate a social configuration unique to the profession, viz., a professional culture. All occupations are characterized by formal and informal groupings; in this respect the professions are not unique. What is unique is the culture thus begotten. If one were to single out the attribute that most effectively differentiates the professions from other occupations, this is it. Thus we can talk of a professional culture as distinct from a nonprofessional culture. Within the professions as a logical class each profession develops its own subculture, a variant of the professional culture; the engineering subculture, for example, differs from the subcultures of medicine and social work. In the subsequent discussion, however, we will treat the culture of the professions as a generic phenomenon. The culture of a profession consists of its *values, norms,* and *symbols.*

The social values of a professional group are its basic and fundamental beliefs, the unquestioned premises upon which its very existence rests. Foremost among these values is the essential worth of the service which the professional group extends to the community. The profession considers that the service is a social good and that community welfare would be immeasurably impaired by its absence. The twin concepts of professional authority and monopoly also possess the force of a group value. Thus, the proposition that in all service-related matters the professional group is infinitely wiser than the laity is regarded as beyond argument. Likewise nonarguable is the proposition that acquisition by the professional group of a service monopoly would inevitably produce social progress. And then there is the value of rationality; that is, the commitment to objectivity in the realm of theory and technique. By virtue of this orientation, nothing of a theoretical or technical nature is regarded as sacred and unchallengeable simply because it has a history of acceptance and use.

The norms of a professional group are the guides to behavior in social situations. Every profession develops an elaborate system of these role definitions. There is a range of appropriate behaviors for seeking admittance into the profession, for gaining entry into its formal and informal groups, and for progressing within the occupation's hierarchy. There are appropriate modes of securing appointments, of conducting referrals, and of handling consultation. There are proper ways of acquiring clients, of receiving and dismissing them, of questioning and treating them, of accepting and rejecting them. There are correct ways of grooming a protégé, of recompensing a sponsor, and of relating to peers, superiors, or subordinates. There are even group-approved ways of challenging an outmoded theory, of introducing a new technique, and of conducting an intraprofessional controversy. In short, there is a behavior norm covering every standard interpersonal situation likely to recur in professional life.

The symbols of a profession are its meaning-laden items. These may include such things as: its insignias, emblems, and distinctive dress; its history, folklore, and argot; its heroes and its villains; and its stereotypes of the professional, the client, and the layman.

Comparatively clear and controlling group values, behavior norms, and symbols, which characterize the professions, are not to be encountered in nonprofessional occupations.

Our discussion of the professional culture would be incomplete without brief mention of one of its central concepts, the *career* concept. The term career is, as a rule, employed only in reference to a professional occupation. Thus, we do not talk about the career of a bricklayer or of a mechanic; but we do talk about the career of an architect or of a clergyman. At the heart of the career concept is a certain attitude toward work which is peculiarly professional. A career is essentially a *calling*, a life devoted to "good works." [21] Professional work is never viewed solely as a means to an end; it is the end itself. Curing the ill, educating the young, advancing science are values in themselves. The professional performs his services primarily for the psychic satisfactions and secondarily for the monetary compensations. [22] Self-seeking motives feature minimally in the choice of a profession; of maximal importance is affinity for the work. It is this devotion to the work itself which imparts to professional activity the service orientation and the element of disinterestedness. Furthermore, the absorption in the work is not partial, but complete; it results in a total personal involvement. The work life invades the after-work life, and the sharp demarcation between the work hours and the leisure hours disappears. To the professional person his work becomes his life. [23] Hence the act of embarking upon a professional career is similar in some respects to entering a religious order. The same cannot be said of a nonprofessional occupation.

To succeed in his chosen profession, the neophyte must make an effective adjustment to the professional culture. [24] Mastery of the underlying body of theory and acquisition of the technical skills are in themselves insufficient guarantees of professional success. The recruit must also become familiar with and learn to weave his way through the labyrinth of the professional culture. Therefore, the transformation of a neophyte into a professional is essentially an acculturation process wherein he internalizes the social values, the behavior norms, and the symbols of the occupational group. [25] In its frustrations and rewards it is fundamentally

[21] The term *calling* literally means a divine summons to undertake a course of action. Originally, it was employed to refer to religious activity. The Protestant Reformation widened its meaning to include economic activity as well. Henceforth divinely inspired "good works" were to be both secular and sacred in nature. Presumably, then, any occupational choice may be a response to divine summons. In this connection, it is interesting to note that the German word for vocation is *Beruf*, a noun derived from the verb *berufen*, to call.

[22] Johnson, *op. cit.*

[23] The all-pervading influence of work upon the lives of professionals results in interesting byproducts. The members of a profession tend to associate with one another outside the work setting (Oswald Hall, "The Stages of a Medical Career," *op. cit.*). Their families mingle socially; leisure time is spent together; "shop talk" permeates social discourse; and a consensus develops. The profession thus becomes a whole social environment, nurturing characteristic social and political attitudes, patterns of consumption and recreation, and decorum and *Weltanschauung* (Caplow, *op. cit.*; and William H. Form, "Toward an Occupational Social Psychology," *Journal of Social Psychology*, Vol. 24, February 1946, pp. 85–99).

[24] Oswald Hall, "The Stages of a Medical Career" and "Types of Medical Careers," *op. cit.*

[25] R. Clyde White, " 'Social Workers in Society': Some Further Evidence," *Social Work Journal*, Vol. 34 (October 1953), pp. 161–164.

no different from the acculturation of an immigrant to a relatively strange culture. Every profession entertains a stereotype of the ideal colleague; and, of course, it is always one who is thoroughly adjusted to the professional culture.[26] The poorly acculturated colleague is a deviant; he is regarded as "peculiar," "unorthodox," "annoying," and in extreme cases a "trouble-maker." Whereas the professional group encourages innovation in theory and technique, it tends to discourage deviation from its social values and norms. In this internal contradiction, however, the professional culture is no different from the larger culture of society.

One of the principal functions of the professional schools is to identify and screen individuals who are prospective deviants from the professional culture. That is why the admission of candidates to professional education must be judged on grounds in addition to and other than their academic qualifications.[27] Psychic factors presaging favorable adjustment to the professional culture are granted an importance equivalent to mental abilities. The professional school provides test situations through initial and graduated exposures of the novice to the professional culture. By his behavior in these social situations involving colleagues, clients, and community, the potential deviant soon reveals himself and is immediately weeded out. Comparable preoccupation with the psychic prerequisites of occupational adjustment is not characteristic of nonprofessional occupations.

IMPLICATIONS FOR SOCIAL WORK

The picture of the professions just unveiled is an ideal type. In the construction of an ideal type some exaggeration of reality is unavoidable, since the intent is to achieve an internally coherent picture. One function of the ideal type is to structure reality in such manner that discrete, disparate, and dissimilar phenomena become organized, thereby bringing order out of apparent disorder. We now possess a model of a profession that is much sharper and clearer than the actuality that confronts us when we observe the occupational scene. What is the utility of this model for social work?

The preoccupation of social workers with professionalization has been a characteristic feature of the social work scene for years. Flexner,[28] John-

---

[26] The laity also entertain a stereotypic image of the professional group. Needless to say, the layman's conception and the professional's self-conception diverge widely, because they are fabricated out of very different experiences. The layman's stereotype is frequently a distortion of reality, being either an idealization or a caricature of the professional type.

[27] Oswald Hall, "Sociological Research in the Field of Medicine: Progress and Prospects," *op. cit.*

[28] Flexner, *op. cit.*

son,[29] Hollis and Taylor,[30] and others have written on the subject, proposing criteria which must be met if social work is to acquire professional status. Whenever social workers convene, there is the constant reaffirmation of the urgency to achieve the recognition from the community befitting a profession. The union of the seven separate organizations into the National Association of Social Workers is generally regarded as an important milestone in social work history, precisely because of its potential stimulus toward professionalization.

In view of all this, it is proper for social workers to possess clear conceptions of that which they so fervently seek. The model of the professions portrayed above should contribute to such clarification; it should illuminate the goal for which social workers are striving. It is often contended that social work is still far from having attained professional status.[31] But this is a misconception. When we hold up social work against the model of the professions presented above, it does not take long to decide whether to classify it within the professional or the nonprofessional occupations. Social work is already a profession; it has too many points of congruence with the model to be classifiable otherwise. Social work is, however, seeking to rise within the professional hierarchy, so that it, too, might enjoy maximum prestige, authority, and monopoly which presently belong to a few top professions.

The model presented above should also serve to sensitize social workers to anticipate some of the problems that continued professionalization must inevitably precipitate. The model indicates that progressive professionalization will involve social workers in novel relationships with clients, colleagues, agency, community, and other professions. In concluding this paper we refer briefly to one such problem. It is no secret that social workers are not all uniformly enthusiastic about the professionalization of social work. Bisno [32] has given verbalization to a prevailing apprehension that social workers might have to scuttle their social-action heritage as a price of achieving the public acceptance accorded a profession. Extrapolation from the sociologists' model of the professions suggests a reality basis for these fears. It suggests that the attainment of professional prestige, authority, and monopoly by social workers will undoubtedly carry disturbing implications for the social action and social reform components of social work philosophy. The anticipated developments will compel social workers to rethink and redefine the societal role of their profession.

[29] Johnson, op. cit.

[30] Ernest V. Hollis and Alice L. Taylor, Social Work Education in the United States (New York: Columbia University Press, 1951).

[31] Flexner considered that the social work of his day was not a profession. Hollis and Taylor regard present-day social work as still in its early adolescence.

[32] Herbert Bisno, "How Social Will Social Work Be?" Social Work, Vol. 1, No. 2 (April 1956), pp. 12–18.

These and other dilemmas flowing from professionalization are bound to tax the best minds among social workers for their resolution. In this connection a proper understanding of the attributes of a profession would seem to be indispensable.

Major Dilemmas of the Social Worker
in Probation and Parole

Lloyd E. Ohlin, Herman Piven, and Donnell M. Pappenfort

When a field of service strives toward professionalization of its training requirements and its practice, two basic problems of general significance occur: (1) those charged with the responsibility for professional education must maintain a close integration between preparation and practice; (2) educators and practitioners alike must create conditions in the field which will make professional behavior possible.

The integration of preparation and practice must be maintained if changing needs of field workers are to be met by appropriate educational revision, consistent with professional goals:

> The function of a profession in society and the demands implicit in its practice determine the objectives of education for that profession. The

Lloyd E. Ohlin, Herman Piven, and Donnell M. Pappenfort, "Major Dilemmas of the Social Worker in Probation and Parole," *Crime and Delinquency* (formerly *The National Probation and Parole Journal*), 1956, pp. 211–225. The article has been abridged. This article draws on a portion of interdisciplinary research which has been carried out under a three-year grant by the Russell Sage Foundation to the Center for Education and Research in Corrections at the University of Chicago. It reflects the collective efforts of the staff of the Center. The authors wish to acknowledge their great indebtedness to the contribution of the late Frank T. Flynn, formerly Professor of the School of Social Service Administration, University of Chicago, and Associate Director of the Center for Education and Research in Corrections. Space limitations have compelled a very general treatment of the problems discussed in this article. These limitations have also prevented a full citation of the supporting evidence drawn from the literature, case analyses, and field interviews. Detailed treatment of these and other problems in the field of corrections will be presented in a book now being prepared for publication.

responsibilities which its practitioners must assume designate the content of knowledge and skill to be attained. They determine also the character of the educational experience which students must have to become the kinds of people required both for competent service and to contribute to the ongoing development of the profession in a changing social order.[1]

This is not difficult to sustain when professionalization of the field of service has gained general acceptance. In such a case, the existing body of theory, principles, and methods will provide appropriate responses for the majority of problems encountered in the field; situations of practice will have been standardized and the roles of practitioners clearly defined. It is then relatively easy to control or modify the content of educational experience to train persons adjusted to the work realities of the field.

The situation is far more difficult when there is no general agreement on appropriate professional functions in the field. This usually occurs where the claim to control over professional education by one group is met by equally strong claims from competing groups who envision different training requirements. In such a case, different precepts and techniques of practice compete for recognition, and the work settings and orientations undergo constant change. Under these conditions the practitioners' need for theoretical, conceptual, and technical support from the centers of professional education is most acute. However, it is also at this point in the struggle for professional recognition that the schools of professional education are least well equipped to provide this support in the form of integration of the service needs of the emerging field of practice into the generic educational curriculum. This problem can be solved only through the coordinated efforts of educators, practitioners, and research workers in an impartial assessment of the problems and needs of the field service and an objective reconstruction of the educational curriculum to meet these needs.

The second major problem involved in the professionalization of a new field of service relates to the organizational arrangement and systems of expectations within which the emerging professional practitioner must carry on his work. The need for reorganization, as well as the amount of conflict and resistance encountered, is likely to be at a maximum when an established system of professional education and practice extends its professional mandate to lay claim to a new field of service. An effort is then made to reorganize the new field in the image of allied services where the profession is generally accepted. This movement focuses the resulting struggle of competing groups on such basic problems as definition of the objectives of the field of service, standards of recruitment, methods of job performance, redefinition of administrative and practitioner roles, and reorganization of the expectations of other agencies and the general public as to the nature of the service to be provided. Conflict develops on these points precisely because the professional cannot work effectively in a setting which does not give him adequate freedom to implement his professional skills and knowledge. In the transition period the professional is faced with special dilemmas and problems that make it extremely difficult for him to work effectively and to retain a professional identification with other members of the profession who are unaware of or relatively unconcerned about his position. The problem is further complicated by the fact that the professional knowledge and skills of the practitioner have not been adjusted to the requirements of the new work setting. Consequently, though the need for reorganization of the work setting to provide greater professional freedom is evident, there is no clear-cut understanding of the form and direction which such reorganization should take. A pertinent example of this problem is the situation of the psychiatrist and other therapists in correctional institutions. Although they have achieved general public acceptance, they feel severely hampered in their work because the custodial and administrative staff, as well as clients, have not properly defined their roles and granted them the power and freedom necessary to function professionally.

SOCIAL WORK EDUCATION FOR PROBATION
AND PAROLE

Since World War II the social work profession has increasingly become a source of recruitment for probation and parole field services. This occupational expansion takes place at a time when social work education is built on a generic program applicable to all social work settings, subject only to specific on-the-job training. The special requirements of correctional work are a dramatic challenge to this program. Practitioners and social work educators interested in the correctional field have pressed for broadening the system of generic social work education to incorporate theoretical knowledge and methodological skills which would prepare practitioners to handle the problems of serving the offender client in the correctional agency setting. They are convinced that social work training provides the best available professional preparation for this work.

> It [probation] is rather a *process of treatment* aimed at effecting a readjustment within the community setting, of the attitudes, habits and capabilities of the offender. If this is the goal of probation, then casework becomes the best method for achieving this goal, since the sole aim and purpose of casework is to strengthen the individual's ability to "regulate his own life" in society.[2]

This concern that social work educators and practitioners have in the professional development of the correctional field has raised many questions. Is probation and parole social work? Does social work education as presently constituted adequately prepare practitioners for the correctional field? Can the theoretical and methodological requirements for correctional work be successfully incorporated into generic social work education?

All these questions call for more detailed exploration than has thus far occurred.

One of the functions of research, under such circumstances, is to inform the educator and the field administrator of the empirical problem of implementing the professional position. It seeks to describe the conflicts and limitations which beset the practitioner and to highlight the discrepancy between what is taught in the schools and what is demanded in practice. The results of such research should provide the basis for the rational development and strengthening of educational programs and a core of knowledge and understanding for the professional reorganization of the field of work itself. This article is an attempt to outline the major dilemmas in which the social worker often finds himself as he tries to carry out his professional obligations as a social worker while fulfilling his job obligations as a probation-parole officer.

The professional in any field is more than the possessor of certain knowledge, skills, and techniques for doing his job. He is identified with a profession which constitutes for him a subculture. This subculture defines for its members the purposes, aspirations, and obligations of the profession as a whole and makes a meaningful pattern of the complex experiences of the occupational life.

> Professional education as a re-educative process has to fulfill a task that is essentially equivalent to a change in culture. Since the individual's attitudes have been formed through his dependence on relationships and through his response to authority pressures within the family and other organized groups, Kurt Lewin holds that one of the outstanding needs for bringing about acceptance in re-education is the establishment of an "in-group," that is, a group in which the members experience a sense of belonging.[3]

Insofar as the practitioner is a professional man he has internalized this subculture, drawing from it the roots of his professional "identity"—his professional "self." The significance of this identification is dramatically experienced by many social workers in the correctional field. Correctional work is generally conceived by the larger profession of social work as a marginal activity [4] and it receives neither the recognition and status nor the educational and organizational support accorded to other fields of service in the profession. Consequently, correctional practitioners often feel that they are alienated from and not accepted by the general profession. This results in a confusion of professional identification which inhibits the continuity and progress of their personal careers and retards the general professionalization and development of correctional services.

The social worker, because of his practical concern with human development, has become especially aware of the fact that he is a man with a mission as well as a technical expert.[5] The social work school deliberately instills in its graduates a set of expectations about the role of the worker in relation to his client, agency, and community. It has consciously organized its curriculum to produce graduates who are oriented to the needs of traditional agency settings (best illustrated by the private family agency and the out-patient psychiatric clinic). These expectations are not always fulfilled in the correctional setting and the discrepancy between expectation and actuality is a measure of the "reality shock" experienced by the new worker. His reaction to the dilemmas in which he is placed has profound consequences for himself, his clients, the probation-parole service, and the wider field of social work.

THE PROBATION-PAROLE SETTING

The probation-parole occupation has undergone continuous change, with the entrance of the social worker representing a significant turning point in its professional development. The social work recruit comes to an agency in which many clients have not voluntarily sought casework service, are not "motivated for treatment," and are limited by lack of capacity even if they could be motivated. In addition, other occupational and interest groups and occasionally general public opinion view him with watchful suspicion, even hostility. Like other public institutions in a democratic society, his agency has organized its directives and structure partly in response to the pressures and counterpressures of public opinion. The nature of the clientele and agency organization poses for him many serious theoretical and practical problems which make his adjustment and the exercise of his professional competence far more problematic than he had been led to expect during his educational and field work training experience.

The social worker often finds the agency organized in terms of presocial work theories of probation and parole. From the point of view of work orientations, two types of probation-parole workers have dominated the field. The "punitive officer" is the guardian of middle-class community morality; he attempts to coerce the offender into conforming by means of threats and punishment and his emphasis is on control, protecting the community *against* the offender, and systematic suspicion of those under supervision. The "protective agent," on the other hand, vacillates between protecting the offender *and* protecting the community. His tools are direct assistance, lecturing, and praise and blame. He is recognized by his ambivalent emotional involvement with the offender and others in the community as he shifts back and forth in taking sides with one against the other.

A third type, the "welfare worker," is entering correctional work with increasing frequency. His ultimate work goal is the improved welfare of the client, a condition achieved by helping him in his individual adjustment, within limits imposed by the client's capacity. He feels that the only genuine guarantee of community protection lies in the client's personal adjustment since external conformity will only be temporary and in the long run may make a successful adjustment more difficult. Emotional neutrality permeates his relationships. The diagnostic categories and treatment skills which he employs stem from an objective and theoretically based assessment of the client's situation, needs, and capacities. His primary identification is with the social work profession.

The three types of workers are often found as colleagues in the same organization, particularly during the period of emerging agency professionalization. Their differing work orientations frequently generate conflict and impose limits on the extent to which any of these work patterns can achieve full expression.

OCCUPATIONAL DILEMMAS

Three conditions structure the occupational dilemmas of the social worker: [6] (1) the nature of the clientele, (2) agency organization, and (3) community expectations.

The Client

By virtue of the control which traditional casework agencies exert over their intake policies, the profession is able to insist on the fulfillment of certain norms which are sometimes inapplicable or opposed to the requirements of probation-parole practice. The model in social casework presumes that the individual applicant selects an agency,[7] asks to become its client for service,[8] defines the service appropriately,[9] and is acceptable to the agency on the basis of his motivation and capacity for treatment.[10] With the possible exception of the last of these criteria, the probationer or parolee appears to be excluded from generic casework consideration as a client. The ramifications of this disparity between social work norms and correctional practice are manifold. The social worker in corrections feels he has not been sufficiently prepared to deal with clients who are unmotivated, who lack capacity for treatment, or who do not require his help. His expectations for providing helpful service are frustrated by clients who refuse help or fail to acknowledge the existence of problems which require help of the kind the practitioner feels professionally equipped to offer. In addition, he is confronted by a work load which does not allow him enough time to concentrate on trying to overcome these difficulties and render appropriate casework service. The basic problem is that his academic training had not given him the skills and guides to action for converting a relationship of control and authority into one of consent and treatment.

The social worker desires a warm, neutral, and nonjudgmental relationship with his client.[11] He recognizes, however, that the client regards him as a participant in the punitive and condemning system of apprehension, judgment, and correction. He knows that the offender is compelled to come to him as a condition of probation or parole and often approaches him with hostility and an interest in concealing facts and feelings. The social worker knows that his authority is real. For example, both he and the client know that the actual decision on revocation usually is the worker's, even though the formal authority is lodged elsewhere. His profession tells him that this is "an initial obstacle to be worked through," but it does not teach him what to do. This is a major though not an insuperable barrier for the recruit who has no specific training to apply.

Failing to find guidance from the social work profession in dealing with this problem, the social work practitioner sometimes turns to older workers or supervisors in the probation and parole system itself. Since many of these persons do not share a common theoretical and conceptual background of training with the social work recruit, the advice he receives often sharpens rather than resolves his dilemma. To meet his own need to overcome client hostility toward him as an authoritarian figure in order to establish conditions requisite to treatment, and at the same time to satisfy the pressures of the community (and, in some agencies, the pressures of his superiors) for client conformity, he frequently attempts to play two roles. On the one hand, he tries to offer a caseworker's sympathetic understanding and help; on the other, he is the agent of law and respectability, attempting to explain one function as separate from the other. Because he has no clear conception of how or when to integrate control and treatment functions, and lacks knowledge of the skills by which they might be made mutually supportive, his attempt to play two roles is frequently unsuccessful.

> Because humans tend to react to any one phase of an agency experience in terms of the total self and in terms of a totality of needs, it may not be a simple matter to render services clearly distinguished one from another. An agency may conveniently divide itself into two sets of services and proffer them like two different commodities. But a man has not two separate sides to his head or to his heart.[12]

This makes his dilemma clear, but it does not resolve it.

The social work recruit brings with him a model of treatment purpose and process from the classroom, casework literature, and field placement experience. He grants the possibility of incorporating the "wise use of authority," [13] but in a work situation where the anticipated traditional process does not unfold he feels bewildered and betrayed because he has never been taught techniques appropriate to other than nonauthoritarian and nonjudgmental relationships.[14]

The social caseworker in probation and parole also experiences difficulty in classifying the problems represented in his caseload. He finds many clients with whom he would have difficulty establishing a treatment relationship even under ideal working conditions because of personality structures and lack of capacities, and because of the paucity of available knowledge and techniques. Many of the types of cases which he encounters in his agency experience have not been included in the theoretical and methodological training with case materials received during his educational preparation. Although he usually learns to classify his caseload and provide service for many who need and can use it, the probation-parole officer trained in casework first goes through the painful process of rebuff, dismay, and experimentation. He often finds it necessary to seek guidance from sources other than social work itself, sources which deal with his specific clients and problems.[15]

The difficulties which the social worker encounters with his caseload are further complicated by lack of familiarity with the criminal and delinquent subcultures from which most offenders emerge. Social casework emphasizes the importance of identifying the social environment with which the client is interacting in order to understand how he perceives and feels about his situation and how he may be helped. This requires knowledge and familiarity with the cultural and social backgrounds from which offenders come, a familiarity which the officer does not usually bring from his own background and knowledge which his formal education does not specifically give him.[16]

Agency Organization

Democratic administration has been defined as the art of compromise through which divergent and contradictory social forces modify one another and reach a final expression simultaneously reflecting the wishes of all but those of no group completely.[17] Because the probation-parole agency must adapt itself to the threat of powerful and antagonistic groups in its environment,[18] it occasionally represents an extreme case of the generalization that every organization displays a discrepancy between its stated purposes and the objective consequences of the actions of its functionaries.

The failures of probation and parole are more spectacular than those in most other professions, and newsmen have the occupational motive of "good copy" to encourage them to scrutinize correctional practice and organize critical public opinion around a dramatically destructive episode.

Elected judges, legislators, and other public officials have a vested interest in being on the popular side of a crisis, and occupational groups whose interests are inherently in opposition to client-centered probation and parole supervision are able to use periods of public excitement to further their own purposes. Consequently the administrator is under pressure to anticipate possible criticism and to organize the agency and its policies in self-protection. The problem is frequently intensified for the social work administrator who feels a professional obligation to expand his program and recruit social work officers, thus requiring support from important officials and citizens not only to protect the agency but to aid in its development.

The accommodation to external threat is expressed in an emphasis on public relations revealed not only in positive educational campaigns, but also in organization of the agency and the development of policies on client supervision and the worker's role in the community.

During this transitional period, however, when the agency is striving for public acceptance of its work through increased professionalization of staff and operation, the interests of the administrator and the caseworker tend to diverge. The caseworker often perceives the public relations interest of the agency as a compromise with enforcement concepts promoted by other occupational groups in the community. He frequently feels that the agency's treatment objectives are being sacrificed for agency protection. He feels that he is under pressure to make nonprofessional decisions on his cases. This divergence of interests between the agency-centered administrator and the client-centered caseworker is illustrated below by problems arising in (1) the area of supervising the caseworker, (2) the rules for supervision of clients, and (3) informal policies about agency-community conflicts.

1. In the eyes of the social work profession, supervision by personnel skilled in imparting knowledge and techniques and in helping workers to recognize and profit by their errors without ego-destructiveness is mandatory for client welfare and workers' professional growth. The emphasis on agency protection in probation and parole, however, often results in promoting men who are successful in public relations rather than skilled in casework supervision. Also, when agencies are in a period of transition, the protection of morale and seniority leads to promotion of older employees trained in fields other than social work. Under these conditions, the social worker feels that the central focus of these supervisors is to prevent him from acting in ways which might embarrass the agency. He feels that treatment problems not involving the possibility of public condemnation are of secondary concern, and that aiding his professional growth very seldom becomes a work function. The limitations imposed by the supervisor oriented to public relations, and the conse-

quent variance in understanding the subtleties of casework, pose for the social worker many problems which penetrate a large number of his daily activities. He has been taught to expect supervision of a learning-helping nature; when this source of support and professional guidance is absent, he feels that he has lost one of the main links to his professional identity and competent professional performance.

2. The "rules of client supervision" are an inheritance from an earlier phase of probation-parole when control over the client was more openly advocated. For the social work administrator, however, they are functional, since they are a formal expression of community expectations concerning control of offenders which can be used as a defense against public criticism that the agency "coddles" its clients, or enforced to achieve other administrative ends with clients and workers. The "rules" sometimes are extended by informal policies and official requirements into a structure unacceptable to the social worker because he cannot interpret it as reasonable and necessary for his client. If a client must, by virtue of court order, parole decision, or informal agency requirement, abstain from drinking or observe a curfew, neither the worker nor the client can escape the realization that these are restrictions from which other adults are formally immune. The effect of this is to deny the client participation in normal activities and to reinforce his conception that he is somehow different *in kind* from other persons in the community. For the worker it reinforces the conception that the agency and the community regard his goals, methods, and clients as different *in kind* from those of other social agencies. The caseworker further feels that the "rules" may prevent individualization according to his client's needs.

3. Agency policy controlling the agent-community system of relationships also has important consequences for the casework task. The degree of emphasis on public relations varies greatly from one agency to another. An urban agency may generally achieve more autonomy than a rural one: in districts of similar population density, community pressure increases from federal to state to county levels of jurisdiction. Two extremes of agency structure exist—the relatively "autonomous" agency and the "restricted" agency.

(a) In the "autonomous" agency the social worker has far greater freedom to reject the control function and to pursue the treatment objectives of casework. For example, he makes definite recommendations for disposition, which are followed with few exceptions, and he feels free to circumvent court or parole board directives which he regards as opposed to his client's welfare. He is in a position to reject pressure from finance companies and to persuade the judge to remit court costs and restitution. He contacts clients as seldom or as often as casework needs and caseload requirements dictate and will usually arrange appointments before making home visits. He feels free to inform clients explicitly that their drinking, sex habits, hours, driving, purchases, etc., are of concern to him only when they constitute casework problems. He frequently feels the obligation to inform the client of discriminatory practices by certain employers and may even encourage him to conceal his criminal record in approaching them for employment.

It is within the "autonomous" agency that the social caseworker feels he can act most consistently with the professional directives received in his academic training. He feels he can confine his role essentially to the treatment function and permit other agencies to discharge the control function as they do with other citizens in the community. In short, he seeks to structure the performance of his work and the organization of his work relationships according to the model of social casework in traditional agency settings.

(b) In the "restricted" agency this freedom to pursue the treatment orientation and to reject the control function as a significant part of the worker's role is impossible to achieve. The social worker in the "restricted" agency encounters many points of conflict in fulfilling agency policy and maintaining a service-treatment relationship in the interests of the client—each of which is a professional norm. A uniform policy of mandatory home visits, for example, prevents individualization according to client needs. Other agency policies forbid undertaking treatment with clients whose problems may require occasional "acting out" as a prerequisite to eventual adjustment, a situation the worker has been trained to anticipate and accept as appropriate to casework. More importantly, the social worker often feels that he is forced to emphasize immediate client conformity to unrealistic standards; e.g., early curfew, abstention from drinking, from sexual relationships, etc. He frequently feels that such action keeps the client from being integrated into his own legitimate groups, prevents the client from viewing him as a treatment resource, and denies the worker the opportunity to move beyond the question of conformity in interviews. He thus has difficulty in "motivating" the unmotivated or strengthening a client's weak capacities. When he also feels compelled by agency policy to make unexpected night visits, to look in bars and poolrooms, to check on clients at work—in short, to practice "surveillance" —the problem is intensified. One social worker reported: "My God! My clients won't talk to me; they don't even want to see me. They pull the curtains when I drive up to the house."

Community Expectations

As generally portrayed in social work education, the "community" is composed of heterogeneous individuals who share certain basic values and interests. Problems of casework clients involving other people are seen as personal problems of the client, and alternative solutions are explored in the counseling relationship to aid the client's decision. The worker-client relationship is conceived as private and confidential, and the only responsibility of the worker is his client's welfare. For example, it would be unusual for a businessman to request the cooperation of a family, medical, or psychiatric social agency in persuading a client to pay a debt, and it would be regarded as clearly improper for a caseworker of such an agency to accept this responsibility.

The social worker in corrections, however, soon recognizes that the community consists of a number of interest groups with varying and conflicting demands upon him and the offender client. He finds that many officials and citizens have a negative attitude toward his client and that this is reciprocated by the client. His task is not only to alter both conceptions, but to deal with the problems raised by these conflicts of ideas and interests during the conduct of the case. He finds himself subjected to various pressures to act in ways which violate his own conception of the proper role and function of a social worker. He feels that his profession has not provided him with realistic conceptions of the "community," expectations of the pressures he will encounter, or prescriptions for appropriate action.

The probation-parole worker feels, for example, that the police pursue enforcement objectives without sufficient regard for the consequences of their actions on the offender's adjustment.[19] Such acts as indiscriminate arrest on suspicion are perceived by the worker as not only impeding the client's adjustment but re-enforcing the offender's conception of himself as a person apart from and rejected by the community. The worker experiences widespread pressure by the police and other official functionaries to define his role as that of an enforcement officer who should use control measures to restrict the client's freedom and coercion to punish him for wrongdoing. When he attempts to resist these pressures, he finds probation and parole interpreted as leniency and himself identified as a "sob sister." Recognizing that police, prosecutors, judges, and others are often guided by values and objectives different from those which he considers primary, he is uncertain as to how to proceed, especially at those points where he is required to commit what he feels are gross violations of professional norms. An illustration is often found in the use made of the worker's presentence report, where the judge not only may dispose of cases on grounds other than treatability and humanitarian equality,[20] but also may violate confidentiality by making the report public. Powerless to prevent police and others from pursuing their own interests in the client in ways which he defines as interference with the treatment and adjustment of the client, yet requiring their cooperation in his daily work, he feels untrained to deal satisfactorily with either the client or the officials.

Social workers have tended to adjust to this situation in a variety of ways. Some have expended considerable effort in seeking to educate and influence officials and citizens to understand the rehabilitative approach of the worker, the nature of the client-worker relationship, and casework methods for effecting client adjustment. Others resort to evasions, sentimental appeals, and "slanted" or safe reports. Still other workers have sought to withdraw in some measure from the norms of client service and confidentiality, accounting for apparent norm violations as limitations of the setting.

A final group of problems experienced by social workers in corrections relates to their identification with the profession. Since community officials and citizens with whom he frequently deals, as well as his own supervisor in many instances, are not social workers, the officer is usually restrained from employing the diagnostic and treatment vocabulary he has been trained to use. This limitation frequently creates anxiety in the worker, who fears the hazards of daily communication and the loss of familiarity with the technical tools of his profession. Probably more important is the difficulty experienced in maintaining a professional identification with other social workers. Not infrequently social agencies look with suspicion and distrust on the probation officer who seeks collateral information from their records. The stereotyped image maintained by social workers in traditional welfare agencies concerning the nature of casework practice in corrections often leads them to share the general community conception of the probation-parole worker as a law enforcement agent. This lack of understanding and acceptance of his position and problems by social work colleagues and educators contributes to a process of professional alienation, thus promoting further anxiety in the worker as to his professional identification.

RESPONSES OF THE SOCIAL WORKER

As a result of these barriers to professional practice in probation-parole, as conceived in traditional social casework terms, many social workers leave the field. Some give up social work entirely, disillusioned and convinced that both social work as a discipline and corrections as an area of practice are without genuine reward or meaning. Some return to more traditional casework settings, convinced that it is not possible, at least for them, to operate professionally in probation-parole work. Others remain in corrections, unhappy with their most recent job experience, but feeling committed to this specialty because of an awareness of casework needs in the field, because of the nature of the contacts and experience they have acquired, and because of a genuine conviction that the necessary knowledge and structure can be created for professional casework in this setting. As to the social workers who remain in corrections, five general types of adjustment have been distinguished, varying principally with the length of time the officer has worked, the nature of the agency organization, and the character of community conditions.

1. One type of adjustment is found in the relatively "autonomous" agency directed by a social work oriented administrator. The worker feels that the agency is moving toward increased professionalization and that he is able to function significantly as a professional in spite of the obstacles. He identifies himself primarily as a social worker but hastens to point out major differences between the ideas and practices of the larger profession and those of the correctional field.

2. In the "restricted" agency, the worker is often harried and bewildered by demands made upon him by clients, supervisors, officials of other agencies, and the community at large for "unprofessional" behavior. He gradually accepts the "protective" definition at various important points and explicitly identifies himself as a probation-parole officer divorced from the field of social work.

3. Also found in the "restricted" agency is the worker who completely rejects what he regards as "anti-professional" demands and seeks to come to terms with these pressures by manipulation and evasion. Since the extent to which he can achieve this by himself is limited and because the effort—itself a violation of social work norms—tends to isolate him from the agency in which he works, he blames both the profession and the agency for his predicament. He derives his ultimate justification for evasion from the social work ideology of client service, however, and therefore retains a professional identity—albeit an alienated one—and he hopes to transfer to a correctional agency where the climate will be more conducive to treatment efforts.

4. Quite commonly the recent recruit to the field of corrections operates as a marginal and ambivalent worker. He experiments with various "new methods and techniques," including client coercion, in attempting to solve his work problems. Seriously disturbed by the "reality shock" of his first contact with correctional work, he already feels disenchanted with social work. The career patterns in the field suggest that he will continue experimenting for a while and will eventually resolve his conflicts by becoming one of the other types.

5. Finally, the social worker may accept the protective measures of the "restricted" agency as more or less natural and necessary for probation-parole work, trying to give service and treatment to clients as fully as possible within the given framework. He sees himself as a special kind of social worker and explains the imposed restrictions on clients as "necessary reality," identifying the client's difficulties in accepting these restrictions as a lack of capacity to adjust "to society."

CONCLUSION

The problems of the social worker in probation and parole have been related to the generic education he receives and to the special circumstances he faces in an area of practice where his caseload differs from that of more traditional settings, where powerful community forces oppose his ideals, and in which his agency attempts to protect itself by demanding of him decisions which seem unprofessional to him. His responses to the unexpected and painful dilemmas include withdrawal to another setting, experimental-evasive-manipulative tactics, and alienation from his professional identification. These symptoms indicate a lag between social work education and the requirements of probation-parole practice.

If social work is to retain probation-parole as an area of application, it will have to participate in the solution of three problems, each demanding revision of social work preparation for the field: (1) community expectations about probation and parole must be modified to allow the professional sufficient freedom to pursue treatment interests; (2) he must be given the knowledge and skills which will enable him to do constructive work when alternatives are limited by public opinion and agency organization; (3) the practitioner must be provided with the knowledge required for work with his particular clientele. . . .

REFERENCES

1. Charlotte Towle, "The General Objectives of Professional Education," *Social Service Review,* December, 1951, p. 427.
2. Ben Meeker, "Probation Is Casework," *Federal Probation,* June, 1948, p. 52. Cf. Arthur E. Fink, *The Field of Social Work,* New York, Henry Holt, 1942, pp. 213–261; Frank T. Flynn, "Probation and Individualized Justice," *Federal Probation,* June, 1950, pp. 70–76; Elliot Studt, "Casework in the Correctional Field," *Federal Probation,* September, 1954, pp. 19–26; *Training Personnel for Work with Juvenile Delinquents,* U.S. Department of Health, Education, and Welfare, Children's Bureau Publication No. 348, Washington, D.C., 1954.
3. Charlotte Towle, "The Contribution of Education for Social Casework to Practice," Cora Kasius, ed., *Principles and Techniques in Social Casework,* New York, Family Service Association of America, 1950, p. 262.
4. Cf. U.S. Bureau of Labor Statistics, *Social Worker in 1950,* New York, American Association of Social Workers, 1952, p. 23.
5. "Competencies expected of social workers were grouped into three categories: (1) Perceptual and Conceptual Knowledge; (2) Skills, Methods, Processes, and Procedures; (3) Personal Professional Qualities. Attitudes permeated all three. The first two of these categories have been referred to graphically as 'must know' and 'must do' items. Perhaps the third should be designated as the 'must be and must feel' category." Ernest V. Hollis and Alice L. Taylor, *Social Work Education in the United States,* New York, American Association of Social Workers, 1952, p. 27.
6. A complete study of probation-parole requires analysis of problems encountered by the "punitive officer" and the "protective agent" as well as the "welfare

worker" as represented by persons recruited from the field of social work. In this article only the problems and dilemmas of social workers will be considered. It should be noted, however, that each of the other types of workers face equally serious and consequential problems in their work adjustment.

7. Helen L. Witmer, *Social Work—An Analysis of a Social Institution,* New York, Rinehart, 1942, pp. 179–180.
8. Swithun Bowers, "The Nature and Definition of Social Casework," *Principles and Techniques in Social Casework, op. cit.,* p. 108.
9. *Ibid.,* p. 11.
10. Delwin K. Anderson and Frank Kiesler, "Helping Toward Help: The Intake Interview," *Social Casework,* February, 1954, p. 72.
11. Cf. Charlotte Towle, "Social Case Work in Modern Society," *Social Service Review,* June, 1946, pp. 168–169, for the casework model of this relationship and the treatment process.
12. Charlotte Towle, *Common Human Needs,* Chicago, University of Chicago Press, 1945, p. 61.
13. Elliot Studt, "An Outline for Study of Social Authority Factors in Casework," *Social Casework,* June, 1954, pp. 231–238.
14. In the article by Charlotte Towle, "Social Case Work in Modern Society," *op. cit.,* it is noted that some clients "become confused, anxious and frustrated" in the neutral casework relationship and that it is then advisable "to be supportive—i.e., . . . to use authority, meet dependency, impose demands, and convey moral judgments in a sustaining way so that the individual may become more self-determining or, at least, less self-destructive in his behavior." The social worker points out, however, that the school has not shown him when or how to do this.
15. In one study, all but one of the social work officers in the probation and parole agency gave as his first reading choice either the NPPA JOURNAL or *Federal Probation,* in preference to social work journals. This is an indication of the partial alienation from the social work profession which practitioners trained in social work frequently experience under the pressure of solving their immediate work problems.
16. Cf. Otto Pollak, "Cultural Dynamics in Casework," *Social Casework,* July, 1953, pp. 279–284; Melitta Schmideberg and Jack Sokol, "The Function of Contact in Psychotherapy with Offenders," *Social Casework,* November, 1953, p. 386; and Elliot Studt, "Casework in the Correctional Field," *op. cit.,* p. 25.
17. Reinhard Bendix, "Bureaucracy: The Problem and Its Setting," *American Sociological Review,* October, 1947, pp. 493–507.
18. Cf. Philip Selznick, "An Approach to a Theory of Bureaucracy," *American Sociological Review,* February, 1943, pp. 47–54.
19. Other major interest groups frequently mentioned with varying degrees of similar criticism by workers are lawyers, judges, finance companies, bonding companies, used-car companies, and institutional personnel. Cf. U.S. Department of Justice, *Attorney General's Survey of Release Procedures,* Vol. IV, *Parole,* Washington, D.C., 1939, pp. 220–221.
20. *Ibid.,* Vol. II, *Probation,* pp. 470–471.

Professions in Process

Rue Bucher and Anselm Strauss

The "process" or "emergent" approach to the study of professions developed in the following pages bears considerable resemblance to a common-sense point of view. It utilizes common language to order the kinds of events that professionals informally discuss among themselves—frequently with great animation. It is even used by sociologists in their less professional moments when they are personally challenged by their own colleagues or by persons from other fields. What is different here is that we shall take the first steps toward developing an explicit scheme of analysis out of these commonplace materials. In addition, it will become apparent that this approach differs from the prevailing "functionalism" because it focuses more pointedly upon conflicting interests and upon change.

Functionalism sees a profession largely as a relatively homogeneous community whose members share identity, values, definitions of role, and interests.[1] There is room in this conception for some variation, some

[1] Cf. William J. Goode, "Community within a Community: The Professions," *American Sociological Review*, XX (1957), 194–200.

Rue Bucher and Anselm Strauss, "Professions in Process," *American Journal of Sociology*, 1961, LXVI, pp. 325–334. The intellectual origins of this scheme of analysis are both our own research and various writings of our predecessors and colleagues. Its specific ideas occurred to us when Miss Bucher, several years ago, had occasion to analyze a number of specialty journals and interview a sample of pathologists. Since then we have both been engaged in a study which brings us much information about psychiatrists and psychiatric nurses in Chicago, and we have had available also Everett C. Hughes's interviews with the medical staff at the University of Kansas medical school. The writings to which we are most indebted are those of Everett Hughes on work and professions (cf. *Men and Their Work* [Glencoe, Ill.: Free Press, 1958]) and the symbolic-interaction position in social psychology (cf. George Herbert Mead's *Mind, Self, and Society* [Chicago: University of Chicago Press, 1934]). Because the materials on occupations, work, and professions are well known and readily available, we have not cited all references to pertinent literature; the files of various specialty journals in all the professions are useful to anyone interested in further illustrations.

differentiation, some out-of-line members, even some conflict; but, by and large, there is a steadfast core which defines the profession, deviations from which are but temporary dislocations. Socialization of recruits consists of induction into the common core. There are norms, codes, which govern the behavior of the professional to insiders and outsiders. In short, the sociology of professions has largely been focused upon the mechanics of cohesiveness and upon detailing the social structure (and/or social organization) of given professions. Those tasks a structural-functional sociology is prepared to do, and do relatively well.

But this kind of focus and theory tend to lead one to overlook many significant aspects of professions and professional life. Particularly does it bias the observer against appreciating the conflict—or at least difference —of interests within the profession; this leads him to overlook certain of the more subtle features of the profession's "organization" as well as to fail to appreciate how consequential for changes in the profession and its practitioners differential interests may be.

In actuality, the assumption of relative homogeneity within the profession is not entirely useful: there are many identities, many values, and many interests. These amount not merely to differentiation or simple variation. They tend to become patterned and shared; coalitions develop and flourish—and in opposition to some others. We shall call these groupings which emerge within a profession "segments." (Specialties might be thought of as major segments, except that a close look at a specialty betrays its claim to unity, revealing that specialties, too, usually contain segments, and, if they ever did have common definitions along all lines of professional identity, it was probably at a very special, and early, period in their development.) We shall develop the idea of professions as loose amalgamations of segments pursuing different objectives in different manners and more or less delicately held together under a common name at a particular period in history.

Our aim in this paper, then, is to present some initial steps in formulating a "process" model for studying professions. The model can be considered either as a supplement of, or an alternative to, the prevailing functional model. Some readers undoubtedly will prefer to consider the process model as supplementary. If so, then there will be a need for a further step, that is, for a transcending model. But we ourselves are concerned here only with sketching the outlines of a process approach, suggesting a few potentially useful concepts, and pointing to certain research problems that flow from our framework and concepts.

"ORGANIZED MEDICINE"

Medicine is usually considered the prototype of the professions, the one upon which current sociological conceptions of professions tend to be based; hence, our illustrative points in this paper will be taken from medicine, but they could just as pertinently have come from some other profession. Of the medical profession as a whole a great deal could be, and has been, said: its institutions (hospitals, schools, clinics); its personnel (physicians and paramedical personnel); its organizations (the American Medical Association, the state and county societies); its recruitment policies; its standards and codes; its political activities; its relations with the public; not to mention the professions' informal mechanisms of sociability and control. All this minimal "structure" certainly exists.

But we should also recognize the great divergency of enterprise and endeavor that mark the profession; the cleavages that exist along with the division of labor; and the intellectual and specialist movements that occur within the broad rubric called "organized medicine." It might seem as if the physicians certainly share common ends, if ever any profession did. When backed to the wall, any physician would probably agree that his long-run objective is better care of the patient. But this is a misrepresentation of the actual values and organization of activity as undertaken by various segments of the profession. Not all the ends shared by all physicians are distinctive to the medical profession or intimately related to what many physicians do, as their work. What is distinctive of medicine belongs to certain segments of it—groupings not necessarily even specialties—and may not actually be shared with other physicians. We turn now to a consideration of some of those values which these segments do *not* share and about which they may actually be in conflict.

The Sense of Mission

It is characteristic of the growth of specialties that early in their development they carve out for themselves and proclaim unique missions. They issue a statement of the contribution that the specialty, and it alone, can make in a total scheme of values and, frequently, with it an argument to show why it is peculiarly fitted for this task. The statement of mission tends to take a rhetorical form, probably because it arises in the context of a battle for recognition and institutional status. Thus, when surgical specialties, such as urology and proctology, were struggling to attain identities independent of general surgery, they developed the argument that the particular anatomical areas in which they were interested required special attention and that only physicians with their particular background were competent to give it. Anesthesiologists developed a similar argument. This kind of claim separates a given area out of the general stream of medicine, gives it special emphasis and a new dignity, and, more important for our purposes, separates the specialty group from other physicians. Insofar as they claim an area for themselves, they aim to exclude others from it. It is theirs alone.

While specialties organize around unique missions, as time goes on segmental missions may develop within the fold. In radiology, for example, there are groups of physicians whose work is organized almost completely around diagnosis. But there is a recently burgeoning group of radiologists whose mission is to develop applications of radiation for therapeutic purposes. This difference of mission is so fundamental that it has given rise to demands for quite different residency training programs and to some talk of splitting off from the parent specialty. In pathology—one of the oldest medical specialties, whose traditional mission has been to serve as the basic science of medicine with relatively little emphasis upon clinical applications—lately a whole new breed of pathologists has come to the fore, dedicated to developing pathology as a specialized service to clinical practitioners and threatening those who cling to the traditional mission.

The split between research missions and clinical practice runs clear through medicine and all its specialties. Pediatrics has one of the most rapidly growing fields of practice, but it has also attracted a number of young people, particularly at some centers in the Northeast, specifically for research. They are people who have no conceptions of themselves as family pediatricians at all; they are in this field because of what they can do in the way of research. In the two oldest specialties, surgery and internal medicine, one finds throughout the literature considerable evidence of this kind of split. One finds an old surgeon complaining that the young men are too much interested in research, and in internal medicine there are exhortations that they should be doctors, not scientists. This latter lament is particularly interesting in view of the traditional mission of the internist to exemplify the finest in the "art of medicine": it is a real betrayal when one of them shows too much interest in controlled research.

Work Activities

There is great diversity in the tasks performed in the name of the profession. Different definitions may be found between segments of the profession concerning what kinds of work the professional should be doing, how work should be organized, and which tasks have precedence. If, for example, the model physician is taken as one who sees patients and carries out the diagnosis and treatment of illness, then an amazing variety of physicians do not fit this model. This diversity is not wholly congruent with the organization of practice by medical specialties, although there are certain specialties—like pathology, radiology, anesthesiology, and public health—whose practitioners for the most part do not approach the model. Within a core specialty like internal medicine there are many different kinds of practice, ranging from that of a "family doctor" to highly specialized consultation, a service to other doctors. These differences in the weights assigned to elements of practice do not begin to take into account the further diversity introduced when professionals assign different weights to such activities as research, teaching, and public service.

This point can be made more clearly by considering some of the different organizations of work activities that can be found within single specialties. The people who organize their work life as follows all call themselves "pathologists": (a) time nearly equally divided between research and teaching, with little or no contact with patient care; (b) time divided (ideally) equally between research, teaching, and diagnostic services to other doctors; (c) administration of a hospital service, diagnostic services and consultations with other physicians, and educational activities. (The objects of educational activities are not only medical students and residents but other practitioners of the hospital. These pathologists may also actually examine patients face-to-face and consult on a course of treatment.)

Again, consider the radiologist. There is considerable range in the scope and kind of practice subsumed under radiology. The "country radiologist" tends to function as an all-round diagnostic consultant, evaluating and interpreting findings concerning a broad spectrum of medical conditions. In the large medical center the diagnostic radiologist either does limited consultation concerning findings or else specializes in one area, such as neurological radiology or pediatric radiology. Then there is the radiologist whose work is not primarily diagnostic at all but involves the application of radiation for therapeutic purposes. This man may have his own patients in course of treatment, much like an internist or urologist.

These illustrations suggest that members of a profession not only weigh auxiliary activities differently but have different conceptions of what constitutes the core—*the most characteristic professional act*—of their professional lives. For some radiologists it is attacking tumors with radiation; for others it is interpreting X-ray pictures. For many pathologists it is looking down the barrel of a microscope; for others it is experimental research. A dramatic example of the difference in characteristic professional acts is to be found in psychiatry, which for many of its practitioners means psychotherapy, an intricate set of interactions with a single patient. This is what a psychiatrist does. Yet many practitioners of psychiatry have as little face-to-face interaction with a patient as possible and concentrate upon physical therapies. Still others may spend a good deal of their time administering or directing the activities of other people who actually carry out various therapies.

Not all segments of professions can be said to have this kind of core— a most characteristic activity; many are not so highly identified with a single work activity. But, to the extent that segments develop divergent core activities, they also tend to develop characteristic associated and auxiliary activities, which may introduce further diversity in commitment to major areas, like practice, research, or public health.

Methodology and Techniques

One of the most profound divisions among members of a profession is in their methodology and technique. This, again, is not just a division between specialties within a profession. Specialties frequently arise around the exploitation of a new method or technique, like radiology in medicine, but as time goes by they may segmentalize further along methodological perspectives. Methodological differences can cut across specialty—and even professional—lines with specialists sharing techniques with members of other specialties which they do not share with their fellows.

Insofar as these methodological differences reflect bitter disagreements over the reality that the profession is concerned with, the divisions are deep indeed, and communication between the factions is at a minimum. In psychiatry the conflict over the biological versus the psychological basis of mental illness continues to produce men who speak almost totally different languages. In recent years the situation has been further complicated by the rise of social science's perspectives on mental illness. Focusing upon different aspects of reality, psychiatrists of these various persuasions do different kinds of research and carry out various kinds of therapy. They read a variety of journals, too; and the journals a man reads, in any branch of medicine, tend to reflect his methodological as well as his substantive interests.

Social scientists must not suppose that, since psychiatry is closer in subject matter to the social sciences, it is the only branch of medicine marred by bitter methodological disputes (we do not mean to imply that such disputes ought to be avoided). Pathologists are currently grappling with methodological issues which raged in some of the biological sciences, particularly anatomy, some years ago. The central issue has to do with the value of morphology, a more traditional approach which uses microscopic techniques to describe the structure of tissues, as against experimental approaches based upon more dynamic biochemical techniques. While the proponents of the two methodologies appear to understand each other somewhat better than do the psychiatrists, they still do not wholly appreciate each other: the morphologists are disposed to be highly defensive, and the experimentalists a little embarrassed by the continued presence of those purely morphologically inclined. Then, in the primarily clinical specialties, those combining medical and surgical techniques offer their own peculiar possibilities for dispute. Men can differ as to how highly they value and emphasize the medical or surgical approach to treatment; for example, an older urologist complained in a journal article that the younger men in the field are "knife-happy." An analogous refrain can be heard among clinicians who frown upon too great a dependence upon laboratory techniques for diagnosis and accuse many of their colleagues of being unable to carry out a complex physical examination in the grand clinical manner.

Clients

Characteristically, members of professions become involved in sets of relationships that are distinctive to their own segment. Wholly new classes of people may be involved in their work drama whom other segments do not have to take into account. We shall confine ourselves for the moment to considering relationships with clients.

We suspect that sociologists may too easily accept statements glorifying "the doctor-patient relationship" made by segments of the medical profession who have an interest in maintaining a particular relationship to patients. In actuality, the relationships between physicians and patients are highly varied. It does appear that an image of a doctor-patient relationship pervades the entire medical profession, but it is an image which, if it fits any group of physicians in its totality, comes closest to being the model for the general practitioner or his more modern counterpart, the family-practice internist. It seems to set an ideal for other physicians, who may incorporate whatever aspects of it are closest to their own working conditions into an image of the doctor-patient relationship peculiar to their own segment.

Specialties, or segments of specialties, develop images of relationships with patients which distinguish them from other medical groupings. Their own sense of mission and their specialized jobs throw them into new relationships with patients which they eventually formulate and refer to in idealized ways. Moreover, they do not simply define the relationship, but may highly elaborate a relation which this particular kind of doctor, and this kind alone, can have with patients. The pediatricians, for example, have created an image of family practitioner to whom not only the child but the parents and the whole family group surrounding the sick child are patients. According to a spokesman of the pediatricians, the peculiar involvement of parents in the illness of the child creates the conditions under which the pediatrician can evolve his relationship to the family unit. Something similar exists in psychiatry, where it is not the mentally ill patient who may be regarded as the sole or even main client but the family. It is probably in psychiatry, too, that the most highly elaborated doctor-patient relationships exist, since the psychotherapeutic practitioner uses his relationship to patients as a conscious and complex therapeutic tool. The most significant point here is that the young psychiatrist, learning the art of psychotherapy, has to unlearn approaches to the patient that he acquired in medical school.

In addition, there are the physicians who only in a special sense can be said to have patients at all. We are likely to think of pathologists, anesthesiologists, and radiologists as doctors without patients: they may have little or no contact with patients, but they do have a relationship to them. The pathologist practicing in a hospital has a well-developed set of obligations to the patient whom he may never confront, and interest groups among the pathologists are concerned with making the lay public aware of the functions of the pathologist behind the scenes. Practitioners in all three of these specialties appear to be concerned with defining their own relationship to patients.

Colleagueship

Colleagueship may be one of the most sensitive indicators of segmentation within a profession. Whom a man considers to be his colleagues is ultimately linked with his own place within his profession. There is considerable ambiguity among sociologists over the meaning of the term "colleague." Occasionally the word is used to refer to co-workers, and other times simply to indicate formal membership in an occupation—possession of the social signs. Thus, all members of the occupation are colleagues. But sociological theory is also likely to stress colleagueship as a brotherhood. Gross, for example, writes about the colleague group characterized by *esprit de corps* and a sense of "being in the same boat." This deeper colleague relationship, he says, is fostered by such things as control of entry to the occupation, development of a unique mission, shared attitudes toward clients and society, and the formation of informal and formal associations.[2]

This conception of colleagueship stresses occupational unity. Once entry to the occupation is controlled, it is assumed that all members of the occupation can be colleagues; they can rally around common symbols. However, the difficulty is that the very aspects of occupational life which Gross writes about as unifying the profession also break it into segments. What ties a man more closely to one member of his profession may alienate him from another: when his group develops a unique mission, he may no longer share a mission with others in the same profession.

Insofar as colleagueship refers to a relationship characterized by a high degree of shared interests and common symbols, it is probably rare that all members of a profession are even potentially colleagues. It is more feasible, instead, to work with a notion of circles of colleagueship. In the past, sociologists have recognized such circles of colleagueship, but from the viewpoint of the selective influence of such social circumstances as class and ethnicity. The professional identity shared by colleagues, though, contains far more than the kinds of people they desire as fellows. More fundamentally, they hold in common notions concerning the ends served

[2] Edward Gross, *Work and Society* (New York: Thomas Y. Crowell Co., 1958), pp. 223–35.

by their work and attitudes and problems centering on it. The existence of what we have called segments thus limits and directs colleagueship.

Identification with segments not only directs relationships within a profession but has a great deal to do with relations with neighboring and allied occupations. We might use the term "alliances" to distinguish this phenomenon from colleagueship within a profession. Alliances frequently dramatize the fact that one branch of a profession may have more in common with elements of a neighboring occupation than with their own fellow professionals. For example, experimentally minded pathologists consult and collaborate with biochemists and other basic scientists, while pathologists oriented toward practice make common cause with clinicians of various specialties.

Interests and Associations

To what extent, and under what conditions, can we speak of professionals as having interests in common? (Here we mean "interests" in the sense of fate, not merely that they are "interested in" different matters.) Sociologists have been overlooking a very rich area for research because they have been too readily assuming unity of interest among professionals. That interests do diverge within a profession is clear enough when the observer looks for it; not only may interests run along different lines, but they may be, and frequently are, in direct conflict.

Pathologists present a particularly striking illustration of conflict of fateful interest between segments of a specialty. The practitioner pathologists are intent upon promulgating an image of the pathologist that undermines the identity of the research-oriented pathologist. The more the practitioners succeed in promoting the notion of the pathologist as a person who performs invaluable services to the clinician, and succeeds in enlarging the area of service, the more do the pathologists who want to do research have to ward off demands from their institutions for more and more service. Fee-splitting in surgery is an example of another kind of conflict of interest: many surgeons can make a living only by engaging in fee-splitting relationships. The more successful surgeons who dominate the professional associations see the practice as tarnishing the reputation of the specialty as a whole and attempt to discredit it in codes of ethics, but they cannot, and even dare not, attempt to stamp it out.

Probably the areas in which professionals come most frequently into conflicts of interest are in gaining a proper foothold in institutions, in recruitment, and in relations with the outside. Here there are recurrent problems which segments and emerging specialties have with their fellow professionals. In order to survive and develop, a segment must be represented in the training centers. The medical-school curriculum today is crowded as the medical specialties compete for the student's time and attention, seeking to recruit or, at least, to socialize the budding professional into the correct attitudes toward themselves. (Some specialties regard themselves as having so little lien on the student's time that they use that time primarily, in some medical schools, to impress upon him that only specialists can safely do certain procedures—in short, how important and necessary is the particular specialty of the instructor.

Then, too, segments require different understandings, even different contractual relations, with clients and institutions. Many a professional association has arisen out of just such conflicts as this. In the 1920's there was a great deal of ferment between the rising specialty of pediatrics and the American Medical Association over governmental ventures into child health legislation, the pediatricians favoring the Shepherd-Towner Act. The pediatricians, recognizing a need for an organization which would represent their own interests independent of the American Medical Association, eventually formed the American Academy of Pediatrics. The big professional associations in the specialty of pathology are all dominated by, and exist for, practitioners in pathology. Therefore, when leading research-oriented pathologists recently became concerned with increasing research potential in the field, and incidentally with capturing some of the funds which the National Institutes of Health were dispensing to pathology, they formed committees especially for this purpose to function as temporary associations. Recently, a Society of Medical Psychiatry has been formed, undoubtedly in response to the growing power of psychoanalytic psychiatry and to the lessening importance, in many academic settings, of somatic psychiatrists.

Looking at professional associations from this perspective, it seems that associations must be regarded in terms of just whose fateful interests within the profession are served. Associations are not everybody's association but represent one segment or a particular alliance of segments. Sociologists may ask of medicine, for example: Who has an interest in thinking of medicine as a whole, and which segments take on the role of spokesmen to the public?

Spurious Unity and Public Relations

There remain to be considered the relations of professions to the lay public and the seeming unity presented by such arrangements as codes of ethics, licensure, and the major professional associations. These products of professional activity are not necessarily evidence of internal homogeneity and consensus but rather of the power of certain groups: established associations become battlegrounds as different emerging segments compete for control. Considered from this viewpoint, such things as codes of ethics and procedures of certification become the historical deposits of certain powerful segments.

Groups that control the associations can wield various sanctions so as to bring about compliance of the general membership with codes which they have succeeded in enacting. The association concerned with the practice of pathology, for example, has recently stipulated specific contractual relations which the pathologist should enter into with his hospital and is moving toward denying critical services of the association to noncomplying members—despite the fact that a goodly proportion of practicing pathologists neither have such contractual relations nor even consider them desirable. But more or less organized opposition to the code-writing of intrenched groups can lead to revision of codes from time to time. Changes occur as the composition of critical committees is altered. Thus, since the clinically oriented pathologists have gained power, they have succeeded in making certification examinations more and more exacting along applied lines, making it steadily more difficult for young pathologists trained for research to achieve certification. Certification procedures thus shift with the relative power of segments, putting a premium on some kinds of training and discriminating against others.

Those who control the professional associations also control the organs of public relations. They take on the role of spokesmen to the public, interpreting the position of the profession, as they see it. They also negotiate with relevant special publics. The outsider coming into contact with the profession tends to encounter the results of the inner group's efforts; he does not necessarily become aware of the inner circle or the power struggles behind the unified front. Thus, in considering the activities of professional associations the observer must continually ask such questions as: Who handles the public and what do they represent? Whose codes of ethics are these? What does the certification stand for? We should also ask, wherever a profession seems to the general public to be relatively unified, why it seems so—for this, too, is a pertinent problem.

SEGMENTS AS SOCIAL MOVEMENTS

Our mode of presentation might lead the reader to think of segments as simple differentiation along many rubrics. On the contrary, the notion of segments refers to organized identities. A position taken on one of the issues of professional identity discussed above entails taking corresponding positions along other dimensions of identity. Segments also involve shared identities, manifested through circles of colleagueship. This allows one to speak of types of pathologist or types of pediatrician—groups of people who organize their professional activity in ways which distinguish them from other members of their profession.

Segments are not fixed, perpetually defined parts of the body professional. They tend to be more or less continually undergoing change. They take form and develop, they are modified, and they disappear. Movement is forced upon them by changes in their conceptual and technical apparatus, in the institutional conditions of work, and in their relationship to other segments and occupations. Each generation engages in spelling out, again, what it is about and where it is going. In this process, boundaries become diffuse as generations overlap, and different loci of professional activity articulate somewhat different definitions of the work situation. Out of this fluidity new groupings may emerge.

If this picture of diversity and movement is a realistic description of what goes on within professions, how can it be analyzed? As a beginning, the movement of segments can fruitfully be analyzed as analogous to social movements. Heretofore, the analysis of social movements has been confined to religious, political, and reform movements, to such problems as the conditions of their origin, recruitment, leadership, the development of organizational apparatus, ideologies, and tactics. The same questions can be asked of movements occurring within professions. Professional identity may be thought of as analogous to the ideology of a political movement; in this sense, segments have ideology. We have seen that they have missions. They also tend to develop a brotherhood of colleagues, leadership, organizational forms and vehicles, and tactics for implementing their position.

At any one time the segments within a profession are likely to be in different phases of development and engaging in tactics appropriate to their position. In pathology, for example, the clinically oriented segment, which one of its antagonists termed "evangelistic" and which is still expanding, has already created strong organizations, captured many academic departments, promulgated codes of ethics, and is closing in on the battle to secure desirable status for pathologists in hospitals. The more scientifically oriented segment, on the other hand, finds itself in a somewhat defensive position, forced to reaffirm some aspects of its identity and modify others and to engage in tactics to hold its institutional supports. Possibly the acme for some expanding segments is the recognized status of specialty or subspecialty. Certainly, this is the way specialties seem to develop. But the conditions under which segments will become formal specialties is in itself a fascinating research problem. (So also is the whole question of relative development, degree of change, influence, and power —matters expressively alluded to when professionals speak of "hot" areas and dead ones.)

We have said that professions consist of a loose amalgamation of segments which are in movement. Further, professions involve a number of social movements in various kinds of relationship to each other. Although the method of analysis developed for studying political and reform movements provides a viewpoint on phenomena of professional life neglected in contemporary research, some differences must be noted between professional movements and the traditional subject matter of analysis. First of all, professional movements occur within institutional arrangements, and a large part of the activity of segments is a power struggle for the possession of them or of some kind of place within them. Second, the fates of segments are closely intertwined: they are possibly more interdependent and responsive to one another than are other kinds of movements. It is probably impossible to study one segment in movement adequately without taking into account what is happening to others. Third, the leaders are men who recognize status within the field, operate from positions of relative institutional power, and command the sources of institutionalized recruitment. Finally, it must be pointed out that not all segments display the character of a social movement. Some lack organized activities, while others are still so inchoate that they appear more as a kind of backwash of the profession than as true segments.

In any case, the existence of segments, and the emergence of new segments, takes on new significance when viewed from the perspective of social movements within a profession. Pockets of resistance and embattled minorities may turn out to be the heirs of former generations, digging in along new battle lines. They may spearhead new movements which sweep back into power. What looks like backwash, or just plain deviancy, may be the beginnings of a new segment which will acquire an institutional place and considerable prestige and power. A case in point is that of the progenitors of the clinical pathologists, who today are a threat to the institutional position of research-oriented pathologists but who were considered the failures, or poor cousins, of the specialty thirty years ago.

We have indicated what new kinds of research might originate from the conception of professions that we have presented. However, this perspective has implications for several quite traditional areas of research.

1. Work Situation and Institution as Arenas

The work situation and the institution itself are not simply places where people of various occupations and professions come together and enact standard occupational roles, either complimentary or conflicting. These locales constitute the arenas wherein such roles are forged and developed. Work situation and institution must be regarded in the light of the particular professional segments represented there: where the segments are moving and what effect these arenas have on their further development. Since professions are in movement, work situations and institutions inevitably throw people into new relationships.

2. Careers

The kinds of stages and the locales through which a man's career moves must be considered in terms of the segment to which he "belongs." Further, the investigator must be prepared to see changes not only in stages of career but in the ladder itself. The system that the career is moving through can change along the way and take on entirely new directions. The fate of individual careers is closely tied up with the fate of segments, and careers that were possible for one generation rarely are repeatable for the next generation.

3. Socialization

An investigator should not focus solely upon how conceptions and techniques are imparted in the study of socialization; he should be equally interested in the clash of opinions among the socializers, where students are among the prizes. Segments are in competition for the allegiance of students: entire schools as well as single departments can be the arena of, and weapons in, this conflict. During their professional training, students pick their way through a maze of conflicting models and make momentous commitments thereby.

4. Recruitment

The basic program of recruitment probably tends to be laid down by powerful segments of the profession. Yet different segments require different kinds of raw material to work upon, and their survival depends upon an influx of candidates who are potential successors. Thus, recruitment can be another critical battleground upon which segments choose candidates in their own image or attempt to gain sufficient control over recruitment procedures to do so. Defection by the recruited and recruiters, by the sponsored and the sponsors, is also well worth studying, being one way that new careers take form.

5. Public Images

We have seen that images beamed to the public tend to be controlled by particular segments of the profession. However, sometimes segments reject these public images as inappropriate—either to themselves, specifically, or to the profession at large. If only the former, then they may require that the public acquire specialized images for themselves. In any case, segments from time to time must engage in tactics to project their own images to the public. The situation is more complicated when the whole profession is considered as a public for particular specialties or for segments of specialties. Segments may be at pains to counteract the images which other people in the profession have of them, and attempt to create alternative images.

6. Relations with Other Professions

Different segments of the profession come into contact with different occupations and professions. They might have quite special problems with other occupations which they do not share with other members of their profession. In considering the handling of relations with other professions, it is thus necessary to ask such questions as: Who in the profession is concerned with this problem and what difference does it make to them? Who does the negotiating and in what ways?

7. *Leadership*

Most leadership is associated less with the entire profession than with restricted portions of it. Certainly, it is linked with intellectual movements, and with the fates and fortunes of certain segments. Leadership, strategies, and the fates of segments deserve full focus in our studies of professionalization.

Part D

Client Relations

CLIENT-ORGANIZATION relations are paramount to the attainment of the goals of most welfare organizations that offer direct services. In agencies that have tasks of deviance reform or of increasing social participation, interpersonal relations between the clientele and the organizational staff are the crucial means for effecting change. Therefore, an analysis of these relations provides a real lever for increasing the effectiveness of welfare organizations.

Client-organization relations in welfare organizations are characterized by several features not commonly found in client relations in other types of organizations. First, because the client usually does not buy the service, the agency personnel (unless they have internalized the client's interest) may be less intent on satisfying the client and meeting his needs. Clients do not possess the monetary means to sanction personnel. Of course, other sanctions may be available to the clients—certainly, clients in totalistic agencies such as mental hospitals and correctional institutions, and even in more segmental agencies such as casework agencies, can affect the ability of the agency and its personnel to do its job.

A second difference between client relations in welfare organizations, as compared to other kinds of agencies, lies in the status of the client. To oversimplify: clients in welfare organizations are often not full participants in the society; they frequently come to the agency as supplicants without full rights or means. Not only are they legally without full rights but, psychologically, they are not full participants; they are the downtrodden and the vanquished. On the one hand, the agency often has more legal control over clients than do many other organizations and, on the other hand, the problems of motivating clients' energies for self-help may be very great.

Finally, client-staff interactions are marked by breakdowns in communications stemming from the differences in psychological perception and differences in class and educational backgrounds.

The articles in this part deal with the general aspects of client-agency relations. However, since so much of social welfare concerns clients from lower socioeconomic groups, the selections in Part E will focus on lower-class clientele.

In the first selection, "Problems of the Person Seeking Help in our Culture," David Landy argues that it is not enough just to understand client-agency relations but we must look to *pre*-client-agency relations—we must understand how the potential client becomes an actual client. Landy shows that there is, indeed, an extremely complicated psychological and social process involved in a person becoming a client. The pre-client must decide that he needs help; he must expose himself to others as needing help; he must find out what kind of services are available through either a lay or a professional referral system; and he must make choices—often with inadequate knowledge as to what services are appropriate—and so on. The whole process can be costly both psychologically and economically. Once a client has made contact, his own expectations and those of the agency may show only slight correspondence.

The selection by John Spiegel, "Some Cultural Aspects of Transference and Countertransference," confirms some of the points discussed by Landy. Spiegel demonstrates how the expectations and values of different groups lead to different problems in psychotherapy. His article represents the application of a very general theory of cultural values to the role of cultural values in family functioning and to treatment problems. Spiegel discusses the correspondence between treatment philosophy and middle-class values. He then shows how the values held by various ethnic group members, and embedded in their social relations, lead to particular defensive problems when treatment is attempted. The article also suggests how treatment might be modified to meet these problems.

The selection by Harold Sampson, Sheldon Messinger, and Robert Towne, "Family Processes and Becoming a Mental Patient," focuses on the role of family processes in determining when women experiencing schizophrenic symptoms actually become mental patients. First, the authors show that family structure and process lead some families to shield and protect the deviance of the mother for long periods of time. Second, they demonstrate how these processes are disrupted, eventually leading to hospitalization.

In this introduction the terms "client-organization relations" and "client-staff relations" have been used interchangeably. In some organizations the dominant tone of client-agency relations may be set by client interaction with one person. But in total institutions, such as mental hospitals and correctional establishments, clients interact with many people. On the one hand, if the agency is to have a consistent program, it must coordinate a wide number of staff personnel in their relations to clients. On the other hand, clients begin to relate to the whole organization, not to any one person.

Problems of the Person
Seeking Help in Our Culture

David Landy

Recent studies of intake in social casework agencies have found that at least one third of the applicants never returned after the intake interview, and all have concluded that "the applicant's understanding and expectations of the agency were not clear." [1] Discussing this phenomenon, Helen Harris Perlman offers for consideration of practitioners this proposition:

> What an applicant will do in the intake phase of a case is heavily conditioned by his conception of what is expected of him and what he may expect, in turn, from the caseworker and agency—in short, *by his conception of his and the caseworker's roles in relation to the problem he brings.*[2]

The phase of casework that precedes the appearance of the applicant before the worker is a decision-making process taking place within the framework of conceptions and misconceptions that the seeker after help entertains. It is crucial in determining whether he will bring his appeal for assistance to a caseworker or to some other resource, or attempt to get along without anyone's help. We shall call this the "preclient" phase of the casework process.[3] That the process may be short-circuited does

[1] Helen Harris Perlman, "Intake and Some Role Considerations," *Social Casework,* XLI (1960), 171. Useful distinctions are made here between the "applicant" role and "client" role.

[2] *Ibid.,* p. 174. Italics in original.

[3] Of textbook writers only Perlman has dealt with the preclient phase in any detail. See Helen Harris Perlman, *Social Casework: a Problem Solving Process* (Chicago: University of Chicago Press, 1957). Gordon Hamilton devotes about three pages to "Attitudes toward Seeking Assistance" in *Theory and Practice of Social Case Work* (2d ed.; New York: Columbia University Press, 1951), pp. 149–53. Other texts con-

David Landy, "Problems of the Person Seeking Help in Our Culture," *Social Welfare Forum 1960,* National Conference on Social Welfare, Columbia University Press, New York, 1960, pp. 127–144.

not obviate the fact that help-seeking, strictly speaking, begins at the moment the preclient or potential applicant first becomes aware of a problem which requires the help of others.

We shall examine the decision-making process of searching for assistance in terms of a number of propositions, viewing the process of seeking help from the perspective of a participant in the intricate and multistructured culture of American society. Just as Perlman has dealt with casework as a process in problem-solving, we deal here with the preclient phase as consisting of a number of decisions which the person in trouble must make before he finally steps into the agency and assumes the role of applicant and ultimately, if he persists, the role of client. A number of assumptions are made or inferred about the culture of this society, including the one that both help-seeker and help-giver are participants in that culture, and the practices and values involved in asking for and rendering help form cultural processes. Some of these assumptions can be fairly well substantiated by studies of American culture and casework. Others are offered as inferences for further testing. Little of what is said will be new to casework practitioners; but perhaps this phrasing of the problem will offer testable hypotheses for research and insights to the practitioner.

1. The help-seeker must decide that something is wrong, that in some way some need has not been fulfilled, some obligation not met, some social or personal standard violated, with regard to himself, his family, his friends, and/or society.

Doubts have been expressed by professionals in the psychiatric field that purely intellectual motives are sufficient to undergo psychotherapy successfully; if the individual does not actually feel urgent emotional pressure, psychotherapy will become an intellectual exercise without ever facing the patient directly with the dynamics and pockets of ego-weakness that govern his personal functioning.[4]

Psychotherapy and casework are predicated upon the principle that a client will recognize, accept, and be motivated to overcome personal and interpersonal difficulties. However, major value orientations of American

---

sulted were: Florence Hollis, *Social Case Work in Practice* (New York: Family Welfare Association of America, 1939); Herbert Hewitt Stroup, *Social Work, an Introduction to the Field* (New York: American Book Co., 1953); Helen Leland Witmer, *Social Work, an Analysis of a Social Institution* (New York: Farrar and Rinehart, 1942). Scant attention to the preclient phase was found therein.

[4] For example, John Dollard and Neal E. Miller, *Personality and Psychotherapy* (New York: McGraw-Hill Book Co., 1950), p. 234; Lewis R. Wolberg, *The Technique of Psychotherapy* (New York: Grune & Stratton, 1954), pp. 232–33; Frieda Fromm-Reichmann, *Principles of Intensive Psychotherapy* (Chicago: University of Chicago Press, 1950), *passim.*

culture militate against the use of help of others in the struggle to fulfill emotional or material needs. Emphasis, beginning quite literally at birth and continuing through the socialization of the individual, is upon independence and achievement.[5] Like casework and psychiatry, the culture teaches that man's worst enemy is himself; it is he who is responsible for his fate. (Casework and psychiatry derive their own value orientation from those of the culture of which they, like their clients and patients, are the creatures, creators, and carriers.) Not only does "man make himself," but he may also correct damage done by himself; he may influence and alter his fate, make success out of failure, make material achievement out of dreams.

Other patterns of the culture to some extent counteract emphasis on individual achievement and responsibility: thousands of voluntary associations at every level of life are evidence of the need of Americans to live in concert with, as well as in isolation from, friends, neighbors and colleagues. It is a tradition of the American way that in times of disaster the community comes to the assistance of the individual and the family. But the fact that these *are* defined as special circumstances underlines their exceptional character and emphasizes the general rules of self-help and self-reliance.

The helping professional considers it his duty to communicate to the person seeking help that the professional function is not to do things *for* or *to* the distressed individual, but enable him to perform for himself. This apparently simple formula of self-determination is in fact quite complex, involving a number of assumptions which are at times contradictory to, or at variance with, each other. Bernstein has brilliantly discussed certain of these contradictions and offered possible corrections.[6] As every practitioner knows, it is not easy to communicate this idea to the client; for it is more than an idea, it is the fundamental rule of the game. Not only is it difficult for the client to grasp the full implications of the rule, much less accept it, but all its complexities are as yet not clearly understood by the practitioners who operate by it. In the context of these cultural demands, the person in need of help will have difficulty admitting to himself that he needs help, much less asking others for assistance.

2. The help-seeker must decide to face the probability that family, friends, neighbors, employer and occupational colleagues will know of his disability so that they may question his capacity as father, husband,

[5] See David Landy, "Cultural Antecedents of Mental Illness in the United States," *Social Service Review*, XXXII (1958), 350–61, and the references to American culture orientations therein.

[6] Saul Bernstein, "Self-Determination: King or Citizen in the Realm of Values?" *Social Work*, V, No. 1 (1960), 3–8.

brother, son, breadwinner, worker, producer, and the many other roles which every individual is called upon to play in a technologically and sociologically complex society.

An accepted truism that each day finds supporting evidence in clinical and social studies is that individual, family and society are causally and effectively interrelated. A disturbance in any member of a family creates reverberating effects in every other part of the family system.[7] Facing the fact of his disturbance with his family may have the effect of clearing the air somewhat of tensions generated by repressed and suppressed conflicts. But once the individual admits his disability, he broadcasts a signal of weakness as well as of strength, a cue that may set off a chain reaction of doubt, fear, suspicion, and distrust that exacerbate the problem.

Despite the cultural theme of so-called "momism" that involves the presumably dependent American male and dominating female, it is the male who must bear the brunt of social expectations in the roles of bread-winner, producer and achiever, as well as in his family and recreational roles. Fulfillment of these roles calls for independence and self-reliance, for the ability to make decisions, and for solutions of personal conflicts within the self. Taking his conflicts to other persons, except in certain clearly defined cultural contexts (same-sex social groups, work groups, clergymen, and to a decreasing extent family physicians), is not some-thing that a man commonly does. He may discuss his problems with close friends, but even here the loneliness and isolation of each individual, and preoccupation of each with cultural demands for achievement and in-dependence, may serve as barriers to mutually close and confidential problem-sharing.

Family and friends may sympathize with the individual, but sympathy may be the last thing he wants or needs. Knowledge by others of his disability almost inevitably will result in urgent questioning of his ca-pacity to continue the role performance upon which he and others depend for economic and psychological survival. If his disability causes the individual to behave in ways which seem overtly bizarre or unusual, his continuance in the family will be determined to a large extent by what Simmons and his collaborators have labeled the family's "tolerance of deviance." [8] The family's tolerating ability may vary from almost zero—in which case they attempt to rid themselves of the patient by pushing

[7] John Spiegel, "The Resolution of Role Conflict within the Family," in M. Green-blatt, D. J. Levinson, and R. H. Williams, eds., *The Patient and the Mental Hospital* (Glencoe: Free Press, 1957), pp. 545–64.

[8] Howard E. Freeman and Ozzie G. Simmons, "Mental Patients in the Community: Family Settings and Performance Levels," *American Sociological Review*, XXIII (1958), 147–54; "Wives, Mothers and the Posthospital Performance of Mental Pa-tients," *Social Forces*, XXXVII (1958), 153–59; "Social Class and Posthospital Per-formance Levels," *American Sociological Review*, XXIV (1959), 345–51.

him immediately into some form of help or institutionalization—to an almost indefinite tolerance and pathological dependence upon the deviant member's presence such that he lives at home for years in a "one-man ward." [9]

Perhaps the most debilitating effect of admitting to himself and others that his interpersonal competence [10] has been seriously impaired is upon the individual himself. He now knows, and he knows that others know, that in vital areas of life he has adjudged himself, and been adjudged to be, socially and personally inadequate; perhaps, where the suggestion of mental illness or insanity has arisen, incompetent. This is a blow so shattering that some individuals are frozen and immobilized, or so depressed that their anger and shame can be relieved only in the ritual of self-destruction or anti-social aggression. If feelings of inadequacy are strong enough, the troubled person may feel, even where he thinks of seeking help, that he is in fact beyond help. And these feelings will be reinforced by fearful, shamed, and angry relatives and friends. Lidz and his co-workers have shown strikingly how the patient's family may interfere with his progress at every stage of the way, from prehospital to posthospital period. For schizophrenics, at least, they feel that a primary aim of psychiatrists and social workers is to neutralize the family's baneful effects and block their interference with the sick member's progress. [11] The parts played by the family and others in obstructing and shunting, as well as in facilitating and encouraging, the help-seeker's journey to the help-giver are still little understood.

3. The help-seeker must decide to admit to the helper that he is in distress or has failed as a person and is not capable of handling and solving his problems unaided.

He must decide whether to take the admission of disability and social-personal disqualification to someone completely alien to him. His previous awesome decision to admit his disability to relatives and friends, having met with the sorts of reactions we have discussed, in turn may have stimulated in him, or reinforced already existing, feelings of distrust of others. If he cannot trust the people he knows, how can he trust with his innermost secrets someone he does not know?

He has no idea, if he applies to a public or private clinic or to a family agency, to whom he will be assigned. He might assume that were he requesting aid because of a physical disability, any professionally quali-

[9] David Landy and Robert S. Albert, "Waiting for Hospitalization: a Study of Persons Placed on a Hospital Waiting List and of Their Families," *A.M.A. Archives of General Psychiatry*, I (1959), 519–29.

[10] Nelson N. Foote and Leonard S. Cottrell, Jr., *Identity and Interpersonal Competence* (Chicago: University of Chicago Press, 1955).

[11] Stephen Fleck *et al.*, "II. Interaction between Hospital Staff and Families," *Psychiatry*, XX (1957), 343–50.

fied doctor would be able to handle the case. While it would be helpful if the doctor's personality were friendly and reassuring, such traits are not indispensable to successful treatment. But the person to whom he is to relate in terms of emotional turbulence must be more than professionally competent. The person must be one in whom in every way the individual can place complete trust. Ordinarily he has a narrow range of choice in determining the specific help-giver.[12]

Suppose the help-seeker is bedeviled with problems of his political as well as his personal life, and suppose he is in conflict over unpopular political views. To espouse these views is socially punishing, and even to appear to sympathize with them may mark one as a dangerous deviant. What kind of audience can he expect for his problems? He does not know whether views which to him are profoundly serious will not be disapproved by the therapist, that the therapist may not feel bound to reprove him, even to report him to authorities.[13] If the values of the prospective helper are sharply at variance with those of the client, will he be capable of suspending judgment, of acting in a "nonjudgmental" way, to use a well-worn phrase?

There will be, of course, other attributes of the prospective helper which the help-seeker may wish to know before making a decision. (That he does not have control over whom he will see in treatment does not mean that these factors do not figure prominently in the pretreatment decision-pondering which every potential client must undergo.) What will be the helper's sex, age, education, religious, ethnic, and other factors that figure in an individual's social status, and which help define and identify him for the help-seeker? [14] Can he relate to an older woman if he has problems of an unresolved oedipal conflict? Can he relate to an older man if he has problems with authority? Can he relate to a younger person when he is concerned about his own maturity and perhaps his ability to be a "good" father to his children?

[12] Recently a prominent psychiatrist publicly urged persons seeking psychiatric help to "shop around" for a therapist who meets their conception of what a psychiatrist or counselor should be like. He cited a number of qualifications for a "good" psychotherapist which, it seems to me, raises doubts about the layman's ability to make such judgments, and the willingness of practitioners in the community to help the prospective client categorize fellow therapists in terms of such qualifications. It is doubtful whether more than a small minority of wealthy help-seekers could afford such shopping around, even if it were practical and workable. See Frederick C. Redlich and Maya Pines, "How to Choose a Psychiatrist," *Harper's Magazine*, March 1960, pp. 33–41.

[13] Irving Sarnoff, "Value Conflicts and Psychoanalysis," *Mental Hygiene*, XLI (1957), 197–98. See also Henry S. Maas, "Culture and Psychopathology," *Mental Hygiene*, XLI (1957), 408–14.

[14] Fromm-Reichmann, *op. cit.*, pp. 62–63, suggests that the prospective patient seek the "right" cultural and personal attributes in his therapist. Our remarks in footnote 12 are applicable here as well.

If the helper is a person of a different religion, will he understand religious problems which may plague the troubled person? If the helper is an agnostic or atheist will he tend to underrate the importance of religious conflicts? If he is deeply religious, will he be able to handle the devastation of an antireligious attack by an atheistic client?

Suppose the client is a working man, with occupational and class values at variance with those of a middle-class therapist. What is there in the therapist's training and experience to enable him to understand the need of a man who has spent a whole day, perhaps a lifetime, at strenuous and grinding labor, to stop in at a tavern to drink away his fatigue before he returns to a substandard neighborhood and a dismal and overcrowded flat? What is there in the laboring man's background and experience to enable him to know that a prim and respectable caseworker or psychiatrist in a prim and respectable office will understand his problems?

The prospective client may come from a social milieu far superior to that of the helper. What is there—besides, of course, their common humanity—to enable an upper-class person with deep psychological conflicts to relate easily to a middle-class therapist? Conversely, what experience and background train the middle-class therapist to relate easily to the socially superior client? Will one or the other be able to overcome distrust, contempt, awe, envy, hostility, deprecation?

I have been told by executives of a large urban social agency that they have been most successful in getting middle-class clients into treatment and that it is upper- and lower-class persons in need who do not seek help there.[15] If it is true that most caseworkers are themselves of the middle class, then reasons for such a state of affairs are not obscure.

4. The help-seeker must decide to surrender enough personal sovereignty and autonomy to place himself in the necessarily dependent relationship of asking for help and relying on the ability of the helper to produce the kind of help he requires.

In a sociological analysis of the attributes of the profession of social work Greenwood contrasts professional with nonprofessional occupations.[16] The latter serves customers, he says; the former, clients. The customer can determine, in so far as he is able to make a decision free of the effects of advertising, what services or goods he wishes, "and he shops around until he finds them." There is an assumption between buyer and seller that he has the freedom to decide for himself, that he is able to

[15] Henry Freeman and Perry B. Hall, of Family and Children's Service, Pittsburgh; personal communications.
[16] Ernest Greenwood, "Attributes of a Profession," *Social Work*, II, No. 3 (1957), 45–55. See also references cited in footnote 3 for further discussion of professional aspects and problems.

know what he needs and to judge whether goods or services he purchases are likely to be satisfactory.

> In a professional relationship, however, the professional dictates what is good or evil for the client, who has no choice but to accede to professional judgment. Here the premise is that, because he lacks the requisite theoretical background, the client cannot diagnose his own needs or discriminate among the range of possibilities for meeting them. Nor is the client considered able to evaluate the caliber of the professional service he receives. In a nonprofessional occupation the customer can criticize the quality of the commodity he has purchased, and even demand a refund. The client lacks this same prerogative, having surrendered it to professional authority. This element of authority is one, although not the sole, reason why a profession frowns on advertising. If a profession were to advertise, it would, in effect, impute to the potential client the discriminating capacity to select from competing forms of service. The client's subordination to professional authority invests the professional with a monopoly of judgment. When an occupation strives toward professionalization, one of its aspirations is to acquire this monopoly.[17]

Greenwood goes on to say that the professional cannot prescribe in areas for which his competence does not fit him, as this is a violation of the authority of other professional groups, nor can he "use his position of authority to exploit the client for purposes of personal gratification. In any association of superordination-subordination, of which the professional-client relationship is a perfect specimen, the subordinate member—here, the client—can be maneuvered into a dependent role."[18] The advantage to the client is not only that he will be assured of the professional's capabilities, but also the authoritative role which the professional takes on, lends security to the client and "is a principal source of the client's faith that the relationship he is about to enter contains the potentials for meeting his needs.[19]

If the help-seeker has been influenced by the cultural prescriptions for independence and autonomy, he will have to decide, should he want to lay his problem at the feet of the caseworker, whether he will not have to surrender a portion of that which it may have taken a lifetime to construct, and which even yet may be incompletely internalized. True, he will have to assume a dependent position whenever he seeks help from a professional of any kind. But regarding many other professionals there is a kind of context of folk knowledge against which he may to some extent gauge the degree to which sovereignty must be relinquished. Members of his family and relevant groupings may not possess formal medical knowledge, for example, but they may know a good deal about it. But

---

[17] *Ibid.*, p. 48.   [18] *Ibid.*   [19] *Ibid.*

the work and techniques of the caseworker may be much more ambiguous and hazy in the minds of the public, even much of the so-called "informed" public. This lack of even folk knowledge (and by this I do not mean stereotypes or caricatures; for some of these are becoming part of our cultural heritage, although not in nearly the same volume as parodies of the psychiatrist and psychoanalyst) will tend to invest the functions of the social worker with an aura of mystery.[20]

If the help-seeker is one who is already suffering from problems of dependency, perhaps the decision in some sense will be easier to make. Yet even here, should there also be some awareness, the decision to take on another dependent role will be made with some misgiving. If the help-seeker has suffered from conflicts about authority, and perhaps has already clashed with authority, then the decision to submit to still another powerful social superior will not readily take place. In so far as lower-class persons may have frequent contacts with public authorities, often in such a manner as to cast the help-seeker in an invidious light, they will not be happy at the thought of submitting voluntarily to a relationship which may bear connotations not only of public or private authority, but of welfare or charity. Even though they may be the most frequent recipients of charitable services, there is no evidence that lower-class clients are any happier about the situation than are clients from any other social class. The upper-class member, contrariwise, may avoid contact with the social worker because he does not recognize, or is unimpressed with the power of, the caseworker as authority. Submission to an authority of subordinate status may carry little appeal. In such cases the need for help will probably have to reach desperate proportions before succor is asked of the caseworker.

5. The help-seeker must decide to direct his search among those persons and resources that lie within his "lay referral system"; the caseworker, it has been shown, may lie outside the lay referral systems of many help-seekers and therefore will not often be chosen for assistance.

In a penetrating series of papers Freidson has reported results of a study of two randomly chosen groups of users of New York City's Health Insurance Plan in which the experimental group "obtained health services organized around professional teams in a medical group and the control group obtained health services organized around individual practitioners."[21] He conceptualizes professional practice as comprising a social

[20] But there is a folklore of social work *within* the field that characterizes its own special culture. See Florence Sytz, "The Folklore of Social Work," in Cora Kasius, ed., *New Directions in Social Work* (New York: Harper and Bros., 1954), pp. 38–251.

[21] Eliot Freidson, "The Role of Social Medicine in the Family Health Maintenance Plan" (dittoed draft of Appendix to forthcoming book reporting findings of the study by George Silver, Montefiore Hospital, New York City), p. 1. See also Eliot

system which must be brought into contact with the social system of which the client is a member if effective help is to be given and received. When an individual perceives symptoms requiring outside help, he begins by diagnosing himself and perhaps prescribing simple home remedies. At some point others in his household are attracted, and diagnoses may be shared and new remedies suggested. If a practitioner is not consulted but symptoms persist, then the circle of diagnosers and prescribers widens to include friends, relatives, and others. All of this is a highly informal cultural process in help-seeking and giving, each discussion and prescription being in effect a referral. Eventually professionals, particularly physicians, are consulted.

> Indeed the whole process of seeking help involves a network of potential consultants, from the intimate and informal confines of the nuclear family through successively more select, distant and authoritative laymen, until the "professional" is reached. This network of consultants, which is part of the structure of the local lay community and which imposes form on the seeking of help, might be called the "lay referral structure." Taken together with the cultural understandings involved in the process, we may speak of it as the "lay referral system." [22]

There are obvious differences in the way such a lay referral system will work in physical as contrasted with social and personal difficulties such as come to the attention of a caseworker. But there are also similarities, and it is easy to see that to some extent the decision to seek help of a psychological nature involves some of the same elements.

The increasingly specialized practice of medicine consists of specialties to which the layman is referred by colleagues, and as such, is largely outside the control of its clients.

> Social work is a good example of such a new dependent profession, sustained by agents for the client rather than by the client himself. . . . Although she [the social worker] was doing things to and perhaps for the layman, she was also doing things to him for someone else. . . . she did not, like the general practitioner, arise from the neighborhood and its lay definitions of problems, but, like the anesthesiologist, arose from the professional community at a period in history when professional knowledge became increasingly divorced from lay "common sense,"—the professional concepts of "neurosis" and "behavior disorders" are eminent cases in point. So, almost from the beginning the social worker was asked to per-

---

Freidson and George Silver, "Social Science in an Experimental Health Program," paper read to Fourth World Congress of International Sociological Association, Stresa, Italy, September, 1959 (dittoed).

[22] Eliot Freidson, "Client Control and Medical Practice," *American Journal of Sociology,* LXV (1960), 376–77.

form services which the layman not only did not himself ask for, but the purpose of which he sometimes could not see.[23]

Participants in the experimental medical program were asked whom they would choose to interpret test results, such as X-rays. The first choice of nearly all was the doctor; the public health nurse was second, the secretary third and the social worker last. For advice about a minor cold they chose in order the doctor, nurse, secretary, and social worker. With two types of problems concerning children (getting a child to go to bed, and getting a child to eat), the same pattern appeared. In a purely interpersonal problem such as "trouble getting along with people, or difficulties in your marriage," the doctor was again chosen first, but close behind were the social worker and the nurse. For school problems, the social worker was chosen first, then the nurse, and lastly the doctor. Thus the caseworker has a clear area of competence in the eyes of the clients, while the nurse "is not perceived as to have any prime domain of her own, being most often second choice in a variety of problem areas." [24]

> In all, the nurse routinely entered the home and became distinguished as the only person who knew what things were really like there. In contrast the social worker rarely visited the home. The nurse routinely visited the schools attended by the children of the family. The social worker rarely visited the schools. The nurse was associated with the aura of healing and could authoritatively suggest remedies for minor medical problems. The social worker was sharply segregated from medical affairs. The nurse was routinely preoccupied with the everyday manifest life of the household—diet, budgeting, the common cold and recreation. The social worker was not concerned with those things unless they had a latent association with personal problems. Thus, in practice, the social worker was so thoroughly specialized in function that she was isolated from what people consider normal and everyday.[25]

This perception of the social worker as a distant specialist means that problems of everyday living ordinarily would not be referred to her. Since many behaviors that the professional caseworker might feel were neurotic or psychotic would lie, in the layman's perception, in the realm of routine life, only in very special instances would the caseworker be called upon. Social work becomes, then, what Freidson calls one of the "specialties without roots," since referrals to it are most often from other specialists

---

[23] Eliot Freidson, "Specialties without Roots: the Utilization of New Services," *Human Organization*, XVIII (1959), 112–13.

[24] *Ibid.*, p. 114.

[25] *Ibid.*, p. 115. For an analysis of psychiatric nursing functions and some striking similarities with psychiatric casework functions see Harry W. Martin and Ida Harper Simpson, *Patterns of Psychiatric Nursing* (Chapel Hill, N.C.: Institute for Research in Social Science, University of North Carolina, 1957).

and agencies. As he uses the term, "specialist" "does not only mean one with particular trained abilities—after all, any technician is that—but also one who stands in a later, more authoritative, more superordinate position in a process of consultations." [26] Unfortunately, once the potential client feels that there is something exceptionally wrong, he is liable to say, with one of the respondents of this study, "If I'm so badly off that I have to see someone special, why don't you send me to a psychiatrist rather than to a social worker?" [27]

Recent studies [28] have indicated that, while the caseworker's position is defined by himself and others as special and authoritative, he does not seem to possess the corresponding prestige so important for bringing him readily into the professional area of the lay referral system. One such study demonstrated that while the social worker is highly status-oriented and feels his status is of crucial importance, his status in the eyes of the lay public ranks lower than that of the public health nurse.[29]

Social workers have been deeply concerned with problems of professionalization during the past several years. Educational and training curricula, journals, and symposia frequently discuss and analyze such issues. Students are urged to maintain a "sense of profession," and other helping services are often told that social casework is a profession in the fullest sense of the word. Several studies have investigated professional aspects of the field. What have not been examined as often or as keenly, it seems to me, are the possible consequences that the status of profession, and in particular the kind of profession it has chosen to be, may have for social work in terms of its goals. Such models as those of the medical or psychiatric specialist could be reexamined to determine whether, in the light of recent experience and results, these are appropriate professional guides.

6. The help-seeker often must decide whether to take time off from his job for what may be a long series of interviews; and whether, in many cases, he can afford to trim his needs and those for whom his income provides sustenance in order to pay for treatment.

For some these can be crucial decisions, and may well in themselves settle the question of whether the help-seeker turns to the caseworker or some other professional for help or postpones this help while hoping that other sources may occur, or the problem will "naturally" dissipate, or he may return again to the less costly sources of the lay referral system.

[26] *Ibid.*, p. 116.
[27] *Ibid.*
[28] Salomon Rettig and Benjamin Pasamanick, "Status, Work Satisfaction, and Variables of Work Satisfaction of Psychiatric Social Workers," *Mental Hygiene*, XLIV (1960), 48–54; Alvin Zander, Arthur R. Cohen, and Ezra Stotland, *Role Relations in the Mental Health Professions* (Ann Arbor, Mich.: Research Center for Group Dynamics, Institute for Social Research, University of Michigan, 1957).
[29] Rettig and Pasamanick, *op. cit.*

An individual's attempt to take time from his job may raise doubts in the minds of employer and colleagues as to his normality or fitness to continue working. It may also increase the troubled person's own self-doubts and fears of inadequacy, since had he been able to avoid breaking into his work rhythm he might have found there an anchor of stability even though he was adrift in other life spheres.[30]

Already he may be weighed down with heavy professional expenses and feel that medical and dental care for his loved ones must come before expenditures for himself for which there may be an uncertain return. To cut into the family budget may indicate that he is making his family suffer for his own shortcomings, and such a thought will hardly reinforce his ego-strength or shore up his self-image.

Should he decide that he does not have the wherewithal to pay for treatment, nor is willing to make economic sacrifices that may affect his dependents as well as himself, then he must decide whether to ask for a lower rate of payment for treatment. Thus seeking help will mean that he is asking not only for psychological assistance but for financial favors as well. If he cannot afford to pay anything for treatment, then he will have to decide whether he is willing to signify this and accept the consequences of beseeching and receiving charity. The stigma of charity will not be easy to face if he has always relied on his own resources. The fact that free social service is not defined by the profession or the individual caseworker as charity does not mean that the help-seeker knows this, or even if he does, that he is ready to accept this definition. Asking for what he may perceive as a "handout" will hardly add to his self-evaluation.

For the upper-class individual such decisions will not be so crucial. One may question, however, whether the upper-class person seeking help ordinarily will wish to turn to the social worker when he can purchase services from the higher-status psychiatrist or psychoanalyst.

7. The help-seeker must realize, should he possess knowledge of casework or psychotherapy, that the treatment will have psychological repercussions that may eventuate in beneficial results, but may also threaten existing relationships by opening to examination life areas to which he has managed to make a precarious and tenuous adjustment—but an adjustment nonetheless. He must decide whether to take this risk.

Whatever conception the help-seeker has of casework is apt to be influenced sharply by its sources, and in particular by casework experi-

[30] J. Sanbourne Bockoven, Anna R. Pandiscio, and Harry C. Solomon, "Social Adjustment of Patients in the Community Three Years after Commitment to the Boston Psychopathic Hospital," *Mental Hygiene*, XL (1956), 353–74; Marjorie P. Linder and David Landy, "Post-Discharge Experience and Vocational Rehabilitation Needs of Psychiatric Patients," *Mental Hygiene*, XLII (1958), 29–44; Jeanette G. Friend and Ernest A. Haggard, *Work Adjustment in Relation to Family Background*, Applied Psychology Monographs No. 16 (Stanford, Calif.: Stanford University Press, 1948).

ences of family members and friends. He may be exposed to a good deal of information about psychiatry from the overflowing stream that each year floods lay as well as professional media. Either knowledge or ignorance or misconception of the facts may serve to delay his application for help. If he knows little, he will fear entering into an uncertain interpersonal relationship; if he knows a good deal, knowledge of what he must undergo may increase anxieties as much before the actual process takes place as it may serve to block the process through intellectualization once it begins. He will know that he is expected to discuss in all frankness personal and social relationships in a way that perhaps he has never done before. This possibility actually may threaten current fragile relationships and psychic adjustments to the point where he makes the decision to cling to them and protect them with the old heavy garments of repression and suppression against questioning and doubts.

Should his knowledge of casework and psychiatry be of a highly sophisticated nature, the help-seeker will know that not all psychotherapy or casework is successful and the risk of failure may be much higher than for many surgical or medical procedures. Even more, he will know that, unlike a kind of statistical probability of success that is claimed for certain surgical or medical therapies, based on previous mortality or morbidity rates, knowledge is not at all clear of the chances for success or failure of psychotherapy or casework as a whole, or for any particular brand of psychotherapy or casework.[31] The success claimed for medical procedures may be more statistical than real, while casework may hesitate to make claims of success without supporting evidence. But the folklore of the culture is such that the layman is likely to be influenced by the sense of near infallibility which typifies popular conceptions of medical practice.

He will realize that for most medical treatments he is a passive participant who offers little more of himself to the process than his physical presence, even where he has the motivation to get well. It is one thing, however, to *want* to get well, and quite another to undergo the changes of role, outlook, and in some cases, even of long-held character traits, which frequently take place in the casework or psychotherapeutic process. The person familiar with social work literature will know that the profession has as a goal changes in the ego-functioning and ego-ideals of the client. For example, a recent article in *Social Work* states:

> The client may be helped, through identification [with the caseworker], to modify his ego ideal to conform more closely to those of individuals who are successfully performing their roles in the community. The change may be facilitated by helping the client substitute ego-models with which he can easily identify. A corollary approach is to help him

[31] Wolberg, *op. cit.*, pp. 230–31, 551–54.

substitute membership and reference groups, the norms and values of which are in congruence with those of the majority of the community, for those with which he has previously identified. In this manner acceptable behavior is reinforced in the client, psychologically and sociologically, by and through his experiences of social interaction. The new standards are internalized by the client, they become part of him, and he communicates better in his interpersonal relationships because he "sees" the world more as others in the community see it.[32]

The social worker is thus construed to be the representative of the community, and to serve as ego and superego model for changes to be brought about in the client. The knowledgeable help-seeker may ask: What social groups in the community are represented by the worker? What subcultures in the larger culture are being used as criteria for values that the worker uses in the reeducative process? Doubts may arise about the ability of the social worker to serve as a model for *all* the many subcultures which comprise the whole. He may also wonder whether, should he represent to him something called "middle-class" society, the worker's values are, in fact, the values that he wants or needs. It is one thing to assume that the social worker's job is to "facilitate" or "enable" the patient to make these changes in himself. It is something else to ask whether all clients should be changed in the direction of whatever the pervasive social norms are supposed to be. Should such a change of values occur for large sections of persons of classes subordinate and superordinate to those of the social worker, the possibility is raised that attempting to apply such new-found values in the social milieu whence comes the client may make for cultural dislocations and value-conflicts. And the client may face the task of attempting in turn to change the values of his family and friends to agree with those which he has recently acquired.

We have attempted to deal with problems of the person seeking help in this culture as a decision-making process, and as the preclient phase of casework. The process of help-giving may take place either within the "lay referral system" of which the seeker after help is a member, or within the system of professional casework. Help-seeking is influenced to some extent by the structure and functions of help-giving. Both are cultural processes which are part of, and influenced by, the culture of American society. We have phrased problems of the help-seeker in terms of a set of propositions or hypotheses each of which frame decisions to be reached and conditions which may shape those decisions.

1. The help-seeker must feel that he is handicapped with regard to himself, family, friends or society.

[32] Robert K. Taylor, "Identification and Ego-directive Casework," *Social Work,* V, No. 1 (1960), 45.

2. He must face the probability that these relevant others will know of his disability and question his role and achievement capacity, thus rendering him culturally disadvantaged.

3. He must be willing to admit to the helper that he may have failed as a person and is incapable of handling and solving his problems unaided as the culture demands and expects.

4. He must be willing to surrender some autonomy and place himself in the dependent client relationship, relying on the ability of the helper to give the help he needs.

5. He must decide to ask for assistance within the lay referral system (comprising all those to whom the person may turn for help, nonprofessionals as well as professionals); the caseworker may lie outside this system.

6. He must make a number of economic decisions, each of which not only has consequences for the way he views his own capabilities, but which influence his path to the helper.

7. He must decide, should he know casework or psychotherapeutic process, whether to risk possible threat to existing relationships by opening them to deep probing, since he may feel they are necessary to his delicate though impaired adjustment.

To decrease casualty rates after intake as much as to reach the troubled person who has not heretofore utilized its services, social casework must begin to learn more of the preclient phase. Pathways to, or away from, the social agency must be explored and new routes charted. The consequences of its professional structure on the process of seeking help should be examined in order to correct misconceptions and ignorance about its functions which otherwise may obstruct the help-seeker's progress and return him to the possibly less capable sources that lie within easier reach in the social and cultural systems in which he lives. The profession of public health has found it necessary to spread knowledge of its services to the community. Perhaps what is needed is systematic public education in social casework.

Some Cultural Aspects of Transference and Countertransference

John P. Spiegel

I am going to discuss some of the cultural aspects of transference and countertransference as these phenomena appear in the course of psychotherapy. I would like to leave classical psychoanalysis out of this discussion. The reason for confining the subject matter to psychotherapy is that my information regarding cultural influences has been gathered in large part through the application of this technique. It has been derived from an investigation of the impact of cultural variations on the interpersonal relations within the family and on the psychologic adjustment of the family members. This study,[1] which I have been conducting with Florence R. Kluckhohn and a number of co-workers, assumes that families can be compared in terms of the factors which contribute to the psychologic "health" or "illness" of the family as a whole. Because we wished to give special attention to the culturable variable, our sample of families was chosen from three subcultural groups: Irish-American, Italian-American, and so-called Old American, all at the working class level. So that we could distinguish emotionally healthy from ill families, we divided this total sample into two parts. The first part, consisting of so-called "sick" families, was obtained through the Outpatient Psychiatric Clinic of the Children's Medical Center, Boston, to which these families had been referred because of an emotionally ill child. The second group, the so-called "well" or "normal" families, were selected from the wider metropolitan community. In most instances, contacts with them were arranged through public health and social agencies.

John P. Spiegel, "Some Cultural Aspects of Transference and Countertransference," in *Science of Psychoanalysis*, Vol. 2, "Individual and Family Dynamics," Jules H. Masserman, ed., Grune and Strather, New York, 1959, pp. 160–182. The investigation has been supported by a grant from the National Institute of Mental Health, and from the Pauline and Louis G. Cowan Foundation. It is sponsored by the Laboratory of Social Relations, Harvard University, and the Children's Medical Center, Boston.

Although in all cases we have maintained contact with the family as a whole, where the "sick" families were concerned contact was carried on through psychotherapy with the mother, father, and at least one child. Because of our interest in observing the social role conflicts in the family: [8] individual interviews in the clinic setting were supplemented by visits to the home. This also permitted us to observe the functioning of the family as a unit. In addition, the therapists have at times attended family celebrations, have accompanied the father to his place of work, and have conducted therapeutic interviews in this setting, as well as in trucks, bars, and other unusual places. It is apparent from this brief description that we have regarded the usual setting of psychotherapy—the office with its desk, chair, couch and other props—as merely one aspect of the cultural definition of the therapist-patient roles. We have experimented with the possibilities of other settings. Thus, the observations which form the basis of this report are drawn from a greater variety of therapeutic contacts than are usually included in the definition of therapy. The reasons for this flexibility will, I hope, become more evident after I have discussed the various cultural issues involved in it.

In recent decades, the cultural anthropologists have brought to everyone's attention the extraordinary variety in patterns of living and in basic values throughout the world. As Florence Kluckhohn has stated,[6] continuous cross-cultural research has demonstrated that although people everywhere face much the same problems and choices between alternatives, they do not find the same solutions for them. Moreover, it has been shown that the cultural value orientations guiding these solutions are not superficial, nor are they present in conscious awareness. On the contrary, although they pervade every area of thought and activity, they can usually be formulated only in the most fragmentary fashion, if at all. They thus represent an example of a phenomenon which has recently been called "behavior without awareness." [1] This phenomenon refers to the making of an unconscious discrimination between two or more choices of behavior when the act of discrimination cannot be brought to the status of a conscious report because it has never at any time existed in consciousness. Since the value orientations of a culture are outside of awareness to begin with and are learned in childhood only through their indirect impact on conscious behavior, they can be expected to have a powerful effect on the therapeutic relationship.

In spite of the difficulties, there have been several attempts on the part of contemporary philosophers and anthropologists to formulate the "philosophy," "way of life," or "unconscious assumptions" of various cultures. The formulation which we have used in our study and which I will describe in a moment has been proposed by Florence Kluckhohn [3-6] as a theory of variation in cultural value orientations. The theory is based on a classification of value orientations which can be used for the description

Table 1 *Classification of Value Orientations* [a]

	Evil	Neutral: Mixture of Good and Evil	Good
Innate Human Nature			
	Mutable-Immutable	Mutable-Immutable	Mutable-Immutable
Man's Relation to Nature and Super-nature	Subjugation to Nature	Harmony with Nature	Mastery over Nature
Time Focus	Past	Present	Future
Modality of Human Activity	Being	Being-in-Becoming	Doing
Modality of Man's Relationship to Other Men	Lineal	Collateral	Individualistic

[a] Since each of the orientations is considered to be independently variable, the arrangement in columns of sets of orientations is only the accidental result of this particular diagram. Any of the orientations may be switched to any one of the three columns.

of the similarities and differences between and within cultures. For the sake of the discussion of transference and countertransference which follows, I am going to give illustrations of the application of the theory to the similarities and differences between the American middle class family and the Irish-American working class family. However, before undertaking this, I would like to present in summary outline the classification scheme itself and the presuppositions on which it is based (Table 1), quoting directly from Florence Kluckhohn for this purpose.[4] "Three major assumptions underlie both the classification system of value orientations and the theory of variation in value orientations. First, it is assumed that *there is a limited number of common human problems for which all peoples at all times must find some solution.* This is the universal aspect of value orientations because the common human problems to be treated arise inevitably out of the human situation. But, however universal the problems, the solutions found for them are not the same. Hence the next consideration is the degree of relativity or, better, the range of variability. The second assumption, then, is that *while there is variability in solutions of all the problems, it is neither limitless nor*

random but it is definitely within a range of possible solutions. The third
assumption, which provides the key to the later analysis of variation in
value orientations, is that *all variants of all solutions are in varying degrees present in all societies at all times.* Thus, every society has, in addition to its dominant profile of value orientations, numerous *variant* or
substitute profiles. And in both the dominant and the variant profiles,
there is always a *rank ordering* or preferred sequence of value orientations rather than a single emphasis."

Table 2   *Ranges of Variability in Value Orientation Categories* [a]

Orientation	Middle-Class American	Italian-American	Irish-American
Relational	Ind. > Coll. > Lin.	Coll. > Lin. > Ind.	Lin. > Coll. > Ind.
Time	Fut. > Pres. > Past	Pres. > Past > Fut.	Pres. > Past > Fut. (but some indication of an earlier Past Pres. Fut.)
Man-Nature	Over > Subj. > With	Subj. > With > Over	Subj. = With > Over (doubt about first order here and some doubt that there is a clear-cut first order preference)
Activity	Doing > Being > Being-in-Becoming	Being > Being-in-Becoming > Doing	Being > Being-in-Becoming > Doing
Human Nature	Evil > Mixed > Good Mixed Evil and Good > Evil Good	Mixed Good and Evil predominantly	Most definitely an Evil basic nature with perfectibility desired but problematic

[a] The following abbreviations are used in the table:
   Coll.—Collateral
   Ind.—Individualistic
   Lin.—Lineal
   Over—Mastery-over-Nature
   Subj.—Subjugation-to-Nature
   With—Harmony-with-Nature

Five problems have been tentatively singled out as the crucial ones, universal to all human societies. These problems are stated here in the form of questions, and in each case there is a parenthetic designation of the name that will be used hereafter for the range of orientations relating to the question:

1. What is the character of innate human nature? (*Human-Nature Orientation*)
2. What is the relation of man to nature or supernature? (*Man-Nature Orientation*)
3. What is the temporal focus of human life? (*Time Orientation*)
4. What is the modality of human activity? (*Activity Orientation*)
5. What is the modality of man's relation to other men? (*Relational Orientation*)

I would now like to illustrate the ranges of variability and the rank ordering of solutions in these value orientation categories through a discussion of their configuration in the case of the urban Middle-class American family, and the Irish-American working class family (Table 2). In the latter case, the value orientations are those brought to this country by the first generation of immigrants from rural Southern Ireland.

HUMAN-NATURE ORIENTATION

All societies have found it necessary to orient in some way to the innately given possibilities for good or evil within human beings. Some have solved the contradictions between these two principles by assuming that man is born predominantly evil in nature but that he is perfectible by the application of effort. Others have regarded man as basically evil and unalterable. Still others have regarded man either as a hopeless mixture of good and evil, or as a mixture subject to change depending on internal and external circumstances. Akin to this position, but distinguishable from it, is the neutral point of view which is characteristic of psychotherapy and all the so-called "helping professions." Finally, there is the view of the romantic philosophers that man is born basically good but can be corrupted by external social circumstances, and the rare utopian view that man is immutably good and only seems bad to the jaundiced eye.

With regard to this value orientation, the American middle class family is in a complicated, transitional state. The view we have inherited from our Puritan ancestors is that man is basically evil, but perfectible. Effort, will power, and constant watchfulness were necessary in order to avert wickedness and temptation. Although there is now much variability here, depending on the religious affiliation of the family, there is considerable evidence of a change which puts the formerly second order mixed position into the dominant emphasis. This is in part due to the ever increasing influence of the psychologic and social sciences and to the concomitant weakening of religious convictions. It is probably fair to say that most middle-class Americans are either in transition or in conflict or both with respect to this orientation.

The Irish family very definitely views man as basically evil and almost immutable. Perfectibility is desired but is regarded as highly problematic —something that will be achieved only by a select few. This results in a rather harsh morality, and a heavy load of guilt and shame. Associated with this are specialized procedures for the relief of guilt and shame whose implications for the transference-countertransference situation will be discussed shortly. The second order Mixed position is much less harsh but is possible for the Irish only in certain social activities such as the consumption of alcohol which is usually described as "a good man's weakness."

MAN-NATURE ORIENTATION

The three-point breakdown of this orientation—Subjugation-to-Nature, Mastery-over-Nature, and Harmony-with-Nature—is rather self evident. The Subjugation-to-Nature position is characteristic of the Judeo-Christian tradition. The story of Job expresses with crystal clarity the essential helplessness and weakness of man. The position requires that man admit his weakness in order to gain any control at all over his fate. The Mastery-over-Nature position is characteristic of science, technology and an industrialized society. It assumes that, given enough time, effort, and money, nature can be tamed to man's will, and that control of his fate resides within his own skill and resources. The Harmony-with-Nature position assumes that there is no real separation or distinction between man, nature and supernature. Accordingly problems of fate and destiny are settled through recognition of and conformity with the patterned wholeness of the Universe. This was the position of classical Greece, and, in recent times, of Chinese and Japanese culture.

The American middle class family puts a first order emphasis on the Mastery-over-Nature position. Subjugation-to-Nature is in second position, the Harmony-with-Nature orientation is in the least favored, third order position, and accordingly has little influence on behavior in this country. This rank ordering is associated with the technologic organization and professionalization of activity in the American family. Since all problems are considered essentially solvable with the help of a suitable expert, there is no sympathy for a fatalistic or tragic attitude toward life. However, some problems, such as chronic illness and death, fit badly into this scheme of things. Their significance must therefore either be denied, or handled by a shift to Subjugation-to-Nature.

In the Irish-American family Subjugation-to-Nature is given dominant emphasis; Harmony-with-Nature is in the second position, and Mastery-over-Nature in the least valued third position. Resignation and a tragic view of life are deeply ingrained attitudes. Problems are not expected to be resolved, but rather, in the absence of supernatural help, to recur over and over again. The strong, but second order emphasis on Harmony-with-Nature appears in the form of a naive, implicit animistic view of life. The "wee folk," animal and vegetable life all share in the joys and sorrows of man's existence, often assuming responsibility for the joy and blame for the sorrow. This orientation sanctions a good deal of active fantasy and, in fact, blurs the distinction between fantasy and reality. How this shapes certain aspects of the transference-countertransference situation will be discussed shortly.

TIME ORIENTATION

The possible cultural interpretations of the temporal focus break logically into the range of Past, Present and Future. Much can be predicted about a particular society, particularly the expected direction of change, if one knows what the rank order emphasis is in this category. The American family places its dominant emphasis on the future, with a second order stress on the Present and the Past a poor third. No American wants to be called "old fashioned." Anything new—a new car, a new song or a new idea—is clearly better than anything old. Children and youthfulness in general are considered important because of their connection with the future while old age is a painful condition and the elderly, without much prestige accorded to their years, do their best to appear young. Planning for a long range future, inevitably conceived as bigger and better, leads the American family to live its life by clock, calendar and schedule. The present can be given importance for certain social activities, but very definitely as "time-out" from the compulsive loyalty to the future.

The Present, on the other hand, is of the first importance to the Irish-American family, with the Past second and the Future a weak third. The future is not expected to be any different from the present, and, therefore, making elaborate plans is unnecessary. It is enough to cope with the exigencies of the present. Furthermore, the second order emphasis on the past is quite strong so that any controversy with respect to change whether in the area of morality or of everyday life is apt to be settled in favor of the traditions of the past.

ACTIVITY ORIENTATION

The threefold range of variation suggested for this orientation is Being, Being-in-Becoming, and Doing. The Being orientation stresses the "is-ness" of behavior, the spontaneous inclination to act in accordance with one's moods, feelings, desires and impulses. In distinction to such wholehearted spontaneity, the Being-in-Becoming orientation emphasizes the rounded, integrated development of the personality, bringing into focus different interests at different times. The Doing variable, on the other hand, puts aside the "inner man" in favor of externally judged successful performance. Thus, in this orientation, inner impulses have to be suppressed if they get in the way of the striving for competence and achievement on the road to success.

It is probably obvious to everyone that the American family puts primary emphasis on the Doing orientation. Parents value each other and their children in accordance with their competence and success in performance. This preference is well suited to the importance of hard work in an industrialized society. The first question an American asks of any stranger is, "What has he done?" or "What does he do?" Husbands and wives busily rate each other's performance as parents, and compare themselves and their children with the Smiths next door and the Joneses across the street. Thus competition becomes the pivot of interpersonal relations. On occasion, however, the extraordinary inhibition of inner impulse demanded by this orientation leads to revolt. Then the second order emphasis on Being is invoked, and impulsive activity is allowed free reign, particularly if aided by alcohol or drugs. The Being-in-Becoming orientation is so weak that activity of this nature is likely to be described as frivolous, dilletant-ish or a waste of valuable time.

In the Irish-American family, Being comes first in importance, with Being-in-Becoming in second position and Doing in third. Thus the Irish family values the free expression of inner states. Fighting, loving, fun-making, bickering and the elaborate expression of sentiment are considered more interesting than work for the sake of work. The Being-in-Becoming second order variable is manifested in an appreciative attitude toward art, drama and poetry and toward the need to express the many facets of life. Thus relations between husbands and wives, parents and children are characterized by rapid transitions of mood. Extreme candor gives way suddenly to disguise and deceit. Humor replaces sadness and leads unexpectedly to anger. Finally, such kaleidoscopic shifts are experiences not only in their own right, but also for the sake of the wonderful tale that can be woven out of them in the presence of an appreciative audience.

RELATIONAL ORIENTATION

The last of the common human problems to be discussed concerns the relation between the individual and the group. The three subdivisions of this orientation are the Lineal, the Collateral and the Individualistic. As might be expected, the Individualistic emphasizes the importance of the individual ahead of any group considerations. The Lineal stresses the significance of the vertically structured group hierarchy while the Collateral values the horizontal, "one for all and all for one" aspect of group loyalty.

In American families the Individualistic orientation is in first position, the Collateral second, while the Lineal is the least favored. Thus, there is a certain amount of resentment felt toward any hierarchy and toward anyone who acts too "bossy." Husbands share authority, as well as other domestic roles, with their wives. Parents hope that their children will voluntarily manifest correct behavior so that the issue of discipline and authoritarian controls can be avoided. Every attempt is made to foster the autonomy of the individual family member and to allow children to make their own decisions. Thus independence and self reliance form an important part of the egalitarian ethos. However, if group loyalty is to be invoked (as in organized games and sports) or when the family is to be represented in the community, then it is the collateral, groupwide emphasis that comes to the fore.

In the Irish-American family the lineal principle holds first rank; collaterality is second and individualism in the third order position. The group, whether the family, a bureaucratic political organization, or the church, always comes ahead of the individual. The ordered succession to hierarchical positions over time is constantly emphasized. For example, the father is very much the head of the family and never hesitates to express his authority over the wife and children. But if his own father is still alive, he owes him the same kind of respect and obedience which he showed as a child. In contrast to the American family, the Irish family trains its children for dependent behavior which is expected to remain a constant throughout life. This tends to backfire in a certain amount of hostility to authority, of which the political rebel in Irish history is a good example. Nevertheless, dependency training is on the whole thoroughly accepted, and is well reinforced through the mutual care and aid offered by the extended family, religious and community networks.

I would like to close this brief comparison of the value orientations in the two family systems with a note of warning concerning the stereotyping it would seem to imply. All ethnic labelling is an oversimplification, and falsifies the degree of variation and nonconformity in any social group. Some of the first generation Irish families in this country have been closer to American values from the beginning while many middle-class American families have held values similar to the Irish. Still, for our purposes, such modifications would represent variations from the modal positions which I have described.

Let us now turn our attention to some of the considerations governing the appearance of transference and countertransference behavior within

the psychotherapy situation.* It is ordinarily held that the word transference denotes behavior which is clearly an inappropriate response to
the behavior of the therapist and which functions as a resistance to
therapy. It is understood to derive from some aspect of the childhood
relation with a parent or some other significant person. It is assumed that
the memory of this earlier relationship has been repressed, but that the
patient hopes to recapture with the therapist some of the actual or hoped
for satisfactions of the original relationship. It is one of the aims of treatment to recover the repressed memory, wish, or fantasy and thus to
dissipate the transference behavior.

There is little to be added to these considerations where the therapist's
countertransference is concerned. It is held that countertransference
describes an attitude in the therapist—whether or not it is actually manifested in action—which is inappropriate and unrealistically related to the
current behavior of the patient. It is therefore presumed to have its origin
in an incompletely resolved childhood relation or wish. The principle
difference is that the therapist alone has responsibility for identifying his
countertransference responses and for exploring their significance.

An objection may be raised at this point that these considerations have
been developed in the context of the standard psychoanalytic technique
and that they can not be applied without modification to the therapist-
patient relation in psychotherapy. The objection derives from the fact
that the heightened activity of the therapist and the relative paucity of
his information make it much more difficult to keep track of what aspects
of the mutual transaction either partner may be responding to. I would
agree with this objection. However, the fact remains that transference
and countertransference responses do occur in psychotherapy and must
be dealt with in some way. I believe that the point of view which I am
about to propose may represent an auxiliary tool for identifying and
controlling such responses.

Let me first ask in what way are we to understand the meaning of
the word "reality" as used in psychotherapy? Reality is a slippery concept,
and the implicit assumptions buried in it are usually left unexamined.
The best way of getting at whatever reality may mean in the context of
psychotherapy is through an examination of the most general and standardized expectations established by professional practice for the behavior
of the therapist and of the patient.

Looking first at the patient, I think it is fair to say that the person is

---

* I am here ignoring the confusions and controversies over the exact meanings of the
words transference and countertransference which have troubled the literature on
these subjects. Excellent historical reviews of the semantic and conceptual problems
involved have been published by Orr [7] and by Zetzel.[10] The topic is further complicated by the almost complete absence of any discussion of the countertransference in
the literature of psychotherapy, as distinct from psychoanalysis.

expected to tell as much about himself as he is able. He is expected to work toward a recovery from his difficulties in a responsible way without depending on outside help from his family or friends. It is hoped that he will not withhold important information or refuse to discuss certain topics because of loyalty to external persons, beliefs or institutions. It is expected that he will want, for the sake of his own emotional health and maturity, to become as autonomous and as independent in the making of choices and decisions as is possible, considering his life circumstances. In connection with this personal aim, it is expected that he will wish to have a future different from his past and present, and that he will wish to take individual responsibility for seeing that it is different. It is assumed that he will perceive the therapist as a professional person who has no ax to grind and nothing to contribute to him but his technical ability. It is assumed that he either begins with or soon develops confidence in the benefits to be expected from communication, from insight into himself, and from the use of words rather than physical action in expressing himself. Finally, it is hoped that he will be able to limit his expressive emotional behavior, both within and without the treatment situation, so that he neither escapes from his thoughts and memories through too much overt action, nor from his feelings through too much inhibition of action.

These are the goals set up professionally for the patient. Because of the operations of "resistance," it is not expected that the patient will actually be able to adhere consistently to these standards. On the contrary, it is believed that a large amount of treatment time will be spent in discovering why he is unable to behave in accordance with such goals. Nevertheless, it is hoped that by the time the treatment has ended, he will have *achieved* many, if not all, of them. For these are the standards, in this country, of what is called "mental health." It should also be clear by now that they represent, in vivid detail, the value orientations of the American middle class family.

Now let us look at the expectations for the psychotherapist. It is expected that, like any expert or professional person, he will confine his activity with the patient to serious, responsible work on the patient's problems. In connection with the "work-oriented" relation he has with the patient, he is expected to exclude the ordinary social, recreational and personal aspects of human relations. Though he is permitted a modicum of so-called "educative" activity, he is expected to refrain from influencing the patient in accordance with his own personal, as opposed to professional, goals, standards or values. Indeed, he is expected to display a "benevolent neutrality" in this area, neither approving nor disapproving anything the patient says or does. In the place of a value attitude, he is to substitute "reality testing," helping the patient to discover the actual consequences in "external reality" and in the "reality" of the treatment situation, of anything the patient does, feels or thinks.

This neutral attitude with respect both to the good and the evil in the patient's behavior is maintained for the sake of helping the patient obtain maximum autonomy and independence in the formulation of his own goals and standards. He is expected to believe firmly in the patient's capacity to master his problems, neither overestimating, nor underestimating the degree to which actual change is possible. Concerning the probability of change, the therapist is expected to keep a weather eye on the future, but to concentrate mostly on the past and the present. There is some difference of opinion and even controversy as to whether the past or the present is to be given greater consideration, but most therapists would emphasize a balanced perspective between the two.

Such controversy, however, is indicative of a wider area of tension and indecision in the definition of the therapist's role. This has to do with the degree to which he should be free to change or modify the techniques he uses. On the one hand, he is expected to express his individuality in the moment to moment exercise of his technique. But on the other, he is expected to preserve the theories, concepts and techniques inherited from the past. Accordingly, he inevitably experiences some conflict between the conservative and the experimental aspects of his role. Furthermore, the tension between these two contradictory goals is heightened by the structure of the organizations with which he is affiliated. These organizations, such as hospitals, clinics and professional associations tend to be more hierarchically structured and more conservative of the past than is altogether congruous with the goals of scientific and technical activity.

If one scrutinizes this description of the standards for the "reality" structure of the therapist's behavior, it becomes evident that they, too, are guided by the American Middle Class value orientations. Slight variations appear in the *Nature-of-Man*, the *Relational* and the *Time Orientations*. The first emphasizes the intensely neutral attitude toward good and evil more than is characteristic of the American middle class family at the present time. The *relational* orientation gives a stronger stress to the Lineal structure than one finds in middle class values, and is probably representative of a value conflict in this orientation. Similarly, the therapist is expected to carry on his technique in an independent and individualistic way, but not to violate the canons of theory and practice imposed by the hierarchically structured organizations to which he belongs. In the same vein, the *time* orientation stresses the tradition and importance of the past somewhat more than is called for in American middle class values.

In spite of these mild incongruities between the values governing the definition of "reality" for the patient and for the therapist, the fit is on the whole a fairly good one. The roles are matched to each other on the basis of their conformity with the dominant American middle class values.

On this basis, it can then be stated that transference and countertransference phenomena will be identified, insofar as they have cultural determinants, on the basis of their departure from these value orientations. This means that resistance, from the cultural point of view, is resistance against dominant American values. One might say, without being altogether facetious, that to resist is to be un-American!

Although this statement of the cultural determinants of transference and countertransference resistance may sound overgeneralized, it is certainly not unexpected, nor does it require any apology or defense. Psychotherapy is a scientific and technical procedure and it is only natural that it should be based on the same set of values which govern the socio-economic class most representative of the scientific and technical outlook of the society as a whole. It may even turn out to be the case that the slight incongruity in the values governing the two roles is necessary to the maintenance of an optimum tension between the patient and therapist.

Good as the matching of the roles may be at this professional level, there is abundant evidence that the goodness of fit is subject to several weaknesses which I would now like to examine. Theoretically, it could be expected to remain stable if both the patient and the therapist come from American middle class families. In such cases there should be nearly perfect agreement about the "reality" toward which both parties are to strive. However, psychotherapists come from all classes and ethnic groups in this country, and, with the increasing development of mental health education and facilities, so do patients. So, one must ask, what happens when the value orientations of the family of origin of both the patient and therapist are discrepant with each other, and with dominant American values?

There is a presumption that the therapist is spared from difficulties in this matter in two ways: through a personal psychoanalysis, and through identification with the professional values and goals which I have just described. A personal analysis is designed to free the therapist from excessive bondage to his archaic super-ego and for this reason he is supposed to be able to remain relatively flexible in the presence of values different from those in which he was trained as a child. Correlated with this lack of anxiety toward new or different values, is the internalization of the "benevolent neutrality" and the other standards of the image of the perfect therapist.

Although there is no doubt, to my mind, about the validity of both these assumptions, there is much question about the extent to which the therapist can actually be freed of his original values. The experiences my colleagues and I have had, working with patients whose cultural backgrounds differed greatly from our own, is that the value discrepancy sets up a very complicated strain within the therapist. The conflict between the original values of the patient and the original values of the therapist stimulates a strain between the therapist's archaic super-ego and his new, professional identifications. A three-way conflict is precipitated in him which becomes fertile soil for the growth of countertransference difficulties. But before examining the details of such value conflicts and their consequences, let us turn to the patient and look at the difficulties he may experience on contact with the therapist.

For purposes of illustration, let us take a father in one of our Irish-American families, possessing the value orientations I have already described. How will he perceive the "reality" of the behavior which the therapist expects of him? He is expected to tell everything he knows about himself. But his training is that one does not tell intimate details about oneself even to family or friends, much less a total stranger. If the details are shameful or guilt-ridden, one doesn't even admit such things to oneself. They are too suffused with evil, and there are only two ways to handle such things. Either deny their existence, or confess them to a properly constituted authority, such as a priest. But isn't the therapist such a properly constituted authority, somewhat different from a priest, perhaps, but a person entitled to hear such things? Certainly not. By virtue of what organization and what authorization would he possess such a right? I must confess that when we hear this question, which is usually implicit rather than directly stated, we are tempted to answer, "On the authority of Freud, the American Psychiatric Association and the Children's Hospital!" However, even this answer would not help since these authorities and organizations are already perceived as either unknown or possibly sinful. To the lineal values of the Irish-American, any hierarchy is better than no hierarchy at all, but one that is unknown or remote is likely to be regarded as hostile until it has proved itself otherwise.

But, one might well ask, how about the "benevolent neutrality?" Won't this neutral attitude help to counteract the fear of sinfulness, and its associated hostility to the sinner? Unfortunately, the answer is again no. In the perceptions of the Irish-American patient, such an attitude is hypocritical. It smacks of the benevolence of the upper classes toward the "deserving poor." It signifies merely that one's real feelings remain undeclared behind a concealing mask of condescension. Hiding one's real feelings is a familiar affair, and, according to his experience, is inevitably followed by brutal frankness when it is least expected. So this "neutrality" is merely a matter of waiting for the ax to fall.

Still, looking at the problem all this presents to the therapist, one might ask whether it is really so different from run-of-the-mill difficulties which always crop up at the beginning of therapy. Won't the suffering experienced by the patient encourage him to continue with therapy despite these hurdles? There are two answers to this question. In the first place, if the patient is the father of a disturbed child, he may very well not experience much suffering in his own personality. The only emotional disturbance he may be aware of is that caused him by his child's illness. But, secondly, even if he is aware of inner disturbance, this will probably not in itself be sufficient to make him want to work hard on the overcoming of obstacles. Hard work in an independent, self-responsible way for the sake of long distance goals has not been a part of his value training. In this area, the Present Time, Being, Lineal value structure are all firmly opposed to psychotherapy as understood by the therapist. Such a patient is not used to working on his own problems for the sake of vague future gains. He is accustomed to being told what to do, right now, in the present. Therefore he repeatedly asks the therapist what he is supposed to be doing, and, if he is not told, he is paralyzed. He feels that nothing is happening and he is wasting his time. And, even if the therapist, sensing this hopelessness, tries repeatedly to instruct him on how to conduct himself in the interview, this will prove to be of little help. For the Subjugated-to-Nature and Present Time Orientation lead the patient to see little possibility of change or improvement in the future. What will be, will be, and evil must be punished. In fact, the only hope of the future, as he sees it, is to cling grimly to the sense of evil, wistful for forgiveness, but never abandoning the sense of the power of evil, since this is his only guide to realistic conduct.

Exposed to these responses, which constitute the "reality" of the patient, how will the therapist conduct himself? For a while he may identify the patient's response as "resistance" and keep on trying to use his usual techniques. However, after a variable length of time, he will feel intensely frustrated. This frustration will stimulate the three-way conflict which I have already mentioned. On the one hand, his therapeutic values will order him to stick to his technique. The strong Mastery-over-Nature position will make him feel guilty if he wants to stop the treatment before the patient appears ready to quit. For the American therapist, unlike the European,* feels that no patient or situation should be identified as "untreatable," at least until all possibilities have been exhausted. But, if he continues under the guidance of these values, he will reach a stalemate, not being able to make progress or to terminate treatment. Meanwhile, the original values attached to his archaic super-ego tend more and more to assert themselves into the gap created by the stalemate. As this happens, a conflict develops between his original values and his newer therapeutic values. In addition, a conflict develops between his original values and the values on which the patient is acting. Since there already exists a conflict between his therapeutic values and the values

---

* See, for example, the contrast between the contribution of an American analyst, Leo Stone,[9] and a British analyst, Anna Freud,[2] to the topic "The Widening Scope of Indications for Psychoanalysis." The difference between the two analysts in value orientations as related to therapeutic indications is striking.

which are guiding the patient, his ego is caught in a three cornered struggle which in most cases proves too much for its integrative capacity. When this point has been reached, the archaic super-ego wins the struggle, though usually concealing its activity behind the facade of the therapeutic super-ego.

For example, suppose the therapist treating an Irish-American comes from an American-Jewish background. The values of this culture, insofar as they can be discerned at present, are characterized by the first order position of Evil, Subjugated-to-Nature, Future Time, Doing, and Collaterality. Thus his Doing and Future Time orientations clash violently, with the Being, Present Time behavior of the patient. The Evil and Subjugated-to-Nature orientations of patient and therapist coincide. Therefore he comes to feel more and more hostile to the patient for not making a sufficient effort, and comes to characterize this default as evil, just as he would originally have characterized such a trend within himself. As the patient comes to stand increasingly for a rejected and bad part of the therapist, his ego tends to give in by finding a way to characterize the patient as deserving of rejection. However, the therapeutic part of his super-ego will still be strong enough to insist that such a rejection be justified on technical grounds, or at least clothed in professional jargon. The final resolution of his inner conflict is obtained through a termination of treatment on the grounds that the patient is too immature, too narcissistic, too dependent, too well defended, or any of a multitude of expressions which indicate that he has found the patient burdensome.

Is this description too cynical, or too cavalier in respect to the psychodynamic issues? The question is valid, because there is always a danger of explaining too much through the use of a cultural analysis. Certainly, much more is involved in the development of the transference-countertransference impasse than the value content of the super-egos of the patient and therapist. I do not wish to ignore the complex questions of ego psychology with which the conflict in cultural values is also associated. Unfortunately, it would take more time and space than is available to go into these questions. If I have somewhat overstressed the cultural analysis at the expense of other psychodynamic issues, it is because it is usually totally neglected. I would, however, like to take up one psychodynamic issue in order to lead into the concluding section of this paper.

While it is perfectly true that one aspect of the Irish-American patient's resistance is associated with the Subjugated-to-Nature value position, this is, as I have just stated, by no means the whole story. The value orientation accounts for the patient's resignation, his inability to conceive of the possibility of change, in the cognitive area. A real change within the personality has not been in his experience and he just does not see that it is possible. However, there is an emotional as well as a cognitive side to this kind of resistance. On the emotional side it is associated with the identification with the angry, critical parents. The attachment to the internalized parental images is intensely ambivalent, and masochistically satisfying. The treasuring of the sense of sin is, from one point of view, a conscious derivative of the highly libidinal, unconscious cathexis of the internalized, scolding parents. In addition, the scolding parent within becomes a tender forgiving parent whenever a confession takes place. The alternation between sinning and confessing is necessary to the maintenance of the internal, libidinal dynamics. Furthermore, sinning or the alerting of the sense of sin in the external object, is the primary way of getting the object's attention.

These considerations are directly pertinent to the transference problem in the management of such a patient. It is not only that the patient remains cognitively unaware of the possibility of change. In addition he has no wish to change in the direction which the therapist expects him to. Giving up the crushing sense of sin means, essentially, renouncing the relation with the internalized parents. This might be possible if the therapist could capture the attention of the patient. It is an accepted fact that psychotherapy cannot take place without the establishment of at least a minimum positive transference. But the value neutrality of the therapist operates precisely at this point to prevent the establishment of a positive transference. The patient feels he cannot get the therapist's attention. Furthermore, he has no other reason to care about the therapist since the latter is not associated with any of his prestige systems or organizations. As a result he withdraws, and the therapist then realizes that *he* cannot get the *patient's* attention. This is the beginning of the therapeutic impasse.

I would like to conclude this paper with a consideration of some suggestions for the handling of this impasse. There are several possibilities. One could resign oneself to the acceptance of defeat. The conclusion then offers itself that not everyone can profit from psychotherapy, and that it is important not to let therapeutic ambition overrule good diagnostic judgment. This view involves a shift from the Mastery-over-Nature position which is difficult for most Americans to effect. Another possibility is to persist, doggedly, neither modifying the technique of psychotherapy, nor abandoning the attempt to help. Some Irish-American families have made a sufficient transition to dominant American values so that they may be able to respond to the standard techniques. However, the payoff in success is low and thus the price of sticking to the Mastery-over-Nature position in this fashion is very high. It can be done only by extremely patient therapists who have a high tolerance for frustration.

A third alternative preserves the Mastery-over-Nature position, but abandons the Past Time orientation insofar as this inhibits change and experimentation. This is the approach we adopted in our work with Irish-American patients. We have experimented with various methods for overcoming the resistance and for establishing a positive transference so that we could be in a position to exert some psychotherapeutic influence. The steps we took, however, were not set up on the basis of trial and error, but arose out of our theoretic point of view. We had already become convinced of the close connection between the pathology of the individual and the interpersonal and cultural value relations within the family. But the modifications which we adopted were made primarily for the sake of carrying on research. Only gradually and secondarily did we perceive their relevance for the handling of transference and countertransference problems.

Our approach emphasizes the importance of the extended family and the community to the functioning of the individual. Although therapy concentrates mainly on the mother, father and child, we attempt to see and make ourselves known to a wide assortment of relatives. This means that we become assimilated, to a certain extent, to the lineal chains of influence which bear upon the pathologic deviations in the family members. In addition, members of the therapeutic team become known, not simply as individuals, but also as members of a readily identifiable organization. This approximation of individuals and organizations reduces the fear of the strange, unknown group and, simultaneously, raises its prestige. At the same time, we have shown our willingness to depart from the routine of regular office appointments whenever this is necessary. Seeing family members when and where they are available is closer to the Present Time and Being orientations. Therefore it is more apt to be perceived as a valid act of attention than strict adherence to a Future oriented appointment book, and other bureaucratic routines.

In further validation of the Irish-American value orientations, we have relaxed to a considerable extent the principle of non-reciprocity. We answer personal questions about ourselves and do not hesitate to reveal our own value attitudes upon a variety of issues. Although our therapeutic standards have made us somewhat uneasy about such conduct, we have gradually become more comfortable with it. Especially has it become easier as we have come to understand how the Irish-American patient perceives non-reciprocity. Failing to answer a question, directing it back to the patient, or interpreting it are perceived as evasive maneuvers. Withholding a personal attitude is seen as having something to be ashamed of. Concealment, evasion and denial are so ubiquitous in Irish-American culture that they are easily projected to the therapist. Such projections can be handled by interpretation only after the relationship has been established.

Finally, we have come to reinterpret the meaning of "benevolent neutrality." As ordinarily understood, this principle involves the adoption of a strictly neutral attitude with respect to the matters about which the patient feels guilty or ashamed. We have found that if the impulses of which the patient is ashamed would also make us feel ashamed if discovered within ourselves, it is best to be quite frank about it. And vice versa. That is to say that, if his impulses would leave us truly neutral and unmoved, we have to be frank about that, too. Since the sense of sin is a primary vector of interpersonal feeling, it cannot be hidden from those who are highly sensitive to its manifestations. Thus the reinterpretation of "benevolent neutrality" involves the recognition and admission that we all think of ourselves as sinners in some way. On this basis, denial is more easily renounced and the evil impulse more easily held in consciousness because the therapist is seen as someone who recognizes the patient's problem and has established his right to deal with it. This point of view also makes it easier to deal with the characteristic denial through the use of humor. Since the therapist is not denying anything through the assumption of "neutrality," he can appreciate the humor and still insist on the expression of the feelings it is meant to conceal.

These are the major modifications which we have used in our research. The results of using them are not spectacular. They have not led to dramatic relief of symptoms. This is not the place to review the results of our work, nor are we ready to report final conclusions. But we have gained the conviction that we have been able to establish and maintain therapeutic contact with patients who would otherwise have been rejected or would have dropped out of treatment. We have been able to produce small increases in insight in individual family members. We have been impressed with the fact that a small gain in one or two family members is registered as a large gain in the total functioning of the family.

I hope it is clear that the modifications in approach which I have described are not to be considered general prescriptions for the field of psychotherapy as a whole. On the contrary, the value of a cultural analysis of the psychotherapeutic situation is that it clarifies the relation between variations in technique and the specific transference (and countertransference) responses which can be expected from members of different cultural groups. The general principle that emerges from this point of view is that modifications in technique should be rationally adapted to the varieties of cultural value orientations which exist among patients. A corollary of this proposition is the need, in the future, to give as much consideration to problems of cultural dynamics as has been given, in the past, to purely psychologic processes. It is my firm belief that such a program is necessary if we have to extend the range of effectiveness of psychotherapy to groups who have, up till now, proved refractory in the face of our best efforts.

REFERENCES

1. Adams, J. K., "Laboratory Studies of Behavior without Awareness," *Psychological Bulletin*, **54**, 383–405 (1957).
2. Freud, Anna, "The Widening Scope of Indications for Psychoanalysis: Discussion," *J. Am. Psychoanalyt. A.*, **2**, 607–620 (1954).
3. Kluckhohn, Florence R., "Dominant and Substitute Profiles of Cultural Orientations: Their Significance for the Analysis of Social Stratification," *Social Forces*, **28**, 276–293 (1950).
4. Kluckhohn, Florence R., "Dominant and Variant Value Orientations," in *Personality in Nature, Society, and Culture*, Clyde Kluckhohn and Henry A. Murray, Eds., New York, Alfred A. Knopf, 1953.
5. Kluckhohn, Florence R., "Variations in the Basic Values of Family Systems," *Social Casework*, **39**, 63–72, 1958.
6. Kluckhohn, Florence R.; Strodbeck, Fred L., et al., *Variations in Value Orientations*, Row Peterson & Co., Evanston, Ill., 1961.
7. Orr, Douglass W., "Transference and Countertransference: A Historical Survey," *J. Am. Psychoanalyt. A.*, **2**, 567–594 (1954).
8. Spiegel, John P., "The Resolution of Role Conflict within the Family," *Psychiatry*, **20**, 1–6 (1957).
9. Stone, Leo, "The Widening Scope of Indications for Psychoanalysis," *J. Am. Psychoanalyt. A.*, **2**, 567–594 (1954).
10. Zetzel, Elizabeth R., "Current Concepts of Transference," *Internat. J. Psychoanalyt.*, **37**, 369–376 (1956).

Family Processes and Becoming a Mental Patient

Harold Sampson, Sheldon L. Messinger, and Robert D. Towne

Becoming a mental patient is not a simple and direct outcome of "mental illness"; nor is hospitalization in a mental institution, when and if it comes, the automatic result of a professional opinion. Persons who are, by clinical standards, grossly disturbed, severely impaired in their func-

Harold Sampson, Sheldon L. Messinger, and Robert D. Towne, "Family Processes and Becoming a Mental Patient," American Journal of Sociology, LXVIII, 1962, pp. 88–96. This report is based on a study carried out by the California Department of Mental Hygiene and partially supported by Grant No. 3M-9124 from the National Institute of Mental Health. Thanks are due to David Ross, Florine Livson, Mary-Dee Bowers, Lester Cohen, and Kate S. Dorst for their substantial contributions to the research for this study.

tioning, and even overtly psychotic may remain in the community for long periods without being "recognized" as "mentally ill" and without benefit of psychiatric or other professional attention. It is clear that becoming a mental patient is a socially structured event.[1] The research reported here is directed to increasing our understanding of the nature and significance of this structuring as it mediates the relations between individuals and the more formal means of social control. The research explores (a) the relationship between patterns of family means for coping with the deviant behavior of a member who later becomes a mental patient and (b) efforts of the future patient or members of his family to secure professional help.

The broad nature of this latter relationship may be inferred from a number of published findings. Yarrow and her colleagues have documented the monumental capacity of family members, before hospitalization, to overlook, minimize, and explain away evidence of profound disturbance in an intimate.[2] The post-hospital studies of the Simmons group have suggested that high "tolerance for deviance" in certain types of families is a critical determinant of the likelihood of poorly functioning and sometimes frankly psychotic former patients avoiding rehospitalization.[3] Myers and Roberts found that few mental patients or their families sought or used professional assistance before hospitalization until the problems they encountered became unmanageable.[4] Whitmer and Con-

---

[1] Erving Goffman, in "The Moral Career of the Mental Patient," *Psychiatry*, XXII (May, 1959), 123–42, discusses a variety of "career contingencies" that may intervene between deviant behavior and hospitalization for mental illness. Also see the articles in *Journal of Social Issues*, XI (1955), ed. John A. Clausen and Marian Radke Yarrow, under the general title of "The Impact of Mental Illness on the Family." August B. Hollingshead and Fredrick C. Redlich (*Social Class and Mental Illness: A Community Study* [New York: John Wiley & Sons, Inc., 1958], chap. vi, "Paths to the Psychiatrist") also emphasize this point.

[2] Marian Radke Yarrow, Charlotte Green Schwartz, Harriet S. Murphy, and Leila Calhoun Deasy, "The Psychological Meaning of Mental Illness in the Family," *Journal of Social Issues*, XI (1955), 12–24. Also see Charlotte Green Schwartz, "Perspectives on Deviance—Wives' Definitions of Their Husbands' Mental Illness," *Psychiatry*, XX (August, 1957), 275–91; Hollingshead and Redlich, *op. cit.*, esp. pp. 172–79; and Elaine Cumming and John Cumming, *Closed Ranks* (Cambridge, Mass.: Harvard University Press, 1957), esp. pp. 91–108.

[3] See Ozzie G. Simmons, *After Hospitalization: The Mental Patient and His Family* (Hogg Foundation for Mental Health, n.d.) and the several studies by the Simmons group cited there.

[4] Jerome K. Myers and Bertram H. Roberts, *Family and Class Dynamics* (New York: John Wiley & Sons, Inc., 1959), pp. 213–20. These findings also suggest that lower-class families are better able to contain an extremely disturbed person for long periods of time than are middle-class families; the latter call on outside help more rapidly when "major psychotic decompensation" occurs. This would follow from the argument presented by Talcott Parsons and Renée Fox in "Illness, Therapy, and the Modern Urban American Family," *Journal of Social Issues*, VIII (1953), 31–44.

over reported that the occasion for hospitalization was ordinarily not recognition of "mental illness" by the patient or his family but inability to cope with disturbed behavior within the family.[5]

These observations and our own permit two inferences. First, both before and after hospitalization some type of accommodative pattern ordinarily evolves between a disturbed person and his family which permits or forces him to remain in the community in spite of severe difficulties. Second, it is the disruption of this pattern which eventually brings a disturbed person to psychiatric attention.[6] An investigation of typical family accommodations to the deviant behavior of future patients, and how these accommodations collapse, should therefore contribute to our understanding of the ways in which individuals and the intimate social networks of which they are members are rendered less and more accessible to institutionalized devices of social control. Specifically, it should provide us with a glimpse of those dynamic family processes which determine a future mental patient's accessibility to community, particularly psychiatric intervention; these same processes determine the accessibility of the family. It should also contribute to our understanding of the meaning of such intervention to the future patient and his family. Such family accommodations pose strategic problems for the persons who constitute and man community remedial facilities. These are problems seldom taken into explicit or systematic account by such persons—problems beyond but related to the pathology of the patient.

We shall be concerned here with two phases in the relationship between the future patient and his family and with the connections between these phases and the course of events leading to hospitalization. The first phase consists of the evolution of a pattern of accommodation within the family to behavioral deviance on the part of the future patient.[7] The second

[5] Carroll A. Whitmer and Glenn C. Conover, "A Study of Critical Incidents in the Hospitalization of the Mentally Ill," *Journal of the National Association of Social Work*, IV (January, 1959), 89–94 (see also Edwin C. Wood, John M. Rakusin, and Emanuel Morse, "Interpersonal Aspects of Psychiatric Hospitalization," *Archives of General Psychiatry*, III [December, 1960], 632–41).

[6] Another inference we have made, and which we discuss elsewhere, is that an important set of effects of community devices of social control pertain to family patterns of accommodation. In important ways, it is through these that individuals are controlled, rather than by direct action (Harold Sampson, Sheldon L. Messinger, and Robert D. Towne, "The Mental Hospital and Family Accommodations" [unpublished manuscript, 1962]).

[7] This phase emphasizes one side of a complicated reciprocity between family relations and the deviance of family members. We have focused on the other side of this reciprocity—family relations as they sustain and promote deviant behavior—elsewhere (see Robert D. Towne, Sheldon L. Messinger, and Harold Sampson, "Schizophrenia and the Marital Family: Accommodations to Symbiosis," *Family Process* (forthcoming), and Robert D. Towne, Harold Sampson, and Sheldon L. Messinger, "Schizo-

phase consists in the disruption of this pattern of accommodation. Our observations are derived from a study of seventeen families in which the wife-mother was hospitalized for the first time in a large state mental institution and therein diagnosed as schizophrenic.[8] We established a research relationship with both patient and spouse at the time of admission and continued to see them regularly and frequently throughout hospitalization, and for varying periods extending to more than two years following first release. We conducted about fifty interviews with the members of each marital pair, including typically one or more joint interviews. Other relatives, psychiatrists, physicians, hospital personnel, and other remedial agents who had become involved with the patient or family over the years were also interviewed. Interview materials were supplemented by direct observation at home and in the hospital, and by such medical and social records as we could locate and gain permission to abstract.

These methods, which are described more fully elsewhere,[9] enabled us to reconstruct the viscissitudes of these marital families from courtship through marriage, child-bearing and child-rearing, eventual hospitalization of the wife, and well into the period following the patient's first release. We shall focus here on a longitudinal analysis of two patterns of accommodation which evolved between these women and their families prior to hospitalization and the disruption of these patterns. The patterns are exemplified by eleven and four cases, respectively; two of the seventeen families do not appear to be adequately characterized by either pattern. In order to present the patterns in some detail, our analysis will be developed in terms of selected families exhibiting each type of accommodation. This does not exhaust the empirical variety to be found even in the limited number of cases studied here. In the concluding section, however, emphasis will be placed on common patterns of relationship between future mental patients and their immediate interpersonal communities, as well as on the conditions under which these patterns deteriorate and collapse.

---

phrenia and the Marital Family: Identification Crises," *Journal of Nervous and Mental Diseases,* CXXXIII [November, 1961], 423–29). There is a large and growing literature on this topic, particularly as it concerns schizophrenia, much of which is referred to in the various citations to be found in *The Etiology of Schizophrenia,* ed. by Don D. Jackson (New York: Basic Books, Inc., 1960).

[8] Detailed characteristics of the families studied may be found in Harold Sampson, Sheldon L. Messinger, and Robert D. Towne, "The Mental Hospital and Marital Family Ties," *Social Problems,* IX (Fall, 1961), 141–55. In two of seventeen cases, a brief psychiatric hospitalization in a county hospital had occurred earlier; in a third case, the woman had been hospitalized in a private sanitarium for one month earlier in the same year she entered the state institution.

[9] *Ibid.*

THE UNINVOLVED HUSBAND AND SEPARATE WORLDS

In the first situation, exemplified by eleven families, the marital partners and their children lived together as a relatively independent, self-contained nuclear family, but the marital relationship was characterized by mutual withdrawal and the construction of separate worlds of compensatory involvement. At some point during the marriage, usually quite early, one or both of the partners had experienced extreme dissatisfaction with the marriage. This was ordinarily accompanied by a period of violent, open discord, although in other cases, the dissatisfaction was expressed only indirectly, through reduced communication with the marital partner. Whatever the means of managing the dissatisfaction when it occurred, in each of these families the partners withdrew and each gradually instituted a separate world. The husband became increasingly involved in his work or in other interests outside the marital relationship. The wife became absorbed in private concerns about herself and her children. The partners would rarely go out together, rarely participate together in dealing with personal or family problems, and seldom communicate to each other about their more pressing interests, wishes, and concerns. The marriage would continue in this way for some time without divorce, without separation, and without movement toward greater closeness. The partners had achieved a type of marital accommodation based on interpersonal isolation, emotional distance, and lack of explicit demands upon each other. This accommodation represented an alternative to both divorce and a greater degree of marital integration.

It is a particularly important characteristic of this type of family organization that pathological developments in the wives were for a time self-sustaining. The wife's distress, withdrawal, or deviant behavior did not lead to immediate changes of family life but rather to an intensification of mutual withdrawal. In this setting, the wives became acutely disturbed or even psychotic, without, for a time, very much affecting the pre-existing pattern of family life. This is exemplified in the following cases:

> In the evenings, Mr. Urey worked on his car in the basement while his wife remained upstairs, alone with her sleeping children, engaged in conversations and arguments with imaginary others. This situation continued for at least two years before Mrs. Urey saw a psychiatrist on the recommendation of her family physician. Another two years elapsed before Mrs. Urey was hospitalized. During this period, Mr. Urey became even less concerned with his wife's behavior, accepting it as a matter of course, and concerned himself with "getting ahead" in his job.

> For two years prior to hospitalization, Mrs. Rand was troubled by various somatic complaints, persistent tension, difficulty in sleeping, a vague but disturbing conviction that she was a sinner, and intermittent states of

acute panic. Mr. Rand was minimally aware of her distress. He worked up to fourteen hours a day, including weekends, in his store, and eventually a second job took him out of the home three evenings a week. On those infrequent occasions when his wife's worries forced themselves on his attention, he dismissed them curtly as absurd, and turned once again to his own affairs.

In these families the patterned response to distress, withdrawal, or illness in the wife was further withdrawal by the husband, resulting in increasing distance between, and disengagement of, the marital partners. These developments were neither abrupt nor entirely consistent, but the trend of interaction in these families was toward mutual alienation and inaccessibility of each partner to the other. In this situation, early involvement of the wife in a professional treatment situation was limited by her own withdrawal and difficulty in taking the initiative for any sustained course of action in the real world, as well as by the husband's detachment.

This pattern of mutual withdrawal eventually became intolerable to one or the other partner, pressure for a change was brought to bear, and the family suffered an acute crisis. In some cases, pressure for change was initiated by the husband. In other cases, such pressure was initiated by the wife in the form of increasing agitation, somatic and psychic complaints, and repeated verbal and behavioral communications that she was unable to go on. However the pre-hospital crisis was initiated, and whether it signaled a desire for increased or reduced involvement by the initiating partner, the change indicated an incipient collapse of the former pattern of accommodation.

In four of the eleven cases considered here, the pre-hospital crisis was primarily precipitated by a shift in the husband's "tolerance for deviance." In two of these cases, the wives had been chronically and pervasively withdrawn from role performances and at least periodically psychotic. One husband, in the midst of job insecurities and a desire to move to another state to make a new start, pressed his wife to assume more responsibility. Another husband, approaching forty years of age, reassessed his life and decided that the time had come to rid himself of a wife whom he had long considered "a millstone around my neck." These husbands sought medical or psychiatric assistance specifically to exclude their wives from the family; the two wives were passively resistant to hospitalization. The explicit attitude of the husbands was that they wished the hospital to take their wives off their hands.

In the other two cases, the disruption of the earlier accommodation was associated with the establishment, by the husband, of a serious extramarital liaison. Here, as in the two cases referred to above, there appeared to be no marked change in the wife's conduct prior to this indication of a desire by the husband for total withdrawal.

Virtually identical family processes were apparent in those cases where the manifest illness of the wife was itself the source of pressure for change, the harbinger of the collapse of the prior marital accommodation. The wife's illness intruded itself into family life, at first with limited impact, but then more insistently, like a claim which has not been paid or a message that must be repeated until it is acknowledged. The wife's "complaints" came to be experienced by the husband as, literally, complaints to him, as demands upon him for interest, concern, and involvement. These husbands, however, uniformly initially struggled to preserve the earlier pattern, that is, to maintain uninvolvement in the face of demands which implicitly pressed for their active concern. Thus, as the pre-hospital crisis unfolded, the wife's manifest illness assumed the interpersonal significance of a demand for involvement, and the husband's difficulty in recognizing her as seriously disturbed had the interpersonal significance of a resistance to that demand. The excerpt cited earlier from the Rand case illustrates this process if we add to it the observation that during these two years Mrs. Rand's difficulties recurrently came to the husband's attention in the form of momentary crises which compelled at least the response of curt dismissal.

In this situation, the husband initially assumed a passive or indifferent attitude toward his wife's obtaining professional help. But if she became involved with a psychiatrist, physician, minister, or social worker who took some interest in her life situation, the husband became concerned with the treatment in a negative way. The treatment "wasn't necessary," it "wasn't helping," it "cost too much money." In addition to these deprecations was a hint of alarm that the treatment would challenge the husband's pattern of uninvolvement.[10] For example, Mr. Rand, whose working schedule was mentioned earlier, worried that his wife's psychiatrist might support her complaint that he did not spend enough time at home. Thus the involvement of the wife with a psychiatrically oriented helper was experienced by the husband, at least initially, as a claim upon himself—for money, for concern, and most centrally, for reinvolvement. We have reported elsewhere [11] that there is some basis for this feeling. The treatment process, especially during hospitalization, does tend to induct the husband into the role of the responsible relative, and thereby presses for the reestablishment of reciprocal expectations which had been eroded in the earlier family accommodation.

In most of these cases, these processes led to more extreme deviance on the part of the wife which eventually came to the attention of the larger community, thereby resulting in hospitalization. For example, Mrs. Urey, who had been actively psychotic for some time, was hospitalized

---

[10] In one case, the psychiatrist urged the husband to seek treatment for himself.
[11] Sampson et al., "The Mental Hospital and Marital Family Ties," *op. cit.*

only after she set fire to her home. In brief, the wife's distress is at first experienced by the husband as an unwarranted demand for his reinvolvement in the marital relationship, he withdraws further, and her behavior becomes more deviant.

We may conclude this section with a few more general remarks. The pre-hospital crisis, in each of these cases, marked, and was part of, the disruption of a pattern of accommodation which had been established between the marital partners. The disruption was in effect initiated by one of the partners and resisted by the other.[12] The former accommodation and the way in which it came to be disrupted were important determinants of the processes of "recognizing" the wife as mentally ill, of seeking and using professional help, and of moving the wife from the status of a distressed and behaviorally deviant person within the community to that of a mental patient. These processes, in fact, can only be understood within the context of these family patterns. The problems of early intervention in cases of serious mental illness and of effective intervention in the later crises which ordinarily do come to psychiatric attention cannot even be formulated meaningfully without consideration of these interpersonal processes which determine when, why, and how sick persons become psychiatric patients.

THE OVERINVOLVED MOTHER AND THE MARITAL FAMILY TRIAD

In a contrasting situation found in four cases, the marital partners and their children did not establish a relatively self-contained nuclear family. Rather, family life was organized chronically or periodically around the presence of a maternal figure who took over the wife's domestic and child-rearing functions.[13]

This organization of family life was a conjoint solution to interlocking conflicts of the wife, husband, and mother. In brief, these mothers were possessive and intrusive, motivated to perpetuate their daughters' dependency, and characteristically disposed to assume the "helpful" role in a symbiotic integration with her. The daughters ambivalently pressed for the establishment or maintenance of a dependent relationship with

[12] Wood, Rakusin, and Morse, op. cit., have arrived at a related conclusion on the basis of an analysis of the circumstances of admission of forty-eight patients to a Veterans Administration hospital. "There is also evidence to suggest that hospitalization can for some patients be a way of demanding that those close to them change their behavior, just as it can be an expression by relatives that they are dissatisfied with the patient's behavior."

[13] This person was the wife's mother in three cases, her mother-in-law in the fourth. This distinction is not critical in the present context, and we shall refer to "the wife's mother," etc.

their mothers and struggled to break the inner and outer claims of the maternal attachment. The husbands responded to anxieties of their own about the demands of heterosexual intimacy and marital responsibility, as well as their own ambivalent strivings toward maternal figures, by alternately supporting and protesting the wives' dependence on the maternal figure. The resulting family organization, in which the mother was intermittently or continuously called upon for major assistance, represented an alternative to both a relatively self-contained, independent nuclear family and to marital disruption with the wife returning to live within the parental family.

In direct contrast to the family accommodation described in the preceding section, the wives in "triadic" families did not quietly drift into increasing isolation and autism. Here, sickness or withdrawal by the wife were occasions for intense maternal concern and involvement. This development was ordinarily abetted by the husband. The resulting situation, however, would come to be experienced as threatening by the wife. She would come to view her mother as interfering with her marriage and her fulfilment of her own maternal responsibilities, as restricting her freedom, and as preventing her from growing up. At this point a small but often violent rebellion would ensue, and the husband would now participate with his wife to exclude the mother from family life. Such cycles of reliance on the mother followed by repudiation of her recurred over the years with only minor variations.

This accommodation complicated seeking and using professional help, but in a distinctively different way than in the family setting depicted earlier. Here, the family accommodation included this patterned response to withdrawal, illness, or distress in the wife: the mother replaced the wife in her domestic and child-care functions, and established with the wife a characteristic integration involving a helpless one who needs care and a helpful one who administers it; the husband withdrew to the periphery of the family system, leaving the wife and mother bound in a symbiotic interdependency.

In this patterned response, outside help was not simply superfluous but constituted an actual threat to the existing interdependency of mother and daughter (by implying that it was inadequate, unnecessary, or even harmful), whereas in the type of family accommodation previously described, treatment was experienced as a threat to the husband's uninvolvement; here, treatment was a threat to the mother's involvement.

It was the failure of this family accommodation which led to the wife's contact with the physician or psychiatrist. This failure occurred when, simultaneously, the wife rebelled against the maternal attachment but could not establish with her husband the previously effective alternative of temporary repudiation of that attachment. The following example demonstrates these processes:

Mrs. Yale became anxious, confused, and unable to cope with the demands of daily life in the context of increasing withdrawal by her husband combined with increasing inner and outer pressure for reinvolvement with her mother. Her mother, Mrs. Brown, was living with the marital family, tending the house, caring for the child, and remaining by the side of her troubled daughter night and day. Mr. Yale had become increasingly involved in shared interests with a circle of male friends, and felt disaffected from family life.

Mrs. Brown later characterized this period to the research interviewer: "I think Mary resented me because I tried to help and do things for her. She didn't want me to help with her work. She didn't seem to want me around—sort of resented me. She kept saying she wanted to be on her own and that she didn't have confidence because I was always doing things for her. She even resented me doing the dishes. I just wanted to help out." At this point, Mrs. Brown considered her daughter to be seriously emotionally disturbed, and thought psychiatric help would be advisable.

In such cases, the behavior which led family members to doubt the young woman's sanity consisted of hostility, resentment, and accusatory outbursts directed toward the mother. In these violent outbursts toward the maternal figure, the daughter was indeed "not herself." It was at just this point that the daughter's behavior constituted a disruption of the former family pattern of accommodation and led toward involvement with outside helpers. The mother might now view outside helpers as potential allies in re-establishing the earlier interdependency. The psychiatrist, however, was unlikely to fulfil the mother's expectations in this regard, and then he became an heir to the husband in the triadic situation, a potential rival to the mother-daughter symbiosis.

Shortly after outpatient treatment began, Mrs. Brown took her daughter on an extended vacation which effectively interrupted the treatment, detached the daughter from her incipient attachment to the psychiatrist, and re-established the pattern of mother-daughter interdependency with the husband at the periphery of involvement.

We may summarize, then, certain connections between this type of family accommodation and the use of professional help prior to hospitalization. The initial response of the family to the wife's distress was to attempt to reinstate a familiar pattern: a drawing together of mother and daughter in symbiotic interdependency, and a withdrawal of the husband to the periphery of the family. This accommodation was disrupted by the eruption of the daughter's formerly ego-alien resentment toward her mother, and at this point the latter was likely to view physicians or psychiatrists as potential allies in restoring the former equilibrium. The psychiatrist, however, was unlikely to play this part and became, for the mother, a rival to the interdependency. For the daughter, also, this meaning of treatment invested it with the dangerous promise of a possible separation from the maternal figure. In this drama, the husband was likely to play a relatively passive if not a discouraging role, affording the wife little if any support in what she experienced as a threatening and disloyal involvement outside the family.

The way in which the hospitalization of the wife came about, in the collapse of this family accommodation, also provided contrasts to the processes depicted in the preceding section. As the pre-hospital crisis developed, the wife sought to withdraw from continuing intolerable conflict in the triadic situation. At first, the wife felt impelled to choose between regressive dependency on a maternal figure and the claims of her marital family, but was unable to either relinquish the former or achieve inner and outer support for the latter. Both alternatives were transiently affirmed and repudiated in the period preceding hospitalization, but in time she came to feel alienated from *both* mother and husband, and driven toward increasing *psychic* withdrawal. This process did not resolve her conflicts or remove her from the triadic field, and in time she herself pushed for physical removal.

Thus, in two of the four triadic cases, the wife herself, with a feeling of desperation, explicitly requested hospitalization. In a third case, the disturbed wife was brought to a psychiatrist in the company of both mother and husband, refused to return home with them after the appointment, and was thereupon hospitalized. In the fourth case, the wife was initially cooperative to a hospitalization plan, but equivocation by the husband and psychiatrist delayed action, and the wife gave herself and her daughter an overdose of drugs, thereby precipitating the hospitalization. This last case resembles the most common pattern described in the preceding section, in which the wife is driven to extreme deviance which comes to the attention of the larger community and compels hospitalization. But the secondary pattern, in which a husband takes primary initiative for hospitalizing a reluctant wife because she has become a "millstone around my neck," was entirely absent.

DISCUSSION

The career of the mental patient and his family ordinarily comes to the attention of treatment personnel during the course of an "unmanageable" emergency and fades from view when that emergency is in some way resolved. Prior to this public phase of the crisis, and often again after it, the disturbance of the patient is contained within a community setting. It is the collapse of accommodative patterns *between* the future patient and his interpersonal community which renders the situation unmanageable and ushers in the public phase of the pre-hospital (or rehospitalization) crisis.

Our analysis has been addressed to ways in which two particular organizations of family life have contained pathological processes, to the ways in which these organizations were disrupted, and to the links between family dynamics and recognition of illness, seeking and using professional help, and the circumstances of mental hospitalization. The analysis carries us beyond the observations that families often "tolerate" deviant behavior, may resist "recognition" that the future patient is seriously disturbed, and may be reluctant to use help, toward a systematic view of "typical" accommodations around deviance and typical patterns of crisis.

It is, of course, by no means evident how typical the patterns we have described may be. Although the analysis is confined to certain marital family organizations and does not entirely exhaust our own empirical materials, we suggest that the presentation does touch upon two common situations encountered in work with the mentally ill and their families. In the first situation, the future patient and his immediate interpersonal community move from each other, effect patterns of uninvolvement, and reciprocate withdrawal by withdrawal. The future patient moves, and is moved, toward exclusion from interpersonal ties and from any meaningful links to a position in communal reality. This situation, as we have seen, is compatible with very high "tolerance for deviant behavior," which may permit an actively psychotic patient to remain *in* the community while not psychosocially *of* it.

The accommodation may be disrupted by a shift in the "tolerance" of the interpersonal community, however determined,[14] or from the side of the future patient by increasing agitation which signals an attempt to break out of inner and outer isolation. Here, hospitalization is a possible route toward further disengagement of the patient from his interpersonal community, or conversely, toward reestablishment of reciprocal expectations compatible with reengagement. Whatever the outcome, a strategic therapeutic problem is posed by the chronic pattern of mutual disinvolvement and withdrawal.

In the second situation, the future patient and a member of his immediate interpersonal community become locked in mutual involvement, effect patterns of intense interdependency, and reciprocate withdrawal by concern. The future patient moves and is moved toward a bond in which interlocking needs tie the participants together rather than isolate them. This situation is also compatible with high tolerance for deviant

---

[14] The determinants may be extraneous to inherent family processes. Thus, in a case not included in the present sample, the movement of a family from farm to city altered the family's capacity to retain a psychotic young man and precipitated his hospitalization.

behavior, but here because the deviance has become a necessary component of the family integration. It is this type of family process, rather than the first type, which has attracted most psychiatric interest,[15] although there is no reason from our data to suppose that it is the more common.

In the cases observed the disruption of this accommodation took the form of an ego-alien movement by the future patient against the claims of the overwhelming attachment. Here, hospitalization is at once a route of escape from intolerable conflict in the interpersonal community, and a potential pathway toward reestablishing the earlier pattern of accommodation. The strategic therapeutic problem posed is the contrasting one of modification of a chronic pattern of intense involvement.

The observations reported do not yield precise knowledge as to how psychiatric intervention might routinely be brought about early in the development of a serious mental illness, whether or when this is advisable, and how intervention might be more effective later on. The observations indicate, rather, that we must confront these questions in their real complexity, and investigate more closely and persistently than heretofore the characteristic ways in which families cope with severe psychiatric disturbances, the ways in which these intrafamily mechanisms are disrupted, and the significance of the family dynamics which form the crucial background of the eventual encounter between patient and clinician.

[15] See Jackson (ed.), *op. cit.*

Part E

Social Welfare Organizations
and Lower-Class Clientele

THE major target of welfare organizations tends to be the poor population. Are there special problems of reaching the poor? What kinds of service do this group actually get? Does poverty cause them to get as good service as other users of welfare organizations? How do staff members react to this client group? These are some of the questions raised in the concluding articles.

The first selection, "Social Class and the Treatment of Neurotics," by August B. Hollingshead and Frederick C. Redlich, discusses the differences in treatment received by neurotics from the five different social classes (class I is the highest class, and class V is the lowest). The authors studied all treated cases of mental illness that originated in New Haven, Connecticut, over a number of years. Their data show not only a difference between the agencies in which neurotic patients of different social classes were treated (the lower the class the more likely a patient was to be treated in a public, as opposed to private, setting), but also that the amount and type of treatment are related to social class within a given agency. Similar findings, varying only in degree, also hold true for the treatment of psychotic patients.

In "Private Social Welfare's Disengagement from the Poor: The Case of Family Adjustment Agencies," Richard Cloward and Irving Epstein ask a related question: Why have private social agencies tended to serve a predominantly middle-class clientele? First, they show that over the last fifty years the voluntary agencies have actually shifted from a lower-class to a middle-class clientele. Then they explain this change. They are not satisfied with the easy answer that the change is the result of the growth of public welfare services; they point out that aside from the granting of money there are other important functions that social work could perform for the poor. Instead, they look to problems in the development of the profession of social work in American society: both the position of the profession in the prestige system and the philosophies of treatment that emerged to justify the science base of the profession led toward the serving of a middle-class clientele.

In some ways the first two selections give pessimistic data and interpretations, focusing on the inadequacies and difficulties of service to the poor; however, imaginative use of sociological concepts may help to bridge the gap. The article by George Brager, "Organizing the Unaffiliated in a Low-Income Area," analyzes the structure of lower-class communities. Given this structure, it proposes a number of mechanisms for reaching groups with whom community organizers, typically, have had little success. Basic to this analysis are three sociological concepts: level of community integration, opportunity and opportunity channels, and indigenous leadership. The program that Brager describes attempts to manipulate the latter two variables to affect the level of community integration and to integrate the community more fully into the larger society. The final article by Peter M. Blau, "Orientation toward Clients in a Public Welfare Agency," discusses the modes of staff adaptation to clients and to bureaucratic procedure in a public welfare agency dealing with lower-class clients. Blau finds that the common stereotype—that as workers stay on the job they become more cynical and detached—does not apply to all workers. Instead, he shows the informal processes and structure that help a worker maintain a commitment to client service.

Social Class and the Treatment of Neurotics

August B. Hollingshead and Frederick C. Redlich

TREATMENT AGENCIES

Theoretically we might expect that disturbed individuals who are diagnosed as neurotic would be accepted for treatment in any available agency. Practically, however, the problem revolves around the question of which agency is available to what patient.

The principal restrictions on each type of agency were pointed out earlier. Nevertheless, we shall repeat the essential eligibility requirements for each one. Veterans Hospitals and Clinics are open only to former members of the Armed Forces. Private practitioners' services and private hospitals are limited to those able to pay their fees. Clinics tend to be restricted to certain groups according to age, economic status, or diagnosis, such as the guidance clinics for children, psychiatric dispensaries for lower income groups, and the clinics of the Commission on Alcoholism for alcoholics. The state hospitals are available only to residents of the state. These limitations mean that particular kinds of treatment agencies are, in fact, more or less restricted to certain segments of the community's population.

Precise knowledge of the many practical considerations involved in the implementation of a decision to refer a disturbed person to a psychiatrist led us to suppose that class status is a meaningful factor in the determination of who is accepted where for treatment. In order to test this idea, the clinical record of each patient had to be studied to learn where his first psychiatric treatment occurred. The results of this phase of the research are summarized in Table 1. A glance at the probability statement for Table 1 will show that where neurotic patients are treated first is linked distinctly with class status. Individuals in classes I–II and III go, in large part, to private practitioners; class IV's go, in about equal

August B. Hollingshead and Frederick C. Redlich, "Social Class and the Treatment of Neurotics" in *Social Class and Mental Illness: A Community Study,* by the same authors, John Wiley & Sons, 1958, pp. 261–275.

Table 1   *Percentage of Neurotic Patients Treated for the First Time in Specific Types of Psychiatric Agencies—by Class*

Treatment Agency	I–II	III	IV	V
Private practitioners	85.7	67.0	47.4	9.8
Private hospitals	9.2	5.3	. . .	. . .
Public clinics	5.1	20.9	30.9	57.4
Military or V.A. hospitals	. . .	6.1	14.3	13.1
State hospitals	. . .	0.7	7.4	19.7
$n =$	98	115	175	61

$$\chi^2 = 131.20, 12 \; df, p < .001$$

proportions, to private and public agencies; class V's go, in very large part, to public agencies. Hospitalized neurotic patients are in the minority in all classes, but the lower the class, the higher the percentage who are hospitalized. Class I–II patients are attracted to private hospitals; class III's go, in about equal numbers, to both private and public hospitals; some two out of three class IV patients first enter a military or veterans hospital; the class V neurotics go to the state hospitals or the veterans hospitals.

CHANGES IN TREATMENT AGENCIES
FROM FIRST TO CURRENT TREATMENT

Thirty-eight percent of the patients are in their second or third experience with psychiatric care, and some have had even more contacts. An examination of where these patients were treated first and where they are treated currently shows a significant change in the use of treatment agencies in each class from the first to the present phase of their illness. In class I–II there is little change in the use of treatment agencies from the first to the current course of treatment, except for patients who received their first treatment in private hospitals. Although only six patients had their first treatment in a private hospital, five of the six changed to other agencies. Two are treated currently in public clinics, one is in a veterans hospital, and two are in state hospitals. Thus, 83 percent of the class I–II patients who were treated first in a private hospital, then were discharged, and at a later time re-entered treatment, are now in a public agency. Private mental hospitals appear to be patronized mainly by persons from class I–II who are in treatment for the first time. Private practitioners hold their class I–II patients from the first to subsequent periods of treatment.[1]

Class III individuals are loyal either to private practitioners or to clinics. If a patient starts with a private practitioner, he tends to stay with a private practitioner in later courses of treatment, although not necessarily with the same one. Likewise, when a class III person starts in a clinic he returns to a clinic when he feels in need of treatment. The private hospitals lose over nine out of ten class III patients who find it necessary to re-enter treatment. Some 76 percent of the class III patients who do not return to private hospitals enter state hospitals. The remainder are treated largely by private practitioners, but a few are in clinics. Among veterans, the largest shift is from first treatment in a military setting to current treatment with a private practitioner. At the time of our field work, not a single class III neurotic patient was in a veterans hospital. In class III the two significant changes in the use of psychiatric facilities between the first treatment and the current treatment involve moves from private to state hospitals among the nonveterans and from military hospitals to private practitioners among veterans.[2] The bills for the private treatment of these veterans are paid by the Veterans Administration.

In class IV there are two marked changes in the use of psychiatric agencies between the first course of treatment and the present one. First, almost every veteran who received his first treatment in military service is cared for now by a private practitioner on an ambulatory basis at the expense of the Veterans Administration. Second, patients who first came into psychiatric treatment either with private practitioners or in clinics are now in state hospitals.[3]

In class V, the same changes occur but in even more marked ways. Specifically, 83 percent of the veterans who are treated currently by private practitioners at Veterans Administration expense had their first psychiatric experience in military service. Class V patients who are treated for the first time in clinics either return to them or go to the state hospitals when a second course of treatment is necessary. If a clinic cannot care for them, the probability is that they will be taken to a state hospital.[4]

These data tell us in a general way what treatment facilities are available to which patients and in what phases of mental illness. Classes I–II and III turn for help to private hospitals and private practitioners when they first become ill. As chronicity develops, they go elsewhere or possibly "shop around." All three classes rely upon private practitioners in later illnesses, but only class I's continue to patronize private hospitals. In classes II and III, the shift from the first to later courses of treatment is from private hospitals to public hospitals. Class IV's tend to utilize clinics and private practitioners first, rather than private hospitals. Later they turn to the state hospitals out of necessity. Class V's are wholly dependent upon public agencies in all phases of their illnesses.

CLASS AND TREATMENT AGENCIES

We have seen that each of the five types of treatment agencies are utilized by sharply different proportions of patients in the classes who have had one and more previous courses of psychiatric treatment. We will now examine the way they are used by all the patients, that is, those who are in treatment for the first time as well as those who have a history of previous treatment. By way of introduction, we shall note that no class I neurotic patient is treated in public clinics, state hospitals, or Veterans Administration hospitals. Conversely, no class V patient is found in a private hospital. Between these extremes a series of significant associations exists between the class status of the patients and the use they make of the different treatment agencies.

Class I individuals are treated exclusively by private practitioners or in private hospitals. Class II persons, for the most part, are treated by private practitioners or private hospitals. Class III's are treated predominantly (71 percent) by private practitioners, but 21 percent are cared for in the clinics; 2 percent are in private hospitals and 6 percent in state hospitals. The percentage of class IV patients treated by private psychiatrists is lower than in class III, as is the percentage in private hospitals. The proportion in clinics is only slightly larger, but the percentage in the state hospitals is twice as great as in class III. Some 20 percent of the class V's are treated by private practitioners. The remainder are treated in public agencies, 52 percent in the clinics, 5 percent in Veterans Administration hospitals, and 24 percent in the state hospitals.

The class profiles of patients in each type of institution (see Figure 1) show that each type of institution draws its patients from selected segments of the status structure. The state hospital is utilized in sharply increasing percentages as the class status scale is descended. The use of Veterans Administration hospitals is not as closely linked to class as the state hospitals. Nevertheless, the proportion of class V patients in Veterans Administration hospitals is almost three times greater than in class IV. The veterans hospitals are used proportionately by many more lower than higher status veterans. The differential increase from class II to class V in veterans hospitals is as one is to five.

The profile for the clinics is similar to that of the state hospitals, but the differential between classes II and III is not as large. However, the increases between classes II and III and classes IV and V are of approximately the same magnitude. For example, 2 percent of the class II's are in the state hospitals, but of the class III's there are 6 percent; thus, the proportion of class III's in the state hospitals is three times larger than class II's. Likewise, 7 percent of the class II's are in the clinics, but 21 percent of the class III's. Between classes IV and V the differences in the

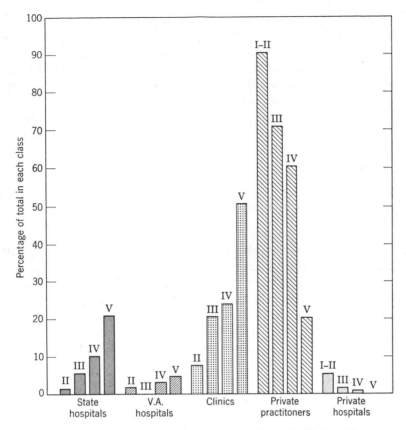

$\chi^2 = 87.98$, *df* 9, $p < 0.001$ (State hospital combined with V.A. hospital and private practitioner combined with private hospital for the χ^2 analysis.)

Figure 1 *Percentage of neurotic patients in different treatment agencies—by class.*

percentage of patients in the clinics and the state hospitals is as one is to two, with the larger proportion belonging to class V. In brief, there is a marked increase in the proportion of patients in the clinics and state hospitals as one goes down the class scale. The gradient for the Veterans Administration is not as steep, but it is, with the exception of class III, in the same direction.

The class profile for the patients in private agencies is the opposite of that in public agencies. Eighty-six percent of the class I–II patients are treated by private practitioners, 71 percent of the class III's, 62 percent of the class IV's and 20 percent of the class V's. Only eight neurotic patients are treated in private hospitals, but half of them belong to class I–II; two are in class III and two in class IV.

The class gradient for neurotic patients in private agencies is far steeper when their use is viewed in terms of who pays the costs of treatment. All class I–II patients pay for their treatment, but only 63 percent of class III's, 39 percent of the class IV's, and none of the class V's do so. Patients in classes III and IV who are treated by private practitioners, but do not pay their own bills, are financed by the Veterans Administration. In class V the private patient's bills are paid either by the Veterans Administration or by compensation insurance carried by employers. In short, when class V neurotic individuals receive treatment it is at public expense. This generalization is applicable also to 60 percent of the class IV neurotic patients.

PRINCIPAL FORM OF THERAPY AND CLASS STATUS

Interrelationships between the principal types of psychiatric therapy administered and the class status of the patients who receive each type of therapy are examined from two perspectives. First, we shall view the data without controlling for treatment agency; then we shall control for it to see if class position is linked to the kind of therapy psychiatrists prescribe for their patients within a treatment agency. The data essential for the first analysis are given in Table 2.

Some form of psychotherapy is the predominant treatment method in each class, but there are distinctly different percentages of patients in the several classes who do or do not receive a particular type of psychotherapy. Psychoanalysis and analytic psychotherapy are concentrated in

Table 2   *Principal Type of Psychiatric Therapy Received by Neurotic Patients—by Class*

	Class			
Type of Treatment	I–II	III	IV	V
Classical analysis and analytic psychotherapy	46.9	20.9	5.1	4.9
Directive psychotherapy [a]	50.0	62.6	69.7	54.1
Group psychotherapy	1.0	2.6	2.9	8.2
Organic therapy (shock, drugs, operations)	2.0	9.6	16.6	9.8
Custodial care	0.0	4.3	5.7	23.0
$n =$	98	115	175	61

$$\chi^2 = 128.72, 9 \; df, p < .001$$

[a] Directive and group psychotherapy combined for χ^2 analysis.

class I–II. Directive therapy is clustered disproportionately in classes III and IV. Only a small number of patients receive group therapy, but the largest percentage is in class V (all group therapy was administered in a state hospital). When the individual psychotherapies are summed, a clearly defined class gradient emerges: All class I's receive it, 97 percent of the class II's, 84 percent of the class III's, 75 percent of the class IV's, and 59 percent of the class V's. The organic therapies, shock, operations and drugs, are relatively rare in all classes, but the class V neurotics receive an organic therapy five times as frequently as the class I's and II's. Custodial care is limited largely to class V. When the patients who are administered an organic therapy are combined with those receiving custodial care, a definite inverse association appears between class position and the receipt of one of these kinds of treatment, namely, class II—2 percent, class III—14 percent, class IV—23 percent, class V—33 percent. These dramatic differences show clearly that the lower the class, the greater the proportion of neurotic patients who are administered therapies which dynamically oriented psychiatrists do not approve. In class V, at least two out of five patients do not receive one of the active therapies developed in this century that are believed to aid in the solution of neurotic difficulties.

TYPES OF THERAPY WITHIN AGENCIES

We will now analyze the therapies patients receive within three groups of treatment agencies, private practitioners, the clinics, and the public hospitals, to see if class position is a significant factor in the kind of therapy when the agency where they are treated is held constant.

Private Practitioners

Forty-two private practitioners are caring for 65.5 percent of the neurotic patients. Individual psychotherapy is the predominant therapeutic method used. The particular subtypes administered, analytic psychotherapy and directive psychotherapy, are related definitely to the patient's position in the status structure. Psychoanalysis is limited entirely to classes I and II. Analytic psychotherapy also is confined, in large part, to the same strata. Directive psychotherapy, by way of contrast, is inversely related to class status. It increases from 53.4 percent in class II to 86.4 percent in class V. This is the only form of psychotherapy which class V patients receive from private practitioners. Even though 90 percent of the private practitioners' patients are treated by some form of individual psychotherapy, the remaining 10 percent who are prescribed some form of organic treatment exhibit class-linked therapy patterns, as a glance at Table 3 shows. The lower the class, the higher the percentage receiving an organic therapy.

Table 3   *Percentage of Private Practitioners' Patients in Each Class Treated with a Specific Type of Therapy* [a]

	Class			
Psychiatric Therapy	I–II	III	IV	V [b]
Psychoanalysis and analytic psychotherapy	45.4	19.0	1.8	0.0
Directive psychotherapy	53.4	72.7	88.7	86.4
Shock and sedation	1.1	8.3	9.5	13.6
$n =$ 88	84	110	12

$$\chi^2 = 89.33, 4 \ df, p < .001$$

[a] Includes eight patients in private hospitals.

[b] The class V patients are combined with the class IV patients in the χ^2 analysis.

Observation of the data on the types of psychiatric therapies administered to patients leads to the conclusion that the private practice of psychiatry in our community is highly correlated with class status. To test the certainty of this idea, the private practitioners' patients were divided according to the therapeutic orientation of the practitioners to see what strata are represented in the practice of each one. The procedure gave us three groups of practitioners: (a) psychoanalysts, 22 in number, (b) analytically oriented psychiatrists, but not analysts, 11, and (c) psychiatrists who utilize either directive, supportive, suggestive techniques or organic therapies.[9]

The psychoanalysts draw 77 percent of their patients from classes I and II, 17 percent from class III, and 6 percent from class IV. The analytically oriented therapists draw 52 percent of their patients from classes I and II, 39 percent from class III, and 9 percent from class IV. Forty-eight percent of the directive-organic therapists' patients are in class IV, 34 percent are in class III, and only 15 percent belong to class I or II. These figures [5] indicate that private practitioners have "class" practices for the most part. Therefore, it is not surprising to find that the type of therapy a practitioner administers to his patients is correlated with the patient's social position.

Psychotherapeutic treatment is aimed toward the re-education of the patient. This is believed to occur as a patient "works through" his personal problems with the therapist or, in the directive psychotherapies, when he accepts and follows the therapists' notions. To rehabilitate a neurotic patient through the use of individual psychotherapy takes the time of the patient and the psychiatrist. The amount of time they actually spend with one another is measured here in three different ways: (1) the number of meetings the patient has with his therapist each month, (2) the length of each psychotherapeutic session, and (3) the length of time the patient has been receiving care from his present therapist.

The number of therapeutic visits per month made by patients receiving individual psychotherapy from private practitioners is definitely linked to class status. As a rule, the higher the class the more frequently treatment is administered. The class gradient is steepest for the patients who see their doctors nine or more times per month. These patients are being treated by an intensive form of psychotherapy. A glance at Table 4 will show that they are heavily concentrated in classes I–II. This is what one would expect from the previously demonstrated strong association between high class status and the prescription of analytic psychotherapy or psychoanalysis. Patients who see their therapists less than once a week are clustered in classes IV and V. Patients who see their therapists once or twice a month certainly are not participating in "re-education" with the same intensity as those who see their psychiatrists more than twice a week.

The folklore of psychiatric practice tells us that the optimal length of a psychotherapeutic session is a "50-minute hour." [6] We are not interested in determining what the length of a psychotherapeutic session ought to

Table 4 *Percentage of Private Practitioners' Patients* [a] *Receiving Individual Psychotherapy Who See Their Therapists a Specified Number of Times Each Month— by Class*

| Number of | Class | | |
meetings	I–II	III	IV–V
1	17.2	18.9	30.4
2	12.6	25.7	39.2
3–4	23.0	31.1	25.5
5–8	13.9	18.9	3.9
9 and more	33.3	5.4	1.0
$n =$	87	74	102

$$\chi^2 = 69.39, 12 \ df, p < .001$$

[a] Patients in private hospitals receiving individual psychotherapy included.

Table 5   *Percentage of Neurotic Patients Treated by Private Practitioners—by Class and Length of Sessions*

	Class			
Length of Sessions	I–II	III	IV	V
50–60 minutes	94.3	81.3	75.8	45.4
30–49 minutes	3.4	17.3	20.9	18.1
15–29 minutes	2.3	1.4	3.3	36.4
$n =$	87	74	91	11

$$\chi^2 = 47.09, 6 \; df, p < .001$$

be. Our interest is in seeing if the amount of time psychiatrists spend with their patients on each visit is related to the class position of the patients. The answer is embodied in Table 5.

Table 5 demonstrates that class position is a definite factor in the determination of the amount of time private practitioners spend with their patients. Approximately 94 percent of the class I–II patients see their therapists for a 50-minute hour. At the other end of the status structure, only 45 percent of the class V's receive treatment for 50 minutes, whereas less than 6 percent of the patients in class I–II are treated by "short time." We infer that this is another manifestation of the subtle intrusion of class status into the practice of psychiatry.

The number of months patients have been in treatment is related directly to class position. In class I–II, two patients out of five have been in continuous intensive treatment with their present psychiatrist for more than three years. In class V, no patient has received any form of treatment for as long as two years. In class IV only one patient out of 14 has received continuous psychotherapy for as long as two years.[7] Unfortunately, we cannot conclude that lower class patients are cured more quickly or do not require long-term intensive psychotherapy. Moreover, we do not know if they would remain in long-term therapy or benefit from twice the amount of time per treatment session.

Differences in the length of time patients remain in treatment with private practitioners may be attributed, at least in part, to the kind of psychotherapy being administered, but the personality characteristics of the class V patient, such as impulse gratification, inability to verbalize, and short span of attention, probably also enter into the process. However, who gets what kind of therapy is a class-linked variable. For example, a psychoanalyst may prescribe either psychoanalysis or intensive analytic psychotherapy for his patients, but these therapies are limited largely to classes I and II. Supportive therapy, by way of contrast, may be prescribed by directive psychiatrists for their patients. It is not a matter of chance that the patients who receive this form of treatment are almost exclusively in either class IV or V. These are the patients who see their psychiatrists once or twice a month for 15 to 30 minutes and drop out of treatment within a few months. In short, class status is inextricably interlinked with what kinds of treatment patients receive from private practitioners.

The Clinics

Seven different clinics treated the 104 patients whose treatment experiences will be examined now. Approximately two thirds of these patients were cared for in the large community clinic. Two other clinics treated most of the remainder. Because of the concentration of so many patients in a single clinic, the general statistical picture will be overshadowed by what occurs in the large clinic. Analytically oriented individual psychotherapy is the acknowledged treatment in this clinic; three of the other clinics also stress analytic psychotherapy, two have a directive-organic orientation, and the orientation of one, at the time of the field work, was indefinite. Unfortunately, the number of patients is too small for us to examine the clinics individually. However, we will present some data in later paragraphs from the large clinic in the community hospital. One final word about the clinic patients: No class I individual is among them.

Within the clinics the class position of the patients is related in significant ways to the types of therapy psychiatrists administer. A glance at Table 6 will show that the higher the class, the greater the percentage of

Table 6 *Percentage of Neurotic Patients in Clinics by Principal Type of Psychiatric Therapy in Each Class*

	Class			
Psychiatric Therapy	II [a]	III	IV	V
Analytic psychotherapy	71.4	33.3	17.0	6.3
Directive psychotherapy	28.6	45.9	65.9	59.3
Shock therapy [b]	0.0	4.2	7.3	3.1
Sedation	0.0	16.7	9.8	31.2
$n =$	7	24	41	32

$$\chi^2 = 18.03, 4 \; df, p < .01$$

[a] Class II is combined with class III in the χ^2 analysis.
[b] Shock therapy and sedation are combined in χ^2 analysis.

patients who are prescribed analytic therapy. While directive psychotherapy is distributed rather evenly in the three lower classes, only a small percentage of class II's receive it. Relatively few patients receive an organic therapy, but in class V over one third are given either sedation or shock.

The significant association of class with the type of therapy psychiatrists give within the clinics is of particular interest, because the treatment prescribed is not connected with the economic factor as it is in private practice. The patients are treated free, or for nominal fees determined by administrative personnel who have no direct connection with the patient's therapy. We may infer, therefore, that the type of therapy given to a clinic patient is related more to social factors than to economic costs. The doctor-patient relationship and communication between the physician and his patient appear to be related, in turn, to the class of the patients and of the doctors.

The intensity of individual psychotherapy, as measured by the number of times a patient sees his clinic therapist per month, is not linked significantly with class position. Nevertheless, there is a tendency for class V patients to see their therapists, once, twice, or three times a month, whereas the class II and class III patients see their therapists once a week. Specifically, 71 percent of the class II patients in clinics, but only 57 percent of the class V patients in clinics, see their therapists more than once a week; none see him as often as twice a week.

The clinics are structured around a 50-minute hour; therefore, there is no association between class position and the length of time patients are seen. Only four patients receive less than this amount of psychiatric time, but three of these four are in class V; the other is in class IV. This slight tendency to give a class V patient less time and attention than a higher status patient is another bit of evidence of the generalized nature of class differences.

The length of time the clinic patients have been in treatment is related to class. The higher the class the longer the patients have been in continuous treatment. For example, 62 percent of the class II patients have been in treatment for more than one year; whereas 79 percent of the class V's have been in treatment for less than six months. Classes III and IV fall into their characteristic intervening positions along this gradient.[8]

Two members of our team, Myers and Schaffer, studied the large clinic in the community hospital to learn as much as possible about interrelations of social factors and the practice of psychiatry within one institutional setting.[9] They found that of neurotic patients in their first course of treatment, who are prescribed analytic psychotherapy, 59 percent of the class II's are treated more than 10 weeks, but only 14 percent of the class V's.[10] They also found that a patient's class status determines the professional level of the therapist who treats him. Class II patients are treated by fully trained staff psychiatrists; resident trainees select class III and IV patients; and class V patients receive treatment from undergraduate medical students or social workers.

Treatment in Public Hospitals

The 12 percent of neurotic patients who are in state and Veterans Administration hospitals do not exhibit the class-associated therapy patterns found among private practitioners and in clinics. However, the data in Table 7 reveal some interesting treatment practices in the public hospitals. Only two patients are treated by analytic psychotherapy, one in class II and one in class V; both are in veterans hospitals. Group psychotherapy, on the other hand, is found only in one state hospital, and it is unduly concentrated in class III. Electro-convulsive therapy is limited, likewise, to the state hospitals. Custodial care and routine administration of sedation are little used, and they are found in about the same proportion in each of the two lower classes.

RE-ENTRY INTO TREATMENT

Approximately 32 percent of the neurotic patients have experienced one or more previous courses of psychiatric treatment. Re-entry into treatment within a year of the time previous treatment was completed is not related to class position although there is a trend toward more re-entry

Table 7 *Percentage of Neurotic Patients Treated in State and Veterans Administration Hospitals by Principal Types of Psychiatric Therapy—by Class*

	Class			
Psychiatric Therapy [a]	II	III	IV	V
Analytic psychotherapy	66.7	0.0	0.0	5.9
Directive psychotherapy	0.0	14.3	12.7	17.6
Group psychotherapy	0.0	42.8	20.8	29.5
Shock treatments and lobotomies	33.3	28.7	45.7	29.4
Custodial care	0.0	14.3	20.8	17.6
$n =$	3	7	24	17

$$\chi^2 = 6.52, 6\ df, p > .05$$

[a] Class II is combined with class III and Analytic and Directive psychotherapy are combined in the χ^2 analysis.

into treatment in classes IV and V than in the higher classes. However, when the interim between courses of treatment is 12 months or longer, there is a distinct inverse relationship between class and the percentage of patients who re-enter treatment. In classes I and II, 12 percent of the patients return to treatment after an interval of at least a year, but 28 percent of the class V's re-entered treatment after a year had elapsed since their previous course of treatment. The intervening classes show percentages between these extremes. It would appear that a functional connection exists between lower class status, short periods of treatment, and periodic recurrences of disturbed behavior requiring further psychiatric care.

SUMMARY

The place where neurotic patients are treated is strongly associated with class status; the higher the class, the higher the percentage of disturbed patients treated by private practitioners. Treatment in public agencies is related inversely to class position; the lower the class, the greater the proportion of patients treated in public agencies. How patients are treated also is linked to class position. Individual psychotherapy is a major treatment in all classes, but the lower the class, the greater the tendency to administer an organic therapy, shock treatment, lobotomy, or treatment with drugs. When the agency where treatment takes place is held constant, the status factor continues to be important. Private practitioners administer analytic psychotherapy to the higher classes and directive therapies to the lower classes. The same class-linked gradient exists in the clinics, but not in the public hospitals. The number of times patients see their therapists per month, as well as the length of the visits, is significantly different from one class to another. The higher classes receive more frequent and longer treatments than the lower classes; the disparity is most marked between classes IV and V.

NOTES

1. A comparison of first and current treatment by public versus private agencies in class I–II gave a $\chi^2 = 5.46$, 1 df, $p < .05$.
2. $\chi^2 = 15.40$, $p < .01$, 4 df, for class III.
3. $\chi^2 = 42.34$, $p < .01$, 3 df, for class IV.
4. $\chi^2 = 9.38$, $p < .05$, 3 df, for class V.
5. $\chi^2 = 86.075$, 4 df, $p < .001$.
6. This is a heritage from the Freudian practice of scheduling appointments an hour apart.
7. $\chi^2 = 25.523$, 4 df, $p < .001$.
8. $\chi^2 = 10.56$, 4 df, $p < .05$.
9. See Jerome K. Myers and Leslie Schaffer, "Social Stratification and Psychiatric Practice," *American Sociological Review*, Vol. 19 (June 1954), pp. 307–310.
10. $\chi^2 = 17.503$, 6 df, $p < .01$.

Private Social Welfare's Disengagement from the Poor:

The Case of Family Adjustment Agencies

Richard A. Cloward and Irwin Epstein

THE PUBLIC-PRIVATE ALLOCATION OF CLIENTELE

The movement of private family adjustment agencies away from low-income people * is nowhere better revealed than in an examination of their patterns of referral of clients to public assistance programs.

Once publicly supported income-maintenance programs came into existence, following the depression, private agencies began to refer economically deprived clients, thus conserving their resources for other

---

* The evolution and magnitude of the trend away from the poor can also be shown with respect to a number of other kinds of private agencies. In the field of group work and recreation, for example, see Elizabeth Douvan and Carol Kay, *Adolescent Girls*, Ann Arbor, Michigan: Survey Research Center, University of Michigan, n.d.; Elizabeth Douvan, *A Study of Adolescent Boys*, Ann Arbor, Michigan: Survey Research Center, University of Michigan, for the National Council, Boy Scouts of America, n.d.; Sidney G. Lutzin, "The Squeeze Out!—Recreation's Abdication of Responsibility," *Recreation*, LV, 8 (Oct. 1962), pp. 390–392; University of Maryland, Division of Social Sciences, *A Survey of Leisure Activities and Interests of Teen-Age Youth in the Washington Metropolitan Area*, Part I, Oct. 1960; *Program of the Girl Scouts of the U.S.A.*, Ann Arbor, Mich.; Survey Research Center, University of Michigan, Sept. 1958. By and large, these studies show a pronounced tendency among agencies to serve middle-income young people.

Richard A. Cloward and Irving Epstein, "Private Social Welfare's Disengagement from the Poor: The Case of the Family Adjustment Agencies." Abridged from *Proceedings of Annual Social Work Day Institute*, School of Social Welfare, New York State University at Buffalo, May, 1965. This paper was originally published in two parts. The first part contained a summary of historical trends in agency clientele from 1900 to the present. It documents the shift of services away from low-income groups by private family adjustment agencies. The second part, reprinted here, represents an effort to explain why this shift came about.

services. The extensive use of referral to public agencies as a way of closing out contact with the poor has been noted in a number of recent studies. Maas, for example, observes that "Proportionately more lower-occupational-status families terminate in consultation or referral" (43, p. 6). Beck notes:

> The proportion of cases closing on a planned basis at the end of the first intake interview increases rapidly as social class declines. To some extent this probably reflects merely increased referrals to public agencies for financial assistance. Probably inappropriate requests for other types of direct service account for additional closings for these groups (33, p. 34).

The emergence of publicly supported income maintenance agencies is sufficient to account for referrals of low income people by private agencies for relief. The emergence of these programs is not sufficient, however, to explain the tendency of private agencies to act as if such referrals fulfilled their responsibility to poor people.

In 1934, Linton B. Swift (46) described the developing relationship between private family agencies and public agencies. Because the Federal Relief Administration had eliminated subsidies to private agencies for cash relief, a huge proportion of the private agency clientele was shifted to public relief roles. The general public, however, was unwilling to support casework service as part of public relief administration. Hence, public agencies turned to the private sector for such services. Swift favored this pattern of simultaneous service, and urged that it be more widely instituted, saying that private agencies should not duplicate but "supplement" public programs. He called for patterns of public-private services that were:

> . . . not mutually exclusive, but . . . related: thus the adequate administration of relief requires [private agency] case work in some of its aspects: good case work in some situations requires relief resources, and so on. And all these elements in our community program grow out of two basic needs: (1) the necessities of life for individuals in distress, and (2) attention to other handicaps, within the individual or his environment, which hamper his capacity for social self-expression (46, p. 18).

This division of labor—that is, private agency supplementation of public service—was, however, short-lived. As the pall of the depression lifted, many private-agency clients became economically independent, with the result that the private agency no longer felt constrained to integrate its program with the public agency. A new conception of private casework began to emerge—one heavily dominated by psychological conceptions of family problems. It tended to eschew the importance of environmental approaches (housing, employment, medical, and other concrete environmental services), leaving responsibility for them to public agencies, despite an awareness that the public programs were inadequate for the task. The private agency began to limit its responsibility for poor people to conducting studies and to giving expert testimony about the current needs of welfare recipients. Now, three decades later, even this "social reform" function often has little priority in the private agency. Jean Rubin (45), of the Public Issues Committee of Family Service Association of America, recently commented on the difficulty of securing the interest of private-agency staff members in issues such as public welfare, equality of opportunity, and other matters which most affect the poor:

> We hope these memoranda and materials [on problems of the poor] circulate among the staff . . . [of constituent agencies], but we have no control over what happens once they have left our mail room. I must confess that I sometimes feel as though I was putting a message in a bottle and launching it upon the high seas (45, p. 7).

There is no question that it is appropriate for private agencies to help the poor make use of public services: only in the public sector are the necessary economic resources available to meet income-maintenance needs. However, many low-income people who have been referred have had a variety of problems extending beyond income maintenance (e.g., housing, health, employment). Who was to help with these problems? As we have noted, one possibility was that the private agency would define its role as giving continuing service *concurrent* with referral to a public assistance program. But this happened only for a short time during the depression itself.

What is the evidence revealing the current lack of simultaneous service? First, we have noted that private agencies now refer a great many low-income clients to public agencies. This finding by itself might suggest merely a recognition that the public agency is far better able to meet the income-maintenance needs of the poor. However, it should be stressed that the early termination of contact does not occur because private agencies believe the poor to be without troubles beyond those of income maintenance. "Clearly," Beck observes, "lower-class clients are somewhat more likely than upper-class ones to have an overwhelmingly large number of problems" (33, p. 28). Nevertheless, disengagement from the poor, as the FSAA study makes clear, "occurs *even though lower-class clients have somewhat more problems and cases with more problems generally receive more interviews*. It also occurs in a setting where inability to pay for service is no deterrent to treatment" (33, p. 33, emphasis added).

Second, these early closings are not at the initiative of the poor. The wealthy are the clients most likely to decide when contact should be discontinued. Where the poor are concerned, it is the agency which plan-fully disengages from the relationship. Here, again, the findings from the Family Service Association of America comprehensive survey should be pondered:

> Except for the top class, closings at client initiative dropped as social class declined. In the upper middle class, nearly six cases in ten took the initiative in terminating in contrast to only one in three of the lowest group. Closings at worker initiative, while unusual at any level, were more than twice as frequent at the lowest level than at any other (33, p. 35).

Referrals to public agencies preclude the necessity of dealing directly with the difficult reality problems which the poor bring to their doors. In the private-agency sector, closing a case after the first or second inter-view is one of the chief ways in which the poor are disengaged. Such closings are typically defined as "consultations" or "referrals." If the for-mer, the case record will usually show that the client was "inaccessible to treatment" or held "unrealistic expectations of the agency's services." Of course, a more effective way of terminating services is to pass the client on to another agency, for the client who is being referred is likely to believe that he is being served rather than simply disengaged, and potential resentment is thus drained off. Such referrals, as we noted, are typically made to public agencies, chiefly to public assistance agencies. As a consequence, the public agencies frequently stagger under virtually unmanageable burdens. Private residential treatment institutions for juve-nile delinquents, having made "errors" in intake, "pass on" their difficult cases to the public training schools; settlements and community agencies arrange to have public detached street workers assigned to the more diffi-cult juvenile gangs; family agencies abandon so-called multiproblem families to welfare departments; private hospitals shrug off the chron-ically ill patients to the back wards of publicly supported custodial hos-pitals. Thus the public programs have tended to become the repository for the poor; private agencies have abandoned the neediest segment of society as their chief target.

WHY THE DISENGAGEMENT FROM THE POOR?

How has this situation come to be? Why have private agencies become disengaged from the poor, as we contend they have?

The private agency, we suggest, did not respond to the development of public programs by defining a new role with respect to its traditional clientele, the poor; instead, it moved toward a new clientele, economi-cally more fortunate than the old. At the same time, a new conception of the private agency began to emerge.

Historically, the field of social welfare has been concerned with social problems arising from large-scale immigration, difficulties in the integration of age and sex roles, massive changes in the occupational structure, the unequal distribution of social and economic opportunities, and the like. Social-welfare institutions arose to ease the disturbances produced in the lives of people by these societal dislocations.

At a given time, of course, there are limitations in the resources to help people, which the society makes available through agencies and other institutional systems. Hence, choices must be made about which problems will be tackled and which will be shelved or ignored. The field of social welfare has generally been guided by the principle that its scarce resources should be allocated for the solution of problems that the people involved cannot be expected to solve for themselves, either because they lack the objective social resources—money, power, etc.—to overcome their problems, or because they have become incapable of resolving their difficulties without organized assistance as a result of their prolonged exposure to destructive social forces and their inability to purchase remedial help. These conditions obviously describe the poor, the powerless, and the dispossessed in the society.

The historic decision to give service to low-income people was not based on a belief that middle-income people could not use social services or had no problems. It was based on the conviction that help should be given where the problems are greatest and the capacity to overcome them least. The point is that the many problems common to all groups in an industrial society are considerably more severe when coupled with extreme and prolonged economic deprivation. Whether the problem in question arises from adolescence, aging, physical disabilities, or any other source, great material deprivation overshadows and worsens it.

In recent years, the profession of social work has been retreating from this position. The literature abounds in statements stressing the private agency's potential for service to all persons, regardless of class, and alluding to the "new mission of private-agency casework." To the extent that it is achieving a representative cross section of clientele, it is said, the family agency is meeting its true purpose—to serve the community as a whole—and thus is becoming a genuine "community agency." There is no discrimination in such an agency against rich or poor. Those who question whether the field of social work ought to be serving the middle- and upper-income groups are told that these groups also have problems, that they too need help, and that social work needs to overcome its historic preoccupation with one class of clientele and give all those in need the benefit of its professional technology. Egalitarianism, in short, has become the guiding ideology of private agencies.

To account for changes such as these in private agencies—whether in ideology or in clientele—it is not sufficient to point to the emergence of massive public programs designed to deal with the problem of poverty. Great economic deprivation and associated problems remained then and remain now. The shift away from the poor has been concomitant, for example, with the migration to urban centers of extraordinary numbers of economically distressed rural Negroes. It hardly needs to be noted that such movements bring with them enormous problems of hardship and adjustment. There was, and still is, ample opportunity for private agencies to continue programs of financial assistance for many emergency situations, for supplementation of inadequate public-assistance grants, and for other purposes. There was, and is, ample opportunity for private agencies to concentrate their resources on problems experienced by the poor which are not dealt with adequately in public programs, especially in such spheres as medical care, homemaking, housing, and employment. Private agencies were dislocated by the emergence of public programs, to be sure; but they still had the option of developing new roles in work with their traditional clientele. The fact that these agencies have increasingly turned away from the poor and have attempted to persuade the public that their services should be used by *all* economic groups cannot, therefore, be explained on the basis of the development of broad public-welfare programs.

PROFESSIONAL STATUS AND THE SELECTION
OF CLIENTELE

Strains in the occupational status of social work have doubtless exerted an influence on the intake policies of private agencies. The community has been niggardly in allocating professional status to social workers—a circumstance customarily attributed to the presumed lack of a coherent body of social-work knowledge, to the presumed lack of distinctive social-work technology, and to other presumed deficiencies in the field of social work.

But the status of any profession is, to an important extent, a function of the status of its clientele, whether that clientele is defined in terms of age, sex, socioeconomic level, or other factors. The dilemma of social workers, like that of, for example, criminal lawyers, is that there is little prestige to be derived from serving groups in the society which are generally defined as lacking moral virtue, ambition, self-reliance, and dignity—indeed, groups which are often viewed as being composed of "free-loaders" and "chiselers." In effect, the brush which tars social work's clients also tars social workers. The prestige of the public-welfare worker is probably lowest among social workers, only a notch above that of his clients on the dole. Thus the image lingers that social workers are soft-headed, sentimental, and "overhumanitarian"—and all this chiefly because of their ostensible concern with the poor.

The field has not been unresponsive to these occupational strains. They are a source of pressures toward private practice, toward "clinical" doctorates, and toward professional and legal certification. These same strains have led to marked status distinctions among types of casework and group-work practice—chiefly between traditional practices and the growing body of therapeutic practices, such as psychiatric social work and group therapy. One caseworker has commented on this tendency as follows:

> The high status in the casework hierarchy of the agency offering counseling services to clients with emotional problems as against the status of the agency supposedly geared to tangible [i.e., concrete] services should give us pause to reflect on the priorities which casework is setting for itself (48, p. 25).

Thus the search for prestige may have led social workers to upgrade their clientele by socioeconomic position. The price of prestige may well be abandonment of the poor.

SOCIAL-WORK TECHNOLOGY AND CULTURE CONFLICT

Social-work technology arose from essentially middle-class conceptions of the universe, and is generally practiced by persons identified with these conceptions. Among low-income groups, however, value patterns arise which are adaptive to poverty. Thus a situation of culture conflict exists, mainly along social-class lines, which permeates contacts between agencies and low-income people. Conflicting cultural values generate strains between client and worker, leading progressively to dissociation if not to estrangement. Culture conflict, in other words, is probably one of the chief mechanisms producing disengagement from the poor. This is not a new idea, although professional thinking has yet to feel its full force. Several years ago, a caseworker put the point as follows:

> The predominantly middle-class identification of the present-day social worker has . . . made him less able to appreciate the client different from himself, whether this difference is culturally based or lies in the different ego capacity of the client. . . . We look for and expect to find in the client's attitude and behavior those norms and deviations that are characteristic of the middle-class society we know, making surprisingly little allowance for different cultural and social orientation. . . . The increasing social and cultural distance between middle-class worker and "other class" clients fosters a communication problem which should be of genuine concern to social work (48, pp. 24–25).

But social agencies have always been dominated by middle-class values. How, then, can a force that has presumably remained constant be invoked to account for the changes in agency ideology and clientele which we have documented? The answer is that the current bases for determining the appropriateness of serving particular groups of clients and judging their receptivity to the services being offered differ substantially from those of earlier eras. Furthermore, the structuring of relationships between agency representatives and clientele has changed greatly. Together, these two changes have enormously intensified a long-standing culture conflict, making it more evident and more irritating. These changes, we contend, account in large measure for the current disengagement from the poor.

The chief manifestation of these changes is in the development of psychologically based, therapeutically oriented casework technology. If, in an earlier era, the field revealed its middle-class biases in its tendency to discriminate between the morally worthy and unworthy poor, it now exhibits these biases in its tendency to discriminate between the psychologically "accessible" and "inaccessible" poor. The field has substituted middle-class mental-hygiene bases of evaluation for the traditional middle-class moral bases (47). Furthermore, the new technology calls for a strategy of help which requires intense interaction between caseworker and client. Concrete services, offered on a relatively routine basis, were once a sufficient attraction to overcome strains arising from a morally based culture conflict; now this inducement is largely gone. At the same time, the intimate, prolonged, and intensely personal character of the new therapeutic casework sharply reveals the differences between caseworkers and low-income people with respect to value orientations. The more deeply caseworkers and low-income people become engaged with one another, the more clearly are these differences revealed. Strains in relationships are the result.

Culture Conflict and Barriers to Treatment

Strong evidence for the argument being made here can be found in the statistics on those selected for continuing treatment from among those who apply for service. If culture conflict is operating, we should find that lower-class clients are selectively screened out.

Coleman, for example, compared the selection of applicants for treatment in a clinic and in a family agency. He found

> . . . no significant differences in the distribution and severity of psychiatric diagnoses in the two agencies. It is important to note, however, that Class V [lowest] patients, regardless of diagnosis, tended to receive less favorable consideration for continued treatment in the clinic, and also in Family Service although to a smaller extent. A surprising, and at this point unexplained, finding was the high rejection rate of Class IV applicants in the family agency (34, p. 79).

We might also expect to find that more lower-class applicants are assigned to waiting lists, as a means of disposing of them short of outright rejection. As it happens, the reverse is true, but this exception to our prediction—Beck to the contrary—unexpectedly serves to buttress the main argument. The FSAA study shows that upper-class persons are most likely to be assigned to waiting lists ["thirty-two percent of the highest class were placed on a waiting list, but only 11 percent of the lowest" (33, p. 32)]. Beck concludes from this finding that the poor are actually being given priority in service:

> The explanation for this seemingly odd finding lies first in the relatively high proportion of lower-class cases involving emergency situations where delay cannot be tolerated. In the second place, many more are referred immediately to public agencies because of their need for financial assistance. It is, therefore, the upper-class families with marital and parent-child problems in their early stages, when casework can be most effective, that most often have to wait for continued treatment. There is certainly no evidence that agencies are favoring upper-clients because they can pay fees (33, p. 32).

To infer that the rich are actually being discriminated against from the fact that they must frequently wait for continued treatment is a marvelous bit of social rationalization because the truth is that low-income applicants are less likely to get continued treatment whether they wait or not. The FSAA report notes, "In general, the average number of interviews decreases as social-class status declines. . . . The drop is from an average of nearly eleven interviews per case in the top class to less than six for the lowest" (33, p. 33). The poor, in other words, are not placed on waiting lists as often as the wealthy, partly because they do not receive continued service as often or as long as the higher classes. Their cases are quickly disposed of without simultaneous continuation of treatment. Placing clients on waiting lists has the effect, whether intended or not, of favoring the wealthy over the poor in access to continued service.

In the Milwaukee Family Service *Study of Continued Treatment Service Cases*, "seventy-five percent [of the 200 cases studied] were in the middle or lower-middle class. The former includes small proprietors, white-collar people and semi-skilled workers. The remaining 25 percent is split between . . . the upper-middle class and the lower class" (39, p. 2). In other words, only 12 percent of the total cases in treatment were drawn from the lower class.

That these selective tendencies are not accidental is suggested by the Milwaukee study, for "the social class of the client seems to affect casework evaluation, diagnosis and prognosis. The worker's judgment of

Table 1 *Distribution of Children Offered Treatment, by Family Income*

Income Structure	Accepted for Treatment (%)	Applicants (%)
High	47.3	29.5
Middle	27.7	33.0
Low	25.0	37.5

Source. Sylvia Stevens, "An Ecological Study of Child Guidance Intake," *Smith College Studies in Social Work,* XXV, 1 (Oct. 1954), p. 82.

treatability becomes increasingly pessimistic as we move from upper-middle class clients to lower-class clients" (39, p. 3).

It should be pointed out that the tendency to select higher-income people for continuing treatment is not limited to private agencies. It has also been noted in public agencies in which the decision to treat is discretionary with treatment personnel. In 1954, to take one illustration, a study was published by the Institute for Juvenile Research, a tax-supported child-guidance clinic available at no cost to all residents of Illinois. Like many of the studies of intake cited earlier, the IJR study shows that a representative cross section of the total population applies for service. However, the characteristics of those who actually receive treatment are far from representative (see Table 1). On the basis of these data, the IJR study concludes, "even though income level . . . [does] not affect intake, [it influences] the probability of entering treatment" (50, p. 82). This evidence strongly suggests that the disengagement from the poor by private agencies may be caused, not by the division of labor between public and private agencies, but by something in the nature of professional technology that exerts pressure for disengagement *whatever the setting.*

Conflicting Definitions of Problems and Solutions

The decision to offer continued treatment probably depends upon a judgment by the agency that the client is accessible, amenable, or otherwise suited to make use of a highly structured casework relationship. This decision appears to be greatly influenced by the class of the client, as we have shown. The direct correlation between social class and chances of receiving continued treatment can probably be explained, in turn, by class differences in socialization. In general, the higher his social class, the more likely it is that the client will exhibit values which, in the judgment of agencies, are congenial to a casework relationship. This decision thus reflects a fundamental class-based culture conflict.

As might be expected, clients from different social classes hold rather different definitions of their problems and the appropriate solutions to them. Maas, for example, concluded from his studies that:

> The managerial and professional workers or college-educated parents tended to expect the "mother-father-child" approach. The white-collar workers tended to expect the "mother-and-child" approach. The skilled, semiskilled, and unskilled workers and "high school and below"-educated parents tended to expect a "child-only" approach (43, p. 68).

In these and other respects, social classes have been found to differ in orientation.

The chief point to be made about such differences is that the typical agency exhibits a point of view which accords more with the view prevailing in the middle and upper classes than with that characteristic of the lower classes. The lower-class emphasis on a "child-only" approach is least congenial with current casework thinking. In this vein, Beck reports:

> Agreement on the principal problem in the first interview dropped from 64 percent in the upper three class groups to 52 percent in the lowest. Agreement on the principal problem was relatively frequent when the problem was in the family relationship area or in such obvious situations as old age, physical illness or handicap, or unmarried parenthood. Worker agreement was low when the client saw the principal problem as one of employment or the personality adjustment of a child (33, p. 30).

The increasing tendency of private agencies to define client-problem priorities in heavily psychological terms has been accompanied by a reduction in the amount of agency resources allocated to the provision of concrete services. But low-income clients are buffeted by many environmental problems, they define their problems in concrete terms, and thus they seek concrete remedies. Hence a broad area of conflict exists which has been noted in several studies.

The FSAA study dramatically documents the lack of congruence between the expectations of agencies held by low-income clients and the actual services offered:

> In general, client requests do not match closely the services offered. Casework service, which is the core service of Family Agencies, is requested by 86 percent of the top class but only 55 percent of the lowest. Perhaps it is hard for a lower-class applicant to conceive of being helped merely by a talking process. Requests for financial assistance follow the reverse pattern and rise steeply as social class declines. Even though few agencies any longer give any substantial amount of financial assistance, 31 percent of the applicants from the lower class still ask for such aid (33, p. 31).

Lower-class people also ask for more help in a variety of other reality areas, including "physical illness or handicap, substitute care of children, housing, old age, etc." (33, p. 29). When Beck compared worker-client agreement levels on all problems, not just on the principal problem, the following results were obtained:

> Agreement on all problems dropped from 49 percent to 34 percent as social class declined. In the areas of family relationship and individual personality problems, workers reported one or more problems in many instances where no corresponding client concern was noted. As social class declined, discrepancies of this type became progressively more frequent. Apparently lower-class clients are less prone than others to define their problems in these terms. Instead they are accustomed to seek solutions through some type of environmental change or concrete service (33, p. 30).

The FSAA report goes on to observe:

> These marked differences between client expectations and the services actually provided pose a real problem for agencies, particularly in relation to services to the lower-class groups (33, p. 31).

These and similar statements in other research reports are extraordinary for several reasons. For one thing, they speak of social casework as a thing apart from concrete services; casework appears to have become a "talking process" in many agencies. Second, the very tentativeness of conclusions about the importance of concrete services in helping the poor bespeaks an unfamiliarity with the problems of people in poverty that is remarkable in a field which has made the elimination of poverty and its consequences one of its central aims.

The tendency of low-income clients to view their problems and the solutions to them in terms of concrete services appears to be an important basis for refusing continued service to them. In a study of 295 initial telephone contacts in 12 family service agencies (where there was no previous information about the callers), it was found that applications focused on problems of family relations were more likely to be made cases than any others (85%). Applications centered on personality problems, old age or physical illness, or substitute care of children were also likely to be made cases. Of the sizable group of applications in which economic problems were central (and these are most likely to be lower-class persons), only 65 percent were made intake cases (37, p. 8).

Ann Shyne, summarizing the results of a number of studies of continuing treatment, lists four factors associated with continuance and four associated with early termination:

Associated with continuance beyond a single interview were: (1) a request by the client for help with problems primarily of a psychological or interpersonal nature; (2) favorable response by the client to the worker's proposal for solution or treatment of the basic problem: (3) indication by the client that he saw the worker as a source of help in working through his own thoughts and feelings about the problem; and (4) movement forward during the interview in acceptance of the worker in a counseling role. Conversely, associated with termination after one interview were: (1) a request for help with problems of other than a psychological or interpersonal nature; (2) noncommittal or negative response to the worker's proposal for solution; (3) a conception of the worker as a source of concrete service; and (4) failure to move forward in accepting the worker in a counseling role (49, p. 225).

The chief point is that conflicting definitions of problems and solutions lead to strains in the relationship between social workers and low-income clients. As a consequence, disengagement occurs—disengagement by workers because they probably do not feel that clients can make effective use of service, and disengagement by clients because they probably do not feel that available services have a significant bearing upon the resolution of their problems.

The general conditions of life among the lower classes tend to produce modes of family structure, sex-role differentiation, values, language forms, ways of relating to one another, and the like, which differ significantly from the more familiar and widely diffused patterns of middle-class life. In particular, the poor people focus on the problem of survival, not because they are personally deficient, but because that is precisely the problem facing them. They often find incomprehensible the belief that natural and social forces can be harnessed and controlled, precisely because the experience of their lives—as contrasted with the lives of middle-class people—tells them that such pressures can only be endured. If their life conditions change—if their opportunities are enlarged—their values will change. But, meanwhile, they will adopt patterns of values and behavior which enable them to adjust, to accommodate in a reasonable fashion to their particular conditions of life. In this connection, Coleman notes:

> It is known to clinicians that psychological self-concern is in a sense a social luxury; that is, that it is dependent on the presence of a certain minimum of material and external security. In the presence of real, excessive deprivations and threats, the individual knows only one imperative, and that is to find ways of obtaining basic supplies and of escaping danger—of protecting himself against the bombardment of external stimuli (34, p. 3).

In short, many low-income people probably regard as impractical the notion that a person in trouble can improve his circumstances through a better understanding of himself and the way in which he presumably contributes to his own problems. Members of this group value skills in coping with deprivation and uncertainty. They lack or do not value the personality attributes and skills required to make effective use of social-work technology—introspection, insight, verbal facility, and the capacity to use formalized, professional relationships. Such skills are much more likely to be the product of middle-class socialization. Thus, in many ways, of which the field has not been sufficiently mindful, casework technology has become class-bound.

These are the terms, then, in which we account for the current disengagement from the poor by private agencies. In addition to status pressures, we suggest that the chief source of this disengagement is a culturally inflexible psychiatric technology. The private-agency field, having developed a new conception of casework, seeks out a clientele who can make use of it. Hence it moves toward those whose socialization is compatible with the new technology—the middle class. The field may know how to deal differentially with various types of small group or various types of personality dysfunction, but it does not know how to deal with people who have not been prepared in advance to use its technology. Coleman, commenting on the high percentage of cases in the lowest class group that were closed at intake singles out as ". . . the most important factor . . . the attitudes of therapists toward their patients . . ." (34, p. 79).

> When a patient does not respond to the characteristic procedures that the therapist has learned to use in introducing him to the therapeutic situation, the tendency seems to be to react to the patient with indifference or veiled hostility and rejection, rather than to question the procedures. A person is apparently expected to meet certain requirements before he will receive approval as a patient. He must recognize that he has a problem relevant to the interest of the agency, that he is concerned about it and that he wants the kind of help the therapist is interested in giving him; furthermore, he must recognize the therapist's authority without its being explicitly imposed upon him. He must be prepared in a sense to do what the therapist wants him to do without having to be told what is expected. . . . In dealing with a great many patients, we shall be clearly at an impasse if we evaluate treatability by the extent to which a patient is able to comply with largely unverbalized requirements, derived from [middle class] sociocultural and educational experience (34, p. 79).

To help lower-class people, social work must construct a strategy of service which grows out of their patterned ways of understanding, perceiving, and grappling with the realities of their lives. A not-inconsiderable literature now exists which describes the life styles of low-income people. In order to reverse the movement away from the poor by private casework agencies, these findings must be used systematically in the revision of problem classifications, the modification of service strategies, and the development of a different pattern of relations between the private and public sectors.

CONSERVATIVE EXPLANATIONS OF THE DISENGAGEMENT FROM THE POOR

It is characteristic of human societies that social problems of various kinds are defined as resulting, not from institutional inadequacies, but from the presumed moral, social, or psychological defects of the people implicated in those problems. To the extent that these definitions are successfully imposed, criticism is deflected from the social order and support is mobilized for the maintenance of the existing system of social arrangements. Hence such definitions are essentially conservative; they tend to preserve the institutional *status quo*. Social-welfare institutions are not exempt from this general tendency.

That a general disengagement from the poor has occurred in the private-welfare sector seems clear. If our analysis has any merit, at least some of the reasons for this disengagement are to be found in various agency practices, such as the decline in emphasis on concrete service and the increasing use of psychotherapeutic techniques, with all that this has meant for intensified culture conflict. But how is the problem of disengagement usually defined? How do agencies typically explain their failure to work effectively with the poor?

For the most part, the field has been content to assume that the sources of the problem reside with the poor themselves. It says that they are "hard to reach"—a definition of the situation which has become extremely popular in recent years. To illustrate this tendency, let us cite some common explanations for disengagement.

A frequently advanced explanation is that the poor generally lack awareness of their problems and of the ways in which professional help can be used to overcome them. For this reason, presumably, they do not seek help. In the Berkeley study, an effort was made to determine whether a relationship exists between social class and awareness of problems. Respondents from residential areas of varying economic characteristics were asked whether they knew of anyone who had problems in the following spheres: marital relationships, emotionally disturbed children, child care, well-baby care, medical care, and use of leisure time. The study findings indicate:

> Although the lower socioeconomic tracts . . . appear to have the highest incidence of problems, there is no greater awareness of problems by persons of low socioeconomic status . . . (44, p. 38).

Wolins draws two "possible conclusions . . . from the noncorrespondence of problem volume . . . and the population's awareness of problems." He notes:

> First, problem rates comprising the social breakdown index are taken from sources which may be more likely to register problems of persons of lower socio-economic status than of higher status. Higher status may, in other words, be a deterrent to an individual's having a problem or attaining recognition as a problem carrier. . . . Secondly, if the first conclusion is a false one and problems are fully reflected in the breakdown statistics, then the lower socio-economic person is less aware of the problems which surround him and/or less likely to express awareness (44, p. 39).

There is, of course, a further possibility. What people come to define as problems may have something to do with their life conditions. Had the classification of problems to which people were asked to respond included unemployment, inadequate housing, and the like, it is possible that low-income people would have expressed greater awareness than other people in their community. Indeed, the studies previously cited make it abundantly clear that the chief problem that the private agency encounters in dealing with low-income people stems from their persistence in making, as the FSAA study puts it, "inappropriate requests . . . for direct service"—which is to say, requests for help with a multitude of concrete reality problems of which they are apparently very much aware (33, p. 34).

Another common explanation is that the poor are so unsophisticated in regard to mental hygiene that they do not seek or effectively use casework services. The FSAA study suggests:

> Probably people who have had the advantage of extended education appreciate more than do those of limited background the importance of seeking professional help on personal and family problems. They may likewise find it a little easier to formulate and explain their problems verbally to a caseworker (33, p. 9).

The Institute of Juvenile Research study takes a similar view of the poor: among low-income groups "the chief concern . . . is with economic well-being and, because of this 'practical-mindedness,' emotional problems are often overlooked" (50, p. 81). But perhaps it is not so much that the poor tend to overlook emotional problems in their inappropriate preoccupation with environmental problems as it is that practitioners tend inappropriately to define the environmental problems of the poor in psychological terms. Differing life conditions produce differing values and patterns of behavior. And such differences, when they are exhibited by people low in a system of social classes, will be regarded as moral or psychological or social defects. Low-income people, for example, often tend to make external attributions of causality—to believe that the difficulties which afflict them are the consequence of outside forces and pressures. Middle-class people, by contrast, are more likely to attribute causality to inner forces. Persons who exhibit the latter value orientation are usually defined by agency workers as psychologically conforming. In particular, agency workers define as "projecting" those who voice a belief that problems of living are generated by arbitrary and capricious external forces. Referring to clients who received only one interview, the bulk of whom were in the lower class, Ann Shyne writes:

> It was found that an overwhelming proportion phrased their problems in terms of the need of another family member or a tangible need, with little more than one in ten phrasing their requests in terms of difficulties in interpersonal relations, although most of the requests were considered [by caseworkers] to stem from problems in family living. This corroborates the [findings of other studies] of a predominance of attitudes of "projection" among one-interview cases (49, p. 225).

To say that lower-class clients "project" is, in effect, to call individual personality into question as an explanation of widespread disengagement. Thus the Milwaukee study reports:

> A continuous increase in the proportion of clients who are [defined by caseworkers as] rejecting, resistant, and evasive as we move from the upper-middle class to the lower class. Of those who are receptive, there is also a continuous increase in the number who are not strongly motivated [as defined by caseworkers] (39, p. 3).

Aside from the pervasive culture conflict to which we have pointed, and which is frequently misinterpreted as representing resistance and evasion, there may be other socially structured sources of strain between private-agency workers and low-income clients. For example, the way in which a person gets to a social agency—whether voluntarily or under duress—undoubtedly is an important determinant of his initial attitudes toward the agency. His attitudes may therefore reveal less about the individual's basic capacity to use agency services than about the processes by which he was led to the intake interview. We may ask, then, how clients are recruited and what consequences different recruitment patterns have for attitudes and expectations. In the FSAA study, the following class differences in recruitment were identified:

To the surprise of many, those coming because they had found the agency listed in the phone book were highest in social status. Those referred by private physicians and psychiatrists ranked second in this respect. Probably upper-class adults are more accustomed than others to locating help on their own initiative either through use of directories or through consultation with the medical profession. Clients coming because of what they had seen or heard through the mass media were predominantly from the middle or lower-middle-class groups. So also were those referred or steered to family agencies by other community organizations, such as schools, churches, and social and health agencies of other types. Over half of those coming on the informal advice of friends or relatives, on the other hand, were from the lower class. About three in four of those sent by lawyers, courts, police, and parole officers were from this same group (33, p. 27).

Concerning the relationship between occupational status and source of referral, the Maas study indicates that:

Self-referrals [to the New York agencies studied] tend to be more frequent than expected in the two higher occupational statuses and less frequent in the two lower occupational statuses; upper-occupational-status families who are medically referred tend to come through a private physician, and lower-occupational-status families, through hospitals and clinics; and court referrals tend to be less frequent in the two higher occupational statuses and more frequent in the two lower occupational statuses. The San Francisco data on occupational status and referral source reveal a comparably significant relationship. Again one finds that self-referrals and referrals by private physicians, hospital clinics, and courts, as well as social agencies, offer families in different occupational statuses somewhat different routes for entry to the clinic (43, pp. 51–52).

Sylvia Stevens, in her study of child-guidance intake in Chicago, also directs attention to this area. She presents data on the sources of referral to different agencies by social class (Table 2). Stevens then concludes

. . . the lower-income group has a disproportionately higher number of referrals from the Juvenile Court, social agencies and the schools, while the upper groups have a disproportionately higher number from private doctors and self-referrals. This would tend to verify the prediction that the upper-class groups are more sophisticated in regard to mental hygiene and utilize available resources voluntarily, while the lower class tend to come to the clinic because of pressure from social institutions. It may therefore be concluded that referral source of the clinic's intake is influenced by income level of neighborhood residence (50, p. 80).

Two points should be made about such findings. First, the resistance and suspicion ostensibly felt by involuntary "lower-class" recruits may

Table 2 *Class Distribution of Intake, by Referral Source*

| | Class of Client | | | |
Referral Source	Low (%)	Middle (%)	High (%)	Total Referrals (%)
Juvenile Court	45.8	33.4	20.8	12.0
Social agencies	49.0	27.4	23.6	27.5
School	48.4	24.3	27.3	16.5
Private doctor	26.3	39.5	34.2	19.0
Self	22.0	40.0	38.0	25.0
All referrals	37.5	33.0	29.5	100.0

Source. Sylvia Stevens, "An Ecological Study of Child Guidance Intake," *Smith College Studies in Social Work,* XXV, 1 (Oct. 1954), p. 80.

have a great deal of basis in reality, since the public agencies of social control (police, courts, etc.) are not noted for their humane and dignified treatment of low-income people. Failure to take the institutional sources of resistance and suspicion into account may lead to invidious definitions of the low-income client as hostile. Second, it is methodologically inappropriate to draw conclusions about the lower-class client, as such, when we are obviously dealing with two rather different groups—those who are in difficulty with the agencies of social control, and those who are not. Findings about lower-class attitudes toward agencies would be much more useful if they were controlled by voluntary or involuntary character of referral.

These are some of the terms, then, in which the current disengagement from the poor is being defined in the private sector. As this disengagement has progressed, a category of persons has been created to whom the field invidiously refers as the "hard-to-reach." But we might also consider whether the problem is not, at least in part, one of "hard-to-reach services"—of a structured incapacity on the part of contemporary agencies to give effective service to the poor. It is all too easy to blame failures in service upon the apparent intractability, recalcitrance, apathy, resistance, or lack of sophistication of the low-income client, when in fact the poor are not necessarily any less capable of being helped than are other groups in the social structure. As one caseworker has said, we "have hidden too long behind the facade of 'client failure' in the problem cases where we have been unsuccessful. . . . We have assumed that our failures were inevitable and have excused ourselves from looking at our contributions to them" (48, p. 29). The problem may be that the field has increasingly developed a strategy of help which is neither practicable for nor congenial to the needs and interests of the low-income person. It should be remembered that the so-called multiproblem family is fundamentally a multideprived family, and the difference in connotation is of no small consequence. Indeed, the multideprived family is all the more deprived because it is denied effective and meaningful service by those in the private sector who speak in its name. If this is true, and it appears to be, there is great cause for concern.

BIBLIOGRAPHICAL REFERENCES

The Trend Away from the Poor

1900–1933

1. Brandt, Lillian, *Charity Organization Society of the City of New York, 1882–1907*, New York: Charity Organization Society, n.d.
2. Brandt, Lillian, *Growth and Development of A.I.C.P. and C.O.S.*, Report to the Committee on the Institute of Welfare Research, New York: Community Service Society of New York, 1942.
3. Rich, Margaret, *A Belief in People*, New York: Family Service Association of America, 1956.

1933–1941

4. Benjamin, Julian E., *Family Life and National Recovery*, New York: Family Welfare Association of America, 1935.
5. Bennett, Ruth, "A Study of Intake in the Family Welfare Society," *Smith College Studies in Social Work*, VII, 2 (Dec. 1936), pp. 135–136.
6. Brown, Maxine, "A Study of Intake in a Family Agency," *Smith College Studies in Social Work*, VIII, 2 (Dec. 1937), pp. 146–147.
7. Cadbury, Olive, *Social Work in Seattle*, Seattle, Wash.: University of Washington Press, 1935.
8. Family Service Association of Wheeling, W. Va., *Intake Study*, Oct. 1938.
9. Family Society of Philadelphia, Pa., *Review of Applicants to the Family Society of Philadelphia*, Nov. 1937.
10. Family Welfare Association of America, *Family Social Work in a Changing World*, New York, mimeo., 1934.
11. Family Welfare Association of Baltimore, Md., *Study of Intake*, Feb. 1934.
12. Family Welfare Association of Springfield, Mass., *Intake Report*, Nov. 1938.
13. Glover, Elizabeth, and Elizabeth Lourder, "A Comparison of the Cases Active with the Family Service Society of Richmond, Va., in 1928 and 1935," *Smith College Studies in Social Work*, VII, 2 (Dec. 1936), p. 139.
14. Hurlin, Ralph B., *Statistics of Family Caseworker Operation*, New York: Russell Sage Foundation, 1938.
15. Hurevich, Miriam, *Studies on Intake*, New York: Jewish Social Service Association of New York, mimeo., Jan. 1937.
16. Intercity Conference of Pennsylvania, *Report of the Special Committee*, Feb. 1937.
17. Klein, Philip, *Social Survey of Pittsburgh*, New York: Columbia University Press, 1938.
18. Lander, Flora, *Analysis of the Applications to the Family Welfare Association of Peoria for the Months of October and November 1938*, Peoria, Ill.: Family Welfare Association of Peoria, Nov. 1938.

19. Patch, Helen, "Trends in Intake and Service in a Family Agency," *Smith College Studies in Social Work*, XV, 2 (Dec. 1944), pp. 153–154.
20. St. Louis, Mo., Provident Association, *Trends in the Volume of Service, January–June 1936*, n.d.
21. Waite, Florence T., *A Warm Friend for the Spirit*, Cleveland, Ohio: Family Service Association, 1960.
22. Witmer, Helen T., et al., "Current Practices in Intake and Service in Family Welfare Organizations," *Smith College Studies in Social Work*, VI, 2 (Dec. 1935), pp. 101–209.

1941–1950

23. Afflech, June F., "Applications Accepted by a Family Agency," *Smith College Studies in Social Work*, XX, 2 (Feb. 1950), pp. 134–135.
24. Albany Jewish Social Service, *The Jewish Communal Survey of Albany, New York*, 1946.
25. Blenkner, Margaret, J. McHunt, and L. Kogan, *A Study of Intake, Community Service Society of New York*, New York: Institute of Welfare Research, mimeo., 1950.
26. Cutler, Jean, "Trends in Intake and Service in a Family Agency," *Smith College Studies in Social Work*, XVI, 2 (Feb. 1946), pp. 144–145.
27. Emery, Marian, *Intake Study*, Indianapolis, Ind.: Family Welfare Service of Indianapolis, August 1963.
28. Jones, Catherine, "The Role of Relief in a Private Agency," *Smith College Studies in Social Work*, XVI, 2 (Feb. 1946), pp. 147–149.
29. Keller, Helen Hafner, *The Relationship Between Length of Contact and Presenting Problem in a Family Service Agency*, Unpublished Master's Thesis, University of Michigan School of Social Work, 1952.
30. Milwaukee Family Service, chart entitled "Compiled Statistics on Intake and Application 1939–1940 through 1946–1947," n.d.
31. United Charities of Chicago, *Report of Situations for 1941, A Study of Intake in the Family Service Bureau of Chicago, Ill.*, 1941.
32. Wilmington, Del., Family Service, *Intake Study, Oct. 1945–Dec. 1946*, n.d.

1950–1960

33. Beck, Dorothy Fahs, *Patterns in the Use of Family Agency Service*, New York: Family Service Association of America, 1962.
34. Coleman, J., Ruth Janowicz, S. Fleck, and Nea Norton, "A Comparative Study of a Psychiatric Clinic and a Family Agency," *Social Casework*, XXXVIII, 1, 2 (Jan., Feb. 1957), pp. 3–8, 74–80.
35. Council of Social Agencies, Buffalo and Erie County, N.Y., *The Buffalo Self-Study of Social Adjustment Services*, Dec. 1957.
36. Eaton, Joseph W., "Whence and Whither Social Work? A Sociological Analysis," *Social Work* I, 1 (Jan. 1956), pp. 11–26.
37. Family Service Association of America, *Study of Telephone Interviews: Part II*, New York, 1955.
38. Family Service Association of Indianapolis, Ind., *Follow-up Study of Brief-Service Cases*, mimeo., 1955.
39. Family Service Association of Milwaukee, Wis., *Study of Continued Treatment Service Cases*, mimeo., Dec. 5, 1960.
40. Hollingshead, August B., *Elmtown's Youth: The Impact of Social Classes on Adolescents*, New York: John Wiley & Sons, 1949.
41. Hollingshead, August B., and F. C. Redlich, *Social Class and Mental Illness: A Community Study*, New York: John Wiley & Sons, 1958.

42. Hollingshead, August B., *Two Factor Index of Social Position*, New Haven, Conn.: A. B. Hollingshead, 1965 Yale Station, n.d.

43. Maas, Henry S., "Sociocultural Factors in Psychiatric Clinic Service for Children," *Smith College Studies in Social Work*, XXV, 2 (Feb. 1955), pp. 1–90.

44. Wolins, Martin, *Welfare Problems and Services in Berkeley, Calif.*, Berkeley Council of Social Welfare and School of Social Welfare, Nov. 1954.

The Public-Private Allocation of Clientele

45. Rubin, Jean, "The Caseworker's Role in Public Issues," speech given at *The Middle and North Atlantic Regional Institute*, Pocono Pines, Penn., June 10, 1964.

46. Swift, Linton B., *New Alignments Between Public and Private Agencies in a Community Family Welfare and Relief Program*, New York: Family Welfare Association of America, 1934.

Why the Disengagement from the Poor?

47. Davis, Kingsley, "Mental Hygiene and the Class Structure," *Psychiatry*, I, 1 (Feb. 1938), pp. 55–65.

48. Lindenberg, Ruth Ellen, "Hard to Reach: Client or Casework Agency?" *Social Work*, III, 4 (Oct. 1958), pp. 23–29.

49. Shyne, Ann W., "What Research Tells Us About Short-Term Cases in Family Agencies," *Social Casework*, XXXVIII, 5 (May 1957), pp. 223–231.

50. Stevens, Sylvia, "An Ecological Study of Child Guidance Intake," *Smith College Studies in Social Work*, XXV, 1 (Oct. 1954), pp. 73–84.

Organizing the Unaffiliated
in a Low-Income Area

George Brager

Community organization efforts generally have one of three broad objectives. In the first instance a substantive area of community change—

George Brager, "Organizing the Unaffiliated in a Low-Income Area," *Social Work*, April 1963, 8, pp. 34–40. This paper grew out of the author's experience as Director of Action Programs, Mobilization for Youth, Inc., New York, N.Y. Mobilization for Youth is an experimental action-research project in the field of juvenile delinquency prevention and control on the Lower East Side of Manhattan. Offering broad-scale services in the fields of employment, education, casework, group work, and community organization, it is supported by the National Institute of Mental Health, the President's Committee on Juvenile Delinquency, the Ford Foundation, and the City of New York.

a needed reform—is emphasized, as, for example, attention to housing needs and inequities. Another goal is the co-ordinated and orderly development of services, as evidenced in the planning of a welfare council. The third focuses upon citizenship involvement, regardless of the issues that engage citizen attention, in order to heighten community integration. These three goals are not necessarily mutually exclusive, although it may reasonably be argued that this is more true than is generally realized. In any event, programs that do not develop objectives in some order of priority risk diffuse and ineffective performance, as well as the impossibility of focused evaluation. There is, of course, some advantage in this nondefinition. One of the three arrows may hit *some* mark, and, in any case, one need not face up to his failures if he has not specified his goals.

An encompassing delinquency prevention effort may rightly concern itself with all three objectives, although perhaps to some degree different programs need to be devised to achieve different objectives. In order to sharpen this discussion, however, focus will be placed only upon issues relating to citizenship participation.

In a study of two lower-income neighborhoods of similar socioeconomic levels it was found that in the more integrated neighborhood (in which people knew their neighbors, perceived common interests, shared common viewpoints, and felt a part of the community) delinquency rates were markedly lower.[1] Participation by adults in decision-making about matters that affect their interests increases their sense of identification with the community and the larger social order. People who identify with their neighborhood and share common values are more likely to try to control juvenile misbehavior. A well-integrated community can provide learning experiences for adults that enable them to serve as more adequate models and interpreters of community life for the young. In short, participation in community-oriented organizations is highly desirable in delinquency reduction efforts.

A program must, however, involve significant numbers of representative lower-class persons.[2] Such an organization ought to enable what has been called the "effective community" of working-class youth—that is, the individuals, families, and groups with whom these youth interact and identify—to exert more positive influence on them.[3] The learning that accrues from the collective process can result in better opportunities or

[1] Eleanor Maccoby et al., "Community Integration and the Social Control of Delinquency," *Journal of Social Issues*, Vol. 14, No. 3 (1958), pp. 38–51.
[2] The word "representative" is used here in the sense of "typical of their group, i.e., class" rather than in the political sense of "functioning or acting in behalf of others." Elsewhere in the literature it has been restricted to the latter use. *See* Chauncey A. Alexander and Charles McCann, "The Concept of Representativeness in Community Organization," *Social Work*, Vol. 1, No. 1 (January 1956), pp. 48–52.
[3] Derek V. Roemer, "Focus in Programming for Delinquency Reduction" (Bethesda, Md.: National Institute of Mental Health, 1961). (Mimeographed.)

more effective models for potential delinquents only when large numbers of working-class adults are members of community organizations.

However, such membership is not very common among the lower class. A considerable number of studies indicate that formal group membership is closely related to income, status, and education; the lower one's income status and educational level, the less likely one is to participate in formal community groups.[4]

Furthermore, in every slum neighborhood there are adults who, in attitudes, strivings, verbal skills, and possession of know-how, are oriented toward the middle class. Although their children are less likely to experience strains toward deviance, these are precisely the parents who tend to join formal community organizations and to have faith and competence in the collective solution of social problems. In most organizations, therefore, persons who are in a minority among slum dwellers (i.e., the upward mobile) unfortunately represent the majority of those working-class members who participate. Because lower-class persons tend to eschew formal organizations, organizers who set out to reach the effective community of the delinquent frequently settle for those slum dwellers who are easiest to enlist.

Although reports of failure only rarely find their way into the literature, the modesty of claims regarding the organization of the deprived population itself indicates a general lack of success. For example, in East Harlem in 1948 a five-block area was chosen for organization. Five trained social workers were assigned to organize these blocks and a program of social action was embarked upon, devoted to housing, recreational, and social needs of the neighborhood. Unfortunately, the East Harlem Neighborhood Center for Block Organization was able to attract only a limited number of participants during a three-year period. Subsequent research indicated that those who did participate were upwardly aspiring. Further, they were isolated from the rest of the community and therefore nonrepresentative.

BARRIERS TO COMMUNITY INTEGRATION

Characteristics of Community Life

Why are representative lower-income adults less likely to become closely involved in community affairs? The source of the barriers to their effective participation rests with all three elements of the interaction: the characteristics of community life, the nature of lower-income adults, and the structure of the community organization effort.

One such community characteristic is residential mobility. Local com-

---

[4] Morris Axelrod, "Urban Structure and Social Participation," *American Sociological Review*, Vol. 21, No. 1 (February 1956), pp. 13–18.

munities have been inundated by new migrants, many of them un-familiar with the demands and opportunities of urban life. Although pub-lic housing mitigates some of the problematic aspects of slum life, the recruitment of single-family units from widely dispersed parts of the metropolitan area collects in one place thousands of deprived families, strangers to one another and to local community resources. Physical re-development programs and the consequent exodus of old residents have in many instances shattered existing institutions, so that they are unable to help in assimilation of the newcomers into the urban system. For ex-ample, the diminishing vitality of some local political machines, with their attentive political leaders, eliminates an important interpretive link to the new world.

Intergroup tensions are also a barrier to community integration, as are the bewildering operations of massive bureaucratic systems. The size, impersonality, concentrated power, and inflexibility of these large or-ganizations makes them seem to local residents hardly amenable to their influence.

The community characteristic that may act as the major deterrent to involvement of lower-income people in community affairs, however, is the opposition of already entrenched organizations. New groups in a community—especially new minority groups—are often confronted with hostility from established groups whose positions of power are threatened by the possibility of forceful action by the newcomers. There is evidence, for example, that some political machines will avoid registering minority group members, even under the impetus of national campaigns. This is so even though the minority group member is assumed to support the machine's national candidates. It is recognized that the new group will inevitably challenge the dominance of incumbent leadership.

This resistance of political parties, governmental agencies, and private organizations is never directly specified. Ordinarily it takes the form of statements such as "the minority groups are not really interested," they are "not ready," "they'll take positions we don't agree with," or they will be "controlled by the left-wing agitators." Whatever its form, the oppo-sition of established community groups is a formidable obstacle to in-digenous community participation.

Lower-Income Life

The circumstances of lower-income life and the nature of lower-income persons constitute another set of obstacles. The realities of lower-class life, i.e., the necessary preoccupation with the day-to-day problems of survival, hardly encourage attention to broad community matters. Fur-thermore, lower-class persons lack the verbal or literary requisites for organizational skills; neither do they tend to be comfortable with the formal methods of doing business in organizations. Their self-defeating attitudes also interfere with community integration. Lower-income groups tend to view life more pessimistically, with less hope of deliverance, and, as a consequence, they tend to retreat from struggle. A Gallup poll conducted in 1959 indicated that a higher percentage of respondents in the under-$3,000 income group expected World War III and a new depression than respondents in any other grouping. As one observer noted, "Seeing his chances for improvement as slim produces in the slum-dweller a psychology of listlessness, of passivity, and acceptance, which . . . reduces his chances still further." [5] Such defeatism, resulting in lack of participation, produces a loss of interest in changing their conditions.

Structure of Community Organization

The community organization itself, while purportedly seeking the involvement of lower-income persons, offers certain obstacles, whether inevitable or otherwise. Most community activities, for example, are staffed by middle-class personnel. To the extent that lower-class people feel that they are being dominated, they are likely to withdraw from collective activities. The predominance of the middle class in community organizations has a number of sources. When community problems become so severe that people are motivated to act, it is generally the middle-class element (or at least those who are oriented toward the middle class) that reacts first. Although lower-class persons may affiliate with the organization, its predominantly middle-class style soon becomes a subtle source of intimidation. Its leaders are likely to be businessmen, professionals, social welfare personnel, ministers, and other members of the middle class. The formality of the organization meetings, with predetermined agendas, concern with rules of procedure, and the like, tends to make the lower-class participant, unfamiliar with these matters, feel insecure and inferior.

Furthermore, organizers who insist on maintaining control of the activities and policies of the organization, subtly or otherwise, inevitably encourage the participation of lower-class persons whose values and skills are congenial with those of the middle-class organizer. Those whose values and skills differ, however, will gradually sense that such differences matter and that the organization exists to serve middle-class ends. They may, therefore, disassociate themselves.

It may be that, because of the disparity between lower- and middle-class "life styles," significant numbers of both groups cannot even be expected to participate together within the same organization. For example, a study conducted by the Girl Scouts, focused upon recruiting volunteers from working-class communities, was forced to conclude that the agency could offer no program suitable to both middle- and lower-

[5] Michael Harrington, "Slums, Old and New," *Commentary*, Vol. 30, No. 2 (August 1960), p. 121.

class groups. As noted by the authors, lower-income adults are less interested in "the joys of fully integrated personality in a democratic society" than in the need to better their standard of living. They do not even object to their children being handled authoritatively if it serves such end.[6]

The tendency of social workers to emphasize the amelioration of conflict and the reduction of tension, while often appropriate and helpful, may, in effect, also discourage lower-income participation. With issues flattened rather than sharpened, differences minimized rather than faced, there may be little to arouse the interest of a group that already lacks the predisposition to participate. Matters sufficiently vital to engage slum residents are almost inevitably fraught with controversy or are challenging to some powerful community interest. If they are avoided by a community organization, it may be expected that the organization will be avoided in turn.

The sponsorship of the community organization effort will also affect the character of participation. The primary interests of a sponsoring group will tend to determine membership selection, organizational form, objectives, and activities. Organizational maintenance requirements of the sponsor will inevitably limit the independence of an action-oriented affiliate. Further, its responsibility to a board of directors with widely varient views and connections to numerous community interest groups will limit a sponsor's freedom to encourage a free-wheeling community action program. When the sponsoring group is an already established community organization, it is likely to contain significant representation from groups that, as noted earlier, actively oppose the effective participation of lower-income and minority group people.

The formidable array of obstacles thus cited does not permit us to be sanguine about the success potential of any program oriented toward community action by representative lower-income adults. We may conclude, as a matter of fact, that the limitations to independence inherent in sponsorship by private or public social service organizations are hardly surmountable. Or we may discover that those obstacles least accessible to the social worker's means of intervention are most centrally required for program success. However discouraging, a specification of barriers is, nevertheless, a requirement of intelligent program planning.

STIMULATING PARTICIPATION

With these points considered, a specific strategy can be developed for a specific area, such as the Organizing the Unaffiliated program of Mobilization for Youth, an experimental action-research project on Manhattan's Lower East Side in the field of juvenile delinquency prevention

[6] Catherine V. Richards and Norman A. Polansky, "Reaching Working-class Youth Leaders," *Social Work*, Vol. 4, No. 4 (October, 1959), p. 38.

and control. While also offering broad-scale services in the fields of employment, education, casework, and group work, Mobilization for Youth proposes, through Organizing the Unaffiliated, to stimulate the participation of lower-income persons in attempts to resolve community problems. It is described here only because it has been designed in the context of the previous discussion, rather than because it provides ready solutions to knotty problems. As a matter of fact, plans for Organizing the Unaffiliated do not overcome a number of the obstacles cited earlier, and as such it is a ready candidate for mixed success. Whatever the risks of failure, however, attempts must be made if debilitating community conditions are to be mitigated or knowledge advanced.

Lower East Side residents who now participate in unaffiliated voluntary associations, such as storefront churches and hometown clubs, will be encouraged to plan collaborative programs of a cultural, social, and social-action nature. Although lower-class persons participate in formal group life less than do members of the middle class, urban slums do not lack indigenous social organizations. In fact, there is evidence of a proliferation of voluntary associations in depressed working-class neighborhoods. For example, in Manhattanville, a community of 100,000 within sixty city blocks, there are an estimated 400 informal groups, most of which have minimal attachments to the institutional life of the community.[7] Similarly, 300 small groups have thus far been identified in the area by Mobilization staff, each with at least a name and a designated regular meeting place.[8]

Focusing particularly upon work within the existent social structure, professionals are contacting leaders of these lower-income groups. Initial approaches have been based upon the similarities of the participants in addition to social class, i.e., ethnicity, race, religion, and the like. One worker, for example, is assigned Puerto Rican hometown groups, sports, and social clubs; another has established relationships with small all-Negro social groups; a third is working with the Pentecostal churches.[9] Ways in which Organizing the Unaffiliated may relate to the group, provide specific help, and assist in the implementation of group purpose have been explored.

[7] Hurley Doddy, *Informal Groups and the Community* (New York: Columbia University Press, 1952).

[8] Excluded from this definition of voluntary associations are amorphous, unattached groups, such as street-corner groups.

[9] Mobilization research indicates a low level of community integration. The small amount of interorganizational collaboration that does take place mainly involves organizations of similar type (e.g., storefront church with storefront church). It would therefore probably be a mistake to attempt heterogeneous groupings in beginning the program. On the other hand, a start toward the integration of groups (and leaders) which now work separately but which have common concerns and share a desire to do something about the Lower East Side must be developed.

Issues of concern to the groups have been identified and particular interest in employment problems, housing, and youth needs has been indicated. Special efforts in these substantive areas are planned to serve the organizations in the program. In the area of employment, for example, a co-operative program with a local union, to upgrade the skills of its members, is contemplated. Programs of job-finding, English language classes, and specialized training will be developed. Finally, action will be taken to modify discriminatory employment practices or to affect legislation.

As contact is established by professionals, promising indigenous group leaders are being selected, given in-service training, and hired as part-time community organizers. Persons who represent—and can also influence—the norms of their group have been sought; the ability to handle forms and to comply with middle-class modes of behavior is considered secondary.

Because lower-income people are accustomed to performing more spontaneously, within a small, highly personal group, the organizational milieu must be informal and flexible, the structure unorthodox and undetermined. The nature of the structure depends, of course, upon the wishes of the groups that choose to participate. Because of the wide diversity of voluntary associations and their current isolation from one another, a somewhat diffuse organizational form is anticipated. A loosely organized Council of Puerto Rican Organizations already exists. Some groups may ultimately wish to be part of a League of Storefront Churches, an Association of Tenant Councils, or an area-wide council. Those groups not prepared to join officially with others will be encouraged to maintain their ties to the programs through the community organizer and will participate on an ad hoc basis. It is also anticipated that some of the groups may ultimately wish to affiliate with a more established community organization, such as the Lower Eastside Neighborhoods Association.

Just as there is a variety of structures or groupings, so is there a wide range of readiness for programs. Some groups want to be involved only in social or cultural programs, others only in such undertakings as a large dance or a campaign against slum landlords. Still others are eager for social action on a number of issues and will concentrate on instrumental activities exclusively.

USE OF INDIGENOUS ORGANIZERS

It is hoped that the use of indigenous organizers will encourage lower-class residents to identify with the project and to perceive that the program represents their interests. In addition, it avoids the problems in communication that sometimes arise between people of different social strata. Leaders of lower-class groups will doubtless be more successful in engaging the interest and interpreting the aspirations of other residents. It is recognized, however, that the employment of these leaders may undermine their influence among group members. Since leadership adheres, in any group, to those with the power to withhold or provide items of value, the influence of indigenous organizers will be buttressed by the services provided by Organizing the Unaffiliated. To the extent possible, however, indigenous leaders will be prevented from molding themselves in the professional image.

Because of the structural and programmatic diversities, these organizers have a variety of tasks. Principally, they act as a group's channel of communication with the organized community and with other small groups. If groups are informed about community developments and about the activities of others, they become a part of the community even if they remain unaffiliated. Organizers are expected to help individuals to exploit the social resources provided by other Mobilization programs, and by the settlements, churches, and other institutions.

Community organizers have often relied solely on what may be called altruism. They have offered the individual participant and the group the psychic satisfaction of contributing to communal betterment. While middle-class persons readily link social action with personal and social gain, most lower-class people have difficulty relating seemingly remote goals to their bread-and-butter problems. Organizing the Unaffiliated recognizes the immediate self-interest of the depressed population and offers members such individual benefits as free legal advice, job referrals, homemakers, and baby-sitters. Such specific aids to groups as providing meeting space and clerical assistance are also proffered. Further, organizers provide assistance in arranging social and cultural activities as well as action on social issues of meaning to the group. Although these immediate gratifications are legitimate in their own right, especially in dealing with deprived individuals, they are viewed, in addition, as an aid to organization.

Significant portions of the slum population do not, of course, belong to organizations of any kind. Another task of the organizers, then, is to encourage and assist existent social units in recruiting unaffiliated individuals. Organizers will also attempt to form new groups that can eventually be drawn into wider participation.

To be maximally effective, this requires a co-ordinated effort by a wide range of professional persons. The program of Organizing the Unaffiliated is advancing this effort in two ways. It has developed a system whereby caseworkers, group workers, and educators assess the interest in group participation of the individuals with whom they have contact, for follow-up by indigenous community organizers. Further, sessions are planned to sensitize non-community organization professionals to community issues and organizational strategies, so that ultimately they may directly assist in the formation of groups around issues of community concern. This moves, of course, to the development of a generic social worker role, concerned primarily with substantive problem-solving rather than primarily with method.

LIP SERVICE OR COMMITMENT?

The assumption has been made that the successful involvement of lower-class persons requires that they be allowed greater freedom of action than is usually permitted low-income participants in community-wide activities. There is, of course, a contradiction inherent in the proposal to establish "independent" lower-class community organizations under Mobilization sponsorship. Mobilization is responsible to a wide variety of groups. Issues with which lower-class organizations deal may threaten some of these groups, which may exert pressure to control the fledgling. Unless they are formed spontaneously under the impetus of an inflammatory issue, lower-class groups cannot be organized without the financing and support of such established (i.e., middle-class) organizations as Mobilization. The fact that Mobilization constitutes a new structure partially mitigates the problem of control. So, too, does Mobilization's expressed intention to protect the organizations' independence. This is scant solution, however; it will be necessary for Mobilization to divest itself of responsibility for the program as soon as feasible. Encouraging the organizations to raise their own funds would be a step in that direction, although this may be hardly feasible. The possible lack of independence constitutes a most serious deficiency of the program.

Plans for indigenous community organization must assess community conditions realistically, including the sources, both direct and subtle, which oppose such organization. It must take into account the life styles, feelings, and needs of lower-income persons, regardless of our own orientation or attitude. Rather than hope to change people to fit predetermined structures, we must be willing to revise the structures in the context of the people we hope to attract. Unless we come to terms with these issues directly and honestly, our much-vaunted desire to organize lower-income groups will inevitably seem more lip service than commitment.

Orientation toward Clients
in a Public Welfare Agency

Peter M. Blau

Public assistance differs in important respects from other branches of social work. Since furnishing financial aid to those in need is legally recognized as a public responsibility, such assistance is administered by public welfare agencies, whereas case work and group work are generally carried out by private agencies. The welfare agencies in metropolitan communities are larger and more complex than private social work agencies, often having one thousand employees or more and consisting of numerous divisions, which provide many services besides financial assistance. Another distinctive characteristic of public welfare is that most of the "case workers" who administer assistance are not professionally trained social workers but have only a college degree and possibly a few courses in social work. Welfare agencies have not been successful in attracting professionally trained personnel not only because of their low pay but also because the ideology of professional social workers depreciates work in public assistance.

This paper is concerned with the orientation of case workers toward clients in a public welfare agency in a large American city, and particularly with the ways in which the organizational and social context of the agency influenced their orientation.[1] Merton's concept of role set calls attention to the "complement of role relationships which persons have by virtue of occupying a particular social status."[2] Thus the status of case

[1] For a study that deals extensively with the orientation to clients in a public employment agency, see Roy G. Francis and Robert C. Stone, *Service and Procedure in Bureaucracy* (Minneapolis, 1956). A study that deals with the influence of the community on the orientations to recipients in a public welfare agency is reported in Edwin J. Thomas, Role Conceptions and Organizational Size, *American Sociological Review*, 24 (1959), 30–37.

[2] Robert K. Merton, *Social Theory and Social Structure* (rev. ed.; Glencoe, 1957), p. 369.

Peter M. Blau, "Orientation toward Clients in a Public Welfare Agency," *Administrative Science Quarterly*, December 1960, Vol. 5, No. 3, pp. 341–361.

workers in the welfare agency involves individuals in role relationships with superiors in the organization, with clients, and with co-workers, and each of these relationships has some bearing upon the way they perform their role as case worker.

The first question to be raised is that of bureaucratic constraints. The administrative procedures that have necessarily become established in such a complex organization impose limits upon role relationships and operations. Training, supervision, and accumulated experience help the case worker to adapt his role to the bureaucratic requirements. What are the consequences of these bureaucratic conditions for his orientation toward recipients of public assistance? A second problem is posed by the role relationship between case worker and clients. How does the experience of meeting recipients and encountering difficulties in dealing with them affect the worker's approach? His relationships with peers and integration in his work group constitute a third important source of influence upon the case worker's orientation toward recipients. Finally, the significance of the absence of a role relationship should be noted. Since they are not professionally trained, case workers are not actual members of a professional group of colleagues (although professional social work is a meaningful reference group for some of them).

The data for the study were collected in 1957 in a large public welfare agency.[3] The agency was responsible for administering general public assistance, but it also provided medical and legal aid, help with employment, industrial training, child placement, and several other services. The main duty of the case worker was to determine whether new applicants were eligible for public assistance and to continue to check whether recipients remained eligible. He was also expected to furnish sufficient case-work service to encourage clients to become self-supporting again and to see that they obtained the services from other departments as needed. These tasks required familiarity with agency procedures and involved a considerable amount of paper work in the office as well as visiting clients in their homes. Case workers spent about one-third of their time in the field. Large case loads and high turnover of personnel created special difficulties for discharging these responsibilities. More than one-half of the case workers were men, and one-third were Negroes.

The research concentrated on twelve work groups, each consisting of five or six case workers under a supervisor. After a three-month period of observation devoted to collecting some systematic data as well as general impressions, pertinent information was abstracted from agency records, and the members of the twelve work groups were interviewed. A central

[3] I am indebted to Philip M. Marcus for assistance in the collection and analysis of the data, and to the Ford Foundation as well as to the Social Science Research Committee of the University of Chicago for financial support. I also want to acknowledge William Delany's helpful suggestions for revising the paper.

focus of the interview, which lasted from one to two hours, was the respondent's orientation toward clients. Only those items which analysis revealed to be salient as well as reliable are used in this paper. Although such interview responses cannot hope to capture all subtle aspects of the case worker's approach to clients, they do indicate some basic differences in approach.

BUREAUCRATIC CONSTRAINTS

Case workers often complained about the bureaucratic restraints under which they had to operate. Many of them felt that the agency's emphasis on following procedures, and particularly the requirement to investigate closely each recipient's eligibility, made it impossible for them to provide the kind of case-work service which would benefit clients most:

> They always talk about social work, but actually you can't do anything of the kind here. For instance, I had one case which I wanted to send to . . . [another agency], but my supervisor said, "You can't. You would have to make a case plan first, and we can't do that."

These were the words of a worker who had been with the agency only a few months. Newcomers not only voiced such complaints most often (although they were by no means alone in doing so), but they also frequently criticized old-timers for having grown callous and inflexible in the course of having become adapted to the bureaucratic organization.

Implicit in the opinions of case workers were two contradictory explanations of compliance with official procedures. On the one hand, compliance was ascribed to externally imposed restraints that prevented workers from following their own inclinations and furnishing good case-work service. On the other, the old-timers' conformity to procedures was attributed to their rigidity resulting from their overadaptation to the bureaucratic organization. As a matter of fact, neither of these explanations is entirely accurate. Bureaucratic constraints actually became internalized, but adaptation to them did not increase rigidity.

The impact of the bureaucratic organization on service to clients cannot be directly determined without comparing different agencies that are more or less bureaucratized. While this is not possible in a study confined to case workers in one organization, an indirect estimate of this impact can be made. Since bureaucratic pressures are, in large part, transmitted to workers through their supervisors, their influence can be inferred from a comparison of the orientations of workers under supervisors who stress strict adherence to official procedures and under supervisors who interpret procedures more liberally. On the basis of their description of a day in the field, workers were classified as being primarily

oriented either toward checking eligibility in accordance with procedures
or toward providing some case-work service. Only 7 of the 29 workers
under supervisors who emphasized procedures were oriented toward
case-work service, in contrast to 19 of the 31 under less procedure-
oriented supervisors.[4]

Some case workers were subject to less bureaucratic pressure than
others, and this was reflected in their work, but few if any escaped the
penetrating impact of bureaucratization. The summer camp program
illustrates this. A number of free placements in children's camps were
made available to the agency each year. Case workers who often deplored the lack of funds that made it impossible to help clients beyond
supplying them with the bare necessities of life, and who sympathized
particularly with the plight of children, would be expected eagerly to take
advantage of this opportunity to provide special services and to compete
for the few placements available. Actually, most workers were not at all
interested in making camp referrals, looking upon it as an extra burden
rather than an opportunity, although the actual amount of work involved
was quite small. Moreover, service-oriented workers were no more likely
to make referrals to summer camps than others.

This general apathy toward the camp program indicates that, although
many case workers complained about being restricted in their endeavors
to serve clients by bureaucratic restraints *externally* imposed upon them,
they had actually internalized bureaucratic constraints to a considerable
degree. To be sure, some workers defined their responsibilities less narrowly than others, partly in response to differences in their superiors'
interpretations of agency policies. But even a broader definition of the
case worker's bureaucratic responsibilities limited their scope to certain
recurrent services, and referring children to camps was an extraordinary
service, not part of the regular routine.

The very complexity of official procedures in this large organization
served to promote adaptation to bureaucratic practice. In order to help
his clients, a case worker had to know agency procedures and to work
within their bounds. But it was impossible in a few days or weeks to
learn to understand, let alone to administer, the many rules and regulations that governed operations. New employees were overwhelmed by
the complexity of their administrative duties and had to devote several
months, often much of their first year, to becoming familiar with agency
procedures. Newcomers who were unable or unwilling to master the
pertinent regulations and perform their duties in accordance with them
either found their job so unsatisfactory that they soon left or, more rarely,

---

[4] Supervisors were classified on the basis of descriptions by their subordinates. But
regardless of how a given worker described his supervisor, the worker was less apt
to be service-oriented if the other subordinates described the supervisor as emphasizing procedures than if they did not.

performed their tasks so poorly that they did not survive the probation period. Most of the case workers who remained with the agency for any length of time had come to accept the limitations of official procedures and, indeed, to incorporate them into their own thinking, because doing so was a prerequisite for deriving satisfaction from the job and performing it adequately.

Internalized bureaucratic constraints tended to govern the decisions and actions of case workers, their protestations against bureaucracy notwithstanding. But as an examination of the data reveals, this does not mean that adaptation to the organization and its requirements increased rigid adherence to procedures at the expense of case-work service. Case workers who had been with the agency for a long time could be assumed to be better adapted to it than newcomers, for reasons already noted. (The fact that less than one-half of the workers with more than one year of employment, compared to three-quarters of the newcomers, mentioned bureaucratic conditions as one of the things they liked least about the job supports this assumption.) Old-timers, however, were less likely than newcomers to confine their work to checking eligibility. Twelve of the 21 newcomers, 10 of the 21 workers with one to three years of service, and only one-third of the 18 workers with over three years of service were primarily oriented toward eligibility procedures. Another finding indicates a similar decrease in rigid compliance with official procedures with increasing experience. Agency rules required workers to be on time, and repeated tardiness was penalized. The time sheets showed that none of the newcomers were late for work more than once every other month, whereas nearly half (19 of 39) of the workers with more than one year seniority were.

Apparently, adjustment to the organization did not lead to greater bureaucratic rigidity; on the contrary, it was the insecurity of the newcomer, not thoroughly familiar with procedures and not yet adapted to the bureaucratic organization, that produced rigid adherence to official procedures. The more experienced worker's greater understanding of procedures and better adaptation to them made him less confined by them,[5] with the result that he was more likely than a newcomer to go beyond checking eligibility in his contacts with clients and provide some case-work service.

REALITY SHOCK

There are two things you learn on this job, particularly if it is your first job. First, you become less idealistic. You realize that people are not

[5] The same relationship between knowledge of procedures and lack of rigidity was observed in another bureaucracy; see Peter M. Blau, *The Dynamics of Bureaucracy* (Chicago, 1955), pp. 197–198.

always honest—that you cannot always accept what they say. Then, you learn to work within a framework of rules. You realize that every job has rules and that you have to work within that framework.

This statement of a perceptive case worker who had been with the agency for not quite one year indicates the two major problems that confront the newcomer. Often fresh out of college, not only is he faced by a complicated set of procedures, but he also encounters clients who are very different from what he had expected and with whom he must establish a working relationship.

Most persons who took a job in the welfare agency were partly motivated by an interest in working with and helping poor people. They tended to look forward to establishing a warm, although not intimate, relationship with deserving and grateful clients, and considered the case worker as the agent of society who extended a helping and trusting hand to its unfortunate members. Newcomers generally deplored the "means test" and cared little about protecting public funds by investigating whether clients meet eligibility requirements, feeling that a trusting attitude should accompany financial aid in the best interest of rehabilitation. While a few case workers were motivated to seek their job by very different considerations, such as a desire to dominate people, they were the exception, and the attitudes of most new case workers toward clients were strongly positive, if somewhat sentimental and idealistic. Contacts with clients put these views to a severe test, which often resulted in disillusion.

Recipients of public assistance constitute the most deprived segment of the population, especially in a period of relative prosperity. In this northern metropolis, disproportionate numbers of them were Negroes, immigrants from the South, unmarried mothers, alcoholics, and generally people with severe handicaps in the labor market. The mores and folkways of most of these people were quite different from those prevailing in the American middle or working class. Strong moral condemnation of desertion, illegitimacy, or physical violence, for example, was not part of the values of their subculture. Such differences in values and customs made it difficult for middle-class workers to maintain their positive feelings for clients, but another factor was even more important in changing their orientation. Clients were in dire need, since the assistance allowance, originally set low, never caught up with the inflationary trend. They were, therefore, under strong pressure to conceal what slim resources they might have had and try to get a little more money from the agency, even if this required false statements. People under such deprived conditions tend to look upon government organizations as alien forces that must be tricked into yielding enough money for survival, and consequently some clients, although by no means all, tried to cheat. In fact, the situation in which recipients found themselves made honesty a luxury.

The new case worker was typically full of sympathy for clients' problems. But as he encountered clients who blamed him personally for not helping them enough, even though agency procedure limited him, and clients met his trusting attitude by cheating and lying, the newcomer tended to experience a "reality shock," [6] just as new teachers do whose first assignment is an overcrowded class in a slum.[7] This disillusioning experience might make a worker bitter and callous, or induce him to leave the job, and even those who did not have either of these extreme reactions tended to change their orientation to clients.

Finding out that people one has trusted have lied is a threatening experience. It implies that one has been made a fool of and that others are laughing behind his back at his naïveté. To protect his ego against these threats, a case worker is under pressure to change his orientation toward clients. If he anticipates deception by distrusting the statements of recipients, their lies no longer pose a threat to his ego. And if he loses his personal interest in them, their attitudes cease to be significant for his self-conception, making his ego still more immune against possible deception and other conflicts. In short, the *situational context* of public assistance, by producing a reality shock, tends to create a distrustful and uninterested orientation toward recipients.

The conception of reality shock implies that case workers lose some of their interest in clients and concern with their welfare during their first year in the agency. The empirical data confirm this hypothesis. Of the newcomers, 57 percent reported that they worried sometimes or often about their cases after working hours; of the workers with more than one year of service, only one-third did (this proportion was the same for those with one to three years and those with more than three years seniority). Personal involvement with clients, that is, the proportion of workers who considered it important to be liked by clients, decreased similarly after one year of service.

A less simple pattern, however, was revealed by the relationship between seniority and deriving satisfaction from clients, as Table 1 shows. Contacts with clients were a major source of work satisfaction for three-quarters of the newcomers; this proportion decreases, as expected, to considerably less than one-half for workers with one to three year seniority; but it increases again to more than three-quarters for old-timers with more than three years of employment. The proportion of workers who in particular enjoyed helping clients manifests the same pattern—a drop

[6] This concept has been introduced by Everett C. Hughes in his studies of professional careers.

[7] See Miriam Wagenschien, "Reality Shock" (unpublished Master's thesis, University of Chicago, 1950).

Table 1   *Seniority and Source of Work Satisfaction*

Major Source of Work Satisfaction	Newcomer (%)	1–3 Years (%)	Old-Timer (%)
Client contacts	76	43	83
Other sources	24	57	17
Number of cases	21	21	18

after one year and a rise after three years. Again, workers with one to three years of seniority were somewhat more likely to think that clients often cheat than either newcomers or old-timers. These findings suggest that the reality shock has some effects that are temporary as well as some permanent ones.

Having come to the agency with idealistic views about poor people, newcomers tended to be much concerned with helping recipients. Contacts with clients constituted the most gratifying aspect of their work, not only because of their positive feelings toward clients, but also because they had few alternative sources of satisfaction on the job. Still unsure about procedures and not yet having become friendly with many colleagues, newcomers were not likely to find much gratification in their work at the office, where the necessity to make decisions and submit them to the supervisor aroused their anxieties, and where the friendly interaction among other case workers underlined their own relative isolation. The disillusioning experience of the reality shock often alienated the case worker from clients. After he had been with the agency for about a year, therefore, he tended to lose much of his concern with helping clients and to derive less satisfaction from working with them. But as the worker learned to adapt to the reality shock by becoming less involved with clients, contacts with them ceased to be a threatening and unpleasant experience. Moreover, as he became increasingly conversant with agency procedures and acquired skills in applying them less rigidly, the worker could furnish more effective case-work service, and this made contacts with clients once more a source of work satisfaction for him. The continuing lack of involvement of the old-timer might be considered a residue of the reality shock. After three years of experience, however, the old-timer was again at least as apt as was the newcomer to find satisfaction in his work with clients. But whereas the gratification of the newcomer was rooted in his interest in recipients and their welfare, that of the old-timer, who generally lacked such a personal interest in clients, stemmed from his superior skill in providing effective service. The workers who did not find the exercise of this skill an interesting challenge probably left the agency in disproportionate numbers, and this selective process may well partly account for the finding that those who had remained with the organization for more than three years obtained more satisfaction from contacts with clients than those with one to three years seniority.

PEER GROUP SUPPORT

The finding that newcomers, despite their positive feelings, were less likely than other workers to go beyond checking eligibility and to offer case-work services to clients has been interpreted by suggesting that lack of experience and familiarity with procedures engendered insecurities and anxieties, and that these anxieties led to rigid adherence to procedures. If this interpretation is correct, then conditions other than experience that lessen feelings of insecurity should also promote case-work service.

Friendly relations with colleagues are a source of social support which helps reduce the anxieties and insecurities that arise in the work situation. Individuals who were somewhat isolated from colleagues, therefore, were expected to be less oriented toward case-work service than those with extensive informal relations with peers. Indeed, this seemed to be the case. Two measures of social support from peers were the caseworker's popularity in the organization (how often others named him as a colleague with whom they were friendly) and his integration in his work group (whether he was called by his first name by other members of his own work group). Whichever index was used, over one-half of the workers with social support from peers were service oriented, in comparison with not quite one-third of those without such social support.

Apparently, friendly relations with peers decreased the tendency of workers to confine themselves rigidly to checking eligibility,[8] just as accumulated experience did. The influence of both social integration in the peer group and experience (seniority) on the service orientation of workers [9] is presented in Table 2. The data in adjacent pairs of columns show that social support from integrative relations with co-workers encouraged case-work service only among workers with less than three

[8] An alternative interpretation of the finding would be that service orientation made workers more popular among colleagues, but other data suggest that the interpretation presented is probably the valid one. Thus this interpretation implies a direct relationship between popularity and self-confidence, and also one between self-confidence and a service orientation, and the data confirm both of these inferences.

[9] The pattern of findings is quite similar if the index of popularity rather than that of integration is used, and also if several other measures of orientation to clients are substituted for the one shown in the table. (Integration in the ingroup rather than popularity in the organization is the measure presented in the tables, because there are too few popular newcomers to make meaningful comparisons.)

Table 2 *Seniority, Integration, and Orientation*

Orientation toward Clients	Newcomer Integration		1–3 Years Integration		Old-Timer Integration	
	Low (%)	High (%)	Low (%)	High (%)	Low (%)	High (%)
Eligibility procedure	67	50	67	33	13	50
Intermediate	11	8	11	0	38	0
Case-work service	22	42	22	67	50	50
Number of cases	9	12	9	12	8	10

years of experience, but not among old-timers. If the two categories of case workers who had been with the agency less than three years are combined, 22 percent of the unintegrated, in contrast to 54 percent of the integrated, were service oriented. But after three years, whether workers were integrated among peers or not, the proportion of service-oriented ones was 50 percent. This suggests that social support from colleagues is significant for service to clients only as long as lack of experience engenders anxieties that impede service. Since the worker who has become fully adapted to the organization and its procedures in several years of employment experiences little anxiety in his work, the anxiety-reducing function of friendly relations with peers has no bearing upon his performance.

Experience decreased rigid concern with procedures considerably among unintegrated case workers but had much less impact on the orientation of integrated workers, as a comparison of alternate columns in Table 2 shows. Among the integrated, the proportion of procedure-oriented workers declined somewhat after the first year only to increase again after the third. Among the unintegrated, in contrast, two-thirds of the workers were procedure oriented for the first three years, but this proportion dropped sharply to one out of eight after three years of experience. This finding probably indicates that experience frees the worker from being rigidly restricted by procedures, and thus fosters case-work service, not simply because it increases a worker's technical competence but specifically because his increased competence lessens his feelings of insecurity and anxiety. The unintegrated worker, whose anxieties are not already relieved by social support from peers, is therefore the one most apt to become less rigid with increasing experience.

Social support from colleagues and accumulated experience can be considered functional substitutes for each other with respect to service to clients. Both seemed to reduce anxieties and rigidities and thus to foster case-work service, but their effects were not cumulative. If workers were experienced, integration did not increase their tendency to be service oriented, and if they were integrated, experience hardly increased service. As a matter of fact, there is some indication that the combined influence of much experience and social support from peers was the very reverse of that of either condition alone. After three years of employment, integrated workers were somewhat *more* likely to be procedure oriented than unintegrated ones. This could be interpreted as showing that a certain amount of anxiety serves as an incentive to go beyond merely checking eligibility. Workers who were too secure had no incentive to do more than that, and those who felt too insecure were too rigid to do more. The integrated workers without several years of experience and the highly experienced but unintegrated ones, on the other hand, whose anxieties presumably had been mitigated without having been entirely eliminated, were most apt to go beyond checking eligibility and provide some case-work service.[10]

While the implication of social integration among peers for case-work service was largely similar to that of years of experience, the significance of integration for the concern workers expressed about helping clients was opposite of that of experience. Fully 28 of the 34 integrated workers were sufficiently concerned to worry, at least occasionally, about their cases after working hours, in contrast to only 12 of the 26 unintegrated workers. Integration in the work group was, then, directly related to this manifestation of interest in the welfare of clients, but experience, as previously noted, was inversely related to it, and this remains true if the associations of both factors with worrying are examined simultaneously, as Table 3 shows. Case workers who were integrated among peers were more apt to be greatly concerned about their cases than unintegrated workers, whatever their seniority (compare adjacent pairs of columns). Experience, on the other hand, reduced the tendency to worry much about recipients, both among integrated workers (from 67 percent for newcomers to 40 percent for old-timers) and among unintegrated ones (from 44 to 25 percent).

These findings suggest that peer group support served to absorb some of the impact of the reality shock. The unintegrated worker, without such social support, experienced the full force of the reality shock, which

[10] Although it is hazardous to venture an explanation of a single reversal, this one deserves to be mentioned, because it calls attention to forces that are often neglected in sociological studies of administrative organizations, including my own. In our reaction against scientific management and purely rational models of administrative behavior, we have tended to overemphasize the significance of informal relationships and paid insufficient attention to the formal administrative structure, the significance of incentives, and related problems. See on this point Alvin W. Gouldner, "Organizational Analysis," in Robert K. Merton et al., eds., *Sociology Today* (New York, 1959), pp. 400–412.

Table 3 *Seniority, Integration, and Concern*

	Newcomer Integration		1–3 Years Integration		Old-Timer Integration	
Concern: Worry about Cases	Low (%)	High (%)	Low (%)	High (%)	Low (%)	High (%)
Often or sometimes	44	67	22	42	25	40
Rarely	44	25	22	25	0	50
Never	11	8	56	33	75	10
Number of cases	9	12	9	12	8	10

constrained him to shield his ego by developing a hardened attitude toward clients. Ego support from integrative relations with peers made a worker less vulnerable, enabling him to cope with disagreeable experiences with recipients without feeling threatened and thus reducing his need for protecting his ego by becoming indifferent toward clients. Among unintegrated workers, therefore, the proportion who never worried increased from 11 percent during the first year of employment to 75 percent after three years, but there was no corresponding increase among integrated workers (compare alternate columns in the third row of Table 3). Social support from colleagues helped integrated workers withstand the reality shock and thus permitted them to maintain a greater concern for clients and their fate. Moreover, workers whose interest in helping clients led to worrying and made them vulnerable had particularly strong incentives to seek social support by fostering integrative relations with colleagues. The data do not enable us to tell whether integration increased concern or concern enhanced the chances of integration, or whether both influences occurred. In any case, however, they point to the conclusion that integration in the work group served to lessen the impact of the reality shock.[11]

Does this finding imply that the colleague groups discouraged a detached approach toward clients? It does not, because professional detachment is quite distinct from lack of concern with helping clients. As a matter of fact, the question about worrying was originally intended as a measure of detachment, but further reflection as well as examination of the answers revealed that it is not a valid indication of an impersonal

[11] The findings permit, however, still another interpretation from which this conclusion would not follow. Perhaps certain personality types, as for example dependent individuals, were more likely than others to worry about clients and also more likely to foster integrative relations with colleagues. The assumption made in the text is that the relationship between integration and worrying is not spurious, that is, not simply due to personality differences that affect both these factors.

professional approach. Professional detachment involves lack of personal identification and emotional involvement with clients, but not lack of concern with their welfare or lack of interest in helping them. How much a worker worried about his cases appeared to be not so much indicative of his emotional involvement as of his concern with providing effective service to clients, as the examples given by respondents of what they worry about showed.[12] The social contacts of 20 case workers with an average of four clients each were observed, and an index of detachment was derived from these observations. To be sure, there was a direct relationship between detachment and lack of concern. However, integrated case workers were more apt than unintegrated workers to remain detached in their interviews with clients,[13] whereas they were also less apt than unintegrated ones to be unconcerned with clients by not worrying about their work after office hours, as we have seen. Although the number of workers directly observed is small, the finding suggests that worrying expresses an aspect of the orientation to recipients that is distinct from, although not unrelated to, lack of professional detachment.

The way the colleague group promoted adjustment to the reality shock was apparently by encouraging its members to displace aggression against clients in conversations among themselves. Case workers often expressed very callous attitudes toward recipients in joking and talking with one another. For instance, when a worker went to interview a neurotic client, a colleague bid farewell to her with the words, "Don't push him over the brink," to which she responded, "Anything to get your case load down." Or, a worker proudly displayed his strictness by telling another about having discontinued assistance for a recipient when finding a Christmas tree and presents at his home, and ended by saying, "A dirty thing to do, right at Christmas." Workers often seemed to be actually bragging to colleagues about how unsympathetic they felt toward clients and how harshly they treated them. Indeed, even those workers who had impressed the observer with their sympathetic and understanding attitude toward

[12] Few examples revealed personal involvement with clients ("Somebody gets under your skin and bothers you . . ."); the majority expressed a more impersonal concern with effective service ("Did I do everything so that they can get their checks?"); and some referred not to clients but only to the respondent's own work or performance ("Too much paper work; we are under great pressure; heavy load"). It is worth noting that newcomers did not differ from old-timers in the proportion of their examples that referred only to their own problems. This indicates that the observed difference between newcomers and old-timers in *extent* of worrying is not simply due to the fact that experienced workers had less reason to worry about their performance, as one might otherwise suspect.

[13] See Blau, "Social Integration, Social Rank, and Processes of Interaction," *Human Organization*, 18 (1959–1960), 152–157. In this paper, which is primarily based on observational data, I mistakenly assumed, on the basis of an inconclusive analysis of some of the interview data, that amount of worry is an index of detachment. I want to correct, and apologize for, the erroneous statement reported there.

recipients joined in this aggressive banter. To be sure, these workers might have deceived the observer by simulating a positive orientation in their statements to him and their behavior with clients when under observation by him; a systematic check, however, confirmed the initial impression. In five of the twelve work groups, a quantitative record was kept of all anticlient statements made during section meetings and conferences with the supervisor. A worker's tendency to make anticlient statements in these interactions with colleagues was not at all related to his attitude to clients, as indicated in the interview.

Aggressive jokes or remarks about clients were typically made at these meetings and conferences after some disagreement or conflict, and the common laughter or indignation helped to reunite the conflicting parties. In other words, anticlient statements were a mechanism for reaffirming social solidarity among colleagues. Since they readily served this function, case workers had incentives to make aggressive statements against recipients, regardless of their attitudes toward them, as a means for healing breaches in interpersonal relations that might otherwise fester and become disruptive conflicts. Moreover, since older workers, who had generally less considerate attitudes toward clients than newcomers, tended to occupy dominant positions in the work groups, newcomers were under pressure to prove that by joining in the anticlient raillery they were "regular fellows" and disprove the suspicion that they were naïve and sentimental about clients.

Displacing aggressive feelings aroused by conflicts with clients in the fairly harmless form of ridiculing them and displaying a hardened attitude toward them in discussions with colleagues may have helped to prevent such aggressive reactions from crystallizing into an antagonistic attitude to clients; but a case worker's opportunity for doing so depended on the extent of his informal relations. The unintegrated worker's inability readily to relieve the tensions produced by conflicts with recipients in this fashion may be one reason why he was more prone than the integrated worker to develop a callous, unconcerned attitude toward clients as a means of avoiding such tensions. Processes of selection, however, may also have contributed to the observed differences in worrying about the welfare of clients. Perhaps workers who worried left the agency in disproportionate numbers, and unintegrated worriers were even more apt to do so than integrated ones, whose friendly relations with peers made the job relatively more attractive. This pattern of turnover could also account for the findings presented in Table 3.

DISCUSSION AND CONCLUSION

Two important components of a professional orientation, in social work as well as in other occupations, are an interest in serving clients and the ability to furnish professional services. These are, of course, not the only elements in professionalism, but they are of special interest in the study of public assistance, because they become particularly problematical in the context of the administration of public welfare. The necessity to adapt to the bureaucratic procedures of complex welfare organizations creates obstacles for service, partly by diverting energies to learning the official regulations and administering them, partly by engendering anxieties and rigidities, and partly by the limitations imposed by internalized bureaucratic constraints. Furthermore, conflicts with clients, resulting primarily from the requirement to check their eligibility for assistance, jeopardize the interest in extending services to them. Finally, since the large majority of the personnel of public assistance agencies are not professionally trained, it is especially pertinent to ask what substitutes for such training, if any, promote a concern with the welfare of clients and an ability to serve them.

To be sure, untrained workers cannot be expected to have the skills to provide intensive case work, and there is no measure of such professional competence available in any case. We are concerned here merely with the worker's ability to cope with official procedures without restricting himself simply to checking eligibility—his ability to maintain an orientation to case-work service. Although newcomers were most vociferous in their criticism of agency procedures, their approach to clients tended to be most limited by them. Experience, including the training that workers received from their supervisors as well as from training officials, was a functional substitute for professional training, which enabled workers to render more extensive services to clients. It apparently reduced the case worker's anxieties about his work and thus freed him from being rigidly confined by procedures. Social support from integrative relations with peers also lessened anxieties and inflexibilities and, consequently, encouraged service to recipients.

Concern with the welfare of clients, too, was reinforced by integrative relations with colleagues, probably because peer group relations mitigated the impact of the reality shock that workers experienced in their early contacts and conflicts with clients, which obviated the need to adapt to such conflicts by developing a callous attitude toward clients. Experience, however, did not contribute to an interest in the welfare of clients; on the contrary, it reduced concern with their welfare.

In sum, experience increased the case worker's ability to serve recipients but decreased his interest in doing so. Peer group support, on the other hand, promoted the worker's concern with helping clients as well as his ability to help them. Friendly relations with peers, moreover, constituted a source of work satisfaction which may well have reduced turnover.[14] This possibility raises the question of how differences in the tendency to leave the agency affected the findings.

The relationships between seniority and the orientations of case workers to recipients were in all likelihood not entirely due to the influence of experience but partly to processes of selection. Since friendly relations with colleagues make the job more attractive, integrated workers have more reason to remain than unintegrated workers. Hence, factors that make the job unsatisfactory would be expected to increase the quitting rate of unintegrated workers, whose interpersonal relations do not hold them back, more than that of integrated workers.[15] One such dissatisfaction might be a worker's inability to extend the scope of his activities beyond the fairly routine and uninteresting task of checking eligibility; another one might be the anxiety caused by contact with severely deprived recipients. If workers who feel restricted by procedures leave the agency in disproportionate numbers, there will be fewer procedure-oriented workers among those with several years seniority than among those with little seniority. And if the restrictions of procedures increase the quitting rate of unintegrated workers more than that of integrated ones, the differences in procedure orientation between old-timers and newcomers will be pronounced among unintegrated but not among integrated workers. This is precisely what Table 2 shows. Similarly, if worry about clients encourages quitting, and if worry exerts a stronger influence on the turnover of unintegrated than that of integrated workers, it follows that there are fewer worriers left after several years, and that the difference in worrying associated with length of service is greater among unintegrated than among integrated workers. This is precisely what Table 3 shows. In short, the pattern of findings may be due either to these processes of selection or to the influence of experience discussed earlier. The most plausible assumption is that both factors contributed to the observed differences.[16]

[14] Over one-third of the integrated workers, but less than one-tenth of the unintegrated ones, spontaneously mentioned friendly relations with colleagues as one of the things they liked best about the job.

[15] Lack of integration in combination with another source of job dissatisfaction might have motivated workers to leave. By itself, lack of integration in the ingroup evidently did not have this effect, as shown by the finding that the proportion of unintegrated did not decrease with seniority (see last row of Table 3). Lack of popularity in the organization, on the other hand, might have induced workers to leave; for the proportion of the unpopular did decrease with seniority (from four-fifths among newcomers to one-third among workers with more than one year of service).

[16] There is still another factor that may have contributed to these differences, namely, promotions to supervisor. Perhaps the promotion chances of procedure-oriented workers were better than those of workers who showed little interest in official procedures; perhaps individuals who worried about their cases were more likely to be promoted to supervisor than those who expressed less concern with their work; and perhaps

Professional training in social work not only imparts knowledge and skills but also has an important socializing function; namely, to inculcate an orientation toward clients that combines impersonal detachment with serious concern for their welfare. The untrained workers in the agency studied probably suffered even more from not having undergone this process of socialization than from lack of professional knowledge and skills. To be sure, beginners were typically much concerned with helping clients, but they were not prepared for the shock of actually meeting recipients and, particularly, for coping with their own reactions to either the sympathy-evoking plight or the threatening aggression of recipients. The worker's untutored response to the tensions produced by these experiences was to become emotionally involved, or to escape by leaving the agency, or, perhaps most often, to lose concern with the welfare of clients as a means of avoiding these tensions. Such ego-defensive reactions would probably have been much rarer if the initial concern of workers with the welfare of recipients had been fortified by a detached attitude which made them less dependent on clients, just as ego support from integrative relations with colleagues reduced the likelihood of such reactions. To produce a detached service approach—the peculiar combination of a strong interest in furthering the welfare of clients and a detached attitude toward them—is an important function of professional training in social work.

---

popularity among colleagues decreased a worker's interest in becoming a supervisor. These processes of selective advancement might have contributed somewhat, though hardly very much, to the observed differences between newcomers and old-timers.

Name Index